Psychology of the Child

Psychology of the Child
THIRD EDITION

Robert I. Watson
University of New Hampshire

Henry Clay Lindgren
California State University at San Francisco

John Wiley and Sons, Inc. New York / London / Sydney / Toronto

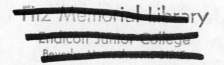

Cover drawings by

Jay Falk, *age 9*

Marybeth Falk, *age 8*

Steven Fletcher, *age 6*

Katy Kretschmer, *age 6*

Library of Congress Cataloging in Publication Data:

Watson, Robert Irving, 1909-
Psychology of the child.

(Series in psychology)
Includes bibliographical references.
1. Child study. I. Lindgren, Henry Clay, joint author. II. Title.

BF721.W33   1973   155.4   72-4538
ISBN O-471-92240-4

Preface

A textbook is, essentially, an attempt to instruct, and there are as many different approaches to textbook writing as there are teachers. As one reviews the various goals and philosophies that characterize various modes of teaching, however, a number of patterns are apparent. Some instructors in child psychology, and some textbooks as well, seem to aim primarily at preparing research workers. They emphasize theory and methodology, and studies are presented and discussed with this intent in mind. Other instructors and textbooks appear to be principally concerned with presenting only the material that seems relevant to the everyday experience of students. Research and theory are introduced only incidentally, and the important goal is that of talking to students primarily in terms of their own experiences. Each of these approaches has its merits and there are excellent teachers (as well as excellent textbooks) that exemplify each of these styles.

We have chosen to use both of these approaches because we find them both equally attractive. Theory and methodology attract us since, without them, psychology may be interesting and anecdotal, but it is not a science. Furthermore, the science of psychology attracts us for its own sake. We consider the scientific study of human behavior a fascinating enterprise, so much so that we have devoted our lives to it.

In our role as teachers, however, we also find relevance attractive. One obvious reason is that we know students learn more effectively when they see how the material is related to their own lives and daily experiences. A more important reason is that we *want* psychology to make sense to students: a student who takes a psychology course (or reads a psychology textbook) without understanding himself and others at least a little better has failed, and so has his teacher (or the author).

The writer of textbooks in child psychology has a number of advantages if he tries to meet both these goals, as we have. One advantage is that there is now a large body of research material and theoretical discussion dealing with many phases of child development. Indeed, the amount of material is embarrassing in its very richness, and the problem becomes that of deciding what to choose. The second advantage is that child development is a part of everyone's experience. We have all been children, and it is difficult for an adult to go about his daily business without encountering some sample of child behavior. Also, most students who take courses in child psychology are looking forward to careers as teachers or as parents, usually both, and this orientation gives them a special incentive in becoming involved in the course material. It is to this group that we dedicate our book.

Essentially, we have tried to bridge the gap between psychologists' views of child behavior and development and students' everyday experiences with children, including their memories of what it was like to be a child. We hope that our writing reflects our bifocal perspectives and goals in ways that are both intriguing and interesting. Our approach is also characterized by a belief that any subject becomes both more interesting and more understandable when it is presented in terms of a number of aspects or dimensions. A child, for example, may be understood biologically, but our understanding is enhanced if we can also see him as a social organism, as a personality, as affecting the behavior and attitudes of others, and as being affected by them in turn. To use a colloquialism, we have tried to present the "big picture" of the child, in the hope that as our readers look at this picture, they will see themselves, the children they were, in addition to the children they encounter.

In developing this book, we have been aided by many people, Gordon Ierardi, Wiley editor, was a helpful and supportive guide, as well as a valued and esteemed friend, before his untimely death. Miss Rosalyn Gill helped during the first edition, and Carolyn Clement aided with this one. We are also indebted to Fredi Lindgren for her editorial assistance, as well as to Leonard W. Fisk, Jr. for his extensive work on the chapter summaries and the instructor's manual. We also mention with thanks the contribution of Dr. Thomas W. Spencer, of California State University at San Francisco, who did a thorough review of the second edition that was of particular assistance in updating the present one. Other helpful reviews were received from William Kessen, of Yale University, Donald L. Peters, of The Pennsylvania State University, and Robert J. Seltzer, of Indiana University.

Durham, New Hampshire   Robert I. Watson
San Francisco, California   Henry Clay Lindgren

September 1972

Contents

Modeling and aggression. **The development of self and social awareness.** *The self.* MEMORY AND THE SELF. SELF-EVALUATION IN THE SELF-CONCEPT. ORIGIN OF THE SELF-CONCEPT. *Children's perception of parents.* PERCEPTION OF PARENTAL ROLES. **Peer relationships.** *Social participation. Socialization: general trends.* MODELING AND PROSOCIAL BEHAVIOR. *Social acceptance. Summary.*

Part 4 The Middle and Later Years

Psychology of the Child

PART I

Principles of Development

1 The History of the Study of Children

Children as Objects of Interest and Concern

When college students who have completed an introductory course in psychology decide to elect a second psychology course, more of them sign up for child psychology than any of the other areas of special interest. Child psychology courses also rate high as attractions in adult education programs. The subject obviously has a strong appeal for both the college student and the employed adult.

Attempting to analyze the reasons for the popularity of child psychology courses may seem like belaboring the obvious. Common sense would tell us that children are *intrinsically* interesting, that people willingly enroll in such classes because the subject matter is in itself interesting. After all, how can anyone resist the appeal of a child?

Early Attitudes Toward Children

A brief review of the history of child study shows us that such explanations are, so to speak, culture-bound. Children are no more intrinsically interesting than sardines or prime numbers or snowflakes. The fact that our forebears lived and died for thousands of years without showing the slightest interest in children as children is witness to that fact. The great interest in children today is not due to any irresistible attractiveness that children have always had for adults, but rather to a special combination of values, attitudes, and percepts that characterize modern Western

3

society today. To be sure, most parents probably loved their children in ages past (although the evidence for that is rather shaky) but they also regarded them in ways that were vastly different from the attitudes we have toward children today. For one thing, Western society from the end of the Roman Empire onward until the rise of the modern middle class was not even certain where childhood left off and adulthood began. As Philippe Ariès (1962)[1] pointed out in his review of childhood through the centuries, medieval children from the age of three or four onward took part in adult activities of all types. When the artists during the Middle Ages depicted a child (the Christ Child, for example), it was portrayed with the face, body build, and garb of adults, only smaller. It was not until 1430 that Luca della Robbia of Florence sculpted a marble choir loft decorated with singing and dancing children, who were *indeed* children; and thus created one of the first and most delightful naturalistic representations of children in modern times. Yet hundreds of years were to pass before children were generally regarded as having unique personalities. Today, proud parents keep pictures of their children in their wallets and purses to show casual acquaintances, and every home has its photographic record of children's progress from infancy to adulthood. During the medieval period, no one bothered: ". . . childhood was simply an unimportant phase of which there was no need to keep a record" (Ariès, 1962).

Ariès points out that it was only toward the end of the nineteenth century that society took steps to separate the world of children from the world of adults. This shift in thinking was symbolized by differences in clothing;

[1] A name followed by a year means that the reference cited or quoted will be found under the author's name in the References and Author Index at the end of the book.

before this, there was little difference between adult and child modes of dress. The change came first in middle- and upper-class families and only slowly and incompletely in lower-class homes, where children and adults dressed alike and there was no distinction between them either working or playing.

Some might explain the great interest in child psychology today in terms of the dictates of necessity—in other words, a parent or teacher *must* understand children in order to cope with them and their problems and to help them grow up properly.

This attitude, too, is a product of our times. In earlier periods, one did not try to understand child behavior, partly because childhood was not recognized as a different period of development, and also because children were not regarded as individuals with inalienable rights, but rather as nuisances and chattels. An Italian visitor to England about 1500 reported that children of both sexes were generally bound out as apprentices at the age of seven to nine for a period of from seven to nine years. Even children of the nobility were often sent away to be trained in the homes of others. So common was this placing out of children that people even gossiped when it was not done (Queen and Habenstein, 1967).

Discipline was swift, severe, and often capricious, even as late as the more enlightened nineteenth century:

"One mother, writing in a woman's magazine in 1834, told what happened when her sixteen-month-old daughter refused to say 'Dear Mama,' at her father's command. The infant was isolated in a neighboring room, where for ten minutes she screamed wildly. She was then taken out and once again commanded to say 'Dear Mama.' When she refused, she was whipped and asked again. This treatment was kept up for four hours, until the child finally obeyed the command" (Sunley, 1955).

Parents as a rule felt quite self-righteous about such treatment, because they believed that one of their responsibilities was "breaking the will" of their children. They seemed unaware that children could be socialized by anything other than harsh discipline. When physical punishment is the method of choice, and is even seen as "good for children," there is little point in trying to understand them.

The Era of Childhood Education

A major change in our thinking occurred when education began to be viewed as desirable and even necessary for children. The industrial revolution created a world with complex economics and complicated occupational roles, roles that could not be learned by imitation and example, as in an apprenticeship. A rapidly changing society called for people who had breadth of understanding and who had a good range of social and intellectual skills, people who could work together as members of organizations, initiate and conduct civic enterprises, and perform a variety of functions in different social settings. The schooling that the elite had been providing for their children and young people served as a first model. Literacy was a first goal in this education, followed by understanding of the world, its customs, traditions, and practices. Thus the modern school curriculum was born.

The harsh family discipline of the times was at first carried over into the schools virtually unchanged, but wiser schoolmasters soon realized that horses led to water do not necessarily drink, even when beaten. Furthermore, not every child of six or seven could read Cicero and do higher mathematics, and some adjustment had to be made in curricular materials, adapting them to children's levels of maturity. Attendance at schools was initially selective, then mandatory. The time occupied by school attendance was minimal at first; today it has come to occupy almost half the waking hours of half the days of a child's life between six and sixteen and beyond. Keeping children occupied at learning tasks for long periods called for increasing amounts of skill and understanding, and teachers began to look to child psychologists for answers to puzzling problems of instruction and classroom management.

The Democratic Tradition in Child Rearing

The difficulties encountered by the teachers were as nothing compared to the trials of the parents. As parents themselves became more educated, they began to entertain doubts about the desirability of the kind of discipline on which they had been raised. Perhaps a degree of competitiveness led them to wish they could be better parents than their own fathers and mothers. Reasoning and understanding became the order of the day, and punishment, when used at all, was an occasion for guilt and a sense of personal failure. Families today function much more democratically than they did a generation or two ago; children are both seen and heard; often they influence family decisions, especially when urged to do so by television commercials advocating the prompt purchase of exotic breakfast foods and new variations of familiar toys. The parent who eschews violence in favor of democratic methods is hard pressed to find ways to get his children to do what is patently best for them and he turns to the writings of child psychologists in the hope that they may show him the way out of his perplexing dilemmas.

In a very real sense, child psychology is a by-product of our striving to become democratic. In more traditional societies, the worth of the individual is more closely tied to his position and status in the social structure. Inasmuch as such societies are adult-oriented and male-dominated, women have subordinate status and children are coddled, suppressed, or ignored—whatever the prevailing custom happens to be—but seldom listened to or treated as individuals. Differences between American and French child-rearing patterns demonstrate this point. Françoise Dolto (1955), a psychoanalyst who has worked with both French and American families, reported that French parents, irrespective of their social class, are absolutely certain that they are bringing up their children "the correct way." When they consult with a psychiatrist, it is to ask that the child be admonished and influenced to accept his parents' direction more willingly, without further resistance. "The parents feel that, by virtue of their very position, their conduct and their demands are faultless" (p. 411). American parents, on the other hand, "are not at all sure about themselves as educators" (p. 411). As a consequence, they consult the psychiatrist both about their child's behavior and their own attitudes toward him. Note that the French and the American parents are both having problems with the child and, as a consequence, consult the psychiatrist, but that the French parents only want the child brought back into line, whereas the American parents are seeking to understand both the child and their relations with him.

Child Psychology and Self-Understanding

This brings us to a third reason for the interest that has been directed toward child psychology in recent years, particularly in America: the desire to understand oneself as an adult.

One of the paths to self-discovery lies through child psychology; through our study of the child, we believe that we can find some of the keys to the mystery that is ourselves—who we are. We all realize that we are in-finitely more than we were at birth, and our exploration of the events and experiences of infancy and childhood holds the promise of filling in the gap between ourselves at birth and what we are today. We examine the accounts of these events and experiences in search of ourselves, in search of explanations for our successes and failures, our inhibitions and capacities, our potentialities for pleasure and sorrow. We are, as North Americans, particularly interested in the environmental factors that impinge on the growing child, rejecting the European idea of biological predetermination. As confirmed environmentalists, we also believe that through understanding child development we can provide experiences for children that will help them realize their best potentials, growing up to become adults who will create a better society. This idealism helps to explain much of the interest we as North Americans have in child psychology, as it also explains much of our confusion and frustration when our children and young people behave in ways that seem less than ideal. At such times we wonder whether they would be behaving in a more satisfactory way had we brought our child-rearing practices closer to the ideal or whether the principles to which we subscribe are valid after all.

Our motives in studying children and their behavior are worth examining partly because they explain why some of the work done by child psychologists is more interesting, and other work, less so. Furthermore, most child psychologists (and most of the studies we will report) are North American, and we shall see that they differ in their approach and interest from European psychologists. For example, European psychologists are inclined to be more genetically-biologically oriented. They want to identify the inborn mechanisms and programs that set the pattern of development at the point of conception. North Americans are more concerned with environmental factors—mothering, stimulation, social class, and the like, as well as with the kinds of behavior that different environments produce. Although both European and North American psychologists are interested in the interplay between the child as a developing organism and his physical and social environment, Europeans tend to be more descriptive and categorical, and North Americans more interested in measurements and correlations. The work of both European and American psychologists can be of value to the student who is interested in child psychology as a way of pursuing a search for self. Both have something to contribute, as we shall discover in the following pages.

Early Theories about Child Development

We noted earlier that until the industrial revolution was under way, society made few provisions for adult-child differences other than size. Even when schooling became widespread, some aspects of these early attitudes lingered on, as reflected by attempts to teach children in terms of adult interests and aspirations. Textbooks were written to interest adults, not the children for whom they were intended. Education was regarded as an indoctrination into the ways of adult life and a means of getting the child to behave like an adult as quickly as possible.

Hand in hand with failure to appreciate age differences went a general obliviousness to other differences among children. Children were regarded much the same, one as another. They were treated the same, expected to behave in the same fashion, and not allowed to differ in any important way.

To the Greeks and Romans, the child was seen as a future citizen and as a member of a family group. With the coming of Christianity another view appeared. As a result of Adam's fall, all mankind is born in sin. A conception of the child as innately depraved arose, to hold sway for many centuries. The warning, "Spare the rod and spoil the child," exemplifies the attitude that was considered appropriate under these circumstances.

One of the first and most influential writers to dispute these early views of children and their treatment was John Locke (1632–1704). In 1693, Locke published his treatise, *Some Thoughts Concerning Education,* in which he recommended that young children should be permitted to give vent to their feelings and be restrained only rarely. He disagreed with the practice of apprenticing children or "farming them out" to other families, for he said that parents have a duty to be interested in their children's upbringing and should keep them nearby as much as possible. Being a good example was the best possible type of influence. Unlike the prevailing Calvinist concepts of child rearing, his attitudes toward children seem most modern: "The chief art is to make all that they have to do sport and play too."

Although Locke's book was intended for the use of English gentlemen, it received a great deal of attention throughout the British Isles and on the Continent and became a classic in educational theory.

Locke was also an influential thinker in the development of the scientific method. He rejected the belief that ideas and knowledge were innate. He maintained that much of our knowledge and understanding is initiated by contact with the environment, and that conclusions should be confirmed through empirical methods. The controlled experiment of modern sciences is a lineal descendant of that idea. Locke's work on sense perception, memory, association of ideas, pleasure and pain, the emotions, and the development of language also laid down the foundations of empirical psychology.

Early influences on child study

John Locke, 1632–1704

Jean-Jacques Rousseau, 1712–1778

Charles Darwin, 1809–1882

Johann Heinrich Pestalozzi, 1746–1827

Another writer who had great influence on attitudes toward children was the French-Swiss Jean Jacques Rousseau (1712–1778) who, like Locke, rejected the idea of original sin and the natural depravity of childhood. Although Rousseau's recommendations regarding child rearing are full of quirks and contradictions, what comes through as one reads them is a great respect for children as individuals. For example, parents should not insist that their child say "Forgive me," because he is innocent of wrong-doing. "Wholly unmoral in his actions, he can do nothing morally wrong, and he deserves neither punishment nor reproof." In another passage, he cautions against "overteaching" a child: "Leave childhood to ripen in your children. In a word, beware of giving anything they need today if it can be deferred without danger to tomorrow." (Rousseau, 1911).

Rousseau also expressed a strong faith in the innate goodness of the child, saying that "he is naturally disposed to kindly feeling because he sees that every one about him is inclined to help him, and from this experience he gets the habit of kindly feeling toward his species; . . ." Somehow, this basic kindliness becomes warped and frustrated as the child is integrated into society. Then he becomes "jealous, deceitful, and vindictive."

Another Swiss, Johann Heinrich Pestalozzi (1746–1827) also recognized the importance of understanding children and their behavior and proclaimed his faith in the inborn goodness of the child. He viewed the mother as the first and most significant educator of the child and urged her to trust her feelings toward it. Although a mother does not consciously teach her child and only intends to quiet him and occupy his time, she thereby opens up the world to him and prepares him to use his senses and powers of observation.

Charles Darwin (1809–1882) is best known for his classic *The Origin of Species,* the state-ment of his theories of evolution. Among his other works, however, he published a paper in which he reported his observations of his own first-born child, in whose behavior he saw supporting evidence of his theories. Incidentally, Darwin showed himself to be a sympathetic, understanding, affectionate father, in keeping with the new spirit of the times.

The work of Darwin and others on the study of evolution did much to stimulate interest in the study of the child. In testing the hypothesis of man's descent from animals, evidence derived from the study of children was utilized. The baby was regarded as a link between animal and man. Closely allied to this source of interest was the theory that the child relived or successively passed through the different stages of animal life (described by a phrase that a modern advertiser might well be proud to have coined—"ontogeny recapitulates phylogeny"). The crawling of the infant replicated the swimming movements of the fish; creeping, the locomotion of mammals; and running, the stage of man's movement. Survival of specific behaviors from prehuman days was sought, as in the grasp or "Darwinian" reflex, which, according to this theory, came about because the primate infant clung to the mother or tall branch for protection.

Today, the child is not regarded as a stage of evolution in the sense these early biological workers used this phrase. And yet childhood *is* a transitional period. Insofar as growth itself is a manifestation of the evolutionary process, the child is one performer in the evolutionary tableau.

The theory of recapitulation, erroneous though it may be, was rooted in the biology of the day. Hence, in it a *scientific* interest in the child was apparent. This helped to pave the way for the advance of modern child psychology, suggesting concepts which lent themselves to experimental test instead of providing merely a loose philosophical scaffolding.

The Beginnings of Child Psychology

Child psychology came into being from the scientific study of the child through the work of investigators from other fields. Even psychologists who contributed to this beginning were drawn from various specialties other than child psychology. These investigators had the characteristic that they were not primarily identified with child psychology when they did their important work. When it was done, they were the first child psychologists.

Preyer and the Baby Biography

Systematic observation is basic to all scientific investigation as the account in Chapter 2 will attest. Although occasionally attempted before the nineteenth century (for example, Rousseau's *Émile*), relatively systematic observations of children reached a position of importance and significance in the later decades of the past century. The first observational procedure used was the so-called baby biography. The observer, often both parent and scientist, made day-to-day observations of a single "normal" child, starting at or near birth.

The work of Wilhelm Thierry Preyer, a physiologist, is one of the earliest examples. In his account of his son's mental development during the first four years, he recorded careful and detailed observations, to which he added information contributed by others as well as comparative data from the behavior of animals. He observed the development of reflexes from birth and the influence of experience and learning. *The Mind of the Child* (Preyer, 1882), the book resulting from

his labors, is one of the great classics of child psychology, although it has been justly criticized for not sharply separating fact from inference. Another pioneer biography, noted earlier, was Charles Darwin's (1877) diary of his infant son, which was begun in 1840 but did not appear in print until almost 40 years later.

These biographies served the useful purpose of indicating clearly the value of carful observation and detailed study for the guidance of subsequent psychological workers. At the same time such intrafamily biographies have certain serious weaknesses. One of these is the fact that a naive observer is likely to see merely what he is looking for; especially desirable characteristics are apt to be noted, while such behavior as would smudge the family escutcheon might be overlooked. Such biographies differ from observational studies carried out today, which define in advance what is to be included and excluded and make provision for a check on the reliability of observations. (Reliability in this case can be achieved through independent and simultaneous observation by more than one person.)

In the baby biography many of the observations were unsystematic and subjective, recorded long after the event had occurred, and were thus subject to memory distortion; furthermore, the children selected for study were not typical of children in general. In spite of these weaknesses the baby biographies helped to lay the groundwork for a scientific child psychology by raising problems which could later be answered more adequately by improved methods.

Hall and the Questionnaire

Preyer's work was introduced to American readers by G. Stanley Hall (1846–1924), the father of the child study movement. As William Kessen (1965, p. 148) points out, "from the Boston kindergarten studies of 1880 until his death in 1924, Hall was committed to the notion that the study of development was at the heart of the problem of understanding man." Hall was stimulated by the theories of biological evolution and recapitulation. He theorized that the normal growth of the mind is to be seen as a series of stages more or less corresponding to those that early man and his ancestors went through in the history of the race. He thus was influenced by the point of view sketched earlier of the child as a stage of evolution. Hall collected data by asking teachers to question schoolchildren and thus was able to accumulate a great assortment of facts about childhood experiences and problems. The findings are exemplified by Hall's paper on children's lies published in 1882 and his study of the contents of children's minds published in 1883.

Shortly after the initial studies by Hall an abundance of efforts along similar lines by teachers, parents, and others appeared in the literature. Societies and associations dedicated to the study of the child by this technique were formed both here and abroad. The period of most intense activity in this way of studying children was from about 1890 to 1915.

It should be noted that Hall's (1891) own original work in this field was methodologically an improvement over both earlier and later studies using the questionnaire. For example, in his first study he used specially selected teachers, trained them to uniform methods of questioning, and met with them frequently for discussion and critique during data collection. However, he and his students later began the practice of circulating questionnaires on various topics to teachers and parents throughout the country. In this way, a great deal of information could be collected in a relatively short time over wide geographical areas. If the questions were too difficult for the children, their teachers and

parents were requested to interpret them to the children.

Still later the scope of the technique was broadened by circulation of questionnaires suitable for adults to record their childhood experiences as they remembered them. Some of the topics Hall studied from questionnaires were appetites, fears, punishments, dreams, memories, toys, early sense of self, prayers, crying and laughing, perceptions of rhythm, and motor abilities.

Only the simplest of statistical devices were used in analyzing the data, and no clearly defined or typical samples were gathered. Often the questions were worded to suggest the desired answer. The questionnaire as Hall used it also had certain inherent weaknesses: direct questioning of children, as he attempted it, often produces careless, evasive, imitative answers of a sort the child thinks the adult wishes to hear. His untrained recorders undoubtedly committed many sins both of omission and commission.

In large measure, the child study movement fell of its own weight. Parents and teachers uncritically, enthusiastically, and dogmatically stated the results of their superficial excursions into child development. Hall himself began to lose enthusiasm and turned his energies toward some of his other manifold interests, especially the psychology of religion and of senescence.

Despite its weaknesses, the child study movement of this period made definite contributions to the psychological study of the child. It led to increased recognition of the importance of empirical study of the child, brought forth a realization of the necessity of a critical evaluation of the methods used, and led to a recognition of the importance of childhood per se. It might also be added that the questionnaire approach fostered by Hall was the forerunner of modern personality testing.

Binet and the Intelligence Test

In 1904, the French Minister of Education named a commission to consider proposals intended to see that mentally retarded Paris school-children receive the best possible educational training. This commission decided that no child suspected of mental retardation should be eliminated from ordinary school classes without first taking a special examination. The task of developing and applying such an examination was taken over by Alfred Binet. The patriarch of all later psychological tests—the Binet-Simon tests—was thus the direct result of an administrative decision in educational practice.

The first great advance that Binet made in intelligence testing was to abandon dependence on the artificially simplified laboratory tasks used in mental testing prior to his efforts. Short, discrete, simple tasks, such as tonal memory, estimation of distance, speed of reaction, and rate of tapping are examples of previously used items. Early tests such as these had been found to have little prognostic value in work with children. Whatever they were measuring, it was not intelligence as the term is used today.

Binet, after many years of preliminary work, chose to use the more complex and realistic tasks of everyday life. In his first, or 1905 scale, done in collaboration with Theodore Simon, there were 30 tests. Illustrative of the content were the tests requiring verbal knowledge of objects such as parts of the body, naming of common objects, repetition of digits, drawing of a design from memory, finding the right word to complete a sentence, and definitions of abstract terms. These tests were arranged in increasing order of difficulty.

Not until the 1908 and the 1911 revisions of the scales did Binet make his second great contribution to mental testing—the grouping of tests as representative of the age at which they are usually passed. Mental age is the degree of intellectual development of an individual found by comparing his performance with that of other individuals of the same chronological age. Thus, a ten-year mental age is the degree of intellectual development attained by the average child of ten years. Through this procedure was established a frame of reference for interpretation of test results. Of course, crude comparisons using something analogous to this concept had been known before, as exemplified in remarks such as, "He has no more sense than a child." It was Binet's work, however, which firmly established this means of assessing intelligence test results in quantitative form.

In the United States, Lewis Madison Terman, a student of G. Stanley Hall, restandardized and extended the original Binet-Simon Scale for American use and published it in 1916 as the Stanford-Binet Intelligence Scale. This version soon became *the* standard testing instrument for measuring children's intelligence. In fact, it is no exaggeration to say that the principal task of many psychologists working with children was to administer the Stanford-Binet.

The scale had the great merit of being carefully and objectively standardized. It was constructed with attention to the standards of scientific rigor of its day. As a tool it proved its value in predicting educational status of schoolchildren, in aiding in the diagnosis of mental deficiency in children, and in serving as a means whereby many problems of child psychology became open to investigation. As Florence Goodenough (1949) pointed out, the rapidity with which Binet testing was adopted in the United States can be traced to a number of conditions that made the times right for its appearance. Compulsory school attendance was beginning to be vigorously enforced and the length of the period of schooling was increased. Backward students in the schools thus became an increasingly important problem. Juvenile delinquency as a social problem was coming into active prominence, and emphasis upon social welfare and prevention of emotional and mental defects was becoming part of the American scene. Such problems called for large-scale assessment by means of a standardized instrument, a commission which was admirably fulfilled by the several revisions of the Binet scales. The revision in current use appeared in 1960.

Montessori and the Freedom to Explore

Maria Montessori (1870–1952) was the first woman to be granted a medical degree by an Italian university. She early interested herself in the education of mentally retarded children, adapting methods devised by the French physician Edouard Seguin, whose techniques emphasized the training of perceptual and sensory-motor skills. She achieved amazing results with her methods, and retarded children trained by her were able to pass the state examinations in reading and writing prescribed for normal children. It occurred to her that the methods might also work with other children, and she opened a number of small schools in the slums of Rome for children aged three to six. As she worked with these children, she found that learning tasks based on simple materials—blocks, beads, rods, and the like—captured their interest to the point where they would work on a problem for an hour at a time.

Montessori stressed the natural development of children in wholesome and regulated surroundings. In her method, the teacher provides each child with appropriate learning materials and leaves the child free to handle them himself, but at the same time watches to see whether his reactions are appropriate. If not, the teacher may intervene and substitute another set of materials that seem more appropriate. Certain apparatus is used for certain types of learning, which in turn are related to "periods of sensitivity"—stages in a child's biological and mental development when he is considered to be more responsive to certain experiences.

Although Montessori's methods seem rather formal in contrast to the practices followed in most nursery schools today, they were revolutionary in her era. Her approach was a refreshing contrast to prevailing practices in Italian schools, which required children of all ages to remain in their seats, memorize facts from textbooks, and complete copybooks that were identical one to another.[2] Montessori attacked traditional educational policies, saying that children taught by such methods were not being disciplined, but "annihilated." School authorities, in their turn, retorted that her approach, which permitted movement and encouraged free exploration, was destructive of discipline. Experience with the Montessori method, however, showed that even problem children were refreshed and quieted through working with the learning materials.

Montessori's challenge to the educational establishment was in the tradition that extends from Locke, through Rousseau and Pestalozzi. Today, this tradition finds its expression in the free play experiences of the nursery school and kindergarten, and particularly in experimental and highly permissive schools started by "communes" of intellectuals in North America, whose educational philosophy stems from A. S. Neill's "Summerhill" in England.

There has been an attempt in recent years to revive the Montessori movement, but it seems out of phase with most current think-

---

[2] Most schools in most countries of the world, unfortunately, are still run more or less along these lines.

ing in America. Laura E. Berk (1971), who conducted an investigation of the effects of nursery-school environments on children's behavior, noted that the Montessori method calls for a high degree of order and routine. In contrast to a more conventional nursery school, the Montessori school in her study provided a prepared environment featuring highly structured materials and ritualized expectations for their use. Whereas children in the conventional nursery school were free to do anything they wished with learning materials, Montessori teachers found it necessary to intervene to demonstrate use of materials and to interrupt when children persisted in using them improperly. There was little interaction among the children in the Montessori school, in contrast to the other nursery schools, because children worked in groups under the direct supervision of teachers or on solitary tasks that demanded concentration. Berk also noted that the kind of child who succeeded in the Montessori school "was an adaptive complaint child, since there were many rules and strictures placed upon him and his progress depended on his conformity to these rules" (p. 865).

It thus appears that the Montessori method, which was radical in its day, now seems traditional and old-fashioned. It is also somewhat ironic that the type of schools that were so successful with the mentally retarded and with children from the slums of Rome are now attended almost exclusively by children of better-educated, affluent, middle-class parents.

Watson and S-R Research

John B. Watson (1878–1958) made a major contribution to the whole field of psychology by directing its attention to behavior that can be observed and precisely measured. Some of his work was on emotional responses in infants. Working with animals, particularly the white rat, and human infants, he found it impossible to use the then current major method of psychological investigation—introspection. Earlier investigators who had relied on the method of introspection had almost ruled out children as suitable subjects for psychological investigations because they could not be trusted to report accurately their conscious experiences. In dismissing introspection, Watson made infants and children legitimate subjects for psychological experiments. He militantly championed an approach to psychology, so-called *behaviorism,* which stressed the behavioral aspects; hence, the name he gave to it. Watson advocated and applied various objective techniques which did not depend on introspection.

One of the techniques he used was that of conditioning. As Pavlov had established, when a dog is making a definite response to a particular stimulus, any frequently accompanying stimulus is likely to be responded to in the same way. Thus, a dog simultaneously presented with food, to which he responds by a flow of saliva, and the sound of a bell will eventually respond by salivating to the sound of the bell alone. Introspection is neither possible nor necessary; the study is performed by presenting the dog with stimuli to which he responds.

Conditioning technique was applied by Watson to new-born infants to demonstrate how emotional responses are acquired. His most famous subject, Albert, aged eleven months, was reared in a hospital. When first tested, Albert showed no fear reaction to such stimuli as a white rat or a rabbit, a mask or cotton wool. He reached for practically everything brought near him. Fear, however, was shown by Albert at the sound of a steel bar being struck sharply.

In one of his experiments, Watson presented a rat to Albert. Just as he was reaching for

Pioneer psychologists and educators who influenced
important trends in child study early in the present century

G. Stanley Hall, 1846–1924

Sigmund Freud, 1856–1939

Alfred Binet, 1857–1911

Maria Montessori, 1870–1952

John Broadus Watson, 1878–1958

the rat, the bar was struck, producing a loud sound. Albert jumped violently, burying his face in the mattress. When the rat was presented a second time, Albert again reached for it, and again the bar was struck. This time, in addition to jumping violently, Albert began to whimper. A week later the rat was presented without the sound from the bar. Although he eyed the rat there was no tendency to reach for it, and when the rat was placed near him he withdrew his hand. Evidently, the two joint stimulations of the sight of the rat and the sound of the bar had had an effect. Thereafter, joint stimulations of rat and bar were made several times. After five simultaneous presentations the rat was presented alone. The instant Albert saw the rat he began to cry and crawl rapidly away from it. A subsequent check showed that the rabbit and the white mask, formerly eliciting no fear, now were reacted to violently. The fear of the white rat had *generalized* to these other objects. (Watson and Raynor, 1920)

This and other studies showed that fears might be acquired by conditioning. Watson also demonstrated a lack of specificity—that is, a generalizing of the stimulus—in the S-R relation; a conditioned response to one stimulus was also capable of being elicited by other stimuli having certain common characteristics with it. Conditioned responses were found to persist over periods of time. In general, Watson demonstrated that many fears of infants were acquired.

Through the work of such men as Preyer, Hall, Binet, Terman, and Watson, scientific child psychology came into being. Although wrestling with different problems in different countries, these men all shared a common desire for objectivity and the conviction that through quantitative measurement this could be assured. Each pioneer turned his back on philosophical and theological explanations of child behavior and worked toward the goal of new explanatory systems based on scientific research. Each is identified with a technique of study of the child which emphasizes to a greater or lesser degree exactitude and replicability of observations—the true beginnings of the scientific study of the behavior of the child.

Child Psychology in the Twenties and Thirties

Beginning in the last century and extending through the first twenty years of the present one, the pioneers carried on their research. During the 1920s and 1930s no longer were there only a few isolated giants as in the past, but rather many capable workers collectively making a considerable contribution to knowledge of child psychology.

The type of research was largely determined by advances in methodology made during the pioneering period. Devices for measuring diversified forms of behavior had been developed, and projects were now launched to measure these behaviors. These decades were thus characterized by specialized studies of the different capacities and traits of the child.

These were the years in which specific traits and capacities were being investigated. Emphasis was placed upon the quantitative and the objective. Specialized studies dealing with learning, intelligence, sensory capacity, motor performance, emotion, language, and thinking were carried on. Studies of intelligence and learning loomed the largest. Many workers would turn to a given field when a promising method or challenging theory was advanced, leaving other areas relatively inactive.

With the advent of the World War I the opportunity for large-scale psychological testing of the intelligence of army recruits arose. As a result, tests were developed which could be applied simultaneously to groups of individuals. Based on this experience tests were extensively developed for peacetime uses in the school systems. From the measurement of intelligence the use of tests spread to other areas of ability and personality.

There was a great deal of interest in behavioral norms during this period. Some researchers, like Arnold Gesell, were concerned with identifying the behavior that a child might be expected to display at various ages or stages in his development. Gesell's conclusions were based on his extensive observations of activity of thousands of infants and children. Gesell's work produced many valuable insights, but his conclusions were marred by a lack of concern for environmental factors. Not only did he assume that a child's developmental fate was entirely determined by his biological heritage but also that normal, healthy children are pretty much alike in the behavioral patterns they display at various ages. In spite of these limitations, Gesell's work produced some valuable data, and we shall be referring to his research from time to time when we discuss infancy and childhood.

Other researchers during the 1920s and 1930s were concerned with measuring more specific aspects of physical development and behavior and produced age and sex norms in the form of height and weight charts, intelligence and school achievement tests, and motor-development scales. Unfortunately, in their preoccupation with measurements, these research workers tended to lose sight of the *child,* who was the object of this measurement.

The investigation of "individual differences" was also typical, superficially appearing to contradict the comment that the individual child was lost to view. These particular studies of individual differences were concerned with variation in only one measure at a time, with the scores on this measure studied to show how the *group* varied. For example, we might administer the Stanford-Binet to 100 children and calculate the average IQ and the spread of scores from low to high. Thus, a given child might be close to the average, another only at the fifth percentile, and still another at the ninety-fifth percentile. Only one psychological measure was obtained from each of these children. All that was available was his score on a test, along with other children's scores on the same test.

At best some investigators administered several tests, and scores on a series of tests might become available for each child. Although a series of separate statements could be made about a child, nothing was known about the relationship of these trait scores to one another. To these investigators the child was merely a series of isolated scores. Norms, useful though they may be, are not explanatory. We must go beyond averages or individual scores to search for the reasons for the child's behavior and experience.

On this issue some doubt was expressed, and still is. "Where in this mass of facts," people asked, "is the child?" The segmented, compartmentalized approach was noted with misgiving by some parents, educators, and others who dealt with children in everyday situations in which the child appeared somehow different from the reactions described in textbooks in child psychology. These critics asked for general principles that would make the child understandable, that would make the isolated facts of his behavior cohere intelligibly. In short, they asked for general principles of personality organization, a theoretical framework into which these facts could fit.

This plea, although justified, was premature. What early critics of this lack of integrative knowledge of the child did not understand was that normative data were essential before a more integrated picture could be assembled. Before developing this theme of personality organization, destined to be a dominant note in the modern period, it is necessary to pause to consider the influence on child psychology of work in other fields.

The Influence of Other Fields upon Child Psychology

None of the pioneers in child psychology confined his interests to this one area. And just as these workers toiled in other scientific vineyards, researchers outside child psychology made substantial contributions to the cultivation of the new field. From its beginnings child psychology benefited from developments in psychoanalysis, child guidance, clinical psychology, pediatrics, education and educational psychology, and cultural anthropology. Let us consider briefly their various legacies.

Psychoanalysis

A major influence upon modern child psychology has been the work of Sigmund Freud, the founder of psychoanalysis, who was more or less a contemporary of Hall, Binet, and Watson. In fact, it was Hall who introduced Freud and his views to American psychologists. His influence is to be found not only in the direct utilization of psychoanalytic concepts and findings in child psychology today but also in the subtle, indirect, and sometimes unnoticed effects upon child-training practices. Bearing the imprint of his thinking are present-day practices concerning the child's experiences in his motivated strivings, parent-child relationships, the effect of unconscious influences, and our understanding of disturbed children.

Psychoanalysis arose as a method of treatment, but almost immediately was seen to be a means of also securing psychological data from patients which, in turn, not only gave rise to a theory of personality but also to a psychological system or school. At this juncture something will be said about psychoanalysis as a means of treatment and of securing psychological information. Psychoanalytic theory will receive detailed attention in later chapters.

Toward the end of the last century, while still practicing as a neurologist in Vienna, Freud became interested in the more psychological aspects of the problems of his patients. He began a search for a method of treatment to help them with their emotional problems. Ultimately he arrived at what is known as the method of free association in which the patient is asked to say anything that comes to his mind, to relate all of his thoughts as they occur, no matter how trivial, irrelevant, or distasteful they may be. His early patients spontaneously reported their dreams to him and, since they bore considerable resemblance to waking free associations, their interpretation was also incorporated into psychoanalytic procedure.

According to Freud, this "verbal mind wandering," with little or no direction on the part of the psychoanalyst, produced one invariable result—the report of childhood experiences. Gradually Freud was led to the conclusion that adult personality maladjustments were directly traceable to unfortunate experiences in childhood. Moreover, these experiences turned out to be predominantly of a sexual nature—feelings of love and hate toward father and mother, sexual encounters, jealousy of a brother or sister regarded as favored by a parent, and the like.

Freud became convinced that these experiences exerted a profound and heretofore unrecognized influence upon subsequent adult behavior and experience. Although the principles and techniques of psychoanalysis developed from work with adult patients, his findings indicated the crucial role of childhood experiences. Freud thus forcibly called attention to childhood as a critical period of development. Indeed, it was not until Freud emphasized that adult neurotic symptoms were the outcome of childhood experiences that these incidents were studied intensively in order to explain present behavior.

Freud was also struck by his patients' inability to see the significance of their free associations and dreams. Whereas it would be clear to him what the free associations signified, patients would deny, often vigorously, Freud's interpretations when he suggested them. The patients thought and lived on one plane, while on another level, that of the unconscious, many extremely important determinants for their behavior were treated by them as nonexistent. Only after many psychoanalytic sessions did the patients gradually begin to have insight into the unconscious meanings of what they were saying and doing.

Thus the extreme importance of unconscious determinants of behavior came to the fore. Freud was not the first to point out the significance of unconscious determinants, but he was the first to advance a method—free association—whereby they could be adequately studied. It is to Freud, then, that child psychology owes its interest in and appreciation of the importance of unconscious experiences in childhood.

Some psychoanalysts, like Anna Freud (1946), began to work directly with children. The method of free association is impossible to use with a young child, since it requires a more advanced verbal level than he possesses. The child psychoanalysts emphasized play activities in securing data for analysis and for interpreting their significance. They drew upon the symbolic significance Freud had found to be appropriate with adult patients.

The psychoanalyst is in a favorable position to develop insights into human behavior and to derive principles concerning it. He spends his professional life examining in minute and exacting detail the behavior and experience of a small number of individuals. Regularities are noted, and any deviation, no matter how trivial, does not escape scrutiny. His training makes him sensitive to the nuances of behavior, the evasions and deceptions so common in our adjustive behavior.

As a method of inquiry, psychoanalysis is essentially a means of reconstructing the individual's past, whether he is an adult or a child. These hindsights and clinical reconstructions may accomplish a great deal in the way of therapy. Psychoanalytic findings are more useful, however, as starting points for research by psychologists than as instances of verified research findings. Their results are not sufficient in themselves, and the further step of scientific verification of clinical finding is necessary.

Child Guidance

The original impetus for the formation of child guidance clinics arose from a desire to combat juvenile delinquency (Watson, 1960). Before the advent of such clinics, the child or adolescent might have had a physical examination by juvenile authorities, but no investigation into why he had performed the delinquent activities was conducted.

The first child guidance clinic was founded in 1909 by William Healy in Chicago. As the child guidance movement spread, the link to delinquency weakened, but not the other major force which led to the clinic's founding —the conviction that delinquency represented a form of psychological behavior that was amenable to modification. There has been a gradual broadening of scope of these clinics, as it was recognized that substantially the same means of treatment applicable to the

" AND IF YOU GET IN TROUBLE, USE THAT PHONE....
ITS A DIRECT LINE TO A CHILD PSYCHOLOGIST "

Like other branches of psychology, child psychology has become an applied as well as a research field.
(Al Johns. Reprinted from *APA Monitor*, December, 1970.)

delinquent could be applied to the emotionally disturbed nondelinquent child. This broadening came when it was recognized that delinquency and emotional maladjustments were different surface manifestations of what might be highly similar causative pictures.

During the 1920s the child guidance clinics were organized in various cities. Maladjustment in school and home, especially that centering upon parent-child relationships, came to the foreground. In many clinics today the influence of psychoanalysis is very evident. Adaptation of psychoanalytic principles and techniques to the setting and personnel of the clinic and to the nature and age of the patients came rapidly. The child, regarded during an earlier period as a passive victim of whatever circumstances were impinged upon him, came to be viewed in the dynamic tradition of psychoanalysis as a very active participant who could be helped by psychotherapy.

The unique characteristic of the child guidance clinic is the use of the so-called team approach, or the coordinated services of the specialists on the staff. Instead of one clinician serving in all phases of work, a flexible division of labor has evolved. In a typical child guidance clinic procedure, the social worker, as intake supervisor, talks to the person requesting clinical services and describes what might be done, provided the facilities of the clinic are appropriate for the child's needs. During the initial contact, a visit of both the parent (generally the mother) and the child is arranged. The child is seen by the psychologist for psychological testing; the child is observed, often in a playroom, by the psychiatrist; and the mother is seen by the social worker who secures a comprehensive family history and an account of the difficulties that the child is exhibiting. Often the psychiatrist also sees the mother.

After sufficient information is collected to make possible some tentative diagnostic appraisal, a case conference is arranged. The psychiatrist, social worker, and psychologist review the information that has been gathered and each discusses his interpretation of the difficulties the child is facing. A general plan of treatment is worked out and psychotherapists are selected for mother and child. In many clinics, the psychotherapist is chosen more for his particular fitness or availability, rather than because he is a representative of one or another of the disciplines. Thus, either a psychiatrist, a psychologist, or a social worker may be the psychotherapist for the child or mother. Later, there are conferences in which the talents of the staff are again pooled in efforts to further the progress of the child and mother.

Clinical Psychology

Some of the influences brought to bear on child psychology helped to shape the history of clinical psychology. The psychological test tradition, the influence of psychiatry and psychoanalysis, and the child guidance movement had their effects upon its development. Clinical psychology, in turn, affected their development.

The opening in 1896 of the Psychological Clinic at the University of Pennsylvania is said by many to mark the advent of clinical psychology (Brotemarkle, 1947). Lightner Witmer, the founder and director of the clinic, became interested in helping the educationally retarded and handicapped child. As a consequence, the great majority of the cases seen in the clinic came from the school systems. Cooperation with special teachers of the blind, deaf, and mentally defective was stressed.

This clinic, the first of many organized at universities and teachers colleges, found its particular area of competence in the everyday problems of the child, particularly those relating to academic success, such as reading. Of course, neither emotional nor nonschool problems were ignored; but less stress was placed upon them—perhaps because at that time there was less understanding of them.

Although clinical psychologists continue to work with schools, their work is increasingly being taken over by school psychologists, clinically trained individuals who specialize in school problems, especially at the elementary school level. As a major specialty in the psychological profession, clinical psychology has outgrown its beginnings in a quasi-educational setting and today clinical psychologists may be found in mental hospitals, child guidance clinics, homes for the mentally retarded, executive training in industry and government, and a wide variety of agencies that deal with intergroup and ethnic minority problems in urban communities. Indeed, it is the clinical psychologist who is taking the lead it what is termed *community psychology*—an applied branch of psychology concerned with treating a broad spectrum of sociopsychological tensions and disorders.

The psychologist who works in clinics, hospitals, or private practice today is likely to carry full diagnostic and therapeutic responsibility not only with educationally or intellectually handicapped but also with the emotionally disturbed child or adult. In the next chapter, these two facets of the clinical method of the psychologist, diagnosis and therapy, will be explored as tools of research in furthering our understanding of the child.

Pediatrics

The pediatrician is interested in the behavior and experience of the child, in health as well as illness. Pediatrics first emerged as a medical specialty in the middle of the nineteenth century. It was initially a field of teaching rather than practice. Even in diagnosis and treatment of physical disease the child presented his own unique problems.

Interest in the psychological aspects of child medical practice was slow to develop, not reaching any proportions until the end of the first quarter of the present century. Pediatric attention first focused on neurological conditions. This was followed by an interest in the testing of intelligence, which later broadened to an appreciation of the developmental sequence (Senn, 1948). In the meantime, knowledge of phenomena of conditioning and learning, particularly as stimulated by John B. Watson, led to theories on how to rear children.

In later years psychiatric-pediatric collaboration became closer, and child guidance clinics made provision for pediatric service. One expression of appreciation of the importance of psychological aspects was the attempt of some pediatricians to combat the prevalent, rigid, impersonal method of infant feeding by the clock and by the ounce. Pediatrics as a branch of medicine is based on physiology and anatomy, but today it is also concerned with the child as an individual person and as a psychological being.

The fields so far discussed as contributing to child psychology—psychoanalysis, child guidance, clinical psychology, and pediatrics—have in common a desire to understand and to treat the individual child. The intimate, face-to-face situations that practice in each field affords serve to provide its practitioners with excellent opportunities for learning about children. Their professional interests are directed toward variables which, when combined, offer some chance of seeing each child as a molar unit. Each child who is a patient presents a unique problem, personality, and array of environmental circumstances, and requires a unique form of treatment. Common strands are created by similarities in age, dependent status in a family or institution, and similar cultural backgrounds at a particular time. Each child, nevertheless, presents a different pattern of personality to the clinician and demands understanding in terms of himself.

Education and Educational Psychology

Child psychology and childhood, as education and educational psychology view it, owe much of their development to the same forces. The early attitudes toward the child previously sketched are as much the heritage of education and educational psychology as they are of child psychology. Preyer, Hall, Montessori, and Binet are part of the history of educational as well as child psychology.

In the more modern period, two individuals stand out as influencing studies of children's learning and of methods of teaching them—John Dewey and Edward L. Thorndike. John Dewey—philosopher, psychologist, and educator—probably had a more profound influence upon education than any other man of this century. His educational philosophy is widely known, though not always put into practice. Through his followers, his work led to the progressive education movement which, in essence, consists of the application of mental hygiene principles to education (Krugman, 1948).

The studies of Edward L. Thorndike on learning and related topics are part of this heritage. Sharing through his own research in learning the discovery of the child as an individual, he did much to document the newly appreciated fact of individual differences. The existence of individual differences was now established by research instead of being part of the intuitive grasp of the gifted few "born" teachers.

The work of the educational psychologists and that of their colleagues in other disciplines has led to a concern with the growth and development of each child, in spite of the educator's responsibility for large groups of children. Differentiated curricula, the activity program, the advent of elective subjects, concern with each individual student's interest and motivation, the appearance of learning readiness programs, and the presence of psychological services in the schools attest to education's concern with the individual child and his emotional as well as intellectual needs.

Cultural Anthropology

Findings in cultural anthropology have also influenced child psychology. Workers in this field attempt to understand man as a social being. In general, they study the so-called primitive cultures throughout the world, although some anthropologists have begun to interest themselves in contemporary cultures such as our own.

Prior to 1920, cultural anthropology used a descriptive and historical approach relatively uninfluenced by events in other fields (Kluckhohn, 1944). E. B. Tylor (1871) in his book, *Primitive Culture,* laid the foundation of the field. His most celebrated doctrine was that of *animism,* the view that primitive man tended to look upon all things as if they had consciousness or "soul." His point of view influenced the thinking of his contemporaries among evolutionists, especially those who viewed primitive man as essentially childlike. Later, this doctrine came under suspicion as being too sweeping and in need of qualification. True, there are primitive cultures that foster the development of animistic thinking, and, since children in our society think "animistically," an analogy is drawn. But the fact is that there are also primitive societies that discourage animistic thinking in an even more rigorous fashion than our own (Mead, 1932). Eventually, we have come to the position that there is no such thing as *the primitive;* rather there are *individuals* in many different so-

cieties. The pattern of living imposes individuality on members of primitive societies no less stringently than in ours.

Many of the contributions of such distinguished anthropologists as Margaret Mead have been impelled by a desire to test psychiatric-psychological hypotheses in other cultures. Often such studies focus attention on younger subjects and are avowedly developmental in character (Mead, 1954). For example, *Coming of Age in Samoa* and *Growing Up in New Guinea* reveal in their very titles a concern with the developmental sequence (Mead, 1928; 1930).

In her Samoan study, Mead was interested in testing the hypothesis that the so-called storminess of adolescence was a result of particular cultural conditions, instead of being an inevitable manifestation of maturational factors as it was generally assumed to be. Lacking power to construct experimental conditions, she turned to Samoa, a culture far different from our own. Careful and intensive study of fifty adolescent Samoan girls supplied evidence that adolescence was not a period of strain in Samoan society.

The finding is an instance of the corrective principle of "cultural relativity"; psychological assumptions may not be universally applicable. The possibility of cultural relativity must be entertained about given psychological phenomena until evidence becomes available that universal applicability is a reasonable assumption. Adolescence may be a period of stress and strain in American society, but failure to demonstrate its same phenomena in Samoa makes it probable that there are particular social circumstances that account for the difference.

Here the task of the anthropologist is the thankless one of gently but firmly indicating that in such and such a cultural setting a particular generalization does not hold, and hence, the behavior in question is culturally relative. To express the same issue more positively, anthropologists test psychological formulations found to hold in our culture in other cultures to see if they also apply, which they must if they are to have universal validity.

Findings of the anthropologists have forced a recognition that we can never observe human beings who have not been subject to cultural influences. Their findings further indicate that cultural factors are important during the formative phase of personality development; hence, the emergence of the problem of the interrelations between personality and culture.

Researchers in child psychology must of necessity be concerned primarily with relatively narrow aspects of child behavior in order to maintain control of the various elements in their research. Persons who *use* the theories and findings of child psychology in their work—psychotherapists, teachers, social workers, pediatricians—must keep the whole child in view. Today the tendency is for professionals to view the child as an individual in a total situation, who functions as the result of individually determined forces and because of the environmental circumstances pressing upon him. The beginnings of this point of view were apparent in the earlier periods, as in Freud's psychoanalytic view which stressed the effect of adverse circumstances upon personality development. There was definite recognition of external influences in the child guidance movement. William Healy's first major work, *The Individual Delinquent,* showed delinquency as a situational phenomenon, not a characteristic of the child himself. Within child psychology itself, this stress upon the total social situation gave impetus to social psychology.

This emphasis on all aspects of the child in a total situation has added impetus to another trend of the modern period—the importance of multidiscipline child research institutes. Often psychologists predominate but the personnel of such institutes may also include researchers from different areas of specialty and interest, such as psychiatrists, pediatricians, nutrition experts, and physiologists. Many of their long-term studies have now been going for so lengthy a period that children evaluated in infancy and early childhood have been seen again as adults. Childhood characteristics can now be related to adult counterparts in the same individuals.

The Institute of Child Study of the University of Toronto received a major impetus in its research when identical quintuplets, born to the Dionne parents in 1934, were housed in a nearby hospital for an extended period of time. Studies were carried on of the physical and cognitive development of these children, which in turn stimulated a variety of long-term research programs in close conjunction with many service and training functions. The Institute has its own affiliated nursery, kindergarten, and elementary schools, keeps in close touch with the parents of its students, and trains not only research workers but also teachers and others in the University who desire training in child behavior. Other leading institutes include those at the Universities of Colorado, California (Berkeley), Iowa, and Minnesota; the Merrill-Palmer Institute in Detroit; the Fels Research Institute in Yellow Springs, Ohio; and Purdue, Yale, Harvard, Stanford, and Cornell Universities. In Europe, Piaget's Institute at the University of Geneva is a major center for the study of cognitive processes in children. Arising from the same recognized need for interdisciplinary collaboration was the organization in 1933 of the Society for Research in Child Development, open to all workers on child research.

The interplay between science and practice is characteristic of the modern period in child psychology. The healthy integrating exchange thus emerging is borne out by many of the facets of history previously outlined. Clinical-child psychologists, or, if you prefer, child-clinical psychologists, are one manifestation. Still other child or developmental psychologists are to be found within education, home economics, pediatrics, parent education, marriage counseling, correctional work, and the gamut of children's agencies. Research stations such as those mentioned above are very sensitive to questions of practice.

This brief review could not do justice to the many influences brought to bear on our knowledge of the behavior and experience of the child. General experimental psychology, most particularly the field of learning, has contributed to child psychology in the modern period. The contribution of sociology, through its study of the family, has not been mentioned; nor have the insights and findings of the linguist, philosopher, artist, or religious leader. These, too, have made contributions to the modern period in child psychology.

The Modern Period in Child Psychology

Child psychology, as an academic discipline, is likely to be included under the larger heading of developmental psychology. Developmental psychologists are concerned with theories and empirical evidence as to developmental trends throughout the life-span, from conception to old age and death. It is also concerned with similar trends in other animals—monkeys, rats, and mice, for example. Some of the work with these laboratory animals has shed considerable light on developmental tendencies in man. Developmental psychology deals with the behaviors that characteristically occur at various ages and stages of development. A developmental psychologist is likely to be interested in intercorrelations among the behaviors that appear at a given stage and in the differences that occur between the behaviors that appear at one stage and those appearing at other stages.

Child psychology is the largest branch of developmental psychology. It is in infancy and childhood that the greatest number of changes take place in the shortest period of time; hence, there is more to observe and more data have been accumulated by researchers. Another reason for our greater store of data may be found in our great interest in children and in childhood today, a topic we discussed earlier in this chapter.

We should also note that children are, by and large, a captive group of subjects. They are highly accessible by reason of their being in hospitals as neonates, in school as pupils, and as patients in child guidance clinics. They are usually quite cooperative and seem to enjoy being interrogated and observed. Unlike adults, they are unlikely to question the motives of the researcher, or are satisfied with such explanations as, "We are going to play a game, you and I." More intelligent than the white rat, and less suspicious or preoccupied than the average adult, a child is in many ways the ideal research subject. It is not surprising that we have gathered more data about children than we have about adolescents or adults. The fact that children are more vulnerable than adults and hence more easily exploited does create ethical problems, of course, and psychologists have to be unusually careful about the way in which they design and conduct their research.

The work of developmental psychologists, like other fields of human endeavor, is characterized by styles and trends. A generation ago, there was much interest in the relative effects of environment and heredity on intelligence, with learned and sometimes heated arguments on both sides. The controversy reached an impasse and faded out, leaving the most vocal groups on each side unconvinced of the arguments of the other, but unwilling to pursue the discussion further, having amassed enough evidence to reassure themselves. Most psychologists resolved the problem for themselves by concluding that intelligence was a function of *both* heredity and environment, with heredity setting the limits to the intellectual potential that could be developed, and the quality of the environment determining the amount that could be developed within the ranges set by heredity. This state of relative quietude continued for about 25 years, when the controversy was reopened by the publication of Arthur Jensen's (1969) observations on racial differences in intelligence. We shall have more to say about this later, but the point here is that the heredity-environment issue, which had lain dormant for a quarter of a century is once again a major topic on the agenda of the developmental psychologist.

Most research in child psychology today can be related or contrasted in some way or another with two major research styles or orientations. These approaches could be labeled as *genetic* or *developmental* and *environmental* or *experimental*. The terms are not mutually exclusive, for geneticists generally concede that environmental factors are extremely important, and environmentalists agree that inherited, biologically determined behavioral tendencies are the starting points for everything that follows. The difference between environmentalists and geneticists lies more in what is emphasized in their research, the research methods they use, the kind of theories or hypotheses they test, and the kinds of assumptions they make before their research is undertaken.

A major force in the environmentalist camp is experimental psychology, with its behaviorist orientation. In a typical experiment, the effects of variations in the organism's environ-

ment are compared, all other factors being controlled. The organism's basic nature—whether it is a two- or a three-year-old child, whether it is a rat or monkey, or whatever—is, of course, taken into consideration, but the chief interest here is its *behavior:* how it *responds* to the *stimuli* in its environment. This focus on stimulus (S) and response (R) has led to the designation "S-R research." S-R research is particularly well adapted to the study of small, precisely thought-out experiments, particularly in the field of learning, and it is a credo of the environmentalist that all behavior is either learned or is modifiable through learning.

The geneticist viewpoint is primarily oriented to the organism as such. It seeks to understand the mechanisms and their programming that produce consistencies and regularities in behavior. A basic assumption is that the regularities *do* exist, and the task of the psychologist is to find out what they are. This leads to a concern with structure, either in psychological or in physiological terms. Piaget, for example, is concerned more with the psychological structure, as paced by physical and neurological development. Other concepts that are of central interest to genetically oriented psychologists are maturation and the identification and description of stages of development.

Sheldon H. White (1970), in a review of the effect of S-R learning psychology on child psychology, maintains that child psychologists prior to the 1950s accepted a viewpoint that was mainly genetic. They were not particularly interested in conducting experiments and were not much concerned with learning. In the end, this led to a kind of sterility or impasse. Roger G. Barker (1951), in the first survey of child psychology published in the *Annual Review of Psychology*, reflected this situation when he complained that there did not seem to be any definitive body of research that could be called "child psychology" and that there was "little evidence of the existence of a professional group of skilled child behavior specialists" (p. 1). In support of this statement, he reported that his survey of the literature had turned up only one paper reporting original observations or experiments for every three papers devoted to programmatic, didactic, or speculative expositions. He noted "a great demand by professional people for scientific information about children," and regretted that "child psychology should be relatively inactive at a time when so much is expected of it" (p. 3).

According to White, the situation was in a state of change even as Barker wrote. American experimental psychology, taking its cue from the behaviorism of John B. Watson, was developing two strong currents of research. One current derived from the work of Clark L. Hull (1943), who developed a learning theory that served as a starting point for S-R research. The other current, best typified by the work of B. F. Skinner (1938), has dealt with what has been called "the experimental analysis of behavior." The intense activity in these two branches of learning research inevitably infiltrated child psychology. Robert R. Sears (1943), who was initially interested in testing the validity of psychoanalytic theories, was one of the first to undertake the development of an S-R learning theory within the context of child psychology. This attempt did not come off as was hoped, according to White, but Sears and his co-workers did succeed in producing an interesting and valuable body of research dealing with children's socialization.

The infusion of S-R research interests and methods also had a revitalizing effect on the entire field of child psychology and led to research in children's learning; a variety of cognitive areas, such as attention, perception, curiosity, stimulation; emotional responses, including anxiety; and the modification of undesirable behavior.

White believes that the influence of S-R learning theories and methods reached its peak during the 1960s and is now on the decline. Although the S-R approach stimulated a great deal of research and enabled child psychologists to get some new and intriguing perspectives on children and their behavior, it failed to provide them with any synthesizing concepts or any central theories. S-R ways of approaching research also have their sterile aspects. Consider this description of a developing child:

"The developing child may be adequately regarded, in conceptual terms, as a cluster of interrelated responses interacting with stimuli" (Bijou and Baer, 1961, p. 14).

Such a formulation is undoubtedly useful in conducting small-scale S-R research, but it is singularly unsatisfying to a child psychologist who needs some overall theoretical framework that he can use to organize and sort out all he knows about children and their behavior.

The child psychologist who confronts the question of whether to use an S-R environmentalist approach or a genetic-developmental approach in his research is in a quandary today. On the one hand, he is attracted by the methods of the tough-minded, empirical S-R experimentalist, who regards with skepticism partially tested theories and unproven speculations about behavior, but on the other hand, he is afraid that close adherence to the S-R line will lead him to lose a great deal of important data and leave him with only a fragmented picture of the behavior he is trying to understand.

A major fact about children is that they are continually changing as they grow, develop, and mature. The S-R psychologist is not particularly interested in those changes, except as they can be related to changes in the environment. In the end, the child psychologist, being more interested in the child than the environment, typically finds himself in the genetics-development camp, but using S-R methods as much as possible to test his hypotheses. As White points out, there is a move toward a cognitive functionalism, in which psychologists conduct experimental studies with cognitive (thinking) functions and, at the same time, try to integrate data from neurological studies. This neurological work has been carried on extensively in Russia, and White sees it as lying somewhat apart from both the genetic and the S-R traditions.

Another trend that appeared in the 1950s was a strong current of interest in personality and socialization. This interest was due in large part to the strong psychoanalytic orientation that was prevalent in clinical psychology and in the child guidance movement. Its earliest manifestations consisted of testing Freudian theories through various kinds of longitudinal and cross-sectional studies. When the results of these studies proved to be disappointing, the focus of interest was broadened to include other approaches, particularly the influence of social factors such as social class, child-rearing practices, and the effect of group norms. There was also considerable investigation of personality traits and "constructs": anxiety, hostility, aggression, level of aspiration, and needs for achievement, affiliation, and dependency. The relative stress given S-R research and personality studies can be seen by an analysis of the contents of a Children's Bureau bulletin in 1961, which showed that 13% of the studies during a recent period dealt with topics that could be considered more or less in the S-R tradition: physical, motor, perceptual, cognitive-intellectual, and learning processes. This proportion was in contrast to 20% for social, familial,

cultural, and personality research. Emotional disturbance in children accounted for 24%, while applied research in education, health, and social service accounted for the remaining 43%.

A decade later, the picture had changed radically. A tally of the number of papers in various categories abstracted in the *Child Development Abstracts and Bibliography* for the first quarter of 1971[3] shows that some 37% of the studies were of the S-R-experimental type, in contrast to 13% for personality, sociology, and social psychology. A statistical breakdown of papers cited by Elkind and Sameroff (1970) in their review of developmental psychology in a recent edition of the *Annual review of psychology* shows much the same picture in that studies dealing with personality and socialization make up only 20 to 25% of the total number listed under the headings of early childhood and middle-to-late childhood. The point made by White relative to the decline of S-R influence is also supported by the fact that only 18% of the studies in these headings dealt with learning research.

The field that is attracting the greatest amount of research interest appears to be cognition: almost 60% of the studies cited came under the headings of cognition, cognitive development, perception, perceptual and motor processes, language, and intelligence. The growing edge of child psychology today seems to be the research into cognitive areas. This trend has come about partly because the nature of the subject—the child—lends itself more to a genetic than an S-R treatment. As White points out, there is no learning theory in child psychology, no learning theory has ever been developed from research with chil-

[3] Vol. 45, Nos. 1 and 2, February–April, 1971, published by the Society for Research in Child Development.

dren, and learning theories were never designed to accommodate the data of children's learning. The fading attraction of Freudian theory has been replaced by a welling up of interest in cognitive development, as typified by the theories and research of Jean Piaget and Heinz Werner. Research activity in the cognitive field has also been stimulated by intervention programs to help children of the disadvantaged poor to develop skills that will enable them to profit from classroom experiences. Although cognitive research is more or less based on maturational considerations, and hence is more biologically oriented, there has been much concern about research design, control of variables, and environmental influences, a concern that gives it a flavor that is decidedly more "scientific" than the fact-gathering expeditions and the speculative theorizing of the period between the two World Wars.

Summary

Although common sense would tell us that children are intrinsically interesting, our forebears had an entirely different opinion. From the end of the Roman Empire until the rise of the modern middle class, Western society did little to discriminate between children and adults. Childhood was merely a period of transition. Discipline was severe and, in some countries, children were bound as apprentices at an early age.

One of the first and most influential writers to dispute these views was John Locke, who recommended that young children be permitted to give vent to their feelings and disagreed with the practice of apprenticeship. Locke also rejected the notion that ideas and knowledge were innate and thus laid the foundations of a modern, empirical psychology. Rousseau and Pestalozzi rejected the doctrine of original sin and, like Locke, believed in the natural innocence of childhood.

These men helped awaken a real interest in children as such. This developing concern, however, seemed to spring spontaneously from society as a whole, as well as from the pens of these writers. One possible explanation for this new interest stems from an increasing need for educated people to fill the complex occupational roles of a newly industrial society. Parents and teachers were forced to adopt a more realistic view of childhood in order to educate their children to fill this need. As parents became better educated, they began to doubt the desirability of the kind of discipline on which they had been raised.

The scene was set for the development of child psychology over a century ago. Darwin looked for support for his theories in the behavior of his infant son. He made the detailed observations that are necessary to a genuinely scientific study of child behavior. Preyer also published a "baby biography" in which he carefully recorded his son's mental development. Although biographies of this sort are useful, they tend to be biased by atypical samples and a lack of observational reliability.

G. Stanley Hall introduced the questionnaire technique, a definite methodological improvement, but still not a refined enough instrument to make any but the most superficial study of children. This advance in quantitative method was continued by Alfred Binet. Asked to develop a tool to diagnose mental retardation, Binet responded with the Binet-Simon intelligence tests. These tests were noteworthy because they made use of realistic tasks from everyday life rather than the simplified laboratory tasks used previously. Binet also grouped and standardized the tests according to the age level at which they were usually passed. Both the test and the concept of mental age have survived, the latest revision of the Stanford-Binet dating from 1960.

In a sense, child psychology is a by-product of our striving to become democratic. In more adult-dominated societies, children are seldom treated as individuals. In France, for example, parents are certain they are bringing up their children in the "correct way," whereas American parents are more likely to question their own behavior and attitudes toward the child.

In this respect, Montessori's educational methods are in contrast to traditional European approaches. Building on the techniques of Seguin, who concentrated on the training of perceptual and motor skills, she achieved amazing results in the training of retardates. Encouraged by her success, she went on to apply the concept of free exploration in a structured environment to normal children, with similar results. Her methods, though revolutionary in their day, now seem dated in comparison to modern preschool practices.

John B. Watson made a major contribution to the whole field of psychology by directing its attention to behavior that can be observed and precisely measured. By dismissing introspection, the behaviorist made infants and children legitimate subjects. In one experiment, Watson used Pavlovian conditioning procedures to demonstrate the acquisition and generalization of an emotional response.

The advent of World War I offered psychologists the opportunity of large-scale psychological testing, a trend that resulted in the collection of massive amounts of normative data. The typical investigation of "individual differences" on single measures reflected the narrow concerns of the psychologists of that era. This information gathering, however narrow, was the necessary precursor of the more integrated science we know today.

The work of Freud, the founder of psycho-analysis, has been a major force in the development of modern child psychology. Freud believed that maladjustments of the adult personality were directly traceable to stressful childhood experiences and that many of the determinants of behavior were unconscious. In order to help patients gain insight into these unconscious processes, Freud developed the free-association technique. Because children are not capable of verbal free association, the psychoanalyst stresses observation of play activities as a source of information. The psychoanalytic findings gained from this sort of procedure are more useful as a source for new ideas than as verification of research findings.

Some of the influences brought to bear on child psychology helped shape the history of clinical psychology. Lightner Witmer, the founder of the Psychological Clinic at the University of Pennsylvania in 1896, was primarily interested in helping the educationally retarded or handicapped child. Since that time, clinical psychology has outgrown its beginnings in a quasi-educational setting and branched out to a wide range of settings.

The child guidance clinic, for example, has played an important part in the history of child psychology. The unique characteristic of the child guidance clinic is the use of a co-ordinated team consisting of social worker, psychologist, and psychiatrists.

The history of educational psychology is inextricably entangled with the history of child psychology: Preyer, Hall, Montessori and Binet are part of the tradition of both. In the modern period, however, two individuals stand out as pioneers in the understanding of childrens' learning—John Dewey, philosopher, psychologist, and educator, and Edward L. Thorndike, discoverer of the basic principles of learning.

Findings in cultural anthropology have also influenced child psychology. Margaret Mead, for example, studied the adolescent period in

Samoa, finding that the storminess of adolescence is "culturally relative." Findings like this serve to remind us that psychological assumptions cannot always be universally applied and that we must view the child and his total environment as a functional entity. This emphasis on all aspects of the child in a total situation has also added impetus to multidisciplinary child research institutes.

Child psychology is included under the larger heading of developmental psychology. The developmental psychologist studies developmental trends throughout the life-span and is likely to be interested in intercorrelations among the behaviors that appear at a given stage and in the differences that occur between the behaviors of different stages. A generation ago, there was much interest in the relative developmental influences of heredity and environment. These two approaches can be labeled genetic or developmental, and environmental or experimental. Experimental psychology, with its stimulus-response analysis of behavior, is a major force in the environmentalist orientation. Where the environmentalist believes that all behavior is learned or can be modified through learning,

the geneticist looks for the innate structure and biological "programming" that produces consistencies in behavior.

The excitement generated by experimental psychologists like Hull and Skinner during the last several decades carried over into child psychology, and has led to a large body of research on children's learning. This approach, however, has failed to provide a unifying theoretical framework and, although the tough-minded S-R methodology remains, the current trend is toward the genetic-development orientation.

Another trend that appeared in the 1950s was a strong interest in personality and socialization. The original focus of research moved from testing Freudian theories to studies of the effects of social factors such as social class and child-rearing practices, and personality traits and constructs, like anxiety, aggression, and need for achievement.

The field that is attracting the greatest amount of current research interest is cognition, the structure of intelligence, language, and perceptual and motor processes. This is typified by the work of men like Piaget and Werner.

2 The Scientific Study of the Child

. . . Spare the rod and spoil the child.
Samuel Butler (1600–1680)

Children and fooles cannot lye.
Proverb collected by John Heywood (1497–1580)

Children learne to creepe ere they can learne to goe.
Ibid.

Burnt child fire dredth.
Ibid.

Children and fools want everything, because they want wit to distinguish; . . .
George Savile (1633–1695)

Children are what their mothers are.
No fondest father's fondest care
Can fashion so the infant heart.
Walter Savage Landor (1775–1864)

The Scientific Approach

All knowledge begins with observation. When many people make similar observations leading to similar conclusions, the result is a consensus and an accepted "fact," which becomes commemorated in common sayings, homilies, old saws, and poetry.

Observations are not, however, independent of the experience of observing. We put something of ourselves—our beliefs, our values, our psychological needs—into every act of observing. The fact that a number of people may come to similar conclusions as a result of observing certain kinds of behavior helps to eliminate individual quirks and variations in the data, but it does not avoid the effect of beliefs held by all the members of a culture. The effect of this systematic bias cannot be overestimated. Until Galileo performed his classic experiments on the acceleration of falling objects, it was an accepted "fact" that heavier objects fell faster than lighter ones. It was, as one might say, "common sense."

Some of the work of a science, particularly a behavioral science like child psychology, is concerned with testing "tried-and-true" behavior principles, like "spare the rod and spoil the child." In order to undertake such an enterprise, a scientist turns to methods that are more objective and that go beyond the simple steps of everyday observation and consensus. Measurement is one of these methods. It was by measuring the time taken by different objects to reach the ground that Galileo was able to refute the common sense of his day.

As science moved from the testing of common-sense "facts" to the investigation of phenomena more removed from everyday experience, it developed a paraphernalia of intricate instruments: microscopes, retorts, finely calibrated equipment of all sorts, electronic devices, and the like. The general public, who viewed the proliferating activities of scientists with awe and wonder, came to associate this "hardware" of science with the entire scientific undertaking. It was a natural step from this association to the conclusion that it was the "hardware" that made science scientific. This is, of course, a misinterpretation, and many a quack and charlatan has capitalized on this error.

What makes any kind of observation or investigation scientific, is the method that is employed. A true scientist is scrupulous about eliminating all possible sources of bias that might interfere with the objectivity of his observation and measurement. If he is investigating a concept that has widespread acceptance, like "spare the rod and spoil the child," he goes to unusual lengths to compensate for biases resulting from his membership in a culture that accepts such a concept as "truth." The test of the scientific value of any such investigation is its *replicability*—that is, any scientist anywhere, who observes the same phenomena under similarly controlled conditions should come to the same conclusions as his.

Conducting scientific investigations under these rules requires a very rigorous kind of discipline—for instance, an ironclad commitment to report whatever findings emerge, irrespective of whether they support or discredit the hypothesis that is being tested.

A formal scientific investigation is likely to begin with a *hypothesis,* a guess about the relationship between two or more classes of events or *variables*[1] say, between "rod sparing" and "child spoiling." Often the hypothesis grows out of theories about human behavior or attempts to interpret the findings of other research studies. Piaget's theories and clinical observations relative to the regularity with which certain modes of cognitive functioning appear before or after other modes has led psychologists to attempt experiments in which children at one stage of development are tempted to use cognitive modes that are ahead or behind them in sequence, for example.

Behavior, as well as variations in behavior, may be understood in terms of their causes, and scientific investigation is concerned with isolating and identifying such causes. The variable that is suspected of being a cause becomes the *independent variable* in a research study, while the variable that is presumably affected by changes in the independent variable is termed the *dependent variable*. If we are testing a theory that children learn a task best by self-directed interaction with their environment, rather than by being instructed, the treatment (noninstruction or instruction) becomes the independent variable and the degree of skill demonstrated becomes the dependent variable.

Experimental Methodology

The experimental method is the classic form of carrying out S-R research. Cause-and-effect relationships are explored by introducing a stimulus (an independent variable) into a

[1] Anything that varies is a *variable,* irrespective of whether we are referring to visible variations, like height and weight, or "invisible" ones, like love, hostility, and anxiety. Height and weight can be measured more or less directly, but love, hostility, and anxiety can be measured only indirectly, by questionnaire responses, behavior toward various objects or persons, changes in heart rate, palmar sweating, and so forth.

controlled situation. The stimulus may be the intensity of sound, the length of exposure to a visual stimulus, or the like. As the experimenter varies the independent variable through prearranged steps, he observes the effect of this antecedent stimulation upon consequent changes in the dependent variable, that is, the response resulting from the stimulation.

The experimenter, it is important to note, exercises a degree of control over the antecedent. He uses this control in such a way that the independent variable is altered in a specific and known manner, and this makes it possible for the original investigator or someone else to repeat the experiment. The need for these "prearranged steps" implies a laboratory situation, which is usually the setting for an experiment. An experimenter causes an event to happen at a certain time and place, and he is thus alerted to make accurate observations by knowing when and where to undertake them.

Laboratory conditions are desirable because they facilitate the scientific control of variables that might confuse the reading of results. Let us examine an experiment to see how the experimenter does this. Cynthia Turnure (1971) was interested in studying the effect of the mother's voice on infant behavior, particularly the extent to which infants could distinguish between various versions of the mother's voice, as well as between the mother's and a stranger's voice. She controlled the stimulus situation by tape-recording the mother's voice and a strange woman's voice. She could, of course, have used a man's voice or a child's voice for the control stimulus, but if she had done that, she would not know whether any observed differences in response were due to the "motherness" of the stimulus or its "adult-femaleness."

Turnure instituted even more intricate controls. The infants heard three versions of the mother's voice: normal, slightly distorted, and grossly distorted. This enabled the researcher to determine the extent to which infants were using a "perceptual-cognitive model" of their mothers as a basis for determining which stimuli could be accepted and which rejected as characteristic of "Mother."

Another type of control was introduced by having several subjects of both sexes. The use of one subject would have raised the question of whether differences in response were caused by the idiosyncratic behavior of a single infant; if she had used subjects of the same sex, her results would have left unresolved the question of whether the observed differences were characteristic of only one sex. The more generally applicable the results of an experiment, the more interesting they are, because they tell us more about human behavior in general and are not limited to the individuals under observation.

Turnure was interested in controlling a second variable: age. As a consequence, her experiment included three groups of subjects, aged three, six, and nine months, respectively. This made her results even more interesting, because they not only told us about three-month-old infants, but also about infants at six and nine months as well. Although her study was a cross-sectional one, in the sense that it studied a tiny sample of infanthood at the three ages and not the same infants at three ages over the six-month span from three to nine months, we can nevertheless assume, in the absence of contrary evidence, that differences in the behavior of the infants at each of the three ages are probably typical of any infants of those ages, and hence are the result of maturational processes. The assumption that cross-sectional studies will give data that permit longitudinal interpretations[2] becomes

[2] That is, changes in the same individuals noted over an extended period of time.

harder to defend for studies of adults, but it seems to be defensible for studies of infants and children.

The dependent variable presented a problem. How can one determine whether infants are responding differentially to various stimuli? Turnure resolved this difficulty by making motion pictures of each infant and by noting all types of movement: smiling, frowning, crying, mouthing, vocalizing, and limb-mouth contact. Controls were also instituted by having 30-second neutral "no-stimulus" periods before and after the stimulus-presentation period. This enabled her to score responses separately for the control and the experimental periods. The scoring of the filmed responses was done by another research worker who did not know the purpose of the experiment—still another type of control. Ordinarily, the scoring would have been done by two or three different observers, in order to determine the *reliability* of the scores. Previous use of this type of observational method showed that it had a high degree of reliability, however, and this extra control was not used.

Turnure's results, incidentally, showed that, with increasing age, infants became quieter during stimulus presentations. Turnure accounted for this in terms of increased attention—that is, the older the infant, the more likely he was to reduce motor activity in order to "concentrate" on the stimuli, presumably to determine their meaning. At three months of age, furthermore, infants mouthed more when they heard their mother's voice than when they heard the stranger, presumably because of the association of "mother" with "feeding." The six-month-old infants cried more when they heard their mother's voice, particularly her natural voice. Turnure suggested that this may be due to the greater attachment that infants this age have for their mothers, perhaps a kind of "separation protest" initiated by hearing the mother's voice without being able to see her. There were some sex differences. Three-month-old girls were more active than boys the same age when the mother's voice was distorted, but at nine months, they were more active when they heard their mother's normal voice.

In this experiment, subjects also served as their own controls—that is, responses made during the stimulus period were compared with responses made when there was no stimulus. In other studies, particularly with older children, another kind of control is instituted by dividing the subjects into two groups in such a manner as to make the groups as alike as possible. For example, suppose that in a study of reading ability one wishes to control (equalize) for the effect on the results of individual differences in intelligence. With scores on an intelligence test available, the top child may be placed in the experimental group, the next highest in the control group, the third highest in the experimental group, and so on, alternating between the groups. Thus, both the average intellectual level and the variability of the two groups are equalized.

The problem of placement becomes more complicated when other matching variables, such as sex, age, socioeconomic status, and race, must also be considered, but basically the way of equating is the same. In general, the intent is to make the experimental and control groups as similar as possible in the independent variables *not* under consideration, but which may, nonetheless, cause variation in the dependent variable being studied. The choice of matching the groups on certain variables depends on whether it is known or suspected that there is a concomitant variation with the dependent variable. For instance, as Anderson (1954) has observed in studying motor skills with all except very young children, it is not necessary to control intelligence or socioeconomic factors, because concomitant variation with motor ability is known to be very low. On the other hand, in studying language, which is positively related to (concomitantly varies with) these factors, both must be controlled.

Now that this necessity of equation of the groups has been indicated, it is possible to elaborate on the nature of the control group study. Two equated groups of subjects are used, differing only in that one group, the experimental, has the independent variable introduced (or has a greater or lesser magnitude, and so forth), while the second or control group does not. In the simplest form of this technique, both groups receive a prior test to establish equality; following this, one group undergoes the experimental procedure, while the other does not. Both then take a final test. The difference in final test results between the two groups is considered the result of the experience undergone by the experimental group which the control group did not undergo, and is the measure of the effect of the experimental (that is, the independent) variable.

Figure 2-1 presents the results of an experiment in which first-grade and fifth-grade boys were exposed to one of three different treatments in that they were praised for their performance on a fairly complex task, were criticized, or were exposed to a neutral stimulus. In this instance, we have two experimental conditions: "praise" and "criticism." The control condition consists of the neutral stimulus. The two types of reinforcement are therefore the independent variables. The dependent variable consists of the mean (average) number of trials the boys in each of the groups needed to learn the task—the more trials, the more difficulty they experienced. As might be expected, the first graders functioned less effectively under all conditions than did the fifth graders. The results show an interesting difference between the two age groups. The first graders were more successful

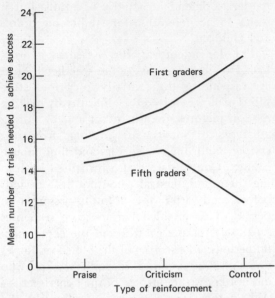

Figure 2-1. *Graph showing differences in performance among experimental and control groups of first-grade and fifth-grade boys working at a discrimination task.* (Spear, 1970.)

when there was some kind of reaction to their performance, either favorable or unfavorable, whereas the fifth graders evidently found praise or criticism distracting and turned out their best performance when neither was present—in the control condition.

To summarize our discussion, then, the independent variable in an experiment is introduced and varied systematically while other variables that might conceivably influence the dependent variable are controlled. Whatever changes occur in the dependent variable are attributed to the changes in the independent variable.

The Differential or Correlational Method

In the experimental method, the distinguishing operation is the manipulation by the investigator of some specific stimulating condition, the independent variable. But there are some problems in which this intervention on the part of the investigator is impossible or even undesirable. There are certain circumstances in which arrangement of conditions by the experimenter is not feasible, and he must seek a different method of carrying on his research. Indeed, there are sciences, such as astronomy and geology, in which experiment is impossible so far as major problems are concerned. The space and time dimensions of these sciences do not permit experimental manipulation. An astronomer cannot vary the orbit of a star to see its effect; a geologist cannot introduce an ice age in order to observe the resultant changes.

Whenever scientists are unable, for one reason or another, to conduct a controlled experiment, they turn to the differential or correlational method to test their hypotheses. In behavioral science, this is also termed R-R (response-response) research, in contrast to S-R (stimulus-response) research, because relationships *between responses,* rather than between *stimuli and responses,* are studied. In this approach, the investigator studies differences or similarities in two sets of variables. Margaret Mead, whose anthropological studies were discussed in Chapter 1, used a differential or correlational method when she compared and contrasted the behavior of individuals in different cultures. The cross-cultural approach, which she used, is therefore a variation of the differential or correlational method. Researchers who test Piaget's propositions are likely to use R-R methods, in that they look for relationships between stages of maturity (as indicated by chronological age) and cognitive styles.

The scope of children's environments, even within a single culture, can be extraordinarily wide. We can find examples of deprivation in the lowest social classes, as well as in institutions for children that are so understaffed that they cannot provide the usual range and intensity of human contacts that children in a family setting receive. The institutionalized child may lack mothering and receive hardly any personal verbal stimulation. Hence he has less opportunities to learn from these experiences. The psychologist would not deliberately create these situations, but when he finds them already present he utilizes them for study.

Many psychological problems do not encourage experimental manipulation. Sometimes to do so would be too costly in time, money, or effort. Sometimes an attempt to study a problem experimentally would involve violation of the personal rights of others.

An illustration would be the attempt to make the independent variable of an experiment the development of an experimental psychosis in a child; so, too, would be the placement of heretofore emotionally stable children in a family environment designed to produce emotional trauma. Moreover, respect for living things prevents workers in all sciences from inflicting unnecessary pain in the course of their experiments. Child psychologists are further limited in their use of the experimental method because of their desire to avoid interfering in any way with the best development of the child's personality. This precaution is followed even when harmful effects are only remotely suspected.

There is, for instance, a question, that is of considerable relevance for the field of child development and regarding which equivocal data have appeared in the literature. The question is whether insufficient oxygen (anoxia) at birth causes lasting damage to the child. The surest, most efficient technique of answering this question would be to subject newborn infants to varying degrees of anoxia and to follow their subsequent development. However, so long as there is even the faintest suspicion that such a procedure might cause lasting damage to the children, such a method is one to be scrupulously avoided. Instead, a differential method—that of following up cases of anoxia that occur in spite of all obstetrical precautions—is the one that is best employed.

In such instances, R-R research, rather than S-R experimentation, is followed out of necessity; in other instances, it is the method of choice. For certain kinds of research in developmental psychology, it is important to observe life as it is actually lived; hence, differential or correlational methods are more useful than are experiments. Studies of normal development, for example, are central to child psychology. Since we are interested in the *normal* changes concomitant with age, we do not attempt to alter the course of development precisely because it is the normal child we are trying to study.

In using the differential method, the investigator finds a situation rather than arranges for it. The children are behaving in ways that are natural to them. The children are already "intelligent," "mentally retarded," or "disturbed" when the differential method is applied.

Independent and dependent variables are still present when applying the differential method. In such research, independent variables are not manipulated, as they are in the S-R type of research. Instead, they are identified as possible causal and preexisting conditions that can be related to consequent or dependent variables. Subjects are chosen according to a criterion, and the measurements themselves form the variable. Inasmuch as the researcher does not manipulate the independent variable, he has less control of it. Nevertheless, the use of various controls, as previously described, are not only possible but also highly desirable.

Control groups can obviously be of value in R-R research. Suppose the problem under investigation is the relationship of aggression in children to attitudes of their parents. By a means irrelevant to the issue at hand, 50 already aggressive children are identified. Let us further suppose that in 32 of the homes from which these aggressive children come, it is established that parental rejection of these children takes place. It would be tempting to conclude that parental rejection is associated with aggressiveness. Actually, the results of this study are inconclusive without a control group. We must also isolate a control group of nonaggressive children to find out how often parental rejection is present in homes of this group as well. Only if the two types of homes differ significantly in the number showing parental rejection can we speak with any degree of assurance about the meaning of the results.

Although to some extent it is loose usage, the independent variable can be called the *causal* variable, and the dependent variable the *effect* variable. The nature of the particular problem under investigation defines whether a particular factor is an independent or a dependent variable. What is a cause in one setting may be the effect in another. Intellectual functioning, for example, may be either, depending on the research design in question. When the effect of lack of mothering upon the infant is discussed, his intellectual functioning will be used as the dependent variable. That is, if children are deprived of mothering (the independent variable), does this influence their intelligence (the dependent variable)? But when considering the schoolchild, the question will be raised concerning the reasons for superior schoolwork, and intellectual functioning will be explored as an independent variable. That is, does schoolwork (the dependent variable) vary as a consequence of intellectual functioning (the independent variable)?

In some of the differential or correlational studies, the investigator looks for differences between two or more groups that are greater than would be expected by chance. Such differences are termed "statistically significant," the cutoff point for significance usually being the 5% level—that is, a difference that would occur by chance not more than 5% of the time. If the differences turn out to be significant at the 1% or the 0.1% level of confidence, there is even less likelihood that the observed differences result from chance, and findings can be considered to be more strongly supported.

Other studies make use of correlational techniques. A common measure of the relationship between two variables in the Pearsonian coefficient of correlation, a statistic that may range between the limits of +1.00 and −1.00. Relationships that are purely chance have values near .00, an indication that the variables under study are essentially unrelated. The magnitude of a correlation, like the magnitude of the difference between two groups of subjects, tells us only part of the story. As in the case of the difference, we are also interested in its statistical significance. A coefficient that is significant at the 10% level is considered only marginal and suggestive of a possible relationship, and the 5% level is the conventional cutoff point for statistical significance for correlations as well as for observed differences.

Minus correlations do not mean lack of relationship, but rather that two variables are *inversely* related: the more of one, the less of the other, and vice versa. In the theoretical study just described, we would expect to find a positive correlation between the amount of parental rejection and children's aggressiveness, just as we would expect a negative correlation between indications of parental acceptance and emotional support, on the one hand, and children's aggressiveness on the other.

Here are some examples of positive and negative correlations. Lindgren and others (1964) found a correlation of .24 (significant at the 5% level) between scores on a question-naire measuring attitudes toward problem solving and scores made on an achievement test in arithmetic, for children in their fourth year in the elementary schools of Pôrto Alegre, Brazil. The implication is that attitudes favorable to problem solving have some effect on success in learning arithmetic. Another possible interpretation is that repeated successes in problem solving facilitate the development of attitudes favorable toward that type of activity, as well as to success in arithmetic. As an example of a negative correlation, we can cite the study of Winder and Rau (1962) who asked sixth-grade boys to rate one another on various traits and characteristics and found that likability correlated −.41 with ratings of depression. In this instance, the findings suggest that there tends to be a relationship between a boy's characteristic mood and the extent to which others respond favorably to him. In other words, depressed moodiness decreases the probability of being liked. The other interpretation may also be valid, namely, that not being liked by others leads to a feeling of depression. Still another viable interpretation is that both being rejected by others and being depressed are interrelated dimensions of a general personality pattern characterized by poor social relations and depression, as well as a number of other negative attributes. Table 2-1 lists some examples of pairs of correlated variables.

A great deal of the research done in child psychology is of the differential-correlational, R-R type. This is consistent with the main currents of research in this field, which are, as we noted in Chapter 1, genetic and developmental, rather than experimental in the S-R sense. In one survey of child psychology research conducted in the mid-1960s, correlational studies outnumbered experimental studies about two to one (Siegel, 1967).

Experimentally oriented researchers sometimes question the validity of R-R research as being "less scientific" than S-R research.

TABLE 2-1. Examples of Correlations Between Pairs of Variables

First Variable	Correlation Coefficient	Second Variable
Number of hours worked each month during the school year 1971–1972 by a nursery school teacher earning $6 per hour correlated	+1.00	with amounts the nursery school teacher earned each month. (The more hours she worked, the more she earned, and the fewer hours worked, the less she earned.)
At the end of each month, the above teacher calculated the number of days she had worked so far during the school year. These end-of-month totals correlated	−1.00	with the number of days remaining in the school year. (The more days she worked, the fewer days remained to work.)
IQs earned by children taking Form "L" of the 1937 Stanford-Binet Intelligence Scale correlated	.92[a]	with the IQs earned by the same children taking Form "M" of the same scale (Terman and Merrill, 1937)
The height of children who were measured at age 4 correlated	.81	with the height they attained as adults (Tanner, 1970)
Amount of vocalization observed in girl infants (0–2 years of age) correlated	.56	with their IQs when they reached the age of 13 (Cameron, Livson, and Bayley, 1967)
Height of fathers correlates	.56	with the height of their sons (McNemar, 1955)
Years of education of Brazilian parents correlated	.28	with measures of their children's popularity in elementary school (Lindgren and Guedes, 1963)
Height of 11-year-old Scottish children correlated	.25	with their IQs (Tanner, 1970)
Scores obtained by fourth-grade children on a test of attitudes favorable to problem solving correlated	.24	with their scores on a test of competence in arithmetic (Lindgren et al., 1964)
The IQs of schoolchildren were found to correlate	−.18	with the number of siblings in their respective families (Anastasi, 1956)
Tendencies of nursery school children to command or order others about correlated	−.31	with their tendencies to comply with others' demands (Berk, 1971)
Ratings sixth-grade boys received from one another on "likability" correlated	−.41	with ratings the same boys received on "depression" (Winder and Rau, 1962)

[a] It is customary to omit the "+" when correlations are positive.

Most psychologists, however, maintain that both types of research have their place. Cronbach (1957) has noted that experiments (S-R research) can only tell us about the effect that the environment has on the organism, whereas correlational psychology (R-R) research can only tell us about differences and similarities among organisms. In order to predict the organism's behavior, we need to understand the organism *and* its environment. Coffield (1970), too, points out that R-R research is needed if we are to develop any understanding of the details that lie behind individual variations in behavior. It should also be added that researchers conducting experiments find it desirable to use data from R-R studies in order to control experiential and personality variables among their subjects. Correlational studies have established the fact that boys and girls tend to behave differently on a wide number of tasks, for example; hence the investigator who does not take sex differences into account when designing his experiment is likely to have his results questioned.

Cross-sectional versus Longitudinal Research

Child psychologists often need to get information regarding the changes that take place in children's behaviors over an extended period of time. For instance, a researcher may be interested in the ages at which children use various linguistic forms: at what age do they use single words, combinations of single words, single sentences, multiple sentences, and so forth. The most convenient way of gathering such information would be to observe children of different ages, record their conversation, and correlate usage with age. Such an approach is termed "cross-sectional," because each age sample is considered to be a representative cross section of children at that stage of development. The difficulty with such research, however, is that it assumes that

children being studied have similar backgrounds. Suppose that the study were made in a rural community into which television had been introduced a year previously. A question might be raised as to whether the language development of children who had not been exposed to television until age 10 would have been different from those exposed to it a year ago at age 3.

The best way to control for such effects is to carry out a series of observations of the *same* children over an extended time span. In this way, each child's linguistic responses serve as a base against which the subsequent appearance of new responses can be compared. Such research is termed "longitudinal" because it proceeds in a "lengthwise" direction in each child's life-span, and does not involve taking behavior samples "across" a number of lives at only one point in time. Longitudinal research gives a more accurate picture of developmental changes. The best example of this can be found in research with intellectual changes in adulthood. When intelligence tests were first developed, norms for each age were developed by taking samplings of the performance of individuals at different age levels—a cross-sectional approach. Inasmuch as individuals from the age of 30 onward were observed to make successively lower scores, researchers concluded that intellectual ability tended to decline from the mid-20s onward (Jones and Conrad, 1933). It was not until sufficient data from longitudinal studies had accumulated that it became clear that verbal intelligence tends to increase, not decline, during the adult years (Owens, 1953). Nonverbal intelligence tends to decline slightly during the later adult years but not as much as the earlier findings suggested (Schaie and Strother, 1968). The reason for the false reading of the earlier cross-sectional research was that the older individuals in the samples had completed less schooling than the younger samples, and years of education has been found to contribute heavily to variations in measured intelligence (Ginzberg et al., 1959).

The Techniques of Child Study

One purpose of research techniques and devices is to increase the accuracy of our observations. A handmaiden of accurate observation is immediate and accurate recording, necessitated by faulty and distorted memory to which all of us are subject. Many of the techniques discussed in this and later chapters —chronoscopes, tests, motion pictures, and so on—are means of making observations more correct and their recording less subject to error. Just as eyeglasses are worn to enhance vision, so, too, are the devices and procedures employed in psychological research the means of making more exact and more acute the observational processes of the investigator; and, just as watches are carried to help us establish the time of events, so, too, are other devices used to help to make sure that what is observed is recorded accurately.

In a sense, all observation is subjective because it depends on the organism of the observer. We attempt to make it as objective as possible by arranging conditions of observation so that the human element can be minimized, although never eliminated. Devices and procedures increasing objectivity are attempts to reach the goal of minimal dependence on subjective impression. It follows that all such devices have varying degrees of objectivity-subjectivity; they represent quantitative differences along this continuum.

In many research situations, especially in clinical settings, the investigator not only passively records observations but also interacts actively with his subject. He becomes, in Harry Stack Sullivan's apt phrase, a "participant observer." This may lend subtlety to the situation, but it also makes it more complex.

In effect, the investigator, because he is part of the research situation, becomes a variable in the research thereby affecting the results. It becomes necessary to consider carefully and precisely what the investigator is to do, in order to make sure that his participation does not cause him to commit errors in his evaluation of the situation.

There is also a more restricted meaning for the term observation. This is so-called "systematic observation," first carried on in the 1920s and 1930s and further exploited in the years thereafter (Thomas, 1929; Wright, 1960). Just as a mining engineer takes a sample of ore, the child psychologist takes a sample of behavior through observing children in one of their natural habitats—a schoolyard, a classroom, a doll-play setting, or a party. It was recognized early that the sample could not be everything the children were doing; samples would have to be directed to be relevant to a particular problem. For example, observations might be made of the popularity of children at a party or their attempts at dominating one another on the playground.

A variety of considerations must be dealt with by the investigator in carrying out research using systematic observations. He must decide upon the time sample to be used; he has to select the particular series of short time periods during which observations are to be made in such fashion that they are representative of the whole period being studied. He must also define the area selected for study and develop a recording scheme for the categories of behavior to be observed. And he must make provision for evaluating the reliability of the observations of his observers. Observer reliability, or more precisely, interobserver reliability, is the extent to which two or more observers agree in independently recording the behavior they are seeing.

A measure of maternal care developed by Rheingold (1960) will serve as an illustration.

A checklist of 30 mothering and 12 infant activities was prepared. The operations of mothers in caring for their infants were then sampled in the setting of homes and an institution. Some of the mothering-caretaking activities were the ones to be expected—patting, diapering, dressing, and so on. Others had to do with the number and location of the caretakers. Infant activities observed included vocalizing, crying, playing with toys, and the like.

The time observation was one in 15 seconds with recording taking place during the remaining 14 seconds. The cycle was then repeated with four observations in each minute for a total of ten minutes. After a break of five minutes, the cycles started again. For each infant this was done for four hours one morning, followed the next day by the same schedule in the afternoon for a total of eight hours of observation. There were three observers in all, but only one observed an infant in a four-hour period. Another observed that same infant the second day. Observer agreement was calculated for each item. For all items it was found to be 90%—thus showing high observer agreement. The instrument in actual use in this research is described in Chapter 8.

The investigator must select the techniques he is going to use on his particular problem. Unless he can demonstrate that a technique measures something relevant to his problem, his findings, even if they are published, would be ignored by those familiar with the necessity of an investigator's taking into consideration the *validity* of his measures. Validity is demonstrated when an investigator shows that what he is doing actually measures what it is supposed to measure.

Sometimes mere description supplies information that is sufficient to establish validity. In learning studies, for example, we arrange for the child to be faced with a new problem, and if after practice trials the child commits fewer errors and takes less time, we can say that learning has taken place. Or an investigator asks a child to tell which of two lights is the brighter, and can then say that he has studied visual brightness discrimination. Or he asks a child to press a key as soon as a light flashes, and can then say that he has measured reaction time to a visual stimulus. In these instances there is some direct, unequivocal connection between what he says he is studying and what he is actually studying.

In a similar manner marks on a weight scale may be used directly to measure weight. But if weight is used *indirectly* as a measure of nutrition, then it is up to the investigator to demonstrate that there is a necessary connection. The relation between the indicator and what it indicates must be determined, not assumed. Only if it measures what it purports to measure is it valid.

As the variables under study increase in complexity, the problem of designing valid measures becomes extremely difficult. The measurement of intelligence is a case in point. Francis Galton, the eminent British amateur of the life sciences, constructed some of the first tests of intelligence, as did James McKeen Cattell, an early American psychologist. Their tests consisted of measures of such variables as tonal memory, estimation of distance, speed of reaction, and rate of tapping. The fact that the researchers claimed to be measuring intelligence added nothing to the validity of the tests, and when the tests were subjected to critical examination, their validity was nil.

Alfred Binet abandoned this approach and instead attempted a more "global" measure of intelligence. The fact that he used a different approach did not in itself make his method more valid. Evidence had to be accumulated to show that Binet's scale produced results that were consistent with other indications of

Psychologists Study the Behavior of Children

A visually and aurally handicapped child is tested on her ability to fit cut-outs into the appropriate spaces in a form board. Interaction during play therapy can be videotaped and the process observed simultaneously through the one-way mirror in the background.

An ambidextrous child shows his ability to trace forms. A school psychologist adminis-
ters an objective test to a seventh grader. Mother and child are observed as they decide
how coded objects should be grouped and sorted.

intelligence. One such indicator was the change in cognitive ability that occurs with age during childhood—that is, six-year-olds can generally solve problems of greater complexity than those that three-year-olds can solve, and ten-year-olds are more competent at this than six-year-olds. The fact that scores on Binet's scale were consistent with this everyday observation was one indication of its validity.

Reliability of a measure, as distinguished from reliability of observers, must also be established. Often reliability is found by measuring the consistency of the results by repeating the measures on the same subject a second time. A thermometer reading of a normal temperature that measures it as 90.1 on one occasion, and as 99.3 on another would be unreliable. So, too, psychological measures that fluctuate because of imperfections of the instrument are faulty because they are inconsistent, that is, unreliable. A psychological measure is considered reliable if it yields substantially the same results on the first and second testings when there is no reason to believe the individual has changed in respect to what is being measured.

Now that certain characteristics have been described, we are in a position to examine some of the techniques used in child psychology. We follow Rosenzweig (1949) in classifying the numerous techniques available into objective, subjective, and projective.

Objective Techniques

Objective techniques depend on the subject's behavior as noted by the observer-investigator. The child does something spontaneously in a free situation, such as in a playroom, or on request, as when he reads from a book, pushes a button when he sees a light, learns a problem, or lifts a weight. Characteristics of his physiological processes, such as blood pressure, may also be investigated. In objective techniques, then, the observer looks at the subject and reports on his observations. Basically, there are two approaches: control of the stimulus situation and observation of responses.

Techniques used in controlling visual stimuli will serve as illustrations. In the study of color vision, representative methods of controlling stimuli include colored cards, yarns of known saturation, hue, and brightness, and colored light stimuli. For the study of brightness and form, light without color, two- and three-dimensional forms on paper and spheres, and cubes and cylinders have been used. With respect to the recording of responses, work with infants has included the use of recording drums, timing devices, conditioning apparatus, galvanometers (instruments for measuring differences in electric potentials, e.g., of the skin), and indeed, the gamut of laboratory devices developed over the years for investigating psychological phenomena.

Cinemanalysis was developed and refined by Arnold Gesell and his co-workers. This technique consists of an analytic study of a motion picture film either as a sequence or individually, frame by frame. Exactitude of original observation and accurate recording can be no more vividly illustrated than by this type of motion-picture study. What the infant or child did is available on photographic film long after the original moment and thus may be studied and restudied. The work of Gesell on the development of behavior, frequently referred to throughout this book, is based primarily on cinemanalysis.

Measuring general activity of the infant is often done through a device called the stabilimeter. The infant is placed on a platform that is so arranged as to be sensitive to the slightest movement. The movements of the platform are recorded by pens writing on a moving tape. To control other unintended sources of stimulation, the apparatus is frequently enclosed in an observation cabinet so that temperature, humidity, sound, and light can be regulated in order to keep them constant.

Objective measures have been devised for a wide variety of behaviors. Often they are the preferred means of study. Many of the studies of infant and child reported in the chapters to come will be found to depend on objective techniques.

Subjective Techniques

Subjective techniques make use of what the subject has to say about himself to an observer. They consist of an introspective account of his experiences, points of view, traits, aims, needs, or interests. These statements are taken by the investigator for what they are—disclosures by the subject about himself. Thus the subject looks at himself and reports to the observer. Asking children what is a good boy or girl, what they think of their parents' disciplinary practices, where the "self" is located, or what is meant by a lie are illustrative of matters investigated by subjective techniques.

Subjective techniques are based on what the individual can reveal and what he chooses to reveal about himself. Some things he does not know and other things he does not choose to tell. In other words, in varying degree, subjective techniques are weakened by selection on the part of the person concerned. Often subjective techniques depend on the subject's interpretation of the meaning of the material at hand without his being given much of a guide or source of reference as to how to interpret it. Subjective techniques nevertheless possess value. It is undoubtedly important to know what a person thinks about himself. An unfounded belief, even if only masquerading as a fact, is still a valuable datum for psychology. In addition, there are certain problems for which subjective techniques are particularly appropriate.

With children the questionnaire and the interview are the most widely used of subjective techniques. Research using the questionnaire has gone through many guises since it was introduced by G. Stanley Hall almost a century ago. The method still has much value, as research findings given later will attest. The interview will be illustrated from the work of Piaget, who has used it as a research tool with revealing and important results. Illustrative of his approach is a quotation from a phase of one of his studies of the development of moral judgment in children, aged five to seven.

"I (investigator): Do you know what a lie is?

C (child): It's when you say what isn't true.

I: Is $2 + 2 = 5$ a lie?

C: Yes, it's a lie.

I: Why?

C: Because it isn't right.

I: Did the boy who said $2 + 2 = 5$ know that it wasn't right or did he make a mistake?

C: He made a mistake.

I: Then if he made a mistake, did he tell a lie or not?

C: Yes, he told a lie.

I: A naughty one?

C: Not very.

I: You see this gentleman (a student)?

C: Yes.

I: How old do you think he is?

C: Thirty.

I: I would say he is 28. (The student says he is 36.) Have we both told lies?

C: Yes, both lies.

I: Naughty ones?

C: Not so very naughty.

I: Which is the naughtiest, yours or mine, or are they both the same?

C: Yours is the naughtiest, because the difference is biggest. . . .

I: Is it a lie, or did we just make a mistake?

C: We made a mistake.

I: Is it a lie all the same, or not?

C: Yes, it's a lie."[3]

From these and a wealth of similar findings Piaget concluded that children of this age, while aware of the distinction between an intentional act and an involuntary mistake, did not stress the distinction and, on the contrary, grouped both together as "lies." It is hard to conceive of other than a subjective technique revealing this particular facet of child life.

Questionnaires and interviews are also used with parents. One instrument used fairly extensively has been the Parent Attitude Research Instrument (PARI) developed by Schaefer and Bell (1958). Each of the 23 five-item scales has been established as empirically homogeneous, and each measures a specific attitude, such as suppression of aggression, strictness, acceleration of development, or fostering of dependency. Satisfactory internal consistency and test-retest reliability have also been established.

Projective Techniques

Projective techniques are concerned neither with consciously held opinions of the subject nor with his overt behavior but with imaginative responses aimed to uncover indirectly the characteristics of the child. The subject reveals something about himself to the observer by the way he organizes the material

[3] Copyright 1948 by the Free Press and published with permission. Piaget, 1948, p. 140.

presented to him—the way he projects meaning into neutral or ambiguous material. This is tantamount to having both the subject and the observer "look the other way" at some neutral object that is capable of permitting the subject's personality dynamics to be "projected" out where they can be observed.

Since idiomatic responses are sought, no external criterion of "right or wrong" is used. Inasmuch as the situation is arranged in such a fashion that the child does not know what precisely is expected of him, he reveals by his spontaneous manner of handling the stimulus materials some of the ways he organizes his view of the world. As he imparts a structure to the relatively unorganized material, the child reveals his principles of structure which are, it is hypothesized, the principles of his personality.

It is evident that the projective approaches put a heavy burden on the interpreter. Since he is dealing with relatively unorganized material, the clinician or researcher must be alert lest he read his own projections into the material. This subjective element in interpretation of projective material has justifiably been a source of criticism. Only through the awareness of this danger, the use of norms, the investigation of validity and reliability, and careful cross-checking can this criticism be partially met.

Projective instruments such as the Rorschach ink blots, play techniques, drawings, and the spontaneous telling of stories to pictures all have in common the fact that they all are relatively unstructured and yet provide a standardized stimulus situation. They are stimuli that readily enable the child to impose upon them his own meaning and organization, private and idiosyncratic though they may be. The stimuli are to some degree unclear or equivocal, allowing the child to interpret or give structure to them himself. The same principle applies to the instructions given to the child. For all of these techniques in essence the instructions reduce to, "Do with or interpret the material as you want to."

The Rorschach test consists of ten cards each bearing an impression of an ink blot. The subject's responses can be scored according to the extent to which he is evidently responding to the form of the blot, as well as its color, shading, details, edges, white areas, and so forth. These scores can be interpreted as indicating the existence of personality trends, anxieties, cognitive styles, and the like. Although the test was used fairly extensively in children's personality studies during the 1950s and earlier, it is employed less frequently today in such research. Its principal use now is in psychodiagnostic studies performed in connection with psychotherapy.

The approach that is followed in the Thematic Apperception Test, or TAT, is used more frequently by researchers. Tests of this type consist of drawings or photographs that are presented to the child one at a time. The child is told that he is to be shown some pictures and that a story is to be made up for each one. In telling his story he is to imagine what led up to the event shown in the picture, to relate what is happening in the picture, and to tell what the outcome will be. Any questions asked by him are answered noncommittally, with the nature of the situation and kind of story left entirely to the child.

The fundamental assumption concerning projection with the TAT approach is that the child identifies himself with a central figure in the story. The way the figure is described, the problem faced, and how it is handled are considered to be reflections of the child's own feelings and attitudes. The TAT approach has been used extensively in research dealing with certain types of psychological needs, such as the need to achieve (n Ach), to affiliate with others (n Aff), and to aggress (n Agg). Research of this type usually

makes use of a limited selection of cards that have been found to evoke responses that can be scored for the presence or absence of the need in question. The more "structured" nature of the TAT type of test gives the investigator more control over the stimulus situation than he has with the Rorschach and may account for the greater popularity of the TAT method with researchers.

Play techniques are also used as projective devices in both research and psychotherapy. Such methods are particularly useful in studying younger children, inasmuch as play is a kind of natural medium through which they can communicate feelings more effectively than they can through words.

In play therapy, the child is encouraged to play in a spontaneous fashion with the toys and play materials (clay, water, sand, etc.), but in research situations, the more usual practice is to present the child with some kind of standard arrangement of materials. The doll-play test, as described by Pauline Sears (1951), has been used by a number of researchers to measure aggressive tendencies. In her research, five easily identified dolls—father, mother, boy, girl, and baby—irrespective of the actual family constellation of the particular child, were used along with realistically designed furniture for six rooms, such as beds, table, refrigerator, and a toilet, and the walls of a house and rooms. The house was presented to the child with the furniture already arranged in an organized fashion, but none of the pieces were stationary, permitting easy manipulation if the child wanted to do so. Two 20-minute sessions of doll play, usually on consecutive days, were given each subject. In keeping with the projective hypothesis, the instructions were general, amounting to nothing more than calling the child's attention to the whole house and the dolls for the house, and saying that he was to play with them as he saw fit. Sears' results, incidentally, showed that boys increased their aggressive behavior between the ages of three and four, whereas girls showed little change.

Also popular with students of personality and psychodiagnosticians are test situations in which children produce something of their own—a picture, for example. A picture drawn by a child not only tells us something about his motor (muscle) control but it also suggests how he perceives the world. If the picture is that of a person, it may also indicate how he views himself. The draw-a-person test thus may be used as a projective technique: a way of finding out what self-perceptions are being "projected" onto the drawing. In treatment situations, the pictures a child draws may thus provide information as to the progress he is making.

Figure 2-2 presents two pictures drawn by a girl in a preschool for neurologically handicapped children. Initially she behaved in a dependent, aggressive manner with the teacher, calling attention to herself in a loud voice, nagging, and acting in a "clinging" manner. She then began to relax somewhat and to pay more attention to the other children. At the end of four months, she showed increasing interest in her work and was able to concentrate on it for longer periods. Picture (a) represents a drawing of a person made before she entered the school. It was so chaotic and disorganized that the psychologist had to label the eyes and mouth. Picture (b) was drawn at the end of four months and is a respectable attempt at presenting a human figure. It not only shows greater concentration and motor control but it also gives us an idea of how she probably saw herself (Abrams and Pieper, 1968).

The Clinical Approach

The clinical approach to child study is more of a therapeutic technique than a research tool. In essence, it is an application of theory and research findings to various kinds of problems—problems presented by patients or clients, or by a group to which the professional person is a consultant. There is likely to be a "here-and-now" aspect to psychotherapy or consultant work: the professional person has been called into the situation to help solve the problem. Much as he might prefer to, he cannot pause, set up a controlled experimental situation, and set about the task of gathering information methodically. Furthermore, he often has to go far beyond the limits of theory and research results to improvise a working hypothesis to use as a guideline for his work.

Professionals who work with children, regardless of whether they are clinical psychologists, counseling psychologists, social workers, or teachers, all share an interest in or focus on the individual child. The nature of the work of these individuals calls for attention to the child as a person in his own right. Psychology, as a science, is a guide to the *general*—that is, it indicates or suggests how *individuals in general* behave. The professional, as an applied psychologist, is interested in the *general* as a guide to the *particular,* in this instance, the particular child or children with whom he is working.

The fact that the professional is primarily concerned with helping others solve problems does not preclude his examining the behavior he observes with the eye of the researcher. Research and practice are, in fact, often difficult to distinguish; the noting of similarities and differences leads to both individual diagnostic and therapeutic skill and to the adroit formulation of fruitful hypotheses. In the course of ministering to his patients, the clinician may originate many promising ideas for research from what the patients reveal about themselves, from the professional contacts through colleagues, and from his readings in the literature. Though vague and ill-formed

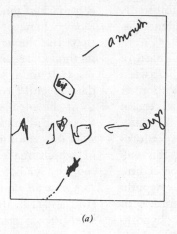

(a)

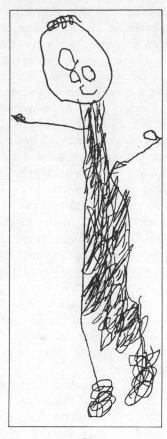

(b)

Figure 2-2. Drawings of a person made by an emotionally disturbed girl (a) before being admitted to a preschool for neurologically handicapped children, and (b) after four months of treatment.
(Abrams and Pieper, 1968, pp. 400–401. Reproduced by permission.)

at first, his idea will serve to sensitize him to other instances he finds in these same sources pointing in the same direction as his "hunch." The primary source is his contact with individual patients.

A specific illustration is to be found in David Levy's account (1943a) of how his work in maternal overprotection came about. He related that in listening to case reports being given at a staff meeting of the Institute of Child Guidance, someone discussed a woman having a child after ten years of sterility. The record also showed that she was very solicitous and indulgent toward this child. These two events were not in any way considered inter-

related at this point. They were merely aspects of a voluminous case record. Levy raised the question to himself: Assuming she wanted the child, would not this ten years' wait cause her to be very solicitous toward him? The idea intrigued him and he began to search the case records of the clinic for cases showing maternal overprotectiveness and then to study the case records to see what other attitudes were shown by the same mother. This is the process of hypothesis forming that takes place in scientific investigation in general. His results, incidentally, showed that overprotective mothers were inclined to be warm and permissive as long as their children were infants, but that they later became unusually restrictive as indications of independence began to appear (Levy, 1943b).

There is always a ragged advance guard of knowledge in that no-man's-land between pure speculation and scientific verification. A clinician may be convinced that a certain explanation of a patient's behavior is valid, and may argue that purely clinical procedures are all that are needed to establish this validity. For example, the clinical procedure that Freud followed to formulate hypotheses was to draw upon his experience with patients, and then to test these hypotheses against later cases. If, in these later cases, consistency with the hypothesis was observed, he considered the hypothesis to be verified. The difficulty with this approach, as Boring (1954) once noted, is that there was no proper scientific control. Freud was, however, unconcerned about the possible influence of factors other than the ones he was interested in.

In sum, the clinician tends to employ looser controls than those used in laboratory research, because he deals with situations and problems that are extremely complex. He is likely to resist suggestions that he eliminate some variables and thus make his task simpler. His objection may be stated in the form of an aphorism: "Research 'contamination' is clinical enrichment." The clinician wants as much information as possible about his patients before arriving at conclusions about them, and he does not want to eliminate any variables prematurely that might possibly shed some light on the problems he is scrutinizing.

As we noted in Chapter 1, there is today a great deal more respect for controlled experimentation among child psychologists than there was, say, a generation ago. Even though the mainstream of research is moving in the developmental-genetic, rather than in the environmental-experimental direction, there

is a marked tendency to use scientific methodology whenever possible. It is for this reason that the looser, more personalized clinical methods are less likely to be employed in research today. This does not mean that the data of child researchers can always be made to fit the ideal scientific pattern. To insist on this would mean the elimination of a considerable amount of interesting material, much of which makes a great deal of sense and suggests leads for future research.

A case in point is a report by Diana Baumrind (1971a) that does not meet the usual scientific criteria, largely because of the small size of her sample. The study dealt with a group of eight families whose control over their children was unusually harmonious. The data were drawn from a larger study that had a sufficient number of subjects to demonstrate statistically significant relationships among variables, but were reported separately in a brief report, because of the unusual character of the child-parent relationship. In many ways, the atmosphere of the families seemed ideal: it was characterized by harmony, a lack of tension, and an emphasis on rationality. Whereas *permissive* parents (in the main study) avoided exercising control over their children, but were angry because they had no control, and *authoritarian* parents willingly exercised control, this group of *harmonious* parents did not seem to be either exercising or avoiding control. The parents concentrated, instead, on achieving harmony in the home and on developing principles that could be used as a basis for resolving differences and for right living. Many of these families were, incidentally, preparing themselves for living in communes, another factor that makes this small study especially interesting.

Six of the eight children in the study were girls. Their behavior in preschool suggested that they were exceptionally well adjusted:

bright, friendly, cooperative, high achieving, and independent. The two boys, however, though cooperative, were particularly submissive, aimless, dependent, and not achievement-oriented.

Baumrind concluded her brief report by noting that it would be interesting to find more families like these in order to study their long-range effects on children's behavior and development.

A study like this stimulates a great deal of speculation. One wonders, for example, whether the "ideal" family is good for girls but not for boys, or whether "harmonious families" can be achieved more readily if the children are girls. It is quite likely that such research will receive considerable attention in the ensuing years. In giving our attention to studies like this brief report we should recognize that the psychology of the child is not a finished body of knowledge, but a vital and rapidly changing structure. All approaches have something cogent to say about the child. It is mandatory to use both the most accurate and the most meaningful contributions to a given problem. It does not follow, however, that accuracy and meaningfulness always reside to an equal degree in the same finding. Experimental-differential evidence found in the traditional fashion should be chosen when such is available and when it appears to be the appropriate method for a particular problem. There should be no hesitation, however, in using clinical findings when they seem more meaningful and relevant than data available from experimental investigations.

Summary

Although knowledge begins with observation, the very act of observing influences the observed event. Our culture provides a background of "common sense" knowledge that tends to bias scientific observation. The use of refined measurement techniques and instruments helps eliminate such bias, but to be called truly "scientific," an investigation must follow a basic set of rules: it must be *replicable,* and it is likely to begin with a *hypothesis* about the relationship of several *variables;* the variable that is hypothesized as causal is the *independent variable,* and the variable that it influences is the *dependent variable*.

The experimental method is the classic form for S-R research. A stimulus (independent variable) is systematically introduced in a controlled situation, and the experimenter observes the subject's responses (the dependent variable). The experimenter must carefully separate the effects of the stimulus he is interested in from other stimuli. Turnure, for example, made sure that her infant subjects were responding to the "motherness" of their mother's voice, rather than to the "femaleness" by measuring the response to a strange woman's voice and comparing it to the response to the mother's voice. Turnure also controlled for sex-specific behavior by including both sexes in her sample. To ensure *reliability* of measurement, she had several observers who were ignorant of which antecedent stimulation the infants had received score the responses. From this she calculated the degree of observer agreement.

The subjects in the Turnure study served as their own control (or comparison) group: each infant was subject to both the experimental and control conditions. Sometimes this procedure is not feasible. When this is the case, matched pairs of subjects are divided between separate experimental and control groups. If the two groups are equal in all important respects before the experimental group undergoes the experimental procedure, any differences afterwards may be attributed to the experimental conditions. To be doubly sure that the posttreatment differences are not the result of preexisting differences between the experimental and control groups, some experimenters test the subjects before as well as after the experiment.

In many cases, practical or moral considerations preclude direct manipulation of the independent variable, and the experimenter must turn to the differential or correlational method. This is also called the R-R method, because relationships between responses, rather than between stimuli and responses, are studied. The cross-cultural approach used by Margaret Mead is one example of R-R research. Deprivation research is another. Obviously, the researcher cannot deliberately deprive any child of stimulation or sustenance, but he can make use of an unfortunate situation and compare the behavior of the deprived child with that of a normal child. In certain kinds of psychological research, it is necessary to observe life as it is lived, rather than in the artificial atmosphere of the laboratory. In such cases, R-R research is the method of choice rather than of necessity.

Although the experimenter cannot manipulate an independent variable while using the differential method, the same precautions taken in the experimental method are still applicable. The careful selection of a comparison group of control subjects is required if the effects of the independent variable are not clearly separable from the influence of uncontrolled variables. With this kind of research it is especially important to remember that the independent variable of one study (intelligence as it affects grades, for example) may serve as a dependent variable in another (maternal care as it affects intelligence).

Research findings are often reported as being statistically "significant" at the 5% level, or at the 1% level, etc. The percentage figure refers to the calculated probability that such findings occurred purely by chance. Some studies use correlational techniques. The "coefficient of correlation" ranges between -1.00 and $+1.00$. The absolute or unsigned value of the statistic reflects the degree of "relatedness" of two variables. A correlation of zero reflects no relationship, whereas an unsigned correlation of 1.0 refers to a perfect relationship. The sign reflects whether the variables are directly $(+)$ or inversely $(-)$ related, and has nothing to do with the strength of the correlation.

Child psychologists frequently need to collect information about changes in behavior that occur at different stages of development. There are two ways to gather this sort of information. The most convenient way is to observe a number of different samples, each a representative of one of the stages or age levels of interest. This is called the *cross-sectional method*. The second and more time-consuming possibility is to follow the development of a single group of children through all the stages one wishes to study. This is termed the *longitudinal method*. Although cross-sectional research is obviously the less difficult of the two, it assumes similarity in background between all samples of children. Unless this assumption is justified, the observed differences may reflect the effect of uncontrolled variables.

All observations are somewhat subjective because they must be interpreted by the observer. Science attempts to minimize this influence with specialized devices and objective procedures. *Systematic observation* is one of these methods. The observer must define the area to be studied, select a representative series of short time periods during which to make his observations, and make a checklist for just those behaviors he wishes to record. The observer using this method, or any observational method for that matter, must also make provision for evaluating *measurement reliability,* as well as *observer reliability.* The former term refers to the agreement between successive measurements and the latter to the agreement between observers. The investigator must also be able to demonstrate the *validity* of his measures. That is, if he is measuring what he intended to measure. An example of an invalid measure would be an IQ test that failed to correlate with grades or any other measure of intellectual function. Some of the early attempts to measure intelligence made this mistake, using such rarified tasks as rate of tapping and tonal memory. The accuracy of objective techniques may be increased by careful control of the stimulus situation, varying saturation, for instance, while keeping hue and brightness constant. Another way to improve accuracy is to use specialized recording devices like stabilimeters or galvanometers.

Psychologists make use of the subject's own introspective observations. We call this *subjective* technique. With children, the questionnaire and the interview are the most widely used of subjective techniques. Another method that attempts to measure conditions internal to the subject rather than overt behavior is the *projective technique.* By observing the subject's responses in an ambiguous situation, the psychologist looks for information of how the subject organizes his view of the world. In such an unstructured situation, the observer must be careful not to project his own personality into the interpretation. The Rorschach test, tests of the Thematic Apperception Test (TAT) type, and play therapy are all examples of projective techniques. The TAT type of test is more structured than the Rorschach, and is often used to measure personality trends, such as the need to achieve (n Ach) and the need to affiliate with others (n Aff). Play therapy and drawings are other examples of projective techniques.

The *clinical approach* has become more a therapeutic technique than a research tool. The professional person is called upon to solve an immediate problem, and cannot pause to set up a controlled experimental situation. His interest is focused on the specific individual and the general case is useful only as a guide to the particular. In his continual and intimate contact with his patients, the clinician is in an excellent position to originate promising research ideas. A great deal of research has followed such educated "hunches." Freud, for example, formulated his hypotheses from experience with his patients. The difficulty with this approach is that there is no proper scientific control.

Although psychologists use scientific methodology whenever possible, clinical methods generate a great deal of useful material. Baumrind's study of the behavior of children of permissive, authoritarian, or harmonious parents is a good example. Although too small and loosely designed to prove anything, the study certainly stimulates a good deal of speculation about the "ideal" family, and will probably lead to further research in the future.

3 The Process of Development

Growth and Development

Observation of the process of development in young children is a fascinating enterprise, and one that never ceases to delight and amaze parents and other participants. The addition of two ounces to the weight chart, the sudden ability of the baby to hold his head in the midplane rather than turned always to one side, the momentous transfer of a rattle from one hand to the other, the solemn embarking on the first solo step, or the articulation of the first distinct word—all provide manifestations of this potential for development. Furthermore, within certain rather broad limits the development is orderly and sequential. Just as a flower proceeds from bulb to stalk to leaf to bud to blossom and never, except under certain artificial conditions, modifies this sequence or short-circuits one or another stage, the development of the child proceeds in a lawful manner according to certain rules established by the fact that he is a living organism and, specifically, a member of the human species.

For example, every parent knows that, in general, a child will sit before he stands, walk before he talks, gain control of his bowel movements before the ability to regulate bladder functioning, and so on. On the other hand, it is unlikely that every parent or interested observer has noted important, if subtler, general trends in the developmental process. One of the purposes of this chapter is to call attention to some of these trends.

Basic to all development is growth. In its specific sense, the term *growth* refers to an increase in size or number of parts of an organism, whereas *development* (literally, "unfolding") refers to changes in character or function. Inasmuch as quantitative changes in a young organism are usually accompanied by qualitative changes, the term *growth* and *development* have taken on overlapping and virtually synonymous meanings in general usage. There are a number of instances, however, where they obviously do not mean the same thing. We think of growth as continuing only to maturity, while development continues throughout the life-span, from conception until death. The term *growth*, too, seems somehow to imply physical changes, although we do speak of cognitive growth. Development is the more general term. It includes the idea of growth, but also that of decline.

Development is observable in every phase of life. Whether the field of observation is at the level of the cell, the organ, the organism, or the person, it is still safe to generalize that some development is always occurring. Although development may be said to begin at the point of conception, we cannot ignore such important preexisting conditions as the socioeconomic status of the parents, their way of relating to each other, and the kind of society into which the child is born. The birth of a baby and the changes that will manifest themselves in all its future behavior represent in one sense a condensation of the entire history of life up to the time of the observation. Reflected in every act will be the evolution of the entire biological drama as performed within the confines of a complex physical and social world.

The fact that development is a *process* rather than a thing makes reliable (i.e., repeatable) observation difficult. In other words, development does not sit and wait for precise measurement of any kind to be made; the organism is constantly changing, and prior conditions can never be exactly duplicated. In actuality no one can claim to have observed the process itself, for development refers to a change detectable from observations made at two or more points on a time continuum. No matter how fine or how gross the temporal units, development itself remains an abstraction, an inference from incremental differences detected by the chosen method of observation. We might take sequential pictures of the metamorphosis from caterpillar to butterfly, project them continuously as motion pictures, and thus apparently compress the development in such a way as to make the *process* itself appear to be the unit of observation. But no matter how much, for purposes of more careful study, we either accelerate or retard representations of development, we can do no more than infer the process from more or less discrete observations made at different temporal points.

Genetic Background and Development

A major concern of the psychologist is that of accounting for variance—that is, attempting to answer the question "How and why do people differ?" Differences between individuals may be attributed to genetic variations, to environmental differences, or to interaction between the two. In former times, it was assumed that interindividual differences were largely the result of inherited traits and that the kind of person the individual became was more or less set at the point of conception. John Locke probably reflected a growing awareness of his day with respect to the importance of environmental influences on the individual. This trend of thought has continued, and today there is a tendency, especially in America, to take a position that is more or less environmentalist.

The support for the environmentalist position lies in the fact that man is an exceedingly plastic organism: no other animal has his capacity either to produce an endless variety of response patterns or to modify response patterns that are initially biologically determined. The acquisition and modification of response patterns comes about through learning, through the interaction of the human organism with its environment. Theoretically, similar environments should produce similar responses. This does seem to occur to some extent. Individuals growing up in the same social environment speak the same language, share many beliefs and values, and even have similar personality traits.

Yet there are some doubts. One is tempted to say that the placid temperament of the Hopi and Zuñi Indians and the aggressiveness of the Apaches and Comanches are the products of their respective cultures, but we cannot be absolutely sure. Clyde Kluckhohn (1949) noted that Zuñi babies who were more than usually active at birth had become placid by the time they were two years old, whereas hyperactive white babies retained their initial hyperactivity. The implication is that while the Zuñi culture emphasizes placidity, the white Anglo culture emphasizes activity, and each culture differentially infuses its children with its own modal personality. This seems to certify the environmentalist's argument, yet we should not overlook another observation of Kluckhohn's, namely, that at birth, the proportion of hyperactive babies was already higher among the whites than among the Zuñis. And so the question is reopened: Are whites more active than Zuñis because their culture teaches them to be active, or are they more active because more of them were born that way? It is beyond the scope of this book to resolve that question, assuming it could be resolved, but it is important to keep in mind that behind our façade of learned similarities and differences, there may be some genetically

acquired tendencies that act on our behavior in ways that usually escape our notice, for one reason or another.

Studies of Twins

The problem of determining the relative effects of environment and heredity in humans is obviously a complex one. At present, the problem has been approached largely through the studies of twins.

Twins are of two types: identical twins, products of a single fertilized ovum, hence *monozygotic* or MZ twins; and unlike twins, products of two different fertilized ova, hence *dizygotic* or DZ twins. MZ twins are always of the same sex, whereas DZ twins may be of the same or different sex. Twin studies have a number of built-in controls and are thus particularly useful for investigators who want to study the interaction of heredity and environment. In the first place, MZ twins share the same genetic elements, whereas nontwin siblings have a similar but not identical genetic background. Siblings, twins or otherwise, differ from individuals from assorted families in that they share a similar family environment: any two siblings are exposed to the influence of the same parents, the same cultural environment, the same neighborhood, and so forth. It would seem that they have the same environment, but strictly speaking, this is not so. Any child's environment includes the attitudes and expectations that others have for him, and these, in turn, are different for each child in the family, depending on his birth order, his sex, the extent to which he is wanted or unwanted, and so forth. These variations are fairly well controlled with like-sex DZ twins, who differ only genetically from MZ twins, theoretically speaking.

Twin studies have dealt with three kinds of variables: intelligence, personality traits, and tendencies toward mental disorder. Studies of intelligence report results that seem to show that intelligence is genetically determined for the most part, for the correlation of intelligence test scores for MZ twins raised in different families is .77, whereas that for similar twins raised together is .76. The correlation for DZ twins raised together is .51 (Shields, 1962). The obvious conclusion could be accepted without question, if it were not for a multitude of studies that show a persistent relationship between environmental quality and intelligence (e.g., Bloom, 1964). We therefore take a second look at the twin research and wonder whether some of the observed similarity was caused by similar environments in the pairs of families in which the separated MZ twins grew up. In another study of MZ twins reared apart, an analysis was made of differences in the educational and social advantages of the pairs of families. Where social differences were small, IQ differences were invariably small, but where social differences were great, IQ differences in seven out of ten cases were also great (Newman, Freeman, and Holzinger, 1937; Johnson, 1963).

With respect to personality traits, Gottesman (1963) compared personality test responses of MZ and DZ adolescents and found that MZ twins were much more similar to one another than were DZ twins on scales measuring such traits as group dependency versus self-sufficiency, confidence versus guilt proneness, and seriousness versus enthusiasm.

Gottesman and Shields (1966) have reviewed a number of studies dealing with the tendency of MZ and DZ twin pairs to develop schizophrenia, a severe mental disorder or psychosis. Their findings were reported in terms of concordance between the pairs—that is, the percentage of times the other twin became schizophrenic if schizophrenia was reported for one twin. What they found was a 58% concordance for MZ twins, in contrast to a 14% concordance for DZ twins.

Taken altogether, these studies suggest that genetically determined biological factors probably do make a considerable contribution to variations in behavior. This does not mean that environmental conditions make a minimal contribution, but rather that a focus on environmental factors is going to tell only part of the story of human behavior. To be sure, the environmental factors are more easily studied and manipulated than are genetic factors, and this in itself is a matter of immense importance.

Trends in Development

The genetic material that makes us different, one from the other, also makes us similar in many ways. One of these ways is the tendency for our development to proceed in ways that are predictable. This predictability is made possible by the fact that developmental changes take place in an orderly, sequential fashion.

A fundamental prerequisite to an understanding of the process is a recognition of the interaction of all developmental phenomena. Although we can observe a great variety of changes that may appear to be unrelated to one another, it is unlikely that this is ever the case. For the only functionally discrete unit of observation *is the whole child reacting to his total environment.* Only with acceptance of the unitary nature of the entire drama of development can we hope to gain understanding of its range. This integrative view does not, however, assert that the forces acting on different organisms are completely identical in their patterning; for, as will be seen, the factors that influence and shape the developmental patterns in each individual child are diverse. Furthermore, these forces do not operate evenly in different individuals.

In selecting a variable for studying the developmental process, we might choose to observe certain physical properties (for example, the size of a muscle) or attributes that will be exhibited only when the organism is in action (such as strength of grip on a hand dynamometer). This is the traditional distinction between *structure* and *function*. In order to understand the complex process of human growth, we should know something about each of these aspects of the process and at the same time recognize that they are not completely separable from one another. That is, structure can often be best understood in relation to the function or behavior which it makes possible, and function obviously does not magically occur independently of a particular structure or set of structures.

To place the terms in a developmental setting, it can be said that maturity of structure —that is, the size and complexity of organization of component parts at a given time in relation to the corresponding organization when maximum development has been attained— has relevance only with respect to the functions to be served. It is frequently necessary to use functional criteria to define maturity of structure; the sex organs are considered "mature" when the individual is capable of reproduction. The digestive tract of the infant changes in structure as he grows older permitting digestion of more complex and varied foods. By feeding him different foods, the mother finds out whether they "agree" with him. Structural readiness, or lack of it, is shown by how his digestion fares when he eats these new foods.

From a study of the development of physical structures, we can learn much about behavior, and vice versa. Indeed, the emergence of certain behavior patterns provides tangible evidence that the destiny of certain physical structures has been fulfilled.

After this declaration of faith in the inseparability of developmental phenomena, it is perhaps safe to say that in this book we shall be more concerned with the development of function or behavior rather than with structure. This emphasis, however, does not imply that these features are any more important than others for an understanding of the general process of development, nor does it mean that they occur independently.

At times a capricious and paradoxical irregularity may appear to be the only predictable feature of development. This impression will most likely arise from a unit of observation too narrow to permit an event to reveal its contribution to the total pattern. But despite the chance factors that may appear to toy with the growing organism and defeat precise prediction, there is apparent in every aspect of development an orderliness which, within broad limits, permits predictability. Some of the patterns that represent the orderliness in development shall be dealt with now.

Developmental Direction

The general direction of growth moves in fairly steady progression from the head region of the organism downward. This directional gradient has been labeled the *cephalocaudal* (literally, head-to-tail) sequence. A correlated type of directionality is the *proximodistal* (near-to-far) pattern, which means that development proceeds from the axis of the body toward the periphery. That growth should so proceed seems determined by the fact that the most rapid embryological development occurs in or near those parts of the cells destined to be nervous structure. There appears to be a heightened sensitivity in these areas that facilitates faster growth.

This directionality is characteristic of both structural and functional change. That is, observation of the human embryo and infant reveals that at any given temporal point, the head is relatively more developed than the legs and feet (see illustrations in Chapter 5). At the functional or behavioral level, this means that the baby will gain control of his eyes and head before the trunk or legs, and that he can coordinate gross arm movements prior to precise and refined finger manipulation. Further exemplification of this trend in development will be found in subsequent chapters.

Differentiation and Integration

The potential for every phenomenon later to be observed must exist in that original cell from which the organism developed. To a large extent, therefore, development must be the creation of differences, or differentiation, and integration, the continuous reorganization into a unitary whole of the differences which thus emerge. Differentiation and integration are facets of the progressive changes in organization of the individual as a functioning system.

The original cell from which a child develops may be thought of as *totipotent,* that is, as possessing the capacity to become any structure that will later be found in the embryo. But if growth is to occur, the cell must abandon its totipotency for individuality, its versatility for specialization. As cell division continues, a milestone is eventually reached at which point a parent cell gives birth to a particular kind of offspring—nerve, muscle, or gland—and these resulting cells will in turn produce only their own kind and no other. Coincident with the increased differentiation, however, is an integration that enables the organism at any stage of development always to act as a coordinated whole. The integration of the ever-increasing specificities increases the organism's ability to adapt by assuring harmony among the interacting parts of the total structure.

A similar process of differentiation and in-

tegration can be found at the behavioral level. In some notable experimental and observational work on the development of aquatic locomotion in the salamander, Coghill (1929) observed that the first movements were gross flexions of the entire trunk initiated in the head region and progressing toward the tail. The flexions may occur either to the right or to the left, and as the reaction becomes more complex, a second contraction in one direction may occur before a contraction in the opposite direction has dissipated itself. When these alternating coils occur rapidly enough, pressure upon the water is exerted and the animal propelled forward, as shown in Figure 3-1.

Walking on land follows a similar pattern, although of course this cannot proceed until anatomical development has progressed to the point at which limbs have emerged. There are at first only mass movements of the trunk succeeded by gradual differentiation or individuation of action of the limbs as they become able to function relatively independently of the movement of the trunk. Myrtle B. McGraw (1946), who studied intensively the acquisition of prone locomotion in infants, aptly remarked on the close similarity between this description by Coghill and the behavior that occurs in the human infant.

Although generalization from the behavior of lower animals may often be justified, it is never judicious to do so when a direct check at the level of human behavior is possible. Some authorities have challenged the explanation in terms of differentiation, stressing the point that individuation from a generalized response may be too simple an explanation of the development of similar patterns of human behavior. In the human fetus no observations have been reported of trunk movements in the absence of associated arm movements (Carmichael, 1954). Certain local reflexes—isolated behavior independent of functioning in other

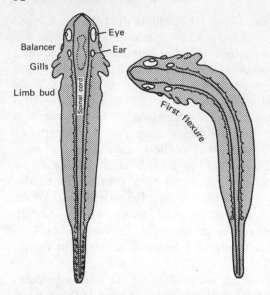

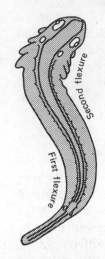

Figure 3-1. The beginnings of aquatic locomotion in the sala-mander (Amblystoma). (After Coghill, 1929.)

parts of the organism—can be observed at a very early stage in the development of the embryo, and more complex patterns of behavior may represent simultaneous individuation from a generalized response and a knitting together of specific local movements. As early as 14 weeks the human fetus has largely abandoned the generalized response and, instead, acquired a variety of discrete responses which can appear either singly or in combination (Hooker, 1943).

Another example of this constant interweaving of differentiation and integration can be found in the development of voluntary prehension in young babies. The infant possesses at birth a grasping—sometimes called Darwinian—reflex. Place your finger in a baby's palm and his fingers will close around it with what sometimes appears to be a viselike grip. This is a clear illustration of a specific response to local stimulation. After about six weeks, however, this reflex begins to disappear or lapses into a relatively static phase during which an object, once grasped, will not be

released until the hand makes contact with another surface which relieves the pull on the tendons. When attempts at voluntary prehension begins, this precise gesture is of little or no assistance, and the new skill must be refined gradually by the perfection of ever more precise movements which become differentiated out of gross movements.

Perhaps the most adequate summary of the conflicting points of view would be one that emphasized the simultaneous refinement of a generalized responsivity and a process of integration of isolated reflexes into a total pattern. These in turn split into behavior patterns that enable the organism to adjust to environmental conditions to be encountered later. There would seem to be little doubt that both processes, integration and differentiation, are simultaneously operative in the morphogenesis of behavior. The almost infinite array of behavioral acts of which the human adult is capable apparently cannot be explained completely in terms of a simple process of differentiation from global, generalized performance. Rather there occurs a constant interlacing of differentiation and integration. As soon as a new pattern emerges it will be absorbed into the total, ever-expanding tapestry of development.

Cumulative Influence

Some events predispose the individual to certain kinds of behavior in later life. Behavior at any moment is a function of the life history of an organism and of the stimuli acting upon it. A significant alteration of either the life history or of the stimulating conditions is likely to produce a different type of behavior. The very concept of development makes it necessary to stress the fact that change is one of the essential attributes of all living organisms and thus by implication that the individual is constantly being altered. Although the events or experiences in the life of the child may themselves be of brief duration, the effects may be stable and permanent. A tornado may last only a few seconds, but its brief visit may leave a permanent scar on the geography of a region.

The principle of cumulative influence is a prosaic way of recognizing the wisdom in the poetic reminder that "The child is father of the man." Development is an irreversible process, just as the flow of time itself is irreversible. The importance of early experiences arises not so much because of their immediate impact but because of whatever residual they leave. A traumatic experience or series of experiences in the life of the child—a serious illness, desertion, or rejection by the parents, consistent favoritism shown to another child in the family—should be evaluated in terms of the possible change in the potential for future adjustment as well as the immediate effects. Likewise, favorable early experiences become important not only because they supply immediate need gratification for the child but also because of their contribution to a life history that will be conducive to continuing good adjustment.

Critical Periods

In the Biblical admonition that there is "A time to be born, and a time to die; a time to plant, and a time to pluck up that which is planted," we find a concise statement of much that is implied in the principle of critical periods. That is, it does provided we interpret it to mean that attempting to plant during the periods when we should be harvesting or vice versa is unwise.

A life history is characterized by a sequence of important formative events sharply etched against a background of seemingly less significant experience. Furthermore, within any given culture, the critical events will show a high degree of similarity. For example, for the American child there are such memorable occasions as the first day of school, loss of the first baby teeth, being permitted to walk to school alone, the first date, graduation from high school, and many, many more. Most of these events will be retained in the memories of the individual; other significant ones, such as the first solo step, the first use of comprehensible speech, and so on, may be remembered only by other family members, but are nonetheless important items on the developmental chart. Another notable thing about such developmental crises is that an inversion in the time schedule is almost invariably a conversation piece. The fact that Mary talked before she walked was long a subject of family discussion; that Harold had not dated a girl during his entire high school career identified him as deviant from the developmental pattern followed by most of his contemporaries.

The critical period hypothesis suggests that

interference with certain developmental phenomena occurring at one point in the life history rather than at another may be of greater significance for establishing future trends. Evidence for this hypothesis will be sought in a variety of developmental phenomena.

We can find support for the critical period hypothesis at virtually every level of observation. Some of the developmental changes occur at the cellular level—the transition from an undifferentiated totipotency to an ordering and constant regrouping of the growing multitude of cells. During this transition certain critical mileposts appear that set the limits to cellular versatility. Up to a point the individual cells are apparently susceptible to diverse influences and, as it were, reveal a chameleon-like adaptability. Evidence on this point comes from transplantation experiments on lower animals during the embryonic stage of development. In such experiments the timing of events is all important.

Suppose some of the cells from the section of the embryo that, if unmolested, would develop into the digestive tract were removed operatively and anchored in the vicinity of the developing heart. If this were done early enough in the life history of the embryo, the cells would develop into a type associated with circulatory functioning, namely, liver cells. Their status at maturity would then seem controlled largely by the situation in which they found themselves. Had the same operation been performed only a day or two later, when the cells of the digestive system had made further headway in their initial surroundings, then transplantation would result only in the juxtaposition of heart and intestines.

What is the significance of such a principle when we look at overt behavior? The answer to that question would require first of all some specification as to the type of behavior concerned and also a defense of the position that a timetable is likely to be followed in any dimension of development. With respect to motor behavior there is some experimental data bearing directly on the question.

It has been demonstrated that salamanders kept in an anesthetic solution during the time when aquatic locomotion should be developing can later acquire precise swimming movements after removal from the solution. However, if left in the anesthesia for longer than a certain length of time (about 13 days), the animals are unable to learn to swim normally (Matthews and Detwiler, 1926). This suggests a critical duration beyond which recovery of normal function is impossible. Likewise, in a famous study of motor development, McGraw (1935) found that attempts to accelerate the acquisition of certain muscular skills were likely to be ineffectual unless introduced at a propitious time in the child's developmental cycle.

From sources as diverse as the animal laboratory, the classroom, and the psychotherapeutic session have come data relevant to the hypothesis. Although these approaches differ in terminology, in the extent to which hypotheses have been put to experimental test, in the populations to which generalizations can be made, and in the kinds of phenomena selected for observation, all nonetheless show an undercurrent of similarity. That is, they all stress the importance of certain events in relation to the time at which these occur.

A good description of the critical-period hypothesis from the perspective of education is that of Robert J. Havighurst (1953). He uses the term *developmental task* to convey the notion of crises in development with which the growing individual must inevitably cope. A developmental task is defined as "a task which arises at or about a certain period in the life of the individual, successful achievement of which leads to his happiness and to success with later tasks, while failure leads to unhappiness in the individual, disapproval by the society, and difficulty with later tasks" (p. 2). In other words, certain developmental tasks *must* be mastered if the child is to develop normally thereafter. These tasks may arise from physical maturation, from cultural pressures, or from the emerging personality that must somehow integrate the forces emanating from the other two sources.

Examples of such tasks that must be faced in early childhood are learning to walk, to talk, and to comprehend and manipulate letter and numerical symbols. Inadequate achievement in any one of these tasks handicaps the individual to a certain extent in his efforts to cope with later contingencies. Consider, for example the problem faced by a child who has not learned to talk but who attempts to establish rewarding social relationships. These learning tasks represent an approach toward integration of the demands made on the child by his physical organism and by the society in which he must develop. They will obviously differ in various social and cultural groups with respect to the manner in which they will be expressed. At the same time, there should be considerable similarity from culture to culture with respect to the tasks themselves if not to the exact manner in which they are revealed.

The Freudian or psychoanalytic description of character development, in which the meaning of the term "character" is actually closer to that ordinarily ascribed to "personality," could legitimately be labeled a critical-period hypothesis. Psychoanalysts postulate several major developmental stages during which the major focus of biological and psychological energy is to be found in one or another bodily zone of development. For example, during the early weeks and months of life, the major source of gratification and, accordingly, of potential frustration, resides in those activities associated with the intake of nourishment. Calling attention to the importance of these incorporative activities, Freud labeled this the "oral" stage. Later the focus of energy was presumed to shift to the anal and eventually the genital zone, at which time the primary source of gratification or satisfaction of important biological and psychological needs was similarly shifted. Freud maintained that insufficient gratification at any one of the periods in effect "freezes" a certain amount of mental energy (his term for this was "fixation of libido") and hampers subsequent normal development. That is, the child who does not receive sufficient gratification of his oral needs presumably is destined to continue to seek substitute (or direct) gratification of such needs and is unable to effect smooth transition to the next developmental stage. In line with this theory a child weaned prematurely or too harshly, or, for that matter, indulged too long in sucking activities, might become fixated at the oral level and be unable to move on freely to more mature developmental levels. In later chapters, we shall examine some of the evidence concerning this contention.

In discussion the importance of timing in the developmental process, it is easy to make the hypothetical timetable sound too rigid, with lengthy barren intervals existing between the critical points. Variability is just as likely to be present in the time schedules of different children as it is in the manner in which patterns of overt behavior are expressed. In order to avoid this implication, it must be mentioned here that the critical period for the development of any form of behavior will be, to a certain extent, unique for each individual and, furthermore, that there is likely to be some overlapping of the periods in whatever conceptual scheme is being considered.

The critical-period concept has received some careful attention in recent years. A major program in President Johnson's "War on

Poverty" in the mid-1960s was Operation Head Start. This program was instituted in order to provide stimulating and cognitively enriching experiences for socially deprived preschool children from poverty homes, with the idea that they would be better able to benefit from regular school experience. Socially deprived children characteristically begin school with IQs moderately below normal, on the average. They make slower and less effective progress through the school curriculum and, by the time they reach adolescence, their mean IQ has declined and they are likely to be retarded two or more years in basic skills. The educators of the 1960s took the critical period to be the preschool years and theorized that if deprived children could be given a "head start," by exposing them to a preschool environment calculated to develop school-oriented skills, percepts, and work habits, they would be able to start school on a more nearly equal footing with children from middle-class homes. However, evaluation studies of Head Start effectiveness have produced mixed results. A common finding is that there is an initial IQ gain of 10 to 15 points, but that it does not hold up beyond the first year of school.

Such results can be interpreted in two ways by proponents of the critical-period theory: either the period selected was not as critical as an earlier one would have been, or else the Head Start programs (many of which had been put together hastily) did not supply what the children lacked. It may also be that there is not one but several critical periods during the preschool years, each of which is important for some skill or percept.

Piaget's Concepts of Development

This latter formulation would be consistent with the theories of Jean Piaget, who has become the most significant figure in child psychology today. His work therefore demands special attention in this discussion of the process of development. Piaget was born in Neuchatel in the French part of Switzerland, in 1896. He early demonstrated an interest in science, publishing his first paper at the age of ten. His earlier interest was in zoology, and by the age of 21 he had published 20 papers on molluscs. In his early 20s, he became interested in psychological problems and worked for a while with Theodore Simon, a collaborator on the Binet scale of intelligence. Piaget was more interested in the responses children gave to the investigator's questions than in the test itself. He was especially fascinated by the incorrect answers and how children arrived at them. During the same period he also studied at Eugen Bleuler's psychiatric clinic in Zurich, where he became acquainted with the *méthode clinique* that later proved so useful in interviewing children as to their processes of reasoning.[1] In 1921, Piaget published four papers on mental testing and was made director of the Institut Jean-Jacques Rousseau in Geneva, now the Institut des Sciences de l'Education (Institute of Educational Sciences). In the years since he has assumed this position, he has published more than 20 books and about 200 major studies, in addition to becoming involved in a great range of scientific and professional activities (Tuddenham, 1966).

Piaget (1970) says that basic to his approach to cognitive development is the idea that each individual's knowledge of the world and its objects is the product of his operations on and with them. Specifically, it is the individual's acting on and transforming these phenomena that enables him to know them. The way in which the child develops his

---

[1] Piaget's use of the clinical method is illustrated by an example we cited in Chapter 2, in which he showed that a six-year-old child is unable to distinguish between a lie and an innocent misstatement.

Jean Piaget observes children dealing with one of his specially designed developmental tasks.

ability to deal with his environment differs at various stages in his life. In his most recent statement, Piaget (1970) has identified three main developmental stages: *sensorimotor, concrete operations,* and *propositional or formal operations.* We shall examine each of them briefly to get a glimpse of the kinds of behavior characteristic of each level of development.

The *sensorimotor* stage occupies the period from birth to about 18 months. Piaget has divided it into a number of substages. During the first month or so, the newborn infant exercises his sensorimotor schemata.[2] These schemata are exercised by sucking, breathing,

[2] *Schemata* is the plural of *schema.* Piaget uses the term *schema* to refer to a coordination of nerves, senses, and muscles that produces a given bit of behavior—an infant reaching toward a colored object, for example.

waving arms and legs, wiggling, gazing, and so forth. The infant next begins to vary his schemata and then to combine them. He sucks and grasps simultaneously and turns his head to follow a moving object. This substage lasts three or four months and is followed by a third substage in which he takes some initiative in responding to his environment. Up until this point he has merely reacted to stimuli; now he begins to initiate involvement. Piaget (1936) described, for example, how his daughter, Lucienne, aged 4 months and 27 days, kicked at a doll that had been hung from the top of her bassinet hood. The doll swung violently. Lucienne was delighted and kicked at it again. The next day, as soon as she saw the doll, she moved her feet. During the next few days, Piaget hung the doll at different points from the hood, and Lucienne attempted to hit it with her foot.

In the fourth substage, which runs from

*According to Jean Piaget, the first 18 months of life constitute the
sensorimotor phase of development*

*After the first three or four months, the infant displays initiative in responding to and
manipulating his environment. He may, for example, kick at a display of toys dangling
above him. Later, when he is able to get around on his own, he begins to explore his
environment. In the preoperational phase of the concrete operations stage, the child
begins to deal with people and things symbolically, especially through linguistic means.*

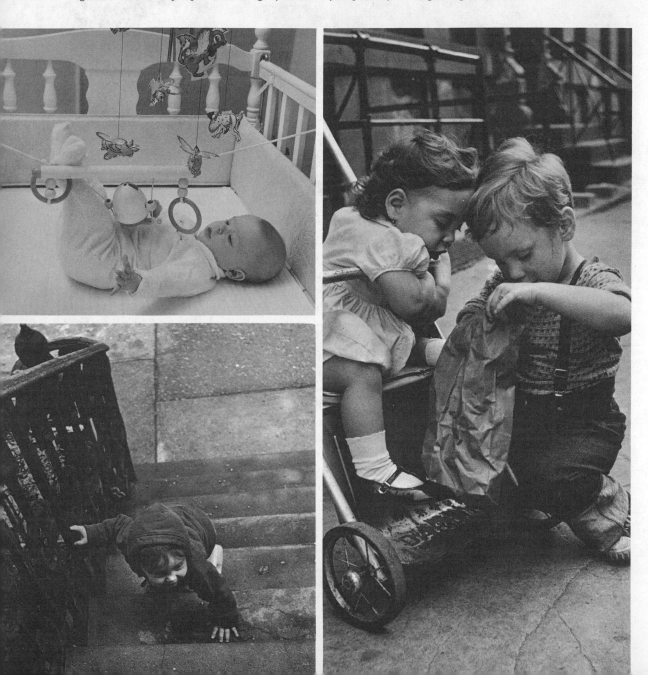

He also investigates and experiments with concepts of form and space. As he moves into the formal operations stage, he learns to deal with complex problems involving probability, logic, and reasoning. Social relations are dealt with on an increasingly complex scale, and the child learns to express the subtleties of dramatic play and humor.

about 8 or 9 months of age to 11 or 12 months, the infant coordinates the secondary schemata that he developed in the third period. He plays games—lets objects fall in order to hear their clatter and to have them picked up again by others and given to him, only to let them fall again. Objects are actively explored and used; space, causality, and time begin to have some meaning; curiosity and interest in novelty appears; the movements of others are imitated. The infant becomes able to locomote during this substage and during the following two substages he begins to walk, to explore his environment in ever-wider circles. Schemata become more and more elaborate and the infant learns to make use of symbols in a rudimentary way.

The second major stage is the stage of *concrete operations,* which begins with a *preoperational* phase, commencing at about one and one-half to two years and continuing until seven or eight years. During the preoperational phase, the child acquires language skills and becomes able to deal with the world symbolically instead of directly, through motor activity. During this period, space and time are seen by the child as centered on him. As Tuddenham (1966) describes it, time is viewed in terms of "before now," "now," and "not yet," and space is located wherever the child happens to be and moves around with him. "When he is taken for an evening walk, the moon follows *him*" (p. 215). He is confused when substances change shape and is hence unable to *conserve* quantity, to use Piaget's terms—that is, he is unable to grasp the concept that water poured from a glass cup into a tall glass cylinder is still the same amount, even though the water level is higher.

In the latter phase of the concrete operations stage, which extends from about 6 or 7 to 11 or 12, the child shows the development of reasoning. He is no longer fooled by the conservation problem just described, and is

able to classify items, order them in series, and number them.

The third stage, *formal operations,* begins where concrete operations leaves off and extends for about two more years. Children in this stage are able to handle abstract relationships, deal with hypothetical situations, understand and use probability, and deal with other complex problems involving logic and reasoning.

Some critics have taken Piaget to task for tying down these stages to certain age ranges, but Piaget maintains that the ages as such are not vital, because it is the *order* of the stages that is important. A child cannot move into the formal operations stage until he has successfully worked through the experiences of the concrete operations stage, whatever his age happens to be. On the island of Martinique in the Caribbean, children are four years behind children in Montreal, Canada (Laurendeau and Pinard, 1963) and some Brazilian Indians evidently never get to the stage of formal operations (Tuddenham, 1966).

Incidentally, some observers have noted that American children apparently attain facility in cognitive processes earlier than the subjects studied by Piaget and his co-worker Bärbel Inhelder (Kooistra, 1963). One reason for this difference may be the tendency of American parents to encourage active, exploratory, and independent behavior in infants and young children.

Although the idea that the behavioral phenomena of development group themselves into fairly well-defined stages seems to have good empirical support, not all psychologists are convinced.

Among the critics of stage theories are Albert Bandura and the late Richard H. Walters (1963a), whose theories on social learning have generated a great deal of experimental research with subjects of all ages. Bandura and Walters maintain that observed similarities in the behavior of children at certain ages can be accounted for primarily by the fact that the children being observed by the researcher are likely to have lived in similar environments and had similar experiences. Whereas stage theories are concerned largely with similarities among children at various points in their development, social learning theorists are more concerned with accounting for differences among individuals and similarities (or continuities) within the modes of behavior displayed by a given individual.

Although the debate between stage theorists and social learning theorists is often heated, the psychologist who listens to them and comes to his own conclusions may decide that both sides have much to offer, that the positions are not as contradictory as they seem at first, and that they are, in effect, reacting to different aspects of the same types of behavior. Although Piaget and his followers do relate certain stages of development to certain ages, Piaget attempts to make it clear that the appearance of a certain mode of cognitive functioning depends on the child's opportunity to have certain experiences. A child cannot, for example, learn the relationships between quantity and volume unless he has experiences that involve these dimensions of reality. Similarly, even the most committed social learning theorist would agree that children are unable to learn certain forms of behavior before they are able to make the necessary discriminations and associations.

Piaget has also been criticized because he uses the clinical method in gathering data, a method that makes it difficult to control for observer bias, as we have noted in our discussion of Freud. Piaget (1929) has maintained that he is very much aware of this problem and routinely subjects his findings to the severest criticism. In his defense, it can be said that experimental tests of his findings and conclusions have generally been supportive, although there have been some exceptions, as we shall note in succeeding chapters. Indeed, one of Piaget's great contributions to child psychology has been the large number of studies and experiments that his ideas have generated.

Discontinuity and Hierarchization. Piaget's own research makes it clear that development is not merely an additive process, but that it leads to schemata or structures that could not have been predicted solely from an analysis of the preceding events. In other words, each stage of development is initiated by discontinuities or abrupt changes from the previous one. The new, emerging forms of behavior are not merely reorganizations of earlier forms. The infant's locomotion will be found to show four stages—lying prone, crawling, creeping, and walking—and each stage involves movements not present at the earlier stage.

This concept of developmental discontinuity is attacked by some psychologists as somehow nonscientific. Properly understood, there is nothing mystical or strange about it. Discontinuity is present in other sciences where it is accepted without question. Water, which is formed of two parts of hydrogen and one part of oxygen, has properties not found in either; the tulip bulb contains the potentialities successively of leaves, bud, and blossom, without their being evident in the bulb. The visible spectrum, which is based on quantitative changes of wavelengths, shows abrupt changes at certain points, when passing from violet to indigo, blue to green, and yellow to orange. Hence there is no special reason why similar discontinuities cannot occur in human behavior and be recognized as scientific facts.

As the structures and functions in a new stage develop, they show an organization that is more elaborate and that includes more elements than do those that appeared in stages earlier in the sequence. This form of discontinuity is referred to as *hierarchization* (Werner, 1957). In the developmental theory of Piaget (1950), for example, the various levels or stages of conceptual development show a hierarchy of progressive differentiation. Each new level of thought, of intelligence, and the like, uses the material of the lower level or levels, but transforms it by greater differentiation and a new coordination so that the new stage draws upon the old, yet becomes a new stage. Each level is an organized totality that is a new entity understandable in terms of itself. A new level is fundamentally an innovation, not derivable from the characteristics of the previous levels.

Maturation and Learning

As we noted earlier, genetic factors have some influence on intelligence, personality, and susceptibility to certain mental disorders. It is also well known that they determine body shape and size, and pigmentation as well. As we also indicated, there is no certainty as to what the precise limits are to this genetic influence, and they probably vary under different environmental conditions.

During the earlier stages of development, certain gross features of the environment, such as insufficient nutrition or extreme over- or understimulation, may have a negative or retarding effect on development. When the child is able to take an active part in interacting with his social environment, the picture becomes more complicated and it is often difficult to decide whether a given type of behavior is more genetically or more environmentally determined. A case in point is the restlessness of children during the primary school years. In North-American schools, we provide for recess periods during the primary grades on the assumption that children cannot concentrate on classroom tasks if they have to sit for long hours. In a great many

Italian schools, however, there are no recess periods (and no school playgrounds, for that matter) and the children sit quietly for long hours working on their assigned tasks. It is difficult to determine which of the two behavior patterns is "normal" and which is learned. Americans who visit Italian schools are likely to view the behavior of the Italian child as "nonnormal" and the result of an unduly constricting environment, whereas Italians are likely to view the restlessness of the American child as resulting from an overstimulating environment, coupled with an excess of permissiveness.

However much the social environment may affect a child's behavior, there is no evidence that even the most ideal environment, whatever that may be, can speed up the developmental processes and cause a child to progress faster than his genetically determined timetable will allow. Any change in behavior brought about by varying the environment will presumably have to take place within the limits set by that timetable. In other words, *learning* is limited (or made possible) by *maturation*. When we use the term *maturation,* we are referring to forms of behavior that appear spontaneously in the developmental sequence, in contrast to learned behavior—those forms that are environmentally instigated.

Many definitions have been proposed for the two concepts: learning and maturation. Of the two, learning has been defined with much less equivocation and with greater community of meaning. Munn (1954) offers the definition "Learning may be said to occur whenever behavior undergoes incremental modification of a more or less permanent nature as a result of activity, special training, or observation" (p. 374). Some of the crucial terms in this definition differentiate learning (*a*) from fatigue (which would involve a performance decrement rather than an increment), (*b*) from sensory adaptation (relatively impermanent modification), and (*c*) from maturation (which should not depend on special activity or training). Changes in function—in ability to do things—are shown by learning. It is not simply a change in physical equipment but in capacity to perform. Details about the learning process are reserved for discussion in a later chapter.

Definitions of maturation have not revealed as much uniformity of thinking. In its original scientific usage the term was used by geneticists to denote the development occurring within the immature germ cell prior to the process of fertilization. Gesell (1933) was one of the first writers to use it in a broader sense, applying it to those developmental phenomena that appear to develop in an orderly fashion without the intervention of any known external stimuli. This usage applies the term to *behavior* as well as to changes in the nerves, muscles, and glands which provide the necessary implements for the execution of behavioral activities.

Carmichael (1951) avoided the formulation of an explicit definition by proposing three criteria by means of which changes attributable to maturation can be distinguished: (*a*) the behavior should be demonstrated as developing universally in all or almost all apparently normal organisms of similar physiological endowment; (*b*) the behavior change must occur in an organism too immature to be able to form stable habit patterns; and (*c*) the behavior should appear in an organism that has had no opportunity to observe the act in question in another member of the species. Rigid adherence to the criteria, especially the third, would virtually preclude application of the term to any type of human behavior. " 'Maturation' is simply development in which commonly observed differences between individuals are correlated with previous differences in the inner organism rather than in the environment" (Howells, 1945, p. 29).

The generally unwieldy nature of the concept of maturation and its resistance to precise definition have led some writers to favor abandonment of it altogether and to encourage instead the adoption of a concept in which outer conditions and inner characteristics merge. As Piaget (1952) has put it, organism and environment form an entity. There is an irreducible interdependence that extends over the subject and object. We can never isolate maturation from learning. Maturation, according to Piaget, is the organism's fundamental tendency to organize experience so that it can be assimilated; learning is the means of introducing new experiences into that organization.

This approach would recognize the inseparability of the maturational and learning processes. Some writers have objected to such attempts on the grounds that fusion of the two concepts makes scientific investigation of the developmental process difficult and shuns precise explanation in favor of global description. Marquis (1930) once asserted that the two concepts can be separated and proposed as the distinguishing criteria the following: "Both processes, it is true, represent an interaction of organism and environment, but learning is distinguished from maturation by this fact: It represents a modification of the organismic pattern in response to specific stimuli present in the external environment at the time of the modification. Maturation, on the other hand, is a modification of the organismic pattern in response to stimuli present in the inter-cellular and intra-cellular environments which at the given moment are independent of external influence" (pp. 347–348).

Although at first glance this definition may appear to emphasize a fundamental distinction, the ambiguity of such concepts as "organismic pattern" and "internal and external environments" soon becomes apparent. Thus we are left with the inevitability of defining both maturation and learning in terms of each other—behavior change not attributable to learning is said to be due to maturation, and vice versa. This is a rather ineffectual way of establishing the independence of either concept. Nevertheless, maturation will be found to be demonstrated primarily through studies in which there is little or no opportunity for learning to take place. Chapter 7, concerned with psychological development in infancy, contains many illustrations of this way of studying maturation.

Maturation (nature) interacts with learning (nurture) to form development (Olson, 1957). It is important to note that they are not additive ($+$) but interactive ($\times$). The formula is

Maturation $\times$ Learning = Development.

In the absence of experience of a specified sort the equation becomes

Maturation $\times$ Zero Learning
$$= \text{Zero Achievement.}$$
Cases in point would be the absence of enuresis (bed-wetting) in a culture where there are no bed clothes to soil or the absence of reading in that same primitive group.

Another formula that applies in the absence of maturation is

Zero Maturation $\times$ Learning Opportunity
$$= \text{Zero Achievement.}$$
Illustrative would be the findings of differences between species. In studying this problem the Hayes (1951) family reared an infant, female chimpanzee in their own home in as close approximation to care of the human infant as possible. The family endeavored to lavish upon her the affection and to give the instruction that might be given to one's own child. Various motor skills, such as pulling the thumb on the hand, holding the feeding bottle toward her, or later, doing the same to a string to which the bottle was attached, were relatively easily developed. Peek-a-boo, hand clapping, and bead stringing were in her repertoire. In these performances the chimpanzee was not to different from a human infant. But in language there was a marked contrast. Here she was very deficient. She never cried, but gave a chimpanzee bark at five weeks and a bark signifying food at fourteen weeks. Only with great difficulty was she taught to sound approximately a few words. Structural and functional differences from the human did not allow the chimpanzee to show maturation in language development. To be sure, another psychologist couple raising an ape were able to teach it a form of rudimentary sign language (Gardner and Gardner, 1969), but the point is still valid: learning cannot exceed the limits set by an animal's physiology.

It has often been said that progress in any field of scientific inquiry is made less by finding the right answers than by asking the right questions. An integrative approach to the developmental process seems to facilitate phrasing questions in such a way that meaningful answers can be found. Viewed in this way, the proper question becomes one *not* of the priority of maturation or learning. Rather it seems more appropriate to inquire into the extent to which the process of development can be influenced or modified by *intervention*. Is development an inexorable, immutable process that will attain realization regardless of the kind of environmental influences to which the organism might be exposed? Or, if it is modifiable, to what extent is this possible? And, as might be predicted from the discussion of critical periods, are there times when modification is more feasible than others? Likewise, if emerging functions are interfered with, is this likely to have a deleterious effect on the total development? To these questions considerable attention will be devoted in later chapters.

The Significance of Age

When children's behavioral manifestations can be shown to correlate with their ages, the psychologist can be reasonably sure that he is dealing with a developmental phenomenon (Kessen, 1960). This relationship can be expressed in the formula $R = f(A)$, in which R (response) is whatever behavior the investigator is studying, and A represents chronological age or some variant, such as mental age. The formula therefore reads "behavior observed (or to be observed) is a function of age." Many problems can be studied in terms of this formula—attempts, for example, to answer the question of what a newborn infant, a child of two, or a child of seven can or cannot do. But this is not enough.

The task of the psychologist is not complete when he demonstrates a relationship between age and a psychological characteristic. To relate a given vocabulary to a given age in children is informative, but it by no means explains the association that has been found. Psychologists want to be able to specify the determinants of this characteristic, to isolate the antecedents that brought about its psychological quality. Something other than sheer age is operative in most of the problems of child psychology.

Size of vocabulary, for example, can be related to age in a reasonably consistent way, but, despite increase with age, there is wide variability at a given age. Other aspects of the child's history must be examined to discover the factors that help to account for its size, rather than saying that his vocabulary is so and so *because* of age. Moreover, knowledge of age alone does not tell how to manipulate the phenomena in question for the best interest of the child and of society. If we wish to deal with variables under manipulable control, we must isolate characteristics other than age itself, a factor that we cannot prevent changing in a given child.

Summary

Growth is basic to all development. Strictly speaking, *growth* refers to an increase in size or number, while *development* refers to changes of character or function. *Development* is the more general term. It refers to a *process,* rather than a thing and must be inferred from differences between observations made at different points in time.

Accounting for differences between people is a major concern of the psychologist. In recent years, especially in North America, the tendency has been to attribute these differences to environmental influences, rather than to genetic factors. Support for this view lies in the fact that man is a plastic organism, capable of an infinite number of adaptive response patterns. Yet there are doubts. It is not certain, for example, whether the Zuñi Indians are placid because they are so conditioned by their culture, or because they are born that way. The traditional approach to this kind of problem has been through the study of twins. There are two kinds of twins: monozygotic (MZ), from a single fertilized ovum; and dizygotic (DZ), from two fertilized ova. MZ twins have identical genetic elements, so differences between them are the result of environmental forces. On the other hand, like-sex DZ twins who are raised under similar conditions show the effects of genetic differences as well as environmental ones. Twin studies have dealt with three kinds of variables: intelligence, personality traits, and tendencies toward mental disorder. Taken all together, the results of these studies suggest that genetic factors make a considerable contribution to behavior.

Developmental changes occur in an orderly, sequential fashion. The forces that come into play, however, are complex, and their interaction makes the whole child reacting to his total environment the only functionally discrete unit of observation. In selecting a variable for studying the developmental process, we might select a measure that reflects either *structure* or *function*. Structure is often best understood in relation to the function or behavior that it makes possible. Sexual maturity, for example, which implies structural maturity, is defined in terms of functional maturity. Observation of the human embryo and infant reveals the general pattern of growth to be both *cephalocaudal* and *proximodistal*. At any given temporal point, the head is better developed than the legs and feet. *Differentiation* and *integration* are also facets of the infant's functional development. The original cell from which the child develops may be thought of as *totipotent,* possessing the capacity to become any structure that will later be found in the embryo. To develop, the cell must divide and differentiate, so that the organism will act as a coordinated whole, the cells must integrate. These simultaneous processes may be found in the development of behavior at almost any level, from the beginnings of aquatic locomotion in the salamander to the development of human prehension.

The critical period hypothesis expresses another important aspect of the developmental process. This hypothesis suggests that certain developmental phenomena are more important at specific points in an organism's life than at others. The chameleonlike adaptability of individual cells at the earliest period of development is a good example. Transplanted cells lose the ability to adapt to their surroundings once this critical period is past. Salamanders kept in anesthetic solution for a certain length of time during and after the period when aquatic locomotion should be developing, never learn to swim. Havighurst uses the term *developmental task* for behavior that must be mastered during certain critical stages in order to permit development of appropriate behavior in the next stage. For instance, every child must learn to walk and to talk, or he will be unable to cope with social demands during childhood.

Freud incorporated the critical period hypothesis into his description of personality development. Insufficient gratification at any one of several developmental stages "fixates" the child at that stage and hampers further development. The child who does not receive sufficient gratification of his oral needs may become fixated at the oral stage.

The critical-period concept has been receiving a large amount of attention in recent years. Operation Head Start is based on the assumption that certain kinds of enrichment during the preschool years is essential to later school-oriented skills, precepts, and work habits. However, evaluation of the program's effectiveness have produced mixed results. A common finding is that there is an initial IQ gain of 10 to 15 points which does not last beyond the first year of elementary school.

Jean Piaget has made extensive use of the critical-period hypothesis in his description of cognitive development. Basic to his approach is the idea that each individual's knowledge of the world and its objects is the product of his operations on and with them. These operations pass through three main stages: *sensorimotor, concrete operations,* and *formal operations.* The sensorimotor stage occupies the period from birth to 18 months, and consists of four phases. During the first month or so, the infant exercises his sensorimotor *sche-*

mata. He next begins to vary and combine them. During the third phase, he begins to initiate behavior rather than merely reacting to stimuli. The infant's sense of curiosity and an active exploratory interest appear during the fourth phase, which fills the last several months of the first year of life. The concrete operations stage begins with the *preoperational phase,* commencing at about one and one-half to two years of age, and continuing until seven or eight years of age. During this period, the child develops symbolic and language skills. He sees space and time as centered on himself and is unable to *conserve* quantity. In the latter phase of the concrete operations stage the child shows the development of reason and is no longer fooled by conservation problems. The third stage, formal operations, begins at age 11 or 12, and extends for about two more years. Children in this stage can handle abstract relationships, deal with hypothetical situations, and can solve complex problems requiring logic and reasoning. Piaget has been criticized for not using more scientific methods of data acquisition, and for tying his stages down to specific age ranges. In response to the latter criticism, Piaget maintains that it is the sequence of stages, not the age at which they occur, which is of importance. Although the former criticism is valid, some of Piaget's ideas have been verified experimentally by others.

Piaget's own research makes it clear that development is not merely additive, but leads to schemata or structures that could not have been predicted solely from preceding events. As the structure and functions of a new stage develop, they show an organization that is more elaborate and which includes more elements than do those that appeared in stages earlier in the sequence. This form of *discontinuity* is called *hierarchization.*

As noted earlier, genetic factors have some influence on intelligence, personality, and susceptibility to certain mental disorders. It is difficult, however, to determine the relative contributions of environment and heredity. Generally speaking, environmentally instigated learning is limited or made possible by *maturation,* the spontaneous appearance of genetically determined behaviors in the developmental sequence. Although most psychologists agree in their definition of learning, the concept of maturation has not generated as much conformity of thinking. Because it seems to resist precise definition, and is difficult to differentiate from learning, some writers have suggested that the concept of maturation be dropped altogether. Perhaps maturation is best defined by the way in which it interacts with learning. The relationship is interactive rather than additive, which means that both maturation and learning must occur for development to take place. For instance, the Hayes' chimpanzee was given the opportunity to learn language, but the limitations of the animal's physical structure did not permit it to achieve maturation in language development.

When children's behavior correlates with what is expected for their ages, the psychologist can be reasonably sure that he is dealing with a developmental phenomenon. This relationship can be expressed as $R = f(A)$. This formula is not enough, however. If we wish to deal with variables under manipulative control, we must isolate the factors that lie behind the influence of age.

4 Socialization, Social Learning, and Personality Development

Each of us resembles *all* other, *some* other, and *no* other individuals (Kluckhohn, Murray and Schneider, 1953). The explanation of how we came to develop these similarities and differences is partly biological and partly environmental, as we noted in the previous chapter. Biological forces set in motion at the point of conception are at first virtually omnipotent, but from birth onward, the environment becomes more and more powerful as an influence that shapes behavior and personality. The physical aspects of the environment are likely to be most crucial in early infancy, for it is important that the baby receive nourishment and be protected against possible injury, but within a few weeks, the social environment begins to intrude and to play an ever-increasing part in the child's development.

Socialization

The process that enables the child to take his place in human society is termed *socialization*. Through socialization, an individual takes on ways of experiencing and behaving that enable him to respond in ways that his society considers to be appropriate. This is an immensely complex process. Society specifies what rewards and restraints are desirable, as well as the conditions under which they will be applied by the child's caretakers. Certain modal patterns of behavior are considered suitable; they relate not only to the way in which the growing child is expected to interact with others and with his physical environment but also to his inner life—that is, to his feelings, beliefs, attitudes, values, and motives. Some deviation from these general patterns is permitted by society, but a child who develops behavior that differs in significant ways will inevitably experience difficulties in his relations with others and in finding his way in the world.

The processes of socialization result in the child's developing a behavioral repertory that is narrower than that of which he is capable. An example of this may be found in language learning. An adolescent who has grown up speaking English and who now enrolls in high school German will have difficulty with such sounds as ö and ü. He is likely to find these sounds "unnatural" and will have problems in shaping lips, tongue, and the rest of his speaking apparatus correctly. When he was an infant, however, these sounds were in his repertory, along with English speech sounds that he has no difficulty in producing. Early in childhood, the ö and the ü dropped out. In learning-theory terms, the English-appropriate sounds were reinforced, whereas the German-appropriate sounds were not reinforced and hence were eliminated.

Curiosity is another example. An infant normally begins exploring as soon as he can locomote. The usual tendency of parents is to discourage or at least limit this behavior, because the child may get into dangerous situations or may become a nuisance. In many middle-class homes, however, exploratory behavior is directed into safe, nondisruptive channels and is encouraged. In effect, the child is rewarded for being curious. When exploratory behavior is discouraged altogether, as it is in some cultures, the child learns to react to novel situations in a passive or even an anxious way. When faced by an unfamiliar problem, he shows little initiative and instead waits for someone to solve it for him or at least show him how to do it. The child whose

exploratory behavior has been reinforced, however, is more likely to try different strategies in attempting to solve a problem and may even be irritated if someone takes over and solves it for him.

By way of an example, Caudill and Weinstein (1969) report that American infants aged three and four months, in contrast to Japanese infants the same age, "are more happily vocal, more active, and more exploratory of their bodies and their physical environment" (p. 42). These differences probably are the result of the fact that American mothers talk more to their infants and encourage them to engage in physical activity and exploration. Japanese mothers, on the other hand, carry their infants around with them and maintain greater physical, rather than verbal, contact with them. A wiggling, exploring baby is naturally harder to manage when carried. Japanese mothers therefore go to some pains to soothe their infants. As a result, Japanese infants become more passive toward their environment. It is very likely that some of the differences between the American and Japanese culture, with respect to environmentally oriented responses, can be related to this early interaction between mother and infant.

Presumably physical activity and exploratory behavior are within the repertories of both American and Japanese infants. In one culture, it is encouraged; in the other, it is discouraged. In both instances, the mother's treatment is consistent with the main culture's general approach to the world and to life in general. Similarly, each culture channels the behavior of its infants in such a way that certain patterns of behavior are discouraged and certain others are encouraged. This shaping of the responses that infants display spontaneously is, however, not the only explanation of the behavior patterns that appear later, as we shall see from the following discussion.

Socialization and Learning

As far as can be determined, differences among cultures with respect to the behavior of newborns are likely to be minimal—that is, there are individual differences within *any* sample of infants, but behavioral differences *between* groups of Saudi-Arab, Ethiopian, Italian-Swiss, or suburban American newborns are probably nonexistent. At this stage of development, all infants sleep a great deal, show the sucking reflex, cry when they are hungry, and so forth. By the time they are two or three years old, however, marked cultural differences can be observed in terms of their behavior toward parents, strange adults, other children, and the objects of their physical environment. Their diets will differ and, as we have noted, their language will differ. These differences in behavior are all learned; they are not inborn.

Classical Conditioning. There are, in theoretical terms, two basic types of learning that can be induced by the manipulation of environmental variables by an experimenter. Both types involve conditioning, that is, the modification of responses. Classical conditioning was the first type to be investigated experimentally. Ivan Pavlov (1849–1936), the Russian physiologist, was doing some research on digestive processes, using dogs whose saliva production could be measured by a tube inserted surgically into the jaw. Salivary flow was induced experimentally by placing powdered meat on the dog's tongue. The dogs developed an annoying characteristic, however; they did not wait for the meat, but began to salivate when they heard the experimenter enter the laboratory. After his initial annoyance with this unexpected behavior, Pavlov became interested in this response tendency and began to experiment with it, using the sound of a tuning fork to initiate the

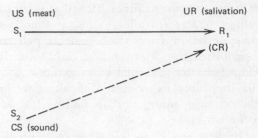

Figure 4-1. Classical conditioning: a new stimulus (sound) evokes a response (salivation) initially evoked by another stimulus (meat).

salivary flow. Figure 4-1 shows the relationship he observed among the various stimuli and responses in the experimental situation. The meat is the *unconditioned stimulus* (S_1 or US); the saliva flow is the *unconditioned response* (R_1 or UR) to the US. When a new stimulus, like the sound of a tuning fork, is repeatedly paired with the US, it may in some instances become sufficient in itself to produce the salivation response—that is, in the absence of the US. If this occurs, the new stimulus is termed a *conditioned stimulus* (S_2, or CS) and the response thus evoked is referred to as the *conditioned response* or CR.

To use an analogous example from infancy, the normal response to the nipple in the mouth is the sucking response. As the infant becomes able to distinguish visual patterns, the appearance of the bottle also stimulates mouth movements, as in sucking. The nipple is the US and the resulting mouth movements is the UR; the appearance of the bottle is the CS, because it appears in connection with (and hence is "conditioned" to) the nipple. The CR is, of course, the mouth movements that appear when the bottle comes into view.

Classical conditioning is a relatively rudimentary form of learning and is used to refer to situations in which the experimenter wants the organism to retain a certain response but to produce it in connection with a second stimulus—a stimulus other than the one that evoked it in the first place. Here is another example: The infant is now several weeks old and the mother wants to introduce some solid food into his diet. At feeding time she prepares a little strained banana and puts it into the infant's mouth with a spoon. The infant is puzzled, not knowing what to make of this strange substance. The stimulation of the lips results in the sucking reflex, however, and some of the banana becomes ingested, whereupon the nipple is presented and the usual feeding routine is carried out. For the next few days, the infant is introduced to mashed banana at the start of the feeding period, and in a short time accepts it as a reasonable form of nourishment, making somewhat the same response to it as he makes to milk.

C. Joan Early (1968) conducted a clever experiment in which attitudes of fourth and fifth graders were changed with respect to their less popular classmates. Early first conducted a survey in order to identify the less popular children or "isolates." Then she asked all the children to memorize a list of word pairs. The first half of each word pair consisted of the name of a child in the class and the second half consisted of another word, such as "neat" or "and." Half the isolates' names were paired with positive value words like "neat" (the experimental group), and the names of the other half (the control group) were paired with neutral value words like "and." The names of all the other class members were also paired with neutral words. Results showed that the children subsequently gave the experimental isolates more attention and interacted with them more, whereas their behavior toward the control isolates was unchanged. In other words, the task of memorizing and associating positive words with the names of the isolates in the experimental group gave the class members a more favorable attitude toward them. The US in this

experiment was the positive word (e.g., "neat"), and the UR was the favorable reaction the children had to the US. The CS was the experimental isolate child and the CR was the class's favorable reaction to him.

Instrumental or Operant Conditioning. In most learning situations we are not so concerned with trying to get the organism to give the same response to a new stimulus, but with getting it to give some new responses. A six-year-old may respond to the stimulus *book* by turning the pages and looking for pictures, instead of trying to read. In this instance, we want the child to substitute some different responses and hence are likely to resort to some form of operant or instrumental conditioning. An initial objective may be getting the child to start figuring out the letters that comprise the words, or it may be that of getting him to identify whole words or phrases. In order to conceptualize what we are trying to do, let us assume that the child has a hierarchy of possible responses to books: looking at the pictures, studying their words, tearing pages out, throwing books at other children, ignoring them. This child looks at the pictures because that response is at the top of the list or hierarchy. The other responses are possible, and we note that occasionally he stops and briefly looks at some of the words and then goes back to the pictures. He may also exchange some shouted words with the child across the table, however, and we can see that it would not take much for them to get into a playful throwing match.

What we want to do, now, is to get the child to attend to the words, at least to the point of asking us some questions about them. In order to accomplish this goal, we use a method termed *reinforcement*. In classical conditioning, reinforcement was accomplished by following the CS by the US—that is, following the appearance of the bottle by the nipple in the mouth. With our present problem, we use the technique of *instrumental or operant conditioning* and follow the appearance of some desired behavior with a reward.

We watch the child, and the next time he stops to look at a printed page, we reinforce that behavior by rewarding him. We could give him a small candy, a stimulus that has been found to be rewarding in working with children, or we might express approval by saying "Good." We decide to do the latter, on the grounds that it is less distracting. We continue to reinforce text-oriented behavior, until we have him spending much more time looking at words. Now we want him to ask questions. If he has been talking about the book, we reinforce talking about the text and ignore whatever he says about the pictures. Gradually we reinforce or "shape" his behavior so that he is spending even more time looking at the textual material and is asking questions about the words. We do not mean to imply that this is *the* way to teach reading, and are only using this example to show how operant conditioning methods can be used to modify behavior, getting a subject to substitute one type of response for another. If motivation and interest in a task are considered important, however, the behavior sequence we have described can be considered as one approach to getting a child involved in a new task.

What we have been describing is the use of reward or positive reinforcement in bringing about learning. Learning can also result from negative reinforcement. In some instances, a child's response—for example, emptying the sugarbowl—may be followed by uncomfortable, painful, or otherwise unsatisfying results, and he learns to eliminate it. Note that the objective of the reinforcer here is the *elimination* of a response, not the acquisition of a new one. Parents, teachers, and other authority figures often attempt to use negative reinforcement in an attempt to get children to try new patterns of behavior, but these attempts usually fail unless there is some positive reinforcing of the desired new pattern. This second step is unfortunately overlooked all too often.

In most of our discussions involving learning we shall be concerned with the acquisition of new behavior patterns, rather than with the discouragement of old ones. For that reason we will be principally interested in positive reinforcement. When we use the term *reinforcement,* we shall therefore be referring to its positive forms, unless we specify to the contrary.

Learning Through Observation, Identification, and Imitation. We come now to a third type of learning, one that calls for some initiative on the part of the learner. Albert Bandura (1969) has pointed out that if we were solely dependent on reward and punishment to accomplish social learning, we would never survive the process. Something more is needed to bring novel responses into the repertory of the individual. Operant conditioning is an improvement over classical conditioning, in that the individual can be guided into more effective modes of behavior, but it does not explain how a child comes to emit a response for the first time. The learning mechanism that enables children to acquire a vast array of responses that are new to them is *imitation,* a process whereby a child matches his behavior to that of another person in a similar situation. The other person thus becomes the *model* for the child, and the imitative process may be termed *modeling.* In his most recent discussion of social learning, Bandura (1969) shows a preference for the term *identification,* which he defines as "a process in which a person patterns his thoughts, feelings, or actions after another person who serves as a model" (p. 214). Bandura then expands this definition to characterize identification as a "continuous process in which new responses are acquired and existing repertoires of behavior are modified to some extent" as a result of direct or indirect experiences with models, real or symbolic whose attitudes, values, beliefs, and motives are revealed by their behavior (p. 255). Although theoretical distinctions are sometimes made between imitation, modeling, and identification, they are not always clear to the nonspecialist, and psychologists themselves differ in the way they use the terms. We shall follow the usual practice and refer to the process as *modeling*.

The child who is about to learn a new segment of behavior first *attends* to the person displaying the behavior—the model. In other words, he orients himself to the model's behavior, ignoring other and potentially competing stimuli in the immediate environment. As the child observes the model's behavior, he recognizes and differentiates what is different between his own responses and the model's responses. There has to be some positive motivation, of course. Merely observing a model's behavior will not in itself lead to learning unless what the model happens to be doing is relevant to some need of the observer. The observer must also be able to interpret the model's behavior in some symbolic way. In other words, if what the model is doing does not make sense to the observer, it will not be learned. Most, but not all, modeling occurs after the child has acquired a measure of linguistic facility, because linguistic interchange enables him to understand the meaning of the model's behavior both in terms of what is being done and why it is important.

The new responses are *acquired* and re-*tained* by the child by his practicing them vicariously (mentally) and in actual behavior. This is most likely to occur when the behaviors lead to satisfying outcomes. This means that the behaviors will be retained if they are reinforced. Sometimes the model (parent or teacher) reinforces the learning through praise or some kind of behavior or gesture that signifies acceptance. At other times, the child notes that the model's behavior is reinforced by others or merely by accomplishing a desired objective. If bicycle riding is the skill being observed, the model's behavior may be considered reinforced by his success in not falling off and in guiding the machine successfully. Most of the time, however, the process is one of self-reinforcement, whereby the learner discovers that his own attempts to duplicate the behavior are satisfying or correct.

The term *identification,* as used by clinically oriented psychologists, carries with it more meaning than mere imitation or even modeling. As used in this way, the term implies positive regard and a desire to affiliate with the behavior model. Such an attitude makes learning even more probable.

If the learner sees the model as someone he would like to resemble in certain ways, he is more likely to attempt to imitate the model's behavior. Identification, too, leads the learner to imagine himself in the model's place—to *empathize* with him—and to behave the way he believes the model is behaving. "Behaving," in this instance, includes the less visible aspects of the model's behavior: thinking, feeling, valuing, and the like.

Psychoanalytic theory also uses the concept of identification, in that the child is thought to use one or both parents as models because of their power to express or withhold love. Freud (1925) maintained that after an affectional relationship has developed between mother and child, the mother may, because of disapproval of the child's misbehavior, threaten to withdraw love—that is, may punish or ignore the child. Such a threat has a powerful effect on the child who has come to expect that the mother's love will be given without conditions or reservations. Experiences in which the mother has indicated to the child that he is not loved when he misbehaves, leads him to take on the mother's behavior and attitudes through a process of imitation, identification, or *introjection,* to use the Freudian term. Bandura (1969) grants that a child of warm, nurturant parents is more likely to imitate their behavior, but explains this tendency in terms of the fact that such parents have more interactive contact with their child than do cold, aloof parents, and hence have more opportunities to reinforce his behavior. Bandura's research has led him to conclude that the important independent variable that leads to imitation is the model's power to reward. His research has shown that children are more likely to imitate the behavior of more powerful than of less powerful models.

In school situations, children will often go out of their way to perform learning tasks for teachers who give them special attention. This is especially true of children from slum homes. Middle-class children are likely to invest some time and energy in school tasks regardless of whether they like the teacher or not, but slum children often do poorly on classroom learning tasks when they dislike the teacher. In effect, middle-class children are largely self-reinforcing in school situations, whereas slum children are more dependent on the reinforcement supplied by the teacher. Teachers who are willing to give them personal attention are therefore powerful models for them, and it is their behavior that slum children will imitate. Colder, rejecting, more socially distant teachers have little reward

value for them and hence do not elicit imitative behavior.

Here is an example of an experiment using modeling as a way of inducing more highly socialized behavior in children. Liebert and Poulos (1971) asked second- and third-grade girls to engage in a judging task in which the payoff for accuracy consisted of tokens that could be exchanged for prizes. The more tokens the child earned, the better the prize. Some of the child subjects worked on the task together with an adult, and results were rigged so that both earned the same amount of tokens: eight. As the two were about to go into an adjoining room to get their prizes, the experimenter asked them if they would contribute some of their tokens for children in another school, who wouldn't have a chance to earn tokens and exchange them for prizes. The adult then deposited four of her tokens and left the room. For some of the children in the experimental condition, the experimenter also left immediately so that apparently no one was there to observe whether the child contributed anything; for others, the experimenter stayed on and watched the child decide whether or not to share her earnings.

The results, as shown in Figure 4-2, indicate that both the opportunity to observe a model and the presence of a witnessing experimenter facilitated sharing behavior on the part of the children. Those who had no model to observe and were also alone when it came time to share earnings, gave the least, whereas the greatest amount of giving occurred when the children saw the model give and were also watched by the experimenter. Inasmuch as giving was entirely voluntary on the part of the girls, the results show what a powerful effect a model has on children's behavior, an effect that is considerably strengthened when an adult other than the model is watching.

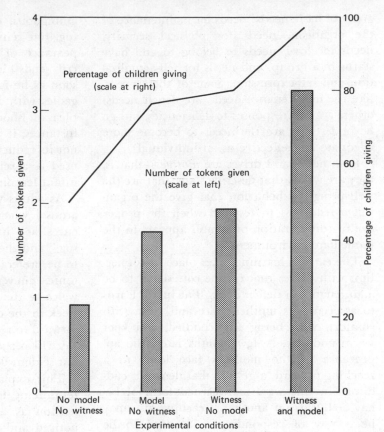

Figure 4-2. Effect of watching a model and being observed on the sharing behavior of primary school girls.
(After **Liebert** and **Poulos**, 1971.)

Motives Underlying Socialization

Drives and Needs. In order for reinforcement to have any effect at all, it must have some relationship to the learner's needs. A food pellet is a reinforcer for a hungry rat, but not for a satiated one. For a slum child, a teacher's "That's very good!" may be a reinforcer, but the same comment from a disliked teacher will have little effect.

What we are saying is that organisms, rats and humans alike, are selective in the way they respond to the stimuli in their environment. Some stimuli evoke responses; others do not. The experimentalist calls this readiness to respond in appropriate ways to appropriate stimuli a *drive*.

A drive is a set of internal conditions in an organism that can be aroused by internal or external stimuli and that lead it to seek some goal. Attainment of the goal reduces the drive and reinforces the behavior leading to the goal. Hunger is a drive that leads to food-seeking behavior, and ingestion of food reduces the drive.

Hunger may also be considered as a *need* for food. Used in this sense, the term *need* refers to a deficiency or deficit in some stimulus that is important for the well-being of the organism. Need may also refer to the tension that results from the deficit; hence we can speak of a need for nourishment or a need for love. Needs can also be quite complex. Abraham H. Maslow (1954) speaks of a hierarchy of basic needs: needs for maintenance of the organism, needs for physical security, needs for love, needs to belong to and have status in a group, and needs for self-actualization and self-expression. Some of these needs, like the maintenance needs, are deficit needs; others are not responses to deficiencies, but go beyond: these are the needs to become more adequate and effective as an individual.

Both needs and drives are *motives*—that is, they are words that describe states that are the wellsprings of behavior, that give the organism a readiness to respond when the proper *cue* or configuration of stimuli appears in the immediate environment.

The earliest learning takes place in connection with drives that can be considered to be maintenance or deficit needs. The infant learns to associate his mother's face and voice with comfort, with being fed, cuddled, and kept warm and dry. A few months later, the appearance of the mother's face leads to a reaching upward, a gesture that demands cuddling. In this way, one learned form of behavior builds on another. Reaching also may be a way of responding to a need to be loved, which many personality theorists consider to be a deficit need, one that must be satisfied if the child is to flourish and develop normal, mature patterns of behavior.

The Need for Arousal. Some forms of goal-directed behavior satisfy the drive-reduction theory very well. This is especially true of physiological drives, like hunger and thirst, as well as of deficit needs, like the need for love. Other motives do not fit so well. In a drive state, the organism is aroused, and attainment of the goal leads to satisfaction and a reduction in arousal. A great many activities in life, however, are satisfying not because they reduce arousal, but because they increase it. As Berlyne (1970) points out, situations that contain elements that are novel, surprising,

ambiguous, or complex are not only arousing, but reinforcing as well. The sudden appearance of a human face over an infant's crib sends him into raptures of delight, and as soon as he is able, he will initiate peek-a-boo games with adults in order to experience the pleasant shock over and over again. In such instances, it is arousal itself that is rewarding, not its reduction. Indeed, peek-a-boo has been used as a reinforcer in research dealing with infant learning.

As adults we recognize the reward value of arousal when we characterize certain experiences as "interesting," "intriguing," "exciting," and the like. Such experiences are likely to be preferable to ones that are quite, monotonic, uneventful, and dull. True, we may welcome the quiet of the woods after a hectic week in the city, but after a few days we look forward to returning to an environment where we will certainly be harassed and frustrated, but seldom bored.

This explains why attention itself can be reinforcing to children. If we conceive of attention as a satisfaction for a drive to be noticed and attended to, we are overlooking the fact that attention has an arousal effect and hence is not a drive reducer. To be sure, adults and children alike can work themselves to a frenzy in order to get attention, in which case attention can have a quieting effect, but in the more usual situation, attention adds interest and excitement to an otherwise ordinary experience. If we take a "needs" approach and say that being attended to fills in a deficit caused by a lack of attention, we have a better understanding of the mechanism, but this still disregards the fact that being aroused seems to be a need in and of itself. The child who unsuccessfully attempts to get his parents' attention turns to some activity that may be less preferred but that is arousing. If the activity is forbidden, it is all the more exciting. It may also lead to punishment, in which case, he gets noticed after all and receives a double reward. Children who are unable to get adult attention for positive, prosocial[1] behavior learn to get it through antisocial behavior. One of the reasons why it is so difficult to unlearn this pattern once it has been established is that both the behavior and the punishment have an arousal effect and hence are reinforcing.

Too much arousal can, of course, lead to satiation and discomfort. This means that the relationship between satisfaction and arousal is a curvilinear one. Arousal is rewarding and potentially reinforcing, but only up to a point. In the middle ranges of arousal, we are likely to oscillate, to move up and down on the scale—that is, we reduce the arousal level, so we can have the pleasure of increasing it again. The child of nursery school age happily puts his picture puzzle together, dumps it out, and puts it together again. This may be repeated for a dozen times. Then he abandons it to listen to a story being read. But a few minutes later he returns to the puzzle with renewed interest.

There are several reasons why we learn socialized forms of behavior. One explanation is that we learn to associate significant others —our mother, for example—with certain basic physiological drives. The mother's voice, face, and presence becomes associated with food and comfort. The mother thus takes on primary value and becomes a stimulus that is associated with other important stimuli. This explanation is, in many respects, a classical one. A second explanation, the operant one, conceives of the parents as taking an active role in socializing their child, in the sense that they reinforce some of his responses and either do not reinforce or negatively reinforce others, in order to get him to display

responses that help him to cope with his social environment and to eliminate others that are irrelevant or that actually interfere. Both the classical and the operant explanations explain socializing partly in terms of its survival value.

The Reward Value of Socialization. A third explanation for socialization, one that is related to our more recent discussion, is that socializing has a reward value in and of itself. In other words, the child becomes socialized not only because he wishes to survive and is rewarded for socially acceptable responses but also because interaction with others is perceived as a satisfying experience in and of itself. Social interaction is likely to be an arousing experience. Of all the activities that are available to the individual, interacting with others has the most potentiality for the novel, the surprising, the ambiguous, and the complex, to use Berlyne's (1967) characterization of experiences that are likely to be arousing. Therefore, being accepted by others and being permitted to associate with them has reward value, and the child learns to seek the company of others and become a member of the group in order to experience this arousal.

An experiment by Irons and Zigler (1969) demonstrates the reward value of one type of social arousal. The subjects in the experiment were two groups of boys, aged 8 and 12, one group from an institution (a California Youth Authority facility) and one from an elementary school in a suburban residential area. The boys were asked to play a simple, monotonous game, consisting of dropping marbles in a hole. Each subject was reinforced with approving comments at two-minute intervals as long as he played, and the dependent variable was the length of time the subject continued to play the game. Because the game was simple and monotonous, the only incentive to continue was the reward value of the reinforce-

[1] Positive, friendly, altruistic; the opposite of *anti-social*.

Cultural influences on learning to become a person

Children are kept close to their mothers in East Asian cultures, like Japan. Fathers are models for occupational skills learned in childhood in India. Even more significant are values and attitudes toward the world and life in general . . .

that parents express through what they do and say and that are imitated by children. According to some theories, children have a universal need to be loved and wanted; according to others, all living organisms have a need for stimulation and arousal. For whatever reason, there is no question but that the attention a child receives is a powerful force in how and what he learns.

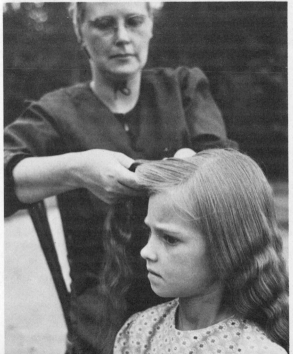

ment. Institutionalized children, in contrast to children living with their families, experience less person-to-person interaction with adults. Hence it is not surprising to learn that the institutionalized children in this experiment worked longer at the monotonous task than did the other children. The Irons-Zigler experiment is one of several conducted in recent years that suggest that children who are deprived of normal interaction with adults build up a kind of a "social hunger" that makes them highly responsive to attention, favorable or otherwise (Gallimore, Tharp, and Kemp, 1969; Tizard, 1964; Dowart et al., 1965).

As an infant matures and becomes a child, changing his relationship to society from that of a passive protégé to that of an active member, he finds that the benefits of membership have their cost. The price exacted by the groups that comprise society is conformity to their norms. This demand for conformity requires that a would-be member of a group must modify not only his overt, visible behavior, but his ways of thinking and feeling as well. To be in a group and not conform leads to rejection. This may take the form of being ignored, in which case the arousal level is too low, or being criticized or punished, in which case arousal is too high. In some instances, of course, the hunger for attention and arousal is so great that the would-be member acts in some outrageous way, in order to experience the arousal that comes from being punished, and may never learn adaptive behavior. For such children, punishment may take on reward value, and the only mode of behavior learned is antisocial in nature. The treatment of choice in such instances seems to be that of ignoring the antisocial behavior and attending to the child only when his behavior is acceptable to the group.

None of these explanations of socialization

tells the whole story; each describes some of the mechanisms that move the child from an asocial humanoid organism to a member of society: (1) the association of the mother with certain biological satisfactions; (2) the reinforcement of prosocial behavior; (3) the imitation of the behavior of powerful models; and (4) learning and conforming to social norms as a way of satisfying a need for arousal.

Learning to Avoid Misbehavior. We have spent considerable time on explaining the development of prosocial behavior, but have said little about another aspect of socialization: the *avoidance* of antisocial, nonconforming behavior. The development of prosocial behavior is the most effective road to socialization. The individual whose attitudes toward others and toward society are positive is likely to find ways of behaving that are consistent with these attitudes.

Much of the literature dealing with socialization, however, is concerned with ways in which behavior that the group considers undesirable can be supressed or eliminated. Part of this concern is due to the fact that behavior which does not conform to group standards is likely to be highly disturbing to group members and is seen by them as a threat to the cohesiveness and psychological integrity of the group. At the very least, it is distracting and disturbing. When young children display behavior that is contrary to accepted norms, we are likely to rush to correct them, seeing the problem as one of getting rid of the undesirable behavior, rather than of teaching them patterns that are more socially acceptable. Busy parents and teachers are likely to be preoccupied with many problems, and the first thing that occurs to them when they see a misbehaving child is to get him to stop doing whatever he is doing. As a consequence, the literature on child socialization is concerned to a major degree with ways of getting children to repress impulses, the development of conscience, the effect of punitive methods of control, and the like.

Of the several theories dealing with this aspect of socialization, the psychoanalytic theory of Freud is the best known. Freudian theory, however, is much more than a concept of socialization: it is a theory of personality development as well as an explanation of psychosexual development.

Psychoanalysis

Freud's work has already been examined as an approach to psychotherapy with patients and somewhat less obviously as a method of research from which to learn about their personalities. At this point interest shifts to the theory of personality that emerged from his labors. From a psychoanalytic point of view, personality is essentially an interplay of reciprocally urging and checking forces (Freud, 1924). Both the nature of these forces and the structure through which their interplay is carried on must be examined.

Dynamics of Personality

Freud (1925) specified the dynamics of personality as a theory of instincts, intrinsic maturational factors. Taken together, the instincts are the sum total of psychic energy. An instinct has four functional characteristics: (a) impetus, the motor element in the amount of force it represents; (b) aim, the satisfaction obtained by abolishing the condition of stimulation; (c) object, that through which the aim can be achieved; and (d) source, the physiological process in a body area in which a stimulus originates.

The cardinal assumption of psychoanalysis is that sexuality is the basic human motive, but Freud and his followers never attributed adult sexuality to the infant or child. Child sexual behavior is not equated with adult sexuality. Instead, they insisted that there was a direct, continuous connection between the behavior of the child in oral and other pregenital stages and his behavior in the genital (adult heterosexual) stage. Infantile sexuality foreshadows but does not completely define the adult pattern.

Just as the ovum contains the adult potentialities, so infantile sexual behavior foreshadows genital behavior. Sexual factors are accepted as the fundamental motivation; nonsexual motivation stems from the sexual.

The libido is the energy for the sexual drives. Almost any impulse to receive pleasure would be an expression of libido, and, hence, considered sexual. In one sense the libido is nonspecific in that it energizes any activity, but in another sense it is quite specific in that the natural expression is sexual. The libido may be defined as that fixed quantity of sexual energy available to an individual from birth onward. Simple physical needs, such as hunger and thirst, are accepted as having drive energy, but these needs are considered relatively uncomplicated and of minor importance in Freudian theory.

Freud (1930) also postulated a second class of drives, the self-preservative drives. In the development of psychoanalysis in still later years, he spoke of life and death instincts in which the latter was invested with a self-destructive quality, including the direction of destructive tendencies upon other persons as expressed in aggressive acts toward them. Aggression is an independent instinctual disposition.

As implied by their acceptance of a relative independence of aggression, psychoanalysts have tended to minimize somewhat in recent years the all-pervasiveness of the sexual motive in accounting for behavior. For the moment, discussion of this point is deferred until we discuss ego autonomy.

Structure of Personality

Freud, early in his work with patients, was struck with the ever-recurring phenomenon of their failing to be aware of certain significant aspects of or events in their lives which, nevertheless, he found had affected them profoundly. Since they behaved as if they were unaware of these determinants of their behavior and aspects of mental life, he referred to them as unconscious. Consequently, in his theoretical formulation he stressed the unconcious aspects of mental life. Freud likened the mind to an iceberg, only its summit of consciousness being above the surface, while its great mass lay below the surface.

Originally Freud adopted a threefold classification of mental life—conscious, foreconscious (capable of becoming conscious but not attended at the moment), and unconscious (repressed, that is, actively excluded from consciousness or instinctual drives that were never conscious). Later, while preserving these distinctions he preferred, on the grounds of greater dynamic possibilities, to speak of structural divisions of personality—the *id*, the ego, and the superego.

In his conception of the structural divisions of personality, the deliberately neutral term *id* (it) was given to the source of unconscious energy. The id's aim is the gratification of its impulses with no sense of morality, logic, or unity of purpose. The major function of the id is to provide free uninhibited discharge of energy. Its activity is in the service of the pleasure principle, that is, the seeking of pleasure and the avoidance of pain with no other considerations entering the picture. This is a kind of animal-like existence with satisfaction only of bodily desires. There is no vestige of "reasonableness" or consideration for the rights of others.

Since the id is unconscious, it has no direct relation with the external world; it can only be known through the ego which does have the characteristic of being conscious (Freud, 1949). Dreams, for example, show the intrusion of id tendencies into consciousness, since the ego is partially relaxed in sleep. Examination of dreams is one way to gain some dim (and frightening) knowledge of id sources. The dreams of even the most straitlaced person are said to contain amoral elements, illustrative of the functioning of the id.

The ego includes the conscious portion of the personality structure. A great portion of the ego exists outside of awareness but can be called into consciousness when needed (the preconscious), while still another part of the ego is unconscious. The unconscious portion of the ego results from repression. Materials once conscious, but unacceptable to the ego, are pushed back into the unconscious. Because of its origin this portion of the ego is called the repressed, and the action of refusing to allow unwelcome impulses to appear in consciousness is known as the mechanism of repression. What is repressed has an "upward driving force," that is, an impulse or drive to break through into consciousness. The ego, under the influence of external reality, controls the entrance into consciousness; therefore, an interplay of reciprocally checking and urging forces is developed in which libido must be expended. To repress requires a continuous expenditure of effort (Freud, 1925, 1935, 1936, 1949).

The ego involves both an awareness of self and the carrying on of executive functions. In connection with the latter, as a representative of reality, the ego serves to mediate among the pressures arising from the id (libidinal pressures), the superego (the conscience and "ego-ideal"), and the demands of external reality. Evaluation of an existing situation, which the individual faces, whatever it might be, and anticipation of the future by him are functions of the ego. Obeying the "reality principle," the ego operates through realistic thinking. Plans are formulated for the satisfaction of needs and carried out (reality testing). In evaluating a situation and in anticipating the future the ego must reckon with the demands of reality as they exist. As an approximation, the ego represents reason, whereas the id represents the untamed passions, although, of course, the latter are represented in consciousness through the ego.

The ego is in control of voluntary movement and is aware of external events. It stores up experiences in memory; it adapts; it learns; it avoids. Thus, it has relation with both the id and the external world. In following the reality principle, the ego mediates between the imperative pressures from the id, the structures of the superego, and the demands of external reality.

Anxiety serves as a signal to the ego, alerting it to danger, internal or external. Although often considered synonymous with fear, Freud preferred the term *anxiety*, because fear is often interpreted as related to something in the external world. Anxiety refers to perception of internal as well as external dangers. The internal conditions giving rise to this anxiety expressed by the ego have to do with unacceptable id impulses or superego demands.

The so-called ego defense mechanisms need preliminary exposition. Anna Freud (1946) who interpreted and extended her father's theories, maintained that each child uses his ego to defend himself in characteristic fashion against anxiety. Each individual has a characteristic pattern for the employment of defense mechanisms, and much variety in personality structures is thus made possible. Repression is one of the major ego defense mechanisms. By preventing the entry of unpleasant thoughts into consciousness, anxiety of a conscious sort is prevented.

Two other illustrative defense mechanisms are *projection,* or attributing to other persons or objects one's own shortcomings as does the inept workman who blames his tools; and *regression,* or returning to less mature forms of behavior than the individual is capable of, as when a ten-year-old throws a temper tantrum. Just as in repression, these defense mechanisms have the characteristic of demanding the expenditure of libido to keep anxiety from appearing. They maintain the status quo but in a manner analogous to a garrison keeping the otherwise restive population in check. At best, they maintain a stalemate; at worst, they express themselves in neurotic or psychotic symptoms.

Sublimation is an important ego mechanism that does not require this continual expenditure of energy. It is the most successful of the mechanisms, since its discharge of energy brings about a significant cessation of impulses without the continued defensive function of the other mechanisms. Sublimations are the socially approved ways of discharging libido without anxiety; they are desexualized expressions of libido. Forms of social behaviors that contain elements of sublimation are social progress, altruism, achievement, and the maintenance of law and order.

A third element of personality is one we have already mentioned in connection with the ego's mediating functions: the *superego*. In a tentative way, it can be said to resemble what in ordinary language is termed "conscience." The superego results from the child's attempts to cope with parental demands that he refrain from behavior that is satisfying but that is also disruptive, destructive, or just "bad." At first, the child responds to direct demands but finds himself unable to refrain from misbehavior when not under parental surveillance. The superego is therefore developed as an internal control entity that represents parental values and behaves toward the ego as the parents once did toward the child. The superego makes the child feel guilty just as did the parents. The reproaches of the superego function as did the reproaches of the parents. Instead of parental criticism there is now self-criticism. The superego has turned aggression against itself.

The prohibitions of the superego must be reckoned with by the ego in expressing id impulses. In this way the superego serves as the vehicle of conscience. However, when the ego and the superego are in harmony, the relationship between the two is felt as pride in accomplishment, and the ego-ideal is manifested. The ego in this case measures itself against the superego and finds that its accomplishment does not fall short of its demands. The requirements of the ego-ideal are being met. The ego-ideal strives after perfection—and occasionally attains it. There are two major aspects, then, of the superego, the moral prohibitions and restrictions, and the ego-ideal. The former is restricting; the latter is satisfying.

The superego serves as an important means of control of those sexual and aggressive impulses, which, if not so controlled, would endanger the very foundation of social life.

Stages of Psychosexual Development

Psychoanalysis posits several stages in psychosexual development. In brief, its view is that the infant shows the capacity to receive pleasure from stimulation of various erogenous zones which assume successive centrality in sequence through the various stages of psychosexual development. An erogenous zone is an area of the body that is sensitive to stimuli and is capable of being stimulated in such a way as to arouse pleasurable libidinal feelings. The lips and oral cavity form one such erogenous zone, the anal region another, and the genital organs still another. Each of these in turn becomes the center of focus of erotic

pleasure in the course of psychosexual development. From birth to adulthood there occurs the oral, anal, phallic, and genital psychosexual stages with the latter two stages separated by the so-called latency period.

During infancy, the obvious source of satisfaction is the mouth. Pleasure comes through taking in nourishment, and displeasure and discomfort come from not receiving it. According to Freudian theory, if the infant is frustrated or dealt with harshly during the oral period, he develops basic fear and anxiety and has problems in dealing with these emotions throughout his life. As a child and an adult, he cannot seem to get enough oral satisfaction and is considered to have been "fixated" at the oral stage of development. If parents overly indulge the infant during the oral period, he may become fixated in a different way—that is, become naïvely trusting and overdependent on others to do things for him.

The next stage, which overlaps with the first, is dominated by problems relating to elimination, hence the term: the *anal stage*. Defecating becomes a source of pleasure during this period, which extends to about age three, but may also be a source of difficulty. This is the period in which society, in the form of the parents, begins to make strong demands that the child conform to proper standards of behavior. Toilet training serves as a focus for this contest of wills, and the child learns that he cannot relieve himself where and when he pleases. Not only does he learn to exercise impulse control when it comes to bowel movements, but he also learns to please his mother by scheduling his movements so they occur at the proper time and in the proper place. Fixation at the anal stage of development may occur if toilet training has been initiated too early or is too strict. If the training has been too severe, personality traits like extreme orderliness, stubbornness, and stinginess are said to eventuate, whereas if the child has been able to "defeat" his parents, he is presumed to develop traits of carelessness, extravagance, and unpunctuality.

During the phallic stage, which extends through the preschool years, children are thought to discover that the genital area can also be a source of pleasure. For boys, this period is marked by the appearance of the *Oedipus complex,* a constellation of behaviors characterized by strong attachment for the mother, coupled with hostile and jealous feelings toward the father, who is seen as a rival for the mother's affection and attention. (The opposite pattern, sometimes called the *Electra complex,* is said to hold for girls). The complex is normally resolved late in the period when the child comes to accept, like, and admire the like-sex parent and to use him (or her) as a model for behavior. When the Oedipal conflict is not resolved satisfactorily, the child may identify with the parent of the opposite sex, with detrimental results as far as his personality development is concerned.

Following the phallic period, children are thought to enter a period of sexual latency, which ends with the genital stage: puberty, adolescence, and the beginning of adulthood.

Freud and his followers felt that the first five years of life were the most significant in the individual's development, and maintained that the main structure of personality was formed then, with further development consisting largely of its elaboration. It is during these five years that children are thought to pass through a number of critical periods, periods in which certain experiences are more likely to affect the course of their later development.

We have devoted a considerable amount of space to Freud's theories because they occupy a very significant place in the history of modern concepts of child development. Freud's ideas regarding anxiety, critical periods, and unconscious processes have a considerable de-

gree of acceptance today, in one form or another, but his ideas about the universality of the Oedipal conflict and fixation at earlier stages of development have not stood up when tested by researchers. For example, William H. Sewell (1952) studied relationships between child-rearing practices and personality traits for 162 farm children of "old American stock" and concluded that psychoanalytically derived concepts were of little or no value in predicting either emotional problems or lack of them.

As a result of studies like this one, developmental psychologists have come to question many of the pronouncements of Freud and his followers. One of the problems with psychoanalytic theory appears to be that much of it is derived from the introspective ruminations of adults about their own childhood, with very little direct observation of the behavior of infants and young children. Psychoanalytically oriented individuals have also been singularly reluctant to test hypotheses with controlled studies, like that of Sewell. Freud's "perceptual set" may also be faulted: he looked at life through the perspective of a middle-class, nineteenth-century Viennese physician and was relatively unaware of the effect that different cultures have on the personality development of children. Nevertheless, he was far ahead of his age and, like Darwin, was able to break the narrow, rigid bonds of the common sense of his day and chart new territory in the study of human behavior.

Other Theories of Personality Development and Socialization

Among the personality theorists who have followed in Freud's footsteps, none has made more of a contribution than Erik Erikson (1963, 1968), whose concepts of development in childhood and adolescence draw on both psychoanalysis and cultural anthropology. Erikson, like most of the successors of Freud,

TABLE 4–1. Schematic Relationship Between Developmental Theories of Freud, Erikson, and Piaget (After Anthony, 1969; and Jersild, 1968)

Stages	Psychosexual Stages (Freud)	Psychosocial Stages (Erikson)	Cognitive Stages (Piaget)	Emotional Problems
0–18m (Infancy)	Oral	Trust vs. mistrust	Sensorimotor	Fear of dark, strangers, aloneness, sudden noise, loss of support. Feeding and sleeping problems; depression, apathy
18m–3 (Nursery)	Anal	Autonomy vs. doubt, shame	Symbolic	Fears separation, desertion, sudden movements, strange sounds. Negativism, constipation, shyness and withdrawing, night terrors
3–5 (Preschool)	Phallic (Oedipal)	Initiative vs. guilt	Intuitive, preoperational	Fears animals, imaginary creatures, injury. Phobias, nightmares, speech problems, bed-wetting (enuresis)
6–11 (Elementary school)	Latency	Industry vs. inferiority	Concrete operational	Fear of school failure, ridicule, loss of possessions, disfigurement, disease, death. School problems, failure to be accepted by peer group
12–17 (Secondary school)	Genital	Identity vs. identity diffusion	Formal operational	Fears being different physically, socially, intellectually; sexual fears; loss of face. Rebelliousness, "acting out," dropping out, destructiveness, apathy, drug-taking

deemphasizes the sexual theme in personality and is more concerned with the *social* aspect of development. His *psychosocial stages* are shown in Table 4-1, together with those of Freud and Piaget, whose developmental system we discussed in Chapter 3. We have also supplemented the lists with examples of emotional problems drawn from the writings of Arthur T. Jersild (1968) and E. James Anthony (1970).

Erikson analyzes and describes each period of development in terms of the psychosocial crises that must be resolved satisfactorily before the individual can go on to the next stage.

In some respects, one can see a similarity here to Havighurst's (1953) developmental tasks which we mentioned in the foregoing chapter. In addition, Erikson takes into account the significant others or "objects" on which the individual's social behavior is focused, the kind of behavior that is appropriate, and the outcome that normally eventuates.

During the years of infancy, the psychosocial conflict is one of *trust versus mistrust*. The social object is, of course, the mother, or whoever happens to play the major caretaker role for the infant. The modalities the infant employs are that of receiving and giving in return. The mother gives nourishment, comfort, attention, and love, and the infant responds with warmth, pleasure, and normal growth and development. If all goes well, the infant learns to have confidence in the orderliness and predictability of his environment; if not, he is likely to become fearful, apprehensive, and panicky.

During the toddler stage, crises are likely to occur with respect to *autonomy versus shame and doubt*. Significant relations are with parental figures, and the basic modalities are holding on and letting go. If all goes well, the child should achieve some measure of self-control and will power. He has learned the rudiments of social behavior and has some degree of independence and self-confidence. This does not mean that all is peace and quiet, however. Self-assertion inevitably leads to friction and negativism. If the crises are not surmounted successfully, the child develops a sense of shame, embarrassment, and self-rejection.

The preschool years are concerned with *initiative versus guilt*. The significant others are the basic family of the child, and the modalities are making, going after, and pretending (in play). If problems are satisfactorily resolved, the child gains direction and purpose; if not, he is likely to be fearful of others, restricted in imagination and play skills, and unduly dependent on adults.

During the middle years of childhood, the crises are related to *industry versus inferiority*, and significant others emerge in the neighborhood play groups and at school. Making and doing things in a group setting are the modalities here. In the North American culture, the world outside the home begins to exert more influence than the family during this period, and social arrangements—rules, regulations, customs, laws, and the like—have an increasing amount of importance. If the crises of this period are dealt with adequately, the child

develops social competence; otherwise he has a sense of personal and social inferiority and inadequacy.

During adolescence, the crises relate to *identity versus identity diffusion*, and the significant others are groups, both peer groups and out-groups, and models of leadership. The modalities during this stage are concerned with becoming oneself and sharing oneself. The adolescent recognizes the complexities of life and human relations, and learns to empathize and sympathize with others. He experiments with various social roles and, if all goes well, learns to avoid roles that carry a "negative identity"—that is, the antisocial or asocial roles of the chronic rebel, the delinquent, the drop-out, or the confirmed "loser."

Erikson's stages number eight in all, the last three covering the adult years and beyond the scope of the present discussion. Like Freud, Erikson's formulations are theoretical and speculative and do not provide many leads for experimental research. All three of the developmental views listed in Table 4-1 are based on clinical research, but it is Piaget's that has had the strongest influence on child psychology and has generated the most research, as we noted in Chapter 3. However, the psychoanalytic theories of Freud and Erikson have had considerable influence in the applied areas of child psychology—particularly on psychotherapy—and they continue to stimulate theories of the broad-gauge, humanistic type in the field of personality.

Social Learning and Personality Theories. In this chapter we have described two major types of explanation for children's social development. The social-learning theories we described in the first part of the chapter tell us, in general terms, that children *learn* the behavior that makes them individuals, whereas the personality theories of Freud and Erikson tell us that there is a kind of inborn mechanism that leads children to develop normally socialized patterns of behavior under favorable conditions and patterns that are less adequate, neurotic, or antisocial when conditions are not favorable. In a sense, we are continuing the theme that appeared in Chapter 3, where we discussed differences between environmentalist and the maturational explanations of child development. It is futile to argue which is the more valid. As far as child study is concerned, both approaches have their value. Environmentalist approaches generate more experiments that enable us to test conflicting hypotheses. They may clarify many points about child development, but the concepts examined are seldom broad enough to present a coherent picture. Personality theories of the developmental type, like those of Freud and Erikson, may falter on details and make some incorrect interpretations, but they give us more generally *usable* concepts of the trends in development. Both approaches are needed; one complements the other. Learning approaches help by correcting the mistakes of the personality theorists, but broad-scale theories are needed to integrate and interrelate the data from isolated observations of children's behavior.

In the chapters that follow, we shall make use of both social learning and personality theory and in each discussion shall use the approach that makes the best sense in interpreting the available data.

Summary

Classical conditioning was originally investigated by Pavlov, a Russian physiologist. In this kind of conditioning procedure, a *conditioned stimulus* (CS) is paired with an *unconditioned stimulus* (US) which arouses an *unconditioned response* (UR). After a number of pairings, the CS evokes a *conditioned response* equivalent to the US. In classical conditioning, the child learns to give the same response to a new stimulus. In *instrumental* or *operant conditioning,* he learns a new response. If the desired behavior is part of the hierarchy of responses already associated with the stimulus, it can be *reinforced,* whenever the stimulus elicits that response. If the response is not part of the hierarchy of responses initially associated with the stimulus, the response may be *shaped* by selective reinforcement of successive approximations to the desired behavior. Although reinforcement is usually used in a positive sense, undesirable responses may be eliminated with *negative reinforcement.* This sort of procedure usually fails unless it is accompanied by positive reinforcement of a substitute behavior.

Bandura suggests that reward and punishment alone cannot account for all social learning. Children acquire new responses through a process of imitation or *modeling.* Initially, the child *attends* to the model. If the observed behavior is relevant and can be interpreted symbolically, it will be *retained* by the child by his practicing it vicariously and in actual behavior. The highest probability of retention occurs when the behavior of the model or modeler is reinforced. *Identification* with the model is also important. Freud used the concept of identification in that the child is thought to use one or both parents as models because of their power to express or withhold love. Bandura prefers to explain the tendency for children of warm, nurturant parents to imitate their parents' behavior by pointing out that such parents have more interactive contact with their children. Middle-class children are more self-motivated in the classroom than slum children. Because the latter are more dependent on reinforcement supplied by the teacher, the teacher's attitude is especially important. The experimentalist believes that

Imitation and the need for attention are important factors in learning.
(Reg Hider in The Christian Science Monitor (c) TCSPS.)

"You, too?"

certain stimuli are reinforcing because they reduce *drives,* which are internal conditions aroused by internal or external stimuli. *Need* is a closely related concept that is defined in terms of a deficit in some necessary stimulus. Both drives and needs are *motives,* and give the organism a readiness to respond to the proper *cue.*

Although most stimuli are reinforcing because they are linked with the reduction of a drive-induced arousal state, some stimuli are sought because they increase the level of arousal. As the use of words like "interesting" or "exciting" would indicate, we all seek novel stimulation to some degree. This need for arousal may explain why it is so difficult to change the response patterns of children who have had to turn to antisocial behavior for attention. The arousing effect of attention and punishment may actually reinforce the behavior. The relationship between satisfac-

tion and arousal is curvilinear, however, and beyond a certain point, arousal becomes unpleasant.

There are several reasons why we learn to become socialized. One explanation is that significant others become reinforcing through their early association with primary reinforcers. Another is that the parents take an active reinforcing role in the conditioning of the infant's social responses. A third explanation is that socializing is rewarding in and of itself. Irons and Zigler demonstrated the reward value of social arousal by asking both institutionalized and normal boys to play a simple, monotonous game and rewarding them with approving comments. The institutionalized boys worked harder, presumably to satisfy their greater "social hunger." As the infant becomes an active member of society, he must pay with conformity for the consequent gains in social arousal. He must either modify his thoughts and feelings (as well as his overt behavior) or be ignored or punished. Behavior that does not conform to group standards is likely to be seen by them as threatening to the cohesiveness and psychological integrity of the group.

Freud's theory of personality development is also a theory of socialization. The cardinal assumption is that sexuality is the basic human motive. In this context, sexuality is not equivalent to adult sexuality. This sexuality is energized by the *libido*. Almost any impulse to receive pleasure is an expression of libido, hence, considered sexual. Unlike the experimentalists, Freud considered hunger and thirst to be of minor importance. Early in his work with patients, Freud was struck by their blindness to certain significant aspects or events in their lives. To explain this lack of awareness, he proposed the *foreconscious* and the *unconscious*. Later he preferred to speak of structural divisions of personality: the *id, ego,* and *superego.* The id merely seeks the gratification of impulse. Since the id is unconscious, it can only interact with the real world through the ego, which is conscious. Dreams are the intrusion of id tendencies into consciousness while the ego is relaxed in sleep. Some portions of the ego exist outside of awareness, but can be called into consciousness when needed (the preconscious). Still other portions are unconscious because they have been *repressed.* The ego operates through realistic thinking, mediates among the demands of the id, the superego (the conscience), and external reality, and carries out all executive functions. Anxiety serves as its signal for internal or external danger. To defend itself against anxiety, the ego may call upon such *defense mechanisms* as *repression, projection,* and *regression. Sublimation* is the most successful mechanism because it discharges libido without anxiety. The superego is an internal control entity that represents parental values and behaves toward the ego as the parents once did toward the child. When the ego and superego are in harmony, the relationship is felt as pride in accomplishment and the *ego-ideal* is manifested.

Psychoanalysis posits several stages of psychosexual development, each identified with an erogenous zone. During infancy, the obvious source of pleasure is the mouth. If the infant is frustrated or dealt with harshly during this *oral* period, he presumably develops basic fear and anxiety. The *anal* stage overlaps with the oral stage, and is dominated by problems relating to elimination. If toilet training has been too severe, personality traits like stinginess and extreme orderliness result. If the child "defeats" his parents, he develops traits like carelessness and extravagance. The *phallic* stage is marked by the appearance of the *Oedipus complex* and the discovery that the genital area can be a source of pleasure. Following this period is a period of sexual latency which ends with the *genital* stage. Psychoanalytic theory was derived from the introspective ruminations of adults about their own childhood and was influenced by Freud's middle-class Viennese "perceptual set."

Among the personality theorists to follow in Freud's footsteps, Erikson has made the most significant contributions to developmental psychology. He deemphasized the sexual aspects of development, and concentrated on *psychosocial* stages, each of which is defined in terms of the crises that must be resolved before the individual goes on to the next stage. During the years of infancy, the psychosocial conflict is one of *trust versus mistrust.* During toddlerhood it is *autonomy versus shame and doubt,* during the preschool years, *initiative versus guilt.* In middle childhood and adolescence, the crises that must be met and solved are *industry versus inferiority* and *identity versus identity diffusion.*

Social learning theories tell us that children learn the behavior that makes them individuals, whereas the personality theories of Freud and Erikson tell us that there are inborn mechanisms that lead to normal socialization under favorable conditions. These points of view reflect a major difference between the environmentalist and geneticist orientations.

PART 2
Infancy

5 The Beginnings of Human Life

It is common practice to date the life of an individual with his birth. Even though we have no recollection of the events of our birth, somehow it seems to mark the point "where we began." It would be more accurate, of course, to date it some nine months before, when we were conceived. Although an individual's age is calculated from the date of his birth in Western cultures, in other cultures—the Japanese, for example—a year is added to reflect the "true beginning" of the individual's life.

From Cell to Organism

This backward extension can be carried even further. Although conception and birth are immensely significant milestones in each individual's life history, the egg and sperm whose union began it all were formed of cells contributed by each parent, and beyond them there is a continuing biological lifeline that extends into infinity, beyond the vague beginnings of human existence. For the purpose of our present discussion, however, we shall confine ourselves to more immediate events.

There are certain uniformities to the biological material contributed by any pair of parents—that is, there are a number of structural and behavioral characteristics that ova and sperm have in common, but there are also elements that are unique. These elements consist of the 46 chromosomes, half from each parent, that provide a kind of a genetic formula or program for each individual's development. The chromosomes are threadlike structures composed of complex double-spiral molecules of *deoxyribonucleic acid* (DNA). Francis Crick, James D. Watson, and Maurice Wilkins won a Nobel prize in 1962 for their research showing that DNA molecules provide the biochemical basis for the genetic transmission of characteristics. It is estimated that there are about a million genetic code units, or genes, in a human cell, which averages out to about 20,000 genes per chromosome. The genes determine the characteristics of another biochemical: *ribonucleic acid* (RNA). The "master program" of the genes is carried out by RNA molecules which serve as "messengers" that determine the structure and functioning of body tissue.

What this means is that the characteristics that any individual displays were set, at least in their initial form, by the DNA molecules in the chromosomes he received from his parents. This fact explains the similarities between parents and children, but it does not explain their differences. The differences come about because of a complex process involving the pairing of chromosomes and the rearranging and trading of genes between chromosomes that takes place shortly after conception. Inasmuch as the number of possible combinations of genes is virtually infinite, we can only speculate as to how children actually turn out to be like their parents and siblings in so many ways. These similarities are most obvious in physical traits, such as the color of eyes, hair, and skin. They are less obvious when it comes to behavioral traits, such as impulsivity, ingenuity, activity level, and the like. The behavior of man is far more modifiable than that of the lesser animals; hence it is far from certain how much of individual differences result from characteristics acquired through biological inheritance and how much through learning. A great many behavioral characteristics that formerly were believed to be the result of biological inheritance now seem to be the products of *social* inheritance. The fact that the members of some families are all acrobats or musicians may be the result of their having learned the appropriate behaviors from one another from a very early age onward. Similarly, the tendency of certain ethnic groups to display one behavior pattern or another may be due to social learning. What each child will become, then, is partly determined before conception by the social environment into which he is to be born, and partly by the genetic contributions of his parents.

Sequence of Prenatal Development. Some time during the middle of the 28-day menstrual cycle of a woman of child-bearing age, one of the two ovaries produces an egg or *ovum* that proceeds down one arm of the *Fallopian tube* toward the womb or *uterus* (see Figure 5-1). If the ovum has not been fertilized by a sperm during its three-to-seven-day journey, it disintegrates and its remains are dispersed. If it has been fertilized, it becomes what is termed a *zygote* and continues to move toward the uterus.

The first two weeks after conception are termed the *ovular* or *germinal* stage, while the period from the second through about the eighth week is termed the *embryonic* period. During this time, the important cellular layers become differentiated, and the various body parts begin to appear. From about two months onward the new organism is termed a *fetus,* and the stage of development, the *fetal* period.

During the earlier stages of the zygote's development, its cells become differentiated into formative and auxiliary components. One function of the auxiliaries is to form a covering for the cells from which the embryo proper will develop. Very soon fluid appears, giving the early ovum the appearance of a fluid-filled sphere. At this stage, it is known as a *blastula*. As this fluid collects, the formative cells are pushed into one side of the blastula and, with

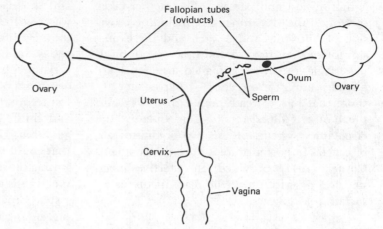

Figure 5-1. A schematic representation of the human female reproductive system showing fertilization.

other cells of the region, form the *embryonic disc,* from which the embryo develops. In this clump of cells, a smaller cavity forms, later to be recognized as the *amnion.* The outer layer of cells, called the *trophoblast,* forms the means of attaching the embryo to the uterine wall and also prepares for the subsequent interchange of nutritive and waste products.

As the trophoblast cells produce a greater accumulation of fluid, the embryo becomes what is known as a *blastocyst* and is now ready for implantation. The inner mass of cells in this rapidly proliferating system quickly produces a new layer of cells, the *endoderm,* which will line the blastocyst and produce another closed space called the yolk sac. This is an extremely important structure in species other than man, as it is the chief source of nutritive materials during early developmental periods. In man, however, its value is transitory and by the end of the fourth week of gestation, it has largely disappeared. Also arising from the endoderm is the *allantois,* a sausage-shaped tube that extends outward toward the periphery of the embryo. The part that remains in contact with the embryonic disc will ultimately constitute the bladder.

Soon a third layer of cells, the mesoderm, spreads out into the original blastocyst cavity

These cells become thickened at one end and form the *body stalk,* which will fuse with the allantois to form the *umbilical cord*—the chief avenue over which maternal-fetal interchange will occur. The outer layer of the entire embryo is called the *chorion.* On the outside of the chorion, little spidery filaments, called *villi,* appear and secure themselves in the lining of the uterus. As soon as blood vessels appear, as they do from the allantois and body stalk, they find their way into the openings of the villi and thence into the uterine walls.

The nutritional demands of the rapidly growing embryo cannot for long be satisfied by materials contained within the ovum, and more permanent arrangements must be made. As soon as the zygote is implanted in the uterine wall, the *placenta* begins to develop. This new and temporary organ will handle the interchange of nutrients and waste products until such time as the new organism can sustain independent existence.

The Biological Mother-Child Relationship

An adequate discussion of the placenta requires clarification of the biological relationship between mother and child during the prenatal period. Essentially this relationship is that of host and parasite. The mother takes care of all the vital functions, including provision of nutrients and oxygen and the expulsion of carbon dioxide and other waste products. The nutrients provided the fetus are already carefully "screened"—that is, they are those that have already found their way into the mother's bloodstream. Consequently, the circulatory systems of the two organisms are of crucial importance for future development. Corner (1944) provided an effective metaphorical description of the placenta-uterus association as follows:

"If the reader has difficulty visualizing the relation of the placenta to the uterus, let him imagine a piece of ground (representing the uterine wall) beneath which is a network of terra cotta pipes (the blood vessels). Dig a hole in the ground, breaking off the pipes as you dig, and make it just large enough to receive the dense roots of a tree (the placenta). Pave the ground over the hole and all about it, the paving representing the chorio-amniotic surface of the placenta. . . . The trunk of your tree is the umbilical cord. The roots will be bathed in fluid from the cut ends of the underground pipes; in like manner the root system of the placental villi dips into a sort of pool filled with maternal blood from the opened ends of small arteries and drained by opened veins. This blood is the source of oxygen and nourishment for the infant and the means of disposal of carbon dioxide and organic wastes which filter back into it from the villi-roots of the embryo."[1]

Should the placenta fail to develop properly, or should its function be seriously impaired at any time during the pregnancy, then damage to the fetus is virtually inevitable. The placenta is truly the lifeline of the new organism,

[1] Copyright 1944 by the Yale University Press, and published with permission.

and, no matter how excellent the seed that was fertilized and that formed the basis for the new life, normal development cannot occur without adequate placental attachment.

Although the placental villi dip into "pools" or sinuses of maternal blood, there is no direct connection between the bloodstream of mother and child. Indeed, during the early weeks of gestation, the infant does not have anything that could technically be called a bloodstream. Rather he has cells that are developing into blood cells and the beginnings of a circulatory system capable of effecting transfer across the placental barrier. Very early in embryonic life the fetal heart begins to pulse and to force its own blood through its own closed vascular system. However, very quickly the outer layer of the embryo begins to form *capillaries* which terminate close to terminals on the maternal side. Actual exchange of chemical materials is accomplished by diffusion through these capillary walls. Thus, although there is no direct connection between the circulatory systems of the two organisms, there is certainly interaction between them.

It is now appropriate to consider the other major circulating and communicating network —the nervous system. Again, there is no direct connection between mother and child in the sense that the nerve fibers of one organism form an open system and become affiliated with fibers from the other system. In order to help demolish certain persistent stereotypes on the influence of the mother on the fetus, it has become customary in recent years to emphasize the lack of direct connection between the nervous system of the mother and that of the fetus. Such assertions, unequivocally made, are based on an inadequate conception of the nervous system, however. Ashley Montagu (1950) once observed:

"A still widely prevalent belief has it that there is no connection between the nervous systems of mother and fetus. This notion is

28 day embryo　　35 day embryo　　42 day embryo　　84 day embryo

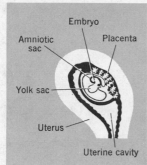
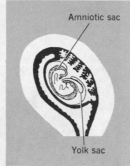

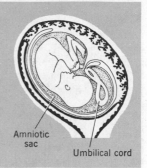

Figure 5-2. The growth of an embryo. (Nourse et al., 1964, pp. 176–177. Reproduced by permission.)

based on a very narrow conception of the nervous system. It is through the neurohumoral system, the system comprising the interrelated nervous and endocrine systems, acting through the fluid medium of the blood (and its oxygen and carbon-dioxide contents), that nervous changes in the mother may affect the fetus. The common endocrine pool of the mother and fetus forms a neurohumoral bond between them. The endocrine systems of mother and fetus complement each other.

All this is not to say that there is anything in the old wives' tale of 'maternal impressions.' The mother's 'impressions,' her 'psychological states' as such, cannot possibly be transmitted to the fetus. What are transmitted are the gross chemical changes which occur in the mother and, so far as we know at the present time, nothing more"[2] (p. 152).

Perhaps an accurate way of summarizing the relationship is that the two systems, although separate and distinct, nonetheless interact.

Prenatal Development

Prenatal development is so orderly a process that it is possible to chart its important features in succinct form. The following brief summary of the more significant events in the prenatal calendar will acquaint the reader

[2] Copyright 1950 by the Josiah Macy, Jr. Foundation, and published with permission.

with a sequence of prenatal growth and will give some idea of the patterning and interlocking of growth during this developmental phase. (See Figures 5-2, 5-3, and 5-4.)

Fetal Changes During Gestation

First Month. Fertilization, descent of ovum from tube to uterus. Early cell division and formation of embryonic disc from which new organism will develop. Early formation of three layers of cells—the *ectoderm,* from which sense organs and nervous system will develop; the *mesoderm,* from which circulatory, skeletal, and muscular systems will develop; and *endoderm,* from which digestive and some glandular systems will develop. Special layer of cells formed in the uterus which will become the *placenta* and through which nutritive substances will be carried to the new organism and waste products carried away. Special layer of cells forms the *amnion* or water-sac, which will surround the developing embryo except at umbilical cord. Heart tube forms and begins to pulsate and force blood to circulate through blood vessels in embryonic disc. Nervous system begins to arise, first in form of neural groove. Development of intestinal tract, lungs, liver, and kidneys begins. By end of one month, the embryo is about one-fourth inch long, curled into a crescent, with small nubbins on sides of body indicating incipient arms and legs.

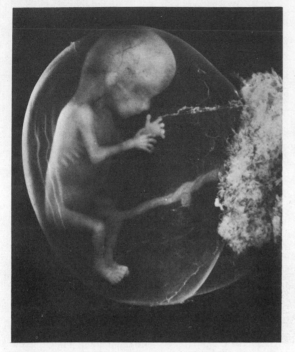

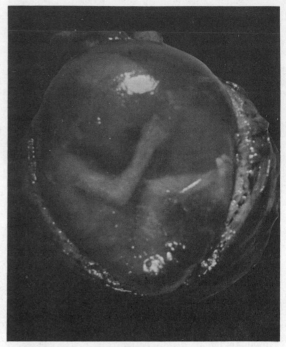

Figure 5-3. Eleven-week-old fetus, showing amnion, chorion, yolk, and umbilical cord.

Figure 5-4. Seven-month-old fetus. By now it is capable of independent life and can survive with special care, if born prematurely.

Second Month. Embryo increases in size to about 1½ inches. Bones and muscle begin to round out contours of body. Face and neck develop and begin to give features a human appearance. Forehead very prominent, reflecting precocious development of brain in comparison to rest of body. Limb buds elongate. Muscles and cartilage develop. Sex organs begin to form.

Third Month. Beginning of fetal period. Sexual differentiation continues, with male sexual organs showing more rapid development and the female remaining more neutral. Buds for all 20 temporary teeth laid down. Vocal cords appear; digestive system shows activity. Stomach cells begin to secrete fluid; liver pours bile into intestine. Kidneys begin functioning, with urine gradually seeping into amniotic fluid. Other waste products passed through placenta into mother's blood. Bones and muscles continue development, and by end of third month spontaneous movements of arms, legs, shoulders, and fingers are possible.

Fourth Month. Lower parts of body show relatively accelerated rate, so that head size decreases from one-half to one-fourth of body size. Back straightens; hands and feet are well-formed. Skin appears dark red, owing to coursing of blood showing through thin skin, and wrinkled, owing to absence of underlying fat. Finger closure is possible. Reflexes become more active as muscular maturation continues. Fetus begins to stir and to thrust out arms and legs in movements readily perceived by the mother.

Fifth Month. Skin structures begin to attain final form. Sweat and sebaceous glands are formed and function. Skin derivatives also appear—hair, nails on fingers and toes. Bony axis becomes quite straight, and much spontaneous activity occurs. Fetus is lean and wrinkled, about one foot long and weighs about one pound. If aborted, it may respire briefly, but will soon die as it seems unable to maintain movements necessary for continued breathing.

Sixth Month. Eyelids, which have been fused shut since third month, reopen; eyes are completely formed. Taste buds appear on tongue and in mouth and are, in fact, more abundant than in the infant or adult. If born, the six-month fetus will perhaps live a few hours or longer if protected in an incubator. During brief extrauterine life, may exhibit "Moro" or startle responses.

Seventh Month. Organism capable of independent life from this time on. Cerebral hemispheres cover almost the entire brain. Seven-month fetus can emit a variety of specialized responses. Generally is about 16 inches long and weighs about three pounds. If born, will be able to cry, breathe, and swallow, but is very sensitive to infections and will need highly sheltered environment for survival.

Eighth and Ninth Month. During this time, finishing touches are being put on the various organs and functional capacities. Fat is formed rapidly over the entire body, smoothing out the wrinkled skin and rounding out body contours. Dull red color of skin fades so that at birth pigmentation of skin is usually very slight in all races. Activity is usually great, and he can change his position within the somewhat crowded uterus. Periods of activity will alternate with periods of quiescence. Fetal organs step up their activity. Fetal heart rate becomes quite rapid. Digestive organs continue to expel more waste products, leading to the formation of a fetal stool, called the *meconium,* which is expelled shortly after birth. Violent uterine contractions begin, though milder ones have been tolerated earlier, and the fetus is eventually expelled from the womb into an independent physiological existence.

Although the fetus has many human characteristics at the beginning of the fetal period, it does not really resemble a human being until about the third month (see Figure 5-2). The head is disproportionately large, with the legs much shorter than they will be eventually, an example of *cephalo-caudal* (literally, head-to-tail) direction of development. The entire course of prenatal development illustrates the principle of differentiation and integration. Even as early as the eighth week, differentiation is exhibited. It shows, for example, in the heartbeat, and in simple body movements, such as the bending of the neck in a prematurely born fetus when stimulated by stroking the cheek with a hair. By about 14 weeks the early predominately generalized responses are less prominent, and less stereotyped forms of activity are being exhibited.

It is clear that there are external and internal environments for the prenatal infant. "Spontaneous" movements are, of course, very much present as any mother can attest. Referring to them as "spontaneous," although carrying a certain air of knowledge, is actually a confession that the stimuli that give rise to them cannot be identified precisely. Evidence of influence from the external environment upon the fetus is also available. Events happening in the external world elicit movements from him. After activity on the part of the mother, fetal activity decreases as compared to such activity when the mother is quiet. This decrease in activity after maternal exercise is attributed to the increased oxygen supply available to the fetus.

Fetal Behavior

In the synopsis of prenatal development, as presented above, it was mentioned incidentally that the conditioning of the fetus could take place. The earlier research of the 1930s and 1940s has in recent years come under some question, because the experiments were inadequately controlled, but their results do suggest that it may be possible to get fetuses to respond to sounds and to maternal movement. If the human organism does respond favorably to stimulation, as seems to be the case, then it follows that within limits the fetus would react favorably to modest increases in activity.

The sheer amount of fetal activity appears to be related to the general activity level of the infant and child later on. C. Etta Walters (1965) had 35 women record the movements of their unborn child during the last three months of pregnancy and then subsequently tested the infants at 12, 24, and 36 weeks, using the Gesell Development Schedules, a scale that enables psychologists to judge the rate at which a child is maturing. Walters' observations were consistent with the findings of an earlier study by Richards and Newberry (1938), who reported a very substantial correlation (.62) between fetal activity and scores on the Gesell schedule at six months. The findings are not too surprising. There is a tendency for there to be a general consistency to the behavior of a given individual. This is, after all, one of the bases on which the science of psychology rests. If people did not behave in consistent ways, it would not be possible to come to any conclusions about them or to make any predictions about their probable future behavior. An active fetus suggests an energetic, healthy organism, one that is likely to develop at an optimum rate after, as well as before, birth.

Environmental Effects

Other environmental influences are at work during the prenatal period. The nourishment available for the fetus is naturally related to the kind and amount of food ingested by the mother. These differences appear most sharply in comparisons of infants born to poor or nonpoor mothers. In one survey, autopsies of 252 infants who were stillborn (dead at birth), or who died within 48 hours of birth, showed that the infants of mothers who were "below the poverty level" were 15% smaller than the infants of other mothers. Furthermore, a higher percentage of the infants who were stillborn were from impoverished mothers (Naeye et al., 1969). Maternal malnutrition may also account for the fact that families from slums and other poverty areas produce a higher percentage of children with birth defects of various kinds than do families where income (and nutrition) are more adequate (Hepner, 1958. Knobloch & Pasamanick, 1958).

In a special message to the Congress, deal- with mental illness and mental retardation, the late President John F. Kennedy (1963) made the following comment:

"Families who are deprived of the basic necessities of life, opportunity, and motivation have a high proportion of the Nation's retarded children. Unfavorable health factors clearly play a major role. Lack of prenatal and postnatal health care, in particular, leads to the birth of brain-damaged children or to an inadequate physical and neurological development. Areas of high infant mortality are often the same areas with high incidence of mental retardation. Studies have shown that women lacking in prenatal care have a much higher likelihood of having mentally retarded children. . . .

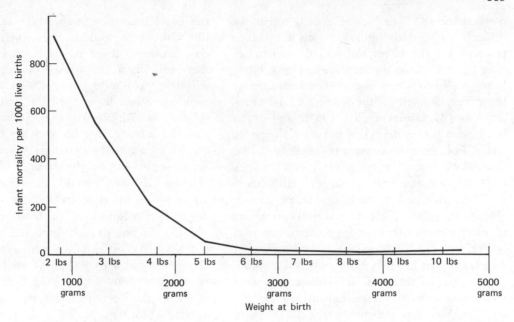

Figure 5-5. Relationship between infant mortality and birth weight. (White House Conference on Children, 1970.)

Among expectant mothers who do not receive prenatal care, more than 20 percent of all births are premature—two or three times the rate of prematurity among those who do receive adequate care. . . . Premature infants have two or three times as many physical defects and 50 percent more illnesses than fullterm infants. The smallest premature babies are 10 times more likely to be mentally retarded."

Insufficient maternal nutrition is a major factor in undersized infants. Surveys show that mortality among infants of subnormal weight is much higher than among those of normal weight, as Figure 5-5 indicates.

Malnutrition, and poor prenatal and postnatal care are not the only problems that affect the health of infants. Particularly dangerous are syphilis, which may kill the fetus or may result in a crippled or mentally deficient child; rubella (commonly known as German

measles), which may lead to deafness and other disabilities; and diabetes, which may cause circulatory and respiratory defects.

Almost anything that causes undue stress to mothers can affect the development of the fetus, although some agents are notably more dangerous than others. Exposure to radiation has been shown to produce birth defects, both in infants born after the atomic bomb exploded in Hiroshima, as well as in infants born to American or British mothers who had received heavy dosages of X rays during pregnancy. A sudden increase in birth defects in Germany during the early 1960s was traced to the mothers' use of a sedative called *thalidomide,* which had been prescribed for the morning sickness of early pregnancy.

In recent years, there has been a considerable increase in the use of psychoactive drugs: the opiates (heroin, opium), lysergic acid diethylamide (LSD-25), cannabis (marijuana, hashish), and the amphetamines, such as methedrine (STP or "speed"). It is obviously difficult for legal and moral reasons to conduct research on the effect the use of such drugs may have on fetal development. There have, however, been some experimental studies of the effect of drugs on the young of laboratory animals (Alexander et al., 1967), and there have been some surveys of human subjects as well. The general consensus appears to be that those drugs that cause hallucinations (LSD-25, for example) produce birth abnormalities when taken early in the pregnancy (Houston, 1969). This observation would be consistent with other findings: anything that is likely to harm fetuses will have its greatest effects early in the pregnancy, when the zygote or embryo has relatively few cells and is most vulnerable. As to preconception effects, one study shows that persons taking LSD-25 are far more likely to have chromosome abnormalities than nonusers (Nielsen, Friedrich, and Tsuboi, 1969). Even if there were no research evidence, it could be argued persuasively on common-sense grounds that the use of substances that create an abnormal physical state in the mother are likely to affect the embryo or fetus adversely.

Incidentally, there are no findings that show unfavorable effects from the use of alcohol or cigarettes, although smoking has been observed to accelerate the fetal heart beat (Montagu, 1950). Common-sense arguments against excessive use, of course, apply to alcohol and tobacco, as well as to other mood-inducing drugs, legal or otherwise.

Still another problem that may affect the development of the fetus is the incompatibility of Rh blood factors. About 85% of all white persons are Rh-positive, which means that a special serum prepared from the blood of rhesus monkeys (hence "Rh"), will cause their blood to clot. The remaining 15% are Rh-negative. If an RH-negative woman marries an Rh-positive man, their first child is likely to be normal. In subsequent pregnancies, however, there is a fair possibility that there may be a miscarriage or that the child will live only a few hours after birth. The problem arises from the fact that the fetus inherits an Rh-positive gene from its father, and the Rh-negative blood from the mother carries an antibody that may destroy the red blood corpuscles of the fetus. Although this type of difficulty would theoretically occur about 5% of the time, in actuality it occurs in .5% of all pregnancies, probably because antibodies do not pass through the placenta in the majority of instances. In any event, if physicians know of Rh problems beforehand, there are various ways in which the problems of incompatible Rh factors may be partially averted (Montagu, 1950).

Pregnancy and the Mother

A moment's consideration will help to show why it is appropriate to examine the question of the mother's attitudes as they exist prior to the child's birth. Pregnancy is a developmental crisis in a woman's life, a "critical period of adulthood," so to speak. Inescapably she must make some major adjustments in her mode of life, not only because of physiological changes that are taking place within her but also because of the impending arrival of the infant. All aspects of her life are directly or indirectly involved. It is completely natural that she should develop some rather pronounced attitudes toward her role as a mother and toward the child-to-be. She develops some expectations of what motherhood will be like and what the child will be like. These preexisting attitudes will carry over into her relationships with the child and will affect her behavior as she attempts to cope with him and guide his behavior.

Maternal Attitudes

Before the birth of the child, these attitudes are likely to develop a certain color or flavor. Are they positive or negative? Resentful or eager? More than likely her feelings are mixed —an overall sense of fulfillment, coupled with a sense of annoyance at her awkwardness and discomfort as she moves around, heavy with child. A mother who was never irritated with the thought of the coming child would be more (or less) than human.

In a survey of a group of 400 mothers, Sears, Maccoby, and Levin (1957) found that 50% were rated as delighted with the coming child, another 18% as pleased but with no evidence of enthusiasm, while 25% had either mixed feelings or were displeased. Those mothers having only their first child included more who were pleased than among those reporting on later children as well. The mothers with more than one child tended to be more pleased the greater the distance between their pregnancies, and to be more pleased if their existing children were girls rather than boys only, or were both boys and girls. Consciously at least, few of the mothers carried over their doubts or displeasure into the period after the child was born. For example, although a mother might have "wanted to wait," once the child was born, her doubts tended to disappear.

To express this question of attitudes in more general terms, a continuum extending from enthusiastic acceptance of the child at one end to rejection of the child at the other is suggested. Even a so-called rejecting mother almost always shows some positive reaching-out, accepting behavior as well. Mothers reject some trends in their children and accept and stimulate others.

These attitudes and behaviors of the mother also shift with changes in the mother, the child, and in the situation. To speak of rejection means merely that negative feelings are dominant in a particular mother at a particular time. Levy's (1942) findings on mothering which follows can be interpreted as consistent with this dimension—with the more maternal subjects toward the accepting end of the continuum and the less maternal subjects toward the rejecting end of the continuum.

There is a suggestion that there is a biologically determined potentiality for motherliness. Levy related favorable attitudes toward mothering to the duration of menstrual flow. Indications of "mothering," used in making the rating, included playing with dolls in childhood, taking care of babies, "baby carriage peeking," number of children wanted, and anticipation of care and breast feeding of their babies. He found that the longer the duration of menstrual flow, the greater the amount of mothering behavior. This was expressed in a correlation coefficient of .58.

For a statistically significant relationship to be found between attitudinal matters and the physiological function of menstrual flow implies either that there is a constitutional basis of maternal attitudes or, conversely, that attitudes are able to bring about actual physiological differences among potential mothers. Regardless of which relationship ultimately proves correct, a close relationship has been demonstrated between the psychological function of mothering and a physiological factor.

Some psychiatrically oriented pediatricians, child psychiatrists, and psychologists are convinced that a considerable amount of the discomfort experienced by mothers during pregnancy arises because they are anxious and expect to have a difficult time. This may be due, in turn, either to not wanting the child or to interpersonal problems or tensions.

Zemlick and Watson (1953) were interested

in learning whether attitudes of acceptance or rejection had an effect on the prospective mother's psychological and physical adjustment during pregnancy. In other words, they wished to know whether a prospective mother who tended to reject her coming child also showed psychological and physical differences from a mother who adopted a positive accepting attitude toward her child-to-be. Mothers expecting their first child were their subjects. Each mother was studied by means of: (1) a selection of Thematic Apperception Test (TAT) cards, through which was established her level of anxiety; (2) a psychosomatic inventory (PS), in which she reported her psychological and somatic symptoms; and (3) a Pregnancy Attitude Scale (ZAR), composed of items which supplied information about her attitudes toward pregnancy, such as the degree to which she wanted the child.

Independently of these data, adjustment to pregnancy, in terms of physical and emotional symptoms, was rated by an obstetrician who saw each mother, on the average, ten times. He also rated the mother's behavior during labor and delivery in terms of her adequacy in meeting this crisis (delivery adjustment rank).

Some of the obtained relationships among these measures are reported in Table 5-1. With the exception of the psychosomatic inventory,

the physical symptom rating given by the obstetrician did not correlate significantly with the paper-and-pencil measures. The emotional symptoms noted by the obstetrician were more substantially correlated with the paper-and-pencil measures, however, and the latter also did reasonably well in predicting the mother's behavior at childbirth.

This positive correlation between attitudes of rejection or acceptance verbalized by the mothers on the attitude scale on the one hand, and emotional symptoms exhibited and delivery adjustment rank on the other, is particularly noteworthy. Mothers with acceptant attitudes tended to have fewer emotional symptoms and higher delivery adjustment, whereas mothers who exhibited rejecting attitudes tended to have more emotional symptoms and lower delivery adjustment. The more the mothers rejected their coming child, the stormier pregnancy they seemed to have.

It is important to note that these mothers were not emotionally disturbed or abnormal individuals. None was neurotic, psychotic, or mentally retarded. And yet, in these more-or-less normal, well-meaning mothers varying degrees of acceptance and rejection were found, thus disposing of the allegation sometimes made that only abnormal mothers reject their children.

In another survey of pregnant mothers,

TABLE 5-1.   *Relationships[a] Between Paper-and-pencil Tests of Mothers' Adjustment During Pregnancy and Ratings Given by an Obstetrician During Pregnancy and at Childbirth (After Zemlick and Watson, 1953)*

Paper-and-Pencil Measures	Obstetrician's Ratings		
	Physical Symptoms	Emotional Symptoms	Delivery Adjustment
Anxiety (TAT)	.29 (NS)	.48	.51
Psychosomatic symptoms (PS)	.54	.75	.50
Attitudes toward pregnancy (ZAR)	.21 (NS)	.59	.54

[a] Except for figures marked (NS), all correlations are significant at the .10 level of confidence or better.

those who were classified as "normal" or "mildly neurotic" tended to react to their pregnancy with an attitude characterized by hopefulness and trust and gave "natural gratification" as their motive for becoming pregnant. Women who were classified as more neurotic tended to react with helplessness, suppressed anger, overactivity, and irrational fears, coupled with low self-esteem. Rejection of the pregnancy was also common in this group, and there was much conflict about dominance and submission between the parents (Wenner et al., 1969).

Barbara A. Doty (1967) made a comparative study of women who were pregnant with their first child (*primiparae* or PP) or pregnant with a child other than their first (*multiparae* or MP). The mothers were also divided into middle and lower socioeconomic groups. Her results, as shown in Table 5-2, indicate that lower-class mothers reported more emotional disturbance and rejection of their pregnancy than did middle-class mothers. On the other hand, the lower-class mothers reported fewer physical symptoms. MP mothers were also more inclined to reject maternal roles than PP mothers, with a slight tendency for attitudes to run stronger with lower-class mothers. Furthermore, MP mothers showed less fear

of pregnancy and childbirth than did PP mothers. Having been through it all before, they were less afraid, but did not particularly welcome the responsibility of an additional child.

There are two explanations for the generally more negative attitudes of mothers from lower socioeconomic environments. One is that the arrival of a child into an already difficult economic and social situation makes its problems all the more troublesome. Another and not unrelated point is that lower-class individuals generally report more emotional problems of all types than do middle-class individuals.

Doty administered additional scales to the mothers in her sample and compared the results with other research in the field. She noted that women who express considerable rejection of pregnancy are also likely to report more problems with their infants, suggesting that attitudes toward pregnancy have their aftermath in mother-child relations. Ferreira's (1960) finding that mothers' rejection of pregnancy is related to excessive infant crying is also relevant here, for it shows that the behavior in question can be noticed by outside, objective observers, and not merely by the mothers.

TABLE 5-2.   *Mean Scores on Scales Indicating Negative Attitudes Toward Childbirth and Pregnancy Reported by Pregnant Middle-Class and Lower-Class Mothers, Both Primiparae (PP) and Multiparae (MP) (Doty, 1967)*

Aspects of Pregnancy Viewed Unfavorably	Middle-Class PP	Middle-Class MP	Lower-Class PP	Lower-Class MP
Emotional disturbance	4.3	4.0	6.9	9.0[a]
Physical symptoms	7.3	6.8	5.0	3.2[a]
Rejection of pregnancy	2.4	3.1	4.0	7.2[a,b]
Rejection of maternal role	3.5	8.7[b]	4.6	8.8[b]
Fear of pregnancy and childbirth	5.4	2.1[c]	4.3	2.6

[a] Significantly different from means for middle-class mothers (p < .01).
[b] Significantly different from means for PP mothers (p < .01).
[c] Significantly different from means for middle-class PP mothers (p < .01).

Doty's analysis of her data showed two main patterns. One group consisted largely of lower-class MP mothers, who rejected pregnancy and the maternal role and also scored high on scales measuring (1) hostile attitudes toward one's children and (2) psychopathic (maladjustive) behavior in general. A second group consisted largely of middle-class PP mothers who were very anxious and who expressed fear of childbirth and pregnancy, were inclined to encourage dependency in children, were fearful of harming their baby, and the like.

As pregnancy proceeds, the mother is apt to become increasingly concerned with the coming birth process of which she is to be so much a part. Considerable effort in recent years has been directed toward inculcating in her a psychologically healthy receptive point of view toward the coming experience. If approached properly, Grantley Dick Read (1959) contends, only a small percentage of births need be traumatic. Perhaps 95% of mothers have no physical abnormalities that would prevent normal childbirth. He maintains that fear is the chief pain-producing agent in what otherwise would be uneventful labor.

Labor is hard work, to be sure, but not intrinsically a fearful experience. The confusion of work with pain is the consequence, he holds, of negative suggestions that lead the mother to view childbirth as a frightening ordeal. The notion that it is the "softness" of modern life that brings on these difficulties is rejected by him as fallacious on the basis of the cogent argument that women's health and longevity are at their greatest in contemporary life. Fear, he says, prevents the balance of effort and relaxation that is an aspect of any hard work. Consequently, teaching the mother correct ways to relax is an important aspect of his methods.

Use of drugs to make the mother less aware of what is happening only on those few occasions when definite medical indications are present allows most mothers to experience to the fullest this important event. Most mothers who follow Read's prescription report that giving birth becomes a profoundly moving, even exhilarating experience. Although Read has produced impressive statistics concerning the value of his method and has won numerous professional supporters and the enthusiastic testimonial of many mothers, it is only fair to add that not all experts accept his methods, especially in their more radically expressed forms.

Another procedure favored in these circles is "rooming-in." This is a hospital arrangement whereby the mother cares for her newborn baby in her hospital room, rather than having the infant lodged in the nursery, except for his visits to the mother at feeding time. This procedure signifies more than mere rearrangement of physical facilities. It recognizes the importance of mother and child as a physical and psychological unit both before birth and thereafter.

Childbirth

A full-term baby is delivered in about 38 weeks on the average, give or take two or three weeks.[3] If all goes well, the birth process, although work for the mother, and always containing some element of danger for both her and her child, is complete in a very large proportion of cases without harm for either.

During the period 1915 to 1935, between 6 and 8% of American mothers died in child-

[3] The oft-cited figure of 40 weeks is the average time elapsing since the last menstrual period. Inasmuch as conception usually occurs during the middle of the menses, this means that the actual period of gestation is about two weeks less than the time from the date of the last menstrual period until birth.

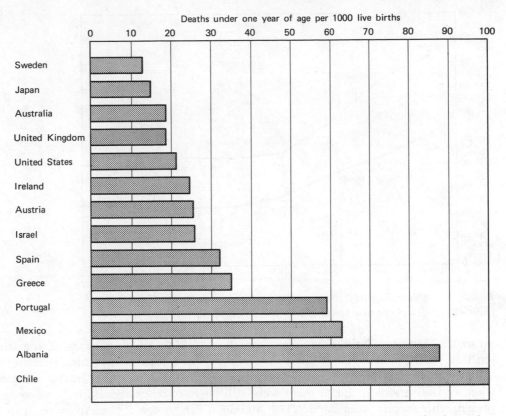

Figure 5-6.   Infant mortality rates for a representative sample of countries in various stages of industrialization. (White House Conference on Children, 1970.)

birth; the rate today is less than .33%. Comparable figures for infant births are hard to obtain, because stillborn figures include pregnancies aborted at less than full term. Statistics for mortality of infants who survive birth and the period directly following it are, however, indicative of the medical progress that has been made. About 10% of American-born infants died during the first year of life in 1915, whereas a little over 2% die during the first year today. The American infant mortality rate compares very favorably with that of most other countries, but is actually a little higher than the Scandinavian countries, Japan, Australia, and the United Kingdom, as Figure 5-6 shows. The infant mortality rate for non-whites in the United States is about double that of whites. (See Figure 5-7.)

Difficult Birth and the Newborn

For the infant, a long and difficult birth may be accompanied by *anoxia,* (a reduced oxygen supply); by toxins in the blood supply; or by direct injury to the brain. The effect of anoxia and other birth traumata has received careful study. The investigators first devised tests differentiating normal newborns, none over seven days of age, from traumatized infants. The measures that differentiated babies from the two groups included threshold for pain, ability to fixate the eyes, maturity,

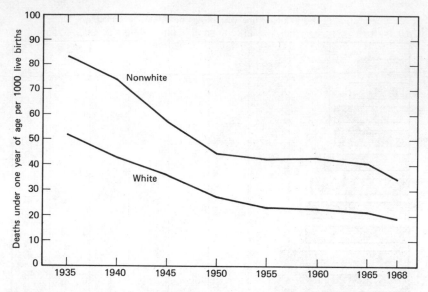

Figure 5-7. Nonwhite and white infant mortality rates in the United States from 1935 to 1968. (White House Conference on Children, 1970.)

muscular activity, irritability, and muscle tension.

The investigators subsequently determined whether indications of impairment were still present three years after birth. The anoxic children were significantly poorer on cognitive measures, such as the Stanford-Binet vocabulary subtest and a concept test requiring the placing of blocks according to color, form, and size. They also exhibited more neurological signs and some differences in personality, with greater distractibility being the most prominent. The damage was seldom severe; few of them were either palsied or mentally retarded. Anoxia did not have an all-or-none effect; but brain damage formed a continuum from a majority of anoxic children who had suffered a minimal amount of impairment to a few at the extreme of severe impairment (Graham, 1956; Graham et al., 1962; Graham, Matarazzo, and Caldwell, 1956).

For the last two decades, professionals who work with children have been using a scoring system, developed by Virginia Apgar

(1953), which consists of the sum of ratings on 5 three-point scales, covering the newborn infant's breathing effort, muscle tone, heart rate, reflex irritability, and color (from grayish to rosy). The Apgar test can be made immediately after birth and has quite a high degree of predictibility as far as infant and child health and development are concerned. Nancy Edwards (1970) found that Apgar scores made one and five minutes after birth were significantly correlated with a number of measures made four years later. For instance, they correlated .45 with fine motor coordination and .49 with gross motor coordination four years later. Apgar scores also correlated .26 with intelligence and .32 with concept formulation. What Edwards' research suggests is that the general health and energy level that is characteristic of a child, and is even in evidence immediately after birth, can be used as an index to his probable physical and cognitive development in the future. Human behavior, as we have noted, tends to be generally consistent, and infants that display above-average health at birth have a better-than-average chance for superiority later on, as Edwards' research suggests.

A poor start at birth often leads to later complications. Daniel V. Caputo and Wallace Mandell (1970) surveyed the literature on infants having a low birth weight—those that are commonly referred to as "premature." A child's normal birth weight is about 7 pounds (about 3500 grams). Infants weighing 2500 grams (about 5½ pounds) were formerly classified as premature, but more lately pediatricians have used the 2000 gram (4½ pounds) figure as being more accurate, unless there is evidence that the gestation period was less than 37 weeks. As a result of their review, Caputo and Mandell concluded that very low birth weight was likely to be associated with significant neurological and physiological impairment. Children who had very low birth weight are likely (1) to score lower on intelligence tests, (2) to be overrepresented among those classified as mentally retarded or institutionalized for various disabilities, or (3) to drop out of high school before graduation. Hyperkinetic (overactive, intense, disruptive) and disorganized behavior is also likely to be characteristic of many such children, although as adults they seem to blend into the general population. Language development is frequently retarded, as well as accomplishment in academic subjects. In addition, there are often deficits in physical growth and motor behavior.

If infants that are markedly below normal weight have more than the usual problems, does this mean "The larger, the better"? Some research into this problem suggests that the answer is "No." One study showed that children whose birth weight (4250 grams for males and 4000 grams for females) was in the top 5% tended to have low IQs when they were four years old. One fourth of the children in this special group had IQs below 80, which

is about twice the proportion one would expect for normal children. (Babson, Henderson, and Clark, 1969)

Anxiety in the Newborn Relative to the Birth Process

Psychoanalytic writers have proposed a number of theories about the possible effects of the birth process on personality development in later years. Freud suggested that the sudden flooding of excitation that strikes all infants at birth was the prototype of later anxiety. After the calm of uterine existence, with its relatively constant temperature, its lack of sensory stimulation other than kinesthetic and vibratory, the newborn infant might be faced with an overwhelming situation with which he cannot cope. Freud, himself, attached only some slight general significance to it. However, Otto Rank, who worked with him for a time, designated birth trauma the major causative factor for later neurotic manifestations of all kinds. Associated with the view that birth is an upheaval, a thrust into the cruel world, is the proposal that this psychological shock produces a permanent unconscious yearning for the protection and security once afforded by the womb. This return to the womb becomes a goal of those who would escape the world. Aside from this, psychoanalytic thinking is not concerned with the neonatal period as such.

Such theories are, of course, not researchable, interesting as they are. One should point out, however, that it is possible to construct theories that make an opposite interpretation, namely, that the fetus is relieved to escape from the womb and become a being in its own right. The latter interpretation would be consistent with the more recent thinking in American personality theory. Robert W. White (1959), for example, maintains that the human organism has a drive to become more effective, more competent. It is only through escaping from the confinement (e.g., womb) that such a drive can manifest itself.

The Neonate

The term *neonate* means, literally, "new-born," and is applied to the first five to seven days of life, the interval between birth and infancy.

It would be fruitless to try to state the sensitivities and activities of which the infant is capable only at the moment of birth. We shall therefore discuss whatever appears in his behavior during the first month of life, even if it is known that a particular function appears earlier or later during the neonatal period. For example, even within the span of the first four days of life, the threshold for pain sensitivity diminishes (Lipsitt and Levy, 1959). Studies of the newborn infant cast in developmental form are not discussed here but in the next chapter concerned with development in infancy. This means that the cumulative influence principle of development does not figure in the discussion that follows. The neonatal period provides the base line of behavior against which to see the later effects of maturation and learning.

Physical Appearance and Bodily Proportions

Even a fond mother may experience a sense of shock at the first sight of the tiny, wizened, red creature that is her offspring. (The "new-born" babies of the advertisements are apparently about two months of age). The eyes are approximately one-half their adult size, and the body as a whole is only one-twentieth of its adult dimensions. The head is about one-fourth of body length as compared to the adult's one-seventh. As a consequence of these proportions the neonate appears all head and eyes. Figure 5-8 shows something of his general

appearance. At birth, the average newborn weighs seven or eight pounds and measures about 20 inches. The range, however, is from three to 16 pounds and from 17 to 21 or 22 inches. Boys are generally slightly larger and heavier than girls.

The Neonate as an Organism

We may speak of the neonate as an organism as distinguished from the person he is to become. The human being may be viewed on various levels. He may be seen as a molecular aggregation, an organism, a person, as an aspect of a diadic unit of two or more persons, and as an aggregate in a group. In other words, he may be viewed in order of expanding perspective at a physical-chemical level, a biological level, a psychological level, a social psychological level, and a sociological level.

The scientific laws laboriously worked out at one level are not necessarily suitable for application at a different level. In scrutinizing the child at a given level, we view him in a different light and see different phenomena than we would if another level were applied.

We shall look at the neonate as a biological organism viewed in cross-sectional perspective. We take our vantage point at the biological level because in the neonate there has occurred a minimum of psychological interaction with others. Psychological laws either of the individual person or of the diadic (social) sort are not relevant in this examination of the neonate's behavior repertoire.

In the light of these principles our organization of the findings on the neonate becomes clear. We must consider reactions to various forms of stimuli and the motor responses of which he is capable.

The Needs of the Neonate

Certain coordinated responses present in the neonate are so vital for his survival and so

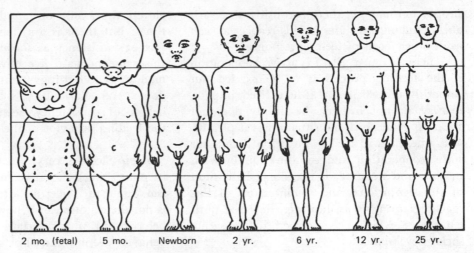

2 mo. (fetal)   5 mo.   Newborn   2 yr.   6 yr.   12 yr.   25 yr.

Figure 5-8. Changes in body form and proportion before and after birth. (Jackson, 1929. Reproduced by permission.)

demanding in their need for satisfaction that they may be conceptualized as *needs* or *drives*.

Hunger and Thirst. Responses such as sucking, swallowing, and head movements, which are aspects of the feeding and drinking responses, have already been mentioned in connection with representative motor responses. Present concern is with coordinated activities expressive of hunger and thirst needs.

Pratt (1930) indicated that neonatal feeding involves a series of three activities: (1) head-mouth orientation—contact stimulation of the neonate's cheek evokes head turning toward the source of stimulation, followed by opening of the mouth and snapping movements; (2) lip reflexes coordinated with head-mouth orientation—pursing the lips to contact with the nipple; and (3) sucking and swallowing movements that form a rhythm. Swallowing imparts its rhythm upon sucking; this combined rhythm is in turn imposed upon respiration so that breathing is not interfered with. General activity is reduced when sucking starts, the neonate becoming relatively quiescent.

When viewed in the perspective of the neo-nate's day-to-day behavior, hunger and thirst are clearly seen not to be automatic reflex activities. Although based on a reflex pattern, sucking is influenced by repeated reinforcement in securing nourishment. If the infant's hunger and thirst are not reduced, and reduced quite quickly, tensions mount and provoke a considerable amount of bodily activity. Consequently, they are important in his learning activities.

These responses, although they form a coordinated series, are not reflexlike in that, once started, the chain is not invariably completed. For example, it has been found that sucking of air may occur without swallowing. It is well known that sucking of some substances, instead of being followed by swallowing, results in spitting out or rejection.

Neonates show individual differences in the efficiency with which they carry out these coordinated activities. Although some authorities insist, as Margaret A. Ribble (1943) once did, that a large number of infants show such feeble sucking movements as to require adult help, the weight of evidence appears to indicate that only a small proportion of infants need assistance or prompting. Whatever the proportion may be, there is considerable variability among neonates in this respect as well as in other facets of feeding responses.

A neonate must give his active cooperation if the feeding process is to be carried out smoothly and efficiently. If he is tired, in pain, drowsy, or not hungry, he simply does not suck. In general, if the situation is a pleasurable one, he will do so. To bring about this state, cooperation and coordination between mother and neonate, is necessary. Discussion of the significance and ramifications of this social relationship is, however, deferred until Chapter 8 which is concerned with psychosocial development.

As prerequisites for arousal of hunger and thirst, the neonate needs to be awake and close in time to a nursing period. The neonate shows his hunger and thirst by crying and restless movements until he is fed. He then tends to quiet down and fall asleep. This cycle of feeding and sleeping is the major cycle of activity that neonates show—restless when hungry, quiescent or asleep when fed.

Healthy neonates demand food about every three hours. Gesell and Ilg (1949) reported that, on the average, newborn babies take seven or eight feedings per day. Nevertheless, there is wide individual variation. Some neonates may reach a peak of maximum activity in as short a time as two-and-a-half hours, while others may go for as long as five hours between peaks. Moreover, neonates who regularly show a given cycle, say, three hours, may have some intervals shorter or longer than the usual interval.

It should come as no surprise by now that individual differences among infants in the number of feedings should vary both between infants and in the same infant from time to time, making relative and tentative these seemingly precise statements. One neonate was fed on self-demand each day between the second and tenth day of life; it was found that on one of these days he demanded to be fed eleven times but on another day, only six times. But there is apt, nevertheless, to be a sort of consistency as shown by the fact that this same neonate five days out of nine demanded nine feedings (Simsarian and McLendon, 1942). Variability, but still with some degree of consistency, seems to characterize the feeding behavior of the neonate.

Sleep. Sleep is very much a need. Without its nourishing restorative function, the organism would die. Sleep is, after all, behavior. It is not the cessation of behavior; it is a kind of behavior in which certain forms of waking behavior are minimized or modified.

Sleep conceived in terms of a gradient of motility seems to fit the situation of the neonate most adequately. We do not have available for use the cultural criteria of adult sleep such as going to bed, closing the eyes, assuming a restful posture, and inability when wakened to give an accurate account of the time intervening. For the neonate the application of these criteria is not possible. What is present is a gradient of motility extending from considerable activity with eyes open to "inactivity," regular breathing and absence of eyelid and mouth movements. It is generally agreed that during sleep, irritability, in its general sense, is decreased and reaction times are lengthened. Responses decrease as depth of sleep increases. However, it is difficult, even for trained observers, to agree in some intermediate stages whether the infant is asleep or awake.

Observations of neonates show that they spend about five-sixths of their time sleeping. Each sleep period is about three hours in length, and there are some seven or eight sleep periods per 24 hours (Gesell and Ilg, 1949). During this period of development, the young infant is, of course, unaware of any distinction between day or night, as any parent of an infant can ruefully report.

Although we tend to believe that we are

relatively quiet and relaxed during normal sleep, observations show that there is much activity taking place and that it can be classified into various levels, ranging from a kind of twilight zone between waking and sleep and a very deep, almost comatose sleep. In one of the intermediate stages, our eyes move rapidly from side to side, under our closed lids, a phenomenon that can be picked up by sensitive electrical devices. This rapid-eye-movement or REM sleep is the stage at which dreaming takes place and seems to play an important part in rehabilitation and physical restoration processes that take place within the body. One researcher maintains that there is even a "need to dream," for when adult subjects were prevented (by being awakened) from engaging in REM sleep on certain nights, they engaged in more REM sleep on other nights (Dement, 1960).

Infants spend proportionately more time in REM sleep than do children, who spend more time than adults. Neonates spend more time in REM sleep than do infants, and observations have shown that the amount of time drops day by day after birth. One male neonate, for example, was observed to have 3.8 episodes of REM per minute during his third day of life, in contrast to 2.3 on the sixth day (Minard, Williams, and Coleman, 1969).

Elimination. Waste products must be eliminated from the body. Three processes are available—sweating, urination, and bowel movements. They are involuntary and automatic in the neonate. Increased pressure in the bladder and in the bowel results in relaxation of muscles and the contents are involuntarily released. The neuromuscular apparatus for voluntary control has not yet developed.

Temperature Regulation. In the fetal period, the environment of the mother's womb supplies a constant temperature. After birth, the neonate faces a fluctuating temperature in the environment. He is exposed to these changes and to drafts. Within certain limits his automatic physiological mechanisms maintain body temperature. However, when these limits are exceeded, adjustment through external assistance by the parents is needed. The neonate, of course, is not "aware" in any true sense of his need for temperature regulation. He, like adults, is aware of it only when something goes wrong. But, unlike the adult, he does not know what he needs when pain and discomfort arise.

Oxygen Needs. Vital to the preservation of life is an adequate oxygen supply. In the neonate this need is intensified by the fact that although respiration is a reflex activity, it is not necessarily stabilized in rhythm and efficiency at the time of birth. In a few days, however, it reaches a level of efficiency quite adequate for ordinary needs. Its relative instability dramatically calls attention to respiration as serving a need of the organism. As in the case of temperature regulation it becomes noticeable as a need only when not met.

Precursors to Sexual Needs. Susceptibility to external genital stimulation in very young infants has been established. Infants are quite responsive to stimulation in the genital area. If an infant is having a crying spell, such stimulation tends to quiet him. Lustman (1956), found that newborn infants were quite sensitive to both manual and air pressure stimulation of the genital region, as shown by temperature increase in this area. In another much earlier study, nine male infants were observed for eight-and-a-half consecutive hours per day for ten days. Tumescence (erection of the penis) occurred at least once every day in seven newborn infants, while the other two showed such behavior on the eighth and ninth day, respectively. These responses were primarily to internal stimulation—strong sucking or a full bowel or bladder setting off the reflex response. Great individual differences were noted, with the actual number of instances of tumescence varying from a median of four to a median of 35 per day. Tumescence was, in general, accompanied by what can be referred to as unpleasantness—restlessness, crying, fretting, and stiff legs—to name the most prominent concomitants. Detumescence, in contrast, was apparently pleasurable—crying during it, for example, was almost nonexistent (Halverson, 1943).

Homeostasis and Neonatal Needs. We have examined the neonate as a biological organism. Like all organisms it is found equipped to survive and to develop. Its behavior repertoire demonstrates its ability to relate to its environment. It shows homeostasis, a maintenance of stability in its biological functioning. Given certain assistance from its environment, particularly from the mother, it maintains its organism through meeting its needs, particularly hunger and thirst, sleep, elimination, temperature regulation, oxygen content, and possibly sexual needs. It preserves its equilibrium in the manner and within the limits sketched in the earlier presentation.

Sensory Stimulation[4]

Reactions to Visual Stimuli. Virtually all parts of the eye are present at birth, but vision takes place only on a fairly rudimentary level. The eyeball is short, the lens large and spherical, coordination is poor, and the optic nerves have only part of the white fatty sheath or *myelin* that is necessary for adequate neural transmission. It is hardly surprising, then, that the neonate's pupils respond to bright light sluggishly, although there is considerable improvement even within the first 24 hours of life. The focus of the eye tends to

be fixed at about 7½ inches, which means that objects closer or more distant are probably seen as blurred (Haynes, White, and Held, 1965). It is questionable whether the neonate can actually see colors, although Fantz (1963) found that neonates looked longer at black-and-white figures than at plain color areas. Not only can newborns distinguish between plain and figured stimuli but they also appear to have preferences. Nelson and Kessen (1969) found that neonates tended to look at the angles and corners in figures, rather than at straight lines. Inasmuch as angles are more complex, this may be the first indication of the preference for greater complexity that appears in many research studies of infants and children.

Neonates also respond to different degrees of brightness. Closing the eyes spontaneously to a flash of light and to objects moving toward the eyes has been noted. Within a day or two after birth the pupillary reflex (widening or narrowing of the pupil in response to light) has been observed. Eye movements of various sorts have also been found. These include: pursuit (following a visual stimulus with movement of the eyes); saccadic (quick jerky fixations as in adult reading); coordinate (eyes moving together); and coordinate compensatory (head quickly moving in one direction, with eye movements in opposite direction).

The eye movement responses just defined are either reflex in character or, at least, of a circumscribed nature. More gross muscular patterns or general mass behavior has also been elicited. Practically any visual stimuli, if sufficiently intense, will release circulatory and respiratory (for example, "catching" the breath) responses in the neonate. The startle response involving coordination of many parts of the body is also elicited by intense visual stimulation. Thus, both reflex and mass activity are reactions to visual stimuli.

---

[4] The present account draws very heavily on that of Karl C. Pratt (1954), with more recent material added where needed.

Reactions to Auditory Stimuli. There is some question as to whether the neonate can hear immediately at birth. Certainly neonates vary in sensitivity, with some showing an imperviousness to the influence of sound, despite later normal hearing. Neonatal infants fail to make pitch discriminations, but they do respond differentially to various intensities of sound.

As in visual responses, both specific reflexes, such as blinking the eyes and gross muscular patterns of response, appear. Wertheimer (1961) found that an infant ten minutes old was able to turn his eyes in the direction of an auditory stimulus. A crude form of auditory localization (coordination of auditory and visual functioning) appears to be possible without learning.

Reactions to Other Sensory Stimuli. In a review of research on sensory and perceptual responses in infants, Spears and Hohle (1967) concluded that evidence showed that the neonate does respond to olfactory stimuli, but only if they are highly aromatic, such as amonia or acetic acid. The responsiveness increases rapidly over the first three or four days of life, with weaker and weaker solutions needed to get some kind of response. Newborns also respond differently to water and milk, as well as to solutions containing acid, glucose, and salt. Sugar solutions tend to elicit the sucking response, which is maintained; acid solutions also evoke sucking, but for a shorter period; salt solutions, after being tried a bit, are not sucked; while bitter solutions, such as quinine, are seldom sucked. There are, however, wide individual differences among neonates. The sucking of fingers, thumb, or hand has been observed shortly after birth and even before the first feeding, and there is even one dramatic photograph of a fetus sucking its thumb (Kessen, Haith, and Salapatek, 1970).

Research reviewed by Spears and Hohle points to the conclusion that pressure and touch sensitivity are present in neonates and even in fetuses several months before birth. Attempts to get neonates to respond to pain had mixed results in early studies, partly because of the problem of measuring the amount of stimulus being applied. More recently it has been possible to use mild electric shock and to control the amount of stimulus. Results show that thresholds for this type of stimulation apparently diminish with each day following birth—in other words, infants respond more quickly to smaller and smaller shock voltages.

Although infants have differentiated responses to various temperatures and hence can be considered as able to distinguish between them, one study suggests that there is no particular value in warming infants' milk formula. The researchers used premature infants, in order to have a conservative test of their procedure. Milk at body temperature was administered to 17 infants, while 16 received milk taken directly from the refrigerator at 45° to 52° F. Observation of the two groups over some 2000 feedings showed no differences, outside of an almost imperceptible drop in body temperature (.2° F) for those receiving cold milk. There were no differences, in other words, in weight gains, crying, sleep patterns, frequency of vomiting, or in behavior while feeding (Holt et al., 1962).

Sensitivity to being moved or changed in position, which stimulates the static receptors, is shown in postural or "balance" responses, by which the neonate rights himself when not too far off-balance. Reactions to internal (organic) stimuli are present. Although the respiratory and circulatory system supply some of these, the preponderance of the internal stimuli comes from the digestive and excretory systems. Regurgitation, hiccuping, urination, and excretion are illustrative of this.

The responses of neonates to sensory stimuli are well-defined and predictable

The Moro reflex can be elicited by laying the infant on his back and suddenly hitting the mattress on both sides of his head. He will respond to this sudden shock by flinging open his arms and extending his fingers, followed by bringing his arms close to his body, as though he were hugging someone. A light touch on the underside of the foot causes it to twist inward—the Babinski reflex.

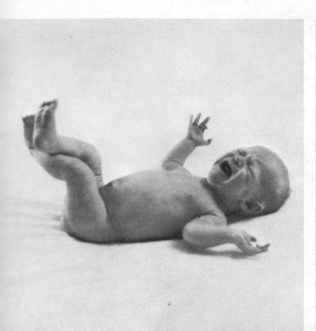
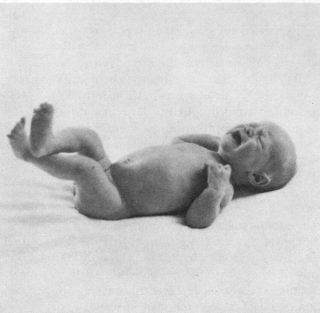
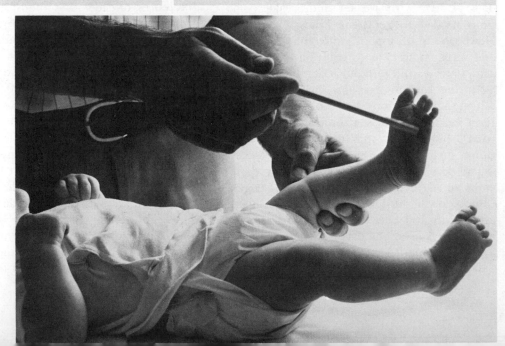

Touching the infant on the cheek or near the mouth sets off the sucking reflex, which can also be elicited by contact with a hand or fist.

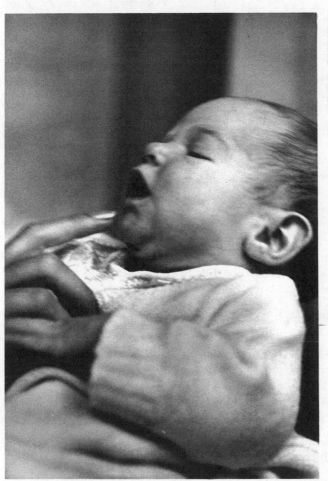

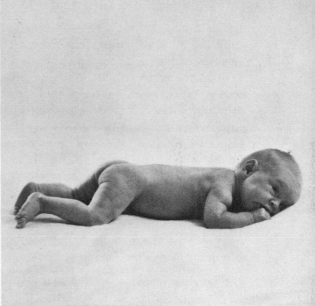

It is apparent, even from this brief summarization, that the neonate exhibits a varied repertoire of reactions to sensory stimuli, both external and internal. Although sensory capacities will increase in sensitivity and scope, a considerable variety is available during the neonatal period.

Motor Responses

The distinction between reactions to sensory stimulation and motor responses, although clear enough in some respects, is nothing more than a matter of emphasis. In the preceding section, focus was on the sensory modality originating the response. Nevertheless, sensory stimulation was known to occur through the responses elicited. We now group responses by the motor areas served. Naturally, many of the same kinds of responses appear again, but they are now in the setting of such areas as the eye, mouth, and trunk.

A succinct indication of some of the motor responses of the neonate is adapted from a summary by Wayne Dennis (1934).

1. EYE RESPONSES—opening and closing eyelids, pupillary, pursuit, saccadic, and coordinate compensatory responses (described in reactions to visual stimuli).

2. FACIAL AND MOUTH RESPONSES—opening and closing mouth, lip movement, sucking, pushing objects from mouth, yawning, and grimacing.

3. THROAT RESPONSES—crying, swallowing, coughing, gagging, vomiting, hiccoughing, cooing, and holding the breath.

4. HEAD MOVEMENTS—upward and downward, side to side, and balancing in response to change of bodily position.

5. ARM RESPONSES—closing hand, arm flexion, rubbing face, grasp reflex, and "random" movements.

6. TRUNK REACTIONS—arching back and twisting.

7. FOOT AND LEG RESPONSES—knee jerk, flexion, extension, kicking (both legs simultaneously), stepping (when neonate held upright with feet touching surface), and toe flexion.

8. COORDINATE RESPONSES OF MANY BODY PARTS—resting and sleeping position (legs flexed, fists closed, upper arms out straight from shoulder with forearms flexed at right angles parallel to the head), springing position (infant held upright and inclined forward, the arms extend forward and legs are brought up), stretching, shivering, trembling, unrest with crying, creeping, bodily jerk, Moro reflex (throwing arms apart, spreading of fingers, extension of legs, and throwing head back).

Despite the list's incompleteness, the neonate's behavior repertoire may still appear surprisingly diversified. Only to the uninitiated eye is the infant a mass of twists and squirms. The neonate starts life with a rather large number of often complicated responses. Potentialities for both differentiation and integration are present. There are both specific movements and mass activity present in his behavior.

The neonate tends to respond to stimulation in a general way, although there are likely to be patterns that are more characteristic of one infant than another. Touching a neonate's cheek is enough to set off the sucking reflex, but some infants will respond with the sucking reflex to all kinds of irrelevant stimuli, such as hair pulling or tweaking the big toe! Others, of course, respond to such stimuli with the crying response or increased body movement.

"General activity," or "mass activity," is also found. The study of these larger patterns of behavior in the newborn was hampered for many years by the lack of a satisfactory classi-fication system of response measures. These categories now include hand-mouth contact-ing, mouthing, crying, and general movement (Kessen, Williams, and Williams, 1961).

Other Responses

Learning in Neonates. The fact that neo-nates have needs and drives and respond to various stimuli suggests that learning can be induced experimentally. Arnold J. Sameroff (1971) reviewed the research in this area and concluded that operant conditioning experi-ments can be carried out, but that it is difficult to demonstrate classical conditioning.

An example of successful operant condition-ing may be found in a study conducted by Einas R. Siqueland (1968), who was able to get one group of neonates to increase head-turning responses and another group to decrease the same type of response.

Classical conditioning, as we noted in the previous chapter, occurs when a previously neutral conditioned stimulus (CS) is associated with a nonneutral unconditioned stimulus (US)—in the case of the dog, the neutral stimu-lus of the tuning fork's sound becomes asso-ciated with the meat powder so that either will produce the salivation response. The problem with neonates, according to Samer-off, is that there really are no "neutral" stimuli for them. The tuning forks, bells, and buzzers used in operant conditioning experiments are all novel stimuli as far as neonates are con-cerned, and they respond defensively instead of giving the more neutral *orienting response* —the "Now, what could *that* be?" reaction. The orienting response is basic to a state of awareness that is prerequisite to classical con-ditioning.

Sameroff suggested two hypotheses to ex-plain the difficulty in instituting classical con-ditioning: either the newborn infant is unable to respond to stimulus changes, or the new-born infant *is* able to respond to general changes, but not the specific ones of the type that are used in such experiments. In order to respond to the stimulus change required in classical conditioning treatments, the infant must develop the ability to perceive differences in stimuli.

Need for Stimulation. A characteristic that humans share with other animals is what might be termed a "need to be stimulated." We noted one aspect of this "need for arousal" in Chapter 4, as well as in the studies showing that newborns show a preference for somewhat more complex visual stimuli, rather than bland stimuli. The need for arousal or stimulation also appears in a study in which five premature infants were stroked five minutes each hour of the day for ten days beginning in the first day after birth. The stroking was administered by a nurse or an aide, who rubbed each neonate's neck, back, and arms. A control group of five premature neonates received only the ordinary hospital care. Results showed that the specially handled infants were more active than those in the control group. They also regained their initial birth weights more rapidly and were described by a pediatrician (who had not been informed as to the nature of the experiment) as being healthier in terms of growth and motor devel-opment when he examined all ten of the infants when they were seven and eight months of age (Solkoff et al., 1969).

The fact that the infants in the experi-mental group responded favorably to tactile stimulation suggests that the stimulation may have met an important need. One study worthy of mention is that of Salk (1960, 1961) who theorized that neonates missed the sound of their mothers' heartbeat and hence broad-cast the sound of a human heart beating at the normal rate to 102 neonates for a four-day period. In contrast to a control group of 112 neonates who did not get this special treatment, the experimental neonates gained weight slightly, whereas the controls lost weight. The experimental group also cried more and were more restless, probably due to a higher level of activity and arousal.

Salk's research was followed up by Yvonne Brackbill and others (1966) who found that there was essentially no difference between the effect of heartbeat sounds and other types of sounds. She did note, however, that infants cried more when there was *no* sound of any kind. She therefore did an experiment in which infants were exposed to 0, 1, 2, 3, and 4 modes of stimuli simultaneously. Stimuli were loud sound, bright light, swaddling clothes, and increase in temperature. Results showed that the more the stimulation, the more the infants slept and the less they cried. Under the maximum stimulation, motor activity, breathing irregularities, and heart rate were also reduced (Brackbill, 1970).

Although common sense would dictate that the more the stimulation, the more the disturbance, these studies, and particularly the last one by Brackbill, suggest that the opposite is true. That is, stimulation facilitates healthy development within limits, because there obviously is a point at which stimulation becomes disturbing, rather than relaxing. It is reasonable to conclude, however, that stimulation is satisfying up to a certain level and also that it is satisfying because it meets some basic need.

Interrelation of Behavior

An important study by Bell (1960) dealt with the interrelation of behavior manifestation. Derived from the rating of filmed observation of 32 neonates, each of 37 behavioral measures was correlated with every other measure. A factor analysis of these intercor-

relations was then performed. Factor analysis, it should be explained, is a means of statistically manipulating the measures until a clear picture of how some are related to others, either positively or negatively. By this procedure, Bell arrived at several patterns and tried to find names that best suited each of the factors that emerged. A requirement for a factor is that it be relatively independent of the others in the correlation table. In short, factor analysis is a means whereby we can find the smallest number of independent factors from a table of intercorrelations. It is an attempt to capture the essence of the relationships among the measures used.

Bell found "level of arousal" was the first factor to emerge. It included the tests concerned with amount, loudness and pulsation (periodic changes of pitch and intensity) of crying, rate of return to sleep, number of movements while awake, hand-mouth contacts, and a negative loading with amount of time spent in sleeping. In other words, those neonates high in these various forms of activity also spent less time sleeping.

The second factor, "depth of sleep," was shown not only by ease of being awakened, length of time to return to sleep, and other measures taken while asleep, but also by waking sensitively to auditory, tactual, and visual stimuli. The three other factors had to do with "tactile sensitivity," "oral integration," (sucking efficiency), and "fetal position." This last factor was derived from the finding that birth length and weight tended to go with a predisposition for the neonate to assume the leg retracted (knees fixed) position, characteristic of that held by the fetus in the womb.

Bell's results do not support the contention sometimes advanced that there is a single unitary "sensory barrier" common to all infants. The infants do not show a general sensitivity level. High sensitivity, he found, is apt to be confined to one or two sense modalities, not all of them. If there are sensory barriers, they are at the level of specific sense modalities, making for an auditorially sensitive child, a visually sensitive child, and so on. That he found an oral factor tended to give credence to the conception of the importance of orality in young infants. Nevertheless, even here not all oral activities formed an entity, some measures being found in the level of arousal factor. Bell considered level of arousal to account for much neonatal behavior, with some infants easy to arouse, and others not.

These factors are larger groupings of behavior characteristic of the neonate. They help us to understand individuality in the neonate.

Summary

The 46 chromosomes, half from each parent, provide a kind of genetic program for each individual's development. *Deoxyribonucleic acid (DNA)* provides the chemical basis for genetic transmission, and *ribonucleic acid (RNA)* molecules are the "messengers" that determine the structure and function of body tissue. The complex rearranging and trading of genes between chromosomes that take place during the formation of germ cells result in a virtually infinite number of possible genetic combinations. Although familial similarities are easy to detect in physical traits, they are less obvious when it comes to behavioral traits. A great many traits that were once believed to be biologically inherited are actually the products of *social inheritance*.

Before conception, the *ovum* proceeds down one arm of the *Fallopian tube* toward the *uterus*. If it is fertilized, it becomes a *zygote* and continues to move toward the uterus. The first two weeks of growth are termed the *ovular* or *germinal* stage. This is followed by the *embryonic* and *fetal* periods. When the zygote is implanted in the uterine wall, the *placenta* begins to develop. The placenta, through which all nutrients and waste products are passed, forms an indirect connection between the closed circulatory systems of mother and fetus. Although the nervous system of the mother is separate from that of the child, the endocrine systems of the two organisms complement each other. Generally, prenatal development is so orderly a process that it is a simple matter to chart the important features in succinct form.

The simultaneous processes of differentiation and integration are evident throughout prenatal development in such phenomena as the development of the heartbeat, and simple body movements. "Spontaneous" movement is most likely to occur when the mother is quiescent. This increase in activity is generally attributed to the decreased oxygen supply available to the fetus. The sheer amount of fetal activity appears to be related to the general activity level of the infant later on. Several investigators have reported a substantial correlation between fetal activity and scores on such tests as the Gesell schedule at age six months.

Other environmental forces influence prenatal development. Nutrition is important. The incidence of birth defects, infant mortality, and related problems are much higher in the poverty areas, where maternal malnutrition is more common. Maternal illness also plays a role. Syphilis, rubella, and diabetes are particularly dangerous. Birth defects have also been traced to radiation exposure and drugs such as thalidomide. Research with animals has shown that hallucinogens like LSD-25 can produce birth abnormalities when taken early in the pregnancy. The incompatibility of Rh blood factors is yet another problem that may affect fetal development.

Pregnancy is a developmental crisis in a woman's life. Attitudes developed during pregnancy will carry over into her relationship with the child, and will affect her later behavior. Sears, Maccoby, and Levin found that mothers who were having their first child and mothers of girls or of both girls and boys tended to be more pleased with the thought of the coming child. Some psychologists have suggested that there is a biologically determined potentiality for motherliness. Levy found a correlation between positive maternal attitudes and duration of menstrual flow. Zemlick and Watson were interested in learning whether attitudes of acceptance or rejection of pregnancy had an effect on the mother's psychological and physical adjustment during pregnancy. Although they found no change in physical symptoms, emotional symptoms and behavior during childbirth were both correlated with attitude. In a related study, mothers who were classed as more neurotic, tended to react to pregnancy with helplessness, suppressed anger, and low self-esteem, and were more likely to reject the pregnancy than normal women. Barbara Doty compared women who were pregnant with their first child (*primaparae* or PP) with those pregnant with a child other than their first (multiparae or MP). The mothers were also divided into middle- and lower-class socioeconomic groups. Lower-class and PP mothers were more likely to reject their maternal roles. Doty also reported that women who expressed rejection of pregnancy were more likely to experience problems with their infants. Grantley Dick Read contends that very few births need be traumatic and that fear is the chief pain-producing agent in labor. He favors a "natural" childbirth method. "Rooming-in" is a related procedure which allows the mother to care for her newborn baby in her hospital room.

Childbirth mortality figures for both mother and child have diminished considerably over the last 50 years. In America, however, the rate of infant mortality is higher than in a number of other countries, and the rate for nonwhites is double the rate for whites. A long and difficult birth process may be accompanied by *anoxia*. Later in life, anoxic children are likely to score poorly on cognitive measures and exhibit greater distractibility. Apgar developed a rating scale that measures the newborn infant's general health and energy level. The Apgar tests correlate highly with future cognitive and physical developments. Research has also shown that unusually low or high birth weight is likely to be associated with significant neurological and physiological impairment. A number of theorists have related birth trauma to later personality characteristics, but their contentions cannot be verified.

The term *neonate* applies to the infant during the first five to seven days of life. The neonate generally weighs seven or eight pounds, and measures about 20 inches in length. The head is about one-fourth of the total body length, compared to the adult's one-seventh, and the eyes are approximately one-half their adult size. Certain coordinated responses present in the neonate are vital to his survival. Feeding behavior, for example, is a sequence of coordinated activities. Although these activities vary between infants, and are initially reflexive in nature, they are subject to the effects of continuous primary reinforcement. It is significant that the infant must give his active cooperation in this, his first social relationship, if the feeding process is to be carried out smoothly and efficiently. Sleep is another important activity. Because the cultural criteria of adult sleep do not apply, it cannot be defined as a state, but must be conceived in terms of a gradient of motility and irritability. Neonates spend about five-sixths of their time sleeping and spend proportionately more time in rapid-eye-movement (REM) sleep than do children and adults. Elimination and respiration are purely reflex activities at this stage of development, although respiration does not stabilize in rhythm and efficiency for several days after birth. Neonates are sensitive to genital stimulation and tumescence generally accompanies restlessness, crying, and other instances of unpleasantness. Like all biological organisms, the neonate strives to maintain *homeostasis*.

The neonate is capable of relatively rudimentary vision. It is questionable whether newborns can distinguish between colors, although they can discriminate between plain and figured patterns and seem to prefer angles and corners to straight lines. Within a few days of birth, the pupillary reflex and some coordinated eye movements appear. Practically any intense visual stimulus will elicit circulatory, respiratory, or startle responses. Neonates show a high degree of variability in their sensitivity to auditory stimuli. The infant is generally incapable of pitch discrimination although he can respond differentially to various intensities, and is capable of a crude form of auditory localization. Taste, smell, pressure, and touch sensitivity are rela-

tively limited at birth, but responsiveness increases rapidly thereafter. Although infants can respond to differences in temperature, research suggests that infants show no preference for either warm or cold milk. Neonates, like other organisms, have a "need to be stimulated." A number of studies have demonstrated a positive relationship between the amount of sensory stimulation and the infant's health. The relationship is obviously curvilinear: there is a point beyond which stimulation is painful.

The neonate's behavior repertoire is surprisingly diversified and contains both specific movements and mass activity. Stimuli may elicit irrelevant and inconsistent responses. Although operant conditioning can take place with neonates, attempts to induce classical conditioning are unsuccessful, probably because there are no stimuli that are "neutral" to neonates and that can be conditioned. Bell did a factor analysis of a number of behavioral measures and found five factors, among which "level of arousal" and "depth of sleep" were the most important. He also found that high sensitivity was usually limited to one or two modalities, and did not reflect a general sensitivity level.

6 Infancy: Physical and Emotional Development

Although we all think we know what an "infant" is, the term actually has a number of different meanings. In its original Latin, the term *infans* means, literally a "nonspeaking being," and the common practice of applying the label "infant" to children of 18 months or younger is literally consistent with that meaning. Not being able to speak also implies an inability to care for oneself, and most of us would also think of this latter characteristic in connection with infancy. In legal terms, infancy can include the entire period from birth to the attainment of one's majority, at 18 or or even 21 years of age. Until the majority is attained, the individual cannot speak for himself in legal matters and cannot enter into contracts unless an adult takes responsibility.

In this discussion, however, we will hold to the everyday meaning of infancy (which is also the psychological meaning) and limit our discussion to the period from birth to the middle of the second year of life.

A tremendous amount of biological development takes place within these few months. Once the relatively constant internal environment of the womb has been left behind, external stimulation plays an increasingly significant part in the life of the young organism. From his experiences with the world, the infant is to acquire new ways of behaving. In fact, the scope and intensity of learning during infancy exceeds that of any other period of development. Nevertheless, the influence of maturation remains very evident, most clearly exemplified in physical growth.

Physical Growth

Consideration has already been given to the physical appearance and bodily proportions of the newborn infant. Attention is now directed to the physical growth that takes place during infancy. It will be remembered that, on the average, the neonate weighs seven or eight pounds and is about 20 inches long. During the first year of life the infant increases his length by over a third and his weight almost triples. Owing to the greater weight than height gain, the infant at one year appears more thickset. The "top-heaviness," characteristic at birth, gradually decreases as legs and trunk increase.

Physical development in the second year proceeds rapidly but at a slower rate than in the first year. At age two, the average child is 32 or 33 inches tall and weighs about 27 pounds (Thompson, 1954). On the average, boys are heavier and taller than girls (Norvall, Kennedy, and Berkson, 1951). Height and weight are correlated about .60, showing a relatively high degree of relationship between the two indices of physique.

Changes in form and proportion are illustrated in Figure 5-8 in Chapter 5, which shows that parts of the body do not grow equally and at the same rate. The directions of development are from head-to-tail (cephalocaudal) and from the center outward (proximodistal). Head development takes place before neck development and this in turn precedes chest growth, and so on. At the same time, upper arm (or leg) growth precedes lower arm (or leg) growth, which in turn precedes hand (or foot) growth. From infancy onward until puberty, the greatest growth takes place at the extremities. Head growth slows down, limb growth is relatively rapid, and trunk growth is intermediate.

Some of the growth changes that take place during these years are illustrated in Figures 6-1 through 6-4. Figure 6-1 presents the growth in weight (expressed on an annual rate) from the 20th week of fetal age onward. Growth reaches its maximum about the 32nd week and then drops off sharply until birth. After birth, there is a sharp rise until about the sixth week, which is followed by a gradual dropping off in growth rate. Figure 6-2 represents growth curves of attained height for boys and girls through adolescence, and Figure 6-3 includes the same data, but presented in terms of the amount gained per year. Inspection of the two graphs shows that gain is very rapid during the first few years, but settles down to a steady rate until the prepubertal period, when it takes a brief spurt and then slows down markedly. Figure 6-4 shows the differential growth pattern of various parts of the body. The brain and head grow rapidly at first and then slow down. The opposite pattern is displayed by the reproductive organs, while the lymphoid glands achieve their greatest growth during the prepuberal period.

These general patterns of growth and maturation are basically the result of biologically determined traits. This is particularly true during the first year of life. Jordan and Spanner (1970) examined the case histories of 353 infants with respect to Apgar scores (at five minutes after birth), birth height and weight, together with various psychosocial factors relating to the mother's age, social status, race, and personality traits. Various combinations of these measures were used in an attempt to predict the weight, height, and general development of infants at 12 months. Results showed substantial correlations between Apgar scores and other biological measures, on the one hand, and height and weight at 12 months, on the other. There was even a modest but significant correlation between the biological measures and infants' general development. The correlations between psychosocial variables and the infants' status at 12

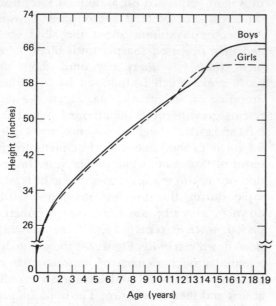

Figure 6-1. Typical curves of height attained by boys and girls from birth to age 19. (After Tanner, Whitehouse, and Takaishi, 1966.) (Reprinted with permission from Mussen (Ed.) Carmichael's Manual of Child Psychology, 3rd ed., Wiley, 1970, p. 82.)

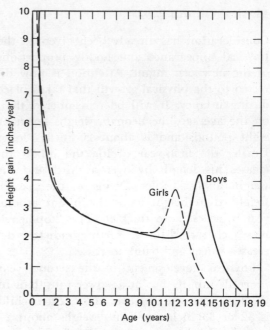

Figure 6-2. Typical curves of gains in height, expressed in terms of inches per year, for boys and girls from birth to age 19. (After Tanner, Whitehouse, and Takaishi, 1966.) (Reprinted with permission from Mussen (Ed.) Carmichael's Manual of Child Psychology, 3rd ed., Wiley, 1970, p. 83.)

months were, however, negligible, suggesting that during this period of development, biological considerations are paramount.

Nutrition. Nutritional intake is, of course, a major factor in normal development and has a significant effect on height and weight. Infants from poverty-stricken families tend to be smaller than normal (Bibring et al., 1961). Eichenwald and Fry (1969) surveyed a wide range of research studies relating to the development of both humans and animals and concluded that malnutrition during early, critical periods may profoundly affect the intellectual and emotional development of the individual. Malnourished infants do not display the curiosity and activity typically noted in normal children, but instead are apathetic and slug-

gish. The degree of apathy in undernourished infants is, in fact, quite similar to that of healthy children who are abruptly separated from their mothers during the first year of life and placed in institutions. A similar lack of emotional responsiveness is also observed in other infants who are lovingly cared for at home, but who have an inadequate diet.

Malnutrition has also been found to be associated with cognitive deficits in young children. Brockman and Ricciuti (1971) administered a simple test of the ability to sort eight simple objects to severely malnourished and normally nourished 18 and 34-month-old children from poverty environments in Lima, Peru. The malnourished children scored markedly below the adequately nourished children.

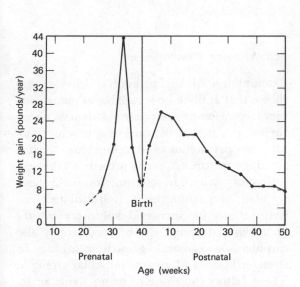

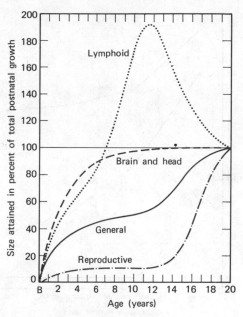

Figure 6-3. Chart of weight gain, expressed in terms of pounds per year, from the 20th week of fetal age until the 50th week after birth. (Estimates were indicated by the dashed lines). (After Tanner, 1963, 1970.) (Reprinted with permission from Mussen (Ed.) Carmichael's Manual of Child Psychology, 3rd ed., Wiley, 1970, p. 91.)

Figure 6-4. Typical growth curves of four different parts or tissues of the body, from birth until age 20. Curves are plotted in terms of total gain and are referred to the size attained at age 20, as represented by 100 on the scale. (Tanner, 1962 and 1970, after Scammon, 1930.) (Reprinted with permission from Mussen (Ed.) Carmichael's Manual of Child Psychology, 3rd ed., Wiley, 1970, p. 85.)

Three months later, after the malnourished children had been put on an adequate diet, a retesting on the same tasks showed that they had made no progress. Observations during the testing sessions showed that both groups of children were equally motivated by the sorting tasks and showed much interest in them. Hence the differences in the scores can only be due to the undernourished children's relative inability to discriminate similarities and differences among the objects and to categorize them properly. Although the researchers were conservative in interpreting their findings, the results can only be explained as resulting from severe nutritional deprivation during a critical period of development.

An experiment with infant monkeys dem-onstrates other behavioral outcomes of inadequate nourishment. In contrast to monkeys having normal nourishment, malnourished monkeys had a slightly higher degree of accuracy with familiar problems, but had difficulty when novel elements were introduced. The difficulty was probably caused by the fact that the unfamiliar elements induced fear (Zimmerman, Strobel, and McGuire, 1970). In view of the fact that learning many life situations involves coping with continually new variations of old problems, it is understandable why individuals from impoverished environments often find they are unable to cope adequately with the problems of everyday life. As the researchers said, "With a decrease in responses to new stimulation and

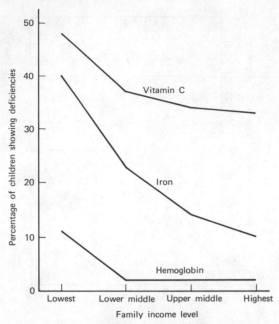

Figure 6-5. The effects of malnutrition: percentage of children aged 12 to 23 months showing the effects of dietary deficiencies. Data are from the first half sample of the Preschool Nutrition Survey conducted by the U.S. Department of Health, Education, and Welfare in 1969. (White House Conference on Children, 1970.)

the development of response patterns which withdraw the infant from the environment, the stage is set for the production of a retarded organism" (p. 198).

As common sense would suggest, it is the children of the very poor who suffer the most from malnutrition. Statistics made available to participants at the most recent White House Conference on Children (1970) show that infants and young children of parents in the lowest income bracket are more than five times as likely to show hemoglobin deficiencies than children from any other income bracket. In contrast to children from families in the highest income bracket, children from poverty homes were also half again more likely to

have iron deficiencies and four times more likely to suffer from Vitamin C deficiencies. (See Figure 6-5.)

Sensorimotor Development

Examination of the neonate's behavior has shown that at birth he is capable of many complex sensorimotor responses. Infancy, nevertheless, is a period of considerable sensorimotor or psychomotor development. Reflex activities mature. A rapid growth of the sensorimotor system in conjunction with both training and autogenous (self-initiated) activity allows for increased voluntary control of activities through the brain; there is also considerable physical growth resulting in stronger bones and greater muscular strength. These factors cooperate to bring about an increase in the scope, precision, and specificity of both sensitivity and response capabilities. Neither the sensory nor the motor phase operates in isolation although emphasis will be placed upon the latter.

Learning and Maturation in Sensorimotor Skills

During infancy a considerable repertoire of skills is developed that the infant uses to manipulate and orient himself to his environment. Both learning and maturation play a part. Some skills are probably more a function of maturation. These include crawling, walking, and finger-thumb opposition. Although we customarily speak of "learning" to walk, neuromuscular maturation is involved and is perhaps the more important of the two conditions of development. If anything, earlier experimenters overstressed the importance of maturation as compared with learning.

A typical illustration is the study of Hopi

Indian babies bound to cradleboards, thus experiencing a good deal of movement restraint during their first year of life. They walked independently about as early as did infants who had had much more previous practice (Dennis and Dennis, 1940). Practice missed by being strapped to the cradleboard did not seem to prevent walking from appearing at the usual age. This finding is interpreted by the particular investigator as indicative of the clear primacy of maturation over learning in the emergence of walking.

Another classic study compared the behavior of 46 week-old twin girls in stair climbing and cube building. The choice of the age of 46 weeks for initial study was dictated by the fact that this was about the age at which infants were at the threshold of stair-climbing and cube-building responses. Twin T (trained) was given a ten-minute practice session each day for *six* weeks. Twin C (control) was given no training until the end of the six-week period at which time she was given *two* weeks of practice. At the end of this practice period, Twin C was performing these activities as well as Twin T who had the four more weeks of practice but at an earlier age. The investigators concluded that the time of appearance of stair climbing and cube building was not influenced by practice but by the ripening of neural structures (Gesell and Thompson, 1934).

Fowler (1962) has taken a critical view of such conclusions, saying that the researchers are overemphasizing the influence of maturation. The roles of perception and experiences, he argued, have been ignored. Moreover there is a strong probability that the more complex the skill concerned, the greater are their roles. Fowler said that there is a receptive phase to any motor activity—perceiving the cubes in three-dimensional space or learning to coordinate visual movement and tactual experi-ence—which has a large perceptual component and which cannot be alleged to be innate. Moreover, there is apt to be opportunity for experience through autogenous practice. In the stair-climbing study, Twin C was not actually permitted to climb stairs or to play with cubes but the constituent activities nevertheless could have been practiced in his day-to-day living. Learning at a given later age may be more efficient than practice at an earlier age, but this does not mean learning did not take place earlier. Even though Twin T had more "practice" than Twin C, he did *learn* at an earlier age. Again we find that maturation and learning interact and that, perhaps, it is futile to try to differentiate precisely their effect.

Major areas of motor development during early infancy are manipulation and locomotion.

Manipulation

The arm and hand are the vehicles of manipulation. The sequence of development of prehension (grasping) has been intensively studied with infants between 16 weeks and one year of age (Halverson, 1931). The seated infant was given an opportunity to grasp a cube. Photographs were studied to arrive at the developmental sequence that had grasping as its culmination. Preceding grasping itself a series of stages of development was found. At 16 weeks the infants generally made no contact at all with the cube; at 20 weeks they made contact, or squeezed it without grasping. From 24 weeks onward, grasping developed. Grasping at first is a clawing type of activity with the thumb inactive, followed later by a nipping pressing kind of closure in which thumb and forefinger dominate, but which is still a form of manipulation that involves much palming.

After one year, however, an entirely new

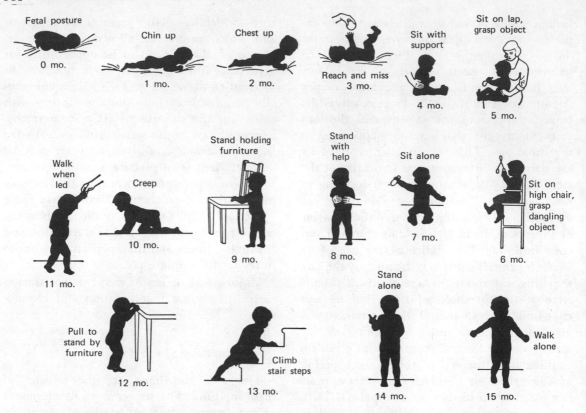

Fetal posture
0 mo.

Chin up
1 mo.

Chest up
2 mo.

Reach and miss
3 mo.

Sit with support
4 mo.

Sit on lap, grasp object
5 mo.

Walk when led
11 mo.

Creep
10 mo.

Stand holding furniture
9 mo.

Stand with help
8 mo.

Sit alone
7 mo.

Sit on high chair, grasp dangling object
6 mo.

Pull to stand by furniture
12 mo.

Climb stair steps
13 mo.

Stand alone
14 mo.

Walk alone
15 mo.

Figure 6-6. Sequence of motor development in locomotion. (Shirley, 1933. Reproduced by permission from Mary M. Shirley, *The First Two Years, Vol. II, Intellectual Development.* Minneapolis: U. of Minnesota Press, 1933. Copyright renewed, 1961.)

level of skill is likely to have made its debut: with elevated palm and a precise plucking motion the pellet is grasped with no waste motion (and, it should be added parenthetically, almost invariably thrust immediately into the mouth). Historically, we might find roots of the eventual precision in the unfailing appearance of the initial reflex grasp, but observation of the entire sequence reveals that much simultaneous integration and differentiation must be accomplished before such refined movement is possible.

Manipulation exemplifies the general orderliness of sensorimotor development; sequential steps follow one another with each stage forming a new level of maturity.

Locomotion

The neonate has no effective means of movement from place to place. From its supine ("face up") or prone ("face down") position it may shift about a bit, but this movement can hardly be called locomotion in the sense of movement from place to place. Mary M. Shirley (1931) conducted careful studies of the development in posture and locomotion of a group of 25 infants. Figure 6-6 shows the steps that she found in the motor sequence. The very fact that we can use the sequence in this figure to represent changes in locomotion shows that again there is a progressive regularity of development despite variability from infant to infant.

The five major stages are very uniform and involve the following order: (1) passive postural control as in sitting with support; (2) active postural control such as sitting alone; (3) active efforts toward locomotion; (4) creeping and walking with support; and, finally, (5) walking alone. The last stage occurred on the average at about 15 months, although some children in the sample walked alone as early as 11½ months, while others did not do so until 17 months. Each major stage has within it several steps. Although these steps may vary in sequence from infant to infant, each stage is a prerequisite for the immediately succeeding one. Walking is the climax of a long series of activities that are not directly locomotor in themselves but which proceed in an orderly fashion in each infant.

Although Shirley's general sequence has been verified, Nancy Bayley (1935) found some reversals of steps. Instead of a regular order of appearance of special abilities there was a more irregular growth in the ability in question. Moreover, the stages seemed to occur at earlier ages. In Bayley's study, the average age of onset of walking was found to be 13 instead of 15 months, which is closer to that recorded by other observers.

The developmental principles of differentiation and integration along with cumulative experience are involved in walking. Not so obvious, perhaps, is the exemplification of the principle of discontinuity and hierarchization in that each stage involves muscular movements not present in earlier stages. Study of Figure 6-6, picture by picture, will show that different muscle groups are being controlled at different stages. First the eye, head, and neck are involved, then the arms and upper trunk, later the hands and lower trunk, and last the pelvic area and the legs—an example of the cephalocaudal direction of development we mentioned earlier.

Beginning to walk has profound psychological consequences. The infant is more able to bring himself in contact with "people, places, and things." This he does because *he* wants to. Others do not have to come to him. To a much greater degree he now may be independent of adult control. He may walk into areas of which his parents approve, but he may also walk into those of which they emphatically do not. To modify a saying, "Fools, and little children, rush in where angels fear to tread." Thus, beginning at about the age of 15 months and continuing to roughly the age of four, there is a period of great locomotor activity. The period, a strenuous one from the parental point of view, is brought about by the simple fact that the infant is able to walk and run.

Motor Development in Later Infancy

Motor development in locomotion has been discussed up to the advent of walking at about 13 to 15 months, while manipulation has been discussed as it takes place during the first year of life. Some later motor behaviors with characteristic age of appearance are given in Table 6-1. Both the older infant's versatility and his steady gain in motor skills are exemplified. Other activities such as language and feeding, too, have their motor components which are progressing rapidly.

Early Stimulation and Psychomotor Development

The rapidity with which infants develop motor skills shows some variation from infant

TABLE 6-1. *Motor Development in the Second Year of Life: Selected Items from the Bayley Infant Scale of Motor Development (Bayley, 1965)*

Item Number	Age in months	Item Name
49	13.5	Walks sideways
50	14.2	Walks backward
51	18.3	Stands on left foot with help
53	18.7	Walks upstairs with help
54	18.9	Walks downstairs with help
57	22.7	Walks upstairs alone
58	22.9	Walks downstairs alone

to infant. Undoubtedly some of these differences are genetically determined, but it is also quite possible that the environment may play a part. Burton L. White (1969) and his co-workers have conducted a number of experiments in which infants were treated to extra amounts of stimulation, through handling or enrichment of the visual environment or both. The results of such studies show that infants given the special treatment begin to reach at objects sooner than those in control situations.

Cross-cultural research shows that African infants, mainly in Uganda, are weeks and months advanced over European children in psychomotor development. One explanation for this precocity is the massive amount of stimulation received by the African children. The Ugandan infant is never left alone by his mother, but is carried with her wherever she goes. In addition he receives a great deal of affectionate fondling, not only from his mother, but from others as well (Geber, 1958).

Although studies like those of White and Geber are suggestive of a possible causative relationship between early stimulation and the facilitation of growth and development, they are by no means conclusive. A great deal more well-controlled, cross-cultural research is needed before we can be reasonably certain that the relationship applies generally to infants in all cultures. The findings are, however, provocative and are consistent with the results of other studies, including those reported in the preceding chapter.

Developmental Changes in Primary Needs

Progressive changes in how often and in what manner the infant satisfies his basic needs are especially prominent and important features of his development. These include feeding, sleep, elimination, and sex. We shall consider secondary needs only insofar as they derive directly from the basic needs, deferring further attention to them until the next two chapters where they are examined in a social setting. This is also the case with exploratory, externally aroused behavior tendencies.

Developmental Changes in Feeding

Gesell and Ilg (1949) observed that neonates require about seven or eight feedings per day. By the time they are four weeks old the number of feedings becomes reduced to five or six, and reduces further to three to five in the following weeks. Beginning at 16 weeks this number of feedings, or a little less, is maintained until toward the end of the first year, by which time the three-meals-a-day regime of our culture is fairly well established, along with one or two snacks.

Diet supplementation in the form of solid foods goes on from about 20 weeks of age. Cup and spoon feeding takes place during this time and by 40 weeks the infant helps himself in feeding, incidentally making a fine mess of it in the process. Preference for certain foods is well defined at one year, for example, certain vegetables, or hot as compared to cold cereals.

Scheduling and Self-Demand Feeding.

Among a large group of mothers, Sears, Maccoby, and Levin, (1957) found the prevalent practice to be neither a self-demand system nor a rigid scheduling but something between. Only 12% of the mothers always fed the infant when he cried and permitted him to eat as much as he wanted, whereas 8% fed him by the clock, waking him for feedings. The remainder followed practices that were between these extremes.

It was the pioneer study of Clara M. Davis (1935, 1939) that probably served as the original scientific impetus for changing adult attitudes in the direction of greater permissiveness toward infant feeding and self-regulation in scheduling. In her study, 15 infants between 6 and 11 months were presented with a variety of foods from which they could choose kind and amount. The foods offered were "natural"—what would be called "macrobiotic" today—and were prepared as simply as possible: finely cut, mashed, or ground; raw, or cooked simply. In the first few days of free choice, the infants showed great individual differences as to the type and quantity of food they ate. They even went on "jags" in which they would eat certain foods exclusively for days at a time. Over a period of time, however, their diets balanced out, in the sense that they consumed the proportions of carbohydrates, proteins, and fats that diet experts agreed would be appropriate for children of that age and weight. The study went on for six years and the grand total of meals consumed by the children was nearly 36,000. Davis reported that none of the children developed feeding problems and that their health and resistance to infection was considerably above average.

Davis's study has often been interpreted as meaning that infants and children should be permitted to eat whatever they want. As she pointed out, however, the subjects in her study were offered only *natural* foods. Most parents today do not have ready access to a full range of such foods and probably do not have the time to prepare them as she and her assistants did. In any event, her study needs to be replicated with a larger sample of infants and with food options that include those available in most homes today: candy, cola drinks, prepared breakfast foods, pizza, and the like.

Despite some tendency toward variability, infants are fully capable of learning to adapt to the feeding schedules introduced by adults. This was neatly demonstrated by Dorothy Marquis (1943) who studied the learning of a feeding schedule by infants during the first ten days of life while they were still in the hospital. The experimental group was on a three-hour feeding schedule, except during the day before discharge when these infants were shifted to a four-hour schedule, while the control group was on a four-hour feeding schedule throughout its hospital stay.

Marquis measured the activity patterns (restlessness) of both groups by a mechanical device that supported the bassinets in which the infants lay. Their activity was the criterion of adaptiveness to the schedule. When the interval of feeding was changed from three to four hours in the experimental group on the tenth day, these infants showed a sharp rise in their activity during this extra hour between feedings. At the end of three hours, their heretofore habitual feeding time, body movements increased abruptly and continued throughout the fourth hour. Apparently, the infants had learned to respond to hunger cues at the end of three hours. Failure to receive their accustomed feeding markedly increased restlessness. Control infants fed on a four-hour schedule from birth to what was now their ninth day showed only their usual gradual increase in activity as feeding time approached.

Having learned a particular schedule, the experimental group became increasingly restless when the accustomed feeding time had passed. Marquis suggests that this is an instance of an early form of socialization. It made a difference for these newborn infants to have to wait an extra hour, whereas the control infants, already habituated to their constant four-hour schedule, showed no increased restlessness.

Breast- and Bottle-Feeding. In the Sears, Maccoby, Levin (1957) study, mentioned earlier, 40% of the infants were breast-fed, the majority for only three months. In view of the large number being fed by bottles and the relative shortness of breast-feeding by those who did receive it, it is of interest, despite its somewhat digressive character, to examine the reasons the mothers gave for not breast-feeding. Over 40% claimed they were unable to breast-feed for physical reasons, such as not having enough milk or the presence of inverted nipples. Another 16% reported that the doctor advised against breast-feeding without specifying any physical difficulty. Thirty-five percent did not want to breast-feed, some for emotional reasons, others because they did not want to be tied down, and still others for unspecified reasons.

The two groups who gave "physical reasons" or "doctor's advice" seem quite large, too large in fact for the reasons given to represent actually the true state of affairs. One suspects that the objections they offered to breast-feeding were rationalizations and that they did not want to for reasons other than the ones given. For example, "inability" may more correctly have been dislike of breast-feeding.

Weaning. The sucking movements of the neonate are adapted for taking liquid foods from breast or bottle. With increased matura-

tion at about the third or fourth month, mouth movements begin to change in a direction suitable for eating solid food and biting movements begin to appear. By seven to nine months these movements have become stronger.

Repeated reinforcement of sucking has occurred during these early months and sucking has become a well-established habit in securing nourishment. The process of weaning means these now habitual patterns must be eliminated and new activities learned.

Weaning at first glance may appear to be a simple straightforward practice; in reality, it is a very complicated one. Even the term is used in more than one sense. Sometimes, weaning refers to a shift from breast- to bottle-feeding. In the sense used here, however, it means the process of giving up sucking for a new mode of food-getting through eating solid foods and drinking (not sucking) of liquids. According to Sears, Maccoby, and Levin (1957), weaning involves five tasks:

"The child must learn *not to want* to get his food by sucking. He must learn to *like* to *drink* the same food he formerly got by sucking. He must learn to *want solid foods*. He must learn the *manipulative skills* required for eating them—biting, chewing, and the use of fingers and utensils, as well as drinking from a cup. He must learn to do *without being held* while he is eating" (p. 69).[1]

Each of these tasks may be presented to the child in an endless variety of ways. For example, solid foods can be thrust at him all at once or their presentation can be spaced almost from birth, long before the process of weaning. Frustrations arising from the tasks of weaning will depend on many things, not very precisely summed up as "weaning."

[1] Reprinted by permission.

In their sample of mothers, Sears, Maccoby, and Levin (1957), found that two-thirds had started the weaning process by the time the infant was 11 months old. For the majority, the process of weaning took four months to complete. Nevertheless, at least 12% took a year or more.

People in Western cultures are likely to think of weaning in purely developmental terms—that is, infants are weaned when they are able to drink from a cup and ingest solid food. Observations of weaning in other cultures shows many different patterns, however. In one series of comparative studies of child rearing in six cultures, it was noted that the American children were usually weaned from the bottle when they were between 9 and 12 months old. Only a small percentage were weaned at more than 18 months. In one study, about 40% of the mothers (all New Englanders) breast-fed their infants, the length of nursing ranging from a few days to five months. In other cultures, which included village societies in Kenya, India, Okinawa, Mexico, and the Philippines, the infants were all breast-fed, and nursing went on for two years or more, usually terminated by the mother's next pregnancy, although not always then. In some cultures, the weaning was accomplished peacefully, and in others, the Okinawan, for example, it was a stormy, angry period for the child. In comparison to mothers in other cultures, American mothers seemed to take a "no-nonsense" approach to weaning, intervening firmly and more or less confidently to terminate bottle-feeding. Mothers in other cultures, as for example the Rajput in India, had difficulty in bringing matters to a close. Some of the Rajput threatened to smear bitter herbs or chili on their nipples, but could not bring themselves to do so. One mother actually held the herb in her hand, while she nursed her infant, but made no attempt to use it (Whiting, 1963).

Taken by themselves, weaning practices are probably of no great significance, but when they are related to other aspects of child-parent relations, they fit into patterns or styles of interaction that have considerable significance for personality development in childhood and even adulthood. The American culture, like other industrialized and urbanized cultures, is highly time-oriented. Things are done according to schedules: society demands that we get to school and work on time, that we do not take up more time than is necessary in our transactions with others, that we have our meals at certain more or less fixed schedules, and so forth. In spite of our preoccupation with scheduling, we also feel that children should be relatively free of such restrictions, in order to facilitate optimal development. This latter philosophy underlies our attempts to be "permissive" with children, to provide opportunities and devices for free play, and to place them on a "demand feeding" basis. These two sets of values create a kind of conflict for us: on the one hand we feel that scheduling of activities is necessary, but on the other hand, we feel that children, and particularly infants, should be exempt from scheduling requirements.

How this dilemma is resolved is suggested by observation of New England mothers in the six-culture series of studies referred to above. Virtually all the mothers in the sample said that they fed their infants on demand. Further inquiry revealed that there was a wide variety of interpretation of "demand." For some mothers, "demand" meant that they permitted half-hour deviations from the schedule. Others reported that they adjusted their own activities to those of the infant. The infant, however, was expected to schedule his own activities within a few weeks of birth, whereupon the mother would faithfully follow his schedule, just as though she had set it up herself. Evidently no infant demanded

Feeding time is the great psycho-social event in infancy

It is the occasion for the closest contact with the mother, learning to cope with the infant's first artifact—his bottle . . .

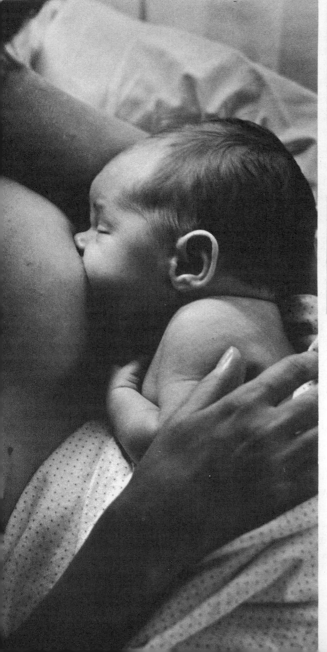
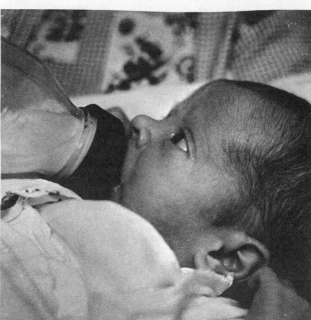

Later, feeding time means learning a basic, complex skill, learning to be independent, and interaction with and integration into the family group.

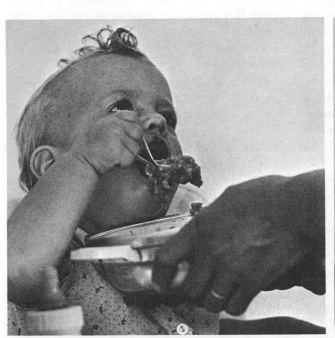

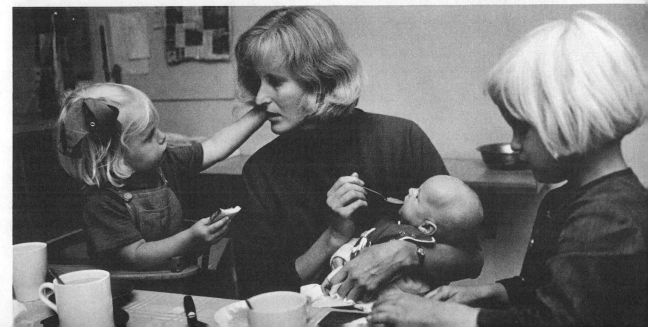

feeding on an irregular basis. If so, no New England mother admitted it (Fischer and Fischer, 1963).

Developmental Changes in Sleep

Gesell and Ilg's (1949) account of the change in sleeping patterns during infancy must be viewed in the framework of the middle-class American culture and reflects the way in which the infant adjusts to family routines as well as to changes in sleep needs resulting from changing biological demands. The researchers noted that at four weeks the infant typically drops off to sleep gradually toward the end of the nursing period. At this age the infant has four to five sleep periods in 24 hours. By 16 weeks he has established something of a night sleep rhythm, falling asleep after the six P.M. feeding and waking between five and six A.M. He does not fall asleep immediately after each feeding and has about three naps during the day in addition to his sleep periods. At 40 weeks he tends to fall asleep after his six P.M. feeding and sleeps through to five to seven A.M. There may be one long midmorning nap or as many as four short nap periods.

Although the total number of hours of infant's sleep is decreasing, the periods are increasing in length. Whereas hunger and pain may awaken him at any time, loud sounds and other stimuli are decreased in our culture at night and consequently, during this period he is less disturbed by environmental stimuli.

The infant must learn to sleep in the same way he learns to creep, stand and walk, and grasp a spoon. He must also learn to stay awake! Although learning is undoubtedly important, maturation is also important. As he grows older he is not so subcortical (without the service of the highest nerve centers of the brain) as Gesell puts it. Millions of cortical cells, previously nonfunctional because they had not matured sufficiently, are beginning to make connections between eyes, ears, and the muscles of the eyes. Their maturation serves to keep his cortex "awake" and thus make him more receptive to his surroundings. Staying awake for longer periods of time with increasing amounts of time spent in acts other than those associated with feeding is an important part of the process of early development. These longer periods of waking afford opportunity for more intensive and varied experiences with the environment.

There are, of course, individual differences in sleep requirements among infants and in the same infant from one time to another. By and large, however, we are not too demanding in our culture and allow the child during infancy to express his individuality in this regard. He generally may be said to sleep as much as he needs. Consequently, sleep is not a vehicle upon which extremes of social pressure are practiced, which accounts for its omission when socialization practices in infancy are discussed later.

Developmental Changes in Elimination

Gesell and Ilg's normative findings (1949) in relation to elimination changes show that at four weeks the infant tends to have three or four bowel movements in a 24-hour period. He may now cry when his diaper is wet, quieting when changed. At 16 weeks there are one or two movements, most commonly after a feeding. By 28 weeks there is apt to be only one movement, usually at nine to ten A.M. Urination is still occurring at frequent intervals. At 40 weeks the infant may be dry after an hour's nap and sometimes an infant may respond to the pot. Changes hereafter will be described in the context of the problem of toilet training which this need engenders.

Social demands in our culture require that the child learn voluntary control of bladder and bowel so as to void at an acceptable time and place. The neonate is cheerily oblivious to these demands. He voids and urinates by the involuntary relaxation of sphincter muscles when pressures have built up to a certain point. Voluntary control of bowel and bladder must be superimposed upon an involuntary activity. Optimally, changes in eliminative processes await the age at which neuromuscular mechanisms have sufficiently matured for them to be voluntarily controlled. As a neonate he cannot do so, even if by some miracle, he "wanted" to do so. Punishment, bribes, and scolding may go on relentlessly, but the learning remains incidental and sporadic until he is maturationally ready for voluntary control.

The importance of maturation in bladder control is shown in a classic study by McGraw (1940) on twin boys. With one of them, bladder training was started at about 50 days by placing him on the toilet every hour. Until about 600 days there was little evidence of learning. After 600 days the curve of success increased sharply, and by 700 days successes were close to 100%. No training whatsoever was started with the other twin until 700 days. His performance was almost immediately as good as that of the twin with the longer period of training. This rather startling difference is not an isolated phenomenon as another record of twins by McGraw shows. Evidently, training started later rather than earlier takes advantage of maturation and is more effective than trying to train earlier.

The results found by McGraw, however, should not be taken as definitive concerning the *date* to begin training or to expect its ending. This is subject to individual variation. Her data are indicative merely of *relative* relationships in these twins and are in no way an index of what happens in sample groups. This normative question will be considered in a moment.

Toilet training may be viewed as a learning situation in which the reward is not in the satisfaction of a basic need. The child's social eliminative needs are, if we may slip into the vernacular, "learned the hard way."

The infant is not repelled by his bodily products. He will play with them when the opportunity arises. Parents vary in their reaction to this situation, but having to face it is inescapable. They may arrange to direct attention elsewhere by diverting the child from this interest, or become angry and repressive, or show any other of a hundred other responses, but deal with it they must. In dealing with the problem they train their infants whether this be formal avowed training or the unacknowledged unintentional facets of their teaching.

The learning of toilet-training practices begins without verbal aids because the infant does not have either the active verbal repertoire or the understanding to deal with training in this fashion. As a consequence, training in cleanliness proceeds by a process of trial and error. To quote Dollard and Miller (1950):

"The child must learn to wake up in order to go to the toilet, though sleep seems good. It must learn to stop its play even when social excitement is strong. It must learn to discriminate between the different rooms of the house—all this by crude trial and error. In this case, "trial" means urinating or defecating in an inappropriate place, and "error" means being punished for the act so that anxiety responses are attached to the cues of this place. In the trial-and-error situation this must be repeated for each inappropriate place—bed, living room, dining room, kitchen, "outside." The function of this training is to attach anxiety responses to the defecation drive so that they win out over the immediate evulsion response. These anxiety responses also motivate and cue off the next responses in the series, such as calling to the parents, running to the bathroom, unbuttoning the clothes, and the like" (138).[2]

This process naturally arouses strong emotional reactions in the child. Anger, defiance, stubborness, and fear appear in response to this situation.

We are now in a position to examine the scheduling of toilet training by parents in our culture. Pediatricians generally encourage mothers to postpone training until the second year. In the "pattern study" of Sears, Maccoby, and Levin (1957) the average age for beginning bowel training was about 11 months and for completion about 18 months. For any 2-month period the greatest percentage started between 9 and 11 months. Almost 75% were trained between 10 and 24 months. A few (8%) were trained between 5 and 9 months and 15% took longer than 24 months. Some mothers claimed it took only a few weeks, but others found it took 1½ years to carry out the process of training. Generally speaking, if begun later it took less time. For example, if begun at 5 months it took 10 months; if begun at 20 months it took only 5 months. This again emphasizes the importance of maturation.

Changes in Sexual Behavior

It is paradoxical to consider this topic since we know almost nothing about its developmental changes; there is even some question if we can accurately speak of a "sex need" during infancy. As was done with the neonate, it is perhaps most fitting to speak of precursors of sexual needs.

Activity in the sex organs of infants is cer-

[2] By permission from *Personality and Psychotherapy,* by Dollard and Miller. Copyright 1950, McGraw-Hill Book Company, Inc.

tainly present, even during the neonatal period. Observation by Kinsey and his associates (1948) showed that in 317 two-to-twelve-month-old male infants, nearly one-third had an orgasm—naturally without ejaculation. The orgasm's reward value may be entirely a matter of pleasurable tactile stimulation. Certainly, it has no heterosexual intent.

We also know from the detailed observations of Halverson (1938) that there seems to be a close relationship between erection and reflex activities associated with sucking. He was concerned with all activities of sucking behavior including measures of general bodily muscular tenseness. Tumescence of the penis was frequently observed when sucking was interrupted by removal of the nipple.

Emotional Development

"Emotion" is a difficult word to define. It may be applied both to an increase in tension or a release from tension, and to sustained high, intermediate, or low levels of tension as well. Inasmuch as our only evidence that an emotional state exists consists of the observable behavior that accompanies or results from such tension states or changes in states, it is probably more accurate to speak of *emotional responses* or *emotional behavior,* rather than *emotion.* The characteristics of emotional responses may be determined from situations in which they occur, as well as from the general direction of the behavior that is displayed. Positive emotions are characterized by a tendency to *approach.* Enjoyment, satisfaction, and love all involve being attracted to objects or persons, wanting to retain them or remain with them, or wanting to stay in their proximity. Negative emotions are of two main types: fear and rage. Fear or anxiety responses have an *away from* quality to them—that is, we want to remove ourselves from offending objects or persons or want them to depart

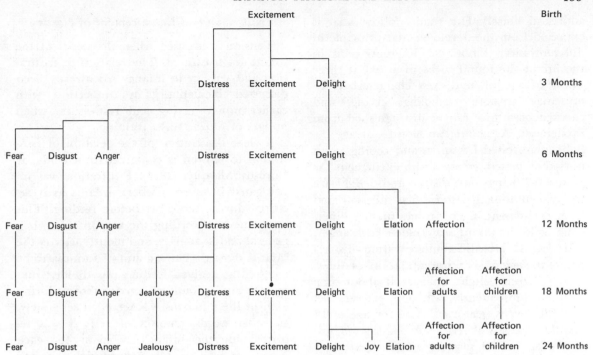

Figure 6-7. Approximate ages of differentiation of various emotions during the first two years. (Bridges, 1932. Copyright 1932 by the Society for Research in Child Development, and published by permission.)

from us. Rage responses have an *against* quality. When we are irritated or angry we want to destroy, humiliate, or injure the offending objects or persons. In very general terms, fear or anxiety responses are characteristic of us when we feel less than adequate to deal with the situation in question, whereas rage or anger responses are associated with a feeling of strength, power, and competence.

With these general outlines in mind, let use examine the development of emotional responses in infants. Psychologists usually take the view that the only emotional response that can be identified in newborns is what might be described as a state of generalized excitement. As the infant develops, its reactions become more specific and more readily focused on certain classes of stimuli. This general idea is consistent with the observations of Katherine

M. B. Bridges (1932), whose conclusions are summarized in Figure 6-7. She noted that neonates displayed undifferentiated excitement or agitation, as shown by uncoordinated overt and visceral reactions to intense stimulation of any sort, internal or external. The vigorous but ill-coordinated movements of the infant's body show little relation to a particular stimulus. Undifferentiated *mass action* is prominent; the baby cries with his whole body. Bridges' finding concerning initial undifferentiated excitement receives support from the fact that there are no distinctive unique patterns of visceral or physiological responses each corresponding to a different emotion (Bridges, 1930).

Despite the presence of generalized excitement it is also an inescapable fact that in the older infant and child other emotions do emerge. It was to their study that Bridges addressed herself. Her results follow what is expected from the developmental principle of differentiation. Emotional differentiations in the infant she found to begin at about three weeks of age when distress characterized by muscular tension, trembling, crying, and checked breathing can be distinguished from excitement. At about two months of age delight, manifested by smiles and cooing when nursed or petted, emerges with excitement. As Figure 6-7 brings out, distress and delight are the two emotional patterns first differentiated from excitement. Each become further differentiated as the infant grows older. Fear, anger, and disgust are differentiated from distress before the age of six months. Elation, as differentiated from delight, emerges at about nine months. Subsequently, affection emerges before 12 months, jealousy before the age of 18 months, and joy shortly after that age. Thus, at the age of 18 months a rather extensive repertoire of differentiated emotional reactions seem to be present in the infant. Although Bridges' scheme is very plausible and fits our general knowledge of how behavior develops, questions must be raised as to whether the "emotions" she observed actually did emerge at the ages indicated. The sequence of their appearance may also be questioned. What is missing in her study is an absence of controls in the form of other, unbiased judges who observed the same children at the same time and who recorded their conclusions independently. One suspects that Bridges' descriptions of behavior suffer from what might be termed "adultomorphism"—that is, a tendency to read into an infant's behavior the kind of feeling an adult would have in a similar situation. These difficulties make her conclusions suggestive and tentative, rather than definitive. There is little question that she was able to establish some differentiation of emotional response; what is not certain are the precise sequence of their appearance and the labels she attached to the responses.

Frustration and Enhancement of Needs

Tension is aroused when the needs of the infant are frustrated. The relation of frustration and tension in infancy has already been discussed incidentally in connection with earlier topics—crying and restlessness when hungry or during toilet training.

A clear illustration of the relation of frustration to tension is contained in a study by Dorothy Marquis (1943). Frustration was investigated in seven newborn infants as it occurred during the delay before feeding. This was done by recording the amount of crying, general bodily activity, and mouth activity the infants showed. The amount of formula to be received at a given feeding was divided into fourths and amount of activity shown during each of these fourths was recorded separately. In other words, amount of activity was recorded for the infant's behavior for each fourth as well as for a fixed delay period without feeding which followed each of the feeding "fourths." As amount of milk consumed increased, there was a decreased amount of activity and increased tolerance of the delay period. To put it succinctly, as frustration from hunger decreased, tension also decreased.

Not only frustration but also that which furthers or facilitates meeting the infant's needs may be provocative of emotion. Delight and affection are emotional responses illustrative of enhancing emotional responses. They may be in themselves tension producing. In fact, if this tension is prolonged or intense it may bring about displeasure. Too many toys can bring about an excited delight which readily passes over into displeasure and crying spells.

Differentiation of Emotional Responses

It is hardly likely that the infant is capable of intense emotional experiences as *adults know them*. We may, for example, see a newborn infant squirming, kicking, and crying. We may infer that the infant is experiencing what we would feel if we were in his place. But we are not in his place. In support of the position that there is considerable difference between infantile and adult emotional experience several points can be offered. We know that neural maturation is still incomplete in the infant, particularly in the cerebral cortex. We also know that there is little if any knowledge of self on the infant's part and that personal reference, so characteristic of adult emotional responses, must be lacking with him. Most important perhaps, certain research studies show that we can be fooled by what we read into the situation when observing "emotional experiences" of infants. Thus when such terms as "excitement," "distress," and "delight" are used, as Bridges did, they should be viewed as if they carried quotation marks to indicate only a tentative similarity to those that adults experience.

This "adultomorphic" tendency of interpreting the behavior of an infant as if we experienced it is at the root of the methodological confusion that occurred in John B. Watson's classic study of 1920 in which he claimed that he had demonstrated the primary emotions of the newborn to be fear, rage, and love, and not others. Fear in newborn infants, he claimed, was produced by loud sounds and loss of support. Rage was brought about by hampering of movements. Love was released by stroking and petting. All other emotional reactions, he went on to state, were the consequence of conditioning of these three primary emotions (Watson and Raynor, 1920).

The validity of Watson's theory rests upon a matter of fact—whether the emotions he described could be identified by others in such a fashion that the three patterns of emotion would be found to be separable and identifiable. Sherman (1927) demonstrated that this was not the case. The situations he used to bring about emotional responses—delay of feeding beyond the usual time, sudden loss of support, restraint of head movements, and pricking with a needle—were first presented to the observers as precludes to the emotional reactions of the infants.

Under these conditions the observers were generally able to offer "correct" identifications of the emotions with considerable interobserver agreement, though some disagreements existed. Thus, observers who saw the infant lose his support and then the emotional reaction which followed tended to label the emotional reaction "fear." But when they saw motion pictures of the infant's emotional reactions cut so that the stimulation period was eliminated, and hence could not know which particular stimulus was being used, they failed to agree on what emotion was being expressed. Moreover, when the film was so spliced as to give the impression that the stimuli preceding the infant's emotion was the actual one to which the infant was responding, the observers tended to ascribe to the infant the emotion appropriate to that stimulus, and not to the one for which it was actually the response. In general, Sherman could find no characteristic emotional patterns that would allow one emotion to be distinguished from another. Rather, there were uncoordinated, unspecialized, and diversified responses with no particular patterns of differentiation. Situations that at a later age arouse a variety of emotions produced the same general undifferentiated emotional reactions in these infants.

Changes in the Mode of Responses and of Sensitivity

As the infant grows older changes in the mode of responses take place—changes in the way the emotion is expressed. Fear in the 20-month-old, for example, is different from the eight-month-old infant. The former now can move away from the feared stimulus, not merely cry. As the infant grows older, more

***In contrast to later stages of development, emotions during childhood
are relatively simple and nonspecific***

*Delight is easy to distinguish. It is usually evoked by some kind of social interaction.
Interest, curiosity, and the orienting reflex are often missing from lists of emotions, but
they nevertheless involve varying degrees of affect, feeling, or arousal.*

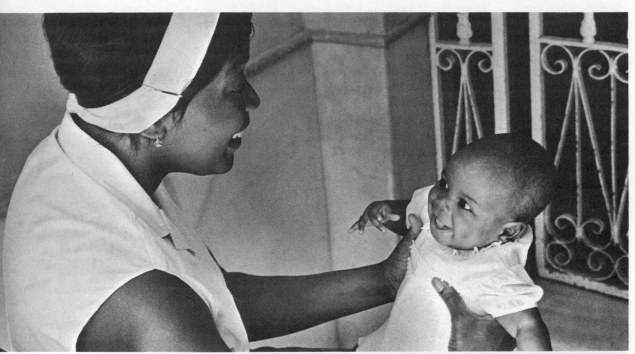

Although indications of distress are as obvious as those of delight, one must know something about the stimulus situation in order to determine whether the infant is apprehensive, angry, frightened, or merely uncomfortable.

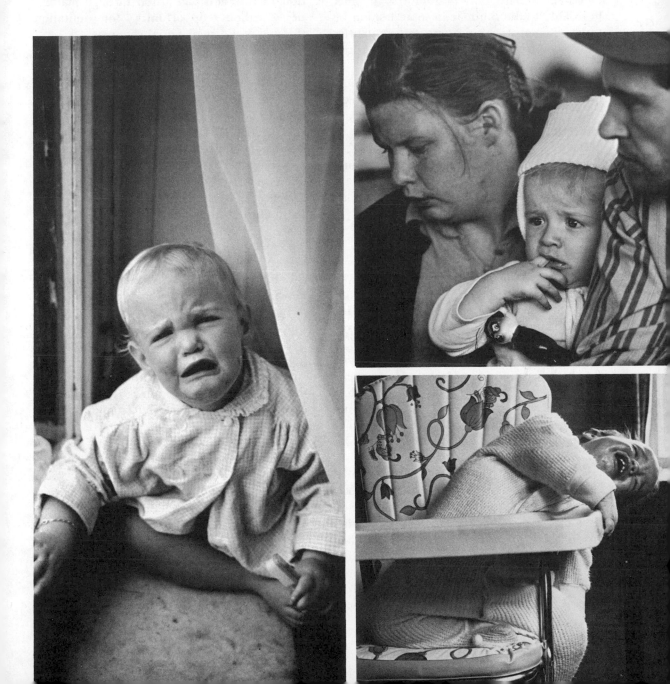

nuances of an emotional situation are capable of being perceived. As intellectual development proceeds, new situations become capable of eliciting the emotion. Emotional reactions are intimately bound with the intellectual stages of maturation reached. An individual reacts emotionally only to situations in which he is able to discriminate in some fashion between their disturbing or satisfying qualities. To respond emotionally he must "interpret" the situation in some fashion.

A young infant is undisturbed by conditions that will later arouse emotion. At ten weeks confinement in a pen is accepted without any indication of emotion, at 20 weeks he is apprehensive, at 30 weeks he cries vigorously. A bright two-year-old may show fear of a strange room or of a snake, whereas a child of the same age and of average intelligence is less likely to be affected.

The Role of Maturation and Learning

The differentiation of emotions, changes of mode of responses, and of sensitivity in emotions with increasing age relate to maturation and learning. An illustration was just given in the differential responses of fear stimuli of a bright and an average two-year-old. Presumably both maturation and learning were operative. The bright two-year-old in responding to stimuli which his peer did not sense not only was expressing a faster maturation, but also that he had learned to perceive what his age peer had not.

Emotion as a product of maturation is shown in studies in which there is no opportunity for the usual learning to take place. This may be observed in differential studies in which restriction on infants or children had already taken place. As an example of differential restriction, a child blind and deaf since birth is not in a position to learn facial or general emotional behavior from others.

Florence L. Goodenough (1932) once studied such a girl, aged ten. Her facial expressions and general behavior under conditions that usually arouse anger, fear, or pleasure in other children were very much like those exhibited by seeing, normal children. Her forms of emotional expression had arisen through maturation without opportunity for imitation through auditory or visual channels.

Goodenough, although considering the primary forms of emotional expression as determined by maturational factors, did admit that a socialization veneer may appear. This was confirmed in a later study by Thompson (1941), who observed a considerably larger number of subjects, both blind and seeing, of ages ranging from seven weeks to 13 years. Their varying ages made it possible to study the effect of socialization with increasing age. In addition to confirming Goodenough's general finding concerning maturation, Thompson also found that beyond two or three years of age the blind subjects showed a decrease in facial activity in smiling and laughing, a change that did not occur among seeing children. Social reinforcement which was lacking with the blind children was operative with them, and the influence of a learning factor was thus apparent.

An experimental study which demonstrates the influence of maturation is that of Dennis (1935). He reared two infants from one month of age until the age of seven months in such a way that the adult voices they heard were not associated with other smile-provoking stimuli. Under these conditions the human voice never caused smiling. Nevertheless, smiling upon *seeing* the adult developed to a marked degree, occurring more markedly when the adult bent over to minister to their needs.

It thus seems that smiling, whose appearance initially is set by the infant's maturational level, becomes associated by learning with certain kinds of stimuli, such as the presentation of an adult face. The smiling response, at first given indiscriminately, becomes more selective. Toward the end of the first year of life, infants reserve most of their smiling for familiar faces and often are disturbed by strange ones. What evidently happens is that infants first are able to perceive differences among faces and then, some months later, are able to form attachments to certain of them (Schaffer, 1963). Similarly, fear responses to strangers depend on the ability to form responses to stimuli recognized by being unfamiliar. Schaffer (1966a) says that fear responses evoked by the unexpected appear in the early months of life, but it is not until the second half of the first year that fear responses become linked to a particular type of person rather than to certain more primitive stimulus events.

Hence the arousal phenomenon that we term "emotion" is present early in life, but until the infant has sufficient maturity to (1) distinguish between various classes of stimuli, and (2) determine what orientation his response to them should have, he is unable to develop the kind of differentiated responses that have the qualities of recognizable emotional states. In short, emotional development depends to a large degree on cognitive development.

Summary

During the first year of life, the infant increases his length by over a third, and his weight triples. By age two, he is 32 or 33 inches tall and weighs about 27 pounds. Height and weight are correlated about .60 and the proximodistal-cephalocaudal trend of development is clearly evident in the relative proportions of different parts of the body. The periods of most rapid growth occur before and immediately after birth as well as during the prepuberal period. Research has shown that biological measures like the Apgar test are related to general development, while various psychosocial factors are not. Nutrition is a major factor in normal development, and malnutrition retards intellectual and emotional development as well as physical growth. Malnourished infants show a marked lack of curiosity and low activity levels. Even after being placed on an adequate diet, tests reflect a permanent decrement in cognitive skills. Experiments with monkeys have lent support to these findings. Although malnourished monkeys are more skillful at solving familiar problems, they have difficulty when novel elements are introduced.

During infancy, both learning and maturation play a part in the acquisition of such skills as locomotion and prehension. The importance of maturation is illustrated by the fact that Hopi Indian babies walk as soon as other infants, even though the Indian cradleboards have prevented an equivalent amount of practice. Studies in which twins are given differential amounts of practice also serve to emphasize the role played by maturation. The performance of the twin who is denied practice rapidly improves to equal that of the trained twin. The simultaneous processes of differentiation and integration are revealed in the evolution of manipulation from the Darwinian reflex to a skilled grasping response. The development of locomotion reflects an equivalent trend. The principle of discontinuity and hierarchization is also exemplified in that each stage requires muscle movements not present in earlier stages. Learning to walk has profound psychological consequences, and marks the advent of a period of intense locomotor activity which continues to roughly the age of four. Studies have shown that psychomotor development can be accelerated by increasing the amount of stimulation infants receive, although at present such findings can be considered as suggestive, rather than conclusive.

Changes also occur in the manner in which the infant satisfies his basic needs. The eight feedings per day required by neonates is reduced to five feedings by 16 weeks. By the end of the first year, the infant is generally accustomed to a three-meals-a-day schedule, along with one or two snacks, and is able to help himself in feeding. In the last 50 years, adult attitudes have shifted in the direction of greater permissiveness in infant feeding practices, and most mothers compromise between self-demand systems and rigid scheduling. Infants adapt readily to the feeding schedules imposed by their parents and become so habituated as to resist changes in their schedules. In the study by Sears, Maccoby, and Levin, 40% of the infants studied were breast-fed. The proportion of mothers who claimed they could not breast-feed for "physical reasons" or because of "doctor's orders" was much too large to represent the true state of affairs.

By the third or fourth month, the infant is capable of ingesting a little solid food. Mouth movements gradually become more suitable for chewing than for sucking. There are a number of ways that a child can be weaned. One study of American mothers found that two-thirds had begun the weaning process by the time the infant was 11 months old. In general, American mothers take a "no-nonsense" approach to weaning, and accomplish the task earlier than mothers of other cultures. Although we are a highly time-oriented culture, we also feel that children should be free of schedules and restrictions. The resolution of this conflict may be seen in the fact that many American mothers who claim to be feeding their infant on "demand" have actually allowed the baby to set the original schedule and regularly enforced it thereafter.

The infant must eventually adjust his sleeping patterns to coincide with family routines. As biological demands change, he sleeps for fewer and longer periods. By 16 weeks, he has developed something of a night sleep pattern. The maturation of cortical cells also helps keep his cortex "awake" for longer periods. Social demands also require the child to learn bowel and bladder control. The infant, however, cannot comply until the necessary neuromuscular mechanisms have sufficiently matured. A classic study by McGraw emphasized the importance of maturation in bladder control. One of a pair of twin boys was trained in bladder control until he mastered the task. He took 700 days of training. The second twin then started equivalent training, and learned almost immediately. Toilet training is generally complicated by the fact that it is a learning situation in which the reward is not in the satisfaction of a basic need. Because the infant does not yet have either the verbal repertoire or the understanding necessary, training must proceed without verbal aids, and becomes a frustrating trial-and-error process for all concerned. Pediatricians generally recommend postponing training until the second year of life.

Emotion is a difficult word to define. Positive and negative emotions may be characterized by the tendency to approach or avoid, whereas rage responses have an aggressive or "against" quality. Most psychologists take the view that neonates are capable only of a generalized state of excitement. As the child grows older, his reactions become more specific and differentiated. Bridges (1930) has identified and plotted the course of development of a number of specific emotions. Critics, however, have pointed out the absence of controls and suggest that Bridges' detailed descriptions of infants' emotional behavior suffer from "adultomorphism." It is doubtful that the infant is capable of intense emotional experiences as adults know them. Watson and Raynor, like Bridges, claimed some success in the identification of basic emotional responses. In fact, further research has revealed that the judges were responding to antecedent stimulus conditions rather than to the infant's behavior. Although we cannot equate the infant's emotional responses with our own, we can identify developmental changes in the mode of expression and eliciting stimuli. As the infant grows older, he becomes more capable of perceiving the nuances of an emotional situation, and has a larger store of response options. Both learning and matura-

tion play a role in these developmental changes. Blind children exhibit the same sort of facial expressions that normal children would exhibit in similar circumstances, reflecting the importance of maturation. The greater frequency of facial activity in smiling and laughing among normal children, however indicates the presence of social learning as well. An experiment with infants suggests that the appearance of smiling and other social responses is determined by maturational processes, and that the increasing discrimination between eliciting stimuli is a matter of learning.

7 Infancy: Cognitive Development

Although the terms perception, language, intelligence, and concept formation are used to describe the experience and behavior of infants, they take on greater exactitude in later years. As with sensorimotor and emotional development, something resembling mass perceptual, intellectual, linguistic, and conceptual thinking seems to take place. Only as the child grows older will there be clear individuation. Let us therefore first consider cognitive development, understanding, or thinking in general.

Cognition in Infancy

To follow this path is to walk in the spirit of Jean Piaget whose developmental concepts we introduced in Chapter 3. He regards cognitive processes as being expressed in thought and intelligence, between which he makes no sharp distinction. For him, they are both aspects of the same central cognitive process. Moreover, Piaget defines perception to cover a much smaller area of psychological phenomena than is customary, while simultaneously making it subordinate to intelligence as a means of individual adaptation or adjustment to the environment (Flavell, 1963).

Interaction Between Infant and Environment

To Piaget, thought is a biological function in that intellectual functioning is a matter of adaptative interaction of organism and environment. Adaptation is expressed in two complementary functions—assimilation and accommodation (Piaget, 1960). Assimilation takes place when the organism uses some object in the environment in the course of its activity. It occurs when the new is drawn into the old behavior repertoire and becomes part of the infant's inner organization. For example, when something new is perceived that resembles an old, already familiar object, it is used as would be the old object. Accommodation, on the other hand, occurs when the old repertoire is adjusted to account for the new object experienced. Hence, new activities are added to the infant's repertoire and the old activities modified to that extent.

In order to aid the reader to "assimilate" and "accommodate" this discussion, the former includes what in old familiar terms we would call generalization and discrimination, whereas accommodation includes differentiation, or the learning of new responses. This adaptational process, embracing assimilation and accommodation as its functions, remains the same as the child grows in age.

Cognitive structures change with age and Piaget's theory of intelligence is primarily a theory of structure. These structures or *schemata* are interposed between the ever-changing contents and the nonchanging functions of intelligence. They are organized through their functioning. To anticipate later discussion, these so-called structures include concepts, such as egocentrism, animism, realism, and artificialism—topics that we will discuss when we take up early childhood and later childhood.

At birth the only organization available to the infant is the congenital sensorimotor responses described in the previous chapter as characteristic of the neonate. During this period the infant's actions are not yet internalized in the form of thoughts (Piaget, 1957). When functioning at this level, the infant as-similates external realities in a fashion corresponding roughly to the problem-solving abilities of the subhuman animals (Piaget, 1952). He exercises these sensorimotor capacities and gropes about in his environment, for example, in showing sucking responses to almost any stimulation of the lips.

Object Permanence. Realities are not yet entities; they are only functional elements—something to be sucked, to be handled, or to be moved. Objects do not yet exist as objects. "Out of sight, out of mind" might be said to characterize the view of the infant. He behaves as if objects that have disappeared from view have ceased to exist. For example, Piaget tells us that an infant of five to eight months of age, already old enough to seize a solid object, will lose interest and turn away if a cloth be thrown over the object before his hand reaches it. At a slightly older age he is capable of seeking an object behind a screen and thus shows the beginnings of the notion of the real exterior permanence of objects. Nevertheless, he is still functioning at the more primitive level.

An infant at the just-mentioned level was given the experience of retrieving an object that he saw placed under the left of two pillows. On the next occasion, he sought the object where he had found it before, despite the fact that the examiner, in full view of the infant, had placed it under the *right* pillow. As Piaget indicates, it is as if his action in reaching under the left pillow was decided by the success of his actions by which he had secured it previously and not by the reality of its external placement under the right pillow on this new occasion. At the sensorimotor level the world to the infant is not that of permanent objects with an autonomy of their own; it is a series of perceptive views which periodically disappear into nonexistence only to be brought back as the function of the proper action on the infant's part.

The infant comes to realize that objects are stable, independent of himself; that they have a shape which remains the same even though as he turns the object its visual appearance varies; that objects retain identity despite varying in apparent size as they approach or recede; and perhaps to him, most surprising of all, that they continue to exist when out of sight. Nor does the infant have as part of his native endowment conceptions of either space or time. Above all, he has to learn about cause and effect. This life-long process begins during the first year. His pushing and pulling make them move, rattle, and squeak. At first he does not realize that it is necessary for him to touch them to cause these effects. He tries magic by waving his hands at them from a distance. It is only during his second year that he seems to realize that in order to make an object move he must touch it.

Piagetian Infancy Scales

Alice S. Honig and Sheila Brill (1970), working with other researchers, have developed the Piagetian Infancy Scales for use in assessing developmental progress made by infants. The scales cover seven aspects of cognition:

I. Object permanence

II. Means-ends scale: development of means for achieving desired environmental events

III. Development of schemas in relation to objects

IV. Development of causality

V. Developmental achievement of the construction of the object in space

VI. Development of vocal and gestural imitation

VII. Prehension

Honig and Brill used the scales to assess the success of an experimental program in which 16 black infants from low-income families participated in a six-month "enrichment program" stressing Piagetian tasks. Atten-

dance varied widely and ranged from 42 to 124 days, with a mean of 84 days for the entire group. At the end of six months of treatment, when the infants were a year old, both they and a control group of infants with comparable family backgrounds were tested. Out of a total possible score of 183, the infants in the experimental group averaged 101.9, while the control infants averaged 94.4, a difference that was significant at better than the .05 level. The most significant difference between the two groups occurred on the object permanence scale.

The results, though interesting, raise more questions than they answer. The mean of 84 days of treatment represents less than half the days in a six-month period, and half the children had less than that. Would differences have been larger if experimental exposure had been greater? Can programs be designed that do the job better? Differences between the two means are statistically significant but are not large in an absolute sense. Does this mean that Piaget is right when he says or implies that cognitive competence can be learned but not taught?

These are intriguing questions, but the answers must wait for still further research. At least the work of Honig and Brill raises reasonable doubts about any hard-and-fast conclusions about the way in which infants develop cognitively.

Criticism of Piagetian Theory. Although Piaget holds that cognitive development takes place through the infant's physical manipulation of his environment, common sense tends to regard cognitive functioning in infancy as basically not much different from cognition in adults. An adult who looks at a road map and notes that a highway runs along the ocean would not have to drive down that highway, hear the surf, and stop to dip his hand in it to grasp the relationship between highway and sea and to remember it adequately enough to inform others. Research with young children shows, as Jerome Kagan (1971) points out, that children, like adults, can acquire perceptual structures or concepts, or alter the form of their overt behaviors merely by watching others or listening to them. Body movement and actual manipulation of the environment are not required in many instances. Even an infant less than three months old "does not have to touch or manipulate stimulus to learn something about its structure" (p. 6).

Kagan does not deny that motor activity facilitates the acquisition of concepts and other cognitive structures. For one thing, activity is accompanied by greater alertness and general arousal, which make it more likely that important features of stimuli will be noted. Furthermore, if a cognitive structure involves new responses, it is likely that some type of manipulation must occur. Even so, the transfer of an existing response to a new situation does not require the display of the behavior in question.

Kagan believes that sensorimotor functioning and coordination are highly significant in the infant's adaptive functioning, but maintains that it has not been proven that they are absolutely essential in cognitive development. In his opinion, if a child whose head and limbs were prevented from moving were exposed to a typical family environment, the child would still be capable of developing cognitively, even to the extent of learning symbolic language.

According to Kagan, the view of Piaget and his followers that "motor action instructs cognition" (p. 178) grows out of the fact that the infant's manipulations may be readily observed, but mental functioning is not. It is all too easy to assume that movements indicate thinking. Kagan theorizes that the child, psychologically speaking, consists of different "systems" that involve action, cognitive structures, and sensing and feeling. As these systems operate together, they make themselves evident in different ways through different kinds of behavior. Much depends on what the investigator is looking for, as well as on the context in which the infant behaves and the investigator observes.

Perceptual-Conceptual Development

Perceptions encompass more than sensations. Perceptions require the presence of stimuli, as do sensations, but they also involve the interpretations of stimuli. This interpretation is, of course, based on the individual's previous experiences.

Perception is a cognitive process in that it assigns some meaning to the stimuli that impinge on the eye, the ear, and the other receptors. In other words, it is not merely a bright flashing, it is a neon sign; it is not merely a clanging, it is the sound of a church bell. In concept formation he goes a step farther. The infant has already perceived objects as shown by his responses. A concept is attained when he can make the appropriate response to stimuli he has not previously observed.

The development of perception is originally dependent on sensory development. If deprived of one or more senses, to that extent the infant is handicapped in the development of understanding. If severely handicapped in several major sensory areas, as was Helen Keller who was deprived of both hearing and vision shortly after birth, the task of "interpreting" the world becomes a very difficult one. Perforce he must learn to interpret the external world through the remaining senses. If completely deprived of all senses, he would have no way of interacting with the world.

Fortunately, in the first few weeks of life the sensory apparatus of a typical infant is in

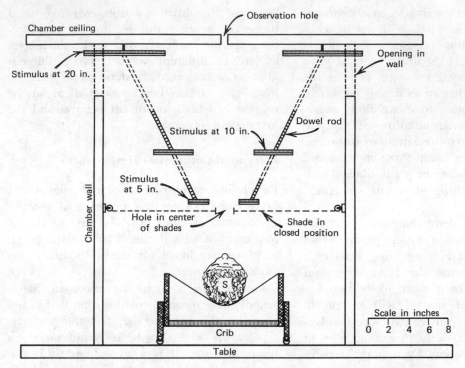

Figure 7-1. Schematic cross section of a testing chamber used to observe infants' preferences for stimuli cards. The infant (S) is placed in hammocklike crib, oriented to the observation hole in the ceiling. When the shades are drawn, pairs of stimulus cards are placed at 5, 10, or 20 inches. Shades are then opened and the experimenter watches through the observation hole to see which of the two stimuli are reflected on the pupils of the infant's eyes and also notes the amount of time each stimulus is looked at. (The drawing is to scale, except for the ¼-inch observation hole at the top of the chamber.) (Fantz, Ordy, and Udelf, 1962. Reproduced by permission.)

good working condition. Nevertheless his understanding of what is going on around him is negligible. When something breaks through his hazy awareness, it produces excitement. Otherwise, when he is satisfied—when his stomach is full, digestion is proceeding smoothly, and he is warm and snug—awareness fades out and he drifts into sleep. Gradually, his periods of wakefulness increase. As he grows older, the infant's understandings come from his active sensory exploration of his environment.

Observation suggests that during the first

year of life the infant spends a considerable amount of time getting acquainted with his world—reaching, fondling, poking, hefting, mouthing, staring, rubbing, tasting, and smelling the objects and persons that come his way. Externally aroused behavior tendencies, then, are very much operative in his beginning to understand both himself and his environment.

The infant seeks out and discovers the qualities of objects—their particular tastes, contours, warmth, and other qualities. His perception of people and objects, his pleasurable

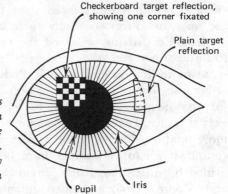

Figure 7-2. Schematic drawing of the eye of an infant who is lying in the test chamber and who has been presented with a checkerboard and a plain stimulus. The reflections cast on the eye show that the infant is looking at the more complex stimulus. This diagram depicts a minimal condition for fixation; usually the reflection of the target stimulus would be more centered in the pupil. (Fantz, 1965. Reproduced by permission.)

recognition of the familiar and his displeasure at the strange, show that objects and persons are beginning to be perceived. Much of what is written about the emergence of the self and social perception in Chapter 9 shows these beginnings.

Preferences for Complexity in Stimuli

We noted earlier that not only can infants distinguish between various stimulus patterns but that they also express preferences that differed according to their sex. There is also a tendency to prefer stimuli of increasing complexity. Robert L. Fantz (1965) conducted a series of interesting experiments to explore the dimensions of this phenomenon. Figure 7-1 shows a schematic cross section of the apparatus he used to present pairs of stimulus cards to infants. Each infant was placed in a hammock-like crib, with its head oriented to the observation hole in the top of the test chamber. The shades were drawn to the position indicated, leaving a two-inch gap that served to attract the infant's gaze to the center. While the shades were in the closed position, the experimenter readied the pair of stimulus cards to be presented. When the shades were opened, the experimenter watched the corneas of the infant's eyes to see which of the two cards was reflected. Figure 7-2 depicts the left eye of an infant who has been presented with a checkerboard and a plain stimulus. The checkerboard is shown reflected on the pupil, indicating that he is looking at it, in preference to the plain card, which is reflected on the edge of the iris to the right.

Some of Fantz's results are shown in Figure 7-3, which compares the preferences of neonates (less than five days old) with infants two to six months in age. Both groups of subjects displayed preferences for the more complex stimuli, but the older infants' prefer-

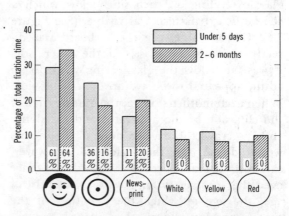

Figure 7-3. Visual responses to three black-and-white and three plain discs by newborn and older infants. Percentage of infants in each group looking longer at a particular target is given at the bottom of each bar. (After Fantz, 1965.)

ences were more pronounced than those of the neonates. Proportionately twice as many of the older infants preferred the newsprint stimulus than did the neonates, and they spent more time in looking at it. Perhaps this is because newsprint may have been blurred for the neonates, appearing as an all-over gray stimulus, or it may be that the older and more mature infants were attracted to its complexity. Fantz's findings have been confirmed by other researchers. Brennan, Ames, and Moore (1966) presented infants three, eight, and fourteen weeks old with checkerboard stimuli of increasing complexity, in addition to an all-over gray stimulus. The three-week-old subjects looked longest at the 2 × 2 stimulus; the eight-week subjects, at the 8 × 8 stimulus; and the fourteen-week subjects, at the 24 × 24 stimulus. No group showed any preference for the gray stimulus.

Depth Perception. Walk and Gibson (1961) have also investigated depth perception in infants. Their research makes use of a clever device termed a "visual cliff," which consists of a center "crawlway" with sheets of glass extending on each side below which a checkerboard pattern was visible. (See Figure 7-4). On one side, the checkerboard was directly beneath the glass; on the other side, it was far below the glass giving what, to an adult, appeared to be a drop off, or cliff side. When each mother stood at the outside edge of the cliff side of the apparatus and asked her child to crawl toward her, none of the infants would do so. On the "safe" side, however, each infant readily crawled toward her. Since even the youngest infants were six months of age, the age at which the essentials of the act of creeping appear, they all had had opportunities for previous experiences from which they might have learned some of the cues to depth perception. Nevertheless, the evidence suggests that at least some aspects of depth perception are unlearned.

Figure 7-4. The "visual cliff" as used in experiments to test depth perception in infants.

The visual cliff has been used to measure depth perception in infants two and three months old—long before crawling age. When infants were placed on their stomachs, with eyes oriented to either the deep or the shallow sides of the stimulus box, significant differences in their heart rate appeared, with location on the deep side producing a much slower heartbeat than the shallow side (Campos, Langer, and Krowitz, 1970). A slower heartbeat is associated with the "orienting response," which occurs when infants (as well as other high organisms) are gazing at a stimulus as though in search of its meaning. The fear response at looking down from heights is one that appears at a later point in the infant's development.

A rudimentary form of depth perception also appeared in an experimental situation in which infants two to eleven weeks of age were seated in front of a screen on which shadows grew rapidly larger, as though a large object were rapidly approaching either on an impending collision course or a "miss" course. In another version of the experiment, a real object was moved rapidly toward the infant in collision and miss courses. Videotapes of the behavior of the infants during these confrontations showed that they moved their heads back and brought their arms toward their face when it appeared that the shadow or object would collide with them. Behavior when the stimulus was on a miss course was quite different and consisted of a slow turning of the eyes and head along the path of the shadow or object. When the stimulus retreated, the typical response was one of relaxation (Ball and Tronick, 1971). The results showed rather definitely that even at this early age infants are able to perceive and react to impending collisions and can differentiate between potential collisions and misses.

Language Development

Perception and Linguistic Development

According to the formulation of learning theorists, perceptions and conceptualizations are cue-producing responses (Dollard and Miller, 1950). Like other types of responses, they are modifiable by further learning. Perceptions and conceptions are thus both a cause and an effect of learning. Language is one of the best examples of the way in which responses produce cues that lead to further responses. The study of Gellermann (1933), which we will discuss shortly, is one example of the influence of verbal cues on form discrimination.

Words are cues. As soon as the child discovers that words have meaning (are cues for something else) and that for every object there is a word (cue), he has made a tremendous step forward in understanding. Words also

exist for conceptions that are independent of objects. Thus, qualities of objects, which may be understood without referring to a particular object, also come to be understood. Roundness, independent of round apples or round balls, is illustrative.

Conceptual discrimination rests on language in the sense that language discrimination improves conceptualization Nevertheless, conceptualization may appear without language. Bing-Chung Ling (1941) demonstrated this in an ingenious study in which the infants showed their conceptual discrimination of a correct form by licking it instead of other forms that were also present. She did this by presenting to infants six to fifteen months old, blocks differing in form, including circles, crosses, and triangles. Successful selection of one form was rewarded by a coating of saccharine it had on its surface. Discrimination shown by licking the correct form was found as early as the sixth month of life. Changing the position of the correct form relative to the others or varying its size had only a slight effect upon accuracy.

Another investigator, Long (1940), showed through a manual response setup that somewhat older subjects in the preschool years also can discriminate forms without being able to name them. He was able to demonstrate that very young children formed a given concept, as shown by going through a test series without error, and yet thereafter were quite unable to give anything approaching a verbal formulation of what they were doing. Thus, form concepts precede ability to verbalize these concepts.

It is significant, however, that some, but not all, of Long's older subjects did use such words as "round" in talking to themselves in the course of their selections.

Language naturally aids a child in concept formation. This may be illustrated by a study of form discrimination by Gellermann (1933) in which he compared two-year-old children

The infant's attempts to learn spoken language are the clearest and most obvious index to his cognitive development

Language learning begins with experimental vocalizations, which can often be encouraged or reinforced by mothers.

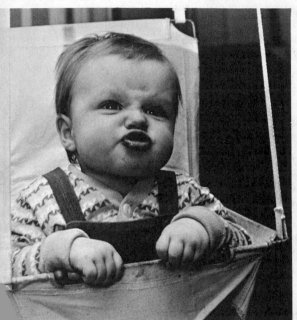

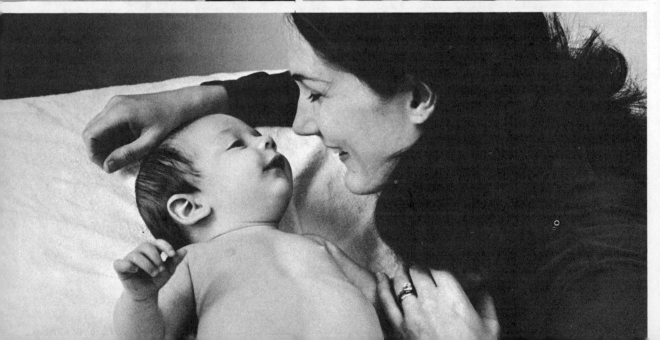

Interaction with siblings stimulates oral self-expression, but parental models elicit the most imitation. As the infant feels the need to make demands on others, language learning begins to move rapidly.

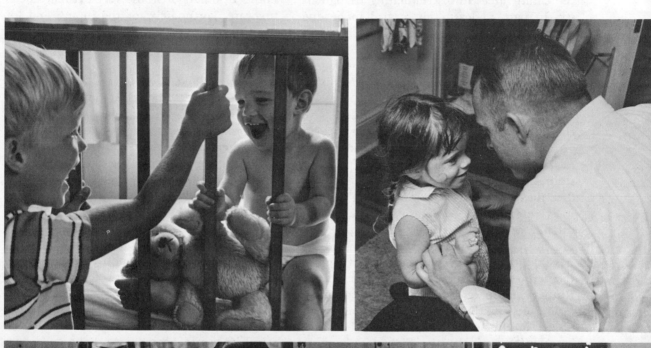

and chimpanzees in discriminating triangularity. The investigator gave no verbal instructions to the children. Some of them formulated the problem, which he had been careful not to verbalize for them, by gestures and verbal behavior instructions to themselves. He found that the children were definitely superior to the chimpanzees in discriminating triangularity. In part, at least, this seemed to be due to their greater verbal facility. The children's verbalizations did seem to help in arriving at conceptualizations as shown by the higher percentages of correct responses in those using them.

Concepts, such as those just discussed, have their beginning in infancy, but they are so grossly inaccurate and so primitive in nature as hardly to deserve the name concepts. The studies of conceptualization which have been described, with the exception of Ling's, either used infants just barely within the age of infancy as did Gellermann or actually used preschool-aged children as did Long. It is possible that these studies may have given too mature a cast to the concepts of the infant. Rather than space concepts, he has poor orientation in space shown in often reaching for an object in the wrong direction. Rather than inaccurate concepts of weight, it is more parsimonious to speak of his making mistakes in weight, such as his being forced to drop too heavy objects when he attempts to hold them.

Early Linguistic Development

Language is perhaps the most peculiarly human characteristic. Out of the vocalization of babes emerges our most powerful vehicles of thought, expression, and communication. Language provides ways of learning other aspects of socialization and is also a means of expressing already established socializations, particularly as these are expressed in interpersonal relationships.

These accomplishments are the goals of language development. They are not the realities of language at the beginning of infancy, inasmuch as infants are so nonsocial in nature as to be called egocentric by Piaget (1926). The infant believes that he *is* the world and has no appreciation of the viewpoints of others of whose very existence he is unaware. Fortunately for the infant, and for us, the world pierces through to him and speech begins to carry on a communicative function.

Language and thought are intimately related. To put it succinctly, thoughts are manipulations of meanings; words facilitate these manipulations, render them more precise and make them more easily recalled. Functionally speaking, language may be said to embrace three kinds of activities—inner, receptive, and expressive (Myklebust, 1956). Some time during the first eight or nine months inner language appears as the infant talks to himself in his private egocentric fashion. Thereafter, until about 12 or 13 months receptive language is in the process of formation. The infant now begins to comprehend others but is not yet able to express himself. Expressive language, the ability to make oneself understood by words, begins toward the end of infancy. Its initial appearance must wait until inner and receptive language have been partially established.

Inner language is a form of play and self-stimulation expressed in babbling just for the fun of it. This activity is an expression of the initial egocentricity that Piaget noted in infants.

Receptive language begins when the infant learns to tease out from the total mass of impression of sounds to which he is exposed those sounds that are the spoken language of other persons. Actions going hand in hand with language are the language units that are probably learned first. Thus, "pat-a-cake," "bye-bye," and "here's your bottle" are accompanied by appropriate actions on the part of adults. At about 12 months the infant obeys simple commands. For example, it is at this age that, on command, he will place a cube in a cup (Gesell and Thompson, 1934). This is a relatively complex activity. Compared to his command of active language, which reference to Table 7-1 will show is only about two words at this age, it is illustrative of his relatively greater receptive language comprehension.

In the infant's earliest vocalizations a considerable variety of basic sounds, or phonemes, appear. The identification of the phonemes were arrived at in the course of many investigations by listening to infant vocalizations and recording them phonetically. Certain phonemes appear in these vocalizations more often than do others, with vowel sounds predominating (Irwin, 1941). Some of these phonemes appear later in English, but many are not elements of any language, let alone English. The infant also utters phonemes used in languages other than English. Thus, an infant in our culture uses sounds corresponding to the German ü and ö, the French u, and the guttural r. This "initial hierarchy" of basic sounds is modified as the infant grows older. With the appearance of teeth and greater dexterity with the throat and tongue, consonant sounds increase, non-English phonemes drop out, and the resultant hierarchy of English sounds comes into being. The emergence of sounds appropriate to the infant's native language may be facilitated by a process of conditioning. Routh (1969) was able to get infants aged two to seven months to express certain kinds of sounds in preference to others. He used smiles, a series of three "tsk" sounds, and a light stroking of the infant's abdomen to reinforce consonant sounds for one group of infants, vowel sounds for another group, and any sounds at all for a third group. Figure 7-5 presents some of Routh's findings and shows that infants reinforced for vowels

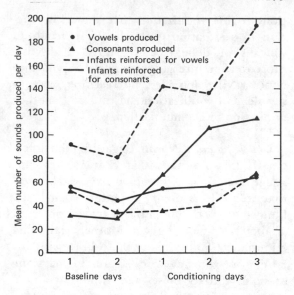

Figure 7-5.   Mean numbers of consonants and vowels per day uttered by a group of infants who were reinforced for vowels and a group who were reinforced for consonants. Each "day" consisted of nine recording sessions of three minutes each. Recordings were made without reinforcement for baseline days, and reinforcement was instituted during conditioning days. (After Routh, 1969.)

markedly increased their vowel production, while their consonant production remained fairly stable. The group reinforced for consonants increased their production of consonants and showed only a slight increase in vowels. Although Routh's findings suggest that reinforcement by adults may play a part in language acquisition by children, this does not necessarily mean that language can be explained entirely in reinforcement terms. We shall have more to say on this topic at the end of this section.

Expressive language development starts, not with the emergence of the first words, but much earlier with the first vocalizations. In a sense, it starts with the birth cry. The presence of overt linguistic activity long before the infant speaks his first word is shown in many ways—calls to attract attention and inflections in his vocalization that show his reaction to a situation quite clearly in scolding, squeaks of delight, and grunts of disgust. Moreover, gesture language such as pointing, hand waving, looking, and reaching serve to supplement vocalization and thus add another dimension to communication.

Developmental Norms. Regarding the differential use of sounds that characterizes language, Gesell and Thompson have established that infantile cries of discomfort, pain, and hunger may be differentiated by the observer at about one month of age. Mothers claim discriminatory ability along those lines with infants even younger. Vocalization in the form of small throaty noises also appear at about four weeks. This and other reports of normative ages for various kinds of vocalization are reported in Table 7-1. These norms are based on samplings of vocalizations at various periods in infancy and have been supplemented by some of Shirley's (1933) observations of infants whose development she followed longitudinally, over an extended period of time.

The researchers whose observations are summarized in Table 7-1 placed the appearance of the first word at about 40 weeks. Shirley reported that her babies used their first word at about 65 weeks, on the average, although there was considerable variation. Some said their first word as early as eight months, whereas with others, it was delayed until as late as two years of age. The mothers themselves credited their infants with a vocabulary of two or three words at 52 weeks, which agrees with the findings reported in Table 7-1. With due allowance for individual variation, it would appear that the average child says his first word before the end of the first year (Darley and Winitz, 1961). Gifted children may use words at an even earlier age, whereas other children are retarded to the point of not attempting words until after their second year.

TABLE 7–1. *Age in Months at Which Vocalizations Are Likely to Occur According to Samplings of Infant Behavior by Various Observers (McCarthy, 1954)*

Age in Months	Vocal Behavior
1.3	Small throaty noises
2–3	Cooing
3	Makes "pleasurable noises"
4	One syllable
4	Self-initiated sound play
6.5	*Ma* or *Mu*
7	Repeats syllables, such as *ma-ma*
8	Vocalizes recognition
8	Vocal interjection
9	Imitates sounds
11	Imitates syllables: *mama, papa, dada*
12	Says two words or more; *jargon*—attempts at conversation in an apparently meaningless language
13	Four words or more
18	*Hello, thank you,* or equivalent
19–24	Names one object or more
21	Repeats things said
21	Joins two words in speech
23–24	Names three objects
24	Simple sentences and phrases

That these findings about the first word seem to vary according to the observer is perhaps because some observers, especially mothers, may be crediting the child with speaking words, basing their reports on utterances which actually are quite far removed from the word in question. Moreover, the word or words for which infants are credited by their mothers may be part of a private language wherein a certain sound, perhaps having no resemblance to the word (such as "yo-e" for water), functions as a word in that particular family.

Shirley found that at 66 weeks her infant subjects used seven comprehensible words. There was little improvement until 86 weeks; she believed that probably this lag was due to the infant's preoccupation with locomotion during this period. By two years of age the average number of words used by her infant subjects was 32. Her observations may be supplemented by returning to those reported in Table 7-1. At two years of age, not only has jargon been discarded but also simple sentences have made their appearance. Considerable development of expressive language ability during the second year has evidently taken place.

Learning Relationships Between Symbols and Objects. The infant's eargerness to speak and to learn names is a major feature of the development of speech. Children have a veritable mania for naming things. Entirely divorced from actual biological needs, this deserves to be called a "hunger for names" since their learning of names is done neither mechanically nor with reluctance, but with enthusiasm.

As most mothers know to their embarrassment, an infant able to use the word "Daddy" may apply it on occasion to any male he sees. Or having learned to use "kitty" for a cat, he is apt to apply it to a dog, a squirrel, or even when playing with the fur collar of his mother's coat. Generalization is operating here as it was in other situations we have examined; it is characteristic of the infant to assimilate the new aspect of a situation to what is now old and familiar to him. As he grows older, his cues for discriminatory decisions increase in precision. Illustrative of his growing discrimination is the use by a somewhat older child of an expression such as "funny kitty" for a squirrel. No longer is it a "kitty" alone but a "funny" one. Some of the cues for kitty are present but also something else. The new

is seen for what it is, assimilated with the old, and the way prepared for cue discrimination. Attaching distinctive cue-producing responses to heretofore similar stimuli tends to increase their distinctiveness.

The infant applies a word to a wide variety of objects or persons that later will be differentiated by different words. "Dog" means many things according to his total reaction conveyed by the tone of voice, gestures, and bodily movements: "I want that dog, I want to pet and hug him," or "there is an interesting object; you should look at it too," or, "I'm scared, hold me, and get me away from here." "Dog" is only one word, to be sure, but with many meanings. The few words the infant does have are made to stand for many objects and actions.

Theories: Reinforcement and Generative. How "dog" loses its excess meanings and becomes attached to the right animal has led to much theorizing and speculation among psychologists and linguists. B. F. Skinner (1957) explained language acquisition in purely operant-conditioning terms saying that children acquire verbal behavior when their relatively unpatterned vocalizations, which have been selectively reinforced, gradually assume forms that produce appropriate consequences. In other words, a child learns to say "dog" in the first instance because something happens to reinforce that particular syllable when he utters it in appropriate context. Presumably, he overgeneralizes at first and applies it to every four-footed animal, but, through being reinforced only for its correct application, learns to discriminate and apply it more selectively.

This formulation of language learning has been subjected to a great deal of criticism. Noam Chomsky (1959) commented that if we had to learn language by Skinner's rules, we would have to spend a lifetime at the task and still not learn its merest rudiments. The idea of an eager adult waiting in the wings for the right syllable to be produced so that it can be reinforced somehow seems more appropriate for the experimental training of pigeons or rats and does not explain the great variety of behaviors that children acquire in so brief a time span. It seems much simpler to assume that "dog" first emerges in the child's vocabulary through imitation. Experiments like those of Routh (1969), which we cited earlier, show that a certain amount of "shaping" of vocal responses can take place during infancy, but so far no one has been able to demonstrate that infants at, say, six months of age can produce "dog" on cue.

Eric H. Lenneberg (1969) takes a "generative" approach and maintains that language forms appear when children are biologically ready to utter them. Indeed, the appearance of various forms is correlated with the appearance of certain motor skills. Sitting and reaching, for instance, is associated with the change from cooing to babbling (about six months). Standing, as well as walking with some assistance, are associated with syllabic reduplication, understanding of some words, application of some sounds regularly to designate persons or objects—in other terms, the appearance of the first words. When the infant has mastered grasping and releasing, is walking with some purpose and without assistance, and is able to creep downstairs backwards, he has come to a point in his language development when he has a repertoire of from three to fifty single words (which he uses as "sentences") and is uttering series of sounds that sound like language but are not ("jargon"—to use Gesell's term). Lenneberg's view, which is also shared by Chomsky (1964, 1967), is that the human organism is biologically "programmed" to generate language. In a study comparing the behavior of infants of normal and deaf parents, Lenneberg found that both groups of infants, through the fourteenth week of life, were producing about the same amount of vocalization. This finding suggests that such behavior is biologically determined and is not dependent on its being reinforced by adults. A similar finding also appears in a study by Tulkin and Kagan (1970), who observed middle-class and working-class mothers interacting with their ten-month-old baby girls. Although the middle-class mothers initiated more interactions with their infants and talked to them much more, there was no difference in the amount of vocalization emitted by the two groups of infants.

Effects of Stimulation. The studies of Lenneberg and of Tulkin and Kagan were done in a normal home environment in which there was a fairly constant amount of stimulation. In institutional environments, where the amount of stimulation in the form of noise and handling is much less, vocalization is also less. Conversely, an increase in stimulation produces an increase in vocalization for such infants. Reinhold, Gewirtz, and Nelson (1959) counted the number of vocalizations made during 9 three-minute periods distributed throughout the day for each of 21 institutionalized infants of a median age of three months. The results for the first two days provided a baseline. These were days when the experimenter merely leaned over the crib with an expressionless face. The second two days the experimenter reinforced vocalizations by smiling, clucking, and touching the infant; the last two days were again concerned with nonreinforcement (baseline behavior). Conditioning (reinforcement) raised the rate of vocalizing to a statistically significant extent over the baseline while nonreinforcement lowered it to a level approaching the baseline.

Environmental restriction, such as occurs with many infants and children living in institutions, presumably has an effect on the learning of language. Characteristically these children do not receive as much individual attention as do children living in the normal family atmosphere. For one thing ratio of infants to adults is likely to be much higher in institutions. Babies under six months of age raised in the unstimulating environment of an orphanage have been found to be retarded in frequency of vocalization and kinds of sounds as compared with children raised at home (Brodbeck and Irwin, 1946). Conversely, enrichment will increase the speech sounds made. Systematic reading of stories to infants from the age of 13 months to that of 30 months leads to a significant difference in the number of vocalizations from this group and another group of infants matched with them for economic status of the father's occupation (Irwin, 1960). After about four months the infants who had been read to showed reliably more speech sounds.

Abrupt changes in the amount of stimulation received by infants can also have an effect on the normal course of development. H. R. Schaffer (1966b) studied infants aged one to 29 weeks whose parents had to send them to a hospital for various types of ailments. As compared to a control group of infants, who had been in an institution since birth, the newly hospitalized infants showed retardation in the development of psychomotor behavior. When they returned to their homes, their rate of development returned to normal.

Intellectual Development

It is difficult to discuss the intelligence of infants in specific terms. Only after the period of infancy has drawn to a close is it possible to be more precise about its meaning and to use such terms as abstract or verbal ability. Aspects of thinking—sensorimotor, perceptual, conceptual, and linguistic activity—are all in-

volved in intellectual activity. When they are used for adaptive purposes to solve the problems the infant encounters, they are being used intelligently. The same active strivings described in the development of thinking are to be seen as operating in intellectual activity. Perception of objects outside of himself is a spur to the infant's intellectual functioning. His tasting, smelling, looking, and feeling show intelligence in operation. Without this active exploration, intellectual development would be stunted. The research findings on environmental restriction described in the next chapter testify to what happens to intellectual functioning when the incentive to carry on this active exploration is stunted in an unstimulating environment.

Developmental Norms

One of the more widely used infant scales will be utilized to demonstrate the changes in performance expected of the younger and older infant. The Cattell Infant Intelligence Scale, developed by Psyche Cattell (1940), is a downward extension of the Revised Stanford-Binet Intelligence Tests (see Chapter 14) and is similar to them in that the items are grouped according to age levels. It is suitable for children as young as two months and, for those who are 30 months of age, it merges with Stanford-Binet tests.

At the youngest levels, the tasks are often perceptual-motor in nature. For example, to receive credit for an item at the two-month level, the child may be expected to show head and eye movements in following a moving stimulus. Beginning at about five months the scale contains a gradually increasing number of manipulatory items. Prior to the age of about 12 months, administration of the items involves neither imitation of the examiner's behavior nor response to verbal requests. Rather, a controlled stimulus is simply presented to the child and his response observed.

For example, does a four-month-old infant become more active at the sight of a toy? When a small one-inch block is placed on the table in front of him, what does he do? Chances are if he is an average three-month-old, he will focus his eyes on it; if he is six months old, he can probably pick it up and even reach for another one. If he is seven months old, he can probably hold two blocks simultaneously. But not before the age of 14 months is he likely to be able to hold three such blocks at one time.

After the age of one year, the items become increasingly dependent on verbal ability. Either the child himself must demonstrate his emerging ability to use speech (be able to say one word at 11 months, two words at 12 months, combine words at 22 months, and so on) or at least be able to respond to verbal instructions given by the examiner. Despite this gradual increase in the use of spoken or comprehended language, manipulatory items still predominate until approximately the two-year level.

With items similar to those in the Cattell Scale, Bayley (1933) found that the mental growth curve was of the sort given in Figure 7-6. The rapid increase in scores during the first year and a gradual leveling off thereafter seem to characterize the changes over the two-year period. It is evident that infancy is a period of considerable mental growth.

Underlying Factors

Intelligence is a sequence of developing functions which differ as age increases (Bayley, 1955). At the youngest ages the intellectual accomplishments of the infant are of the sort attributed to them by Piaget as presented in the account of cognition. Indeed, Honig and Brill (1970), in the study we mentioned

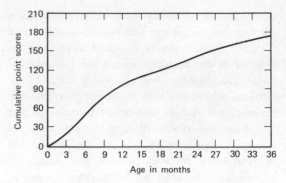

Figure 7-6. Mental growth curve in terms of cumulative point scores. (Bayley, 1933. Reprinted by permission.)

earlier in this chapter, found that total scores on their Piagetian Infancy Scales correlated .43 with IQ as measured by the Cattell Scale. At later ages, measurements of intelligence are more concerned with adaptive behavior of a more abstract nature.

Two independently conducted research studies lend support to these contentions. Richards and Nelson (1939), using items developed by Gesell for infant testing at 6, 12, and 18 months, found by statistical manipulation that two factors accounted for the interrelations they obtained. They called one factor "alertness" and the other "motor ability." The two factors were more closely intertwined than is usually the case with factors found with older subjects. They noted that the motor factor is present practically in all test items. Alertness is considered to be present when, in addition to motor activity, there is also distance perception, as when looking for a fallen object, or playfulness, as in laughing at the sound of music. Findings somewhat consistent with those of Richards and Nelson were reported by Hofstaetter (1954), who found that one factor, "sensory motor alertness," predominated in the intelligence of infants. It may be that a common element in both these factors is "energy level." If so, this might explain the results of a longitudinal study in which the cries of infants aged four to ten days were measured for outburst frequency during their most active period of crying. The resulting scores correlated .45 with the children's Stanford Binet IQs three years later (Karelitz et al., 1964).

Predicting Later Intellectual Development

Except for a few isolated instances, such as the study just cited and another we will mention shortly, developmental tests administered in infancy are not very predictive of later intellectual attainment as measured in preschool ages or later. Despite the standardization of the Cattell Scale as a downward extension of the Stanford-Binet, it is essentially nonpredictive of later results on the Stanford-Binet. For example, the correlations found between Cattell (1940) measures for three, six, and nine months and the Stanford-Binet at 36 months are respectively .10, .34, and .18, all quite low. For older ages the correlations become progressively greater. Using the same standard of 36 months on the Stanford-Binet, those for 12, 18, 24 and 30 months are, respectively, .56, .67, .71, and .83. Predictions of intelligence measures obtained before the age of one year against measures in later years are so low as to be essentially meaningless, but are more adequate thereafter.

The reasons for their relatively poor predictive value generally are not hard to establish. The young infant is not interested in his own performance because he is not even aware of it as a performance. He cannot be guided by verbal instructions to any great degree. His attention is not easily directed to the tasks selected and he is easily distracted. His behavior repertory is much more restricted than is the older child's. Another reason for the low correlations is that measurements and observations made during the first year of life tend to have low reliability. In other words, tests given a day or so apart during this stage tend to produce results that are less consistent than tests given a day or so apart when the child is older. In actuality, the tests are probably as reliable as they can be: it is the infant himself who is unreliable. Any parent knows that an infant is often unexpectedly unable to do something today that he "learned" last week. For example, a child will begin crawling, and may crawl for several days, whereupon he suddenly stops crawling for several weeks. Such phasing in and out of behavior makes it difficult to determine exactly where on the scale an infant is.

Most important, however, is the still unresolved question as to whether intelligence, as we conceive of it in older children and adults, can be said to have emerged before some competence in understanding and using language has been established. In that connection, it is interesting to note that about the only form of infant behavior that appears to have any sizable correlation with later childhood and adult IQ is vocalization. The correlation of verbal items of the Bayley Scale administered during the first year of life with scores on intelligence tests administered between the ages of 13 and 18 proved to be .33, which is higher than most of the correlations between Cattell test scores for the same period and Stanford-Binet IQs at age three, as we noted above. Unfortunately, however, this correlation between early vocalizations and IQs obtained during childhood and adulthood applies only to girls and is essentially zero for boys (Cameron, Livson, and Bayley, 1967).

In spite of the limitations of testing procedures employed during infancy, this does not mean that testing during this period is useless and should be abandoned. If an infant scores consistently below the norms for his age, something is likely to be amiss. An infant's current status is an important source of information, even though his score has only limited predictability for future status (Bayley, 1958).

Individuality and Consistency

The Infant as an Individual

The neonate shows only the barest beginnings of individuality; he cannot be said to have a personality in the sense that he has characteristic organized ways of behaving. Rather, he has the potentiality for such behavior expressed in certain forms of individuality already noted in the previous chapter. There is no question that personality in the sense just mentioned makes its appearance during the two years of infancy, even though it is fruitless to try to give it a more precise date.

The unequal rapidity of various forms of development is a major factor in the appearance of individuality of the infant. The development process is not uniform. In some respects an infant may be in advance of what may be expected of him; in other respects he may be behind. True, this happens later as well, but never again will the contrasts be so great. This individuality of development is attributable to inheritance and environmental opportunities to which the particular infant is exposed. With further development these individualities become patterned and a characteristic personality emerges in the infant.

Infants show persistent variabilities in psychological characteristics. Variability in amount of crying among infants is considerable. Aldrich, Sung, and Knop (1945) found that within a 24-hour period time sample, infants varied in amount of crying from 48 to 243 minutes. Among the infants studied by Marquis (1943), and referred to in connection with the relation of frustration to emotion, one infant showed five times as much bodily

activity in the frustrating situation as did another in the same situation.

Margaret E. Fries categorized differences in activity among infants and noted that markedly active infants tended to be markedly active at later ages as well, and that neonates who were relatively quiet tended to remain relatively inactive individuals in childhood (Fries and Wolff, 1953).

Unusual sensitivities among infants to external stimuli have been noted. One sleeping infant may be awakened by sounds through which other infants sleep undisturbed. In sensitive infants, a startle to sound may appear and the infant may seem to "wince" as if stimuli only moderately intense by usual standards are actually painful. Escolona and Bergman (1949) considered that these sensitivities may be conceptualized as showing in these infants that there are weak barriers between the stimuli of the external world and the infant. If ordinary stimuli are overwhelming, the sensitive infant may have to withdraw from stimulation to a greater degree than the ordinary infant. Bell's (1960) results, reported in Chapter 6, would make it appear that the barrier is confined within one sense modality, and not a general sensitivity extending across all modalities.

Not only variability from infant to infant but also consistency within a particular infant has been observed. In a study based on cinema records, speed of creeping and climbing and manipulating was measured at monthly intervals. A remarkable constancy of psychomotor tempo of activities was found. The infant who crept fastest manipulated fastest, with a similar constancy in other infants (Ames, 1940).

Shirley (1931, 1933), who closely studied 25 babies from birth to three years, described characteristics distinguishing one infant from another in terms of irritability, tone, and timbre of crying, and motility and tonicity of muscles. This individuality in expression of emotion tends to be maintained within particular gross limits as the infant grows older. For example, she described certain infants in which timorousness and irritability had appeared earlier and persisted throughout the ensuing months of her study. Moreover, when "profile charts" were prepared involving a variety of characteristics, differences were so pronounced that the examiner could identify the infants from the charts alone.

This particular study assumes even greater importance because 16 years later these same children were restudied. Without seeing the personality sketches made by Shirley, Patricia Neilon (1948) restudied the adolescents and prepared new personality sketches. Judges then matched the infant and adolescent personality sketches with success far above chance expectation. Temperamental qualities noted in infancy still characterized these individuals when they were adolescents.

Early Indications of Sex Differences

In view of the widespread belief that sex differences in personalty and behavior during childhood and adulthood are entirely the product of social learning and the expectations of others, it may be well to examine the question of whether differences appear during infancy. Presumably, if such differences do appear, they are likely to be the result of genetic influences and not of social learning. Garai and Scheinfeld (1968) reviewed almost 500 studies dealing with sex differences throughout the lifespan. Their conclusions regarding differences appearing during the first year of life may be summarized as follows.

1. Studies are not in agreement as to whether boys are more active than girls at birth, but the evidence is clear that activity differences appear within a few days. For instance, at the age of 23 hours, boys and girls spent approximately the same amount of time in hand-mouth contact and hand sucking, but by 71 hours, boys were clearly ahead of girls (Hendry and Kessen, 1964). The fact that boys' tendency to greater activity is not as evident at birth as later may be related to the fact that there is a greater probability for male infants to be weaker at birth and to have more birth complications.

2. Female neonates are more responsive than males to pain, changes in temperature, and electric shock, a tendency that appears to be related to greater tactile sensitivity and pain reactivity among females of school and college age.

3. By the middle of the first year, boys show more interest in complex geometric stimuli presentations, whereas girls show more interest in representations of faces. Studies of the effectiveness of various types of reinforcement in learning experiments indicate that girls respond more to tonal stimuli, whereas boys respond more to visual stimuli. The reviewers concluded that infant boys tend to show an inherently greater interest in objects and visual patterns, while girls are congenitally more responsive to people and faces.

Infant boys and girls also differ in their responses to the manipulation of objects by the experimenter. At six months, boys are more likely to reach for an object that has been placed behind a barrier, whereas girls the same age are likely to react more passively, by looking away from the object and barrier (Kaye, 1969).

The fact that these differences appear in early infancy or even at or near birth does not mean that all sex differences in behavior and personality observed in childhood and adulthood are inborn and not learned, but it does suggest that the usual patterns of sex-related behavior have some genetic component. Man is a highly plastic animal, as far as behavior is concerned, and the fact that there is so much variance in personality among the individuals of any given sex seems to indicate that basic sex tendencies present at birth may be markedly modified through learning.

Summary

To Piaget, thought is a biological function in that intellectual functioning is a matter of adaptative interaction of organism and environment. This interaction is expressed in the complementary functions of *assimilation* and *accommodation*. If a new situation cannot be assimilated into the old behavior repertoire, the repertoire must accommodate itself to the new environmental circumstances. The cognitive structures are interposed between the changing contents and static functions of intelligence. To the infant, realities are functional elements and are not yet entities. "Out of sight, out of mind" characterizes his point of view. The infant must learn that objects are stable—the concept of *object permanence*. He must also learn to understand the concepts of space, time, cause and effect. The idea that motoric responses involving manipulation of the physical environment is essential for cognitive development has been questioned by Kagan, who points out that infants can also pick up information merely by watching and listening.

In any event, whatever an infant learns must come from his interaction with his environment, and perceptions are a major component in this relationship. Perception is a cognitive process in that it assigns some meaning to the stimuli that impinge on the organism. Observations suggest that during the first year of life the infant spends a considerable amount of time getting acquainted with his world. This active exploration forms the library of experiences upon which his future perceptions will be based.

Fantz conducted a series of experiments to explore infant reactions to stimuli of varying complexity. His results revealed that infants of all ages preferred to look at complex stimuli, but that this preference increased with age. The classical "visual cliff" experiment by Walk and Gibson investigated depth perception of infants. The results suggest that some aspects of depth perception are innate. Even infants too young to crawl show differences in heart rate when suspended over the "deep" side of the stimulus box. A rudimentary form of depth perception appeared in another study when infants attempted to avoid expanding shadows that appeared to be on collision courses.

According to the formulation of learning theorists, perceptions and conceptualizations are cue-producing responses, and thus both a cause and an effect of learning. Language is one of the best examples of the way in which responses produce cues that lead to further responses. Conceptual discrimination rests on language in the sense that language discrimination improves conceptualization. Children seem to be better able to learn conceptual discriminations that they can verbalize (i.e., triangularity). On the other hand, several experimenters have shown that children can form conceptual discriminations without benefit of language.

Language and thought are intimately related. Simply stated, thoughts are manipulations of meanings; words facilitate these manipulations, render them more precise, and make them more easily recalled. Language may be said to embrace three kinds of activities—inner, receptive, and expressive. Inner language is initially a form of play expressed in babbling just for the fun of it. Receptive language begins when the infant begins to discriminate some of the sounds of the spoken language of others and associates them with some of the stimuli that normally accompany them. The infants earliest vocalizations contain the phonemes of many languages. With maturation and learning, the child gradually narrows the range of these phonemes to just those of his own language. Routh (1969) has shown that the frequency of certain sounds uttered by infants can be altered by a kind of social reinforcement.

Expressive language begins as early as one month, the age at which observers can discriminate between infantile cries of discomfort, pain, and hunger. The child generally says his first word at the end of the first year, although there is considerable variability between children and observers. The infant's eagerness to speak and learn names is a major feature of the development of speech. Initially, he applies a word to a wide variety of objects or persons that will later be differentiated by different words. How these words lose their excess meanings and become attached to the right object has led to much speculation among psychologists. B. F. Skinner explains language acquisition entirely within an operant-conditioning framework. Chomsky and others are critical of this approach and believe that conditioning cannot explain either the speed with which language is acquired, or the great variety of resultant behaviors. It seems that language forms appear when children are biologically ready to utter them, and their appearance is correlated with the appearance of certain motor skills. This observation suggests that the human organism is biologically "programmed" to produce language. This view has been supported by research which shows that the amount of infant vocalization is relatively unaffected by the amount of parental vocalization. However, this does not mean that the amount of infant vocalization is totally independent of environmental factors. Institutionalization and other forms of social and sensory deprivation have a very definite influence.

The Cattell Infant Intelligence Scale is a downward extension of the Revised Stanford-Binet Intelligence test that attempts the difficult task of defining the intelligence of infants in specific terms. At the youngest levels, measurement is often confined to perceptual-motor tasks, like the eye and head movements shown in following a moving stimulus. Beginning at about five months, the scale contains a gradually increasing number of manipulatory items. At 12 months, the items also become increasingly dependent on verbal ability. As measured by this sort of scale, the mental growth curve increases more rapidly during the first year and levels off thereafter. Infant intelligence is qualitatively very different from adult intelligence. We cannot even be sure that the young infant is capable of adaptive behavior of a more abstract nature. Several studies that support this contention have found that factors of "alertness" and "motor ability" tend to dominate in the intelligence of infants. Generally, tests like the Cattell Scale are not very predictive of later intellectual attainment. The reasons for this lack of predictability are not hard to establish. The infant is easily distracted and his own behavior is so variable as to make observations somewhat unreliable. It is also questionable whether intelligence, as we conceive of it in older children and adults, can be said to exist before some competence in understanding and language use has been established. In that connection, it is interesting to note that vocalization is one of the few infant behaviors that has any sizable correlation with adult IQ.

Infants show persistent variabilities in psychological characteristics. There are marked differences between infants with respect to amount of crying and total body activity. Some infants are more sensitive to certain kinds of stimulation than others. These differences between infants also show remarkable consistency for particular infants. In a study by

Shirley, the unique tempermental qualities noted in infancy still served to characterize the subjects when they reached adolescence.

Although the belief is widespread that sex differences in personality are the result of social learning, research shows that they appear in infancy, even during the neonate stage. This does not mean that learning does not enter into childhood and adult sex patterning, but rather that there are genetic components that tend to orient development in different ways, according to the sex of the child.

8 Infancy: Parental Influences

Roles of Fathers and Mothers

In this chapter we shall examine the effects that the parents have on the infant, with particular reference to their long-range implications. The parent we shall be most concerned with is the mother, partly because it is the mother who has the most intimate and most frequent contact with the infant in virtually all cultures, and partly because research has focused on her behavior and attitudes during this period of the child's development. This does not mean that the father does not play a part in child development at this stage. His importance as a psychological influence is most keenly felt, especially when he is absent. We know this from research showing the effects of father absence during infancy on childhood behavior patterns, and we shall discuss this topic in later chapters. The father's immediate effect on infant development has, however, been little studied. One can speculate that his interaction with the infant has much the same effect as that of the mother, provided his handling of the infant is consistent with hers. If it is not, the infant may, during the stage when he is differentiating between familiar and strange adults, actually express discomfort and irritation when handled by the father. Perhaps this occurs more often in homes in which mother and father roles are more sharply differentiated.

Today there is a trend in middle-class homes, particularly in urbanized societies, for the roles of fathers and mothers to merge to some degree. This means that fathers are performing many services for infants that were formerly provided only by mothers: feeding, diapering, bathing, burping, cuddling, and the like. Mothers, too, often leave the house or the apartment for shopping or employment, while fathers take care of the children. Because of the trend toward the merging of roles, we should make it clear that when we use the term "mother" in general discussions (not research reports) we are referring to the person who happens to be playing the role of mother, be it the father or an adult relative of the infant.

Older siblings can also play maternal roles. The effects of sibling caretakers on infants have not been researched, partly because variations in the age, sex, and duties of sibling caretakers make it difficult to conduct properly controlled studies, and partly because infant care by siblings is less characteristic of industrialized, Western cultures. Hence we know very little about the differential effects of mother care versus sibling care.

There are many approaches that could be used to analyze the effect that mothers and mother figures have on infants, but for the sake of convenience, we are organizing our analysis into stimulation, love (or attention), and teaching relationships. The stimulation aspect is a more general category than the other two. Anything that a mother does with respect to an infant has some effect on the kind and level of stimulation in the infant's environment. Love or attention constitutes a particular kind of stimulation that is concerned with meeting the infant's needs or with expressing the mother's needs to care for or attend to the infant. The teaching relationship may involve maternal responses that could also be included in the love-and-attention category, but her general intent here is that of socializing the infant, helping him to deal with aspects of his environment, helping

him to become more independent, expressing the values of the culture, and the like. In very general terms, love or attention relationships have a higher emotional or affective content, whereas teaching relationships are more cognitive, didactic, matter-of-fact, or disciplinary in nature.

Early Stimulation

In Chapter 4 we introduced the idea that attention has reward value in learning situations, particularly in socialization, because it has an "arousal effect" on children. In Chapter 5, we discussed Yvonne Brackbill's (1970) research showing that infants one month old responded favorably to moderate increases in stimulation, and in Chapter 6 we cited research suggesting that stimulation has some kind of facilitative effect on psychomotor development. We shall now pursue these themes further and relate them to the course of development in infancy.

All living organisms require some form of energy input. In addition to the ordinary and obvious needs for nourishment, air, and water, there is also a need for warmth, light, and something more—something that actually stresses the organism in ways that are appropriate to its structure and functioning. It is these stresses to which we give the general term "stimulation" and that lead to some kind of arousal in the organism. As we move up the phylogenetic scale, the kind of stimuli that organisms can respond to, and actually seek to respond to, become increasingly varied and complex. Variety and complexity, of course, reach their maximum with man. In a typical hour on a college campus, a student will be stimulated by the sight of grass, trees, buildings, sky, and other people; he may taste a Coke and a hamburger, and smell the fertilizer newly applied to the flower beds; he feels the sun or the wind outside the buildings, the air currents set up by the air conditioner or furnace inside; he hears the babble of voices, scraps of conversations, lectures, music from transistor radios, distant planes and trucks; and so forth ad infinitum. Sometimes, when he is trying to concentrate on his studies, these noises can be distracting, but ordinarily they form a pleasant obligatto to daily activity.

In this, our student is like the rest of us: he finds stimulation enjoyable. Although there are times when we long for peace and quiet, our general tendency is to be attracted toward stimulation. Animals also find stimulation attractive, but man far exceeds them in his search for stimulation and arousal. In the words of D. E. Berlyne (1966), "the central nervous system of a higher animal is designed to cope with environments that produce a certain rate of influx of stimulation, information, and challenge to its capacities" (p. 26). He goes on to say that an overload of stimulation can be stressful, of course, but that "we also have evidence that prolonged subjection to an inordinately monotonous or unstimulating environment is detrimental to a variety of psychological functions" (p. 26).

Animal Research

The work with early stimulation of subhuman species suggests that the need for arousal may be universal. In a number of experiments, Seymour Levine (1960) handled (picked up, petted, stroked) certain pups in rat litters but ignored others. At maturity, the handled rats were more relaxed in novel situations, displaying active exploratory behavior, whereas the unhandled rats cowered in corners, or crept timidly about, urinating and defecating freely—all signs of stress. The manipulated rats also exhibited a more rapid rate of development: they opened their eyes earlier and achieved motor coordination

sooner. They gained weight more rapidly than the unhandled control rats, and continued to gain more rapidly even after the stimulation regimen had been terminated.

Somewhat similar results were reported for kittens that were handled daily from birth until they were 45 days old. Handled kittens approached strange toys and humans more readily. Some of the kittens had also been exposed for five hours a day to a stimulating environment consisting of a large playroom containing kittens from other litters, boys, boxes, a scratching post, and stairs. These kittens also showed superior performance in solving maze problems (Wilson, Warren, and Abbott, 1965).

In another study, young rats were given one of three types of treatment: (1) stimulus enrichment, consisting of playpen experiences; (2) "normal" laboratory environment; or (3) stimulus deprivation, in the sense that they were kept in solitary cages in the dark corners of the animal's room. Results showed that the more stimulation that rats had experienced by the end of their treatment period, the more successful they were in solving maze problems. When the rats were killed, and their brain structure analyzed, researchers found a positive relationship between the amount of stimulation received and the amount of *cerebral cortex* they had developed. The cerebral cortex is the outer layer of the brain—the "thinking area." The findings therefore suggest that stimulation enrichment promotes the development of cerebral cortex. Analysis also showed that the brain tissues of stimulated rats were richer in *acetylcholine* and *cholinesterase*, biochemicals that facilitate the transmission of neural impulses (Bennett, Diamond, Krech, and Rosenzweig, 1964).

Research with somewhat similar results has been reported by Norman D. Henderson (1970) who contrasted the brain size of mice raised in standard cages with that of mice raised in a "playpen" type of cage. Not only did the rats receiving the experimental treatment have larger brains, but their progeny had still larger brains, especially when they, too, enjoyed a stimulus-enriched environment.

Some interesting research with handicapped animals shows that stimulus enrichment facilitates their rehabilitation. Under some experimental conditions, mother rats will deliver pups that have abnormally small heads (*microencephalic*), a condition that is accompanied by a reduction in intelligence, as measured by problem-solving ability. Rabe and Haddad (1970) raised microencephalic and normal rats in stimulus-deprived or stimulus-enriched environments. Rats raised in the enriched environment did better on maze problems than did those raised in deprived environments. What is particularly interesting is that stimulus enrichment enabled the microencephalic rats virtually to "catch up" with the normal rats. In another experiment, monkeys were raised in environments in which they were physically restrained, to the point where they could not view their limbs. Some of the monkeys were visually stimulated by permitting them to see what was going on around them in the laboratory, but others were not, or were permitted to view the laboratory only briefly each day. On release from the confinement, those monkeys who had been deprived of visual stimulation showed marked retardation in picking up the usual motor skills displayed by monkeys their age, but the visually stimulated ones had less difficulty. The more visual stimulation they had received, the quicker they were to adjust to their environment (Levison, Levison, and Norton, 1970).

Research with Human Infants

Research with animals is of particular interest when results seem relevant to human behavior. The work we have cited all sug-

gests that early stimulation has facilitative effects on development during infancy and childhood and that it may even have a noticeable effect on the structure and functioning of the brain. The findings appear consistent with what can be observed in human infants. A study that actually shows a relationship between stimulus enrichment and cognitive functioning was conducted by Ottinger, Blatchley, and Denenberg (1960). In their experiment, human neonates were stimulated by rocking, "mother talk," having their backs rubbed, and watching a rotating color wheel and an appearing and disappearing face on a revolving disc. The treatment consisted of 140 minutes of stimulation spread over three days, while the neonate was still in the hospital following birth. On the fourth day, the babies who had received the experimental treatment and a matched control group were tested, using the Fantz observation box we discussed in Chapter 7 (see Figure 7-1). In contrast to the control babies, the experimentally treated babies kept their eyes on the target for longer periods. Inasmuch as the ability to orient and fix one's gaze is a first step in the cognitive sequence, the findings suggest that stimulus enrichment facilitates human infants' cognitive development, much as it facilitates the development of young animals who have experienced early stimulation.

Research with animals suggests that stimulation does not necessarily have to be pleasant to facilitate development, and at least one investigation dealing with human infants points to a similar conclusion. Landauer and Whiting (1963) conducted a survey in which they rated various cultures on the stressfulness of their child-rearing practices. Stressfulness was rated by the presence of such procedures as binding and swaddling, frequency of loud noises, abrasion (such as scraping the child's skin with shells), the administration of emetics and irritants, the employment of pain, exposure to extremes of heat and cold, and shaping (through binding) of various parts of the body (the head, for example). Their findings suggest that, contrary to what might be expected, such stressful methods may have some kind of facilitative effect, for they found a correlation of +.33 (p. < .01) between the height attained by adult males in the various cultural groups and scores based on the intensity and frequency of stress during infancy.

Although it is relatively easy to institute a regimen of stimulus enrichment in infancy, just exactly what constitutes "stimulus deprivation" is a rather controversial question for which there are no easy answers. Dennis and Dennis (1951) once tried to raise a pair of twins under what amounted to a condition of "minimum social stimulation." Human contacts were kept at a minimum, with the intent of not fondling, playing with, or talking to them during the first six months or so of life. Conditions of social isolation were eased during the remainder of the first year.

The infants showed a record of early development very much like that of infants reared in an environment with the usual social contacts and experiences of fondling, play, and talking. They even responded by smiling when an observer attempted to preserve a pronounced stolidity. These infants emerged from their first year as healthy, alert, and happy.

Stone (1954) studied this issue and concluded that the conditions under which the twins were raised actually represented minimum adequate social stimulation and was at a much higher level than that provided in many institutions. There is also some clinical evidence suggesting that it is the *second* six months that is crucial with respect to the damage produced by isolation. The most marked isolation of the infants was during the first six months. Moreover, Dennis and Dennis did see a lot of the infants, both from sheer decent human impulses and from the fact that they were interested in them too much as "subjects" to stay away. On the average one or both were in their room for a total of two hours a day. The study, it seems, provides information not about deprivation, but about the lower limits of adequate social stimulation.

Dennis himself concluded that (1) practically all the common responses of the first year of life may be developed autogenously, that is, from self-initiated practice; (2) social responses, as such, prior to the second year are few and unimportant; and (3) if his physical well-being is cared for, the infant's behavioral development will proceed along normal lines without intercession from adults.

A well-executed study designed to see the effect of increased "mothering" was carried on by Rheingold (1956). Her infant subjects were drawn from an institution where it was evident that considerable effort in giving this care was expended. Volunteers and hospital personnel were encouraged by the Sister in charge of the floor to talk to the babies and to hold them. Her research situation, then, was unlike more impersonal institutional situations, and did not, by any means, represent the extremes of emotional deprivation that may be found. She was using a situation somewhat closer to that normally prevailing in an infant's home. Hence, if she were to find differences in the infants because of the increased "mothering" she introduced, she would be submitting her hypothesis to a more difficult test than if she had used a more impersonal institution for her study.

Sixteen infants between five and seven months of age were her subjects. She cared for the experimental group four at a time for nearly eight hours per day, five days a week for eight weeks. Adapting herself to the individual needs of each infant, during these hours she alone bathed, diapered, held, talked to, and soothed these infants. She repeated the procedure for the second group of four.

Two control groups, each time numbering four, were cared for in the usual hospital routine.

Observation by an independent observer showed that Rheingold gave the experimental group much more in the way of care than the control subjects received. For the first experimental group, by way of example, caretaking acts were recorded for 23% of the observations, while in a comparable period of time with the control infants caretaking acts occurred during only 7% of the observations, these acts being performed by seven different persons. In other words, this established an experimental situation in which infant subjects received more intensive care and attention from one caretaker than the infants in a control situation received from all seven of their caretakers.

When the effects of this differential treatment were assessed, Rheingold found that, in contrast to the control infants, the experimental infants: (1) were more socially responsive to her; (2) were more responsive to another person (the examiner); and (3) made slightly higher scores on postural tests, cube manipulation, and the Cattell Infant Scale. In other words, Rheingold showed that increased stimulation in the form of "mothering" has a considerable effect on the social development of infants.

Rheingold and Bayley (1959) did a follow-up study of these infants at 19 months of age, after they had been placed in adoptive homes. Their investigation turned up no significant differences between experimental and control infants. It may be that the more stimulating atmosphere of the adoptive homes was sufficient to bring the control infants up to the level of the experimental group.

Significant gains by retarded children, when given the intellectual stimulation of an experimental nursery school, are described by Skeels and others (1938). This investigation by Skeels and his colleagues demonstrates how much devoted, interested adults can do to give support to children so they can be free to explore, be curious, and reach out for the environment. At the start of the study these children, although previously left to shift for themselves, were less able to care for themselves than children raised in a family. They had to be shown how to use the equipment of the playground; they had short attention spans and were destructive of property. About six months of intensive contact with adults was necessary before these children were able to profit from the nursery school; at this point they began to hold their own or even gained in IQ. By way of contrast, the control group with whom they were matched actually showed an IQ loss.

Still other research that shows how a move from a less to a more stimulating environment can lead to developmental changes is a longitudinal study conducted under the direction of Wayne Dennis (1967). Since 1955, Dennis and his associates have been gathering data on the mental development of foundlings housed in a crèche, or orphanage, in Beirut, Lebanon. Children come into the crèche about two weeks after birth and ordinarily remain until five or six, when they go to an orphanage for older children. During the period of study, the crèche staff consisted of five nuns who distributed their attention among some 100 infants and young children. The adult-child ratio was hence very low, much lower than it would be even in a very large family, and lower than it would be in most orphanages in industrialized countries. The mean IQ of the children in the crèche was 53, which is, as Dennis observed, probably the lowest mean IQ reported for otherwise normal children. Follow-up tests of the crèche children who attended a nursery school between the ages of four and six showed that there was also marked behavioral retardation.

During the earlier phases of the study, few children went to adoptive homes. Adoption had not been a common practice in Mediterranean countries, and particularly in the Middle East, but as families became more affluent during the period after World War II, the practice grew. By the late 1960's virtually all the crèche children were being adopted. When Dennis and his associates conducted follow-up testing of those crèche children who had been adopted, they were surprised to find that their average IQ was 81. This is considerably below the 100 IQ norm for the general population, but was almost a 30-point gain over the crèche IQ. Gains were greater when children were adopted younger. Children adopted before one year of age made normal intellectual gains, whereas those adopted beyond the age of four and a half gained at a much slower rate.

The Mother as a Source of Love or Attention

The question that naturally arises in connection with Dennis' study of adopted children is whether the increase in IQ is the result of the greater stimulation in the adoptive home, as contrasted to that of the crèche, or whether adopted children are getting something over and beyond stimulation. The term "stimulation" has mechanical and manipulative implications, and it does not seem to reflect very adequately the full range of possibilities in the "tender, loving care" that a devoted mother renders her infant.

The most obvious thing about the behavior of any newborn infant is his complete helplessness. When a need arises, his only means of tension reduction is random motor discharge. Unable to move about, to keep warm, to feed himself, to avoid danger, the infant is entirely dependent on his mother or some other person who takes her place. Since he is unable to cope with his needs, she ministers to him. The infant is a member of a household or an institution which forms his universe. The infant's universe is mediated to him through the one who fulfills his needs—his mother or his nurse. Other individuals are to be found in his social environment, but they are as a shadowy background to the emerging foreground of the mother figure.

The average infant is in continuous contact with his mother. "Fed," "fondled," "talked to," "changed," and "carried about" express only a few of these forms of contact. This contact is a constant source of stimulation. The infant is encouraged to babble, to form words, to move about, and eventually, to sit up, to stand up, and to walk. He is carried about through a house, filled with many interesting objects and persons. In this atmosphere of contact between mother and child, the infant learns to reach out to his environment, to make his wants known, and to become a social creature.

It should be apparent by now that what a mother does in caring for an infant is more than simple carrying out of a series of acts. She is also communicating something of herself. Contact between infant and mother is, of course, partly verbal. Sensitivity on the part of both mother and infant to one another's touch, bodily tensions, and (later) expressions are an important source of communication between them.

Sybille Escalona (1953) distinguished between communication, a purposive attempt to convey information, and contagion, the process by which a feeling state is transmitted from the mother to the infant. A tense and anxious adult may engender crying in an infant who, if shifted to a relaxed adult, may quiet down. Contagion is not entirely subject to voluntary control. A worried mother trying to convey assurance to her infant may find that he responds to her actual feeling state and not to what she wants him to feel.

Breast-feeding Practices and Maternal Attitudes

The most intimate interaction between mother and infant takes place when he is breast-fed. It is for that reason that psychologists and other researchers have for many years used breast-feeding practices as a variable to explore the relationship between mothering and later psychological development. As a consequence of that interest, a wealth of studies appeared concerning breast- versus bottle-feeding, short versus long breast-feeding, gradual versus abrupt weaning, self-demand versus scheduled feeding, gradual versus abrupt toilet training, and the effect of these infantile experiences on subsequent development. In a careful review, Orlansky (1949) demonstrated that many of these studies were inadequate in research design, in small number of subjects used, and in control of other variables that might affect the results. Moreover, even the most carefully conducted studies turn out to be contradictory in their findings. In one study children breast-fed less than six months or more than ten months showed more behavior problems than did children who had been breast-fed between six and ten months. But in another study the most "secure" college students were those either breast-fed little, if at all, or breast-fed for over a year; these results flatly contradicted the first study.

Subsequent to the Orlansky review, Sewell and Mussen (1952) reported the infant training practices that had been used with about 160 five- and six-year-old children. They hypothesized that better adjustment and fewer oral symptoms would be found in (1) children who were breast-fed as compared with those bottle-fed; (2) children who were fed on a demand schedule as compared with those on a regular schedule; and (3) children who were weaned gradually as compared with those weaned abruptly. Data on infant training practices were obtained from interviews with the mothers. Indices of present adjustment were also obtained from these interviews, along with personality test scores and teachers' ratings of adjustment. In all, there were 26 adjustment or symptom items showing adjustment of these children. No direct relationship was found between any method of feeding gratification and later good or poor adjustment.

The evidence concerning specific practices appears to be contradictory and to lead to no reconcilable results. Perhaps a partial explanation is found in a study that indicates little relationship between the mother's permissiveness in one aspect of socialization, such as feeding, and later aspects, such as toilet training[1] (Sewell, Mussen, and Harris, 1955). This

---

[1] Another reason why these earlier studies of the relationship between breast-feeding and later personality development may have produced contradictory and confusing results is the failure of researchers to control for the social class of the mothers. Martin Heinstein (1965) found that among California mothers, the highest percentage of breast-feeders occurred among mothers with eight years of education or less (53%) and mothers with four or more years of college (46%). Mothers who attended high school, but did not graduate, were least likely to breast-feed (37%). In view of the fact that a great deal of research shows that the development of positive traits of adjustment is positively related to a child's socioeconomic background, Heinstein's findings would suggest that the homes of breast-fed infants provided either the best or the poorest conditions for later psychological development.

finding suggests that we must look beyond specific practices for maternal influences that affect the personality adjustment of infants.

These contradictory results indicate why it is futile to search for practices that will give the one "right" way to raise children. There are many patterns of mother-child interaction. A particular mother, a particular child, a particular set of environmental and hereditary circumstances combine to produce a particular result. A search for simple correlations between characteristics of the mothers and the "consequences" in their children simply does not work.

It appears likely that the specific form of treatment is not ordinarily of critical significance in and of itself. More plausibly a specific practice may be regarded as part of a larger pattern in which it is imbedded. Child-rearing practices and consequent personality development may be indirectly related in that, say, self-demand feeding and gradual weaning reflect a warm reaching-out for the infant on the mother's part. It may be that specific practices are but facets of a general attitude toward the infant.

Martin Heinstein's (1963) longitudinal research with 94 boys and girls suggests that these conclusions are valid. Although psychoanalytic theorists would predict that oral habits, such as thumb sucking, should be present in children who had been bottle-fed and not breast-fed, Heinstein's data showed that the greatest amount of thumb sucking occurred in girls who had been breast-fed and whose mothers, incidentally, had not only achieved a good marital adjustment but also had a better-than-average degree of emotional stability. Other than this, there were no very consistent patterns of childhood behavior problems that could be related to whether the child had been breast- or bottle-fed. Heinstein concluded his report by observing that the zeal displayed by some people in urging that chil-

dren be breast-fed apparently derives from "an oversimplified interpretation of psychoanalytic theory or a long held idyllic picture of mother-infant oneness" (p. 97). He noted, further, that nursing was only "one aspect of the total life space of the infant or child" (p. 97). His data also show that certain maternal characteristics (such as whether the mother is "cold" or "warm") seem to be more related to a child's later adjustment than is the kind of nursing he received as an infant.

Maternal Attitudes and Infant Behavior

The research generally shows that maternal attitudes have a significant effect on the kind of behavior patterns and personality a child will develop. If we ask how these broad general attitudes can be communicated to an infant, we must remember that attitudes are *constructs*. The infant still is stimulated by maternal behavior that manifests the attitude the mother holds, not the attitudes themselves. The evidence presented in the chapter on prenatal maternal attitudes would seem to bear this out.

The results of the study of Marjorie L. Behrens (1954) are relevant and important because she studied *both* specific practices and general attitudes in the same group of mothers. Her subjects were 25 lower middle-class families who were coming to a mental health clinic. Her small sample and other selective factors make suspect wide generalization of the results she obtained, but the results she found are clear-cut and apparently unequivocal. She investigated infant-rearing practices in feeding, weaning, and toilet training in their relation to adjustment of these children at the age of three. She found no correlation betwen the three infant-rearing practices and the children's adjustment. So far, this study bears out the previous studies using the same approach in that the findings were negative.

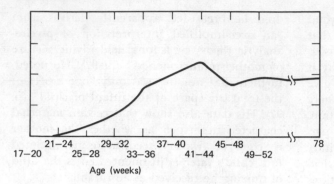

Figure 8-1. Development of attachment to the mother, as indicated by intensity of distress in separation situations. (After Schaffer and Emerson, 1964a.)

Behrens went another step. She investigated what she called the "total mother person," her term for general maternal attitudes and conduct. This was divided into three components based on what she considered to be the mother's underlying attitudes, the manner of meeting the maternal role demanded of her, and observed conduct toward the child. This last has reference to consistency, overprotection, and adaptation of her behavior to the child's needs rather than to specific practices.

Behrens' results, stated in general terms, showed a very high correlation between these various dimensions of the "total mother person" and the children's emotional adjustment. In other words, specific child-rearing practices were not related to adjustment, but overall, global scores of maternal attitudes were predictive of adjustment.

Maternal Deprivation

Among child psychologists, a controversy has continued for some years as to whether infants can be emotionally crippled by being separated from their mothers and, if so, at what age the separation has its most significant effects. One concept that figures prominently in discussion of this topic is that of *separation anxiety*—the feeling of panic or acute depres-

sion that overwhelms an infant on the occasion of an unexpected or prolonged absence of the mother.

Schaffer and Emerson (1964a) traced the course of social attachment in Scottish infants from early infancy to 18 months of age, by observing their reactions to a range of "separation situations"—that is, situations in which the infant was put down after being held, in which the mother left the child alone in a room or in a pram, or the like. As Figure 8-1 shows, signs of distress on such occasions tended to appear in some strength about midway through the first year, although there was considerable individual variation, with some infants showing distress at 22 weeks and others not disturbed at being separated until they were over a year old. The greatest distress occurred, on the average, between 41 and 44 weeks, as Figure 8-1 shows.

Infancy, as David Elkind (1967) points out, is not only a period in which the child makes social attachments, it is also a period in which he establishes a fundamental feeling tone about the world and the people in it. As we noted in Chapter 4, Erikson (1963) has described this attitude as one of *basic trust*—the expectation that people are reliable and that they will meet one's needs. This expectation develops out of the normal experiences of being cared for on an "unconditional-acceptance" basis. When needs are not met or acceptance is given only conditionally, the child may get the feeling that the world is unreliable or even a dangerous place. His characteristic attitude becomes one of mistrust, which undermines all subsequent attempts to establish healthy relationships with others.

If one accepts Erikson's interpretation of this phase of development, then it becomes obvious that mothering plays a crucial role in infancy, as far as later personality development is concerned.

One dramatic way in which the crucial significance of mothering has been demonstrated arises from the study of infants deprived of maternal care. Maternal deprivation is quite different in atmosphere and in effect from that experienced by the rejected child. In rejection, hostility is directed toward the child by one or both parents. He is made to feel unwanted. There is a severity rather than a lack of stimulation. A rejected child meets adults, and, although they may block him, he is stimulated to meet and solve problems even though his solutions are distorted.

A number of different situations are covered by the term maternal deprivation. It may be that a child is frustrated by being deprived even when living at home with his mother, or he may be looked after by a relative stranger in a foster home, or he may be almost completely deprived, as in many institutions. The differences in degree of maternal deprivation are signalized by distinguishing between partial and total deprivation.

Partial deprivation refers to those children who, after establishing a satisfactory emotional relationship with the mother for the first six months of life, are thereafter frustrated by being separated from her. This is supposed to lead to a condition which René Spitz called *anaclitic depression*. A case description derived from Spitz (1948) follows:

There is first what is described as a 'search' for mother. Such infants cannot be quieted, some cry bitterly, others less vehemently but they cannot be soothed. Nevertheless, at this stage they cling to the available adult.

The picture changes on failure of the mother to return. He becomes quiescent, does not look up when adults enter the room, does not play and does not grasp at objects. Along with passivity and dejection he develops eating difficulties, loses weight and shows sleep disturbances. In general, the level of development does not proceed normally or even drops.

This occurs often enough, according to Spitz, to be considered a disorder of infancy attributable to frustration brought about by partial deprivation.

In total deprivation, the infant does not have, early or late, anything resembling emotional ties with a mother figure. The importance of these maternal contacts for normal development is dramatically illustrated by infants almost completely deprived of these experiences.

In infancy, a condition called *marasmus* is said to develop from the frustrations of total maternal deprivation. The following case adapted from one described by Margaret Ribble (1943) illustrates not only the conditions but also something of the general situational background from which it is said to come.

The child was full-term and weighed six pounds, three ounces at birth. The two weeks' stay in the hospital was uneventful. On returning home the mother discovered her husband had deserted her. Thereafter her milk did not agree with the baby. Since the infant refused the breast and began to vomit he was hospitalized. The mother did not come to see him at this time or later, thus deserting him.

He was in a crowded ward, and received little attention or handling. He became a finger sucker and a ruminator (regurgitating food). At two months of age, he weighed about five pounds and had an appearance of a seventh month fetus with arms and legs wasted, large head and large protruding abdomen.

He was transferred to a small children's hospital, where a thorough physical examination revealed nothing of an organic nature. Concentrated nursing care was given him, with his being held in the nurse's lap for a feeding of one half hour duration, his position changed frequently and his being carried about whenever possible. After some slow improvement, a volunteer 'mother' began to come to the hospital twice daily. Her visits were gradually lengthened until she was spending an hour with him on each visit. She had been told the infant needed loving care and physical contact which she gave him.

The results were such that by five months of age he weighed nine pounds. He was now alert and vigorous, although some remnants of his difficulties remained, such as retarded motor coordination and finger sucking.

When the writings of Spitz and Ribble appeared, about a generation ago, they stimulated a great deal of similar research. A number of studies appeared in the United States and elsewhere that affirmed the pernicious effects of maternal deprivation. Further support for this view had also been furnished by observation of infants in adverse conditions, particularly those in Great Britain who were evacuated to the country during the Second World War and those living in institutions. In general, it had been found that infants living in their own homes suffer from considerably fewer personality difficulties than those living in the impersonal environment of an institution (Goldfarb, 1943). Almost needless to add is the fact that the extent and

quality of the damage vary with the age of the child, the specific kind of deprivation, its severity, the length of time it continues, and other relevant factors. When these infants are older, although still within the range of childhood, they seem to be characterized by superficial relationships with other persons, lack of emotional responses in situations where it would be normal to display them, lack of concern about most matters, and pointless deceit and evasion. After examining the literature on maternal deprivation, under the aegis of the World Health Organization, John Bowlby (1951) wrote an eloquent defense of the thesis that an essential of mental health was the necessity for the infant to experience warm continuous relationship with a mother or mother surrogate.

Recently there have been sobering second thoughts about these findings. When critically examined, the studies reveal a host of methodological weaknesses which cast doubt on their conclusions.

The criticisms, presented in devastating reviews, preclude the use of these and many other studies as evidence. Inadequacies of design, uncontrolled factors, lack of precise measurement, failure to report crucial data, and many other errors render the conclusions suspect. The criticisms include the clinical pictures of anaclitic depression and marasmus derived by Spitz. Other clinical patterns or *none at all* may appear as a consequence of institutionalization (O'Connor and Franks, 1961; Pinneau, 1955; Yarrow, 1961; Wolins, 1970).

Despite this negative criticism, something included under the rubric of maternal deprivation seems to have been confirmed. The varieties of study, each with specific inadequacies but of a kind varying from study to study, still led the investigators to reach the same general conclusion. It behooves us to take a more cautious, specific, and rigorous approach to this problem by examining more precisely what went wrong in the earlier studies, and then to turn to some studies that seem to help clarify the problem.

So-called maternal deprivation is a jumble of conflicting and confusing ideas which mean many and different things from one study to the next. Often the situational factors have been studied, not the component psychological factors. It is now recognized that maternal deprivation is not a single homogeneous variable. The events presumably illustrating such deprivation must be more precisely defined for their effects to be predicted. The sheer breadth of characteristics shown by deprived children also suggests not some isolated effect on some specific aspect of personality, but a vast complex that may well have a complicated etiology.

The oft-repeated finding of a significant relationship between the development of the infant and the nature of his early mothering experiences cannot be denied. Gross neglect or prolonged institutionalization with insufficient "mothering" apparently *does* have a pernicious effect. But even here the causal factors have not been precisely identified and isolated. Our best tentative guess is, in light of the considerable research on early stimulation, that maternal deprivation and institutionalization are most deleterious when there is insufficient stimulation and social contact.

Some support for the contentions of Spitz, Ribble, and Bowlby have come from studies of maternal deprivation in monkeys. R. A. Hinde and Yvette Spencer-Booth (1971) conducted experiments in which infant rhesus monkeys 21 to 32 weeks old were separated from their mothers. This is an age at which a rhesus infant still gets milk from its mother but is also capable of feeding itself. The separation period varied betwen 6 and 13 days. During the first few days of the separation, the infants called out a good deal at first and

also showed depressed locomotor and play activity, a condition that persisted up to a month after mother and infant were reunited. Even at the age of 30 months, the behavior of the experimental monkeys was quite different from that of the controls, for they engaged in less exploratory behavior, were less actively social, and more inclined to sit and engage in nonsocial play. In one test situation, year-old monkeys observed a mirror or a banana placed in an adjoining cage into which a narrow passageway had been opened. In contrast to the control monkeys, those who had experienced the separation some five or six months earlier were more reluctant to enter the strange cage, and once having entered it, spent less time there investigating the object. Not only were they less curious, but they showed a greater degree of apprehensiveness.

Kaufman and Rosenblum (1967) conducted a similar set of experiments with macaque monkeys aged five to six months, who were separated from their mothers for a four-week period and then reunited. At the start of the separation period, the infants behaved in a very agitated manner. There was much pacing, searching, frequent trips to the door and window, short bursts of erratic play, and frequent movements toward the other members of the cage group. There was also an increased amount of finger sucking, mouthing and handling of other parts of the body, and cooing —the rather plaintive distress call of the young macaque. These reactions continued during most of the first day, during which time the infants did not sleep.

After 24 to 36 hours, the behavior pattern of three of the four infants changed considerably. They sat hunched over, rolled almost into balls, often with their heads between their legs (see Figure 8-2). Such movement as did occur seemed to be in slow motion. They rarely responded to social gestures made by other infants, and play behavior virtually

Figure 8-2. *The effects of maternal separation. The infant at the right is in a depressed posture that is characteristic in the infant macaque monkeys after the first day of separation from their mothers. The infant at the left is clinging to his mother in a way that is normal for five-month-old monkeys.* (Kaufman and Rosenblum, 1967. Reprinted by permission.)

ceased. They appeared disinterested in and alienated from their environment. Occasionally they would look up and coo. Kaufman and Rosenblum observed that the behavior of the infants at this stage of separation was strikingly similar to the "anaclitic depression" that Spitz reported in his studies of maternal deprivation.

After about a week, the depression gradually lifted, although never completely. Play with peers was still interspersed with periods of depression, although in an abated form. By the end of the month of separation, the infants appeared alert and active much of the time, yet they still did not behave like typical infants their age. The fourth infant, a female, did not go into the depression phase. She spent much time with the adult females in the pen group, was active in exercise play and exploration of the cage. Nevertheless, she

showed many of the behavioral changes displayed by the other deprived infants.

When the mothers were reintroduced into the cage, another major change occurred in the infant's behavior. Clinging behavior and nipple contact increased dramatically, an effect that continued even until the third month after separation. The persistence of this behavior is significant, because this is a period in which infant monkeys generally reduce such close contact with their mothers.

Humans are not monkeys, of course, and one should not "overinterpret" the findings of the Kaufman-Rosenblum study, even though it parallels in a number of ways the studies of maternal deprivation of human infants. One difference is that monkey infants can move about and play more readily than human infants; Kaufman and Rosenblum observed that this ability may have made it possible for the monkey infants to recover to some degree from their depression. Another difference is that human adults may take some initiative in providing care and attention to infants that are not their own, whereas monkey adults do not, as Figure 8-2 suggests. Nevertheless, there may be some general principles underlying the effect of maternal deprivation in both humans and monkeys. Harry F. Harlow (1962) in a series of studies we shall discuss next, found that monkeys reared under mother-separation conditions became neurotic and maladjusted sexually as adults, but that some of these deleterious effects can be avoided if the infants are not reared in isolation, but are permitted to interact with their peers. What this suggests is that while maternal deprivation may be initially disorganizing for monkeys, it may be compensated at least in part by other types of stimulation.

It may well be that the clinical signs of marasmus and anaclitic depression reported by Ribble and Spitz were the results of insufficient handling and stimulation. Consider the situation prevailing in some of the institutions studied by Spitz (1945, 1946). The sides of the infants' cribs were covered by blankets, and no toys were available, so that the only visual experiences came from staring at the blank ceiling; certainly these were conditions making for visual deprivation. There was, furthermore, infrequent opportunity for tactile or kinesthetic stimulation.

Harry F. Harlow's (1958) experiments with monkeys lend support to the idea that stimulation in the form of tactile contact is sought by infants.

The infant monkey is particularly suitable for study because it is more mature at birth and develops its motor skills much more rapidly than does the human infant. It can carry out complicated motor behaviors at an age at which human infants can do no more than twist and squirm. Despite this, there are close similarities of behavior patterns in monkey and human babies, not only of affection but also of fear, anger, and even intellectual growth.

Young monkeys separated from their mothers were "mothered" by the two kinds of surrogate mothers illustrated in Figure 8-3. One figure was made of a block of wood covered with rubber and cloaked in terry cloth. The second figure, made of wire mesh, differed only in being unable to supply "contact comfort," but in one series of trials it supplied the milk for the infant from a bottle's nipple protruding from the figure's front. Light bulbs supplied warmth to both figures. When allowed free access to either mother, the "lactating," wire mesh mother was sought less and less, whereas the terry-cloth mother, who provided no milk, was sought more and more. When frightened or placed in a strange situation, the monkey rushed to the cloth mother, clung to her, and caressed her. When the terry-cloth mother was present, the infant monkey would venture out to explore a fear-arousing stimulus; when the wire-mesh mother was present he tended to explore neither the surrounding space nor the strange object. It was found that this seeking of the cloth mother, "affectional contact," was retained for long periods of time.

Harlow concluded that the stimulation obtained from the terry-cloth mother was innately satisfying and led to an emotional attachment to it. Since the wire-mesh mother was entirely adequate to supply nourishment and physical support, contact comfort was the only essential way in which the two differed. Tactile sensory contact, as such, has been demonstrated to be significant in the behavior of infant monkeys, and it is plausible to suppose in human infants as well.

In later research, Harlow and Suomi (1970) experimented with various models of surrogates. Wire-mesh mothers were electrically

Figure 8-3.   Cloth and wire mother surrogates used in maternal deprivation research with infant rhesus monkeys. (Harlow, 1958. Reprinted by permission.)

heated 10°F above the surrounding air, but infant monkeys still preferred the room-temperature cloth mother. When the infants had a choice between a cloth mother that rocked and one that was stationary, they preferred the rocking mother. Further reactions to fear stimuli were also observed. One female infant was raised on a cloth mother that had a simple ball for a head. When the baby was 90 days old, the ball was replaced by a head like the one on the cloth mother in Figure 8-3. When the baby saw what had been done, she screamed, fled to the back of the cage, and cringed in a corner. After several terror-stricken days, she solved the problem by turning the head around so that she once again faced a bare round ball. When the experimenters tried turning the face to the front again, she turned it back. Harlow and Suomi report:

"Within a week the baby resolved her unface-

able problem once for all. She lifted the maternal head from the body, rolled it into the corner, and abandoned it. No one can blame the baby. She had lived with and loved a faceless mother, but she could not love a two-faced mother.

These data imply that an infant visually responds to the earliest version of mother he encounters, that the mother he grows accustomed to is the mother he relies upon. Subsequent changes, especially changes introduced after maturation of the fear response, elicit this response with no holds barred. Comparisons of effects of babysitters on human infants might be made" (p. 164).

Interpretation of Research on Early Stimulation and Deprivation

A clarification of many of the confused issues concerning the effects of restriction and stimulation on infantile behavior is provided by Gewirtz (1961a, b) in his analysis couched in instrumental or operant learning terms. In keeping with a variety of our earlier incidental comments and with our later analysis of exploratory, external behavior tendencies, Gewirtz argues that the infant actively seeks stimulation. In privation the environment fails to provide the functional stimuli necessary for what is usually learned during the infancy period. It is not only a question of whether stimuli are present, it is more whether they are functional or not; that is, does the particular state of development of the infant allow him to respond to these stimuli when they occur?

Gewirtz conceives deprivation, in contradistinction to privation, to be a state of frustration arising when stimuli, once present, are no longer available to the infant. To illustrate this distinction, infants fed by cup from birth may show privation in sucking responses; other infants, first fed by sucking from the breast or bottle, and then put on cup feeding, are exposed to deprivation. Using these distinctions, Gewirtz (1961a) formulated a variety of kinds of privation and deprivation:

"Under *total privation,* the environment provides few stimuli that might evoke or reinforce behavior. Hence, neither learning nor emotional response habituation would occur, and the infant would develop as unresponsive to stimuli (i.e., passive and asocial), except to those eliciting emotional-startle behaviors. Under *functional privation,* there may be abundant stimuli, but, because they are not discriminable or in proper timing or sequence relationships, they rarely function effectively. Some emotional behaviors may habituate, but little learning would occur. Hence, the child develops as unresponsive to stimuli generally, despite an abundance of access to them. Under the *functional privation of specifically social cue stimuli,* abundant stimuli for effective learning contingencies are provided, but without discriminable social cues. Like the normal child, he can become habituated for most emotional responses and generally responsive to stimuli, but not as such to social conditioned reinforcers and cues available from people (i.e., he would appear 'autistic'). For the *normal* child, there would be available from the beginning evoking, cue, and reinforcing stimuli for behavior, functional for effective learning. These stimuli need not be available in great abundance. In this case, the child's emotional behaviors habituate and he becomes responsive to his environment and oriented toward attaining conditioned social reinforcers. For deprivation, the general case of a major shift in reinforcing-maintaining environment (e.g., from a home to an institutional environment) was illustrated; after which the sub-case of an extreme environmental shift which *separation* from an attached (object) person constitutes was considered."[2]

Whether it be in terms of Gewirtz's formulation or not, there is no question that one of the tasks of future research is to formulate in precise terms the stimulus and response factors involved in privation and deprivation. We shall then be in a position to evaluate more clearly, accurately, and concisely this very active research issue.

Imprinting

In the cross-disciplinary field of ethology, concerned with comparative study of animal behavior, the phenomenon of imprinting has excited considerable research effort that promises to be relevant to the problem of human infantile stimulation and lasting attachments. For some time it has been known that various species of animals, particularly birds, who

[2] Reprinted by permission. © Barnes and Noble, Inc.

have their first social contacts with humans rather than with members of their own species, tend as adults to prefer social contacts with humans over those with their own kind. K. Z. Lorenz (1952), a European naturalist, intensively studied this phenomenon in greylag geese. He divided a clutch of eggs laid by a goose into two groups; leaving one group with the mother, but hatching the second group from an incubator. The goslings hatched by the mother immediately followed her; the incubator raised goslings saw Lorenz only, and followed him. When both groups were intermingled, with the mother and Lorenz present, they immediately headed for their respective "parents." He found this preference for humans to be invariable, provided only that they be the first postnatal social contact.

Lorenz and others extended the work to other species, such as guinea pigs, deer, buffalo, and sheep. ("Following like sheep" is now seen as an instance of imprinting.) It has been established that imprinting is a positive approach on the part of newly born animal infants either seeking proximity and or following the first animate object seen. A great variety of information on a variety of species, some of it anecdotal in nature, has made its appearance. Lorenz (1955) tells of a human imprinted male bittern in a zoo who would chase his mate from the nest when the zoo director appeared and show by his actions that he expected the director to sit on the nest with him to incubate the eggs!

After this naturalistic phase, more precise work followed. The carefully controlled work of Eckhard H. Hess (1959a, b) is outstanding. With suitable apparatus controls, a duckling is placed on a circular runway behind a movable model of a male duck wired so as to emit a sound, an arbitrarily chosen human rendition of "gock, gock, gock" occurring all the while the duckling is in the apparatus.

The procedure consists of two parts. First there is imprinting itself, usually taking less than an hour, during which time the newly born duckling is exposed to the moving and sounding male duck model which it tends to follow. At a later time a test series is given during which the duckling is released from a box midway between two duck models placed four feet apart. In one test the stationary male model used for imprinting was paired while emitting his "gock" call with a stationary model bearing female markings and emitting the real mallard female call to her young. Other paired test conditions included both models stationary; a silent, stationary male and a stationary, calling female; and a stationary, silent male and a moving, calling female. If the duckling made positive response to the male model under all conditions, imprinting was considered complete (100%) and correspondingly less if the duckling failed under one or more conditions.

In the study by Harlow, we noted that the appearance of a new face on a surrogate mother led to considerable anguish on the part of a monkey infant. Her reaction suggests that imprinting plays a significant part in the early lives of monkeys. A study by Green and Gordon (1964) with young monkeys also shows the importance of early visual experiences. They separated infant monkeys temporarily from their mothers and placed them in chambers whose single window could be opened by pressing a bar. Previous experience with infant monkeys had shown that they quickly learn how to operate the device and do so repeatedly for the reward of looking briefly through the window into the next room, even though it may be empty. In Green and Gordon's experiment, there were two bars and two windows, each looking out into different rooms. This arrangement enabled the researchers to determine the relative preference of the infants for various types of stimuli. Results showed that when anything was placed in one of the rooms, the infants chose that room over the empty room, preferring to look at something rather than nothing. The stimulus that evoked the greatest amount of bar pressing, however, was an adult female monkey. The infants worked harder to see this "mother figure" than they did for views of food, other infants, or plastic forms.

To return to ducklings, imprinting is most effective if it takes place 13 to 16 hours after hatching. This seems to be the critical period for its occurrence. In other words, if imprinting does not take place within a circumscribed period, differing from species to species and animal to animal, it fails to appear. In the duckling, decrement in imprinting after 16 hours has been attributed by Hess to fear of new objects, a response seen at this age for the first time. Onset of fear seems to signal the end of imprinting, suggesting that in the human species maximum imprinting should occur before five-and-a-half months, since that is the age of onset of fear. He does caution that imprinting in the human infant is certainly more complicated than this suggestion might seem to imply.

Gray (1958) interprets "human imprinting" as a disposition directed toward attachment to the parent, shown by smiling. Functional equivalence of smiling in human beings and following in lower animals is postulated, and therefore something resembling imprinting is considered to have taken place. Gewirtz (1961b), on the other hand, interprets imprinting as an instance of especially rapid, efficient, instrumental learning. Smiling then becomes one, but only one, among the responses that make for attachment. Any responses (reaching, talking, even crying) which enable contact with another individual would be instances of imprinting. All cause the mother figure's behavior to be continued and maintained.

The rapidity with which imprinting takes place and its relative insusceptibility to ex-

tinction characterizes the process. Massed trials seem to be more effective than spaced trials, and primacy more effective than recency. It is different from conditioning in these respects where the reverse of these characteristics hold, as Gray points out. There is no evidence for the immediate formation of attachment a certain number of hours after birth. Nevertheless, imprinting in the future may be shown to play a part, even an important part, in the process of human socialization.

Effect of Mother Substitutes

Although Gray (1958) has made a case for imprinting in the human infant, evidence is lacking so far that imprinting actually occurs in the same way that it does in the lower animals. The question as to whether changes from one mother figure to another have a disturbing effect has been explored to some extent. The collective Israeli farm settlements, or *kibbutzim,* are a natural laboratory for investigation of this problem. Here the prevailing social structure calls for care not only from the working mother but also from the caretaker or *metapalet,* who has charge of the infant while the mother works (Rabin, 1965).

Comparison with control children from ordinary Israeli villages showed that although there was relative intellectual retardation of the kibbutz-reared infants, it was not observed among children 9 to 11 years of age who had been originally reared in *kibbutzim.* Instead, there was clear superiority both in intelligence and in social and emotional maturity. The environment of a *kibbutz* is both warm and stimulating. Despite the discontinuity of her presence, the child is not deprived of his mother who sees him at regular intervals. He does not experience anything resembling the deprivation of the infant in an institution with a large caretaker-infant ratio.

During infancy, it is the child's caretaker who is the major influence in his psycho-social environment

Conventionally, we think of this source of influence as being the mother, but often overlook the fact that caretaking is often shared by: fathers, siblings, relatives, and workers in various kinds of child-care centers.

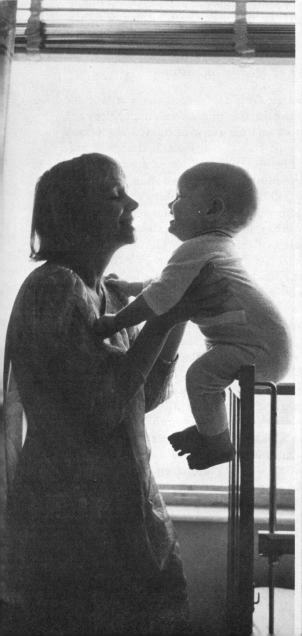

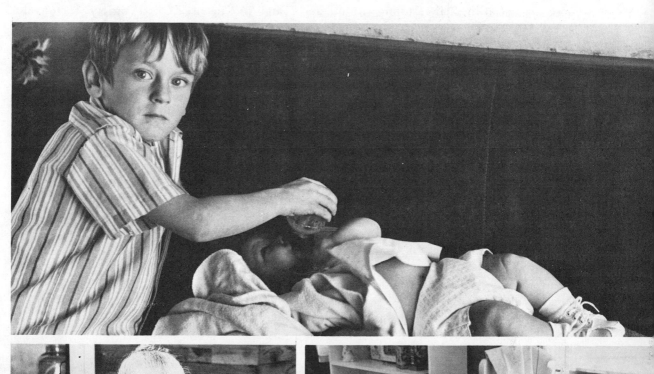

In reviewing research dealing with communal raising of children, Robert A. LeVine (1970) commented that the evidence regarding the effects of the *kibbutz* experience on children's psychological characteristics is conflicting. Although it is fairly clear that the children are within the normal ranges of mental health and intelligence, they also seem to be more superficial in their relations with others, more other-directed with respect to their peers, and better suited to army life in adulthood, in contrast to children raised under more usual circumstances, although observers are not in agreement on these latter points.

Another form of noncontinuous mothering is created by college courses in home management wherein the class members in rotation share in the care of infants for a few days at a time. Taking advantage of this setting, one study involved three groups of infants 24 months of age: (*a*) home-management course infants for their first four months who were then adopted; (*b*) foster home children on a boarding arrangement for the same length of time prior to being adopted; and (*c*) a control group living with their parents the entire time. In addition to an array of psychological tests given at frequent intervals, each infant was placed in two controlled stress situations; the first consisted of trying to place wooden pegs into circular openings that were actually too small to contain them ("peg-frustration") and the second, occurring immediately thereafter, left him alone in the testing room into which a stranger came a few moments later ("stranger-relationship"). The reports of their behavior in these situations were supplied for ratings of frustration and stress to judges who did not know into which of the three groups a given infant fell. There was no clear evidence of effects from either stress situations or from the tests which could be associated with early residence in the home management course group, despite the wide differences

from infant to infant in all of the groups (Gardner, Pease, and Hawkes, 1961).

In another study a group of children aged 8 to 17 who had lived in a college home-management house during infancy and had subsequently been adopted were paired with children from the same communities and school classes and matched individually on sex, age, and intelligence. On a variety of tests for school achievement, personal adjustment, anxiety level, and responses to frustration, no significant differences between the groups were obtained. Investigators concluded that on none of these characteristics could differences be attributed to discontinuity of mothering in infancy (Gardner, Hawkes, and Burchinal, 1961).

Another pattern of discontinuity of mother-infant interaction contrasts families in which mothering is provided by one person, the mother (monomatric), with that by more than one person, such as older sisters, grandmothers, hired caretakers in their own or other homes (polymatric). The investigators collected information by both interview and observation and found only slight differences between the two groups of infants. These differences were consistent with the interpretation that those infants raised by one adult found it easier to relate to other people and were more comfortable in strange surroundings. Developmental data, such as obtained from the Cattell Infant Intelligence Scale, yielded no significant differences. There was no suggestion that infants raised by more than one mother figure were handicapped by this particular experience (Caldwell et al., 1963).

From these various studies it would appear that multiple discontinuous adult care per se is not damaging to the infant although personality differences have been found between monomatric and polymatric infants.

Communal infant rearing is rare among subhuman animals, where attachment to a single mother is the general rule. In some species of mice, however, females may combine their young in a communal nest, which they may share for several consecutive litters, even including the litters of their daughters. Pregnant mice housed in the same cage may build one nest, combine their litters after birth, and nurse them simultaneously, often taking turns at feeding all the pups in the commune. Sayler and Salmon (1969) conducted a controlled longitudinal study of a number of mice litters, in which single mothers nesting alone raised 7 or 14 pups, groups of two mothers nesting communally raised 14 pups, and groups of three mothers nesting communally raised 14 or 21 pups. Results showed, as might be expected, that a low pup-to-mother ratio produced faster growth and higher body weights, presumably because of the greater availability of milk. When the pup-to-mother ratio was held constant, however, the communal pups made proportionately greater gains, as compared with those raised in single-mother nests, and three-mother communes produced better results than two-mother communes.

The authors speculated that the superiority of the communal condition could be attributed to more efficient nursing, greater warmth, and more tactile stimulation. It is difficult to say, of course, how much of the growth advantage can be assigned to each of these variables, but the similarity between the results of this study and those of early stimulation is obvious. As such, Sayler and Salmon's research adds an interesting footnote to the studies of human infants reared monomatrically and polymatrically. In view of the recent interest in communal living arrangements among young adults, we can expect additional research on the effects of communal living and infant care on the development of children. Problems of instituting adequate controls are always difficult in such studies, but each one adds something to our understanding of the effects of social stimulation on infants and young children.

Mothers and Mother Substitutes as Motivators. Before we leave the topic of maternal influence during infancy, it may be well to consider one more animal study that has interesting if puzzling implications.

Different breeds of the same or similar animal often behave differently under similar circumstances. Beagles are ordinarily less active than terriers; when terriers have been kept in isolation, they become more active when released, whereas beagles become less so. (Fuller, 1967) Wild Norway rats tend to be quite aggressive, but laboratory rats are tame, placid, and docile. Laboratory mice, on the other hand, will characteristically fight when placed in a box together. This is species-specific behavior and is usually thought to be instinctive or innate.

Victor H. Denenberg (1971) conducted an interesting series of experiments in which mice pups were raised by laboratory rat mothers. Experience has shown that rat mothers treat foster mice pups appropriately and even tenderly, nursing them, grooming them, and retrieving them when they fall out of the nest. What is of great interest here, however, is that pairs of inbred mice, when raised by a rat mother do *not* fight when placed in a box. Evidently, something happens during their infancy that extinguishes their normal fighting tendencies. That "something" is not the difference in mice and rat milk, for mice pups raised by rat "aunts," whose nipples had been surgically removed, were also likely to refrain from fighting, even when they had been raised with other mice "siblings."

This effect apparently applies only to *inbred* laboratory mice and does not obtain with Swiss albino mice, whose fighting tendencies are undiminished by experience with rat foster mothers or aunts. Another mouse tendency, however, was affected by foster care. Mice show a great deal more open-field activity—running around, exploring, etc.—than do laboratory rats. When the amount of open-field activity was taken as a dependent variable, both inbred and Swiss albino mice who had been reared by rat mothers or aunts showed less activity. The lower activity level was also positively correlated with lower levels of corticosterone in the blood plasma of the experimental animals. Corticosterone is released by the cortex of the adrenal gland. Its level in the blood may be taken as an index of emotional reactivity. In other words, both the overt behavior and the blood chemistry of the experimental animals were evidently modified by their experience as pups.

Denenberg confessed that he was surprised at the results he obtained and commented:

"Even though I am a firm believer in motherhood, I must admit that when we started this set of experiments I did not expect to find that the mother's behavior during the nursing period would have such a powerful effect upon so many different biobehavioral systems of the animal. Clearly, if these results have any degree of generality to other mammals, the subtle and not so subtle behavior patterns of the mother during the early stages of the neonate's development have very profound and far-reaching effects" (p. 91).

Summary

The influence that mothers and mother figures have on infants can be separated into stimulation effects, love or attention effects, and teaching relationships. Stimulation is the most general category, and love and attention are really a specific kind of stimulation. All organisms require some stimulation. As we move up the phylogenetic scale, the kind of stimuli that organisms can respond to, and actually seek to respond to, become increasingly varied and complex. Although an overload of stimulation can be stressful, there is evidence that prolonged subjection to an unstimulating environment is detrimental to a number of psychological functions. A large number of animal studies have lent experimental support to this contention. Levine showed that rat pups developed more rapidly when handled regularly. The same results have been reported for kittens. The handled kittens also showed superior performance in solving maze problems. Rats raised in an enriched environment have been shown to have a more highly developed cerebral cortex. Surprisingly enough, even the progeny of such rats have larger brains. Microencephalic rats normally suffer a reduction of problem-solving ability. However, when such rats are raised in stimulus enriched environments, they virtually "catch up" with normal rats. Stimulus enrichment, in the form of visual freedom, also helped monkeys that were raised under physical restraint acquire normal motor skills.

These findings appear to be consistent with what can be observed in human infants. Neonates given four days of enrichment stimulation keep their eyes fixed on a visual target for longer periods of time. Although it is relatively easy to institute a regimen of stimulus enrichment in infancy, just what determines "stimulus deprivation" is difficult to determine. Dennis and Dennis tried to raise a pair of twins under "minimal social stimulation." Evidently the little social stimulation the twins did receive was sufficient for normal development to occur. Because moral considerations prevent experimenters from subjecting infants to truly severe deprivation conditions, most studies make use of preexisting circumstances. Rheingold for example, gave increased "mothering" to institutionalized infants. After eight weeks of treatment, the infants were more socially responsive both to her and to another person, and made higher scores on the Cattell Infant Scale, postural tests, and cube manipulation. Retarded children have also shown significant gains when given the intellectual stimulation of an experimental nursery school. Dennis and his associates conducted a longitudinal study of children in a Lebanese orphanage. Although the children generally scored considerably below average on IQ tests, those who were adopted younger suffered a smaller decrement.

The question that arises in connection with Dennis' study of adopted children is whether the increase in IQ is due simply to increased stimulation, or to the "tender, loving care" of a mother. Breast-feeding is perhaps the most intimate interaction between mother and infant. For this reason a number of researchers have explored the relationship of feeding practices to later psychological development. Unfortunately, their findings have turned out to be contradictory, at least as far as specific practices are concerned. It appears that general maternal characteristics are much more important than whether the infant is breast- or bottle-fed. A study by Behrens confirms this supposition. She found that specific practices of toilet training, weaning, and nursing were not correlated with the child's later emotional adjustment, but that global scores of maternal attitudes could predict later adjustment.

Among child psychologists, a controversy has continued for some years as to whether infants can be emotionally crippled by being separated from their mothers and, if so, at what age the separation has its most significant effects. A study of Scottish infants revealed that separation anxiety begins about midway through the first year, and reaches a maximum some time before the end of the year. According to Erikson, the experience of being cared for on an "unconditional-acceptance" basis is essential if the infant is to develop the attitude of *basic trust*. Partial deprivation refers to those children who are separated from their mothers after establishing a satisfying relationship during the first six months of life. Spitz believed that this resulted in a condition called *anaclitic depression*. A condition called *marasmus* is said to develop from total maternal deprivation. Both conditions are characterized by developmental retardation. A number of studies, especially of the infants evacuated from London during World War II, reported that children raised in normal homes suffered fewer personality difficulties. More recently, however, reviewers have uncovered an overwhelming number of methodological errors in this research, and in the original work by Spitz. Because institutionalized children often lack more than "just mothering," it is difficult to charge their inadequacies to this factor alone.

Some support for Spitz' contentions have come from studies of maternal deprivation in monkeys. Hinde and Spencer-Booth found that monkey infants separated from their mothers for a few days and then reunited showed depressed locomotor and play activity, a condition that was evident even two years later. Kaufman and Rosenblum separated four infant macaque monkeys from their mothers for a four-week period and reunited them. At the beginning of the separation period, the infants behaved in a very agitated manner. This was followed by a phase of deep depression which gradually lifted. When the mother was returned to the cage, clinging behavior increased dramatically. Harry Harlow's classic experiments with infant monkeys lend credence to the suggestion that some of the effects of maternal deprivation are the result of sensory deprivation. Harlow provided two kinds of surrogate mothers for his infants. One "mother" was made of wire and the other of padded terry cloth. The infants seemed to gain emotional security from their contact with the cloth mother, even though the wire mother was their source of milk. Harlow concluded that the stimulation obtained from the cloth mother was innately satisfying, and led to emotional attachment to it. From infant reactions to physical changes in their "mothers," Harlow also concluded that the infant responds to the earliest mother he encounters.

In *imprinting*, a gosling literally does respond only to the earliest mother he encounters. Lorenz, a European naturalist, was one of the first to investigate this phenomenon. He divided a clutch of eggs laid by a goose into two groups. He left one group with the mother and hatched the other in an incubator. The goslings hatched by the mother immediately followed her; the incubator-raised goslings saw Lorenz only, and followed him. When both groups were intermingled, with the mother and Lorenz present, each group headed for their respective "parent." Further experimentation has established that imprinting can occur with almost any kind of animate object as long as it is present during the critical period. In ducks, for instance, this period occurs 13 to 16 hours after hatching. As suggested by the Harlow study, imprinting may play a role in the early lives of monkeys. A study by Green and Gordon, in which infant monkeys worked harder for views of adult female monkeys than they did for views of a number of other alternate subjects, shows the importance of early visual experiences.

Although Gray has made a case for imprinting in the human infant, evidence is lacking so far that imprinting actually occurs in the same way it does in the lower animals.

Kibbutzim provide a natural laboratory to study the effects of the communal raising of children. Children raised on a kibbutz have been observed to be superior to children raised in ordinary Israeli villages both in intelligence and in social and emotional maturity. LeVine notes that they also seem to be more superficial in their relations with others, and more other-directed with respect to their peers. Studies of home-management house infants confirm these general findings. It appears that multiple discontinuous adult care per se is not damaging to the infant, although personality differences have been found between monomatric and polymatric infants. Research with species of mice that practice communal raising of litters reveals that multiple mothers produce faster growth and higher body weights among the pups, even when the pup-to-mother ratio is held constant. Other research with laboratory mice has found that certain behavioral tendencies thought to be innate—fighting and open-field activity—are significantly weaker when mice pups are reared by laboratory rat foster mothers. The fact that laboratory rats are much more placid than mice suggests that some of the foster mothers' behavior pattern had been transmitted to the mice when they were pups. The transmission was so effective that even the blood chemistry of the mice was affected by their contact with the foster mother.

9 Personality Development in Infancy

Having reviewed the infant's behavior in the perspective of maternal influences, we now examine it as it is expressed in certain behavior tendencies, self and social awareness, and relationship to peers.

Behavioral Tendencies

Dependency

The degree to which infants are attracted to and attached to their mothers is shown by an experiment by Smith, Zwerg, and Smith (1963), who placed infants in a playpen in such a way that each infant could see his mother, a stranger, or a neutral stimulus on a television screen. The playpen revolved slowly, so that the infant could, by crawling, keep the image in view. Results showed that infants between 10 and 20 months of age would spend about 35 seconds of a one-minute experimental period crawling to keep in visual contact with the image of the mother, in contrast to about 30 seconds for a stranger, and 15 seconds in a control condition. Infants between 22 and 26 months however, spent 52 seconds in visual contact with the mother image, 45 seconds with the stranger, with the control contact at 16 seconds. With infants older than 26 months, the orienting behavior toward the mother continued to increase, whereas the interest in the stranger dropped off somewhat. The experimenters also noted that the sharp increase in attempting to keep in contact that occurred between 22 and 26 months, coincided with the age at which crying at environmental changes reaches a peak.

In some respects, this study resembles that of Green and Gordon (1964), mentioned in the foregoing chapter, in which macaque infants worked harder at bar pressing in order to see a mother figure than they did to view their peers or other visual presentations. In Harlow's (1958) study, too, monkey infants worked harder to view their "cloth mother," and were no more interested in seeing their "wire mother" than they were in looking into an empty room. Their emotional attachment to the cloth mother also showed in other ways. It will be remembered that when the cloth mother was not present, and infant monkeys were confronted by strange surroundings or objects, they showed pronounced fear. When "she" was present, they fled to her protection and comfort, getting over their fears so quickly that they soon could leave her and explore the feared object.

The human infant during the second year of life also becomes fearful and anxious when the mother leaves him temporarily. Arsenian (1943) noted that infants and young children placed in a strange room without their mothers showed anxiety; those whose mothers were present played adaptively. The mother's presence produced security; her absence evoked anxiety, thus indicating the infant's dependency upon her. The infant learns to be dependent on the mother and expresses this dependence by showing anxiety when she is not present.

One aspect of dependence is a tendency to rely on the help of others in striving to reach one's goals. Or to put it another way, dependence is the tendency to seek nurturance—attention, care, and support from other people. Dependent behavior has its beginning in infancy: each infant must be dependent because of his helplessness. He may be, as the psychoanalysts say, in the period of infantile omnipotence, but he is learning to be dependent, not all-powerful. He is not born with a need for dependency: helplessness thrusts dependence on him.

The mother is the agent for meeting his needs despite his helplessness. His mother satisfies his needs and, in operant conditioning terms, becomes a source of reinforcement. She is the configuration or pattern of stimuli that is consistently associated with the reduction of his needs—she feeds him when he is hungry, changes him when he is wet, and warms him when he is cold. He learns to be dependent on her as the instrument for meeting his needs. This aspect of dependence occurs when the infant learns to seek help from others. He is learning, to use a term of Glen Heathers' (1955), *instrumental* dependence. The goal here is *help*.

There is another aspect of dependence— *emotional* dependence. This may be illustrated by considering what happens after instrumental dependent tendencies have begun to be learned. After the first few days or weeks it is observed that an infant will cease crying when picked up *before* he is relieved of his hunger or other discomfort. His mother's mere presence has acquired reward value for him. The goal here is *relationship*. Her comforting presence has become a secondary drive in itself.

The infant not only learns to discriminate among persons but he also shows differential reactions to them. One facet of his differential behavior toward persons can be referred to as affectionate behavior. (The other facet, hostile behavior, will be described in connection with aggressive tendencies.) He learns to find pleasurable responses in his relations with others, to have affection for various people, and to wish to be near them. What are the antecedents of this affectionate behavior? It may have a sexual component, and probably has a tactile component, as we have seen from the study of Harlow, but the greatest stress can be placed on emotional dependence. The mother's presence has acquired reward value. The infant reacts with affection because of emotional dependent tendencies.

Katherine M. Banham (1950) observed the development of affectionate behavior in 900 infants between four weeks and two years of age. These observations were made incidental to the giving of intelligence tests and, consequently, she reports in an anecdotal, qualitative fashion.

The infant's affectionate behavior is first shown at about four months by outgoing strivings and approach—his smiling gaze fixed on the person's face. He waves his arms and tries to rise from the crib. Without coordination or too much success, he strives to get closer to the attractive person. At about six months, he reaches out to pat the person. This is roughly the same age as when he begins to discriminate between persons. This is also the age when he responds to affectionate cuddling. As memory develops, so, too, does anticipation. Toward the end of the first year he shows anticipation of the mother coming for feeding, and laughs, squirms, and wiggles with delight on her approach, anticipating pleasurable stimulation. Some infants enjoy being cuddled, but others do not and will squirm and wriggle to avoid hugs and kisses. Schaffer and Emerson (1964a) noted this tendency in their study of babies of Scottish working-class mothers. Of the 14 girls in their study, 11 were cuddlers; of the 14 boys, 8 were cuddlers. The difference is not statistically significant, but it is consistent with the observed tendency of boys to be more active and girls to respond favorably to social interaction of all kinds.

Independence Strivings. Almost as fast as the infant learns to seek help, he learns to get along without it. Independence becomes an end in itself. Rheingold and Eckerman (1970) note that as soon as the infant is able to move, he begins to separate himself from his mother. At first, he does so by inching along on his belly.

"Later he creeps, and then walks away from his mother. He goes out the door and enters another room. In time he walks out of the house, plays in the yard all morning, goes to school, goes still farther away to high school, then to college and to work. He crosses the country, and now he may even go to the moon. Eventually he sets up his own home and produces infants who, in turn, repeat the process" (p. 78).

Rheingold and Eckerman point out that the infant's separation from his mother is of great psychological importance, because it greatly widens his opportunities to interact with the environment. As long as he is in physical contact with his mother, his universe is limited to her person and the adjoining environment. There are limits to what even the most attentive and indulgent mother can bring to an infant. Even when he is carried about, his contacts with the environment are severely limited. Hence the universe can only be explored and understood if the infant becomes separated from the mother.

It makes considerable difference whether the separation is done voluntarily or not. As we noted previously, human infants who are separated from their mothers after the age of six months or so express fear or resentment, and infant monkeys go into a stage of restlessness and random hyperactivity, followed by depression. Infants, whether they are human or monkey, can enjoy separation from their mothers only if they initiate it and if they are free to return at any moment. When monkey infants leave their mothers, the mothers at first make repeated attempts to retrieve them, but yield after a few weeks. Human mothers

Patterns of dependence and independence

Infants are functionally and absolutely dependent on their mothers, but it is a relation-ship that normally both enjoy. The fact that the infant feels secure in his mother's presence gives him the courage to respond to motives to be independent.

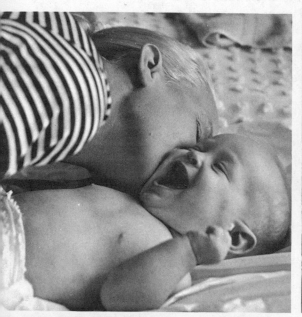
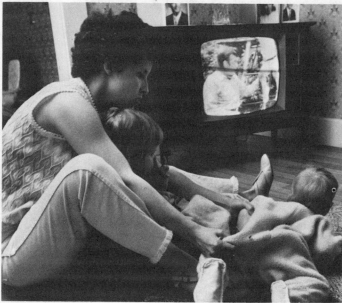

Escaping from one's mother would not be so much fun, if one were not free to return at will. Independence is fostered, too, by the freedom to explore in sheltered situations. In cultures where mothers carry their infants with them at all times, independence strivings tend to be discouraged.

make little attempt to retrieve infants, as long as they are not engaging in activities that are dangerous or injurious.[1]

Rheingold and Eckerman set up a number of experimental situations in which mothers and their ten-month-old infants were placed in one of two adjoining rooms. About two-thirds of the infants were in a crawling stage and, of the remaining third, half could scoot on their bellies and the other half were already toddling. The experimental manipulations consisted of placing one or more toys in the adjoining room which was connected to the first room by an open door, through which an infant could see his mother, should he decide to explore the second room. Even when there were no toys in the second room, infants spent about a third of the ten-minute observation period in it. When a toy was placed in the second room, the infants spent a little more time in it, often bringing the toy back to the first room. Infants who visited the second room did not stay there, but instead went back and forth, as though testing the situation and trying their freedom.

In the next phase of the experiment, infants who had participated in the first phase without the toy were now retested with a toy in the adjoining room. The familiarity of the experimental environment was evidently reassuring, because they now spent considerably less time with their mothers and about half of the ten-minute observation period in the second room. Those infants who had experience with the toy in the first observation did not increase their time in the second room on the second trial when one toy was present, but did increase it considerably when three toys were available.

The results were consistent with the idea that infants are attracted by novelty and seek to maximize their stimulation, at least under conditions where they can maintain visual contact with their mothers and feel free to return to them at any time.

In his second year, the infant is able to move about. In doing so, he shows the overwhelming importance of independence. He is enthusiastically everywhere and on his own as much as possible. He walks, climbs, jumps, and trots; he pushes his stroller instead of riding in it; he carries things, wants to put on and take off his own clothes. Most of the time he does what he is told, but may nevertheless show his dawning independence in saying, "no," "no," to anything and everything persistently and vehemently. This tendency toward independence is also brought out when we reconsider the evidence about the emergence of self during infancy. The infant has the sense of being a person, a bit fuzzy as to the boundaries of the self, to be sure, but he is a person for all that and *he* wants what *he* wants when *he* wants it. It will be found that one of the factors making for the emergence of the self is the oppositional quality of many of the infant's activities. In emerging as a person, he wants to be independent. In addition to protesting against help, there is the obvious pride he takes in doing something on his very own, which also points to independence tendencies.

But in all of this pushing out into the world, in his seeking of independence, there

[1] We must qualify this statement as applying primarily to Western, and particularly to the North American, cultures, in which infants and children are encouraged to behave and act in independent ways. In many Asian and Mediterranean cultures, independence is discouraged, or at least is not encouraged. Sibling caretakers in these cultures often act as extensions of their mothers in encouraging dependence and punishing independence. The underlying motive, however, is not necessarily one of wanting the infant's dependence for its own sake, but is an expression of the prevailing attitude that regards the world as generally hazardous and heartless, an attitude that may be fairly realistic.

is vacillation. The infant takes two steps forward and one step backward, sometimes literally. Off on some gallant adventure, but just out of mother's sight, he bursts into tears and flees back.

Frustration and Dependency. Intruding then, upon the idyllic scene so far sketched is the fact that there is discomfort and pain in the life of the infant, too. He becomes hungry or experiences a pain of one sort or another. The mother is not always there at the instant he wants help. Frustration results. The process is very well illustrated by J. W. M Whiting (1948) in discussing frustration in a primitive group, the Kwoma of New Guinea. Whiting observed that Kwoma infants are cared for by their mothers almost exclusively. During the first three years or so, the Kwoma infant sits in his mother's lap by day and lies by her side at night. During this period, it is the mother's duty to care for all the needs of her child. When frustration does occur, in spite of this constant care, the child cries and the mother does her best to comfort him—with food, if he is hungry; by warming him, if he is cold; by soothing him, if he is ill or in pain. In effect, the Kwoma mother rewards crying as a response to frustration. When the child begins to talk, toward the end of infancy, he asks for help when frustrated, and the mother satisfies his request if it is possible for her to do so. "Thus during infancy a frustration-dependence sequence is established" (p. 138).

This picture is quite different from that of the middle-class Western world, in which a child is expected to show increasing independence in caring for himself and solving his own problems to the best of his ability.

Determinants of Dependence Tendencies. A variety of reasons have led psychologists to postulate that a relation would be found between the severity of frustrations in infancy and later magnitude of dependence tenden-

cies infants exhibited. Although the dependence tendencies under consideration are those learned in infancy, their effects are apt to be more evident when the child is somewhat older, that is, when he is of preschool age or older.

Some early research by Sears and his associates (1953) noted a positive relationship between tendencies of children to behave dependently in nursery school and severity of weaning during infancy. Girls who were on rigid feeding schedules during infancy also tended to be more dependent. Contrary to what might have been expected, however, the investigators found no relationship between dependency tendencies and the severity of toilet training the children had experienced as infants. We will refer to this study from time to time as the "antecedent" study.

A few years later, Sears, Maccoby, and Levin (1957) conducted a survey of patterns of child-rearing practices, a study we will refer to in the future as the "pattern" study. We will describe it in some detail at this point.

The mothers studied were chosen from those living in two suburbs of a large metropolitan area in New England. One suburb was primarily residential and the occupants were mostly of middle-class occupational level, whereas the other suburb contained considerable heavy industry with the population mostly working-class people. Eight schools supplied the sample. Standardized interviews were conducted by ten trained women interviewers with nearly 400 mothers of five-year-olds. These interviews were recorded for later analysis. Information about both mother and child was secured. The investigators chose to describe various dimensions which will be referred to as they become relevant in the topics considered here. These were based on interview schedules or rating scales. Analysis of the interviews was made to decide on the ratings to be given and ratings made by ten advanced graduate students. Each interview was rated independently to test the reliability of rating. Final scores were on pooled judgments of the two raters. Dimensions concerning the mother had to do with (1) her disciplinary technique; (2) her permissiveness; (3) her severity in applying techniques; (4) her temperamental qualities; and (5) her positive inculation of more mature behavior in her child. We are at present concerned with their findings on dependency in infancy.

In the antecedent study, Sears and his associates found that severe weaning practices in infancy were associated with dependent patterns of behavior during the preschool years. Furthermore, dependent behavior in preschool girls was also related to mothers' insistence on rigid feedings schedules during infancy. The Sears pattern study, however, did not confirm the results of the earlier antecedent study. Either negative or even diametrically opposite results were found. No general connection between severity of weaning and dependency could be elicited. Instead of girls showing a relationship of scheduling and dependency, none was found, but boys fed on self-demand (nonrigid) scheduling were more dependent.

The contradiction between the findings of these other two studies is not surprising. Seymour Feshbach (1970) concluded, in a review of research related to childhood aggression, that studies relating weaning and toilet training experiences to later patterns of behavior produce only weak and conflicting findings and he cautioned against attempts to relate this or that specific type of child-rearing behavior to later outcomes. What seems to be more important is the mother's *general attitude* toward the child. In the Sears' "pattern" study, for example, it did not seem to matter whether the toilet training was severe or mild, as long as the mother was rated high on warmth. When the mother was rated as rela-

tively cold, however, severity of toilet training did make a difference.

Aggressive Tendencies

It will be remembered that Bridges (1932), in exploring the emotional process in infancy, found that both undifferentiated and ill-defined positive *and* negative feelings were prominent. As the infants grew older, they gave way to the emergence of focused positive and negative feelings directed toward specific persons.

Important in aggression are anger responses —the vigorous reactions of crying, hitting, screaming, thrashing, and striking out—described in Chapter 6. Constitutional and hereditary factors seem to give us such responses to restraint and to discomfort. Frustration was found to be an antecedent of anger; anger comes about when the infant is frustrated. The frustrating character of weaning and cleanliness training can hardly be doubted.

Florence L. Goodenough (1931) asked 45 mothers of children between the ages of seven months and eight years to record all expressions of anger over a one-month period. When she analyzed the reports, she found that about one-fourth of the outbursts for children less than a year of age occurred in connection with routine child care—dressing, bathing, putting the infant in his crib, and the like. Another fourth were caused by minor physical discomforts. By two years, the establishment of routines, such as toilet training, was the most frequent cause of anger outbursts, followed by clashes with parental authority over other matters.

It is clear from this that the socialization of the infant leads to restrictions in his freedom that he finds frustrating and to which he reacts in a direct way. During this period, too, children resort to tantrums—outbursts of rage expressed through kicking, screaming, rolling on the floor, holding the breath, and so forth. Goodenough found that disagreements with playmates were only a minor source of anger. Parents attempted to deal with these displays of temper by ignoring, spanking or slapping, distracting, coaxing, and removing the source of irritation. Yielding or giving in to the child's demands led to more frequent outbursts of anger, showing the effect of reinforcement. When anger responses were reinforced, they led to aggressive tendencies—to what Sears and his associates (1953) refer to as instrumental aggression—hurting someone to obtain some goal.

At first, the aggression is more or less crude striking out, but with age the child becomes more skilled and more sophisticated. He discovers that he can injure others by hitting or biting them and he also learns other aggressive techniques in dealing with his parents: noncooperation, turning his head away when asked for a kiss, making his body stiff when clothing is being removed, and the like. None of these involve striking out at others, but are aggressive in a passive way.

In middle-class homes, aggression and any expression of anger are likely to be discouraged. Parents serve as models for their child in keeping their temper reined in, speaking in a low tone, and the like. They do not always succeed in this, and when they do become angry, they are likely to feel guilty afterward. How much of this is communicated to the infant is conjectural, but it is important to note that the feeling tone of the middle-class home is concerned with dampening down and subduing anger and aggression. We shall have more to say on this topic in connection with development in the preschool years and in the later stages of childhood.

Fear and Anxiety. Like aggression and anger, fear and anxiety are responses to perceived threats. Whereas anger and aggression lead to an "against" response, the reaction in fear and anxiety is "away from" the source of stimulation. Fear is a more intense, agitated reaction to pain, danger (being dropped, for example), or shock (hearing a sudden loud noise). Anxiety is a more diffuse and attenuated response to a feeling of insecurity, loss, or deprivation. After infancy, it becomes more associated with anticipated events and with interpersonal problems as well.

Benjamin (1963), a psychoanalytically oriented writer, speculated that anxiety, as expressed through irritability toward the end of the neonatal period, may be due either to the mother's overstimulating the infant or her inability to quiet him and reduce his tension. Tension also appears in a number of "threat experiences" during infancy. Gesell and Thompson (1934) reported that more than half the infants they observed responded with "sobering" to strangers as early as four months and that there was a peak of withdrawal from strangers between eight and eleven months. Morgan and Ricciuti (1963) do not interpret this sober examination of strangers as necessarily a sign of fear. It may, however, involve some apprehensiveness and tension and as such may be one of the earlier indicators of anxiety.

Tennes and Lempl (1964) did a study to test a hypothesis of Benjamin's that anxiety resulting from seeing strangers and anxiety at being separated from the mother are basically different in character. Anxiety toward strangers expressed itself in behavior characterized by sobering, turning away, visual avoidance, "freezing," fussing, and crying, whereas separation anxiety was expressed by extremes of activity or inactivity—that is, by extremely hard crying or furious anger, or by reduced activity, overwhelming sadness, and mild, fussy

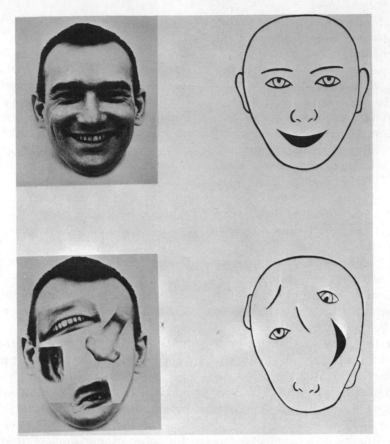

Figure 9-1. Representations of normal and "scrambled" faces used in experiments with infant attention.
(Kagan, 1970. Reproduced by permission.)

protest. Their results showed that stranger anxiety reaches its peak at seven to nine months, whereas separation anxiety is just beginning to appear at eight months and rises to a peak period that usually lasts from 13 to 18 months. They found no sex differences with respect to stranger anxiety, but boys showed more separation anxiety.

Curiosity and Exploratory Tendencies

We have noted that attention to unusual stimuli occurs very early in infancy and that there is an increasing tendency to prefer novel and complex stimuli to the familiar and simple. The "sobering" with which the infant regards the stranger may be on the border between anxiety and curiosity; the unfamiliar face presents the infant with a considerable amount of new information that must be sorted out. Tension and arousal are present as he applies himself to the task.

Schemata, Hypotheses, and Discrepant Stimuli

Jerome Kagan (1970) has done a considerable amount of research on the behavior of infants who are confronted with novel stimuli consisting of photographs and drawings of normal human faces and "scrambled" faces. (See Figure 9-1.) Kagan maintains that children, as they encounter the stimuli of their universe, develop schemata or visual concepts that serve as reference points or models which aid in the understanding of each new confrontation with stimuli. Some time during the second month of life, the amount of attention that an infant will bestow on a stimulus configuration will become related to the extent to which the configuration varies or is discrepant from the schemata he has developed. Kagan's discrepancy principle states that stimuli that vary moderately from a schema receive longer periods of attention than do stimuli that either are familiar or are so different that they appear to have no relationship to the schema. The relationship between discrepancy and attention is therefore a curvilinear one, as indicated schematically in Figure 9-2.

An eight-week-old infant gives approximately equal amount of attention to a three-dimensional representation of a face and an abstract three-dimensional form, but at four months, he spends more time looking at the

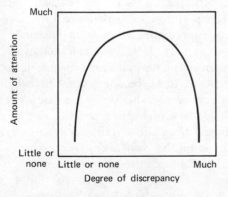

Figure 9-2. Schematic representation of the curvilinear relationship between stimuli's discrepancy relative to an infant's schema and the amount of attention they will evoke from an infant.

face than the abstract form. By now, according to Kagan, the infant has acquired a schema for human faces and rejects the abstraction as being too discrepant from that schema or any other he has developed. When infants this age are shown one of the scrambled faces in Figure 9-1, time spent attending is less than for the picture of the normal face, because the scrambled face is too discrepant.

After six months of age, fixation (attention) times for photographic representations of faces drop by over 50%, because such photographs are not discrepant enough to evoke extended gazing. Kagan has also done similar work with masklike representations of human faces. As with the photographic representations, fixation drops markedly during the second half of the first year. From 12 to 36 months, however, the fixation time increases dramatically. Kagan maintains that this change comes about because of the emergence of a new cognitive *structure* toward the end of the first year of life. This structure, which Kagan terms a *hypothesis*, is different from the schema. Schemata permit a child to recognize a stimulus configuration, but hypotheses enable him to understand and interpret it. Therefore the stimulus that previously got relatively little attention, because it was recognized as familiar, now commands more attention because it is identified as a source of new information. As the child matures, he develops an increasingly greater repertory of hypotheses. The more hypotheses in his repertory, the longer he will work at the task of understanding and the more prolonged will be his attention.

The task of assimilating information from a display of stimuli leads to some arousal, which may be expressed in a variety of ways. As the infant looks at the stimuli, he may vocalize, be quiet, thrash about, or smile. These reactions may also be accompanied by changes in the heart rate, respiration, or electrical impulses from the cerebral cortex of the brain.

After the information has been assimilated, smiling may often occur.

Exploratory Behavior

The attraction of the novel and the complex leads to exploratory behavior as well as fixation. These are activities in which the infant engages for their own sake. One cannot explain such behavior in terms of the usual drive-reduction theory, because such behavior, as we have noted, increases arousal. Instead of seeking to reduce tension, he seeks to increase it. This is also true of the outgoing, exploring activity-seeking, trying-out behavior that we call play. These behavior tendencies are insatiable; when one palls he turns to another play object. This becomes almost all-absorbing. Hunger or the need for elimination are often disregarded unless the infant is reminded by an adult. Of course, this cannot go on indefinitely—he suddenly screams from hunger pangs that have been building up unnoticed, or he has an "accident" and must be changed. He does not get involved in exploratory behavior because of a schedule of reinforcement—he does it because he *enjoys* it.

More systematic observational reports corroborating the presence of exploratory play tendencies are available. Gesell's (1940) normative studies illustrate the appearance of behavior patterns at a given age. Many of them are typical of kinds of behavior under discussion. At one year of age an infant shows gross motor activity, playing with buttons attached to a garment, putting objects in and out of other objects, and reciprocal nursery games, such as "Where is baby?" At 18 months he climbs, moves furniture, plays with pull toys, teddy bears, dolls, pots and pans. At two years he feeds and toilets a doll or a teddy bear, takes them for a ride, plays with sand and water, filling and emptying dishes, and uses little cars and blocks. However, since these are iso-

lated bits of behavior with no information provided about their origin, it cannot be said that they arise independent of more primary drives.

Stott (1961) kept a careful behavior diary of his infant son from birth to 18 months from which he eliminated items bearing a relation to either an organic or a social need. Those individual behaviors remaining, apparently unrelated to any organic or social need, formed the basis of the report. They were classified into five general categories—recognition (looking at the headboard, bending back head to do so); completion (fitting lid on kettle); control (standing in a high chair and shaking until it nearly falls over); exploration (watching movement of adult's feet and hands); effecting change (studying and hand movement). There seemed to be progressive effectiveness in the child's behavior as the child sought new ways of doing things. The observer could see no connection with either organic (primary) or social needs of these behaviors in his own infant. He could, of course, be mistaken. Nevertheless, in Russia, Federov (1951) independently reached the same conclusions as Stott.

Piaget (1951) gives an interpretation of play compatible with considering it a nonreinforced, externally aroused behavior tendency. Play is assimilation for the sake of assimilation, the incorporation of experience for the sake of that experience. Its most primitive beginning stages are seen in accommodation-free sucking movements, without presence of breast or bottle. If there be some question whether this is play or not, this is not the case with the next stage in which prior practice can be distinguished from the activities shown in carrying it on for its own sake. Illustrative is an infant who adopts the habit of throwing back his head to look at objects. At about two months of age he continues to do this "with ever-increasing enjoyment and ever-decreasing interest in the external results."

Piaget observed a seven-month-old infant

who had learned to remove an obstacle in order to secure an object. When this kind of barrier continued to be put before him, the infant would push aside the cardboard and burst into laughter, completely forgetting the toy that was the original incentive for his learning. A still older infant was fond of pretending a piece of cloth was a pillow, or of "eating" paper, laughing aloud as she did so. Here symbolization has emerged as a play activity for the infant. Inadequate stimuli were treated as if they were adequate—as if they were something else.

In the dyadic unit of mother and infant, one aspect of the relationship, the mother, has been emphasized. Now the focus shifts. The child is brought into the foreground, with the mother in the background. Infant social relationships from the perspective of *his* behavior and experience come to the fore. An "infant's-eye" view of this business of infancy is now to be stressed.

The Development of Self- and Social Awareness

The nucleus of self appears to be that which is experienced as "I" or "me," as distinguished from everything else that is "not me." The newborn infant does not have this awareness of "I" and "not I." In addition, there is no awareness of the outside world and, therefore, no self-awareness by which to distinguish himself from that world. The whole world is wet or hungry or cold when he is wet, hungry, or cold. "I" and the "rest of the world" are intermingled.

Conducting research with respect to the development of the self-concept in infancy is difficult. Self-awareness and language facility appear to be interrelated. Inasmuch as linguistic ability in infants is extremely limited, they are understandably hampered in attempting to tell us about their attitudes and feelings

with respect to themselves. A number of theories have been developed, however, to explain the early, virtually prelinguistic beginnings of the self.

The Beginnings of Self-Awareness

The psychoanalytic theory of the ego has already been discussed in Chapter 4. It will be remembered that ego is broader than awareness of self since it also includes carrying on executive functions. At the moment, only awareness will be considered.

The infant at birth has no appreciation of the distinction between world and ego. Libidnal energy is directed upon himself. This state is referred to as primary narcissism, a term derived from the legend of Narcissus, who fell in love with his reflection in a pool. The infant loves himself with supreme egoism because he is unaware of anyone or anything else. Sexual aims are autoerotic, that is, they are concerned with self-love.

The ego of the infant as a sense of self-awareness becomes differentiated when his needs are *not* met. If all of the infant's needs were to be gratified, he would continue to have no sense of ego as differentiated from the world. Anna Freud (1953) offered an explanation in these terms. She maintains that the inner world of the infant at birth consists essentially of the contrasting feelings of pleasure and pain. Pain arises under the impact of bodily needs from within or irritations from without; pleasure comes when the needs are satisfied or the irritants removed. The contrasting nature of frustration and gratification leads to the beginning of the ego.

True, under the ministrations of the mother, the painful tendencies of the infant give way to relief. But his needs are not always met immediately. For example, when feeding is delayed, the inability to summon the breast or bottle immediately helps the infant to differentiate self from nonself. The mother's failure to meet his needs and the inevitable delays in ministering to his wants lead to his growing recognition of "I" and "not I." Awareness comes that for his needs to be met, to have his tensions reduced, something must be done by "mother." Thus, awareness of the mother's presence comes when she is not there! This leads to his losing the sense of omnipotence and the recognition of his dependence on others. He begins to realize that "others" must do something before his needs can be met.

The Beginnings of Social Awareness

There is social awareness, too, in the beginnings of ego development as indicated in discussing the "separation" of child and mother. The quality attributed to this other person is also produced in emerging social awareness. Taking feeding as central to this stage, what happens when the infant is fed? If the mother fondles him, is gentle in the process, helps him learn to suck, his first adjustment to what, as ego-awareness continues, is his first perception of another person is experienced as good. Consequently, he expects other people to be friendly as well. To use the phraseology of Erikson (1963), a sense of trust is developed. But what if the mother is unfriendly and rough, forcing the bottle or breast? The infant does not "think" of her as an enemy; his mental processes are not yet developed to this extent. But he does react with fear, tension, and psychosomatic upsets, such as inability to suck, vomiting, and random bodily movements. The little world for him, which is the here-and-now of the mother-child interaction, is bad and hateful in the primitive beginnings of these terms.

Piaget makes no particular systematic use of the concept of self. Berlyne (1957), in his analysis of Piaget's theories, points out that

Piaget's interpretation of problems relevant to the self rests upon his conceptualization of the sensorimotor stage. The infant receives impressions and reacts to them, but there is not yet a "self between." There is only a shapeless absolute of self and environment intermingled without fixed boundaries. The infant's initial egocentrism is shown by his inability to distinguish the self from the world. In adapting to the external world, he thereby creates it. The Freudian and Piagetian views are not incompatible. In fact, they may be considered complementary.

It is evident that the task before the infant is to mark off the separate specific objects in his environment from himself. He is learning to specify the contours of his body, the sound of his voice, and to identify the various sensory kinesthetic processes from his own body. Simultaneously he also has the task of perceiving or learning to know other persons *as* persons. The mother's gentle voice, soothing touch, and warm body emerge from the fog of his impressions. Also emerging from this total matrix is a sense of the unity of his own person. Gradually, it is not pain but *my* pain, not hunger but *my* hunger, not hunger being fed but *mother feeding me*.

There are some scraps of evidence that help to understand the nature of infantile self-awareness. Using as his data several infants' responses to mirror-reflected images, Dixon (1957) concluded that self-recognition appeared at about one year of age as shown in such behavior as alternately observing arm-finger movements and their reflection in the mirror.

A few behavioral indices related to emerging social awareness are available. Examination will show that some of the items concern the beginnings of the perception of other persons, others concern a recognition of the need for cooperation and communication, and still others concern the use of words that have self-reference. It has been observed that at about the age of four weeks responsiveness to social surroundings begins to appear (Gardner, Pease, and Hawkes, 1961). The infant reacts to social overtures by a reduction of bodily activity. For example, the infant ceases crying, at least for the moment, if held in someone's arms. At eight weeks his face shows signs of animation on seeing other persons and at 12 weeks he may vocalize his reply to their speech. Since the smile is one of the earliest socially instigated responses of the human infant, it has received considerable study.

The smiling response is subject to reinforcement just as are other social responses. If the infant's smile is rewarded by his being picked up, he is likelier to smile on subsequent occasions than the infant not so rewarded (Brackbill, 1958). The positive nature of social responsiveness in infancy is also noteworthy. For 16 infants, observers kept a weekly record for eight weeks of positive responses—smiling, laughing, rolling, and reaching toward the adult—and of negative responses—frowning, crying, turning head away, and rolling and crawling away. Of a total of 527 social contacts, only 65 instances were negative (Rheingold, 1956).

Murphy et al. (1937) expressed the opinion that the self is based in part on experience the infant has in the use of proper names. The use of the pronoun, "I," and related terms such as "me" and "you" are characteristic, according to Gesell et al. (1940), at about 24 months of age. In keeping with this, the sequence might be first "Jimmy does this," to, "Me do this," and, then on perceiving self as doer, "I do this." In language, then, we find evidence of an emerging sense of self.

Independent Strivings and the Self

Another means whereby the self and social awareness emerge in the infant is found in the development of independent, oppositional behavior (Levy, 1958). At age 18 to 24 months he is "into everything." He knows where things are kept and gets them out in what appears to some mothers an alarming profusion. He darts everywhere, and refuses to allow his arm to be held. If restrained, he often resists strenuously and vocally. A specific illustration from Levy is appropriate:

The child, aged two, tries to fill a sink with water, struggling to turn on the faucet. Although his efforts are persisting and exhausting, they are fruitless. The father, observing, turns on the faucet easily, without a word. The two-year-old utters a loud scream, bursts into angry tears, and runs from the bathroom, refusing to be washed or bathed. Everything has been spoiled for him. His father's effortless turning of the faucet is perceived as an obstacle thrown into his path for the purpose of blocking him from attaining his goal—that is, completing his own task, "to be done by himself alone, without the slightest help, or suggestion, or interference" (p. 114).

Mothers can supply countless similar illustrations of behavior having this flavor of opposition which seemingly serves to sharpen the child's sense of being an individual person. These same ways of behaving show the pronounced influence of what earlier has been described as independence tendencies. His growing self-awareness leads to demands for independence.

The Self and Others

The self always develops with respect to others. Its main outlines, according to theories developed by J. M. Baldwin (1904) and George Herbert Mead (1934), are formed by processes of imitation and role playing. Baldwin maintained that imitation enables us to develop "ejective" behavior toward others—that is, the projection of one's own feelings into others. The "ejective" phase of development takes place during the second year of life, when the child shows indications of attributing feelings to others, shows things to others, and attempts to communicate with others. Role taking is made possible in part by imitating the behavior of others and in part by becoming aware of the expectations that others have for one. A boy learns the behaviors appropriate for boys partly by copying things his father and older brothers do and partly through being reinforced for doing some things but not others. He learns something about his status and position as a child by being led by the hand, catered to (or ignored), by the order in which his turn comes when others are being served, and so forth. He lives in a veritable ocean of social stimuli, many of which are concerned with directing and shaping his behavior and telling him, directly or indirectly, who he is. By being responded to as a self, he behaves like a self and thereby becomes a self. He also learns to develop attitudes toward the self that is he. He talks to himself, taking the role of the other and himself interchangeably. During the early stages of superego development he may actually slap himself when engaging in forbidden behavior.

This does not mean that the infant is the completely passive victim of his social environment. As Rheingold (1969) has pointed out, the very event of his arrival makes changes in the lives of his parents, as well as his siblings, if any. He requires constant attendance; room must be made for him, and there are, as a consequence, changes in the physical arrangements of the dwelling. Parents, especially middle-class American parents, worry about the wisdom of their behavior toward him. As his parents modify their behavior and even their entire life style, the infant teaches them, in effect, what he needs to have them do for him.

". . . Of men and women he makes mothers and fathers" (p. 783).

We ordinarily think of the parents as the power-wielding rewarders and punishers. This is, to a large extent, true, particularly during the latter stages of infancy, but Rheingold points out that the infant's behavior also shapes the behavior of his parents. Through his cry, he reminds them of his needs and their responsibilities to him. Crying noises are aversive; the cessation of crying is rewarding to all within earshot. The smile also socializes caretakers: it is as rewarding to them as the cry is aversive. Parents all report that "with the smile, the baby now becomes 'human'" (p. 784), and the smile on the infant is irresistible: it evokes the smiles of the caretakers.

"With the smile, too, he begins to count as a person, to take his place as an individual in the family group, and to acquire a personality in their eyes. Furthermore, mothers spontaneously confide that the smile of the baby makes his care worthwhile. In short, the infant learns to use the coin of the social realm" (p. 784).

Peer Relationships

In a review of research on peer relationships in childhood, Willard E. Hartup (1970) concluded that interaction with peers adds an important dimension to early childhood experiences, perhaps even in infancy, in the sense that it adds to or supplements the social contributions of adults.

Note should be taken, also, of the effect of siblings. They are not usually peers, in the strict sense of the word, because they are likely to be older than the infant, yet they, too, have an effect on his psychological development, particularly if they serve as caretakers.

Studies of family size indirectly measure the effect of peer relationships. Anne Anastasi

(1956) reported that the correlation between intelligence and family size tends to be negative—that is, the larger the family, the lower the intelligence. Such findings may reflect socioeconomic factors, however, inasmuch as individuals from lower socioeconomic levels tend to have lower IQs and larger families as well. The likelihood that large families may have a deleterious effect on the psychological development of their members appears more probable as a result of research by Tuckman and Regan (1967), whose samples were unbiased by socioeconomic effects. Their study showed that children from families of four or more were more likely to be referred to mental health clinics for psychotherapy. Only children were much less likely to be referred for therapy —about half of what one would expect by chance—whereas children from families of three or more were 14% more likely than chance to be referred. Referrals from smaller families were more likely to display neurotic behavior and anxiety, whereas those from larger families were more likely to be referred for school problems and antisocial behavior. It may be that such effects are due to the fact that children in larger families receive less individual adult stimulation, because such adult attention as there is has to be shared with a larger number, or it may be that siblings are less effective caretakers than adults. Such interpretations, though plausible, are speculative and must wait for further research.

Before the infant is four or five months old, there is little response to other infants, although crying on the part of one can set off crying on the part of another. At this age, however, an infant may smile at another infant or cry if the other infant receives attention instead of him (Buhler, 1931). Maudry and Nekula (1931) conducted a study of peer reactions of infants six to 25 months of age, using the technique of "baby parties."

Two infants of approximately the same age were placed together in a playpen, first, without play material, then, after a time, with hollow cubes introduced, followed by a drum and drumstick for each, and, lastly, a ball was given them, preceded by showing them how to roll it between them. Each infant was paired with other infants at different observational periods and the reactions of each recorded. For each period, the findings are those for a typical infant at the designated age.

Six to Eight Months. One-third of the time the infant turns immediately to the surroundings, not to the partner or the play material. Nearly half the attempts of the partner to interact with him are ignored. Friendly contacts, when they occur, are limited to looking, smiling at, and grasping the partner. Games are few and short. Often they consist of unspecific manipulations of the same object without the partner receiving attention. Fights are equally impersonal, consisting of a blind attempt to get hold of the play material.

Nine to Thirteen Months. Play material is responded to first. Since the partner often becomes an obstacle to getting it, fighting is at its maximum at these months. Conflicts now become personal; though it is not yet genuine hostility since nonpartner material (his own toys and clothing, hair, and so on) is still much preferred.

Fourteen to Eighteen Months. This is a transitional period wherein the infant shifts his attention from the play materials to his partner when his desire for playthings is satisfied. There is a pronounced decrease in fighting for material.

Nineteen to Twenty-five Months. The infant integrates his social interest in the partner with his interest in the playthings. Games show a considerable increase in frequency and length. The play becomes personal with much looking, smiling, and grasping, with a modification of his behavior in adjustment to that of his partner.

Disregarding the transitional 14 to 18 months' interval, the investigators concluded that the infant regarded the partner first as play material in itself (6 to 8 months), then as an obstacle to play material (9 to 13 months), and finally as a playmate (19 to 25 months). In other words, the infant has progressed from passivity to social contact, albeit crude, during the first two years of life.

The finding that infants of 19 months typically are more interested in their playmates than in the material suggests a primary social orientation at a very young age. Moreover, cooperation and competition in their crudest beginnings are apparent.

These findings indicate nothing about the factors responsible for the infant's social responsiveness; nor is there other research to which to turn for information. Presumably, the infant's first social relationships in the home, particularly with the mother, play an important part in determining his attitude and behavior in his relations with his peers. Behavioral generalization from the home setting would be expected.

We may lack understanding of their origin, but we do have evidence of individual differences in social reaction. Buhler, as a result of observation of infants' social settings, concluded that three patterns could be discerned —the socially blind, the socially dependent, and the socially independent. She describes them as follows:

1. *Socially blind.* When in the presence of another child, the socially blind infant behaves as if no one were there. He looks at the child, but makes no emotional response. He takes toys, plays, and moves about without any regard for the other child, paying no attention to the other's movements.

2. *Socially dependent.* The socially dependent child is inhibited or stimulated by the other's presence. If inhibited, he will not move, but will watch the other or copy his movements, will obey him and even give signs of fear toward him. If stimulated, he will make gestures and show objects to the other, try to rouse him, and even get enthusiastic or excited. In both instances, the infant's behavior is dependent on the other child's presence; he observes the other's behavior, as if looking for reactions to his own behavior.

3. *Socially independent.* The socially independent child is aware of the other and responsive to him, but is neither intimidated nor inspired by him. He reacts to the other child, may ward him off if necessary, but does not behave aggressively toward him. "He may or may not join the other in play, is not inconsiderate, but sometimes even consoles the other, encourages him, takes part in his activities; yet, for all that, he remains independent in his movements; for instance, he may suddenly turn away and do something for himself" (p. 394).

These types of social reactions in infants are congruent with the social development trends of the preceding study. Presumably, all infants are first socially blind. Even those who can still be so characterized, when other infants are more "dependent" or "independent," show change with increased age in the direction of greater outgoingness. Social dependence presumably is heavily influenced by the age of the other child. If the other child is older, dependence through dominance of the older is expected. By no means can these three characterizations be considered as hard and fast, unalterable by events. The three patterns are, nevertheless, suggestive of the emerging personality differences shown by infants in peer interaction.

Although there are social reactions to peers during infancy, it must be emphasized that social situations are almost completely confined to the family setting. Social interactions with adults far outnumber peer interactions. The "baby parties" after all were arranged by psychologists, not by the infants themselves!

An Ecological Approach

An increasing number of children now spend much of their time in nursery schools and day care centers, and their presence makes it possible to observe interaction patterns at different age levels. Honig, Caldwell, and Tannenbaum (1970) have developed an observational technique they term APPROACH (A Procedure for Patterning Responses of Adults and Children), which involves recording behavior occurring in naturalistic settings and coding the records as to emitted behaviors and behavior settings. Each of these categories is further subdivided in terms of the type of interaction taking place, the setting, and the individuals involved. The records are coded, transferred to computer punch cards, and constitute an ecological description of the total activity of the schools.

Figure 9-3 presents data relevant to our present discussion which show how verbal interaction patterns change from infancy through the preschool years. Infants one year old at day care centers address about 60% of their conversational statements to themselves. Except for tiny percentages addressed to objects and to peer groups, the balance of the statements are addressed to adults. Virtually no conversational statements are made to other children as individuals, but this increases to about 10% with two-year-olds. With four-year-olds, the largest proportion of statements are addressed to other individual children, who by this time are assuming some importance in the social life of the nursery school child. Figure 9-3 also shows that the greatest proportionate reduction comes in conversation with oneself, as children

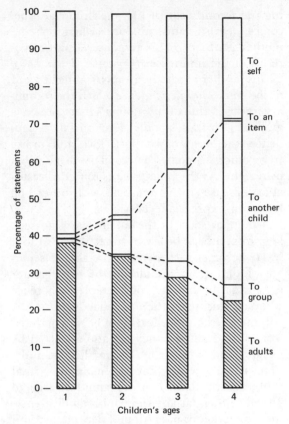

Figure 9-3. Percentages of conversational statements uttered by nursery school children aged 1 to 4 and classified according to addressee. (After Honig, Caldwell, and Tannenbaum, 1970.)

move from egocentric to more other-centered concerns.

Summary

Experiments in which infants are required to work for glimpses of their mothers have indicated a high degree of emotional attachment. These findings have been verified with infant monkeys, as well as with human infants. In human infants, this attraction seems to reach a maximum between 22 and 26 months. During the second year of life, the infant also becomes fearful and anxious whenever the mother is absent. This response is partially a result of the infant's *instrumental dependence* on his mother to satisfy his physical needs, and of the *emotional dependence* which the secondary reward value of his mother's mere presence gradually brings about. This social dependence, the need of comfort, love and praise from others, becomes a secondary drive in its own right. As the infant learns to find pleasurable responses in his relations with others, he learns to express affection.

Almost as soon as the infant learns to seek help from others, he learns to get along without it. He becomes successively more able to separate himself from his mother by ever greater distances. It makes considerable difference whether this separation is done voluntarily. Although infants are fearful of being separated from their mothers, they are also attracted by novelty and seek to maximize their stimulation, at least when they can maintain visual contact with their mothers and feel free to return to them at any time. This ambivalence, the simultaneous operation of dependence and independence urges, is typical of the infant during his second year.

A certain amount of discomfort and pain is inevitable in the life of any infant. The mother is not always there at the instant he wants help. Frustration results. In some cultures, the Kwoma of New Guinea, for example, the mother rewards crying as a response to frustration, and establishes a frustration-dependence sequence. Although this does not typically happen in middle-class Western society, researchers have postulated a relation between frustration and dependence. The "antecedent" study by Sears and his associates revealed that dependent behavior was correlated with rigidity of feeding schedules and severity of weaning. Unfortunately, the "pattern" study of Sears, Maccoby, and Levin failed to verify the results of the earlier studies. It appears that any attempt to relate later behavior tendencies to weaning and toilet training experiences produces contradictory results. Feshbach has suggested that the mother's *general attitude* is more important than these specific practices.

The connection between frustration and anger is more direct. Florence Goodenough found that, by two years of age, the establishment of routines such as toilet training was the most frequent cause of anger outbursts. When such outbursts are reinforced by giving in to the child's demands, the frequency increases, and the child is likely to turn to instrumental aggression. In middle-class homes, aggression and any expression of anger are likely to be discouraged. Like aggression and anger, fear and anxiety are responses to perceived threats. Where fear is an intense and specific reaction, anxiety is a more diffuse and attenuated response to a feeling of insecurity, loss, or deprivation. Infants seem to experience anxiety when they respond with "sobering" to strangers, or are separated from their mothers. Not only do these two anxiety-provoking situations cause different kinds of responses but they also reach peak effectiveness at different points during infancy.

It is possible that the "sobering" response to strangers is more an indicator of curiosity than anxiety. Kagan has studied the behavior of infants who were confronted with various novel stimuli. He maintains that children develop schemata as they encounter the stimuli of their universe. The amount of attention an infant will bestow on a stimulus configuration is a curvilinear function of the discrepancy between stimulus and schemata. Stimuli only moderately different from the schemata receive more attention than familiar or extremely novel stimuli. Fixation times for photographic representations of faces drop after six months of age, but increase dramatically after one year of age. Kagan interprets the decrease as an effect of the curvilinear function. The increase, however, is interpreted as evidence of a new cognitive structure, called a *hypothesis*. Play is another form of curiosity and exploration, and cannot be explained purely in terms of drive reduction. Several observers have attempted and failed to find a connection between play and organic and social needs.

Research with respect to the development of the self-concept in infancy is difficult. Quite obviously, infants cannot tell us about their attitudes and feelings concerning themselves. The psychoanalytic theory of personality holds that the newborn infant cannot distinguish between world and ego and that libidinal energy is directed upon himself. The ego of the infant as a sense of self-awareness becomes differentiated when his needs are not met. The mother's delays in meeting his needs lead to his growing recognition of "I" and "not I." Social awareness also stems from this dawning "separation" of mother and child. Piaget makes no particular systematic use of the concept of self, although his conceptualization of the sensorimotor stage is complementary to the Freudian viewpoint. The infant is at first unable to distinguish himself from the world. In adapting to the external world, he thereby creates it.

A few behavioral indices related to emerging self and social awareness are available. By observing infants' responses to their mirror-reflected images, Dixon concluded that self-recognition appears at about one year of age. The smile is a social response and subject to reinforcement just as other social responses are. The use of proper names and personal pronouns is also an indicator and possible cause of the emerging sense of self. The development of independent, oppositional behavior is yet another. The self develops with respect to others, and role playing and imitation play a major part. According to Baldwin, "ejective" behavior is a result of imitation. It must also be remembered that the infant's behavior influences that of his parents, just as their behavior serves to shape his: the smile also socializes caretakers.

Peers and siblings also play a role in development. Anastasi has reported negative correlations between intelligence and family size. Children from large families are also likely to be referred to mental health clinics for psychotherapy, whereas only children are less likely to be referred. Referrals from small families are more likely to display neurotic behavior, while those from larger families are more likely to be referred for antisocial behavior. Maudry and Nekula conducted a study of peer reactions of pairs of like-aged infants. From age six to eight months, the infants generally treat each other purely as play material. From nine to 13 months, each infant tends to see the other as an obstacle to play material. Only from age 19 to 25 months do the infants treat one another as playmates. The findings that infants of 19 months are typically more interested in playmates than in play materials suggests a primary social orientation at a very young age. Buhler, as a result of observation of infants' social settings, concluded that three patterns could be discerned: the socially blind, the socially dependent, and the socially independent. Presumably, all infants are socially blind at first, and then move in the direction of either dependence or independence. Ecological studies of infants and preschool children in day care centers show that one-year-olds address most of their conversational statements to themselves and to adults and virtually ignore other children. Two-year-olds address about 10% of their conversation to other children. By the time children are four the proportion of statements addressed to oneself has dropped markedly, and the proportion addressed to individual children has increased to over a third, showing that children are becoming less egocentric and more socialized.

PART 3

Early Childhood: The Preschool Years

10 Individual Development: Physical and Emotional Aspects

The period of early childhood begins with the final stages of infancy, somewhere in the second half of the second year of life, and ends about age five, when children are ready to embark on their school career and enter kindergarten. Inasmuch as an increasing number of children today, particularly in urban areas, are enrolled in nursery schools or play schools, this period is also referred to as the "nursery school years" or the "preschool years."

Physical Growth and Development

In their review of the status of child research during the preschool period, E. Robert La Crosse, Patrick C. Lee, and their associates (1970) noted that most of the research on physical growth and development during this period is reported in medical publications rather than psychological journals. In another review, Alfred Steinschneider (1967) observed that most of the studies on physical development deal with neonates, probably because these subjects are the ones that are most readily available. A great deal of the material that has been gathered is also concerned with sensory and perceptual processes, rather than with hand-eye coordination, large-muscle activity, and other aspects of physical development. There are, nevertheless, some data available that serve to outline physical development during this period, albeit roughly and sketchily.

We can say, to begin with, that the years of early childhood continue the rapid physical growth in height and weight so obvious in infancy but at a somewhat slower pace. Different parts of the body, however, have different periods of rapid and slow growth so that the proportions are changing throughout childhood with the skeleton remaining more stable while fat deposits increase and diminish. There are anatomical changes that can be classified as changes in kind, as in prenatal life with the appearance of new types of cells; changes in number, as in the sheer quantity of cells, in organs, teeth, and bones; changes of position, as in that of the heart and the teeth which shift position at different ages; changes in size, shape, and composition, as in darkening in eye color or skin (Meredith, 1957).

At five years of age the average child will have gained about nine inches in height from that of age two. A weight gain of about four or five pounds per year will also be found. Here again there is variability between the slow-growing and fast-growing child. At five the average American boy weighs 43 pounds and is 44 inches tall. The girl is slightly shorter and lighter. By five a child's stature is a fairly good indicator of his final mature height since the correlation between the height measures at five and at maturity has been found to be .70 (Watson and Lowry, 1958). It should be noted, however, that these statistics may not apply under some conditions. For example, poorly nourished children do not grow at the same rate as those who are adequately nourished, and there seems to be a negative correlation between the number of children in a family and their height and weight toward the end of the period of childhood (Tanner, 1970).

The preschool period is the time when childhood illnesses are at their peak. This is particularly true of colds and other respiratory diseases, which increase during the second year of life and then drop off during the sixth

year. Boys seem to be somewhat more prone to respiratory infections during this period; for girls, the vulnerable period seems to be the years from six to eight. Gastrointestinal complaints and other abdominal disorders are at their highest during the first year of life and then drop off sharply to the sixth year, rising somewhat during the middle years of childhood. Allergies follow a somewhat similar course, with the incidence being much lower. Figure 10–1 gives a schematic representation of these trends (Bayer and Snyder, 1950).

Parents characteristically worry a great deal about childhood diseases. They come on very suddenly: a child may be playing vigorously and energetically during the afternoon and then have a considerable fever by bedtime. Fevers can quickly reach dramatic heights: 105°F is not unusual. At such times, parents torment themselves with guilt feelings: "Did I dress him warmly enough?" "Perhaps I shouldn't have let him go into the water so soon after eating," and the like. They are inclined to feel that the illness is their fault, that if they had done their duty and been

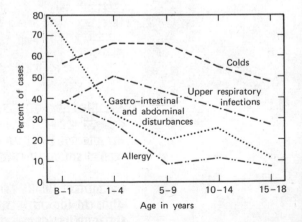

Figure 10-1. Relative incidence of various illness categories for a group of normal children. (Bayer and Snyder, 1950. Reproduced by permission.)

more protective, the child would not have become ill.

The fact of the matter is, however, that a high incidence of illness of various types during childhood is the normal experience. One might even hypothesize that a certain amount of experience with infectious ailments is probably a good thing, since they enable the child's body to develop antibodies that help it cope with recurring infections.

Childhood diseases also have their psychological aspects. Emotional stress has sometimes been identified as a precipitating factor in infections, and some ailments, such as allergies, are strongly suspected of being caused by stressful relations with parents. Research evidence for these contentions tends to be somewhat sketchy, however, and the usual treatment is medical rather than psychological. Prader, Tanner, and von Harnack (1963), however, report the interesting case of a child who had two episodes of *anorexia nervosa* during early childhood. This is an emotional disorder in which there is a marked loss of appetite for no discernible physical reasons. Figure 10–2 consists of a "smoothed curve," representing the average height for normal children, and a more irregular graph representing the height of the young patient. The child's growth was considerably slower than the norm during the episodes of anorexia nervosa, but the termination of each episode was followed by a growth spurt, in which it seemed to "catch up" with the norm.

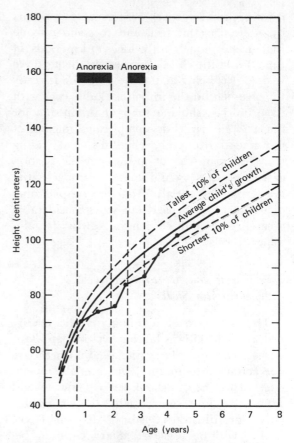

Figure 10-2. The effect of poor nutrition on growth. Graph showing height gains of a young girl before, during, and after two episodes of anorexia nervosa, *as contrasted with the normal range of height increases for this age span. (After Tanner, 1970, as redrawn from Prader, Tanner, and von Harnack, 1963.)*

Sensorimotor Development

During the preschool years, the child shows increasing mastery over the skills developed in infancy and picks up many new ones as well. Gesell and Ilg (1949) noted that the five-year-old, is poised and controlled, with an economy of movement and an adeptness with

fingers and hands—a far cry from the clumsy, uncoordinated two-year-old. Indeed, by the age of three most of the traces of the clumsiness of the infantile patterns in motor behavior have disappeared.

Gesell and his associates (1940) mentioned as characteristic of the three-year-old his ability to accelerate and decelerate in walking and running, to turn sharp corners, to go upstairs by alternating his feet, and to stand on one foot, even though only for short periods of time. From the child's perspective, being three years old is being at the age when he is ready to leave behind the infantile "kiddy car" with its primitive, shoving form of propulsion for the tricycle with its complicated means of movement. Jumping, climbing, and riding tricycles occupy a not unconsiderable portion of the preschool child's time. Such activities are derived essentially from the simpler ones of infancy, but carried out with considerably greater ease and efficiency. New skills also appear.

Learning and Maturation in Sensorimotor Skills

The influence of learning may be readily seen in such skills as talking, writing, and buttoning clothes. Maturational influences are not confined to infancy, but are also operative during the preschool period. Since several studies produce substantially similar results, only one illustrative study, that of Hicks (1930), will be reviewed. Sixty children between two-and-one-half and six-and-one-half years of age were divided into two groups on the basis of their initial ability in throwing balls at a moving target. The experimental group practiced ten throws once a week for eight weeks. Thereafter, both groups were retested and found to have made gains. However, the experimental group was not significantly better in performance than was the control group who received no practice. It would appear that improvement in skill did not result from the specific practice in throwing balls, which the one group had, but resulted from maturation and autogenous (i.e., self-originated) learning.

Autogenous learning refers to the fact that children, whether or not they were actually throwing at a moving target, were, in the course of their daily living, practicing many of the coordinations of body, eye, arm, and hand which are utilized in the complex skill of hitting a moving target. As far as clarity of results is concerned, this complicating factor of autogenous learning appears to be an insuperable obstacle to a clear demonstration of maturational effects with children. Specific practice may be instituted by the experimenter or parent, but the child continues to live and learn (practice) in ways which probably affect the results obtained. Nevertheless, it is plausible to believe that maturation is still taking place.

Stages of Motor Development

A given motor skill may be considered as passing through stages beginning with non-achievement, or absence of skill, through various degrees of proficiency. Mary V. Gutteridge (1939), in connection with some research to be considered in a moment, developed a rating scale defining steps of motor development. Specific motor skills of a child may be evaluated against this scale. Table 10–1 is adapted from her work.

Four general stages of major motor development are indicated: the first stage in which no attempt is made to carry out the motor skill in question; the second stage in which the skill is the process of formation; the third stage in which the basic movements have been achieved; and the fourth stage in which there is skillful execution with variation in its use. Within each stage there are various degrees of skill. The use of initial letters beyond the first ten numbered degrees of skill indicates Gutteridge's recognition that beyond the point in the scale which indicates skilled performances, the child uses his skills in all sorts of variations of the activity executed, despite no further increase in proficiency. It is only in

TABLE 10-1. Scale of Degrees of Motor Skill Displayed in Children's Activities (After Gutteridge, 1939)

Stage		Degree of Skill
I. No attempt made	1.	Withdraws or retreats when faced by opportunity for activity.
	2.	No approach or attempt, but does not withdraw.
II. Skill in process of formation	3.	Attempts activity, but seeks help or support.
	4.	Tries without help or support, but is inept.
	5.	Makes progress, but uses unnecessary movements.
	6.	Practices basic movements.
	7.	Refines movements.
III. Basic movements achieved	8.	Movements coordinated.
	9.	Performs easily and shows satisfaction.
	10.	Displays accuracy, poise, and grace.
IV. Skillful executions, with variations in use	A.	Tests skill by adding difficulties or taking chances.
	B.	Combines activity with other skills.
	C.	Speeds, races, or competes with self or others.
	D.	Uses skills in larger projects, such as dramatic play.

the first three stages that we have degrees of increase in skill in any strict sense. A rating of eight or better on her scale is considered as indicating the child is proficient in the particular motor skill. Although another investigator might use another way of formulating the stages and degrees of motor skill, her scale has enough generality to be of significance quite apart from the research in which it has been used. These four major stages and their related, more precisely defined degrees of motor skill may be considered applicable to the motor skills of childhood in general.

Some Changes in Motor Skills. Gutteridge (1939) used ratings of these degrees of motor skill in an investigation of various activities of nearly 2,000 children, most of whom were four, five, and six years of age. The motor activities studied were climbing, jumping, sliding, tricycling, hopping, galloping, skipping, throwing, bouncing, and catching balls. Teachers, trained as raters, made the necessary observations in the natural settings of classroom and playground. No attempt at special training in these skills was given; the chil-

dren's own "methods of attack" were studied. The degree of proficiency exhibited by the children at each age level was ascertained for each activity. Four of these activities exemplify her results.

Climbing was "proficient," as defined for the test, at the end of the third year in nearly 60% of the children. By the end of the sixth year, 97% were proficient. Considerable variability was found; a child or two in the sample was proficient before reaching two years of age, and three per cent of them were still not proficient even at the end of the sixth year. The children climbed on every conceivable piece of equipment whether it was designed for this purpose or not. Anything with height might become a challenge to climb. Most of them climbed as high as opportunity afforded. Some "stunting" occurred even at as young an age as two years.

Jumping was proficient in 40% of the children by the age of three-and-a-half, whereas about 85% were efficient by the age of six. There was a sharp rise in the percentage of proficiency from the youngest child to that of the four years, six-months-old children for

Development of complex skills

During the years following infancy, a great many complex skills are picked up, not only those involving gross movement and large-muscle activity, but also those requiring poise and a sense of balance and a high degree of small-muscle coordination as well.

whom the median rating was nine points. From this age on, there was relatively little increase in proficiency since for the oldest, six-year group, the median rating was only a little over nine. Variability was considerable at all ages. In the five-year group the range covered nine of the ten possible points, while even in the six-year group it still covered six points.

Tricycling was an accomplishment in which at three years of age, 63% of the children were proficient, while by four years of age 100% were proficient. Doing tricks on a tricycle was very evident as most mothers know; riding backwards, turning corners, and navigating narrow spaces were common.

Ball-throwing was a motor skill in which even some of the two- and three-year-old children showed proficiency. By the end of the sixth year, about 85% were proficient. Range of achievement at all ages, even the oldest, extended from awkward to excellent.

These, then, are some representative findings on the development of some motor skills in preschool children in relation to chronological age. It is pertinent to consider comparative skill among the activities at a given age. In general, Gutteridge's study indicates that a fair proportion of children are proficient in some motor activities before the age of three years, ranging from 17% in tricycling to 50% in sliding. However, proficient use in the throwing and catching of balls and control of movements in such activities as hopping, skipping, and galloping do not appear before age four or five.

Sex differences and variations were found within the individual child. Boys are ahead of girls in climbing, jumping, sliding, skipping, and ball-throwing; girls are more proficient in tricycling, galloping, hopping, bouncing and catching balls. Variation within each child from one skill to another was also noticeable, although Gutteridge states there is some evidence of consistency of pattern. This consistency appears to be tendencies for each child to use certain kinds of motor movements to the relative exclusion of other kinds.

Interrelation among Motor Skills

Some workers would argue that there is a high and positive interrelation among motor skills. For example, Louise Bates Ames (1940), as a consequence of studying manual and loco-motor behavior in infants, stated that slow creeping means slow climbing and slow prehending. Nancy Bayley (1951) found considerable evidence of substantial correlations among infant motor abilities. However, she suggested there was a possibility that motor functions at later ages were more discrete and independent than in infancy.

The evidence tends to bear out Bayley's suggestion that there is greater functional independence of motor abilities at the preschool ages than during infancy. A representative study is that of Doris M. Hartman (1943) who studied a variety of gross motor coordinations in about 60 boys and girls who were between four and six years of age. The motor tests she used were the hurdle jump, jump-and-reach, standing broad jump, baseball throw, and the 35-yard dash. After establishing the proficiency of each child, she intercorrelated the achievement scores of the children. She found intercorrelations ranging between only .36 and .56.

Hartman concluded that different motor abilities were being sampled rather than a general motor ability. A child who is high in one motor skill may not be high in another motor skill. A child may even be quite unskilled in one motor performance and still do quite well in others. Or, to put it in terms of specific skills, knowing a child's skill in throwing a baseball does not enable us to predict with any degree of certainty what he would do on the hurdle jump. We cannot speak of "motor ability"; rather there are motor abilities with a child excelling in one not necessarily excelling in another.

This point of view receives support from studies identifying significant factors. If motor ability were a unitary matter, then such analysis should show the existence of a general motor factor. Instead, often several group factors emerge when this matter is studied in children. For example, using 250 children from the first three grades, aged six through ten as subjects, Aileen Carpenter (1941) applied a battery of motor tests and then performed a factor analysis. She found three factors—a strength factor, a speed factor, and a factor of sensory-motor coordination that was associated with ball-handling. Disregarding this last more limited group factor, a speed factor and a strength factor were isolated. It would seem that at least two of the major components of motor ability are speed and strength. Strength measures seem to be interrelated and speed measures seem to be interrelated, but there appears to be much less relation between those for strength and those for speed.

Presumably other factors, perhaps not yet isolated, are operative in determining motor ability. At any rate, we would expect that more elusive possible determinants, such as interest or lack of interest, willingness or unwillingness to take a chance, intrepidity or timidity in the face of a challenging activity, and self-confidence or the lack of it, might influence proficiency in motor skills. However, the evidence concerning the influence of these determinants is either nonexistent or confusingly contradictory. Thus, little more is possible than to assume that these factors do influence motor skill. Speed and strength, at any rate, are factors in the motor skills of early childhood.

Emotional Development

The emotions of young children continue to show the differentiated patterns already established in infancy. As in infancy, the two streams of emotion differentiated from excitement, the unpleasant, disruptive emotions such as anger and fear, and the pleasant, integrative emotions, will again provide a framework for discussion. Maturation continues to play a part. Nevertheless, the topics to be discussed, appearance of these emotions, developmental changes in expression, frequency, and duration, and the immediate causes for their appearance, all indicate the relatively great influence of learning during the childhood years.

Anger

The physiological responses in anger, such as change in heart rate and blood pressure and tenseness and crying, are not learned, but appear to be innately determined. The relationship, however, between these responses and what at one time in the history of the child were neutral (nonemotional) cues is a matter of learning. Stimuli which originally did not elicit the physiological responses now do so. The child learns to be angry about certain situations that previously did not arouse these responses.

The classic study of anger in young children was conducted by Florence L. Goodenough (1931), who analyzed records for 45 children, aged 12 months through four years. The mothers of these children kept daily records of the anger incidents that occurred, noting the time, place, and duration of the outburst, the immediate cause, and the kinds of behavior they exhibited. From records kept for periods extending from about one to four months, Goodenough collected over 1800 instances of anger outbursts. Inasmuch as her work is the major

The anger of preschool children is usually touched off by some element of blocking or frustration—threats to the ego or self

Being restrained is a common source of anger. Another source is the discovery that things are not working out as anticipated.

Wanting to express dependency needs on inappropriate occasions disturbs both the child and the parent. Disagreements with siblings over possessions are certain to evoke mutual feelings of outrage. One of the more "civilized" ways of expressing angry feelings is to displace them on some inanimate object.

study in this area and subsequent research tends to corroborate her findings, we shall report them in some detail.

Developmental Changes in Expressions of Anger. Goodenough's first classification of the expressions of anger was more global and consisted of classification in terms of the direction the energy was expended—(1) undirected energy—anger not directed toward any end except that of an emotional outlet, such as in kicking randomly, holding the breath, and screaming; (2) motor or verbal resistance—anger expressed in opposing doing what was asked, such as verbal refusal or resisting being held; and (3) retaliation—anger expressed in motor or verbal attempts at revenge, such as biting the agent or giving him a verbal scolding.

As the children increased in age from about two to five, there was a steady decline in expression of anger in mere random discharge, no consistent trend in connection with expression through motor or verbal resistance, but an increase in expression through retaliating behavior. These age trends appear to verify common observations concerning undirected discharge of anger as characterizing younger, immature children and an increase in retaliative behavior with increasing age. Failure to separate motor from verbal resistance may have obscured the possibility that motor resistance decreases with age as verbal resistance increases. Thus, with increasing age expressions of anger are less random and more directed toward something or someone.

The second approach that Goodenough used took the form of a study of the various specific acts associated with anger. Crying was the most frequently encountered form of vocal behavior up to about four years of age. Nevertheless, crying decreased fairly regularly with increase in age. Kicking decreased as well, but stamping increased slightly, whereas striking in-

creased regularly, and throwing self on floor increased until age three and four and then decreased. Goodenough found that these were the major specific acts during anger. Contrary to popular opinion, jumping up and down, stiffening the body, making the body limp, refusing to budge, and glaring "defiantly" were some of the less common forms of expressing anger at these ages. Holding the breath also belongs in this less common category, since only four instances occurred in the 1,800 outbursts that she studied.

Developmental Changes in Frequency and Duration of Anger Outbursts. Figure 10-3 presents Goodenough's findings on age and sex differences in the frequency of anger outbursts. Omitting the findings for children under one year of age because of the small number of cases (two children), rapid decrease is found in anger outbursts with increasing age from the initial high point at the age of one-and-a-half years. The sharp decline in anger with increase in age probably reflects the older child's increasing sensitivity to social demands and increasing ability to meet frustration by forms of behavior other than anger. A consistent sex difference, with girls showing fewer anger outbursts, is also apparent. The results help us to understand the contention, often made, that boys are more difficult to raise than girls. It also represents a difference in the sex roles, with boys showing the expected greater amount of aggressiveness. (See Figure 10-3.)

According to Goodenough's findings, the duration of specific anger outbursts underwent little change during the first eight years of life. In other words, there was no particular evidence of decrease or increase in duration as age increased. Fewer than one-third persisted for as long as five minutes.

Developmental Changes in the Immediate Causes of Anger. Goodenough found certain

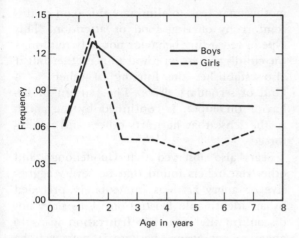

Figure 10-3. Frequency of anger outbursts per hour of observation for a sample of young children. (After Goodenough, 1931.)

categories of immediate causes of anger to encompass adequately her findings—(1) *conflicts over routine physical habits,* such as objection to going to the toilet, to bed, to coming to meals, or to having the face washed; (2) *conflicts with authority,* such as the child's response to being refused permission to carry out some activity, to being forbidden some activity in progress, to being punished, and to having to take the logical consequences of his own act; and (3) *problems of social relationship,* such as being denied attention, inability to make desires understood, a blocking of desires to share in the activities of others, an unwillingness to share, or a desire for someone else's possession. In terms of the percentage of the total number of anger outbursts at all ages, those in connection with routine physical care made up over 20%, conflicts with authority nearly 20%, and problems of social relationship nearly 30%. These three immediate causes of anger totaled nearly 70% of all the incidents the mothers reported.

A few of Goodenough's subjects were under two years of age, making possible a comparative account involving later infancy as well as childhood. During the second year, she found the major source of anger to be conflict over establishment of routine physical habits. Almost equally prevalent was anger brought about by conflict with authority.

In children between the ages of three and four, social difficulties, particularly difficulties with playmates, reached their maximum, accounting for nearly 45% of all outbursts. Conflicts with authority and over routine physical habits account for an additional 35%. In children four years and older, social problems continue to be the largest single category. Conflict with authority accounts for 35% of the anger outbursts.

General Conditions for the Appearance of Anger. The nature of the immediate disturbing circumstances giving rise to anger has been examined. Let us turn now to the general conditions that cause anger. The activity that the child is engaged in at the moment affects his response to the immediate disturbing circumstance. In other words, it is not simply some stimulus to anger alone that we must consider, but also the activity and state of the child at the time the immediate cause for anger occurs. A hungry child playing desultorily is not angered by the call to lunch, but a child not so hungry and engrossed in his play as well may be angered by this same call. Other factors, such as his general physical condition, may also enter. For example, a hungry child who has a cold may react angrily to the call to lunch even if not particularly wrapped up in his playing.

Goodenough found a variety of general conditions that lower the threshold for anger. Frequency of anger outbursts was positively related to: (1) *the time of day,* in the sense that more anger outbursts occurred at certain hours, namely, either just before mealtime or after eight in the evening when fatigue had set in; (2) *condition of temporary poor health,* such as the child having a cold or being constipated; and (3) *atypical social conditions,* such as the presence in the home of visitors.

Individuality in Anger. Individual differences in expressing anger must also be noted. Anger in each child will differ in its direction, frequency, duration, and susceptibility to general conditions. Goodenough listed, among other specific forms, kicking, stamping, jumping up and down, throwing oneself on the floor, holding one's breath, pulling, struggling, pouting, frowning, throwing objects, grabbing, biting, striking, crying, and screaming. No child would be "talented" enough to display all these forms of becoming angry in one or in many settings. He would have his own particular repertoire with a definite preference for some and not for others. Moreover, with the passage of time, he would show his own unique changes in his repertoire of the acts used in expressing anger.

Anger, Frustration, and Aggression. The most general conclusion to be drawn from the overall results of the Goodenough study is that the most common sources of anger are situations that interfered with the goal-seeking behavior of the children. In short, anger may be seen as the product of frustration, which in turn leads to aggression.

In a review of personality development in family settings, Robert R. Sears (1953) theorized that aggression has the function of producing pain in others in order to remove their interference with goal-directed behavior. For example, if a mother fails to provide a child with food when he is hungry or with attention when he is seeking affection, he may react by striking her or by crying loud enough to cause her discomfort.

To continue this theoretical analysis, the mother may seek to eliminate this pain or discomfort by offering food or attention. This type of rewarding behavior not only reinforces the child's aggression toward his mother but it also establishes the hurting of others as a kind of secondary drive. The pattern of behavior thereupon is continued by the child, in the sense that he hurts others and is reinforced.

Sears also observed that Goodenough and other researchers found that not every aggressive or angry act was immediately preceded by an identifiable frustration. This does not disconfirm the idea that frustration leads to anger or aggression, because it may well be that "other stimulus aspects of the frustrating situation besides the fact of frustration itself, that is, the mother, mealtime, cross talk between parents, are sufficiently often associated with frustration to become the instigators to aggression" (p. 231).

Fear

Fear in young children will be discussed in almost the same sequence as anger. As a means of centering discussion, the classic studies of fear by Jersild and Holmes (1935) will serve in the same fashion as did Goodenough's study of anger. In their work there were two major phases, the observational and the experimental study. In the first study they had parents record on observation forms all situations in which their children displayed fear during a specified period. The nearly 140 children ranged in age from under one year to slightly over 12 years of age. The procedure in this study was much the same as Goodenough's. In a second or experimental study, other children, aged from two to six years, were invited to enter into situations, such as coming into a dark room, which were known to be effective in causing fear in at least some children of this age.

In Chapter 6, it was indicated that fear was found by Bridges to differentiate from the "distressed" pattern at about six months of age. As might be expected on the basis of our knowledge of the work of Bridges (1931), fear in later infancy is expressed in a global fashion. Crying, along with general bodily distress, characterizes fear at this age.

As children become older, fear responses become increasingly specific. With increasing maturity fear becomes more often expressed in a withdrawing from the fearful situation. The preschool child runs away, avoids fear-provoking situations, or, when faced with such situations, uses verbal responses such as, "Take it away."

In the Jersild and Holmes parent-observation study they had mothers report any fears which they had noted in their children during a 21-day period of observation. After two years of age the number of fears sharply declined. For the group of two-year-olds, the average daily number of fears was about six, but for the next year group the average number of fears was only 3.7. For the four-to-five-year group only two fears per child were reported. Variability, however, at any one age level is so great that some children at all ages deviated considerably from the average.

The decrease in frequency of fear needs to be related to developmental changes in the expression of fear. The diminution of overt signs of fear—the characteristic crying, trembling, shrinking away or retreating—does not necessarily mean that there is no longer as much fear as before in the life of the child. This decline may be a decline only in *overt* expression of emotion similar to that already noted in the case of anger. In our culture social pressures against displaying fear are operative. Moreover, many of the more symbolic fears characteristic of the older child leaves him with nothing to "flee" from, since such fears do not have as definite a locus as do the ear-

lier, more specific fears. Transitory feelings, a minor tremor soon concealed, a slight trembling of the lip, clammy hands, and the like may for him be the only expressions of fear displayed. These manifestations of fear are easier to overlook than are the more frank, obvious, open ones shown at a younger age. Fear is still shown; the overt manifestations produced have declined in frequency.

In the experimental study of Jersild and Holmes, intelligence and sex differences were found to be related to the number of fears the children expressed. There was a correlation of .53 between intelligence and number of fears for the children in the 24 to 35 months' range. In other words, the smarter the child was at this age, the greater the instances of fear. This relation may be seen as to be expected if we consider that fear may arise after appraising the dangerous qualities of a situation. Some children, more advanced intellectually than the others of the same age, were able to perceive danger where other children did not. Since intelligence is at least partly a matter of maturation, it suggests that maturation plays a role in children's fears. A precocious child is afraid of situations that do not disturb other children of the same age.

The fear of the infant and younger child is of the tangible events and situations in his immediate environment (Jersild, 1936). As he grows older, his perceptual and intellectual prowess increases. The preschool child is afraid not only of more things but also of different things than the infant. As intelligence increases, he begins to recognize potential, real, and imaginary danger that he had not recognized before. Meanings, not before open to him, become part of his behavior repertoire.

For the specific situations Jersild and Holmes studied, the correlation between fear and intelligence declined to almost zero by the age of five. By that age all of the children were able to perceive the fearsome aspects of these situations, so intelligence was no longer a factor. This may be true only for the specified situations. Other situations might be found where the relation between intelligence and number of fears again became a positive one.

As the child's linguistic and conceptual prowess increases, the nature of his fears changes, as shown in the increase in fears of imaginary creatures, the dark, and of being alone. By the same token, an increase in intelligence and in general knowledge renders him less susceptible to fears of tangible objects, noises, and falling. The fear of strangeness decreases in that not so many things are strange any more. The bell of the ice cream vendor may startle the infant, but is known for what it is by a five-year-old.

Incidentally, in almost every situation of the Jersild and Holmes study, the percentage of girls at a given age who showed fear was higher than the percentage of boys. This finding is in keeping with general observation that girls tend to show more fear than do boys.

Up to this point fear has been examined as if its expression were independent of any other elements in the situation (with the exception of intelligence). This omission has painted too simplified a picture. Aspects of the situation other than the "fear" stimulus itself help to determine whether fear will or will not be shown. Consider for a moment the percentage changes with age found for fear of snakes. As Jersild and Holmes noted, the fear of snakes rises substantially between three and four years of age from what it was before. Then this particular fear declines. At first (in infancy) there is no fear of snakes, then at the age of two or three a snake is perceived as a potentially dangerous, noxious stimulus which increases to a peak at three or four. With increasing experience the still older child recognizes that the snake is nondangerous *in the particular situation in which it is seen*. A

similar explanation could be offered of the situation, "being alone," which shows a similar rise and fall. Both seeing a snake and being alone might, under other situational circumstances, bring about fear in these same children.

Since most fears are learned, it is plausible to believe that some fears that children show are acquired from the behavior of their parents. Hagman (1932), on investigating this hypothesis, found a relationship between the fears of the mothers and those of their children. He interviewed the mothers of 70 preschool boys and girls about their own and their children's fears. There was a distinct tendency for the child to have the same fears as his mother, particularly fears concerning dogs, insects, and storms. Consider a specific example of what might be happening in the situations that give rise to these complementary fears. Suppose a child unexpectedly hears a barking dog. No matter what, he will be afraid for just a moment if the situation is new or strange. But if the mother handles the situation calmly, the fear passes rapidly. But suppose she, too, is frightened by dogs. His fear is likely to persist thereafter.

In a summarization of the studies of fear with which he has been associated, Jersild (1943) observed that there are three major ways in which fear is aroused in relation to the fear situation. First, there is a specific relation in which persisting fears can be traced to the event itself. For example, a child is bitten by a dog and thereafter fears that dog. Second, a child may respond with fear not only to the specific stimulus, but also to aspects of the situation in which the fear took place. A child bitten by a dog not only fears the dog, but also is afraid to go into the neighborhood where he was bitten. Or he may be afraid, not only of the dog who bit him, but of other dogs as well. Third, the child may respond in an indirect and generalized way. Bitten by the dog, he has a bad dream that night, and, thereafter, is afraid to go into his bedroom in the dark. This formulation of the ways in which the stimulus situations and fear are related suggests that a great deal of fear is a learned response.

Fear and Anxiety

Anxiety may be conceived as fear in which the source of the fear is vague or somehow obscured. In other words, the person, child or adult, is not clearly aware of what he is being fearful. In this sense the source of the fear, although not the emotional state itself, may be said to be unconscious. Since awareness of the source is not present, it follows that the situation about which one is fearful is not directly and immediately present to consciousness (at least not in the form that generates the emotion). Hence anxiety is anticipatory. The child is *anxious* about the coming visit to the dentist but *fearful* in the dentist's chair. It is this anticipatory element that was stressed by Mowrer (1939) in his analysis of anxiety. He argued that anxiety is a learned response that enables individuals to face potentially harmful events in advance of their occurrence. Sometimes, then, anxiety is adaptive in that the child is led to do something about the situation. One investigation from which it was concluded that anxiety may be constructive was conducted by relating anxiety shown by preschool children to the quality of their play. Anxiety correlated *positively* with constructive play, thus suggesting that mild anxiety facilitates learning (Amen and Renison, 1954).

Often, however, anxiety is debilitating, causing avoidance of the situation or fruitless anticipation of situations that are not really dangerous. In such instances, anxiety is even more generalized than it is in less pathological forms.

Anxiety may pervade almost all aspects of life. Anxiety described as "free-floating" catches this latter aspect of the meaning of the term quite aptly. Such anxiety is "in the air," and is related to something or somebody that cannot be precisely specified and that is not yet being directly encountered.

Rosenthal (1965, 1967) conducted an interesting experiment in which preschool girls were exposed to two types of situations in the presence of their mothers or a strange female. In one situation, which was calculated to arouse a minimum of anxiety, the child was placed in an observation room that was supplied with toys and decorated by smiling faces. In the situation calculated to arouse a maximum of anxiety, there were few toys, the room was decorated by sad faces, and a phonograph in the next room emitted sounds of a child crying, a loud banging on a metallic object, and a shriek. There was a lighted alcohol lamp in the room near a red door; 12 minutes after the child and the adult had entered, the red door opened, and a hand in an armlength black glove reached in slowly, extinguishing the lamp. Behavior of the children was observed in terms of their attempts to attract the adult's attention and to remain in her proximity. As might be expected, the high-anxiety condition led the child to engage in far more proximity-seeking behavior than did the low-anxiety condition. There was no difference, however, in the amount of attention-seeking behavior between the two conditions.

The Relation of Fear and Anger

Anger and fear are related in a variety of ways. Clinical observation often demonstrates that apparent anxiety or fear in a child, on closer examination, is really a mask for suppressed or repressed anger and aggressiveness. Conversely, a belligerent child may be found essentially to be a very frightened child. Quite apart from such admixtures, sometimes an individual vacillates between fear and anger as when he faces a disagreeable situation first by attack but, on this failing, flees from it only to return to attack later. Or, on "being cornered," a child previously afraid may find himself angry and therefore attack.

This intimate relationship between fear and anger is useful in describing conflict in learning on the part of children. Dollard and Miller (1950), for example, traced how fear becomes attached to anger cues. Anger on the part of the adult produces punishment, and hence the situation becomes one in which the fear of punishment may outweigh the anger. It is their contention that this often happens during the period of toilet training. Anger may presumably become attached to fear cues as well, as in an instance where a child who was originally afraid of an older child finds his fear unnecessary and becomes angry instead.

The relative frequency of fear and anger in preschool children was investigated in an early study by Felder (1932). He found that anger outbursts were far more frequent than were displays of fear. It is plausible to believe that we live in a society in which we protect our children from fear situations while at the same time we expose them more to anger-provoking situations. Also it is probable that the higher incidence of observed anger is caused by our relatively greater emphasis on a child concealing his fear coupled with our permissiveness in allowing him to express his anger more openly.

The physiological changes occurring in anger cannot clearly be differentiated from those of fear (Kahn, 1960), but the overt behavior expressive of these emotional patterns is dramatically different in direction. As Goodenough (1931) put it, "Fear is emotional avoidance; anger is emotional attack" (pp. 48–49).

In general, fear behavior takes the form of avoidance or escape, whereas anger is characterized by approach-attack in motor or verbal aggression.

Violence in Children's Fantasy Material

Although comic books and television programs are often blamed for introducing themes of violence into children's lives, there is some evidence that their effect has been exaggerated. Children show interest in violence at a very early age. Louise Bates Ames (1966) analyzed the stories told by children aged two to five and found that violent themes outnumbered nonviolent ones three to one. The most frequent themes were associated with violent accidents (e.g., getting killed), with aggression (e.g., being eaten by a rabbit) a close second. Although boys produced more violent themes than girls, the actual differences were not very large: 76% for boys versus 68% for girls. The highest level of fantasy violence was reached by three-and-one-half-year-old boys, who told stories in which 88% of the themes involved some kind of violence. The lowest point for both sexes was at age 5, when about 67% of the themes were violent.

Ames' method of gathering material was quite simple. She merely took the child aside from his nursery school group and asked the child to tell a story. If the child hesitated, the interviewer prompted: "What could your story be about?" This was usually enough to get the child started. Here are a couple of examples:

"Little bunny rabbit went in the woods and he found a wolf and the wolf ate him all up. But a man heard the bunny rabbit squeaking so he tied the wolf to a railroad track. The train ran right over the wolf" (girl, 4½ years) (p. 377).

"Pussy cat. . . . He got a crashup from the cars. Then the pussy cat went on the sidewalk and saw another car and he had a crashup. And then a crashup again. Then he had another crashup" (boy, 3 years) (p. 371).[1]

Sears, Rau, and Alpert (1965) conducted a series of studies with children of nursery school age and found a negative correlation between punishment by parents and aggressive themes expressed by children in doll-play situations. We shall discuss this research further in connection with aggressive behavior of children, but the reason for mentioning it is to make the point that children did not seem to have learned their predilection for violence from their parents. Quite the contrary: those children who expressed the most violent themes in doll play were the ones who experienced the gentlest treatment from their parents.

It appears, then, that violence appears in children's fantasy in a spontaneous fashion: it does not have to be stimulated or instigated by outside intervention. The explanation of this phenomenon is quite simple: violence has a high arousal value. It is interesting and exciting, and it is understandable how a child whose life has been relatively sheltered and stress-free might wish to invent crisis material to liven things up.

It is a common observation that fantasies have a degree of reality for children that they do not have for adults. A psychologist was looking through a news magazine with a gifted three-year-old, when they came upon a picture showing some soldiers aiming an antiaircraft gun. The child asked what they were shooting at, and the psychologist suggested that perhaps they were shooting at a tank pictured on the opposite page. This possibility disturbed the child considerably. After some discussion the two agreed that the soldiers had decided not to fire the gun, but had changed their minds and gone home to dinner.

[1] Reprinted by permission.

An advertisement in the same magazine depicted a fire cheerfully blazing in a fireplace. The child was fascinated by the fire and asked a number of questions about it. After the magazine had been put aside, and the two were engaged in a play situation, the child suddenly stopped and asked if the fire was still burning. The psychologist suggested that maybe it had been put out by now. The child looked very doubtful, went over to the magazine, opened it, and pointed out that the fire was still burning.

In both these instances, the child was attracted to the stimulus and was fascinated and aroused by it. The arousal quickly reached the point where it was no longer comfortable, however, and some degree of anxiety ensued. At this point, the child began to have some difficulty in distinguishing between reality and fantasy, and sought reassurance.

Affectively Pleasant Emotions

It will be remembered that Bridges (1931) found that delight was the first of the affectively pleasant emotions to differentiate from excitement. This occurred somewhat before the third month. She also observed elation, affection, and joy in infants younger than 24 months. It is to these positive emotions that attention is now directed. Unfortunately, not very much research has been devoted to the study of emotional changes with growth in the affectively pleasant emotions and most of it was conducted some 40 years ago or more. This relative lack of interest may be the result of their having a less dramatic character than anger and fear. Certainly, they are not marked by as severe or as extreme behavioral signs. Often their expressions are less spectacular, partaking more of the character of pleasant feelings than of the pronounced changes of fear and anger. Indeed, anything resembling the pronounced visceral changes accompanying the disruptive emotions is not generally apparent. The visceral changes, although present in the affectively pleasant emotions, are often of so mild a character that they go unnoticed.

Smiling and laughter are the major external behavior indices of the pleasant emotions. Since these indices are observable and quantifiable, research has tended to focus on them.

In our discussion of psychological trends in infancy, we have already made brief reference to the development of smiling and laughter. That account, however, by no means exhausted the important relevant research literature. Consequently, one or two studies will be briefly described so as to make it possible to consider communalities among the causes of laughter and smiling. Leuba (1941), studying laughter in his own two infants, found that at about six or seven months smiling and laughter appeared in response to mild, intermittent tickling. Before the end of the first year, the laughter and smiling had been conditioned to the sight of the moving fingers (preparatory to tickling). Ruth W. Washburn (1929) observed the development of laughter and smiling of 15 infants from eight weeks to one year of age at monthly intervals. By means of a check list, facial responses to a standard set of stimuli were obtained at each monthly observation. Some of the "stimuli" she used were (1) smiling, "chirruping," and talking to infant; (2) peek-a-boo; (3) threatening head (lowering of head toward infant and saying "ah boo"); (4) hand clapping; (5) sudden reappearance from under table; and (6) tickling. All of the stimuli she used were effective in producing smiles at one or more of the monthly age levels. However, some were more effective in producing laughter than others. Laughter in one-half or more of the subjects was produced by peek-a-boo, the threatening head, and hand clapping. The study by Dennis and Dennis (1951) described earlier also attests to the importance of the adult's pre-sence in producing smiles in infants. Smiling is, as we have noted, a social response. Hence it is not surprising to learn that it is very highly correlated with vocalizing in infants— another indicator of socializing tendencies (McCall, 1970).

Florence Justin (1932) designed a study to test the various major theories of laughter: (1) surprise-defeated expectation; (2) superiority-degradation; (3) incongruity and contrast; (4) social smile as stimulus; (5) relief from strain; and (6) play. She devised test situations for each of these categories and then applied them all to nearly 100 children between the ages of three and six. She found that *some* children laughed in *all* of the situations.

Insofar as the situations she devised were tests of the theory on which each was presumably based, each theory accounted for some laughter. Some were more effective than others, but as she indicates, she may have been more adroit in preparing situations appropriate to one theoretical position than she was in another. At any rate, the most effective were the social smile and surprise situations which produced laughing in more than 90% of the children, whereas the least effective was the relief from strain situation, which, however, still produced laughter in about 50% of the children. Quite apart from the groupings by theory, she noted that situations in which the children were active participants, instead of being spectators, were the most effective in producing laughter.

Three other relevant studies of laughter were based on the observation of younger children in the nursery school-kindergarten situation. No attempt was made in any of them to direct or change the situations from which they derived their findings. Instead, the observers unobtrusively, but systematically, observed the children with particular attention to laughter-provoking situations.

Catherine W. Brackett (1934) found that

laughter occurred most often in social situations—situations in which the children were interacting with one another. Brackett found that almost 85% of the laughter of her groups occurred in social settings. Moreover, laughter in a given child was predominately found when laughter occurred in the other children who were present. Laughter was much less frequent when the children engaged in solitary play or parallel play (the latter being play in which both children use the same material, such as a sandbox, but do not apparently pay attention to or react with one another).

Ding and Jersild (1932), in addition to noting the social setting of laughter, also collected considerable evidence that laughter occurred predominately in connection with physical activity on the part of the children. The children they studied laughed most often when they were engaged in active physical play. Laughter, then, seemed to be related to having a motor outlet.

Blatz, Allen, and Millichamp (1936) also studied laughter in the nursery school setting. They were particularly interested in laughter associated with performing certain activities —falling, using the swing, climbing on the jungle gym, going down the slide, and the like. They found that almost always the laughter occurred *after* the completion of an event, that is, after the child had reached the bottom of the slide, after he had jumped into the pool, after he had fallen, after a toy he had thrown actually landed in the water, and so on. They consider that their results indicated that laughter comes when a conflict of some sort has been resolved. That is, the activity the child was engaging in had reached a solution and the conflict about whether the desired result would happen was resolved by its completion. At the top of the slide, for example, there is a tiny element of danger. When a child arrives at the bottom unhurt, he laughs.

In summarizing the major findings it would seem that there is some research support for the following statements concerning smiling and laughter, and, consequently, concerning the affectively pleasant emotions of which these are the indices: The sheer presence of sensory stimulation, especially sudden stimuli, seems to be important in infants (Leuba, Washburn). As sources for the pleasurable emotions in both infants and preschool children, physical activity seems to be very prominent (Brackett, Ding and Jersild, Blatz, and probably Leuba and Washburn). The presence of others in the social situation, the parents in the case of the infant (Washburn, Dennis and Dennis) and other children in that of the preschool child (Justin, Brackett, Ding and Jersild), seems to be operative in producing pleasurable emotions. Another source seems to be the resolution of conflicts (Blatz). It seems that relief from strain (Justin) may be related to this same source. Other sources, such as surprise-defeated expectation, superiority-degradation, incongruity and contrast (Justin) may be operative as well. Ambrose (1963) has proposed a theory that is not inconsistent with these views. He sees laughter in infancy as a means of both maintaining and terminating stimulation and arousal.

Piddington (1963) took a view that derives from social psychology, suggesting that laughter serves the child in social situations as a way of resolving conflicts or dilemmas and of simultaneously meeting social needs. The validity of this analysis is supported by the fact that the sudden stimuli that produce laughter in young children are the same ones that would produce anger or fear responses under other circumstances. It is quite possible that the child is unable to decide initiallly whether to be afraid or to be angry and resolves this conflict or dilemma by concluding that he is not really threatened. The qualities of the stimulus situation enable him to come to that conclusion. What these situational characteristics may be cannot be specified with any degree of precision; it is plausible, however, to consider that the foreground stimuli (such as the sudden ones just mentioned) are pleasant or unpleasant, just as the general backgrounds for the stimulation are pleasant or unpleasant (a trusted adult versus a strange person). In any event, the situation helps to determine whether laughter and smiling do or do not appear.

Although laughter and smiling are emotional responses, they appear to depend on cognitive elements as well. Kreitler and Kreitler (1970) showed five-year-old children pictures involving absurd situations and found that they laughed or smiled when they were able to identify absurdity with criticism, mockery, or wonder. Some cognitive strategies did not produce humor responses: describing the details of the pictures, criticizing them in irrelevant ways, stating the theme without noting the absurdity, resolving the absurdity through fantasy, rationalizing the absurdity in terms of reality, and denying the absurdity.

Sexuality in Young Children

When Freud launched his theories at the turn of the century, he upset many people by his observations about sexual drives in infants and young children. His comments were denounced and ridiculed because (1) sex was considered to be dirty and disgusting, and (2) everyone "knew" that little children were pure and innocent and hence could not have dirty and disgusting impulses.

Subsequent investigation in more liberal-minded times suggests that Freud was on firm ground, as far as the existence of sexually toned motives in early childhood is concerned. When Kinsey and his associates (1948, 1953) conducted their surveys of sex behavior, they found that about half their adult respondents

reported that they engaged in "sex play" during childhood. In the study by Sears, Maccoby, and Levin (1957), which we have mentioned from time to time, about half the mothers interviewed reported some activity on their children that could be classified as sex play. The incidents they reported involved children of the same or different sex, and participants were siblings and neighbor children. Sometimes the episodes were revealed through a child's guilty confession or chance remarks, but sometimes the mother was a direct witness. In some instances, the behavior consisted of some form of masturbation; in other instances, curiosity and exhibitionism were involved. About a quarter of the mothers were inclined to be extremely strict about sex play; somewhat more than half expressed varying degrees of not wanting to make a fuss about it, but at the same time were really disapproving. Less than a fifth expressed views that indicated moderate to complete permissiveness.

The extent to which sexuality is a factor in the emotional life of children depends largely on the culture in which they grow up. Where adults are preoccupied with sexual expression, it is likely that children will develop an interest in it as well. In certain South Pacific cultures, for example, adults expect children to engage in a great deal of sexual experimentation and exploration, particularly during the prepuberal years. In the United States, children in some subcultural groups are likely to be more sexually informed and to have earlier sexual experiences than the average middle-class child.

For most children, it is doubtful whether the sex drive is a major factor in their everyday life. If it is, researchers have been notably unsuccessful in picking it up. To be sure, manipulation of the genital area is often a source of pleasure, even for infants, and enough information about adult sexual behavior is around these days to excite the curiosity of even young children. Hard data are lacking, however, to show that either of these motives are strong enough to have significant effects on the behavior of most children. Puberty and adolescence are another story, of course, because it is then that the sex drive becomes a force to be reckoned with, both in terms of personality and social behavior.

Summary

The period of early childhood begins with the final stages of infancy, between 18 and 24 months, and ends at about age five. During this period, rapid physical growth continues, although at a somewhat slower pace than in infancy. By five years of age, the average American boy weighs 43 pounds, and is 44 inches tall. The correlation between his height at age five and his mature height is .70. The preschool period is the time when childhood illnesses are at their peak. This is particularly true of colds and other respiratory diseases, which increase during the second year, and drop off during the sixth year. Allergies and gastrointestinal complaints reach their highest point during the first year of life, and then drop off sharply at the sixth year. Emotional stress has sometimes been identified as a precipitating factor in infections and some ailments, such as allergies. However, research evidence for these contentions tends to be somewhat sketchy.

During the preschool years, the child shows increasing mastery over the skills acquired during infancy, and picks up many new ones as well. Jumping, climbing, and tricycle riding occupy a considerable portion of the preschooler's time. Although some skills are learned, others are the result of maturation. An experiment by Hicks showed that children given supplementary practice in ball throwing were no more skillful than children who depended purely on maturation and autogenous practice to acquire the skill. The child passes through four general stages of motor development in learning a skill: (1) when no attempt is made to carry out the motor skill; (2) when the skill is in the process of formation; (3) when the basic movements have been achieved; and (4) when there is skillful execution with variation in its use. Gutteridge used this scale to chart proficiency of nearly 2000 children in a number of motor skills. In general, she found that some skills, like tricycling and sliding, are learned before age three, and others, such as ball throwing and skipping, do not appear before age four or five. Although there are substantial correlations among infant motor abilities, the interrelation of motor skills during the preschool period is much less pronounced. This is supported by factor analytic studies. If motor ability were a unitary factor, only one general motor factor could be isolated. In fact, research has uncovered at least two major factors: speed and strength. It is assumed that additional factors remain to be isolated.

The emotions of young children continue to differentiate in the patterns established in infancy. The physiological responses in anger appear to be innately determined. The child learns to be angry about certain situations that previously did not arouse these responses. Goodenough asked mothers to keep a developmental record of their children's anger incidents. She noted that early expressions of anger were more global. As the children increased in age from about two to five years, random discharge was replaced by increasing retaliative behavior. Crying and kicking decreased in frequency, while striking increased. The frequency of all kinds of anger outbursts reached an initial high point at 18 months, and declined sharply thereafter. There were consistent sex differences, with girls showing fewer outbursts, and pronounced individual differences in the mode of expression of anger.

Goodenough also found several categories of immediate causes of anger: (1) conflicts over routine physical habits; (2) conflicts with authority; and (3) problems of social relationship. The first category proved to be the major source of anger for younger children. By age three or four, social difficulties became the largest single cause, accounting for nearly 45% of all outbursts. The general circumstances also influence anger. Goodenough found that that the frequency of anger outbursts was positively related to: (1) the time of day; (2) a condition of temporary poor health; and (3) atypical social conditions. The most general conclusion to be drawn from the overall results of the Goodenough study is that the most common sources of anger are situations that interfere with goal-seeking behavior. In short, as Sears has suggested, frustration leads to aggression. For example, when the mother fails to provide the child with food or attention when the child desires it, he may react by striking her or causing her discomfort. When the mother attempts to soothe the child, she actually reinforces this behavior, and helps establish the hurting of others as a secondary drive.

Jersild and Holmes conducted a study of fear similar to Goodenough's study of anger, and followed up their findings by studying children's fears in experimental situations. As with anger, the expression of fear became more specific with increasing maturity. The frequency of observable fear reactions diminished with age. One possible reason for this decrease is that the more symbolic fears of the older child leave him nothing to flee from. Another reason is that social pressures suppress the overt expression of fear. There was a correlation of .53 between intelligence and number of fears for children two to three years old. Presumably, this can be attributed to an in-

creased ability to recognize potential, real, and imaginary dangers. The same correlation is reduced to almost zero by the age of five. In some cases, for example, the fear of snakes or of being alone, the fear increases to a maximum at age three or four, then declines as the child becomes even more proficient at discriminating between dangerous and nondangerous situations. Most fears are learned and some may be acquired from the behavior of parents. Hagman has found a relationship between the fears of mothers and those of their children. Some fears may become linked to the general circumstances surrounding an event, as well as to the specific fear-producing stimuli. Anxiety may be a form of fear produced by such a source. Although the emotional state itself is conscious, its source is unconscious. Mowrer's analysis characterizes anxiety by its anticipatory nature. Although it is generally debilitating, "free-floating" anxiety has been shown to correlate positively with constructive play. Rosenthal exposed preschool girls to anxiety-arousing situations. The general finding was that the children exposed to high-anxiety conditions stayed physically closer to their mothers or the unknown adult present.

Anger and fear are related in a variety of ways. Clinical observation often reveals that anxiety and fear merely mask anger and aggressiveness. Part of this admixture may be a result of learning. Angry outbursts on the part of the child may consistently precipitate punishment by his parents. Eventually, his anger will be tempered by fear of punishment. Felder has found that outbursts of anger are more common than displays of fear. This may be due to a relatively strong cultural emphasis on concealing fear as compared with anger. The physiological changes occurring in anger cannot be clearly differentiated from those of fear.

Although television is often blamed for introducing violence into children's lives, research has indicated a seemingly natural fascination with violence in children aged two to five. Ames found the highest level of fantasy violence in three-and-one-half-year-old boys, who told stories in which 88% of the themes involved some kind of violence. Sears, Rau, and Alpert found a negative correlation between punishment by parents and aggressive themes in doll-play situations. This suggests that violence appears in children's fantasy in a spontaneous fashion, probably because it has a high arousal value. As with other forms of arousal, a surfeit of fantasy violence can become uncomfortable to the child.

Affectively pleasant emotions have not stimulated as much research as have fear and anger, possibly because they are not marked by the severe or extreme behavioral and visceral changes that characterize the latter emotions. Research has tended to focus on smiling and laughter because they are both observable and quantifiable. Leuba noted that at age six months, his own two infants smiled and laughed when tickled. By the end of the first year they had been conditioned to laugh at the mere sight of moving fingers (preparatory to tickling). Justin attempted to isolate the general kinds of situations that stimulate laughter. She found that the social smile and surprise-defeated expectation produced the most laughter. Other research has revealed a connection between laughter and both social setting and physical activity. Piddington takes the view that laughter is socially useful because it resolves conflicts and simultaneously meets social needs. The validity of this analysis is supported by the fact that many of the stimuli that produce laughter in young children may produce anger or fear responses under different circumstances. Initially the child may not be able to decide whether to be angry or afraid and resolves the conflict by deciding that he is not really threatened.

The findings of Kinsey and his associates have lent some support to the Freudian view of infant sexuality. It is nonetheless doubtful whether sexuality is a major factor in the development of most children. Although stimulation of the genital area can be pleasurable, even for infants, there is very little evidence that these motives are strong enough to have a major effect on the emotional life of most children. Within this general framework, however, the importance laid upon sex in the adult culture will very likely influence children's attitudes toward it.

II Individual Development: Cognitive Aspects

About the middle of the second year of life, the infant begins to make internal symbolic representations and to invent solutions to problems, rather than relying entirely on random, trial and error approaches (Flavell, 1963). At this stage, he is passing into the early stages of what Jean Piaget calls *preoperational thought*. Thinking cannot occur without symbols—that is, there must be some mentalistic devices that represent objects and behavior and that can be manipulated in abstract fashion. Language is the most obvious symbol system, and preoperational thought develops together with the child's acquisition of this mode of behavior.

Piagetian Concepts of Cognition

According to Piagetian theory, the child, two to four years of age, uses preconcepts or representations—that is, stimuli to represent other objects—that are midway between the concept of an object (this table) and that of a class (all four-legged tables). For example, a child of this age was observed in a walk through the woods to say "snail" each time he sighted one, but questioning showed that he did not know whether he saw the same snail or a succession of different snails. In fact, this particular distinction meant nothing to him—they were all "snail." Or, to use another illustration, a person without clothes does not have the same name as the person clothed.

During the preschool years, the child is

passing through a subperiod preparatory to to that of concrete operation. His conceptual operations have not yet taken on stability and coherence which should occur from about ages 7 to 11. This preceding subperiod of preparation includes three stages: beginnings of representational thought (2–4); simple representations (4–5½); and articulated representations (5½–7). This last stage creates a certain awkwardness since it extends beyond the age limits set for this chapter, but in the interests of achieving a greater unity of exposition, it, too, will be considered. Rather than labor over the subdivisions, it is possible to summarize them by saying that preconcepts are first used at two to four years; that simple, global representations appear by four years, and that thereafter the representations are more complex, having subparts and relations of one subpart to another.

The important issue is not these steps, but the shift in representation that takes place. The preschool child learns to manipulate representation, that is to use symbolic function in which *signifiers* (a word, an image) are differentiated from *significates* (a perceptually absent event). He becomes capable of internally evoking a signifier, a word or image that symbolizes a significant, a perceptually absent event, as well as being able to differentiate the two clearly. Although infants possess the ability to use cues, usage brought about by symbolic functioning differs in several ways. Infantile sensorimotor ability makes them capable of linking actions or perceptual states one by one; representation allows considering a broader sweep of events simultaneously. Second, sensorimotor ability allows action, whereas representation permits contemplation or reflection as well. Representation, moreover, permits cognition to go beyond the immediate present to include past and future, and enables persons to share with others through use of language the steps through which their thinking has gone.

If left at this point, the description of preoperational thought might give an impression of a much greater maturity than, in fact, the young child possesses. Although knowing the permanence of concrete objects, he has as yet no fully developed concepts of matter, weight, movement, number, or logic. He is approaching, but has not reached, operational thinking. His cognitions are preoperational as shown by a considerable variety of characteristics which help to bring out clearly the lack of maturity.

Egocentrism

The child is egocentric in his representations, just as he was egocentric in his sensorimotor actions. He cannot put himself in the perspective to another person. He has passed from initial egocentricity of the sensorimotor stage to logical and social egocentricity. Piaget illustrated this new level of egocentricity by the existence of the inability of a preschool-aged child to take the perspective of another person. A child in this age range was shown a model of three mountains and asked to select from a number of pictures of these mountains the one that showed the way it looked to the *doll* who was placed in the mountains. The child, instead of selecting from the perspective of the doll, selected the one showing how it appeared from his own vantage point. As the doll was shifted from one place in the mountains to another, he persisted in selecting the picture that showed his own view of the mountains. He did not understand that an observer sees the same mountains quite differently from various points of view. An everyday example of the same phenomenon is the difficulties children have with personal pronouns. To put it in doggerel, "I am I and you are you, and how can you be I and I be you?"

The young child's own personal perspective is absolute, not relative.

Animism

The young child is also animistic—he tends to attribute life to inanimate objects, such as clouds. Although research investigations tend to use older children, the evidence will be examined here since Piaget considers it characteristic of early childhood.

Piaget (1926) distinguished four definite stages. In the first stage, everything is alive (unless broken or damaged) for children between four and six years of age; in the second stage, everything is alive which moves for six- and seven-year-old children; in the third stage, everything that moves by itself is alive for eight- to ten-year-old children; in the fourth stage, life is reserved for animals and plants, or animals alone, by children aged eleven or older.

Nearly 800 children 6 to 15½ years of age were interviewed by Russell (1940a,b) concerning animism. Ninety-eight percent of their answers could be classified into one or another of the stages of animistic thinking. Furthermore, examination of the classification by stages at each chronological and mental age showed that probably they passed through the series in the sequence suggested by Piaget. Although the fundamental validity of Piaget's classification was accepted by Russell, he could find no evidence that the age range for each stage was limited in the sharp fashion thought by Piaget to exist. Instead, each of the concept stages was found throughout the entire chronological and mental age range covered in the study.

The question of whether these results might merely be an artifact of the child's usage of the terms "living" and "dead" was also investigated by Russell. In other words, a child might be saying something is living because he is not familiar with the essential meaning of the term itself. Some of the children on whom he had information about animistic thinking from the previous study were now questioned whether the same objects used in the earlier study were capable of "knowing" and "feeling." Classification by Piaget's stages of "knowing" and "feeling" and then correlating them with the findings on animistic stages for the same children showed a substantial degree of relationship among animism, knowing, and feeling. This would seem to be rather convincing evidence that if confusion about the meaning of living did exist, it also extended to the most specific meanings of knowing and feeling. In general, it would appear that the children do know what "living" means when they give animistic answers.

Despite this impressive array of evidence, there are some studies whose findings are negative. Typical is the study of Huang and Lee (1945). They asked children aged three-and-a-half to eight years of age not only whether the objects in question were living but also whether they had life, felt pain, were capable of wanting, and the like. They found only a slight tendency to attribute life to such objects as a tree, river, pencil, bicycle, and watch. The children did not attribute feeling pain, wanting, or the like to these objects to as great a degree as they said they were living. The term "living" was applied more loosely than "having life." Evaluation of these disparate results will be considered in a later chapter in the setting of a general critique of Piaget's conceptions.

Centering and Conservation

The child also tends to "center," that is to attend to a single striking feature of the object of his reasoning, disregarding other features, and thus, to distort his thinking. For example, on seeing two identical thin containers, he will agree that they both contain identical amounts of liquid. But when the contents of one is poured into a short, broad container, he will now deny that the remaining twin and the broad container contain equal amounts, arguing either way according to whether he "centered" on the "tall" or "broad" container, to wit, *B* contains more because it is broad or *A* contains more because it is tall.

The ability to recognize that transferring liquid from one container to another of a different shape does not result in a change in the volume of liquid, is what Piaget terms *conservation,* or, in this specific instance, *conservation of volume.* This ability is not fully developed until later in childhood, when the child is no longer misled by appearances and has sharpened his judgment and is willing to trust it. The ability to conserve comes through maturation and through experience with the physical world.

Piaget's ideas on conservation have aroused a great deal of interest, partly because he places a great deal of stress on its importance as a foundation for all rational activity (Piaget, 1965), and partly because his research methods for identifying the phenomenon seem rather unorthodox by Anglo-American standards. For one thing, his data have been reported only in an incomplete, anecdotal, and illustrative form; for another, he has not maintained a consistent approach from time to time and subject to subject (Braine, 1962).

In spite of these deficiencies, experimental work using standard research techniques has tended to confirm Piaget's conclusions (Lovell, 1961a; Elkind, 1961, 1964; Uzgiris, 1964). These and other studies, corroborate Piaget's sequence of cognitive stages, although they have suggested that his age norms do not apply to English and American children (LaCrosse, Lee, et al., 1970). In general, Piaget's norms appear to be too low, and this has, in turn, en-couraged attempts to accelerate the development of logical operations in young children. Some of these attempts seem to have succeeded, but LaCrosse, Lee, et al. (1970) raise some question about the methods used and suggest that researchers who claim to have succeeded in accelerating cognitive development may have only taught children how to verbalize more effectively. Actually, children are able to *predict* conservation at an earlier age than they are able to judge it in a formal test situation. In other words, before the experimenter has actually poured the water into a different shaped container, children will say that volume will be the same. It is only when the pouring has occurred, and they are faced by the apparent change in volume, that their grasp of conservation wavers and slips away from them. The task of determining whether cognitive stages can actually be accelerated is a complex one, and the technical problems of finding acceptable criteria have not yet been resolved (LaCrosse, Lee, et al., 1970).

Rothenburg and Courtney (1969) conducted a study that both confirms Piaget's contentions about the way conservation evolves and also shows how the child's ability to use terms like "same" and "more" is related to the concepts he is developing. The task they employed dealt with *conservation of number,* in which a child is asked to say whether one row of blocks has the same or more blocks than a comparison row. The investigators found that only 2% of their sample of children aged two years and five months to four years and four months were able to conserve numbers. They did notice, however, that subjects aged four years and three months to six years had a better grasp of conservation of number, although in this age range their ability was still limited. There were no sex differences in the abilities demonstrated, but children from lower socioeconomic homes scored significantly lower than those from middle-class homes,

The Piagetian approach to testing cognitive development in children

The investigator presents his subject with a series of tasks. Shown here, Professor Gilbert A. Voyat of the City University of New York, City College, probes the child's level of development by such questions as: What do you think will happen? Why do you think so? How do you explain that?

The child's conception of space: *visual-motor tasks, rotation of landscape and coordination of perspectives, direct and inverse order.*

Conservation: *of liquid, of volume.*

even among children who were only two and three years old. The investigators concluded that serious cognitive deficits appear among lower-class children at this early age. Their finding would suggest that if there is a "critical period" for cognitive development, it occurs very early in life.

A question sometimes arises as to the role of experience in the development of conservation. This theme was studied by some ingenious researchers who administered Piagetian tests of conservation of liquid, number, substance, weight, and volume to two groups of Mexican children, all boys. One group was composed of children of potters and had considerable experience in making pottery; the other group had no experience of this type and constituted the control group. Their results, in general, showed that the potters' children were better able to conserve, particularly with regard to substance. The children were in the age group six to nine, when conservation is more likely than in the preschool period, but the point is that interaction with materials in problem-solving situations apparently did facilitate the development of this ability (Price-Williams, Gordon, and Ramirez, 1969).

Logical Structure. It is difficult to separate logic from other aspects of Piaget's research. As Flavell (1963) has noted, logic is a factor in virtually all of Piaget's experiments. In this section, however, we shall focus on the origins of children's learning classification.

A typical experiment testing development of classification consists of giving the child a collection of different objects and asking him to sort them in terms of those that are similar or "go together." In the first stage of the development of logical structures, which occurs between two and one-half and five, the child does not organize the objects into classes and subclasses, but rather in terms of what Piaget and Inhelder (1959) call *figural collections.* The child proceeds in a relatively planless, step-by-step manner, frequently shifting his criteria of what goes with what as new objects catch his eye. The collection of items that finally emerges turns out to be not a logical class, but a complex figure, hence the term, figural collection. A three-year-old who was asked to sort some objects first selected some circles and piled them; then put some squares next to the circles and added other objects. What he had in mind soon became evident when he looked at this assemblage and said, "Un train, tsch, tsch, tsch!" (p. 40).

Piaget says that there are several difficulties that prevent a child this age from classifying objects logically: he cannot form logical classes or wholes that have a certain inner logic and cannot differentiate or coordinate the qualities that serve as the basis for class membership. Because of these lacks, he is highly distractible and keeps shifting his criteria for sorting.

In another experiment, the child is shown a display of red squares, blue squares, and blue circles and is asked if all the circles are blue. To his question he gives the interesting answer that they are not, because there are blue squares as well. The problem here is that of confusing the concepts "some" and "all," as applied to different classes and subclasses. The child can use these words "some" and "all," of course, and sometimes appropriately, but in actuality it seems that his ability to express himself linguistically has developed faster than his ability to deal with the concepts the words represent.

Perceptual-Conceptual Development

The principle of differentiation is clearly operative in perceptual development among young children. A five-year-old is able to discriminate to some degree among the objects of a classroom, the blackboards, chairs, books, windows, and the rest, whereas the infant sees them as a conglomeration of color and shapes only beginning to be separated as recognizable objects. However, this is only a relative differentiation on the part of the young child. He may perceive a "big" book and a "little" book but not realize that the former is an atlas and the latter the teacher's record book, a discrimination an adult would be able to make at a glance.

A lack of differentiation sometimes extends to the point of fusing the data from the various sense modalities. Although by no means present in all young children, so-called *synethesia* occurs when a specific stimulus arouses not only the corresponding sensation but also another sense-modality united with it. Color-tones and color-smells are illustrative: a three-year-old boy "smelled green" and a girl from her third to sixth year had to be often corrected in her expression of synesthesias since she persisted in referring to the "gold and silver striking of the hour" and "light-and dark-red whistling." This phenomenon tends to disappear with increasing age, suggesting that it is related to increasing differentiation (Werner, 1940).

Differentiation in perception is also shown by less subjective research procedures. As an example of increased discrimination with age, children of four to six were better able with increasing age to judge from photographs the age of adults pictured (Kogan, Stephens, and Shelton, 1961).

Concept Formation

Let us now turn to another aspect of the developmental process—concept formation. Unlike the infant, the young child is capable of using concepts that make him different from the infant he has been. Above all, concepts facilitate the ease and accuracy of thinking of children (and adults). Concepts (1) reduce the complexity of the environment; (2) provide the means by which the objects of the environment are identified; (3) reduce the necessity of relearning at each new encounter; (4) help provide for direction, prediction, and planning of any activity; and (5) permit ordering and relating classes of objects and events as in cause and effect. In short, conceptualizing makes reasoning possible (Bruner, 1956).

Granting that the beginnings of conceptualization occur in infancy, what are some of the conceptual tasks the young child emerging from infancy has before him? He enters early childhood with very hazy conceptions of space, time, weight, number, form, color, and size. It is during early and later childhood that he makes his greatest strides in mastering these classes of concepts.

It is impractical to discuss all of these major classes or aspects of concepts. Instead, discussions of space and time concepts will serve to illustrate conceptual development during early childhood. Some of the findings of Gesell and Ilg (1949) on space conception receive attention first.

Even at one year of age there is enough appreciation of space dimensions to perform gestures for up and down and to play "peek-a-boo." By two years of age the child has in his vocabulary such expressions as "up high," "in," "out," and "go away." By the age of three he can tell what street he lives on, but usually not the number. At the age of five he is still very much literal and factual, although capable of taking simple routes through the immediate neighborhood. He is beginning to appreciate the significance of maps and even may make simple maps indicating the route he takes to school, and so on.

These facts, however, tell us nothing about how these conceptualizations came about. One plausible but as yet not thoroughly documented theory that helps in this regard was advanced by Piaget.

To Piaget, space is not immediately comprehended but must be constructed through experience. Spatial representations are built up by the child's acting on the object in space. First there are the sensorimotor activities of the infant, but later internalized activities take over as more efficient and economical (Piaget and Inhelder, 1956). In very broad outline, this is the theory he advances. Suppose we examine it in more detail.

As we stated earlier, Piaget held that during the sensorimotor stage the infant constructed objects from his experiences. He learns that objects retain identity even when out of sight and that he, the infant, can influence objects by touching them. Space, then, is not independent of objects.

During the preschool years the child moves on to a level in which objects in space are apprehended as related to one another, independent of the perceiver. He is now free from the egocentric illusion and can take into account movements of objects when they go through positions in which he, himself, does not participate. To use as an illustration of Piaget's—Jacqueline had thrown a ball under a sofa. Instead of looking under the sofa, she realized it had passed under and beyond the sofa to another part of the room. Since the way the ball passed was blocked by furniture, she turned away from where the ball disappeared to go around the sofa to find the ball. She had followed a path different from the ball and had elaborated an independent, organized spatial concept through representation of the displacement of the ball; and by detour she found it again. This detour behavior showed her ability to apprehend space in which bodies other than her own had travelled.

In the preschool years this process of moving toward objectivity repeats itself, this time in terms of the preoperational stage. This again includes the child's egocentricity of a logical and social sort. The inability of a child of four or five to conceive that the mountain would look different from the other side is again illustrative.

Concepts of time are among the most abstract, more so than space, for example, in part because of the lack of obvious clues on which to build them. Nevertheless, some development of the conception of time takes place during infancy. Gesell and Ilg (1949) noted that the child of 18 months lives very much in the present. It is characteristic that he finds it difficult to wait and the only time word that is used is "now." Only the slightest indications of any sense of timing have yet appeared; for example, the sight of juice and crackers may bring him to the table. At two years of age although he still lives chiefly in the present, he has begun to use words denoting the future, as for example, "gonna" and "in a minute." He is also beginning to comprehend simple time sequences as implied in "have dollie after juice."

Ames (1946), studying 18- to 48-month-old nursery school children, found that within those ages words indicating the present came first, then those for the future, and, lastly, those indicating the past. Parts of the day, morning and afternoon, were understood before the day of the week. By the age of three the child knows his own age, and most basic time words are now in his vocabulary. He can be persuaded to wait for things. Although he shows only pretense of telling time, the very fact that he does so shows a dawning conceptualization in this area. During these years he is still living very much in the here and now, as shown by the fact that even at five years it is very difficult for him to conceive of not being alive, of dying, or of anyone living before him. At this age he can name the days of the week and is interested in clocks and calendars, although by no means adroit in handling these time phenomena.

Doris Springer (1952), in studying clock time conceptualization with four-, five-, and six-year-olds, found a developmental progression to exist. The youngest children could relate time in descriptive terms to regular events in their preschool schedule; those somewhat older used imaginative but not unreasonable clock time, such as fifteen o'clock in the afternoon; still older children expressed reasonable but incorrect time; and the oldest conceived of the correct time.

Hours are learned first, then half-hours, and finally, quarter hours. Time is first conceived as a sequence in relation to activities, then as outstanding divisions of time, such as morning and afternoon, followed by an understanding of the days of the week, and thereafter calendar and clock time. This sequence seems to be the order of development. The young child seems to be moving from a concrete action level toward levels of greater and greater abstraction.

Piaget (1969) has expressed theories about children's development of time concepts that are in some ways similar to his ideas about the way concepts of other environmental dimensions are evolved. Temporal concepts, like concepts of space, do not merely emerge but must be *constructed* by the child. For example, the child must learn how to retrace the course of certain events and to coordinate their beginning and end with other events. The complications involved in such reconstructions often lead to interesting errors. A six-year-old told Piaget that it took him ten minutes to go home, that he would get home more quickly if he ran, but that it would take *longer*. This response demonstrates the child's confusion about time and velocity. Piaget analyzed the child's reasoning along these terms: "(1) if you go quickly you will necessarily cover more space: (2) if you cover more space, you need more time to do so; and (3) if you go more quickly you need more time because you cover more space" (p. 88).

The development of concepts proceeds by stages, in which each higher level of abstraction includes within it lower and more specific levels. *Fruit* is at a higher level of abstraction than *apples, peaches,* and *pears.* Welch (1940) proposed a hierarchical organization to account for these levels.

There is first the concrete or object level of, say, *this dog.* Beyond this concrete level there are varying degrees or levels of abstractness. The first hierarchy level is that of *collie;* the second, *dog;* the third, *animal;* the fourth, *living substance*; and the fifth, *substance.* These are levels of increasing abstractness on a logical basis. The logical order is based on the fact that the next higher hierarchy includes the lower and so on to the highest level. The first order, *collie,* is included in the second, *dog,* and this in turn in the third, *animal,* and so on.

The developmental order, however, may be quite different from the logical. Welch noted that a child when learning language may begin by using words that properly belong at the second or third hierarchical level. This does not necessarily mean that the child is using second- or third-order concepts, but rather that he is applying the appropriate words erroneously. The reverse may also occur. If *dog* is his first class concept, then he may mistakenly assume that all four-legged animals are *dogs.* He may then learn another concept from the first level, that of *cat,* but will have difficulty in realizing that both dogs and cats belong to a higher level category *animals.* Welch speculates that a child may react to this difficulty by complaining:

"You call all of these things animals. That means they are the same. Then you turn around and call one a dog and another a cat. That means they are different. Why don't you make up your mind! Are they the same or are they different?" (pp. 203–204)

Welch (1947) maintained that there are two kinds of abstract concepts—(1) first-order, those representing classes as, for example, a chair; and (2) second order, those showing characteristics divorced from any object, such as number or justice. The second kind of abstract concept is illustrated in the learning of arithmetic. Progressing from two apples and two apples equaling four apples to $2 + 2 = 4$, the child is also moving from the first to the second order of abstract concept.

To find out when children begin to grasp concepts, Welch (1940) gathered data from about 80 children aged between 21 and 72 months. His procedure consisted of two parts. First the child was faced with objects consisting of a toy dog, a cow, a horse, a pig, a soldier and a nurse, a hat, coat and shoes, a chair and table, a carrot and a potato, an apple, a banana and an orange. One at a time he was asked to group together two animals, the man and woman, two vegetables, and two pieces of fruit when given their species name (first order concepts).

The second part consisted of questions designed to show whether the child had knowledge of *games, color, food, weather,* and the like. An overall maximum score of 21 for first-order concepts was possible. In Figure 11–1 the number of first-order abstract concepts at various ages is given. Knowledge of abstract concepts increases steadily from two to six years of age. There appears to be an

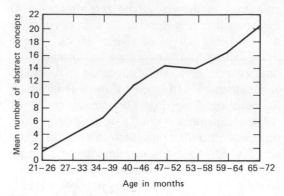

Figure 11-1. *Gain in knowledge of first-order abstract concepts during the preschool years.* (Welch, 1940. Reprinted by permission.)

evolution of concepts with gradual changes rather than a saltatory, discrete series of levels.

Welch found that at the age of 21 to 26 months a group of children manifested an average of little more than one first-order abstract concept. The trend of development with increasing age was linear with an average of about six concepts at age 34 to 39 months, an average of about 14 concepts at 53 to 58 months, and 20 concepts at 65 to 72 months. Second-order concepts made their first appearance in a few children at three years of age. By five years of age practically all knew at least one second-order concept, such as apples are fruit and potatoes are vegetables.

A significant point concerning the acquisition of the names of things has been made by Roger Brown (1958). On the basis of the developmental principle of differentiation we would expect that children's vocabulary would build from relative lack of differentiation to increased differentiation. As a matter of fact, there is evidence that some of the child's vocabulary is learned this way—*milk* and *water* are acquired before *liquid, apple* and *orange* are learned before *fruit, mother* and *father* before *parents,* and the like.

Some concrete terms appear in the vocabulary before abstract or superordinate terms. But this is by no means always the case; the child also learns *fish* before *perch* or *bass, car* before *Chevrolet* or *Ford, house* before *bungalow* or *mansion*. This point need not be embarrassing, as Brown points out, even though it seemingly contradicts developmental principles. The child's vocabulary is being determined in part for both trends by the naming practices of adults. Sometimes they want children to know first the subordinate words, *orange* or *father*, before the superordinates, *fruit* or *parents*. Sometimes they want them to know the superordinate word first, *fish* or *car*, before the subordinates, *perch* or *Chevrolet*. Primarily the parent chooses the word that meets the child's and his own needs, and this is the commonest name at its usual level of utility.

Language Development

Speech is a major factor in concept development. As we indicated earlier, children cannot engage in thinking without the use of symbols, and the richest source of symbols may be found in the language the child is acquiring.

Learning and Speech

The responses that children acquire in the process of learning are touched off by *cues*—that is, by configurations of stimuli that serve the function of signaling that a certain response is appropriate. Among the earlier theories relating cue production and language are ones proposed by Miller and Dollard (1941), whose point of view has been ably summarized by Hall and Lindzey (1970):

"One of the most important cue-producing responses is the labeling or naming of events and experiences. The individual may immediately increase the generalization or transfer between two or more cue situations by identifying them as having the same label, for example, by identifying two completely different situations as 'threatening' the individual may greatly increase the likelihood that he will behave in the same manner in both situations; or he may build up a sharp discrimination between two similar situations by giving them different names, for instance, two individuals who are objectively very much alike may be labeled respectively as 'friend' and 'enemy' with the result that they will be responded to in a highly individual manner. Within any culture there will be critical generalizations and discriminations which are emphasized and thus made easier by the structure of the language. The often repeated examples of tribes where a given commodity, such as cattle or coconuts, is of great importance and where the language contains a tremendous number of differentiated labels for such objects illustrate this principle.

Not only may words serve to facilitate or inhibit generalization, they may also serve the important function of arousing drives. Further, words may be used to reward or reinforce. And, most important of all, they serve as time-binding mechanisms, permitting the individual to instigate or reinforce present behavior in terms of consequences which are located in the future but susceptible to verbal representation in the present. It is clearly the verbal intervention in the drive-cue-response-reinforcement sequence which makes human behavior so complex and difficult to understand and at the same time accounts for much of the difference between man and lower species" (pp. 436–437).[1]

Language as a product of learning can be seen as an important aspect of development. Without the learning of language much that

[1] Reprinted by permission.

makes us characteristically human would be lost.

The preschool years show an enormous increase in the use of words. This is significant not only because of the ease and subtlety of communication, but also because it facilitates other learnings. Even in infancy the increased efficiency of subjects who use words was found in the study of Gellermann (1933) noted earlier. A considerable number of studies have shown that children learn to discriminate among stimuli presented to them if prior to the study itself they are given experience in naming the stimuli. In other words, possession of verbal facility allows ease of learning.

The study of Weir and Stevenson (1959) is representative. They studied this problem with children of three, five, seven, and nine years of age divided into two groups. Both groups gave a pushing response to register their choice of the "correct" picture of two common animals shown together. Before making the response the children in one group were instructed to say the name of the animal they thought fitted the correct picture. The children in the other group were exposed to the same pretraining procedure but nothing was said about giving a name to the stimulus. Both groups practiced to the same level of proficiency. Then they faced a more complicated but similar task. Those who had been asked to verbalize in pretraining showed consistently better learning at every age studied.

The idea that thinking is a form of subvocal or covert speech would help to explain the findings of Weir and Stevenson, but difficulties are present. Conrad (1971) points out that before the age of five, children do not use covert speech to memorize, reason, or plan. Instead, they seem to use speech in socially communicative ways to respond impulsively to specific situations, including the naming of objects to other people. Language is also used in social contexts in a way that is essentially devoid of conventional meaning, as when a child babbles, using real words, but does so apparently because he enjoys their sounds. Conrad observed a three-year-old child engaged in a task involving the selecting of a card from one group and matching it with an identical card from another group. The child talked to himself as he performed the task, but his words were not consistent with his actions. For example, he would say "Cat goes with cat," while he correctly matched "bat" with "bat." It is clear that the child was not using language labels in a way that would be considered logical or appropriate. It was as though his problem solving and his language usage were proceeding on separate tracks, unrelated to each other.

Indeed, the entire concept of verbal functioning as essential thinking seems suspect. Hans G. Furth (1971), in a review of research relating to the thinking of deaf individuals, concluded that language plays little part, if any, in their ability to function cognitively. The thinking processes of deaf children and adolescents have been found to be similar to hearing subjects, although with few exceptions, individuals deaf from birth are severely deficient in linguistic skills. The deaf person who can read lips, for example, is a rarity, and few deaf individuals can read above the fourth-grade level, in spite of 10 to 15 years in schools where linguistic skills get maximum stress. In view of the fact that deaf people attain normal levels of cognitive performance without anywhere near comparable linguistic ability, it would appear that language competence is probably not a requisite for cognitive development in normal children as well. Furth points out that such a conclusion would be consistent with Piaget's position that language is not involved in the development of logical thinking in children (Inhelder and Piaget, 1964).

Still further support for this line of reasoning comes from research by Jerome Kagan (1971), who showed four-year-olds pictures, one at a time. Later, when each picture was shown to the children, together with one they had not seen, they were able to pick the one they had seen with 90% accuracy. Language could not have played a part in their thinking, because many of the pictures involved objects they had never seen in their lives (like a slide rule or an unusual lathe); hence this performance could not be explained by the assumption that each picture had been supplied by the child with a language label.

Theories of Language Development

In Chapter 7 we referred briefly to the controversy between proponents of the operant-conditioning explanation of early language learning (e.g., B. F. Skinner) and those favoring a biologically based theory (e.g., Noam Chomsky). Chomsky (1965, 1968) argues that langauge development in children can be explained only if one assumes that there is an innate language capacity. He says that the linguistic environment in which children find themselves is deficient in many ways. First, the language that children hear is *degenerate*, because adults talk to children in ways that are different from the way they address each other. Children often hear sentences that are ungrammatical—for example, baby talk, fractions of sentences, and the like—as well as grammatical. For all they know, ungrammatical and grammatical sentences are on a par with one another. The language children hear is also *limited*, for it consists of only a small sample of the statements that are possible in language. Furthermore, their linguistic stimuli are *scattered*, in the sense that they are not organized appropriately for children's learning.

In spite of these deficiencies, Chomsky argues, children everywhere learn to speak about the same age and make progress at a rate that is roughly much the same. Chomsky concludes, therefore, that human beings are born with what might be hypothetically conceived of as a *language acquisition device*, which enables them to process whatever linguistic data that come their way and achieve a grammatically sound competence in their native language.

In a review of the various competing theories of language development, Harry Osser (1971) notes that there is some support for the Chomsky position, because children from various language communities seem to use much the same approach in learning their native tongue. That is, Russian- and English-speaking children in early stages tend to use similar, simplified grammatical construction that is actually "ungrammatical" by usual standards, but that serves as a kind of bridge between their prelinguistic state and later grammatical competence. The fact that children literally invent a working grammatical structure for themselves shows, according to Chomsky, that it is not learned but is generated by processes that are maturational or *nativistic*, to use a term frequently employed to designate Chomsky's position.

Osser cites an unpublished study by Drach et al. (1960) that tends to support Chomsky's theories. These researchers recorded conversations between a mother talking to another adult and between the same mother and her 26-month-old son. They noted that the mother used much longer and more complex sentences in talking to the adult than she did with her child.

The environmentalist position taken by Skinner (1957) does seem to be too narrow, because more seems to be involved in language learning than adult reinforcement of proper language forms, as we noted in Chapter 7. However, other environmentalist explanations seem to be more valid. Imitation seems to be a fairly obvious explanation of the way in which children acquire language. Osser notes that when children and adults interact, adults often repeat what children say, reinforcing and at the same time adding some grammatical niceties. For instance, the child says "Daddy go work," and the mother replies, "Yes, Daddy has gone to work," whereupon the child counters, "Daddy *gone* work," picking up a new language mode and moving a little closer to standard English. Brown and Bellugi (1964) conducted a longitudinal study of the speech of two children from infancy onward, however, and concluded that the linguistic knowledge they developed could not be accounted for entirely by imitation, reinforcement, and parental expansion of the type we described.

One explanation that the environmentalist or learning-theory proponents make for the appearance of new forms in the child's speech is that he learns principles, such as the formation of plurals for nouns, which he then *generalizes* to other forms. Once having learned to discriminate between "shoe" and "shoes," he can then extend the same rule to "boy," "girl," and so forth. Braine (1963) uses this principle to account for language forms learned by young children. He says that children begin by learning two classes of words: *pivot* and *open*. Pivot words are key words that can be used to frame two-word sentences with words from the open class. A two-year-old may be able to say, for example, "My ball," "My horsie," and "My boat." "My" is a pivot word, and "ball," "horsie," and "boat" are open-class words. According to Braine, the child learns to use a word in a particular way and then generalizes its use to similar positions or relationships in new sentences.

Sociolinguistic learning theory goes beyond the mere learning of words and sentences and is concerned with how children learn linguistic styles (whether to say "I" or "we," when to speak, when to be silent, etc.) that prevail in their families. Inasmuch as families are ex-

tensions of the subculture within the main culture, each child learns the language appropriate to his socio-economic status and the ideas and values that are appropriate to it (Bernstein, 1972). These interlocking speech-and-thought structures constitute his way of reacting to others outside the family and in in turn modify their reaction to him. His speech patterns therefore announce who he is, in terms of social class and ethnic group, and suggest the way in which he looks at life and its problems. A five-year-old child with a rich vocabulary and precise grammar identifies himself as a member of an educated family that values ideas and individual differences; a child the same age with minority group dialect thereby identifies himself as a member of the group in question and one who subscribes to their life view, whatever it may be.

Bernstein notes that language serves a different function for a working man and a business executive; the former uses language in here-and-now situations for manipulation and control, whereas the latter uses it for decision making in the context of complex organizations. These two styles of communication carry over to their family relationships and inevitably affect the kind of language forms their children learn. The working-class child will therefore learn to use language in ways that may help him to deal with material objects in a very direct way, but will not enable him to deal with complex, abstract phenomena. This will, in turn, give him difficulties at school. Bernstein also believes that if a child from a working-class home is successfully taught the more elaborated linguistic mode of the middle class, this may alter the relations between him and the members of his family and the working-class subculture.

In essence, the nativistic position explains language acquisition in maturational terms, and the environmentalist position explains it in learning terms. Experts engage in long arguments as to which position is correct, but the evidence suggests that both are valid. L. R. Goulet (1968) reviewed the extensive research dealing with verbal learning in children and concluded that it was virtually impossible to separate the effects of maturational and experiential variables in developmental studies dealing with verbal processes, irrespective of whether the research was cross-sectional or longitudinal. It is not a question of "either-or," but "both-and."

Egocentric and Sociocentric Modes of Speech

Two of the earlier students of language development in preschool children are Dorothea McCarthy (1930) and Jean Piaget (1926). McCarthy investigated several related aspects of language by obtaining 50 consecutive verbal responses from each of 140 children, 20 at each of seven age levels from one year and six months to four years and six months.

In the main, Piaget relied on about 1500 remarks made by two children, aged six-and-a-half, supplemented by other observations of Swiss schoolchildren between two and eleven years of age. By American standards his work is considered to be relatively unsystematic and "loose." Even his classification of the speech of his subjects bore within it contradiction from one part to another (McCarthy, 1954). Nevertheless, it was the work of Piaget that focused contemporary attention on the functions of language as being both a means of communication with self and with others—the egocentric and socialized functions of language respectively. This distinction between egocentric and socialized speech has been generally accepted, despite disagreement over definition, relative proportion, and age at which they make their appearance.

As Piaget described it, egocentrism refers to the infant's isolation within himself. In an infant, egocentrism is epitomized by his inability to distinguish the self from the world. In a preschool child it is shown in egocentric speech—in his talking without knowing to whom he is speaking or whether he is being listened to. Egocentric speech may be expressed in any one of three forms: (1) repetition, or talking for the sake of talking; (2) monologue, or talking to oneself as though thinking aloud; and (3) collective or dual monologue, or the other person serving both as stimulus and as recipient of the speech, although that person's point of view is not being considered.

Extending the concept of egocentrism beyond its manifestation in language, it means that an egocentric individual shows no consideration of the other person's point of view. This is in contrast with socialized speech in which the talker addresses the listener, considers his viewpoint, at least to some degree, and tries to communicate with him. Piaget seems to regard adult speech and thought as highly socialized and egocentrism as a characteristic of immaturity.

In studying egocentric speech in the manner mentioned earlier, Piaget found that the speech of children showed considerable egocentricity, but with a decrease in the proportion of egocentricity and an increase in sociocentric speech as age increased. He classed 38% of the 1500 remarks in the egocentric category with about 45% classed as spontaneous social speech. (The remaining 17% was made up of answers to remarks or questions and hence were not spontaneous.) He found even higher percentages of egocentric speech for less intensively studied children ages three to five as well as lower percentages for children ages seven and eight. It is only at about the age of seven or eight that he considers true social maturity to appear simultaneously with the virtual disappearance of egocentric speech.

This work of Piaget has stimulated a considerable number of research studies both here

Language learning

Parents, and especially mothers, are the child's first models for the learning of words and phrases. Children learn to perceive their environment not only through parents' eyes but also through parents' verbalized concepts. Language is a social technique, and it is in social situations that the most language is generated.

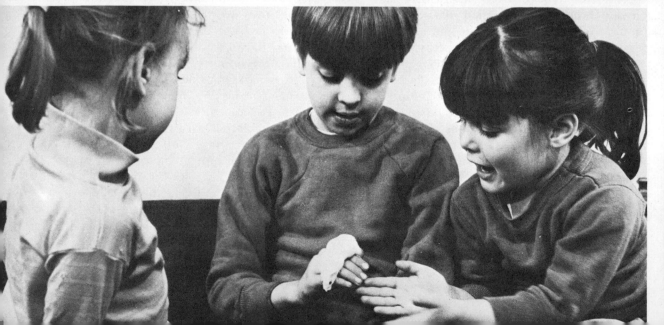

Communication phenomena from the world outside the family also have their influence on language development in the form of television and books. Beginning with the concrete action level, the child moves to levels of greater and greater abstraction.

and abroad. McCarthy (1954), in summarizing these investigations, found that some studies which tried to follow Piaget's approach literally, or at least very closely, defined the meaning of egocentricity differently from Piaget. Usually the definitions of egocentricity adopted by the latter group of investigators were based on considering the sentence either egocentric or not egocentric on the basis of the grammatical subject. For example, when the sentence had the self as subject, it was considered to be egocentric in nature. Paradoxically, in studies using these other definitions of egocentricity, they found percentages that agreed rather closely with those Piaget found following his own definition. Others using his definition found much less egocentricity.

In her preschool study McCarthy (1930), with due attention to reliability and objectivity, followed Piaget's meaning of egocentricity closely in classifying her samples. She found the percentage of egocentric speech to range only between 1.3 and 6.5% for children aged one-and-a-half to four-and-a-half. The average for all ages was 3.6%, a proportion considerably less than that reported by Piaget.

Rather than explore other specific research findings concerning egocentric speech in children, an attempt will be made to offer a summary. It would appear that there is general agreement among investigators that a certain proportion of the young child's speech is egocentric. There is similar agreement that a decrease takes place in this proportion with increasing age. Turning now to the magnitude of this proportion, even if we accept as more valid those studies finding the highest percentages, they never reach 50%.

Egocentrism in the speech of young children does exist, but it does not predominate. The present evidence indicates that the percentage of egocentric speech in children is less, perhaps considerably less, than reported by Piaget.

Egocentric speech, it should be indicated, does serve a useful function. By naming things to himself, the child is learning to communicate with *himself*. He is learning the names of objects and properties. His first active use of words—omitting the use of interjections, "bye-bye," "hi!" and so on—is learning to name people, acts, and things such as "mama," "doggie," "baby," "milk," "eat," and the like. He develops a great interest in names and is always demanding (in his own version, of course), "What's that?" Talking to himself does not mean he is not still learning. Is it any wonder, then, that he repeats words to himself? Naming seems to make an experience his very own. If he can name what he is doing to himself in egocentric fashion, he can use them better later for social communication. Despite this, egocentric speech is primarily an indication of immaturity.

The shift from egocentric to sociocentric speech with increasing age reflects the influence of socialization. It is plausible to believe that the change from egocentric to sociocentric speech partly stems from rewards for such speech from persons in the child's environment, whereas egocentric speech is simultaneously discouraged. The socially oriented verbalizations that the child learns bring with it rewards. Through sociocentric speech rather than egocentric speech he can manipulate his environment. Moreover, everyday observation would indicate that egocentric speech is actually discouraged as the child grows older and hence not rewarded.

As McCarthy (1954) indicates, it is more than accidental that a marked degree of socialization occurs in the behavior of older preschool child. Language is becoming a more efficient means of communication and it plays a considerable role in the socialization taking place during the period. When the child can understand instructions, when he can ask and answer questions, when he can defend a course of action, when he can tell what he is doing, then he is in a position to profit expeditiously from the socialization efforts of those around him. Every parent knows how much more facility there is in controlling a child's behavior when his understanding of spoken language improves.

Growth of Vocabulary

The size of children's vocabularies grows extensively during the preschool years. The figures reported in a number of normative studies on the average size of a child's vocabulary vary considerably for reasons not hard to identify.

First, there is difficulty in getting agreement on what is meant by "knowing" a word. One investigator may ask only that a word be recognized in context, another that it be used in a sentence, and still another that it be defined. Although all of these methods have some claim to legitimacy as indices of the growth of vocabulary, they yield different size vocabularies. Second, quite apart from how it is to be measured, there is the ambiguity created by the various meanings a given word has; the same word is apt to have different meanings, as anyone consulting a dictionary knows. Differing standards toward the variety of meanings to be counted also result in differing estimates of the size of the vocabulary.

Fortunately, there seems to be some agreement that an early study performed by Medorah E. Smith (1926) is, to some extent more definitive than most of the other studies. Smith standardized a vocabulary test on children one to six years of age. She did so by selecting every twentieth word from a list developed by Thorndike containing the 10,000 words most frequently encountered in writing samples. The meanings of these words were elicited by Smith from her subjects by carefully probing for their meanings by using objects, pictures, and questions. Consequently, more than usual

care was taken by her to find out whether the child did or did not know the word meanings. The total words correctly known by a child was multiplied by twenty, since every twentieth word from the list of 10,000 was used. This gave the child's oral vocabulary. As distinguished from McCarthy's procedure in her preschool study, yielding vocabulary of use, this study gave a vocabulary of recognition.

The vocabulary sizes Smith obtained for various ages are reported in Figure 11-2. A logarithmic scale is used in this figure in order to show how each word learned in the earlier stages is, relatively speaking, a major gain, whereas single words learned later only represent minor additions to the vocabulary. When children are around a year old, gains may be

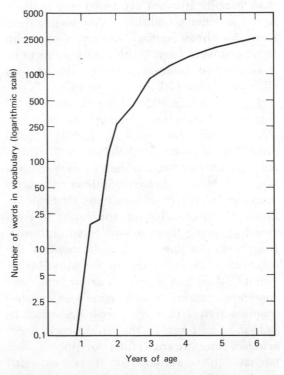

Figure 11-2. *Logarithmic growth curve of the acquisition of recognition vocabulary by children from infancy to six years of age.* (After Smith, 1926.)

measured in terms of single words, but in a few months, gains come in the tens of words, then hundreds. When children are five years old, they are learning to recognize about a hundred new words every three months, but the gain, in proportion to the number they already know, is relatively small.

One fault that may be found in Smith's study is that her estimates may be too low. For one thing, she had no way of determining how many words not on Thorndike's list were known to a child. For another, studies done more recently suggest that children today are familiar with a larger range of words, probably because they are exposed to more media of mass communication, such as television and radio (Templin, 1957). Furthermore, today's parent has completed more years of education than parents 50 years ago and hence is likely to use a richer vocabulary. With some adjustment for these factors, however, the growth curve resulting from Smith's work seems to be a reasonable representation of the rate at which children pick up new words.

The underestimation of the ability of small children to make verbal progress seems to be characteristic of many developmental psychologists. The Russian psychologist, A. R. Luria (1961), theorized that children's ability to regulate their motoric behavior follows an orderly sequence. As the child grows and develops, he increases his capacity for responding to commands, relating them to signals, and externalizing them. In stage 1 (12 to 18 months), the infant's speech is inadequate for his self-regulation. Others can direct his action, but their commands cannot arrest or reverse an ongoing motor activity. In stage 2 (two-and-a-half to four-and-a-half years), the child progressively achieves an internalization of speech and partial self-regulation, but it is not until stage 3 (four-and-a-half to five-and-a-half years) that the semantics or "meaning"

aspects of words become more important than their activating aspects and permit the child to develop a reasonable degree of self-regulation. Luria's theories were put to the test by Bates and Katz (1970), who observed children in a day care center. Their conclusions were that the process of interrelating language and action is more complex than conceived by Luria and that the stages were not as well defined as he described them. For instance, even three-year-olds showed the beginnings of behavior that Luria said they should not be developing until they were about five.

The Emergence of Grammatical Form

Growth in clearness of articulation, in the integration of words into sentences, in the sheer length of sentences, and changes in the relative usage of the grammatical parts of speech take place during the preschool period. Ability to give the sounds of their language correctly increases as children grow older. Wellman and others (1931) reported that the correlation between age and clearness of articulation is .80. In their study the average two-year-old child was able to articulate correctly only about 32% of the sounds he made. At age three the most marked increase was made to an average correct of 63%. As age increased the percentage of correct articulation rose steadily; at age four it was 77%; and at age five it was 88%.

Growth in language skills with age is shown in changes in the integration of words into sentences. There seem to be four relatively distinct stages. Stage one, the single word stage, begins at approximately the end of the first year and lasts from four to twelve months. The second is the early sentence stage. Only one or two words are used by infants, with a preponderance of nouns. Even if the infant uses but a single word, he still uses it to convey differences of meaning to others. This single word may function as a sentence, although not yet having its grammatical form. Mothers soon learn of single words functioning as whole sentences. Even the same word may, on different occasions, serve as several sentences. For example, the word, "mama," used with varying inflections and gestures means "mama look," "mama is here," and "mama come quickly." A small vocabulary, using one word at a time, may still go a long way. This stage lasts until about 28 months of age. The next stage, the short sentence stage (three to four words), is one in which nouns and verbs are used by the young child, but tenses, comparatives, and other inflections are not mastered. This stage lasts until approximately the fourth year. Beginning at this age, the last stage, the "complete" sentence stage, involves six to eight words and is also characterized by a fairly precise use of inflections.

Closely related to the integration of words into sentences is the sheer length of the verbal response which also increases with age. Mildred C. Templin (1957) observed that at three the average number of words per remark was 4.1, increasing to 5.4 at four, and 5.7 at five. Her findings showed significantly longer responses, however, than the earlier McCarthy study of similar design. Again there is the implication that verbal skills have increased for present-day children as compared to those of the recent past.[2]

[2] There have been a number of indications that American children are becoming more adultlike in their speech. Robert H. Koff (1965) administered the Kent-Rosanoff word-association test to children aged eight to twelve and compared their responses with those recorded for children 50 years earlier. In 1916 children were inclined to give responses that were similar to the stimulus words (e.g., king–ruler), but in 1963 children tended to give more

Changes in relative usage of the different grammatical parts of speech are related to age. McCarthy found that nouns which constitute about 50% of the speech of the 18-month-old children decrease to about 19% in the 54-month-old sample. Verbs increase from 14% to 25% over the same age range. Although this is an increase, it is relatively slight as compared to that for adjectives and pronouns which almost double during the age range in question. Prepositions do not show up at all until about 24 months of age and connectives are hardly found until children are 30 months old.

These various developmental differences in the speech of children help to explain its particular so-called childish quality in the younger preschool child. This is most apparent in their usage of grammatical parts. Relative to adult speech the younger preschool child uses many nouns, a fair number of verbs, but very few pronouns and adjectives, and hardly any prepositions or connectives. Speech is direct and bald without the later nuances he learns with age. It is essentially disconnected and lacking in, what to adult ears is, rhythm and fluency. When to this differing grammatical usage is added three properties of relatively poor articulation, shorter sentences, and a small vocabulary, we have the speech of the younger preschool child. Over the years of this period profound changes take place, the nature of

responses that were opposites (e.g., king–queen). Only 3% of the responses were opposites in 1916, whereas 46% were opposites in 1963, a figure that compares with the response pattern of adults, whose responses consisted of 57% opposites. The responses given by children in 1963 were also closer to adults in other ways. In view of the fact that cognitive and speech processes are closely linked, these findings would suggest that children today are also becoming more adultlike in their way of looking at the world in general.

which has just been sketched. These changes take the five-year-old, on his leaving the preschool period, a great distance in the direction of adult speech. Certainly, the preschool years are the period of the greatest changes in speech development of the child. By the same token he advances in the degree of his socialization.

Bronowski and Bellugi (1970) maintain that children extract rules of grammar from the sentences they hear and restylize them in their own speech forms. Children are not taught and do not need to be taught in any specific way the underlying rules of grammatical structure, yet careful examination of their evolving speech shows that they gradually reconstruct the system used in their mother tongue. In initial stages of language acquisition, their system is not precisely the same one used by adults, but bit by bit it approaches the adult system in form and complexity. The way in which they learn these rules is shown by their tendency to pick up a rule and apply it to more instances than is proper. Three- and four-year-olds say things like "He comed yesterday," "It breaked," "Two mans," and the like. These are not phrases that the children have learned, but rather ones that they have generated using the *rules* they have learned but applying them incorrectly.

The approach used by small children is, according to Bronowski and Bellugi, similar to that which they employ in "reconstructing" (i.e., giving structure to) their physical environment. They structure their environment partly by giving objects names, a process that is not merely a matter of learning labels used by adults but is, instead, a way that children use to analyze the environment into distinct parts, which can then be treated as separate objects. The sentences constructed by children imply a view of the world as being separable into things that have an identity and that can be manipulated mentally. This manipulation is made possible by the fact that not only objects but also actions and properties can be symbolized by words.

Individual, Group, and Sex Differences in Language Development

Children of five years of age differ considerably in their facility with oral language. Some are chatterboxes, talking from the moment they wake up in the morning until they fall asleep at night. Others are quiet, almost silent children, economical with words, speaking only when spoken to and often using a nod or a shake of the head where a flow of words would be forthcoming from another child. Some children speak with a variety of good and poor articulations, a sparse or rich vocabulary, and so on.

To put the matter in terms of the specific aspects of oral language, there are individual differences among children of the same age in size of vocabulary, clarity or articulation, ability to integrate words into sentences, length of verbal responses, and the relative usage of different grammatical parts of speech. In fact, from time to time we have drawn attention to these differences. Nevertheless, stress was placed on changes with age. Attention was focused on individual differences, but on differences in speech brought about by differences in age. In one sense, age was tacitly treated as the source of differences, although it is, of course, recognized that changes are a matter of maturation and learning concomitant with age, not age itself. It is only in this sense that age is a source of differences. Other sources of differences in speech skills during the preschool period are individual, group, and sex factors.

Individual differences among children in language skills reflect the importance of practice and reinforcement. Several lines of evidence may be mentioned. Sudies of institutionalized children show vividly the importance of lack of reinforcement. Because of lack of contact with others, institutional children do not have as many reinforced speech responses as compared to the other children—those living in foster homes. The speech of the institutional children was found to be impoverished. There are other sources of evidence for the effect of lack of reinforcement (Goldfarb, 1943, 1945). For example, twins and triplets are slower in learning speech than singletons. Presumably, they are not so highly motivated to learn language because many of their reciprocal social needs may be met by means other than verbal communication which results in less language reinforcement.

There are also situations that increase exposure to reinforcement of language responses. Increased vocabulary development may be associated with new experiences and exposure to words for new objects and processes. Thus "tractor" or "harvesting" may be learned from a visit to a farm. Upper (or upper middle) socioeconomic circumstances tend to facilitate vocabulary growth. Exposure to the material things that go with middle-class life, such as magazines and the encyclopedia, help to broaden the language horizon (Davis, 1937). Only children are also more advanced in vocabulary than others. They tend to associate more with adults than do other children and are thus exposed to more opportunities for reinforcement of new language responses.

Sex differences in language skills have often demonstrated that girls show superiority over boys in nearly all aspects of speech development. One aspect of speech development, length of response, will illustrate. McCarthy (1954) summarized 14 major, carefully controlled studies of length of speech responses at preschool ages. Of the 64 comparisons, 43 favored the girls. The exhaustive study of Templin (1957), however, raises some question about this contention, since she found the sex differences in favor of the girls to be much less pronounced.

Difference in intelligence is another potent factor related to differences in language ability. In fact, size of vocabulary as measured by the Stanford-Binet Intelligence Scales is generally considered to be the most important single test of intelligence among the scales. Indicative of the popularity of the vocabulary section is the common practice that when a relatively short intelligence measure is wanted, the vocabulary test is used alone. The correlation between the vocabulary test and the total Stanford-Binet Scales is about .70 or .80, thus showing a remarkably high degree of relationship between the two (McNemar, 1942).

Much of what we have said in the last few paragraphs has been brought into question by some recent analyses made by workers in sociolinguistic fields. Hymes (1972) suggests that lower-class children may actually excel middle-class children in some aspects of communicative ability that has not as yet been determined by research. Osser (1971), who has reviewed the research in this field, maintains that linguistic differences in social class groups reflect differences in rule-systems of their language. Lower class children, for example, tend to be less *explicit* in their verbal communication than are middle-class children. This tendency, of course, penalizes them when they encounter the linguistic modes that prevail in a classroom. Lower-class children also use forms of language that are quite different from those used by middle-class children. A middle-class child is likely to have little difficulty when he encounters the word *something* in his reading, but a lower-class child may puzzle over it in vain until someone tells him that he is looking at the word for *sump'n*.

Osser notes that there are two conflicting points of view with respect to the effect that nonstandard dialects have on children's speech. One is that lower-class dialects do not by themselves interfere with a child's conceptual development. The other point of view is that such dialects (black English, for example) impose serious limitations on the child's ability to develop logical operations (Bereiter and Englemann, 1966). The preponderant view in education, according to Osser, is that black English and other lower-class dialects render children essentially nonverbal or verbally destitute and hence lead inevitably to academic failure. The argument continues along these lines: irrespective of whether a child remains in lower-class surroundings or whether he moves into the middle class, he must still deal linguistically with a world in which middle-class language, values, and ways of doing things are normal. Furthermore, unless he develops some competency with middle-class language forms (preferably as a *user*, but minimally as a *consumer*), he is doomed to a life of alienation and isolation from the mainstream of the social and economic life of the land in which he lives.

The sociolinguistic viewpoint, according to Osser, holds that research showing that lower-class children are cognitively deficient has not been conducted adequately. Lower-class children are likely to be inarticulate when queried by middle-class interviewers who use middle-class language and middle-class ploys to get them to perform. When the lower-class child is with people he knows and feels comfortable with, he is often as verbal and as articulate as any middle-class child. What is needed, according to Osser, is a school program that will start where the child is linguistically and will go on from there, and he cites some studies to show that the lower-class child will make a good showing when educational programs are presented in the language with which he is familiar.

However, the question is still open. Research by Lorene C. Quay (1971) tested the hypothesis that Negro children would perform more adequately if tested by friendly, supportive Negro psychometrists who used Negro dialect, instead of standard, "establishment" English. Subjects were 100 four-year-old Negro children from Operation Head Start programs, who were given the Stanford-Binet test in either Negro dialect or standard English, and who were reinforced either with candy or with praise for correct answers. The results, as presented in Table 11-1, show virtually the same

TABLE 11-1. *Stanford-Binet IQ Means for Four-Year-Old Negro Children Who Took the Test Under Standard-English or Negro-Dialect Conditions and Were Rewarded for Correct Answers Either with Praise or with Candy (Quay, 1971)*

Reward	Negro Dialect Version	Standard English Version
Praise	97	96
Candy	95	96

mean IQ under all four conditions. It appears that the children understood standard English as well as the dialect they were used to, and that concrete rewards in the form of candy did not facilitate their performance. Other tests of the sociolinguistic position will have to be made, of course, before firm conclusions can be drawn, but the rather definitive results of Quay's research, suggest that we must look for reasons other than linguistic ones for the difficulties that lower-class children experience in school learning.

Intellectual Development

English and English (1958), noted that there are three concepts basic to *intelligence*, as the term is used by psychologists: the ability to deal with tasks involving *abstractions*, the ability to *learn*, and the ability to deal with *new situations*. Intelligence tests characteristically include all three of these concepts: they confront the child with problems that can be solved abstractly; they measure what he has learned (on the assumption he has been exposed to an environment similar to that of most children); and the items themselves are often novel and unlike anything the child will have encountered in his daily life.

An intelligence test, therefore, attempts to tap a number of different areas of cognitive functioning. Children who have been slow to develop cognitive facility for whatever reason will therefore score low on intelligence tests, whereas whose who are advanced will score high. The question of how much of the variation in intelligence test scores can be attributed to genetic factors is, as we indicated earlier, an open question, but the evidence that environmental factors make heavy contributions is impressive. Anything that interferes with normal growth and development is likely to lead to cognitive deficits and a lowering of IQ: malnourishment of the child, particularly during infancy, and birth abnormalities all take their toll. Nonstimulating environments are apparently detrimental. Nutritional deficiencies can, of course, be prevented, and conditions contributing to general health can be improved, but exactly what kind of stimulation should be undertaken for maximum cognitive development is not clear, although much research is now being conducted in this area.

Facilitating Intellectual Development

One trend common among children of poor and uneducated parents is the tendency for IQs to decline after the first year in school. Characteristically, the child from a poor family starts school with an IQ of about 90, which then declines in eight or nine years into the 80s. In rural areas, the IQ is likely to start in the 80s and then drop to the 70s and even below (Green and Hofmann, 1965). If the preschool years can be regarded as a critical period for cognitive development, we might hypothesize that intervention at this stage could forestall IQ declines of such a magnitude.

One of the most successful intervention programs has been organized and supervised by Susan W. Gray and Rupert A. Klaus (1970) of George Peabody College for Teachers in Nashville, Tennessee. Gray and Klaus have for some years been developing a number of longitudinal programs for socially and economically deprived Negro preschool children in Tennessee. Their program has been aimed at helping these children develop the kinds of skills and work attitudes that would enable them to maintain normal IQ levels and attain a reasonable level of success in school. They are particularly interested in encouraging the development of what has been termed *achievement motivation*, especially as it relates to school activities. This includes such characteristics as persistence, the ability to delay gratification and work for postponed rewards, and interest in working with typical school materials: books, crayons, puzzles, and the like.

The George Peabody program has been built around a ten-week summer school experience, in which children are exposed to a variety of new stimuli and are reinforced for attempting and persisting with new tasks. The program is also supplemented during the entire year by paraprofessionals—mothers from the Negro community—who visit the homes of children and encourage parents to behave in supportive and facilitative ways with respect to their children's developing interests and skills. The Gray-Klaus program has met with some success, as indicated by IQs that run significantly higher than those of a control group of children. After the children have gone through a few years of elementary school, however, most of the initial advantage appears to dwindle. This is not the fault of the experimental program, which takes the children only as far as the first grade: instead, it reflects the deficiences of a conventional educational program in a racially segregated school system. Incidentally, the few children who attended desegregated schools seem to have been able to maintain their initial advantage better than those who attended segregated schools.

Predicting Future Intellectual Development

Tests administered during infancy have, as we noted previously, relatively low correlations with later development. The skills that we recognize as being major factors in intellectual functioning are but poorly developed then. Once children learn language skills, however, the scope of their cognitive activities is enlarged, and at the same time it becomes easier to test their intelligence. It is not surprising, therefore, that tests administered during the preschool years are much better predictors of later intelligence than earlier tests.

As part of the Guidance Study of the University of California Institute of Child Welfare (described in Chapter 1), 250 children were given periodic intelligence tests, beginning at the age of 21 months. Follow-up research with these children (who are now adults) continues at the present time. Correlations between test performance at 10 to 17 months and measures made during the preschool years run from .34 to .48 for certain scales or subtests. The ability to make perceptual discriminations seems to be a key skill that has a significant effect on children's vocal-verbal and manipulatory behavior (Bayley, 1970).

Figure 11-3 shows the correlations between the verbal knowledge subtest of the California Preschool Mental Scale administered between two and six years of age to children in the California Growth Study and the IQs of the same individuals in later years. This subtest,

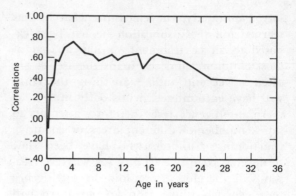

Figure 11-3. Correlations between verbal precocity (as indicated by scores on the Preschool Verbal Knowledge portion of the California Preschool Mental Scale) and IQs of California Growth Study subjects from infancy to adulthood. (After Bayley, 1966.)

a measure of what Bayley calls "precocity," is a particularly good one for this purpose, because verbal skills appear to play a more crucial role than any other factor with respect to school learning, problem solving, and cognitive functioning in general. The graph in Figure 11-3 shows a correlation that is negative during the initial months, which quickly rises to a positive correlation of about .40 and then to .70 about four years of age. After that the relationship between IQ and precocity settles down to .50 to .60 during the school years and then drops to about .40 during the early adult years. The data reported in Figure 11-3 represent the midpoints of correlations for both male and female subjects. The relationships are fairly close during the school years, but about age 16, the correlation with precocity begins to be lower for women than for men. From age 25 onward, the correlation for men actually increases slightly to about .58 at age 36, whereas that for women drops off to about .18. This latter trend may be a reflection of the culturally determined fact that the occupations of men generally tend

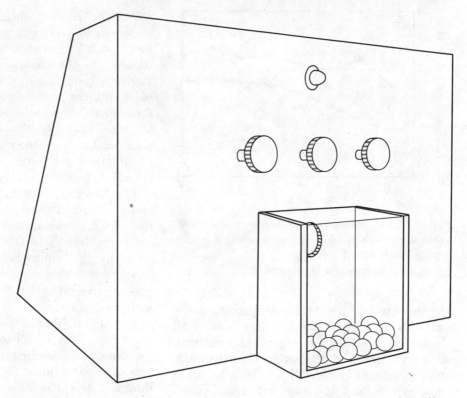

Figure 11-4.   Line drawing of marble-dispensing device used in research dealing with simple problem-solving strategies.
(Weir, 1967. Reproduced by permission.)

to be more intellectually demanding than those of women.

Problem-Solving Ability

During the preschool years, children quickly develop the ability to deal with simple manipulative problems. In fact, there is evidence to show that the approaches used by preschoolers are sometimes more effective with certain types of laboratory problems than are those used by school children and adults.

Morton W. Weir (1967), for example, used the device displayed in Figure 11-4 to present subjects with a very simple type of game or problem. The object of the game was to get as

many marbles as possible out of the machine. The subject did not know that only one of the three knobs (always the same one) was connected to the release mechanism, which was programmed to pay off only one third of the time and at random intervals. In other words, the subject was rewarded only if he pushed the correct knob and then only 33% of the time. Three-year-olds, in dealing with this problem, quickly found that only one knob paid off and settled down to pushing that one most of the time. Older children and adults, however, were puzzled by the frequent lack of payoff and kept trying to figure out a strategy. They were more likely to believe that the other knobs were involved and kept test-

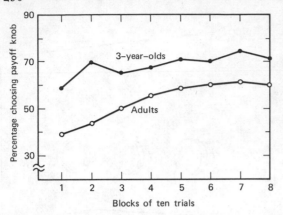

Figure 11-5. Performance of three-year-olds and adult subjects in playing a game involving a simple strategy with a 33% payoff.
(Weir, 1967. Reproduced by permission.)

ing them to be sure. As a consequence, three-year-olds were consistently more successful than older individuals. Figure 11-5 demonstrates the trend very clearly. Three-year-old subjects achieved almost 70% success between the eleventh and the twentieth trial, while adults at that stage were plodding along at about 40%. Adults made steady improvement during the remainder of the experiment, but never achieved the success of the three-year-olds.

Somewhat similar results were obtained by Tracy and Howard Kendler (1959) with a marble-dispensing device rigged somewhat differently. In their experiments, subjects had to choose between one of two levers that were coded by two different symbolic elements, say, color and shape. After their subject had figured out which symbolic element paid off, the Kendlers, without warning, changed the basis of the payoff. A change in one of the two elements, say from one color to the other, called for a change in strategy that the Kendlers termed a *reversal shift*; a change in *two* elements, say from a color to shape of a symbol, demanded what they termed a *nonreversal*

shift. The reversal shift required a partial alteration of strategy; the nonreversal called for a complete abandonment of the former strategy and the learning of a brand new one. Logically, one might think that adults and older children would figure out both types of shifts more successfully than young children, but the results of the Kendlers show that young children learned nonreversal shifts more readily than did older children and adults (Kendler, Kendler, and Wells 1960).

The Kendlers theorized that older children and adults attack the problem verbally whereas the younger ones do not. A number of the older children actually talked aloud when faced by the sudden change in the payoff arrangement. Verbalization evidently helps in making reversal shifts, but tends to interfere with nonreversal shifts.

Although neither of these two sets of studies have any direct or obvious relevance to the problems that children face in growing up, they do shed a little light on the way their thinking develops. As more of such studies are undertaken, we will gain a better understanding of what steps we can take to facilitate the learning of problem-solving skills both for children in normal circumstances, as well as for those who are socially and economically deprived.

Summary

About the middle of the second year of life, the infant begins the early stages of what Piaget calls preoperational thought. During this stage, the child uses preconcepts or representations that are midway between the concept of an object and that of a class. He becomes capable of internally evoking a *signifier* (a word or image), and differentiating it from a *significate* (perceptually absent event).

This new ability for internal representation dramatically increases the scope and complexity of the child's associative skills. The child is egocentric in his representations, just as he was in his sensorimotor actions. Piaget has illustrated this in his account of the preschool child who cannot imagine viewing a scene from any vantage point other than the one he is currently at. The young child is also animistic. Piaget distinguishes a number of stages in the reduction of the range of things the child judges to be "alive." Investigators have suggested that children are not genuinely animistic, but merely misuse or misunderstand the term "alive." The research findings, however, are mixed and do not confirm either point of view.

Piaget also believes that the preschooler tends to distort his thinking by "centering" or attending to only one feature of an object. This leads to confusions in *conservation*. One of a pair of equal volume containers will be judged to hold more liquid if the child "centers" on its greater width. Although a number of psychologists have criticized Piaget for his incomplete and anecdotal research methods, research tends to confirm his conclusions. English and American children follow the general stages of cognitive development described by Piaget, although they do so at an accelerated pace. Roth and Courtney confirmed Piaget's contentions about the evolution of conservation, also finding that the child's ability to verbalize concepts is important. Researchers have investigated the influence of experience in the development of conservation. One such study utilized the special experience the children of Mexican potters had with volume and substance. Results showed that the potters' children were better able to conserve, especially with regard to substance.

Although the preschool child is much better at discriminating between objects than the infant, this ability is far from fully developed.

The lack of differentiation sometimes extends to the point of fusing the data from different sense modalities. This so-called *synesthesia*, characterized by the child's statement that something "smells green," tends to disappear with increasing age. As the ability to differentiate improves, the ability to form concepts also improves. The child's conceptualization of space is one example. According to Piaget, space is not innately understood, but must be *constructed* through experience. Eventually, the infant learns that objects retain identity, even when out of sight, and the child frees himself from his initially egocentric perspective. Piaget cites the example of the child who reveals his growing concept of space by moving around furniture to fetch a ball, rather than following the ball's path directly. Concepts of time are more abstract than those of space, partly because there are few cues on which to build them. Generally, words referring to the present appear in the child's vocabulary before words referring to the future, which in turn are learned before words indicating the past. Children first become able to relate time in terms of regular events. They next pass through two stages in which they learn to relate imaginative but not unreasonable clock times, then they give reasonable but incorrect times. Finally they attain accuracy. Hours are learned first, then half-hours and quarter-hours. The fact that the child must *construct* his own concepts of space and time can lead to some basic confusions, such as the six-year-old who told Piaget that if he *ran* home it would take *longer* than usual.

Concepts may be arranged in a logical hierarchy, ranging from concrete to abstract. The order in which the child develops and names his concepts, however, may not follow the logical order at all. He may, for example, assume that all four-legged animals are *dogs*, and be further confused when told that *dogs* and *cats* are both animals. Welch differentiates between first- and second-order concepts. A first-order concept represents a class, for example, a *chair*. The second order concept is divorced from any object, for example, *justice*. Research indicates that children begin learning first-order concepts when they reach two years of age. In contrast, second-order concepts did not appear until age five. Speech is a major factor in concept development, because it is the richest source of symbols available to the child. Words may not only facilitate or inhibit generalization but may also arouse drives and reinforce the behavior of others. A considerable number of studies have shown that verbal facility enhances ease of learning. A representative study, conductd by Weir and Stevenson, required children to verbalize the correct stimuli. The results showed that these children learned a discrimination task more quickly than the control subjects. There is a question, however, whether verbalization is essential for cognitive functioning. This conclusion is supported by the fact that congenitally deaf people reach normal levels of cognitive ability without corresponding competence in language. Furthermore, children are able to perform tasks with elements for which they have no words in their vocabularies.

There are several opposing views as to how language is acquired. Skinner and other environmentalists favor an operant-conditioning explanation. Chomsky and the geneticists argue that the facts that the language which children hear and use is limited and *degenerate*, and that their linguistic stimuli are *scattered*, combine to make the acquisition of language difficult. Operant conditioning alone cannot explain the rapidity with which children surmount such difficulties. Chomsky concludes that human beings must be born with a sort of *language acquisition mechanism*. The fact that children literally invent a working grammatical structure for themselves to bridge

the gap between their prelinguistic state and later grammatical competence tends to support the maturational or "nativistic" view. Learning theorists other than Skinner include imitation in their explanations of language acquisition. To explain the appearance of new forms, environmentalists also have recourse to the principle of generalization. Once a new rule or *pivot word* is learned, it can be generalized to a variety of new words from the *open class*. Every child learns the language appropriate to his socioeconomic status. The kind of language he uses will, in turn, influence the way he looks at the world, and the way other persons react to him.

Piaget was the first to point out the egocentric and sociocentric functions of speech. Egocentric speech may be expressed by repetition, monologue, or collective monologue. This is in contrast to socialized speech, in which the speaker is genuinely concerned with communicating with another. Piaget found that the speech of children showed considerable egocentricity, which decreased with a concurrent increase in socialized speech, as the child grew older. Although other researchers have not agreed as to the relative proportion of egocentric speech, most agree that it is present, and that it decreases with age. This decrease is probably the result of differential reinforcement on the part of persons in the child's environment.

The size of children's vocabularies grows extensively during the preschool years. Although there is some disagreement between researchers as to what "knowing" a word really means, a study by Smith seems more definitive than the others. Her results show that the rapid absolute gains in vocabulary made later in childhood are not shown to be as large in the relative sense, as the small absolute gains made in the early stages of language acquisition. Because contemporary children's vocabularies are expanding and because Thorndike's list may not be a representative sample, Smith's estimates may be too low. Luria has theorized that, as the child develops, he increases his capacity for responding to commands, relating them to signals, and externalizing them. Research has shown that internalization of speech and self-regulation develop much earlier than Luria expected and in a much more complex manner. The course of language development is revealed in a number of observable changes throughout the preschool period. The correlation between age and clearness of articulation is .80. The child also passes through several distinct stages in the integration of words into sentences. He first progresses beyond the simple use of single words to the point where one or two words function as sentences. By 28 months, he has expanded his sentences to several words, and uses nouns and verbs, although tenses, comparatives, and other inflections are not yet mastered. This stage lasts until the fourth year, when the "complete" sentence stage begins. The average length of the verbal response also increases with age, and the relative proportions of the grammatical parts of speech change. The nouns, which make up 50% of the speech of 18-month-old children, decrease dramatically along with a corresponding increase in most other parts of speech. Bronowski and Bellugi maintain that children extract rules of grammar from the sentences they hear, and restylize them in their own speech forms. The gradual progress they make in this process is revealed by the systematic misapplication of grammatical rules, as in "he comed yesterday."

Five-year-olds differ considerably in language ability. These individual differences reflect the importance of practice and reinforcement. Studies have shown that the speech of children in institutions, twins, and triplets, all of whom suffer decrements in reinforcement, is impoverished. Girls show a clear superiority over boys in almost all aspects of speech development, and language ability is also highly correlated with intelligence. A great deal of attention has been directed in recent years to the influence of socioeconomic factors on language. Osser, for example, has suggested that the linguistic differences in social class groups reflect differences in the rule-systems of their language. Rather than taking the view that lower-class dialects interfere with the child's ability to develop logical operations, Osser feels that lower-class children may be the intellectual equals of middle-and upper-class children. The problem is one of communication, rather than of development, and the child may do perfectly well if taught and tested in the language with which he is familiar. Quay, however, has found that Negro four-year-olds from Operation Head Start programs make virtually the same IQ scores, no matter what dialect the tester used.

Psychologists conceive intelligence as consisting of ability to solve tasks involving abstractions, the ability to learn, and the ability to deal with new situations. Intelligence tests attempt to tap all three of these cognitive abilities. Anything that interferes with normal growth and development will inhibit cognitive development—poor nutrition and birth abnormalities are examples. Environments that are not stimulating may also retard cognitive development.

There is a common tendency for the IQs of the children of poor and uneducated parents to decline after the first year of school. This would seem to indicate that the preschool years are critical for cognitive development, and that intervention at that stage might forestall such decrements in IQ. Gray and Klaus have organized such a program for socially and economically deprived Negro schoolchildren, concentrating particularly on the development of achievement motivation as well as on cognitive skills. The program has met with considerable success, indicated by higher IQs. Unfortunately, most of the gains seem to be lost after several years of attending segregated schools.

Intelligence tests administered during the preschool years are better predictors of later intelligence than are scores on tests administered in infancy. The California Preschool Mental Scale reveals that verbal skills play the single most important role with respect to later cognitive functioning. The graph in Figure 11-3 follows the relationship of preschool verbal skills with IQ from infancy to adulthood.

Preschoolers are sometimes better able to solve simple manipulative problems and games than adults. Both Weir and Kendler and Kendler made this observation. The common factor in both of their experiments was the fact that the required solution was so simple as to elude the adults in their search for a subtle strategy. The Kendlers theorized that this was because older children and adults attack the problem verbally, whereas younger children do not.

12 Parental Influences

The Family and Its Structure

As we have noted earlier, experimental studies of children's behavior have increased in number during the past two decades, with a growing amount of attention directed toward cognitive functioning. In relative terms, interest in personality development has declined. This does not mean that studies of personality are no longer being conducted. As a matter of fact, there has been a steady output of such studies, and some of them have tackled some rather fundamental problems. Indeed, it may be said that the newer studies have produced findings that render some of the earlier studies obsolete.

In very general terms, one might say that earlier researchers tended to emphasize psychoanalytic themes and seemed to be intent on proving that love, parental warmth, and permissiveness are about all that are needed for healthy personality development. The findings of the newer studies do not diminish the importance of love and warmth, but they do raise some questions about unconditional permissiveness and tend to find more evidence favoring firmness and even some strictness. The term *structure* comes to mind in describing such family relationships. Structure, as used in this sense, refers to the predictability and stability of social relationships. In a group that has a relatively high degree of structure, members know what their roles are, which means that they know what to do in different kinds of situations and what to expect of other members. Structure also implies some kind of hierarchy of status and power, with persons at the top able to assign roles and to exact penalties from members who do not perform adequately. The traditional authoritarian family, in which father is supreme, and mother is the second in command, is an obvious example of a highly structured group. It is possible to have a fairly high degree of structure and not be authoritarian, but as parental power diminishes, structure becomes harder to maintain.

Family structure is, like other social forms, very sensitive to psychosocial trends outside the family. Society at large may be very supportive of structure or may undermine parental attempts to impose it. By way of example, it is more difficult for parents to impose a high degree of structure in an urban setting than in a farm setting. The multitude of tasks that must be performed on the farm by all members of the family virtually dictate a highly structured social arrangement. In an urban setting, the family makes relatively fewer demands on the time of family members, whereas society outside the family not only makes more demands but also offers more distractions. As a result, attention is directed away from the performance of familial roles.

Today's families are likely to be less structured than the families of a generation ago. Urbanization is one reason for this change, but increased amount of education of parents, which tends to be associated with greater permissiveness, is another reason. The temper of the times is also more in favor of reducing status differences within groups of all kinds, including the family. Furthermore, North American families tend to be less structured than families in Europe and Asia. This is true even when factors like urbanization and education are held constant. The reason for this difference seems to be the distance between a culture and the roots of its tradition. European and Asian families are likely to be closer to an authoritarian tradition, whereas North American families are more removed.

When our forebears left the "Old Country" and came to the New World, they consciously or unconsciously attempted to purge themselves of traditional ways and set about building a society that incorporated some elements of the Old World but that was innovative in many respects. As a result, we have the evolving phenomenon of the North American family, which is unlike families in any other culture. This is not a recent phenomenon. De Tocqueville and other European visitors commented on the uniqueness of American family life when they visited this country early in the nineteenth century. Because the North American family is not like others, we must be cautious in extrapolating research findings based on American and Canadian children to children elsewhere. The reverse of this also holds true. As we have noted earlier, Piaget's age norms seem somewhat high for North American children, perhaps because the stimulus "input" for European children is more restricted, and they are less likely to be encouraged to experiment, test, and explore things on their own.

This does not mean that there are no "universals." The fact that Piaget's sequence of stages seems generally applicable shows that there are things that children have in common almost everywhere, but when we get into dimensions of behavior that are subject to social influence, we are less likely to find that research-based conclusions can cross cultural boundaries. We see this even in our own country: we are increasingly reminded that generalities based on research with middle-class children do not necessarily apply to working-class children or to children from the poverty class. And even in the latter instance, it sometimes makes a difference whether the home is Negro, white Appalachian, Latin-American, American Indian, or whatever. It is the major task of cross-cultural research to sort out differences and similarities.

The Home as a Social Environment

There are, basically, two major effects that the home has on the life of a child. First, it provides the conditions that facilitate some kinds of behavior and inhibit others. A home environment may be rich or poor in stimuli. Some homes are rich in stimuli and also have order and focus—that is, the stimuli may be directed at the child in the form of conversation, attention, caressing, fondling, and playing. Ordinarily such stimuli have a facilitating effect on the appearance of more mature forms of behavior. Other homes are also rich in stimuli, but the stimuli are more diffuse and are not focused on the child's needs. In such a home, the television may be going full blast 16 or more hours a day, adults may be engaged in loud talk or fighting, and traffic or industrial noises may be intense. Heavy exposure to such stimuli may have an inhibiting or confusing effect on the child's cognitive and affective development.

The second effect consists of the ways in which the child's personality is shaped. Here we are concerned principally with the interaction between the parents and the child, and, secondarily, between the child and his siblings. It is the area of parent-child interaction that has received the greatest amount of attention from researchers.

Child-rearing Practices. Diana Baumrind (1967) has done some work that shows significant relationships between children's personality and child-rearing practices. In her initial project, she did an intensive study relating the behavior of three groups of middle-class children to the modes of child rearing used by their parents. Her subjects consisted of a sample of 32 children drawn from a larger population of 110 three- and four-year-olds enrolled in the nursery school at the Child Stuty Center, Institute of Human Development, University of California at Berkeley. The 110 children were assessed on five personality dimensions: self-control, tendencies to approach or avoid others, self-reliance, subjective mood, and peer affiliation (tendencies to relate positively to other children). Children were ranked on these five dimensions by their nursery school teachers and an observer staff of psychologists. Children who received the highest or the lowest ratings were further screened in a test situation designed to assess their responses to success and failure in solving problems. The 32 children remaining after being screened demonstrated rather clear-cut patterns on the personality dimensions and fell into three well-defined groups: Pattern I children consisted of 13 who ranked high on mood, self-reliance, and approach or self-control;[1] Pattern II children consisted of 11 children who ranked low on peer affiliation and mood[2] and who were not ranked high on "approach"; and Pattern III children consisted of eight who ranked low on self-reliance, as well as on either self-control or "approach." Some of the behavioral tendencies that characterized the children in the three groups are listed in Table 12-1.

Measures of parental behavior toward each child were secured by visiting the home on two separate occasions. The first period oc-

[1] *Approach* refers to tendencies to move toward stimuli that are novel, stressful, exciting, or unexpected in an explorative and curious fashion, in contrast to tendencies to avoid such stimuli or to become anxious when challenged to approach them.

[2] *Mood* refers to tendencies to display zest, pleasure, and bouyancy, and to become happily involved in nursery school activities.

TABLE 12-1. Behavioral Tendencies Characterizing Three Groups of Nursery School Children Selected on the Basis of Clear-cut Personality Differences (Baumrind, 1967)

Pattern I (The self-reliant, self-controlled, approach-oriented, buoyant child)	Pattern II (The anxious, restless, depressed, and disaffiliated child)	Pattern III (The immature child)
Confident	Retreats from situation involving physical risk	Impetuous
Accepts blame	Acts too mature for age	Fatigued at school[a]
Withstands stress	Does not enjoy self at nursery school	Omnipotent attitude[a]
Gives his best to play and work	Has difficulty in relating to adults, other than mother	Self-abusive[a]
Follows standard operating procedure	Does not regret wrongdoing	Apprehensive[a]
Helps other children to adapt	Tattles or informs on other children	Becomes more childish or hostile when hurt[a]
Enjoys other children's company	Guileful	Irritable[a]
	Needlessly disrespectful toward adults	Exploits dependency[a]
		Cries easily[a]
		Sets easy goals for self[a]
		Inconsiderate[a]
		Boasts[a]
		Obstructive[a]

[a] Characteristic of children of both Patterns II and III.

curred from just before dinner to bedtime, in order to observe the home during a period that is likely to demonstrate the maximum interaction and stress. The second period was chosen by the mother as one in which she thought the situation was the least stressful for herself and the child. Each visit lasted about three hours. A second set of measures were derived from observing mother-child interaction in two structured situations. In the first, the mother was requested to teach the child some number concepts, using Cuisenaire Rods (rods whose color and length vary with the numbers they represent); in the second, the child was permitted to engage in a free-play situation, with the mother participating and enhancing his enjoyment or withdrawing

to read a magazine if she preferred. Finally, each parent, mother and father, was interviewed separately in two sessions, the first on beliefs and attitudes, and the second on the child's performance.

The material gathered in the course of these various observations was analyzed and scored, and the results were grouped under four headings: parental control, maturity demands, communication, and nurturance. A graphic representation summarizing the relationships between these variables and the three patterns of child behavior may be found in Figure 12-1. The term *parental control*, as used in these graphs, was evidenced by parents' accepting (i.e., not retreating from) power conflicts with the child, not giving in to child's

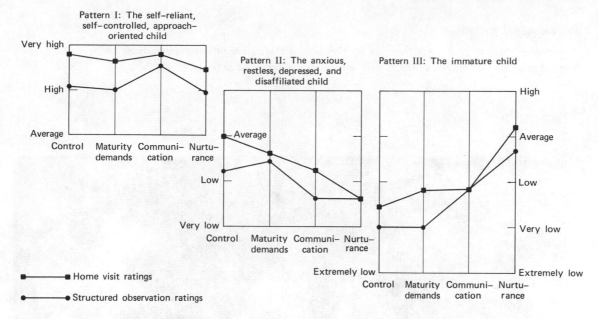

Figure 12-1. Parental behavior associated with three personality patterns in nursery school children. (After Baumrind, 1967.)

"nuisance value," using incentives and reinforcement, and persisting to obtain positive outcomes. *Parental maturity demands* were evidenced by parents' respecting the child's decision, granting independence, and engaging in independence training through control and noncontrol situations. *Parent-child communication* was shown by parents' using reason to get compliance, encouraging verbal give-and-take, and making it clear that they were the source of power. *Parental nurturance* was indicated by parents' supporting and satisfying the child and using positive incentive and reinforcement.

As Figure 12-1 shows, parents of the most adequate children (Pattern I) tended to rate high on all four variables of behavior. Parents of anxious children (Pattern II) had average to low-average ratings on control and maturity demands, communicated less, and were not very supportive or nurturant. Parents of im-

mature children provided very little control, made few demands for mature behavior, and communicated little, but showed average support and nurturance. Figure 12-1 also shows a strong tendency for the ratings of family life and maternal behavior in structured situations to be quite consistent.

Baumrind's results are, to some extent, consistent with common sense, for they show that the best adjusted children get both firm control and love. Their parents expect mature behavior and engage in considerable communication to make this clear. Furthermore, the immature child (who resembles the "spoiled child" stereotype in many ways) gets very little control and few demands for mature behavior. Contrary to common sense, however, he gets only an average amount of attention in the form of nurturance and emotional support. The anxious child perhaps fits the common-sense stereotypes least. He gets a moderate

Parental influences

Personality patterns that persist are set by the way in which parents characteristically restrict, comfort, admonish, instruct, and express acceptance and warmth.

amount of control and demand for maturity; his parents interact with him less and are not supportive. In short, the well-adjusted child gets more of everything, and the anxious child and the immature child gets less of everything.

Baumrind (1971b) conducted a more extended survey of children in the nursery schools of Berkeley, California, studying other aspects of the relationship between parental behavior and personality traits of children. In general, her findings were consistent with her 1967 study. One dimension she studied was *independence,* the tendency of a child to behave in ways that are not stereotyped but are unique to his personality, to make up his own mind on matters, and to question adult authority on occasion. Children scoring high on this dimension were likely to show behavior characterized by dominance, resistance, purposefulness, and achievement orientation. Although psychologists a generation ago tended to believe that firm parental control and demands for maturity were detrimental to the development of independence and led to passivity and overdependence on the part of children, Baumrind found no data to support these contentions. "It appears," she commented, "that children are not that easily cowed by parental pressure" (p. 96). This does not constitute an endorsement for *authoritarian* methods, which Baumrind distinguishes from *authoritative* methods.

The *authoritarian* parent attempts to shape, control, and evaluate the child's behavior according to some set or absolute standard of behavior. Obedience is regarded as a prime virtue, and punitive, forceful measures are invoked to suppress deviations. The authoritarian parent does not encourage verbal give-and-take with the child, insisting that the child should not question parental demands, but should accept them as final.

The *authoritative* parent directs the child in a rational manner that is oriented to issues, rather than the formal aspects of behavior. Verbal give-and-take is encouraged, and the child is shown the reasoning behind parental policies and demands. Although firm control is exercised when parents and children cannot come to an agreement, the child is not hemmed about by restrictions. The parent demonstrates self-respect, but also respects the child as an individual with interests and special ways of his own.

Permissive parents behave in nonpunitive, accepting, and affirmative ways with respect to the child's impulses. They consult with him on family decisions, give explanations for family rules, and make few demands for responsibility for household routines or orderliness. The parents avoid roles as active agents in shaping the child's behavior, but present themselves as resources to be used as he wishes. The child is permitted to regulate his own activities and is not controlled or encouraged to obey externally defined standards. Reason, but not power is used to accomplish such parental aims as seem necessary.

In Baumrind's research, the children of authoritative parents came off much better than those of either authoritarian or permissive parents. They tended to be friendlier, more cooperative, more purposive, and more achievement-oriented than the other children. The girls also tended to be more independent. These findings led Baumrind to conclude that socially responsible behavior in children is facilitated by parents who themselves behave in socially responsible ways, who have a strong involvement with their children, and who exercise control over and make use of reinforcement contingencies. Parents can, furthermore, serve as more potent models and reinforcing agents if they do not act in rejecting ways toward their children, as often happens with authoritarian parents.

Baumrind also explored dimensions of nonconforming behavior and attitudes on the part of parents. Her findings showed that authoritative parents who were themselves nonconforming tended to have boys who were more independent, purposive, and dominant. Nor was parental nonconformity associated with a lack of social responsibility. On the other hand, the coupling of nonconformity and authoritative behavior on the part of parents was associated with hostile, resistive behavior on the part of girls.

Baumrind's findings are consistent with other research studies into the relationship between parental attitudes and children's behavior. Michael Zunich (1966) found that nursery school children were more likely to make positive contact with other children and play interactively with them if their parents were generally approving of their activities, encouraged their verbalization, and shared experiences with them. Those parents, however, who were overly concerned with discipline, and who believed in "breaking the child's will," had children who were inclined to criticize other children, dominate them, and show signs of anxiety. Anxiety was also characteristic of children whose parents were generally irritable and strict in dealing with them.

Maternal Practices and Attitudes

The studies by Baumrind that we have just described are particularly interesting because she made an attempt, through home visitation at supper time, to assess the total atmosphere of the family with respect to its impact on child behavior. This means that the effect of the father as a functioning member of the family group was observed. Furthermore, she also included fathers in her interview schedule.

Although a few other studies of parental attitudes and behavior examine the interaction between both parents and their children, most of them focus on the mother. This practice can be justified to some extent because it is the mother who has the most intimate contact with the child. Furthermore, looking at the matter from an entirely practical angle, it is the mother who is most available and most eager to cooperate with a researcher.

Effect on Cognitive Development

Some of the most interesting research regarding the relationship between maternal behavior and behavioral outcomes in children has been conducted by the group of researchers at the University of California who have since 1928 been studying the children (now adults) who participated in the Berkeley Growth Study. Because the Growth Study has generated so many data gathered over a long span of years, it is an exceedingly rich mine for exploring trends and relationships. One promising lead has to do with the kind of maternal behavior that is more (or less) likely to facilitate cognitive growth. Bayley and Schaefer (1964) correlated several dimensions of maternal behavior, drawn from observations made when the child was three years old and younger, with measures taken when the child was older. We have presented a sample of their findings in Figure 12-2, which reports the relationships between maternal behavior during this early period and scores on intelligence tests administered when the subjects were 16 to 18 years of age. (We could have included IQs taken at earlier ages, but selected the later scores because they are the most removed, in point of time, from the period of infancy and early childhood, and hence are more meaningful in terms of the kinds of predictions that might be made.) We will have more to say about other personality factors shortly, but have selected intelligence as a relevant variable for Figure 12-2, because it is one that is responsive to many dimensions of mental health and personal adequacy.

Several things can be noted in Figure 12-2.

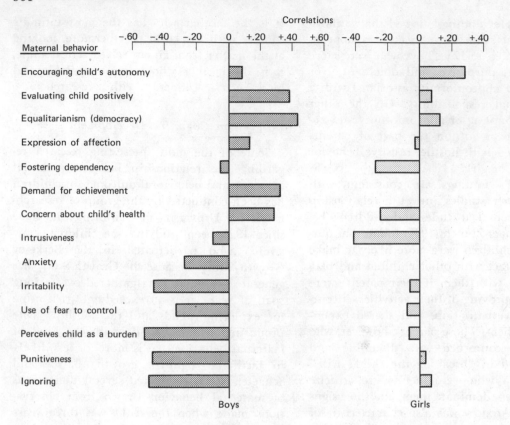

Figure 12-2. Relationship between maternal behavior experienced by children from birth to three years of age and their intelligence at ages 16 to 18. (After Bayley and Schaefer, 1964.)

In the first place, if the sizes of correlational coefficients are any indication, maternal behavior has more of a long-range impact on the cognitive growth of boys than it does on girls. This is particularly true with respect to the more negative forms of maternal behavior. The data also suggest that girls are, if anything, somewhat "tougher" and more resilient, psychologically, than boys, although there are a few exceptions to this trend. Girls appear to respond more to maternal encouragement for autonomy than boys do. It seems to be less important, as far as their cognitive development is concerned, whether their

mother treats them democratically or not, nor is their IQ much affected by the mother's expression of affection. On the other hand, they appear to be most vulnerable to maternal attempts to foster dependent behavior and to intrude on their life space and privacy. Concern about the child's health appears to facilitate cognitive growth in boys, but has the opposite effect in girls. Maternal expectations and demands for achievement seem important for boys, less so for girls. As far as negative and rejecting attitudes of mothers, they seem to have a severe effect on boys and little, if any, on girls. To generalize for a bit, it appears that boys tend to benefit from intense "mothering," but girls respond negatively to it.

Bayley (1970) noted an interesting and puzzling phenomenon in her data for boys. Measures of boys' intelligence made during the first year of life showed a *negative* relationship with democratic, affectionate behavior on the part of mothers, and a *positive* relationship with hostile and rejecting maternal behavior. It is as though a more stressful mother-child interaction facilitates cognitive development during this early age. The relationship does not hold over the years, however, as we can see from Figure 12-2. Bayley found that from the second year of life onward, democratic, affectionate behavior tended to be positively correlated with boys' intelligence, and hostile, rejecting behavior tends to be negatively correlated. The latter effect was even more pronounced with girls four years and under, but by the time girls were ready for school, much of the correlational effect had faded, and the picture from then on was much as it appears in Figure 12-2.

Effect on Social Development

Bayley (1964) also studied relationships between maternal behavior patterns and children's personal-social manifestations of Berkeley Growth Study subjects. Figure 12-3 consists of a graphic presentation of the correlations between certain forms of maternal behavior experienced by boys during the first three years of life and the amount of friendliness they demonstrated when they were between six-and-a-half and seven years of age. Again, mothers' affectionate, equalitarian (i.e., democratic) behavior appears to facilitate friendliness, whereas hostile, punitive, and rejecting behavior appears to inhibit it. Similar relationships were also found between mothers' behavior and boys' cooperativeness and atten-

tiveness. Patterns and relationships for girls are also similar, particularly below the age of three, although the correlations diminish somewhat beyond that age. The general impression is that girls are more self-sufficient and somewhat less affected by maternal behavior than boys are.

Bayley's findings were also consistent with some research done by Kagan and Freeman (1963), who correlated children's IQs taken at ages three, five, and nine with maternal behavior during the preschool years. Maternal restrictiveness, severity, and coerciveness tended to be correlated negatively with IQs for both boys and girls, with maternal stress on the importance of intellectual mastery correlated positively. In addition, interviews turned up the intriguing statistics of a high negative correlation with daughters' IQs and mothers' erotic activity. In other words, the greater the mother's interest in sex, the lower her daughter's IQ was likely to be. Another interesting datum was a positive correlation between girls' IQs and their mothers' tendency to criticize. Kagan and Freeman's research also produced the usual finding of a high correlation between children's IQs and mothers' educational level. There was an equally high (.41) positive correlation between fathers' education and IQ for nine-year-old girls, but other correlations between IQs and fathers' education tended to be somewhat lower for both boys and girls. Fathers are important, as we shall see later in this chapter, but there is little doubt about the psychological impact of the mother on cognitive and affective development in children.

Maternal Influences on Creativity

A study by Dreyer and Wells (1966) produced some interesting findings relative to the development of creativity in children aged four and five. Creativity was measured by

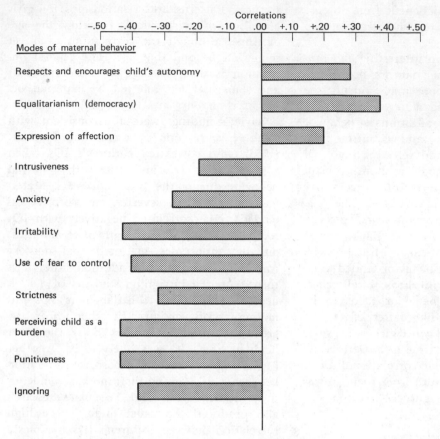

Figure 12-3. Correlations between the friendliness of boys aged 6½ to 7 years and modes of maternal behavior they experienced before 3 years of age. (After Bayley, 1964.)

three subtests taken from the Minnesota Tests of Creative Thinking: Ask-and-Guess, Picture-Improvement, and Picture-Construction. Questionnaires administered to both parents showed no particular behavior patterns as far as fathers were concerned, but the mothers of high-creative children tended to be more willing to grant independence and at the same time emphasized achievement more. For instance, they said that children were ready to make bedtime decisions when they were 11, whereas mothers of low-creative children did

not think children were ready for such decisions until they were 15. Mothers of high-creatives felt that children were ready to go out on a "date" with a crowd of friends when they were 11, whereas other mothers believed that they were not ready for this until they were 14. Mothers of high-creative children believed that 14 was a good age to begin thinking about adult careers, whereas mothers of low-creative children were inclined to postpone such discussions until age 17.

With respect to husband-wife relations, the

parents of high-creative children showed more tension with respect to marital roles and there was also more disagreement on what values should be stressed in the family (e.g., companionship, personality development, place in the community, etc.). One interpretation is that there may be more discord in the families of high-creative children, but another is that such parents are more "open" to their own feelings and those of others and hence are likely to report more negative characteristics. The researchers noted that the parents of high-creative children put less stress on companionship as a family value, an orientation that suggests a higher degree of independence.

Children's Influences on Mothers' Behavior: Sex Differences

In examining the relationship between early patterns of maternal behavior and later behavioral outcomes, it is easy to make the assumption that the child is passive and plastic and that maternal behavior is the major independent variable. Such an assumption, however, overlooks the fact that the mother's personality and behavior style are only a part of the picture. What the mother does is often a reaction to the child's behavior. Maternal hostility may be a reaction to a very aggressive, hyperactive child. Just as mothers shape children's behavior, so do children shape mothers' behavior.

Some variations in maternal behavior are undoubtedly produced by personality differences among mothers, but there are differences even in neonates that undoubtedly produce a patterning of maternal behavior. Children differ from the very beginning. We have noted that premature infants, for example, behave differently from full-term infants and that differences in the newborn's behavior and appearance are important indices to his later development.

Sex differences are also significant, with boys being more active and exploring, once they are able to locomote, and girls showing a higher degree of social interest in early infancy, a precursor to the more rapid development of social skills. Parents with the best intentions in the world of wanting to treat siblings alike find themselves being more restrictive and punitive with energetic, aggressive, resistant, and often destructive sons and being more kind and indulgent to obedient, affectionate, and charming daughters. American behavioral scientists for a number of years tended to explain sex differences in children's behavior in terms of environmental variables—in other words, boys were more aggressive because parents expected that kind of behavior from their sons, tending to reinforce aggressive behavior and to ignore passive or cooperative behavior. Girls, conversely, were expected to be more agreeable and cooperative and were reinforced for the style of behavior considered appropriate for their sex.

Are these differences between girls and boys the result of differences in the way parents treat children of different sex, or are parents responding to differences that are "already there"? One of the ways of resolving this question is to look at primate research. Presumably the behavior of monkeys is uncontaminated by culturally toned attitudes and values. If young monkeys display sex-related behavior patterns similar to those displayed by young humans, this finding would strengthen the conclusion that such responses are not learned but are biologically foreordained.

One such study that supports this line of reasoning is that of Mitchell and Brandt (1970), who observed the behavior of rhesus monkey mothers toward their infants and noted that they were more punitive toward their male offspring and more protective toward their female infants. The behavior of the monkey infants provided some clues as to the reason for the differential treatment. Male infants tended to be "doers," in that they were more likely to play with other infants, to explore their environment, to run and jump (thus leaving the mother), and to threaten other infants. Female infants, however, were more inclined to be "watchers" and to play passive roles.

Harry F. Harlow (1962) made similar observations regarding sex differences in the behavior of his monkeys. He noted that male infants and adolescents were more likely to make threatening responses, to engage in rough-and-tumble play, and to initiate such play with their own and opposite sex. Female monkeys, on the other hand, were more likely to engage in grooming other monkeys, a socialized behavior involving stroking and patting. It is hardly surprising that monkey mothers behave in different ways toward their male and female offspring, in ways that are remarkably similar to the behavior of human parents.

Some data gathered by the Early School Admissions Project in Baltimore shows how mothers of girls and mothers of boys not only have different perceptions of the behavior of their children, but also tend to become involved in different ways in the life of their community. Table 12-2 lists some of the questions asked by Project researchers and the replies given by over 500 mothers of children four and five years old. Although the families

TABLE 12-2. *Differences in Replies Given by Mothers of Four- and Five-Year-Old Children to Questions Posed in Interviews, Classified According to Sex of Child (Galfo, 1971)*

Questions	Reply tendencies of mothers of:	
	Girls	Boys
Does the child bring home books from the library?	Yes	Too young
Is there printed matter in the home? (Mothers named books)	More often	Less often
What are child's favorite programs?	Children's shows	Cartoons
Does the child like to listen to the radio?	Yes	No
Does the child have many friends?	Yes	No
Does child carry out chores and errands?	Yes	No
Does child obediently put away clothes and playthings?	Yes	No
Does child obediently wash, bathe, and brush teeth?	Usually	Sometimes, or No
Does child come obediently when called?	Usually	Sometimes, or No
Does child ask to be taken places?	Often	Sometimes
Does child need to be punished?	Rarely	Often, or Sometimes
Does child show curiosity as to origin of babies?	Yes	No
Does child ever touch himself on privates in public?	No	Yes
Does child suck thumb?	Yes	No
Does child stutter or stammer?	No	Yes
Is the child overactive?	No	Yes
Does child ever get wild or uncontrollable when playing with friends?	No	Yes
Do you attend meetings of groups trying to improve the neighborhood?	Yes	No
Do you belong to any organizations?	Yes	No

were all located in a lower-class or slum environment, many of the sex differences reported would probably be consistent with the views of mothers living in middle-class surroundings. The mothers' replies suggest that girls this age are behaving in ways that are more mature, more socialized, and more passive than boys. One explanation may be that the girls are actually behaving this way; another may be that mothers are biased in favor of girls and tend to expect the worst of boys. A decade or so ago, most behavioral scientists might have preferred the latter interpretation, but today they are more inclined to take the view that sex differences in behavior, particularly in young children, are largely biologically determined.

Paternal Influence on Child Behavior

The research with respect to the influence of fathers on cognitive and affective development of children can be summed up very simply: fathers are important, especially if they are not there.

There is now a fair amount of research data relating to father absence and its effect on children's behavior. One of the earlier studies was conducted by Walter Mischel (1958), who asked West Indian children to do a small task for him. He offered them a choice of rewards: a small candy immediately or a large one a week hence. Children from homes in which fathers were not present tended to prefer the immediate reward. The implication of this finding is, of course, that children from father-absent homes are less able to postpone gratification of needs and wants, and perhaps have less confidence in the reliability of adults.

Lynn and Sawrey (1959) compared Norwegian boys whose fathers were at sea for periods of nine months to two years at a time with those whose fathers were land-based and who remained at home. Father-absent boys tended to be more infantile and dependent, had poorer relations with their peers, and were less secure in their masculinity than the other boys.

Martin L. Hoffman (1971) studied moral values and indexes of aggression for two groups of seventh graders that had been matched as to IQ and socioeconomic status. In one group fathers had been absent from the home for at least six months prior to the study; in the other, families were intact. Boys from father-present homes scored higher than those from father-absent homes on measures of guilt, internal moral judgment, moral values, and conformity to rules. Teachers also reported a greater tendency toward overt aggression on the part of boys from father-absent homes. Somewhat similar tendencies were also observed for girls, but differences were slight and not statistically significant. Hoffman concluded that the absence of the father has adverse effects on the conscience development of boys, at least in part because of the lack of an appropriate parental model. There was also some indication that women without husbands express less affection for their sons than do women whose husbands are present.

Still another study by E. Mavis Hetherington (1966) compared lower-class preadolescent boys from father-absent and intact homes. The boys whose fathers were absent because of divorce, desertion, or death were more emotionally dependent on their peers than were the other boys. Furthermore, those boys whose fathers had left before they were five had difficulty in developing behavior that was appropriately masculine.

Blanchard and Biller (1971) used teachers' grades and school achievement measures in studying third-grade boys who were divided for purposes of comparison into four groups: father absence beginning before the boys were five (early absence); father absence beginning after the boys were five (late absence); father

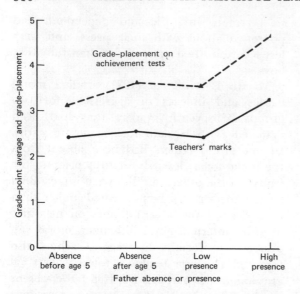

Figure 12-4. Relationship between academic performance and the initial point of father absence or the degree of father presence for boys in the third grade. (After Blanchard and Biller, 1971.)

presence in the home less than six waking hours a week (low presence); and father presence in the home more than two waking hours per day (high presence). Results showed that early absence had the most deleterious effect, as Figure 12-4 indicates, but that low presence also interfered with academic performance. In fact, the low presence group's grades were no better than those for the early absence group. The researchers concluded that fathers who were highly available provided models of achievement, perseverance, and competence for their sons. The data also suggest that the preschool years are a more critical period, in that father absence then has a more disabling effect.

The reason behind the father's absence appears to be important. Santrock and Wohlford (1970) compared fifth-grade boys, mostly from lower-class homes, whose fathers either were present, were absent because of death, or were absent because of divorce, desertion, or separation. Boys in the latter group tended to be more aggressive than the others on a variety of measures and were less tolerant of a delay of gratification, in a test situation like that devised by Mischel, noted above. The latter finding was particularly true of boys whose fathers had left home when the boys were between three and five years of age.

Are Parents Necessary? It is a routine finding that children from broken homes tend to have more adjustment problems than those from intact homes. K. M. Koller (1971), for example, found that over 61% of delinquent girls in a state training school had suffered some kind of parental loss or deprivation. Over half were deprived of both parents, and an additional third had lost their fathers. By way of contrast, only 13% of girls in a matched control group, drawn from the general population, had suffered parental deprivation.

There is no doubt that parents play key roles in the upbringing of children, but the question still remains whether parent substitutes can do as well. The common-sense answer to this question is that they cannot, and that individuals providing group care in children's institutions can never make up the deficit suffered by parental loss.

Some contrary evidence to the assumptions of common sense comes from some recent research by Ruth Goldman (1971), who studied 65 youngsters who had been raised in group-care settings in Austria, Israel, Poland, and Yugoslavia. The psychosocial maturity of the children was assessed by the Raven Progressive Matrices (a nonverbal intelligence test), the Thematic Apperception Test (TAT), a value inventory, and a sentence-completion test and compared with the maturity of 65 children who had been reared at home in intact families. Results were analyzed and classified according to the following categories: cognition, egocentrism, manifest (emotional) conflict, social conformity, and relationship with peers. Here are a few brief summaries of the way in which immature and mature children were described:

COGNITION. One immature subject was characterized as having limited intellectual ability, finding it difficult to function well in many situations. His ideas were stereotyped, simple, and unformed. A mature subject was observed to be "extremely aware of and concerned about her interactions with others" (p. 415) and also to have a "quick, perceptive, analytic style of cognition" (p. 415).

MANIFEST CONFLICT. One imaginative adolescent was rated as immature because of much anger, aggression, and pessimism. Outwardly conforming, he concealed his suspicion and distrust of others. Another more mature child was described as being comfortable with his aggressive impulses and having the ability to express them through socially acceptable forms of competition.

RELATIONSHIP TO PEERS. One immature subject was said to be limited by suspicions toward and mistrust of others. Although he was accepting of the more general social values of his community, he had little concept of sharing, cooperation, or even of competition. A mature subject was observed to be concerned with giving, sharing, and cooperating and to be socially at ease with others.

Goldman was unable to find any differences in psychosocial maturity between group and family-reared children in her Austrian, Israeli, and Yugoslavian subjects, but family-reared children were rated superior in Poland. On the other hand, those children who were group-reared in Israeli *kibbutzim* were superior to those receiving home care. Age at entrance into group care was not significant. In Austria, 80% of the children had entered group care (a "children's village") before they were six, and in Yugoslavia children entered group care at even earlier ages and were judged as psychologically mature as later entrants. Goldman concluded, as a result of her survey, that group-care settings do not necessarily have a deleterious effect on children's psychosocial development, and that much depends on the attitudes and practices prevalent in the institution.

Influence of the Family's Social and Economic Status (SES)

During the earlier years of child research, the socioeconomic status (SES) of parents was largely overlooked. It was not until the work of sociologists in the late 1930s that behavioral scientists had firm evidence that well-defined behavioral trends were associated with various levels of SES. The study of Yankeetown (Newburyport, Mass.) by Warner and Lunt (1941) was an important landmark during this period. Warner and his co-workers observed the behavior of all individuals in this small seaport town, noted who associated with whom, and asked each individual to characterize and describe as many of the other residents as he knew. The researchers analyzed these observations and interpersonal descriptions and classified the townspeople into three major social classes: upper, middle, and lower. Each class was further subdivided into an upper and a lower category, making six subclasses in all.

Sociologists have made extensive use of Warner's methods, with some modifications. The upper class in many communities may be considered to be an extension of the middle class; in any event, it is too small to be of much research interest. The upper-lower class is often termed the "working class," and the lower-lower class as the poverty class or "slum class." Although the main basis for determining social class continues to be one of association—who associates with whom—the resulting classifications are so highly correlated with occupational status and educational level that these two variables are usually used by researchers as valid indices of SES. This is particularly true of educational level, which is easily quantifiable and readily manipulated statistically.

In educational terms, the upper-middle class today may be considered to be comprised largely of individuals who have some substantial amount of college education. Most of these individuals have also achieved some degree of occupational status: they are in the professions, in managerial positions, or are owners of businesses. The lower-middle class is composed of individuals who are in clerical work, the highly skilled trades, technicians, or small businesses. Their education is usually no more than high school, often with additional business school or technical training. Members of the working class usually have completed some high school and are employed in skilled, semiskilled, or unskilled occupations of various types. Individuals in lower-lower or poverty class have little education, are employed sporadically at low-level, unskilled jobs. Negroes and Latin Americans are heavily represented in this class, but most of its members are white.

According to standards used by the U.S. Department of Health, Education, and Welfare, about 13 or 14% of the children in the United States are from poverty families. In numbers, this proportion amounts to three million children under age six and seven million between the ages of 6 and 17. Of the total number of children living in poverty homes, six million are white and four million are nonwhite, and 40% are from fatherless families. Most children from poverty homes live in rural, rather than urban, settings. Among Indians living on reservations, 80%

are in poverty. In 1940, one million children were in families receiving financial aid under the program now known as Aid to Families with Dependent Children. Thirty years later, in 1970, the number was between five and six million, 80% of whom were in families without fathers (White House Conference on Children, 1970).

SES and Child-rearing Patterns

The attitudes and values that are associated with various social-class levels generate parental behavior that affects children's development in several ways. Melvin L. Kohn (1963) has observed that middle-class (MC) parents are inclined to prepare their children for occupations in which they are likely to make their own decisions and work cooperatively with others, whereas working-class (WC) or lower-class (LC) parents are inclined to prepare their children for occupations in which following explicit rules is stressed. For these reasons, MC parents are likely to emphasize independence and social skills. Keeping one's temper plays a key part in social skills, because free expression of anger makes cooperation difficult and jeopardizes one's right to act independently. Hence, child training in MC families is likely to stress reasoning, understanding, discussion of problems, and the like, whereas WC and LC families are likely to emphasize obedience and to punish severely for deviations from the rules. To put this in other terms, MC families are inclined to behave in equalitarian or democratic ways toward children, and WC and LC families to adopt modes that are authoritarian and traditional.

The study by Kagan and Freeman (1963), which we cited earlier, yielded some data that support this position. The education of the mothers was negatively correlated with restrictive, severe, and coercive behavior, and was positively correlated with tendencies to stress intellectual mastery and to give children reasons for demands and for disciplinary action.

The Kagan-Freeman survey is only one of many that associate high levels of parental punitivity and harshness with LC status and more egalitarian or democratic treatment with MC status. Some research by Ostfeld and Katz (1969) suggests the kind of behavior that results from these two modes of treatment. LC and MC preschool children were permitted to select a toy from an array and then were allowed to play with the other toys but not the one they had chosen. The orders not to play with the chosen toy were either given in a mild tone or a harsh, angry tone. Afterward, each child was asked which toy he would prefer if he were buying one in a store. The researchers were most interested in determining which type of admonishment would be more likely to get children to change their mind about the toy initially chosen—that is, to "devalue" it. Results showed that MC children were more likely to devalue the toy when admonished mildly, whereas LC children were more likely to devalue it when admonished harshly. The researchers explained the difference in terms of the fact that MC children are used to receiving mild verbal threats, whereas LC children are usually admonished more harshly.

SES and Intellectual Stimulation

One interesting study of social-class differences in child-rearing patterns was conducted with 76 LC and 38 MC mothers and their children, aged four or five years of age. Each mother and her child participated in a 90-minute session, which began with a 10-minute wait in a "waiting room," where the two were observed through a one-way mirror. The room was furnished with many toys and the floor was marked out with quadrants so that observers could plot the child's movement. Observations were coded in such a way that it was possible to score the behavior of both the mother and the child. Results showed that LC mothers made more disapproving statements to their children and made more attempts to get them to modify or stop whatever they were doing.[3] Both MC mothers and their children made more informational statements. LC children were more inclined to accept their mothers' control and disapproval, but they were more restless, shifting from one toy to another and moving about more.

After the waiting-room session, each mother and her child were brought into another room, where the child was given the task of building a house from blocks. The mother was told that she could give as much help as she wished. Again, there were differences in the two groups of mothers. MC mothers made more suggestions overall and also expressed more approval of the child's performance; whereas LC mothers expressed more disapproval and were inclined to become more actively involved in the building task in a physical way—that is, handing blocks to the child, putting blocks on the house, and the like.

The researchers concluded that the observations gave them a rather clear picture of social-class differences in maternal behavior, particularly in terms of helping to explain differences in school performance of LC and MC children. For example, the typical MC mother tended to allow the child to work at his own pace in the problem-solving situation, offering

[3] The fact that LC mothers were more disapproving does not mean that their children's behavior was poorer than that of the MC children. Researchers were unable to detect anything about the LC children's behavior that would call for the greater amount of control or disapproval they received.

Poverty takes many forms and has different effects on children

It can produce defeatism and alienation. It can mean growing up in crowded conditions. It can mean getting along with the bare minimum or less and having to share it. It can mean the sharing of tasks and responsibilities. It can mean the absence of adult male models. It can also mean a feeling of being friendly and close to family, friends, and neighbors.

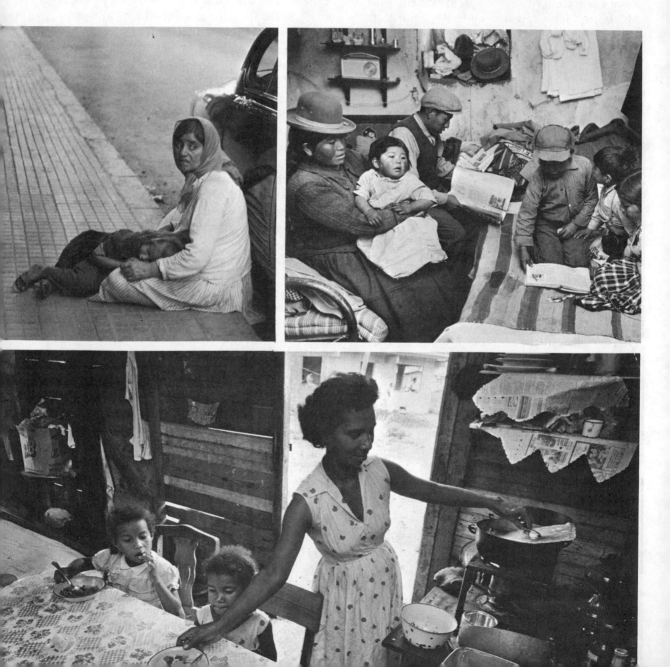

many general structuring suggestions on how to search for a solution to the problem, and spoke approvingly to the child whenever he was doing something correct. She permitted the child to take as much time as he wanted and seldom worked on the problem herself. This approach seemed to encourage the child to explore the problem independently and did not focus his attention on his failures. The typical LC mother, on the other hand, made suggestions that were highly specific and that did not provide any clues to problem-solving strategies. Often she deprived the child of the chance of solving the problem on his own by working on it herself. The MC strategy seems calculated to help children with future problem-solving situations, whereas the LC strategy makes it difficult for children to learn anything that they can generalize to other situations (Bee et al., 1969).

As we have noted previously, both children and laboratory animals respond favorably to increased inputs of stimulation. A number of research studies show that intellectual stimulation varies with the SES of the home. One of the more recent studies was conducted by Emmy E. Werner (1969) who correlated the IQs of almost 500 children (97% nonwhite or non-Anglo) from different cultural and ethnic backgrounds in rural Hawaii with the intellectual stimulation potential of their homes. Intelligence tests were given twice: at 20 months and at age 10. Figure 12-5 presents the results for age 10. They show that correlations between children's IQs and family background are all positive. The relationship is quite similar for parental IQs, parental education, and socioeconomic status, but what is particularly interesting is that educational stimulation produces the highest correlation and evidently is the most significant variable. This latter variable consisted of a composite rating of the opportunities available in the home for enlarging children's vocabulary; the quality of the language models available for the children; the intellectual activities and interests of the family; the kind of work habits emphasized in the home; the availability of learning supplies, books, and periodicals; and the opportunities for children to participate in and explore various aspects of the larger environment through libraries, special lessons, recreational activities, and the like. The intelligence tests given at 20 months showed positive relationships with parental education, IQ, and SES, but correlations were generally lower, which is characteristic of correlations between situational variables and intelligence test results at earlier ages.

All these variables are interrelated, of course. Parents with more years of education are likely to have higher status jobs and be more affluent. They are also more likely to create an environment that is intellectually stimulating for a child. This "hidden curriculum" at home depends partly on economic factors, because it costs money to buy books, subscribe to magazines, pay for music lessons, and participate in a wide range of recreational activities. But educational stimulation is not entirely dependent on economic support, for it also includes such variables as the work habits of the family, the complexity of the language the children are exposed to, and the like. In other words, the parents' attitudes and values are also significant factors. In any event, these variables tend to be correlated with socioeconomic status: the higher the status, the greater the amount of educational stimulation to which the child is exposed; the lower the status, the less the stimulation. Much of the work of the intervention programs, like Operation Head Start and the Early Training Project of Gray and Klaus (1970), which we described in Chapter 11, is concerned with creating situations in which socially deprived,

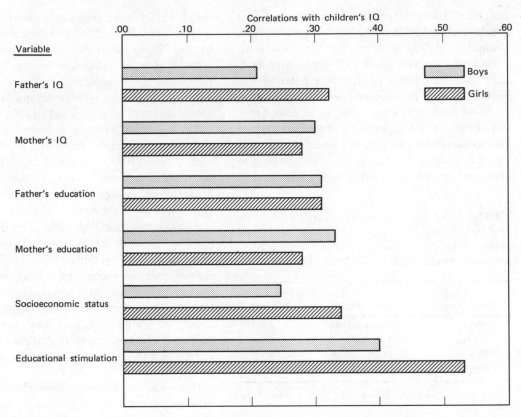

Correlations with children's IQ

Figure 12-5.   Correlations between IQs of children aged 10 and (1) measures of parental ability and (2) environmental ratings. (After Werner, 1969.)

poverty-class children receive greater exposure to stimulation of the type we have been discussing.

It can be argued, of course, that even slum children receive a great deal of stimulation and reinforcement, and therefore should do as well intellectually as MC children. The answer to this is that life in the slum tends to be less predictable for children. Bresnahan and Blum (1971) asked the question: What would happen if reinforcement were as chaotic for MC children as it is for lower-class children. They gave first-grade children from MC and LC homes a series of cognitive tasks

that were preceded by trial sessions in which they experienced random reinforcement at zero, moderate, or high levels. MC children did better than LC children on the tasks, but when the task was preceded by random reinforcement, the performance of the MC children deteriorated until it was at the same level as that of the LC children. Their findings suggest that one of the reasons why lower SES children have more problems in the cognitive area may be that the schedules of reinforcement in their homes are not as orderly or as dependable as they are in MC homes.

A particularly interesting study showing

differential effects related to mothering was conducted by Willerman, Naylor, and Myrianthopoulos (1970), who conducted a follow-up survey of children born to Negro-white matings in urban areas in different parts of the United States. Intelligence tests administered to these children when they were four years old showed some interesting differences when results were classified as to mother's race and marital status. As Table 12-3 indicates, the children of mothers who were Negro and

TABLE 12-3. *The IQs of Four-Year-Old Children of Negro-White Matings, Classified According to Mother's Race and Family Status (Willerman, Naylor, and Myrianthopoulos, 1970)*

Race of Mother	Family Status	Mean IQ of Children
Negro	Unmarried[a]	83
Negro	Married	98
White	Unmarried[a]	98
White	Married	102

[a] Essentially, "unmarried" means "father-absent" in this study.

mothers of both races who were unmarried[4] tended to have lower IQs. These differences cannot be explained genetically, because all children had both Negro and white parents and hence were part Negro and part white. There were essentially no educational differences among the parents, all groups having a mean of about 11 years of schooling. The researchers favored an environmental explanation of the differences, suggesting that Negro and white mothers differ in child-rearing practices and language. In other words, even though the two groups of mothers did not

[4] "Married" covers both legal and common-law unions; "unmarried" includes single, divorced, widowed, or separated and, in essence, refers to a "father-absent" home.

differ in years of education completed, they might have differed in SES. Schools attended by the Negro mothers were undoubtedly segregated along racial and SES lines for the most part, and there is strong evidence that such segregation is associated with markedly lower achievement (Coleman et al., 1966).

Evidence for racially different patterns of child rearing comes from the study by Bee and others (1969) we mentioned previously. In their lower-class subjects, there were no differences between Negroes and whites on two thirds of the variables they analyzed, but the measures that did yield a difference all involved verbal interaction between mother and child. The fact that verbal skills play a crucial role in success in taking intelligence tests suggests an additional reason for the lower IQs of the children of Negro mothers shown in Table 12-3, and one that is consistent with the hypothesis that their SES origins were lower than those of the white mothers.

Influence of Minority Subcultures. One of the reasons why children from lower-class or poverty homes have difficulties in school is that the subcultures of which they are members use reward systems that are different from those used by the middle-class individuals who serve as teachers and play other supervisory roles in the larger society. Robert J. Havighurst (1970) notes, for example, that American Indian children respond to praise and blame from members of their families and their peer groups but tend to ignore outsiders. The norm in some Indian groups is that of being quite intolerant of members who show superior knowledge and understanding. Often a teacher will be unable to get Indian children to volunteer an answer, even though several of them may know. "In oral reading, the whole class tends to read together in audible whispers, so that the child who is supposed to be reciting can simply wait when he comes to a difficult word until he hears it said by his classmates." (p. 317).

Havighurst makes the point that "an effective reward system in a complex, changing society must be based on a strong ego." (p. 319) Id rewards—that is, rewards oriented toward the satisfaction of primitive, infantile impulses—may have immediate and short-term value in learning situations, but what enables children to develop appropriately mature forms of behavior is a system of rewards based on long-range reality considerations. The id rewards must therefore be supplemented by superego rewards, rewards that carry a "child from learning for fun to learning even if it is hard work." Children from cultures that emphasize id rather than ego rewards are likely to have a great deal of difficulty in adapting to life in a "complex, changing society."

Havighurst is critical of experimental programs like those of Kohl (1967), who got 36 slum children to be interested in school by encouraging them to write about their fears and hates, likes and dislikes, and the things they experienced in their homes and in the streets. Havighurst admits that Kohl had made a good start in getting the children to accept school, but raises the question as to the next step, and asks "How far can a slum child (or a middle-class child) go toward mastery of arithmetic, of English sentence style, of knowledge of science and history, if he is motivated only by his desire to express his feelings, or possibly also by his desire to please his friendly and permissive teacher?" (p. 319). What is needed to carry a child onward, Havighurst says, is the inculcation of an ego-reward system that enables the child to promise himself "a future reward for doing something unpleasant at the moment and through making the child take the blame for the future consequences of his mistakes of judgment or his mistakes of self-indulgence" (p. 319). In other terms, a child who attains

such a goal can be considered to be self-reinforcing and therefore less dependent on others to stimulate and pace his learning activities.

A related characteristic that differentiates successful from unsuccessful students is self-esteem or ego strength, as expressed in the firm belief that one has some control over his fate and his environment. Research by James S. Coleman and his associates (1966) shows that Negro students (most of whom were from low SES homes) were more likely than other students to agree with such statements as "good luck is more important than hard work for success." Such findings led them to comment that children from more advantaged groups appear to believe that they can affect their environment, whereas other children believe that nothing they can do will affect their environment, for "it can give benefits or withhold them but not as a consequence of their own action" (p. 321).

Havighurst cites other research showing the effect of ethnic group's values on their children's behavior. Gross (1967) studied two groups of Jewish boys in Brooklyn, all aged about six, and all middle class. The families of one of the groups were Sephardic (Mediterranean in origin), and the other group's families were Ashkenazic (Northern European). The mothers were all native Americans, and English was the household language. The Ashkenazic boys showed a higher level of cognitive development than did the Sephardic boys, as indicated by a 17-point difference between the mean IQs of the two groups. An intensive study of the family training and background of the homes yielded no difference except one: Ashkenazic mothers were more likely to say that their son's future earnings were "unimportant" as compared to other aims in life, whereas the Sephardic mothers were much more likely to say that they wanted their sons to be "wealthy." This difference suggests that the two groups of mothers very likely had different reward systems in dealing with their sons and were also using these systems to reinforce different kinds of behavior. On the surface, it would seem that the Sephardic mothers had the highest level of aspiration for their sons, but in actuality they were not interested in their son's *intellectual* attainments as were the Ashkenazic mothers, and it would appear that although the SES of the two sets of mothers was similar, the Sephardic mothers' outlook was more working class, whereas the Ashkenazic mothers' orientation was more middle class.

The question can be raised as to which of the two types of differences, SES or subcultural, is the more significant when it comes to psychosocial development. Most of the evidence suggests that SES differences are the more significant. Tulkin (1968) found that white schoolchildren tested higher in achievement than Negroes in the same grade, but when white and Negro students were matched according to social class and family situation (e.g., broken homes, maternal employment, crowdedness of home), the differences between races disappeared at the middle-class levels. In actuality, even without controlling for family situation, there were no significant differences between white and Negro middle-class girls, thus suggesting that Negro boys are more vulnerable to environmental stress than are girls. Differences favored white children at lower SES levels, but other research suggests that as difficult as the social environment is for white lower-class individuals, it is even more difficult for lower-class Negroes.

Eleanor Rosch Heider (1971) asked ten-year-old children to describe abstract and face stimuli from sets of six similar items as accurately as possible so that another child could pick out items just from hearing their description. She found that middle-class children were generally superior both at description and at understanding other children's descriptions, irrespective of whether the describers were lower class or middle class, black or white. Lower-class children, however, understood descriptions by other lower-class children better than those of middle-class children. Heider was unable to find any consistent racial differences in the ability to describe or understand, the major difference being attributable to SES.

Questions about SES Research

We should note that not all behavioral scientists accept the idea that SES makes any important difference in child-rearing practices and in the socialization of children. Edward Zigler (1970) reviewed a large number of research studies and took issue with most of their conclusions. He was inclined to favor a genetic explanation, pointing out that lower-class children tend to perform at a lower Piagetian level than midde-class children. They also have poorer impulse control and are less problem-oriented. Zigler also pointed to inconsistencies in SES research, noting that in the 1940s it was stylish to say that middle-class people were more anxious and more overcontrolling of their children, but that today researchers' conclusions are the opposite. Whether this is a valid criticism of SES research is open to question, however. It can be argued that researchers are more sophisticated now than they were a generation ago, but the possibility that experimenter bias is as much a problem today as it was then is not easily dismissed.

In spite of Zigler's misgivings, the weight of the evidence appears to favor SES differences in child-rearing patterns as the most reasonable explanation of why children from the two types of homes turn out differently. There seems to be no doubt that middle-class parents tend to relate to their children and treat them differently than lower-class parents do. The reasons for such differences are complex, but the most logical place to find them is in the backgrounds of middle-class and lower-class parents. Surveys of adults of the two classes show many differences—economic, attitudinal, social, behavioral—but they are all related to education. Differences in education are related to and appear to explain most of the social-class differences, to the extent that most investigators who are conducting research into social-class differences use the number of years of education as the most convenient single index to SES. Perhaps it is going too far, considering the present state of our knowledge, to say that differences in education *cause* SES differences, but the persistent relationship between education and the whole complex of SES-related variables suggests that there may be a causative relationship. Those individuals who have completed a fair number of years of education and who live in ways that are essentially lower class, together with those whose attitudes and behavior are essentially middle class and who have completed only the rudiments of education, constitute a relatively small percentage of the whole. The conclusion seems to be inescapable that if more education does not "create" higher SES, it certainly appears to facilitate movement to higher SES levels.

A major problem with the genetic explanation of SES differences is that it leaves unexplained a number of phenomena that could be explained environmentally. Here is one. A century ago, most of the people in the United States were lower class; today the majority is middle class. Genetic theory would predict that the proportion of individuals in the two classes either would have remained unchanged over the period or that the proportion of lower-class individuals would have increased, because of their higher birth rate. The great increase in middle class can be explained in environmental terms by a reciprocal interaction between economic and educational development. Expanding industry and commerce demanded educated employees, and such employees were available because of the greater accessibility of education. Each better educated wave of parents took on the child-rearing patterns characteristic of the educated middle-class of their times, and their children and their children's children were raised democratically and in home environments that were intellectually stimulating.

The effects of increased exposure to education are demonstrated by a comparative study of the intelligence of soldiers in World Wars I and II. The median Army Alpha score of a sample of World War II recruits was 104, which compares to a midpoint of 62 for enlistees during World War I. The World War II score corresponds to the 83rd percentile on World War I norms. In other words, the "typical" soldier in World War II scored higher than 83% of the soldiers in World War I (Tuddeham, 1948).

Such a difference cannot be explained in purely genetic terms. If genetics were the only significant factor, we would have predicted that the two groups of soldiers would have made comparable scores. The difference can, however, be explained in terms of the greater exposure of the World War II soldiers to education. The average soldier in World War I had a bare eight years of schooling, whereas the typical World War II inductee had completed more than ten years. Furthermore, the number of days in the typical school year was much less at the turn of the century than it was during the 1930s, and school days were shorter as well. Today, the average young adult has completed more than 12 years of education, plus preschool.

Birth-Order Effects

Researchers have paid a great deal of attention in the last decade or so to what might be termed "the birth-order effect." Stanley Schachter (1959) noted that college students who had been first-born and only children tended to be more eager to be with others in stress situations. Other researchers have found that students who were first-born were more inclined to volunteer for psychological experiments (Capra and Dittes, 1962).

Such findings suggest that birth order is a psychologically significant variable. It causes problems for psychological researchers who use adolescents and adults as subjects, because much research makes use of volunteers, and the fact that first-born individuals are likely to be overrepresented in their samples raises questions about hidden bias in their results. In this discussion, however, we are more concerned with the early beginnings of the personality traits that make first-borns "different."

Birth-Order Differences in Childhood Experiences. It is quite likely that the difference results from the fact that first-borns are treated differently by their parents than are children who come later. For one thing, the first-born has a monopoly of parental attention and love until the appearance of the second-born child. As the first-born's siblings take their place in the family, he has to share more and more of this attention, but he always remains "the first" and achieves a degree of primacy from that fact alone. He is more mature than the other children, more responsive, and more can be expected of him. When he becomes old enough, siblings are placed in his charge, and he learns to play the role of the parent substitute, with all the opportunities for social learning that that position implies.

Personality Trends in First-Borns. Hence it comes as no surprise that research shows that individuals who were first-born in their families are likely to be more socialized, more responsible and more favorably disposed to persons in authority than those who were later-born (MacDonald, 1969a,b). Laosa and Brophy (1970) conducted a survey of kindergarten children and found that some of the birth-order-related differences that have been noted in adolescents and adults are also present at this early age. Measures of creativity showed first-borns to be more fluent, and they also tended to be slightly more popular with the other children. In general, the effects were more pronounced with girls, which is in keeping with other research showing girls to be more responsive than boys to environmental variables during the preschool years.

Not all the characteristics of first-borns are positive. Helen L. Koch (1955) secured teachers' impressions of kindergarten children and then sorted out their ratings according to the children's birth order. Results showed that first-borns were inclined to show more anger, to be more intense emotionally, to make excuses when things went wrong, and to be less responsive to sympathy and praise from adults. On the other hand, they tended to articulate more clearly in speech than second-borns. First-borns with opposite sex siblings rated higher on leadership, exhibitionism, and jealousy than those with same-sex siblings.

Parental Behavior Toward First-Borns. The behavior of pairs of mothers and four-year-old children drawn from different birth-order positions was observed by Irma Hilton (1967). The mothers of first-born children, in contrast to those of later-borns, were more likely to start the child working on puzzles, to offer suggestions, and to generally interfere with the child's activities. Mothers of other children were more inclined to let them start puzzles on their own. Mothers of first-borns were more likely to make overt gestures of love or emotional support (hugs, kisses, etc.), especially when the child was succeeding on the task assigned by the experimenter. As far as the children themselves were concerned, first-borns tended to be more dependent (i.e., were more likely to run to their mother's side during the intermission between testing sessions) than later-borns and were more likely to ask their mothers for help.

"Have you lost all interest in your first-born?"
(Drawing by Whitney Darron, Jr. © 1971 The New Yorker Magazine, Inc.)

Mary K. Rothbart (1971) conducted a similar study with first- and second-born five-year-olds, in which mothers supervised a number of tasks. All the first-borns had same-sex siblings two years younger than they, and all the second-borns had same-sex siblings two years older. Results showed that mothers were inclined to put more pressure to achieve on first-borns. In the picture-memory task, each mother showed her child an animal picture for three minutes, discussing it as much as she cared to. She was then instructed to turn the picture over and ask the child to recall as many animals as possible. The mothers had been told previously that the average child could name ten animals; hence they felt a degree of stress which, as Figure 12-6 suggests, was communicated more readily to the first-born children.

While the mother was talking to the investigator before the observation period began, the child had been admitted to a playroom full of interesting playthings. When the observa-

tion period began, the mother was requested to ask the child what it had seen in the playroom. As Figure 12-6 shows, first-born children were able to remember more playroom items than were second-born children.

After these and other tasks were completed, the mother was asked if she and the child would straighten out the room before the next subjects arrived. The observer then noted the extent to which the child participated in the cleanup. Scores indicating the extent of the children's involvement in cleanup tasks are indicated in Figure 12-6. Such tasks are "feminine" in our culture, as they are in most others, and there is no difference in the involvement of the two groups of girls. It is interesting to note that first-born boys, however, are just as involved as girls are in this task (willingly or otherwise—the experimenter does not say) and much more so than are second-born boys.

After reviewing these and other data gathered in her observations, Rothbart concluded

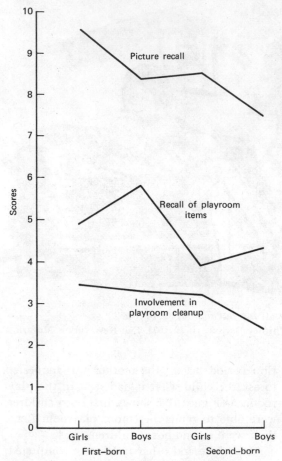

Figure 12-6. Achievement differences between first- and second-born girls and boys as reflected by (1) the number of animals in the animal picture they could recall, (2) the number of playroom items they could recall, and (3) the extent to which they were involved in cleaning up the playroom after the observation session.
(Rothbart, 1971.)

that the mother of a first-born is more likely to be "intrusive" in the achievement behavior of her child, and speculated that the greater success that the first-born tends to have in school later on may be the result of his willingness to accept performance standards that others have set for him.

In another survey, dimensions of parental behavior were related to a number of child variables. An analysis of intercorrelations showed that the higher the birth-order rank in the family, the more attention and guidance the child received from his parents, the more interest they showed in his intellectual needs, and the greater the likelihood that family resources would be placed at his disposal (e.g., to send him to nursery school). There was, however, no relationship between family rank and the extent to which the child was accepted by the parents (Freeberg and Payne, 1967).

The fact that first-borns turn out differently from later-borns shows how differences in parental attitudes and treatment can result in personality differences. The overall impact of differential treatment is not great and probably does not contribute more than a few percentage points to the variance among personality traits. The interesting thing for our purposes is that the first-born serves as a kind of a guinea pig for theories of child development because it is possible to identify the ways in which first-borns differ from other children and to trace the differences back to early childhood experiences which are, for the first-born, systematically different than the experiences of later-born children.

Summary

Earlier researchers tended to emphasize psychoanalytic themes and seemed to be intent on proving that love, warmth, and permissiveness are sufficient for healthy personality development. Current research has raised some questions about the effects of unconditioned permissiveness and tends to favor firmness and a well-defined family structure. Today's families are likely to be less structured than the families of a generation ago. Urbanization and increased education have both contributed to this change. Our rejection of "Old Country" values has also played a part in making the North American family unique. As a result, we must be cautious in extrapolating research findings between cultures, or even between different groups within our own culture.

Baumrind has uncovered some significant relationships between children's personality and child-rearing practices. By careful screening, she was able to find three well-defined groups: self-reliant children; anxious, restless and depressed children; and immature children. Baumrind observed parent-child interaction and found that self-reliant children had parents who rated high in parental control, parent-child communication, parental nurturance, and parental maturity demands. The parents of the second group of children scored lower on control and maturity demands, communicated less, and were not very supportive. Parents of immature children showed average support and nurturance, but scored negatively in all other respects. These results are consistent with common sense. The well-adjusted children get both firm control and love and the immature child gets very little control and few demands for mature behavior.

In a second study, Baumrind explored other aspects of the relationship between parental behavior and children's personality traits. One dimension she investigated was *independence*, characterized by dominance, purposefulness, and achievement orientation. Baumrind found that firm parental control and demands for maturity are not detrimental to the development of independence. She differentiated several types of parents. The *authoritarian* parent evaluates the child's behavior according to some set of absolute standards and demands unquestioning obedience. The *authoritative* parent directs the child in a rational manner that is oriented to issues. Although firm control is exercised, the child is respected as an individual. The *permissive* parent is nonpuni-

tive and accepting with regard to the child's impulses. The children of authoritative parents were friendlier, more cooperative, and achievement-oriented. Baumrind also observed that authoritative parents who were nonconforming tended to have independent, purposive, and dominant boys. Their daughters, however, tended to be hostile and resistive. Baumrind's findings are consistent with those of Zunich. Zunich found that nursery school children were more likely to make positive contact with other children if their parents were generally approving of their activities. On the other hand, the children of parents who were overly concerned with discipline, tended to be anxious and critical of other children.

Although the Baumrind studies attempted to assess total family atmosphere, most research has focused exclusively on the mother-child relationship. Bayley and Schaefer, for example, correlated several dimensions of earlier maternal behavior with IQs taken when the child was older. Their findings show that boys tend to benefit from more intense "mothering." Girls, on the other hand, respond negatively to the same situation, but respond better to maternal encouragement for autonomy. In another study, Bayley found a *negative* relationship between measures of boys' intelligence and democratic and affectionate maternal behavior. This unusual relationship, however, applied only to the first year, and was reversed from the second year onward. Bayley also studied maternal influence on personal-social aspects of child behavior. Affectionate, equalitarian maternal behavior appears to facilitate friendliness, just as it facilitates intelligence. A study by Kagan and Freeman produced similar results. Maternal restrictiveness and severity were negatively correlated with IQ. In addition, interviews turned up a strong negative correlation between daughters' IQs and mothers' erotic activity. Dreyer and Wells made some interesting observations relative to the development of creativity in four- and five-year-olds. Although the father's behavior had no observable influence, the mother who emphasized achievement and granted early independence was likely to have a highly creative child. The parents of high-creative children also showed more tension with respect to marital roles. This could reflect either more discord or greater freedom of expression.

The child is not just a passive organism: what the mother does is often a reaction to the child's behavior. Maternal hostility, for example, may be a reaction to an overly aggressive and hostile child. Although behavioral scientists once tended to explain sex differences in terms of parental and social expectations, recent research has provided evidence that many of these differences are inborn. The differential treatment received by boys and girls may therefore be a result, rather than a cause, of sex-linked personality traits. Mitchell and Brandt verified this hypothesis by observing the maternal behavior of rhesus monkeys. The mothers were generally more punitive toward their male offspring because they were more explorative and aggressive. Harlow made similar observations. Data gathered by the Early School Admissions Project revealed that the mothers of girls tend to have different perceptions of their child's behavior than do the mothers of boys. The mothers also become involved in different ways in the life of their community.

Fathers are important, also, especially if they are absent. A number of studies have demonstrated that boys from homes in which the fathers were not present tend to be dependent, immature, aggressive and less able to postpone gratification of needs and wants. Boys from father-present homes score higher on guilt, moral values, and conformity to rules. Blanchard and Biller found that the academic performance of boys whose fathers were present less than six waking hours a week was as poor as the performance of boys whose fathers were totally absent before the child turned five. Both of these groups did more poorly than boys whose fathers were present at least until the child reached the age of five. Boys whose fathers are absent because of divorce or separation are generally more aggressive than those whose fathers were absent because of death.

Some cross-cultural research by Goldman shows that group care for children is not necessarily deleterious, for children who were reared in children's villages and other group-care arrangements in three out of the four countries surveyed appeared to be as well-adjusted as children raised by their families. The fact that group-reared children in Poland were not as mature as those reared in families suggests that much depends on the attitudes and practices prevalent in the group-care institution.

Socioeconomic status (SES) is determined by association and correlates with education level and occupational level. This measure is related to child development in a number of ways, for example, in differences of child-rearing methods. Working-class and other lower-class familes are likely to emphasize obedience and severely punish deviations from rules, whereas middle-class families are likely to stress reasoning, discussion of problems, and the like. Kagan and Freeman noted that the mother's education is negatively correlated with restrictive or coercive behavior. An experiment by Osfeld and Katz found that middle-class children respond better to mild verbal threats, but lower-class children must be admonished more harshly. One interesting study observed the interaction between mother and child in a problem-solving situation. The lower-class mothers were more critical and restrictive and were inclined to make specific suggestions. Middle-class mothers were approving and encouraged an independent solution.

A number of studies show that intellectual stimulation varies with the SES of the home. Research by Werner showed that the single most important determinant of IQ was a variable called "educational stimulation," a composite rating of home work habits, family intellectual activities, availability of books, etc. Positive relationships were also found for parental IQ, education, and SES. All of these variables are interrelated, for both financial and social reasons. Some people, however, maintain that slum children receive as much stimulation and reinforcement as other children, and that class and racial differences are genetic in origin. This argument can be countered by the observation that reinforcement in the slum is inconsistent. Experiments in which middle-class children have been exposed to chaotic reinforcement schedules have resulted in the expected decrements in performance. A particularly interesting study compared the children of mixed black-white couples. The fact that children of white mothers averaged higher in IQ argues strongly for the environmentalist position. Havighurst maintains that children need to respond to systems of ego rather than id rewards, if they are going to find their way in a complex, changing society. Some ethnic groups emphasize id rewards and thus make it more difficult for their children to adapt, but the main differences in this respect tend to be SES rather than ethnic. For example, differences in school achievement between black and white children can be better explained in terms of more of the black children coming from lower SES homes, rather than in ethnic or genetic terms.

Not all behavioral scientists accept the idea that class differences are environmental, rather than genetic, pointing to past inconsistencies in SES research. Nonetheless, the weight of the evidence favors environmental factors as the source of personality and cognitive differences.

During the last decade or so, a number of researchers have focused their attention on birth-order effects. Schachter noted that first-borns were more eager to be with others during stress situations. Others have found that students who were first-born are more likely to volunteer for psychological experiments. These differences are probably the result of differential treatment during childhood. For one thing, the first-born has a monopoly of parental love and attention until the second child is born. The first-born also learns to take responsibility for his siblings. For these reasons, first-born children are likely to be more socialized, more responsible, more favorably disposed to persons in authority, more creative, and more popular. This is especially the case with girls. They are also more inclined to show anger, to be emotionally intense, and give alibis when things go wrong. The mothers of first-borns are more inclined to take an active or interfering role in the child's activities, and make overt gestures of love or emotional support. This tends also to make first-born children more dependent. On a more general level, the higher the birth-order rank, the more attention and guidance the child receives from his parents.

13 Personality and Peer Relationships

In the young child, as in the infant, the expression of behavior tendencies is a factor of vital importance for psychosocial development. So too are further acquisition of self and social awareness and the broadening scope of peer relationships that are characteristic of this particular age.

In this chapter we will systematically examine three classes of behavior tendencies: dependence-independence, aggression, and achievement.

Dependence and Independence Tendencies

During infancy dependence tendencies become firmly established. The same cannot be said for strivings for independence. Moreover, it would be incorrect to assume without evidence that dependence and independence were merely opposite ends of the same continuum. For this reason changes in dependence occurring in infancy were described as moving from dependence to less dependence, rather than from dependence to independence. The ages three through five appear to be the critical period for optimal normal development of independence. Dependence was a necessary condition of infancy; independence is a task of the younger child.

Certainly, the diminishing dependence of the child as he grows older is a fact. It must be, in part at least, the result of positive development of more independent ways of responding to the same situations which, when younger, elicited dependent reactions. The preschool child appears to be motivated to perform independently, and a series of studies shows how real this independence behavior tendency is.

As components of independence behavior, Beller (1955) suggested the following five: taking initiative, overcoming of obstacles, persistence, just wanting to do something, and wanting to do things by oneself. Using these as the components of independence, Beller constructed rating scales based on each component. Children about three to nearly six years of age were then rated on these scales by their nursery school teacher. Highly significant relations among the rating scales were found. The five indices of independence were found to "hang together" in that most of the children were consistent from one to another of these scales, thus demonstrating the reality of an independence drive so far as these components were concerned.

The second phase of his study was concerned with specific behavior components selected to furnish evidence of a general dependence drive. Rating scales were constructed for five components, namely, seeking help, physical contact, proximity, attention, and recognition. He used the same subjects, raters, and procedure as in the previous phase of the study. A highly significant degree of relationship among components was again found. Children differed consistently from one another in composite dependency scores. Thus, at least for these five components, there was evidence of a dependence drive.

Beller next performed the third phase of the study which is crucial to the issue of whether dependence and independence are separable. The correlation between independence and dependence, as he had measured them, was calculated for this group of children. If dependence and independence were merely opposite ends of the same continuum, a correlation approaching (but because of errors of measurement not reaching) a perfect negative correlation of —1.00 would be expected. The correlation he did find was a moderately negative —.53. This correlation suggests that assuming dependence and independence to be merely bipolar ends of the same continuum is not indicated. Instead, they should be treated as separate, although related, tendencies. He confirmed his own results in a repetition of the study with different subjects (Beller, 1957a).

Dependence and independence are best conceived as separate components of child behavior. It is proper, therefore, to speak of the child while learning to depend on others as simultaneously learning to be independent. He shows both tendencies.

These incompatible behavior tendencies can involve the child in considerable conflict. Beller's (1959) measures of dependence and independence were constructed to permit investigation of the balance between the two. His measure of conflict was the degree of similarity between dependence and independence scores. Those children with a higher level of conflict were more inhibited and inconsistent in their expressions of dependence. Inhibition and inconsistency were measured by placing the child in a situation where he and an adult were in a room with toys on the shelf within the reach of the adult, but not the child (Beller, 1957b). The measure of inhibition was the inability of the child to ask for the toy outright. Moreover, such children showed more behavior problems, such as difficulties in toilet training, defiance, and compulsive behavior.

The Influence of Situational Factors on Dependence Tendencies

Manifestations of dependence may be affected by the immediate situation so that the child's more or less consistent degree of dependence is changing temporarily (and perhaps permanently).

One of the factors causing temporary fluctuation is situational insecurity which increases dependence on the mother. In childhood, strangeness evokes fear and is considered to be one of the conditions of insecurity in childhood. In Arsenian's (1943) research on this problem, the insecure situation was a room strange to the children but containing many toys. The investigator observed through a one-way screen the influence of the mother's presence or absence on the one- to three-year-old child's reaction to this strange room. She hypothesized that security was a function of the mother's presence. She systematically varied the presence or absence of the mother with the child.

Some of the children were accompanied by their mothers, some were not. Children left alone in the room for the first few sessions spent most of their time crying as well as showing agitated nonadaptive movements such as hanging around the door, and the like. When children were accompanied by their mothers from the first, they played with the toys in the strange room with little evidence of insecurity. Her presence made it possible for the child to react adaptively to the new situation. Security was felt by the child because of his dependence on the mother. The situation of being left alone temporarily increased his dependence tendencies. The absence of the mother created a stress situation for the child which increased dependency.

Another approach to stress was used by Beller (1958, 1959). He took the position that since the parental figure had reduced painful stimulation during the child's infancy, her presence and attention was synonymous with relief in his later (preschool) years. Actual or even anticipated deprivation would produce a heightened level of dependence. In his study, Beller not only confirmed the hypotheses that

dependent behavior would be higher in a dependency stress situation than in a nonstress situation, but also found that the higher a child's initial dependence, the greater would be his increase in the stress situation.

Using a sample of some of the children described earlier, Beller compared the children on the number of times they would look at an adult or at an adult-child interaction in free play in which the adult was relatively less available to any one child (dependency stress situation) with the number of times they would do so in organized work and play where the adult was readily available (nonstress situation). His measures were based on direct observation of the child's eye movements in looking at adults or at adult-child interactions during ten two-minute time samples in the two situations.

Initial dependence correlated significantly with the amount of increased looking at adults and of adult-child interactions in the dependency stress situations. This finding was verified in the setting of eight psychotherapy sessions for each of 16 children. The dependency stress situation used in this study was the occurrence of "separation experiences," that is, the therapist's canceling, postponing, or being late to a session. The nonstress sessions lacked these experiences. The number of requests for help coming from the child was the measure of dependence. Again, initial dependence scores correlated significantly with the magnitude of increase of dependency responses in the stress situation.

Deprivation of adult social contact can heighten a child's dependence. Frustration of dependency needs through withdrawal of friendly, rewarding, encouraging, affectionate behavior from an adult (nonnurturance) has an effect on a child's behavior. Willard W. Hartup (1958) compared two groups of preschool children, each of which was composed of equal numbers of subjects rating high or low on dependency rating scales of the type used by Beller. In one group, each child was given ten minutes of consistently nurturant attention (was smiled at, talked to, and so forth) by a female experimenter. In the second group, each child had five minutes of nurturance, which was followed by another five minutes in which the investigator withdrew from interacting with the child with the excuse that "she was busy." This group we shall call the Withdrawal group. After the ten minutes of treatment, each child in the two groups was assigned two cognitive learning tasks.

The children in the two groups differed in their learning efficiency. In the Withdrawal group, both the High and Low Dependent girls and the High Dependent boys were the more efficient learners. It appears that attending to children and then withdrawing that attention is more likely to supply a higher degree of motivation for learning than consistent nurturance. The findings are consistent with those of Beller in that again it was found that dependency behavior was higher in a dependency stress situation than in a nonstress situation.

Changes in Dependence Tendencies with Increasing Age

The mothers' attitudes toward dependence are important in connection with age changes. Parental attitudes about the desirability of dependency are subject to change with time. Mothers expect the infant to be completely dependent, but also expect that he will become gradually less dependent as he grows older. The mother, as the principal agent of socialization during infancy, fosters dependence in some degree and manner, but as least in later infancy also introduces training with the aim of decreasing dependence. The infant is expected under his own direction to learn to

feed himself, to keep himself clean, and in general to adapt to certain rules of the game of living in the family. The goal of socialization is first to foster complete dependence and then to bring about less and less dependence.

It is probable, though not backed by specific definitive research, that during younger childhood emotional dependence takes a different course from instrumental dependence. The mother wishes to lessen instrumental dependence. But with emotional dependence her goal is not so much to lessen dependence as it is to bring about in her child culturally approved and suitable "mature" expressions of emotional dependence.

Consider the two-year-old and his manifestations of affection. He is most direct and open, hugging, kissing, and clinging, and tugging at his mother's dress. But adults believe there is something "infantile" about such behavior. Their goal of socialization, whether they are conscious of it or not, is to bring about a foundness for the mother, a pleasure in her company, and not this embarrassing, demanding, passionate attachment. Above all, the child's incessant demands for proofs of affection must somehow be curtailed. Modification of emotional dependence rather than elimination is the goal. In addition to modification of emotional dependence on her, the mother teaches her child to seek affection and attention from other adults and from his peers.

Changes with age in dependence tendencies during these years have been investigated empirically. Sears and his associates (1957), in their "pattern" study, found that physical clinging decreased during early childhood, but that more verbal forms of seeking attention from the mother were still quite strong at the age of five.

In a study by Stith and Conner (1962), seven categories of dependent behavior—seeking information, help, recognition, praise, affection, reward, and permission—were summed together. Dependency scores were contrasted with seven categories of helpful behavior—giving help, reassurance, permission, praise, affection, reward, and information. Observations during 1300 two-minute periods were collected for 30 boys and 35 girls in a university nursery school and kindergarten. For purposes of analysis of age trends, there were four groups, 38–46, 47–55, 56–63, and 64–75 months. As age increased, dependent contacts with adults decreased in frequency and proportion whereas helpful contacts with both adults and children increased significantly.

Glen Heathers (1955) systematically studied changes with age in dependence (and independence) tendencies of two different groups. One was composed of 20 two-year-old children, the other of 20 four- and five-year-old children. Teachers in a nursery school observed the behavior of the children in both groups toward their teachers and toward other children during play, recording their findings on a variety of relevant variables. Included were four emotional dependence categories. For dependence tendencies directed toward both children and adults, the categories were clinging to and seeking affection, and seeking attention and approval. Two hypotheses concerning the relation of age to the development of emotional dependence were investigated. The first hypothesis was that during the early years of childhood emotional dependence on adults declined relative to emotional dependence on children. The second hypothesis was that emotional dependence as expressed in seeking reassurance and affection tended to decline with age relative to its expression through seeking attention and approval.

Results supported both hypotheses. In general, there was a decline with increasing age in tendencies to behave in dependent ways toward teachers, coupled with an inclination to turn toward one's peers in search of attention. As Heathers put it, ". . . in the process of socialization, emotional dependence tends to shift away from a passive, 'infantile' dependence toward a more active and assertive dependence on one's peers" (p. 56). Thus, changes in dependence tendencies with increasing age have been established.

Determinants of Independence Tendencies

As dependence declines and independence increases the child at each point in time must strike a balance. He must learn and relearn the areas and manner in which he is expected to be independent and dependent. A ratio of dependence versus independence must be struck. Otherwise, overdependence of the sort described earlier or too great independence may result.

This age of three through five seems to be the period that is critical for the development of optimal balance. Research definition of this assertion still is necessary. Consequently, this statement is not to be considered as anything more than plausible. At least, problems of independence-dependence balance appear important to the behavior of the young child.

Resistant behavior towards adults when encountered in a setting of proffered assistance may be interpreted as an instance of the young child testing his capacities for independence. Social resistance expressed in saying, "No!", or "Don't" is a way that socially inept children have of dealing with attempts of others to direct their behavior. Sometimes their resistance is an essential feature of healthy growth.

It has been observed that resistant behavior, or negativism, reaches a high frequency when the child is about two or three years of age. Ausubel (1950) offers the interpretation that this is due to the frustration suffered by the child when his parents slow down their nurturance and begin to make demands for independent behavior. This phenomenon he called "ego devaluation."

In their cross-cultural study, Whiting and Child (1953), investigated what they called severity of socialization arising from dependence and independence training, and socialization anxiety. None of the societies they studied seriously tried to begin independence training before the age of two and the median age of serious efforts was about three and a half years. The American group began somewhat earlier at about two-and-a-half years. Severity of independence training in the American group received a rating at the median. Two aspects of severity of independence training were isolated—freedom to act on his own initiative without adult surveillance and responsibility for taking on the adult role. As compared with other societies, ratings emphasizing the former were on the severe side in the American group, the latter on the mild side. The measure of severity of socialization involves the behavior of parents. But from another point of view, and one more fundamental to Whiting and Child's intent in connection with this particular problem, it is also an index of socialization anxiety aroused in the child.

Consider the four aspects used in arriving at a judgment of severity of socialization or socialization-anxiety—brevity, severity of punishment, frequency of punishment, and signs of emotional disturbance in the child. Each of these is potentially an arouser of anxiety in the child: the briefer the transition, the stronger is the anxiety; the more severe the punishment, the greater is the subsequent anxiety; the more frequent the punishment, the greater is the anxiety developed; and the more signs of disturbance, the greater is the anxiety.

Training for and encouragement of independence increase independence. Striving for independence takes place in areas where moderate difficulties still exist for the child. If the activity in question has been thoroughly mastered, neither parent nor child sees in it anything of a challenge to striving for independence. Thus, a child strives for independence in areas where his ability is still marginal. In this sense, strivings for independence are reflected as an aspect of level of aspiration, that is, the level toward which a person is striving.

Fales (1944) studied nursery school children in the course of their activity of putting on and taking off their wraps. The percentage of refusal of help was taken as an index of "rudimentary aspiration." Next, one group of children was trained in taking off its wraps. Afterward, it was compared with another group not so trained. The group receiving the training increased considerably in its percentage of refusal as compared to the control group. In another related study by Fales, a group of children was praised (encouraged) in connection with its endeavors whereas another group was not. The praised group increased considerably in independence.

It would appear that both training and praise increase independence. Both these incentives are probably important in accounting for the learning of independence. Increase in independence tendencies with age probably reflects the effect of both incentives. Conversely, if the parent and other adults engaged in socialization give no training or actually discourage independence tendencies, a less independent child may be expected.

It may be well to introduce some additional cross-cultural material here, because it may highlight some of the dynamics involved in the development of independent and dependent behavior. Gallimore, Howard, and Jordan (1969) compared the behavior of Hawaiian and Haole (i.e., Anglo-American) preschool children who were given a difficult puzzle to solve. The children were showed the puzzle completely assembled and given directions as to how it could be solved. The puzzle was then disassembled and the children were told: "Go ahead and play with the puzzle and if you want me to help you, just ask and we will play with it together. This is a very hard puzzle." There were clear-cut differences between the two groups of children: 93% of the Haole group spontaneously asked for help, in contrast to only 23% of the Hawaiian group. The typical Hawaiian reaction was to work with interest and attention for three or four minutes, whereupon activity gradually decreased and then stopped. The 77% of the Hawaiians who did not ask for help often appeared to be apprehensive and uncomfortable. The children requesting help in both groups tended to stop working abruptly after three or four minutes and ask for help clearly and in an openly dependent fashion. In other words, in a situation clearly calling for dependent behavior, the Hawaiian children seemed unable to solicit it.

The background to this behavior pattern may be found in the way in which Hawaiian mothers deal with their children. When children are infants and toddlers, they are indulgent to the point of fostering extreme dependency. After a child becomes mobile and verbal, the mothers tend to find the dependency burdensome. The child's requests for attention and help are increasingly punished, and he is forced to depend more on his own efforts or the capricious aid of older children. The child initially responds to the withdrawal of nuturance with increasing demands, to which the mother becomes even more punitive and rejecting.

The transition from dependency to self-reliance would be facilitated if the Hawaiian mother would reward independent behavior, but unfortunately she does not: the child has to become self-reinforcing and never really learns how to respond to reinforcement from adults. When Hawaiian mothers were asked what age children should be able to do such things as eat alone, stay home alone, and the like, they tended to give ages at least a year younger than those given by Haole mothers. In school, Hawaiian children tend to be poor students at all grade levels and seem unaffected by the performance-reward contingencies teachers typically employ. Other research has shown, incidentally, that poor first-grade achievement is associated with early pressure for independence (Chance, 1961). As adults, Hawaiians tend to be more peer-oriented and less independent than other ethnic groups. They seem less able to fend for themselves economically and constitute a very high percentage of welfare cases in the state of Hawaii.

What this research shows, then is that independence in children is not likely to be facilitated when mothers merely discourage dependent behavior. It is as though a child must learn to be properly dependent before he can become independent, and a too early insistence on independence, without accompanying rewards for success along these lines, appears to interfere with achievement later on.

Changes in Independence Tendencies with Increasing Age

Independence, as differentiated from lessened dependence, was also investigated by Heathers (1955). His measures of emotional independence included those meant to be measures of self-reliance as evidenced in nondistractibility, namely, the extent to which children: (1) ignored stimuli from teacher; (2) ignored stimuli from a child; and (3) played alone. He also included measures of self-assertion or dominance in social interaction with other children as other criteria of independence, namely, the extent to which they: (1) organized another child's play (telling him what to do or showing him how); (2) interfered with another child's play; and (3) resisted another child's interference or aggression. Of all of these measures only ignoring stimuli from teacher and organizing another child's play showed an increase with age. Some support, although meager, is thereby given to the hypothesis that independence increases with age.

Aggressive Tendencies

Aggression is widely prevalent in young children. Many of the phenomena of their anger can be seen to have had an aggressive component. Young children direct aggression against the persons in their environment, including their parents. Every one of the 379 mothers studied by Sears, Maccoby, and Levin (1957) had to deal with aggressive episodes, and 95% reported experiences of having strong aggression directed against them by their children.

A preliminary view of the meaning of overt aggressiveness is given in the scales developed by Beller and Turner (1962). These had to do with threatening others, derogating others, destroying materials or possessions of others, attacking adults physically, and attacking children physically. Not only do such scales seem plausible as constituents of aggression but also a factor analysis of them showed they possessed many elements in common. Thus, they supply evidence that aggression is a unitary construct.

From the point of view of socialization, it should be apparent that our society encourages aggression in certain forms. Under some circumstances we expect the individual to be aggressive and "to defend his rights," although the reverse also holds—there are occasions in which parents punish aggression. Most parents will not tolerate physical aggression directed against themselves, whereas they permit it on occasion in aggression against peers.

The strength of tendencies to be aggressive is only one aspect of aggressiveness in relation to socialization. The other aspect is the nature of control or inhibition of tendencies to be aggressive. All societies and individuals have ways of controlling the expression of aggression. Without such controls on in-group aggression, life in a society could not long endure.

In various ways aggressive behavior draws punishment. Punishment for aggression means the extent to which the child is pained or thwarted because he acted in an aggressive manner. Of course, any punishment is a kind of frustration, but for the sake of clarity it may be distinguished from other frustrations. Punishment for aggressiveness during infancy seems hardly likely. Quite probably the child learns during early childhood that aggressive behavior brings punishment. What happens when this occurs needs scrutiny.

Determinants of Overt Aggressive Tendencies

The constitutional determinants of aggressiveness are very evident, though definitive research has not isolated their· exact effect. Consider how at the age of four, height, weight, strength, and sheer activity may be crucial in determining the winner (and the loser) in preschool shoving contests. Consider further how reinforcement or lack of it affects aggressive tendencies. These characteristics are, to a great degree, attributable to a constitutional factor. As we have noted earlier, boys are characteristically more aggressive than girls. This is perhaps the single most thoroughly documented finding on childhood aggression (Buss, 1961). The constitutional factor does not tell the whole story, however. There are wide variations in aggressiveness within each sex, as well as an overlapping of the distributions. In other words, although boys tend to be more aggressive, there is a sizable minority of girls who are quite aggressive, as well as a sizable minority of boys who are very unaggressive. In addition, there are some general trends in aggressiveness that characterize the preschool period of development.

From knowledge of the socialization process of aggression in infancy, we should expect the experience of the young child to contain instances in which frustration would serve to breed aggression. In accordance with learning theory, a child will express aggressive responses to the extent that his past history includes reinforcement or nonreinforcement for such responses.

Let us evaluate the proposition that frustration leads to aggression. Before examining new evidence, it should be pointed out that the principle already has received support. Earlier discussion attests to its operation during infancy. If rejection may be viewed as a form of frustration, which seems reasonable, then research showing that parental rejection leads to aggressiveness also fits this mold (McCandless, 1969).

A study by Barbara A. Merrill (1946) is relevant here. Through a one-way screen she observed each mother in interaction with her child. The first session served to develop behavior categories relevant to the mother's behavior toward her child. Divided into two groups, one group of mothers was told that its children had not shown their full capabilities; the other was treated in the same way as in the first session. The mildly criticized mothers tended to assume more direct control of their children's behavior in directing, interfering, and criticizing. Merrill found that the frequency of maternal restricting and controlling of behavior was positively correlated to indices of frustration in the children during these sessions, namely, their irritable or com-

plaining behavior. Or to put it another way, at one extreme were the more controlled children who manifested considerable irritability and complaints; at the other extreme were the less controlled children who showed less irritability and complaints. The study demonstrates not only that frustration breeds aggression in the form of irritability, but also that there are individual differences in the extent to which children are exposed to frustrating reinforcements of aggressive behavior.

Another finding emerges from this study. Generalization of aggressive tendencies to other situations is shown by the finding that the children who were more restricted by their mothers were more complaining when they played in other sessions with an unfamiliar young woman rather than with the mother. This woman had been deliberately trained to be equally neutral toward all children so that her behavior would be as constant and as similar as possible toward them. The children who were more aggressive with their mothers continued to be more aggressive than other children in the presence of this neutral young woman. Habits of aggressiveness established with the mother tended to carry over into this new situation. Moreover, in a second session when each child was more familiar with the woman, the child's behavior became even more similar to that he had shown toward his mother. Evidently, experiences with the mother established habits that carried over into other situations. The young woman by a process of stimulus generalization elicited similar degrees of aggressive behavior.

A considerable number of studies have been concerned with age changes in aggression. The observations that Florence Goodenough (1931) made many years ago in the course of her classic study are still the best summary of the relationship between age and aggression. Over the preschool years her subjects showed a decrease in random discharge of aggression and an increase in retaliatory behavior. The latter is aggression under a more circumscribed name. This form of behavior with intent to injure seems more in keeping with what is meant by aggression than does blind striking out. Thus, it may be concluded that within the age limits under consideration, aggression increases with age, provided Goodenough's measures are accepted as representative. Her information on parental methods of control is also relevant. She found that with increasing age, use of physical punishment (such as spanking), coaxing, and ignoring diminished and parents shifted to use of scolding, threatening, and isolation. For these and other methods of control, some mothers were successful, whereas others failed. Later research by Walters, Pearce, and Dahms (1957) also confirmed Goodenough's observations. They found that both physical and verbal aggression tend to increase between the ages of two and four and then level off about five.

Fantasy Aggression

The studies of aggressiveness in preschool children reported so far have used indices of behavioral aggression exhibited in day-to-day situations at home or in preschool, or in specially contrived settings as in the Merrill study. Other studies have been performed that are dependent on indices of covert or fantasy aggression expressed in play.

Much of the research in this area was done by Robert Sears and his colleagues. They used the standardized doll-play equipment described in Chapter 2. At each session, instances of aggressive behavior shown by a particular child were noted by trained observers.

The greater aggressiveness of boys is again the single most thoroughly documented finding here (Levin and Wardwell, 1962). This is a definitive finding in almost all studies of doll-play aggression. Hence, it can be considered as well established that sex is a determinant of aggressive behavior.

Increase in aggression in the second as compared to the first doll-play session with the same experimenter present has been found in several studies (Hollenberg and Sperry, 1951; Levin and Sears, 1956; P. S. Sears, 1951). The children, nevertheless, maintain about their same relative rank position. The increase in aggression has been interpreted as resulting from the child's discovery that the usual restraints against aggression do not apply to doll play. By the second session, permissiveness to be aggressive, tacitly given by the experimenter, is interpreted by the children as actual encouragement to be aggressive. Consequently, permissiveness to be aggressive is still another determinant of fantasy aggression.

The Relation Between Overt and Fantasy Aggression

The relation between overt and covert (fantasy) aggression needs clarification. Let it be stated at the outset that fantasy aggression expressed through play does not have a very high correlation with independently derived indices of aggression obtained from interview or observation. Korner (1951) and Sears (1950), for instance, found correlations of only .13 to .21 between overt and fantasy aggression. This lack of appreciable direct relationship, then, is a fact and should not be ignored. The inference, however, is not to be drawn that overt and fantasy aggression are unrelated. Both are forms of behavior; both tell us something about the child. Since a simple linear relation does not hold, investigators have tried to find out if there are more intricate ways of relating the two kinds of expressions of aggression.

Let us start with the assumption that some,

but only some, of the fantasy aggression reenacts aggression a child would actually display in home or school. Let us make certain other assumptions. Some fantasy expression reflects aggression directed toward himself, as when he reenacts some punishment that actually did happen to him. Some of his fantasy aggression represents aggression he feels he would like to indulge in but cannot, as when he stuffs the father doll down the toilet. Moreover, conditions will be present which *inhibit* expressions of fantasy aggression. Although he would like to express them, for some reason he cannot. The most obvious source of inhibition is punishment by the parents for aggression. Their punishment does not necessarily eliminate aggression; it may merely inhibit him in his expression of it in play. Thus, fantasy aggression expressed in play may have several different meanings and implications. These assumptions are subject to empirical investigation.

Sears (1950) has related fantasy aggression and overt aggression in preschool on the basis of the following expectations. Child punishment serves to frustrate a child and hence to increase his aggression. More severe punishment at home would tend to inhibit aggression there because of fear of punishment, but increase aggression elsewhere. This was the finding of Hollenberg and Sperry (1951) in a study reported later, namely, that punishment of aggression decreases aggression in the situation in which it occurs and increases it in dissimilar situations.

Two response tendencies instigated by the parents have now been established: aggression and fear of punishment for aggression. They operate in opposite directions. Sometimes, if punishment is mild, aggression wins out. Their relative influence will depend not only on the strength of the opposing tendencies, but also on the similarities of the home situation to a new situation. It will be agreed that the school with its parent surrogate, the teacher, is similar in many respects to the home. The child may make the same response in school as he does in the home because of stimulus generalization. On the dimension of similarity, doll play lies further out on the gradient, that is, it is less similar than the school setting. If anxiety created by inhibition and punishment generalizes less extensively than aggression, then the inhibition of severe punishment would be expected to affect behavior toward the preschool teacher; aggressive doll play is not inhibited, instead it is increased because of the increased frustration created by the punishment.

This was neatly demonstrated by Robert R. Sears (1951) among preschool children, divided into three groups based on estimates of the amount of punishment of aggression in the home. The first group came from homes low in punitiveness, the second from homes moderately punitive, and the third from homes highly punitive. The moderately punished group showed the most aggression in school. The low and high punished group were found to be approximately the same in mean frequency of aggression. Both were reliably lower in aggression than the moderately punished group. This corresponds to the expectancy outlined earlier.

The same children were placed in the doll-play situation. In their doll play, the children from highly punitive homes showed more aggression than either of the other two groups. Thus, the more severely punished group was highest in fantasy aggression but inhibited in overt aggression. Fear of punishment did not show enough generalizations to reach the doll-play situation, so aggressive tendencies, inhibited in the preschool situation, were permitted to appear.

To return to the issue of the relation of fantasy and overt aggression, the group in which a linear correlation of only .13 was found between the two forms of aggression was now found to show an intelligible high interrelationship when the additional factor of the mothers' punitiveness was taken into consideration.

Levin and Sears (1956) investigated identification as a determinant of fantasy aggression. They advanced various hypotheses having to do with identification, arguing that fantasy aggression was in part a function of the child's identification with aggressive role models. Several measures other than those for aggressiveness were necessary to test their hypotheses.

First, they found the degree of identification of the children with their parents through questioning about how the child acts when he has done something naughty; for example, "What does he do when he is naughty?" "Does he tell you about it?" "What do you do if he denies something you are fairly sure he has done?" They proposed that identification could be estimated from the stage of development of internalized control the child had reached. An example they give of high control (super-ego) for this age was a child whose mother recounted that when he did act naughty he held out for a while, but after a short time came to her and, without prodding, admitted he had done something naughty. Second, the severity of punishment for aggression toward parents was assessed. Third, which particular parent usually punished the child was ascertained from interviews. Two sessions of doll play with 126 boys and 115 girls of five years of age were carried out to provide information on the amount of aggressiveness displayed, through recording the frequency with which it appeared in the play session.

In view of the complexity of their design it is worth while to summarize information Levin and Sears acquired about these children and their parents. On the one hand, they knew the degree of identification the child exhibited along with related findings and, on the other, they knew the frequency of doll-play aggression he or she showed. To test their hypotheses they had merely to relate these two sets of data, treating the data for the boys and girls separately.

Their results supported the hypotheses they had advanced. Boys who were highly identified with the father and had the cue for male aggressiveness by being usually punished by their fathers showed the highest frequency of doll (or fantasy) aggression. The boy's identification with an aggressive male model is then a determinant in the frequency of fantasy aggression. For girls, identification was related to high aggression only when it was associated with the mothers' being the agent of severe punishment. In other words, when the girls, as well as the boys, were identified with an aggressive model, then identification was related to high aggression.

Modeling and Aggression

The prevalence of aggressive models in delinquent subcultures and the opportunity for identifications with them to develop has helped to explain delinquency. It is not surprising that the influence of aggressive models has been extensively investigated in recent years.

Bandura and Walters (1963b) in summarizing their own and other studies indicate that the increase in the number or intensity of aggressive responses involves two rather different effects. There is the *modeling* effect in which the child reproduces the novel response of the model, and there is the *disinhibiting* effect in which observation of the model results in weakening the inhibition of those aggressive responses already in the repertoire of the child.

An investigation demonstrating the generalization of imitative aggressive responses to a setting in which the model was absent was performed by Bandura, Ross, and Ross (1961). Twenty-four nursery school boys and girls were so situated as to observe adult models, either of the same or opposite sex, behave aggressively toward an inflated five-foot clown doll. These adults punched it, tossed it up and down, and hit it with a mallet, along with making verbally aggressive remarks. In the first minute of the session in which the child observed him, the adult had busied himself with a Tinker-Toy assembly. Another 24 children were placed in a nonaggressive condition in which the adult model spent the entire period with the Tinker-Toy, ignoring the clown doll. A control group of the same size had no exposure to the models at all.

Thereafter, in another room each child in the three groups was first exposed to a situation conducive to arousing some degree of aggression. This arousal experience was necessary in order to make sure that the children entered the test for delayed imitation somewhat predisposed to aggressive activities. This condition was produced by each child's being shown attractive toys (fire engine, doll set), allowed to play a sufficient time to get involved, and then told that these were the very best toys, and that it had been decided to reserve them for the other children.

The test series followed immediately in another adjacent room. This room contained a variety of toys, some nonaggressive in character (tea set, crayons, cars, and the like) while others were conducive of aggressive responses (three-foot clown doll, mallet, dart gun). Each subject spent 20 minutes alone in the room, his behavior being noted through a one-way mirror. Measures rated included imitation of physical and verbal aggression, imitative nonaggressive verbal responses (remarks made earlier by the adult model. such as "he sure is tough"), and nonimitative physical and verbal aggression, including use of the guns. The subjects previously exposed to the aggressive models reproduced a great amount of aggression, differing significantly in this respect from the nonaggressive and control groups. Subjects who had observed the nonaggressive model were less aggressive than the control subjects. Boys showed more aggression than girls, following exposure to the male model.

It would seem that observation of cues for aggression from the behavior of models is effective in eliciting the same forms of responses in nursery school children. Subjects not so exposed only rarely performed in this fashion. That aggressive behavior was disinhibited by the communication of permissiveness increased the probability of aggressiveness. That the subjects expressed their aggression in ways clearly modeled on the novel patterns of the adult offers evidence of learning by imitation of the model.

In another experiment involving modeling, preschool-age children watched an adult female perform such aggressive acts as pounding a doll on the head with a mallet, using a knife to chop off the head of a clay figure, and using a fork to jab the legs of a clay figure. Another adult female praised the model for her behavior (reward), criticized the model (punishment), or alternatively praised and criticized the model. A fourth group of children did not see the model and constituted a control group. As Figure 13-1 indicates, the extent to which the model was rewarded or punished was reflected in the amount of imitative aggression displayed by the children when they had a chance to play with the same items. Such results are what might be expected: the rewarding of another's aggression encourages one's own aggression, and the punishment of another's aggression inhibits it.

An interesting effect occurred, however, when the children were divided into younger

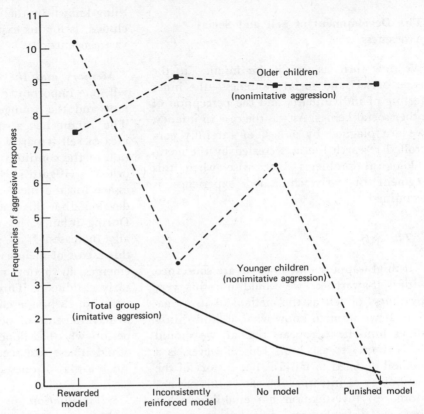

Figure 13-1.   Aggressive response frequencies for children who saw (or did not see) the aggression of an adult model who received one of three styles of reinforcement. (Rosekrans and Hartup, 1967.)

(36–58 months) groups and older (60–71 months) groups and their *non*imitative responses were tallied. As Figure 13-1 shows, those younger children who had seen the rewarded model behaved in a decidedly aggressive manner, whereas those who viewed the inconsistent reinforcement of the model were somewhat inhibited.

The younger children who saw *no* model were quite aggressive. This effect could have been predicted from the implements that were available for play purposes: a mallet, a knife, and a fork. Pounding, cutting, or jabbing are

natural responses when one handles a mallet, knife, or fork. The young children who saw the model reprimanded for aggressiveness, however, were totally inhibited. The older children responded differently. Their nonimitative aggressive responses were generally unrelated to the model's treatment. The authors explain this result in terms of the older children's ability to make finer discrimination among various kinds of aggression and to match their responses only to those categories for which the model was rewarded or punished.

The Development of Self and Social Awareness

We now turn, as we did for infancy, to the issue of self and social awareness—the inner feeling of individuality and the perception of other social beings. As was the case in infancy, we are plagued by a lack of carefully controlled research findings created by the methodological problems that arise when this segment of early childhood experience is examined.

The Self

It might appear that since we are concerned with self-awareness we would use this very awareness of self as the method of investigation. If we want to know what a child thinks about himself, it appears that all we should do is simply to ask him. This, however, is a method doomed to failure. The history of the psychology of introspection shows this clearly. Moreover, investigation has established that there are distortion and deception created by the defensive stratagems of the personality. It is for this reason that introspection failed as a technique of psychological investigation (Hilgard, 1949). True, by such procedures we may get some crude approximations of what children think they think about themselves, but little more.

The vague, yet expansive, boundaries of the self in the young child further complicate the matter. Already familiar from the work of Piaget is the inability of the young child to take the position of the other person, or, to use Piaget's terminology, to show reciprocity. Confusion over "me," simultaneously representing both the child himself and someone else speaking of himself, is illustrative of the child's inability to see the mountain scene model in any but his own perspective. Every-

thing known by the child, moon and stars included, is for his express benefit, showing his vast egocentricity.

Memory and the Self. In considering the self, one important difference between the infant and the younger child must be noted. The infant has a very poor memory. The idea of self is partly as a unifying generalization of the continuity of one's personal memories, as Hilgard (1949) once noted. It is necessary for the memory capacity to be better developed for this generalization to take place. During infancy this memory capacity gradually increases. It is probable, however, that this factor of memory as a contributor to self emerges in major importance only during early childhood. Through continuous memories of one's past, a child (and an adult) is led to have a sense of personal identity. He is a person who has done this and that and the other. These are seen as personal and very much a part of oneself.

Self-evaluation in the Self-concept. Self-evaluation or self-criticism is considered by Hilgard (1949) as a necessary feature in understanding self-organization. Self-evaluation is shown through guilt feelings. The presence of guilt feelings indicates that the individual considers himself an active agent responsible for what he does. If he fails to do that which he considers worthy and right, he develops self-reproof in the form of guilt.

On the other side of the coin is the effort of the self to protect against criticism in order to reduce guilt. In trying to keep a good opinion of ourselves we are capable of self-delusion. We try to make our motives acceptable to ourselves. Self-respect (even if we cannot always give it) is important to children and adults. The individual strives but does not always succeed in keeping a sense of self-worth. He values his opinion of himself and goes to great lengths to protect his favorable view of himself.

The self itself is a value. We expect desirable things from ourselves and expect to behave in ways that are admirable. We are ever ready to defend our evaluation of our self. We become aggressive or show other defensive maneuvers when something threatens our self-evaluation. If something does not fit these values or we fall short of our view of ourselves, we are apt to explain by saying, "I was not myself." We have self-esteem to the degree to which we have self-confidence or satisfaction with our behavior. True, there are varying degrees of self-acceptance. Sometimes we do not value ourselves very highly. We may on occasion dislike or even hate ourselves, and we may even be among those who take so jaundiced a view of ourselves that this disparaging view prevails. By and large, however, our self is something we hold dear.

Parental attitudes contribute to the child's self-evaluation. For example, in earlier discussion considerable emphasis was placed on parental rejection. From the child's point of view, rejection is something he experiences. He feels unwanted, despised, unattractive, or somehow found lacking. Fortunately, he also comes in contact with other parental attitudes and atmospheres. The prevalence of positive fostering attitudes helps to establish in children self-evaluations which are of a more healthful nature than the one chosen for illustration. Whatever their outcome, parental attitudes are experienced by the child and affect his self-evaluation.

Origin of the Self-concept. There emerges in the child a concept of himself—an awareness of what he thinks he is like. It is his conception of who and what he is. Whence comes this self-concept?

To a highly significant degree, the self is a social product. The self-concept, as Harry Stack Sullivan (1947) once said, is composed of the "reflected appraisals" of others. Through learning the opinions, attitudes, and expectations that others have for him the child learns "who he is." It is therefore understandable how either gross overevaluation or derogation can have deleterious effects on the child's self-concept or self-image. Hence, if a child's parents regard him as clumsy or bad or whatever, it should come as no surprise that the child believes them and acts to some degree in a way to correspond to their view. More often than not, however, a child's self-concept is less of a consistent pattern than these illustrations imply. After all, the way he is viewed differs from person to person even in a short space of time. He may be seen as mother's "darling," to the neighbor boy as a "sissy," and to his big sister, a "pest,"—all in the same hour. How he assimilates these pressures and makes his own is contingent not only upon this factor of attribution of traits but also upon the other sources of the self and the effect of past experience.

Inner pressure as a determinant of the self-concept acts through the aspirations or ambitions the child holds. A girl with operatic ambitions may distort her inner evaluation to fit more in line with these ambitions. A boy who conceives himself as an athlete may be under self-pressure to try to fit this conception. These inner pressures may, of course, be reinforced by outer pressures from adults and others who hold similar expectancies for them. Inner pressures also act through interpretation of the situation. The view the boy holds may or may not correspond to the situation as others view it. A child may feel that a parent favors a brother or sister or is unduly harsh toward him when from the parent's point of view such is not the case. But the child's inner pressures will influence him whether they reflect reality or not.

Comparison of the self with others enters

How does a child become a self?

By learning one is a person. By giving and receiving attention. By expressing oneself. By falling down and getting hurt. By being comforted. By being in a group and apart from it at the same time.

through comparison with members of the groups in which the child finds himself. A bright child with even brighter older siblings will think of himself (as will others in the family) as less smart than if he were closer to them in intellectual ability. A child, actually average in height, may perceive himself as rather large if all of his classmates and playmates happen to be short. A child's self-concept is based partly on comparison with other persons.

In that connection, research with Negro children during the 1930s found indications of self-rejection. When black children were shown groups of black dolls and white dolls, they tended to prefer white dolls and to reject black ones. (Clark and Clark, 1947). Other and more recent research has produced similar findings for preschool and primary school Negro children in Newark, N.J. (Asher and Allen, 1969).

A number of other studies, however, suggest that there is an increasing degree of self-acceptance on the part of black children. For example, Hraba and Grant (1970) undertook a replication of Clark and Clark's 1947 study. Their sample consisted of over half the black children aged four to eight in the public schools of Lincoln, Nebraska. The children were shown four dolls, identical in every respect, except that two were black and two were white. The questions were the same as the ones used by the Clarks, which asked the children to indicate the doll they would like to play with, the one that is a nice doll, the one that looks bad, etc. The responses of the children were a complete reversal of the findings of the Clarks and of Asher and Allen (1969), in that about two-thirds of the children expressed preferences for black dolls, although some three-fourths of the children showed some inconsistencies in their responses, occasionally showing preference for a white doll.

Hraba and Grant explained the differences between findings of studies like theirs and those of other researchers as indicative of a growing race pride on the part of black people, a trend that is not as yet universal across the country. Indeed, the results in their study may have been affected by a black pride campaign conducted in Lincoln during the two years prior to the gathering of data. At any rate, the idea that "black is beautiful" did not in this study imply any rejection of whites, for those children who had white friends were actually *more* likely to choose black dolls than those who had only black friends.

Children's Perception of Parents

In early childhood social awareness may be viewed as the problem of social perception. Emphasis will be placed on the child's perception of parental roles. In brief, the issue at hand is what do children think about parental practices and about their parents as parents.

Differences between parents' reports of home situations and children's perceptions are very apparent.

Using a sample of preschool children, Neill (1946), as reported by Hawkes (1957), found considerable difference between what the parents reported the situation to be in their household concerning punishment and their children's perceptions of the same issue in the same home. Fifty percent of her children named corporal punishment as what they expected from their parents; parents reported using corporal punishment only as a last resort. Only about 10% of the children seemed aware that their parents expected them to take the consequences of their acts; about 70% of the parents said they used this practice. Twenty-five per cent of the children agreed that their parents might put them to bed forcefully; 50% of the parents said that, if necessary, they would do this. Even from these brief illustrations it is possible to sense the vast difference between parental practices and the ways in which these children perceived the same situations.

Perception of Parental Roles. The children's perception of parental roles was investigated by Helen M. Finch (1955). Subjects were children between three and seven years of age drawn from 20 professional families. Among other techniques, a set of photographs was used, each of which showed both a father and a mother following some child care routine. From each picture the child told a story, at the conclusion of which the boy or girl was asked whether the mother or the father should carry out the task shown in the particular picture. Responses were categorized as mother, father, or both. It was found that, instead of either parent alone, the children spoke more frequently of both mother and father as performing 10 of the 13 roles—bedtime, baths, meals, prayer, companionship, affection, discipline, teaching, illness, and protection. Almost unanimously the father was seen as economic provider and the mother as housekeeper and contributor to the children.

Before knowing the children's replies, the mothers had been asked what they expected them to reply. Some roles which the mothers expected the children to consider to be those of the mother—bathtime, meals, and care during illness—were roles for which the children chose both father and mother. In response to the direct question, "What is Daddy?" about 75% of the children replied in terms of his being an economic provider. To a similar question about the mother, 50% fell in the category of household duties and 25% in that of caring for children. It would seem that the child sees the roles of the father in the home both as more numerous and as more important than general opinion might lead us to expect.

The egocentricity of the young child shows itself in his relative inability to recognize how others feel in a specific situation. A clear-cut study by Burns and Cavey (1957) compared one group of children, age three to five, and another of five to six-and-a-half in their empathic ability, that is, the ability to infer the feelings of others. Empathic responses were contrasted with egocentric responses or those in which the child imputed his own feelings to pictured figures.

Four crucial and four noncrucial pictures were used, one set for boys, another for girls. Crucial pictures showed (1) a birthday scene complete with cake and presents, (2) the same scene with the addition of a boy (girl) with a *frown* on his face, (3) a doctor with a long needle standing behind an empty chair, (4) the same scene with the addition of a boy (girl) with a *smile,* sitting on the chair. The noncrucial pictures showed a boy catching a fish, a girl pushing a doll carriage, and the like. The children in the two groups were told there was a boy (girl) in the picture, and asked, "How does he (she) feel?" An egocentric response would be scored if the child described the frowning boy at the birthday party as happy, and the smiling boy in the dentist's chair as unhappy. The results found appear in Table 13-1.

The number of empathic responses in which they correctly judged the feelings of the children was significantly lower in the younger children than in the older. The older children

TABLE 13-1. *Number of Empathic Responses to Incongruous Pictures (Burns and Cavey, 1957)*

Groups	N	Number of Empathic Responses		
		0	1	2
Younger (under five years)	17	8	8	1
Older (over 5 years)	22	2	7	13

recognized that the children were not experiencing the same feelings that they themselves would have felt in the situation; the younger children, with few exceptions, failed to do this and attributed to the pictured child what their own feeling would have been.

Peer Relationships

During the preschool years, the young child begins to disengage himself from the home circle and to interact with his peers, sometimes directly, and sometimes in a parallel, side-by-side relationship. Relationships in and with groups are inclined to be somewhat tentative, because the child at this age lacks the skills and probably the motivation required for group-oriented behavior. Opportunity has much to do with this, of course. The child who can play with neighbor children has opportunities to learn social skills that are denied the child on a lonely farm, and the child who attends nursery school or spends much time in a well-run day care center is in the most advantageous position.

Social Participation

Social participation with a child's peers increases in versatility and complexity between the second and fifth years. These increases with age are shown by the more cooperative nature of their participation. Mildred B. Parten (1932), 1933) studied the size of the groups in which children played and the nature of their play activity by a technique of time sampling.

Playing in groups of two occurred 30% of the time for the children two- to two-and-a-half years of age, whereas groups of five occurred only 9% of the time. For children aged four- to four-and-a-half the picture had changed considerably, since groups of five had increased to 24%. Thus, the size of the play group increased with age during the preschool

years. Parten also classified the play behavior of the children into the following categories: (1) *unoccupied;* (2) *solitary* (independent play); (3) *onlooker;* (4) *parallel activity* (playing alongside, but not with other children); (5) *associative activity* (common activity with borrowing, lending, and turns taken); and (6) *cooperative* (working toward some common goal; different roles by various members that supplement one another).

The youngest children tended to engage either in solitary or in parallel play. The older children tended to engage in associative or cooperative play to a much greater extent than the younger children. To bring together the results of the classification of their behavior, each category was given an arbitrary weight for cooperativeness with the highest category, *cooperative* play itself, considered the most cooperative and given the highest weight, and *unoccupied* considered the least cooperative and given the lowest weight. The weighted social participation score correlated with age of the children was found to be .61. As age increased the preschool child engaged more in associative and cooperative play and less in idleness, solitary play, and serving as an onlooker. Parallel play was the only category that did not change materially over the years. It is evident that with increasing age social participation increased.

The proportion of time that preschool children typically spent in various categories of play was recorded by Debra Fatheree (1971), who observed 15 three-year-olds and 20 four-year-olds on a nursery school playground in Berkeley, California. The observation period for the two groups was 16 minutes, with recordings made at two-minute intervals. The percentage of the observation period that the average child in each group spent in the various Parten play categories is reported in Figure 13–2. Fatheree's results confirm Parten's observations in that the older child spent proportionately more time in parallel, associative,

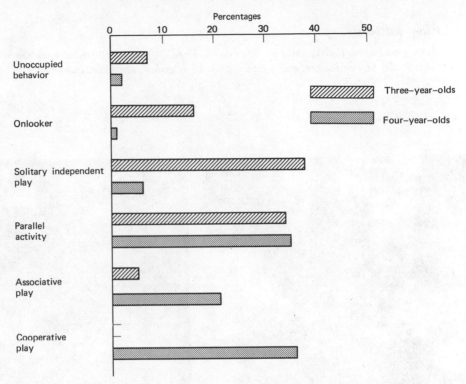

Figure 13-2.   Percentages of time spent in various kinds of play by 15 three-year-olds and 20 four-year-olds during a 16-minute playground observation period. (After Fatheree, 1971.)

and cooperative play than did the younger ones.

Changes in these play patterns can be explained in terms of socialization theory. As we noted previously, the two-year-old tends to be egocentric, and that during the preschool period, socialized responses increase. In social behavior, in the peer group, too, during the preschool period, there is a transition from egocentricity to increased socialization in the sense of increased cooperation.

Socialization: General Trends

The child's increasing tendency to involve others in his play during the preschool years can be explained partly in terms of his at-

tempts to cope with the social dimensions of his environment and to try out new skills, especially those involving the use of language. This increase in social maturity can also be explained in terms of a drive to seek ever more complex stimuli. The introduction of the social element makes any situation more unstable, more unpredictible, more complex, and hence more arousing. Therefore, the child who seeks arousal is likely to seek interaction with others in order to satisfy his need to be stimulated and aroused.

Because it satisfies this need for arousal, association with others is likely to be reinforcing, and any behavior that leads to social interaction is likely to be rewarded. The learning of socialized behavior is also enhanced

Play patterns

With growing maturity, children become involved in play patterns at ever more complex levels: first onlooker, and solitary play, then associative play, and finally, cooperative play.

when children reinforce one another directly through expressions of approval, collaboration on problems, and the like. Charlesworth and Hartup (1967) observed four types of positive social reinforcers in groups of nursery school children: giving positive attention and approval, giving affection and personal acceptance, submitting to others' demands, and giving things to others. As might be expected, the actions described occurred more frequently in the behavior of four-year-olds than three-year-olds. The researchers also observed that giving social rewards to others was associated with receiving them, and there was a tendency for children who engaged in much positive reinforcement to interact with a relatively large number of children in this way.

In a review of socialization research for this period of development, Willard W. Hartup (1970) noted that even negative social actions may have positive reinforcement value for some children. In other words, inasmuch as the attention of others has psychological value, negative attention is better than no attention at all. Hartup also observed that there are wide variations in the extent to which nursery school groups provide social reinforcement. Much depends on the kind of activity taking place: dramatic play provides more opportunity for reinforcement by peers than do eating activities.

Hartup noted six categories of social behaviors that change with increasing age during preschool years:

1. Dependency directed toward peers increases; dependency directed toward adults decreases.

2. Sympathy and altruism increase. (We noted earlier that a related skill, empathy, also increases).

3. Ascendancy (tendency to take the lead) increases.

4. Competition increases, particularly under conditions inviting comparative evaluation of performance with others.

5. Quarreling decreases, but quarrels tend to last longer.

6. Aggressive activity increases but tends to decline after the nursery school years are over (as we noted earlier).

Socialization skills are learned not only as a result of reinforcement but also because other children serve as models. Hartup and Coates (1967) found that "learning to share" could be facilitated by exposing young children to the behavior of a model who did much sharing. It is important not to make too much of this, however. Preschool children are still very immature when it comes to social skills. In contrast to school-aged children, they are less aware of the "group effect," and group involvement per se does not have the value that it assumes a few years later. For that reason, preschool children are less aware of social norms, which is the major factor that binds groups together psychologically and gives them cohesiveness and stability.

E. Paul Torrance (1970) studied the effects of five-year-old children working independently or in pairs on a task designed to measure creative output. He found that the fluency, originality, and flexibility of their responses were all higher in the group situation, thus showing that the interaction was rewarding and stimulating. When contrasted to college students who worked alone or in pairs, however, the increase contributed by group interaction was not as great. In other words, the college students were even more responsive to the effects and the possibilities inherent in the group situation.

In another study, Torrance (1969) observed the behavior of five-year-olds who attempted a difficult task alone, in pairs, or before their class. The children did much better when they worked in pairs than they did when working alone, but the performance before the class was the poorest of all. These findings show that by this age, children are responding to others much as older children and adults do: a single observer provides enough arousal to improve the performance, but the presence of a large audience is so arousing that performance deteriorates.

Modeling and Prosocial Behavior. We noted earlier how the observation of the consequences of models' behavior can facilitate or inhibit the production of aggressive responses. One would assume that the principle involved would work in other ways as well, and that models can influence prosocial as well as antisocial behavior.

A number of research studies suggest that such an assumption is valid. One type of study that has been used to observe the presence or absence of helping behavior in adults makes use of a contrived situation in which a subject is led to believe that he hears someone get into a difficult or dangerous situation and call for help. Ervin Staub (1971a) has used this technique to study prosocial behavior in children as well. In one experiment, Staub preceded the test situation by preparing kindergarten children with one of four treatments: (1) pairs of children enacted situations in which one person needed help, and another provided it; (2) similar to Condition 1, except that situations were described and not enacted, and children were asked how help could be provided; (3) a combination of role playing and discussion; (4) control—children enacted roles unrelated to helping.

During the testing phase of the experiment, an experimenter took each child to a playroom and left him there briefly while she went into an adjoining room to "check on a girl who is playing there." Then she returned and told the child that the girl was playing next door and that he (or she) could play with any-

thing in the playroom. Shortly after she left, the child heard a crash from the adjoining room, followed by sounds of distress and sobbing (actually tape recorded). While this was going on, the experimenter was watching the child's behavior through a one-way mirror. If the child went to the adjoining room to help, the experimenter appeared and explained the experiment to the child. If not, the experimenter waited for a minute and then entered the room to elicit his reaction to the sounds of distress. Each child who participated also received a bag of candy—his choice out of three kinds available. The child was then told that if he wished, he could donate some of his candy for another child who was ill and whose parents were unable to buy him anything for his birthday.

Results indicated that role playing and discussion of helping behavior had some tendency to facilitate helping of the fictitious child in distress. Although results were not clear-cut, girls were more inclined to offer help than boys.[1] When it came to sharing of candy, however, boys were more inclined to do so than girls, particularly when they had engaged in role playing.

It is possible that the rather minor effect that role playing and discussion of helping had on children's behavior in this study was the result of their not seeing the relationship between the altruistic values expressed in the role playing and discussion sessions and a test situation in which they heard a call for help. Another study by Staub (1971b) made use of

---

[1] This finding is contrary to results obtained in similar experiments with adults, in which men are more likely than women to volunteer help. Taking the initiative to extend help to a stranger is, of course, more consistent with the adult male role (Wispé and Freshley, 1971; Schwartz and Clausen, 1970).

a type of preparatory treatment that made the relationship clearer.

The subjects again were kindergarten children. Each of them played a bowling game with an experimenter who either responded warmly to their efforts (nurturant) or was merely matter-of-fact. For those children who were to be exposed to the "modeling" condition, crying sounds (actually tape-recorded) were heard in the next room. The experimenter then left, presumably to attend to the crying child, whereupon the sound stopped, and the experimenter returned saying that a child had slipped and fallen, but that she had helped her up and comforted her. The rest of the experiment was conducted like the one described above, except that there was no candy-sharing sequence at the end. The response of each child was scored on a three-point scale: 3, if the child attempted to go into the next room to help the stranger in distress; 2, if the child did not leave the playroom, but volunteered information in response to the experimenter's query whether everything was all right while she was gone; and 1, if there was no help and no volunteering of information.

The results, as shown in Figure 13–3, indicate that the combination of modeling and nurturance produced the greatest amount of helping, and that modeling or nurturance separately were also effective in eliciting helping behavior from boys, but not from girls. A further interesting sex difference also emerged when teachers were asked about the children who served as subjects in the study in terms of their tendencies to initiate activities in interaction with others, competence on tasks, expression of affection toward other children, and need for approval. Teachers' ratings were all correlated positively for boys' helping behavior, but negatively for girls. In other words, boys who were the most helpful with respect to the "distressed child" were also perceived

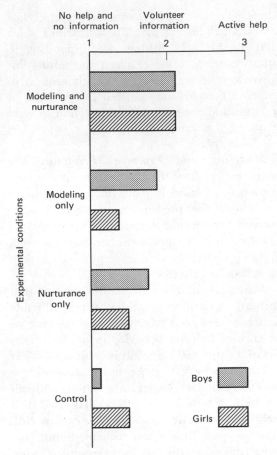

Figure 13-3. *Effect of modeling and/or nurturance on the willingness of kindergarten children to help a strange child in distress.* (Staub, 1971b.)

by their teachers as possessing desirable social traits, whereas girls who were the most helpful to the distressed child, were likely to be seen as not possessing them. What we may be getting here is some evidence that even at this age helping people in distress is viewed as "aggressive" and hence "unfeminine."

Social Acceptance

One of the tools used to study social acceptability and other forms of group interactions has been called sociometric tests by their originator, Moreno (1934). Sociometric tests have in common the fact that they may be used to elicit positive or negative or mutual responses about members of a group by other members of that group. They may be used to select or exclude companions for any group, actual or potential, of which the child might become a member. These positive or negative responses are shaped by a particular investigator to suit his needs. The test of social acceptability is concrete. Not mere liking in general, but the liking for someone in a particular setting or particular activity is found to be most conducive to precise results—a seat mate, a playmate, fellow TV watcher, a party guest, or what you will.

The work of Marshall and McCandless (1957a,b,c,d) has been outstanding. Their picture sociometric technique was an attempt to overcome some of the difficulties plaguing earlier studies. All of the pictures for a particular group of subjects were fastened to a white background cardboard. After finding and pointing to their own pictures, each child pointed or named the others on the card. Then came the sociometric choices. The child was asked, "Whom do you like to play with outdoors?" until three preferred playmates were selected. The same procedure was followed for the three he would prefer to play with inside, and for three children with whom he would like to listen to stories. Either three or four separate sociometric sessions were held about ten days apart for three different groups. A child's sociometric score was the sum of weighted (first choice, five points, and so on) choices of the child as a playmate by all subjects for all sessions.

Teachers' judgments of best friends were also acquired. Three to five teachers for each group listed for each child choices of their four best friends in order of closeness. The two measures, children's sociometric choices and pooled teachers' judgments, correlated significantly, demonstrating that sociometric choice was a useful devise for studying friendships among preschool children.

In addition, social behavior in a free play situation was observed in a series of two minute observations in order to give a score on social interaction. This score was based on ratings of associative play of the sort used by Parten—friendly approach, hostility, such as interfering or snubbing, and conversation—and the best friend was identified by finding the child with whom the most associative play and friendly approaches were carried on.

Social acceptance and social participation were also related to dependence on adults. Dependency on adults was measured by observing the social interactions with adults in the free play situation. A negative relationship with sociometric choice was obtained. The higher the dependency on adults, the lower the social acceptance, and vice versa. Dependency on adults is accompanied by both low social status and participation.

Concerning sex differences in general, girls had higher sociometric scores than boys, but no other sex difference could be demonstrated through teacher judgments of social acceptance, observed social acceptance, or degree of interaction with peers. By using three consecutive testings over time as a measure of progress of acquaintance, no consistent sex difference in sociometric scores emerged (McCandless, Balsbaugh, and Bennett, 1961).

In his review of research on peer relations in preschool years, Hartup (1970) made a number of observations regarding popularity and unpopularity in children. Contrary to earlier reports, the social relationships of children this age are not unstable and everchanging. Indeed, the contrary is likely to be the case. One group of researchers found a correlation of .68 between sociometric readings taken five months apart (Hartup, Glazer, and Charlesworth, 1967). Being liked is highly stable; being disliked, less so, because the kind of behavior that underlies being rejected is less likely to be reinforced either by the peer group or by adults.

In contrast to unpopular children, popular children tend to be rated as more friendly, sociable, outgoing, altruistic, and positively reinforcing to peers, Hartup noted. Low popularity can mean one of two things: either the child is making friendship overtures and is being rejected, or else he is merely being ignored. Popular children tend to be more socialized in their behavior; this does not mean that they are submissive, because actually they are likely to be quite independent, but rather that they are effective mediators in their social group and are responsive to the needs and wants of others.

Along with their independence, popular children also know when and how to be dependent. Their dependency is likely to be of a socially mature type (e.g., the seeking of approval or help), rather than immature (e.g., seeking indications of affection or showing off). They are not less aggressive than unpopular children, but are likely to use their aggressiveness in a more direct and reality-oriented way. This observation holds only when they are compared with *all* nonpopular children, however. When popular children are contrasted with those that are actively *disliked*, the latter are clearly more aggressive.

Summary

Dependence tendencies become firmly established during infancy. The critical period for independence strivings occurs between ages three and five. Dependence was a necessary condition of infancy; independence is a task of early childhood. Research has suggested that these behavior tendencies are not merely opposite ends of the same continuum. Beller correlated a number of measures of dependence and independence, finding a coefficient of $-.53$ rather than the perfect -1.00 which one would expect if the two tendencies were true opposites. Dependence and independence therefore seem best conceived as separate components of child behavior.

Dependency may be influenced by situational variables. Arsenian observed the reactions of preschoolers to a strange room. The children accompanied by their mothers showed little evidence of insecurity and adapted to the situation. Children who were not accompanied by their mothers spent most of their time in agitated nonadaptive behavior. Beller has found that dependent behavior is higher in a dependency stress situation, and that the higher the initial dependence, the greater the increase of dependent behavior in the stress situation. Deprivation of adult social contact can also heighten a child's dependence. An experiment in which an experimental group experienced nurturance withdrawal is consistent with this expectation. The nurturance withdrawal group showed a higher degree of motivation for learning the cognitive tasks assigned to both the experimental and control groups. The mother, as the principal agent of socialization during infancy, fosters dependence to some degree, but in later infancy also introduces training intended to decrease dependence. It is possible that the mother differentiates between emotional and instrumental dependence by trying to lessen the latter and alter the mode of expression of the former. The mode of expression does change. A number of studies have verified that physical clinging is gradually replaced by verbal behaviors, and that seeking the reassurance and affection of adults declines relative to seeking the attention and approval of other children.

Resistant behavior, or negativism, reaches a maximum when the child is about two or three years of age. Ausubel feels that this phenomenon, which he calls "ego devaluation" is the result of frustration suffered by the child when his parents simultaneously slow down their nurturance and demand independent behavior. In a cross-cultural study, Whiting and Child found that although American parents begin independence training fairly early, the severity of training receives a rating at the median. As compared to the children of other cultures, American children are much encouraged to act on their own initiative, but not expected to take an adult role. The child generally strives for independence in areas where his ability is still marginal. As experiments by Fales have shown, training and encouragement both serve to encourage independence. A study comparing the problem-solving behavior of Hawaiian and Haole (Anglo-American) children highlights some of the dynamics of the development of dependent and independent behavior. When told that the experimenters would help them if asked, only 23% of the Hawaiian group requested aid, as opposed to 93% of the Haole group. The reason for this difference may be found in the way Hawaiian children are raised. After extreme indulgency during infancy, the Hawaiian child is subjected to harsh withdrawal of nurturance. The child would make the transition from dependency to self-reliance if the Hawaiian mother would reward independent behavior. Unfortunately, she does not. It is clear that independence is not likely to be facilitated if mothers merely discourage dependent behavior. Aggression is widely prevalent in young children. It should be apparent that our society encourages aggression in certain forms and controls it in others. The constitutional determinants are evident. During early childhood, height, weight, strength, and activity level all con-

tribute to whether the child finds aggressive activities rewarding. From knowledge of the socialization process of aggression in infancy, we should expect frustration to breed aggression. A study by Merrill supports this view. By telling one group of mothers that their children had not shown their full capabilities, Merrill precipitated critical maternal control of the children's behavior. The children who were rigidly controlled responded with considerable irritability. These aggressive tendencies also generalized to interactions between the children and a neutral female observer.

A great deal of research on aggressiveness, especially that done by Sears and his colleagues, is dependent on indices of covert or fantasy aggression. The greater aggressiveness of boys is again the single most documented finding. An increase in aggression between the first and second doll-play session with the same experimenter present has also been observed in several experiments. Fantasy aggression as expressed through play does not correlate very well with indices of overt aggression. This does not necessarily mean that the measures are unrelated. Obviously the child can do a great many things in fantasy aggression that he cannot do in reality. It has been found that severe punishment tends to inhibit aggression in similar circumstances and increase it in dissimilar situations. Thus severe punishment at home can be expected to decrease overt aggression at school, but increase fantasy aggression. This expectation has been confirmed by Sears. Levin and Sears have suggested that fantasy aggression was in part a function of identification with aggressive role models. They found that boys who identified with punitive fathers showed the highest frequency of fantasy aggression. Bandura and Walters have identified two effects that increase aggressive behavior: (1) the modeling effect in which the child reproduces observed behavior, and (2) the disinhibiting effect in which observation of the aggressive model merely releases preexisting aggressive responses. Later research shows that if models' aggressive behavior is rewarded, children are more likely to display aggressive behavior in subsequent situations.

Throughout this phase of development, the child's sense of self is gradually emerging. One of the most important prerequisites for this process is good memory. Self-evaluation, indicated by guilt feelings, is another. Self-respect is important to both children and adults, and both are capable of self-delusion to maintain a good opinion of themselves. Where does the child's concept of himself originate? To a large degree, the self is a social product, in Sullivan's words, composed of the "reflected appraisals" of others. If a child's parents regard his as clumsy or bad, it should come as no surprise to find that he has a similar opinion of himself. The individual child, however, is many things to many people, and his role is far from consistent. A child of average height will consider himself tall if all of his friends are short. The child will be heavily influenced by his social perceptions. Black children's preferences for white dolls may indicate a degree of self-rejection. However, recent research shows an increasing preference for black dolls, suggesting a corresponding increase in self-esteem.

Differences between parents' and childrens' reports of home situations are very apparent. Children, for example, seem to think that their parents use corporal punishment far more often than the parents themselves report. Finch investigated children's perceptions of parental roles. The father was seen almost unanimously as economic provider, and the mother as housekeeper. It would also seem that the child sees the roles of the father in the home both as more numerous and as more important than general opinion would lead us to expect. An experiment by Burns and Cavey served to illustrate the basic egocentricity of young children. When shown pictures of frowning children in happy circumstances, and asked to describe how these children felt, the younger children responded to the situational stimuli rather than to the pictured children's expressions.

During the preschool years, the young child begins to disengage himself from the home circle and to interact more with his peers. The size of the groups in which children play changes dramatically from age two to age five. In one study, for instance, playing in groups of two occurred 30% of the time for two-year-olds, and only 9% of the time for five-year-olds. Older children also spend more time in parallel, associative, and cooperative play than younger ones. Part of the child's increasing tendency to involve others in his play may be the result of a need for more complex and arousing stimulus situations. Giving social rewards to others is associated with receiving them and becomes rewarding in its own right. As Hartup has noted, even negative attention may be more rewarding to some children than no attention at all. Socialization skills are not only learned as a result of reinforcement but also because other children serve as models. Torrance studied the creative output of five-year-olds as they worked either individually or in pairs. Although the children worked best in pairs, their performance in a large group situation was the poorest of all. Modeling has been used to induce prosocial as well as aggressive behavior. After exposure to a model, children are placed in situations in which they hear another child crying as if in trouble. Effects of modeling and other experimental treatments can be observed in their reaction to this situation. One of the tools used to measure the intricacies of group interactions is the sociometric test. In this sort of test, children are asked to list who they would especially like to be with in a number of specific social situations. Socio-metric scores correlate with a number of important social variables. Sociometric choice, for example, is negatively correlated with dependence on adults. Another interesting observation made with the aid of sociometric techniques, is that popular children, in contrast to unpopular children, tend to retain their social standing. Popular children also tend to be more socialized in their behavior and their dependency is likely to be of a socially mature type.

PART 4

The Middle and Later Years

14 Individual Development

The middle and later childhood years span the period from the entry into the first grade until junior high school, from the end of the pre-school period to adolescence. In terms of age, the period runs from about 6 to 12 for girls, and from 6 to 14 for boys, on the average. This is a period in which children begin a major involvement in the world outside the family and the immediate neighborhood. The school plays an important role as a socializing agent, supplanting the parents to a considerable degree.

The sensorimotor development of children during this period approaches adult standards. Emotional expressions and the situations eliciting them take on a new direction and subtlety. Cognitive, language, perceptual, and intellectual processes not only continue to develop but also acquire characteristics closer to those of adults than were shown by infants and younger children. As a beginning to the study of the psychological aspects of later childhood, this chapter explores these various facets of individual development.

Physical Growth

About the end of the third year of life, the growth curve for the average child settles down to a steady rate that continues until the pre-puberal growth spurt at about 11½ for girls and 13 or 14 for boys. Changes in body build are relatively slight during middle and late childhood.

There are, of course, many individual deviations from these general trends. Some girls reach their full adult height at 13, and some boys do not attain it until the early twenties. Although girls reach full maturity about two years earlier than boys, variations of four or five years are still within the normal range.

Scientists have in recent years become aware of what is termed the "secular trend"—that is, a continuing tendency for children at any given age to be taller and heavier than children were at the same age in previous years. The trend shows up in two ways. First, children and adolescents are maturing sooner. This means that ten-year-olds today are likely to be taller and heavier than ten-year-olds even a decade or two previously. Tanner (1970) reports, for example, Swedish school boys aged ten averaged about 52 inches tall in 1883, but in 1938 the average height was 55 inches. Second, the absolute gain is more: adults are slightly taller and heavier than they were in past generations. French university students born in 1925 were about 66 inches tall at age 17, but those born in 1931 were 67½ inches tall when they were 17. At age 22, however, there was only about a quarter of an inch difference in the heights of the two groups.

The best evidence to explain the secular trend, according to Tanner, points to improved nutrition, although emotional stress has been shown to interfere with growth. Recordings of the height of German children show that the secular trend tended to reverse itself somewhat during the two world wars, the probable result of stress, poor nutrition, or both.

The fact that children are maturing faster also means that the period of childhood is growing shorter. The age at which the girl's first menstrual flow, the menarche, occurs has been dropping year by year. In Norway, in 1850, it occurred at age 17, according to Tanner, whereas in the 1950s it was occurring shortly after age 13. In the United States it has dropped since 1895, when it was a little over 14, to less than 13 in the early 1950s. The point at which boys enter puberty is more difficult to determine, inasmuch as its arrival is signaled by a number of changes (ejaculation of seminal fluid, pigmentation of pubic hair, appearance of underarm hair, growth of beard), but there is every indication that it is occurring younger for them as well as for girls.

As far as the trend toward increased size in adults is concerned, Tanner suggests that genetic factors, as well as better nutrition, may be involved. It is quite possible that tallness may be a dominant trait, genetically speaking, in which case outbreeding, or matings between various social and ethnic segments of the population, could lead to an increase in height. Tanner continues: "There is increasing evidence that such dominance does in fact occur. As for outbreeding, that has been increasingly steadily since the invention of the bicycle" (pp. 147–148).

As we have noted, the computing of averages overlooks wide individual variations in maturity and growth, thus making it possible for researchers to compare early with late maturers. In general the method has been to compare early and late maturing boys or girls of the same chronological age on a variety of personal and social characteristics. Differences found were then related to differences as mature adults. Boys who matured earlier showed greater self-confidence, more matter of factness, and more maturity in social situations. Late maturing boys were expressive, talkative, eager, and attention-getting (Jones and Bayley, 1950). When they reached the age of 33, the physical differences had almost disappeared, as had many of the personality differences, but those differences that remained were still in the directions observed in the original study (Jones, 1957). Although earlier studies present equivocal findings with respect to girls, subsequent research has shown that early maturing girls tend to enjoy advantages similar to those of early maturing boys (Jones and Mussen, 1958; Faust, 1960).

Childhood Diseases

In Chapter 10 we noted that the incidence of illnesses of various sorts dropped off sharply during the preschool years and continued to decline well into adolescence. This is, indeed, the general trend, but there are some exceptions. The incidence of communicable diseases (measles, chicken pox, mumps, etc.), according to Bayer and Snyder (1950), actually rises during the preschool years, reaching a peak between five and nine years of age, dropping off sharply thereafter. Gastrointestinal and abdominal disturbances also increase during the middle childhood years, reaching a peak for boys at age 10 and declining to a low point at age 16. The incidence of this type of disorder rises for girls as well, reaching a peak at age 11, then declining somewhat, only to rise to another peak at age 18. As Figure 14-1 shows, girls from mid-childhood onward tend to be more susceptible than boys to such disorders. There are probably psychological implications to these differences, inasmuch as emotional upsets and stomach upsets often go together. Boys during this period are more likely to get into fights and accidents, suffering contusions, breaking limbs, and the like. Each sex has its own psychologically attractive outlet at times of stress.

Sensorimotor Development

In the course of the school-age period children refine and extend their sensorimotor skills. During the earlier years of the period girls delight in such games as jacks and hopscotch which call for precise use of the musculature. Boys become interested in such sports as base-

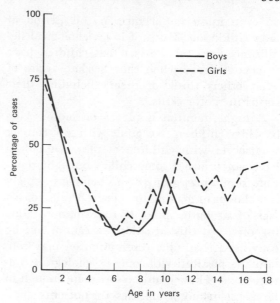

Figure 14-1. Incidence of gastrointestinal and abdominal disturbances among children in the Berkeley Guidance Study from birth until age 18. (After Bayer and Snyder, 1950.)

ball and basketball which likewise call for greater refinement of eye-hand-muscle coordination. Bicycling and roller skating occupy both boys and girls. They naturally are not equally adept in fine-muscle coordinated activities, as any child of six will tell you when asked about his writing skills in keeping his "e's" from looking like "i's." Nevertheless, there is increasing skill with the smaller muscles, such as those of the hand. In fact, it often is said that this is the age to begin learning to play a musical instrument or to type if these skills are to become highly developed.

Most children keenly enjoy motor activities. They delight in constantly being on the go. "Spectators" among them are still very much in the minority. Although considerable advance in motor abilities has taken place during the infancy and preschool years, the psychological significance of motor development takes on even more importance in this period of later childhood. Much of its psychological significance rests on the fact that children have reached the age when they become aware of what others think of them, including their status in motor skills.

A high premium is placed on motor skills by older children. No adult with any contact whatsoever with children at play can fail to have noted either some child's outright rejection from a play group or his being grudgingly last chosen in making up a team because of his lack of strength, speed, or coordination. Having observed this situation we cannot but be convinced that such discrimination may contain the possibility of some psychological consequences. Those children fortunate enough to be adept in motor abilities are not only more acceptable to their playmates, but because of these skills are also more apt to be chosen as leaders. This choice may be made not only in tasks where their motor skills are important, but also may generalize to leadership functions essentially independent of motor skills, such as being elected as a class officer.

Age Trends

It will be remembered from the discussion in Chapter 10 that Aileen Carpenter (1941) found two motor ability factors of general significance—strength and speed. These two factors will form the basis for discussion of age trends in motor development during later childhood.

Speed of response shows a regular increase with age. A study by Florence L. Goodenough (1935) is relevant in this connection. She had children from age three-and-a-half through eleven-and-a-half respond to a test whereby each made a voluntary movement on hearing a sound. At three-and-a-half years of age they took about five-tenths of a second to respond; at four-and-a-half years of age about four-tenths of a second. This increase in speed

continued steadily, until at age eleven-and-a-half the children were responding in two-tenths of a second. This and other evidence indicate an increase in speed with age during these years.

There is a similar increase in strength with age according to Metheny (1941). Up until the age of puberty boys are superior to girls at most strength tests. In both boys and girls there is found to be a general positive relationship between the indices of strength and height and weight and health status. Thus among measures of motor development there is a tendency for the stronger to be taller, faster, and healthier than the weaker child. These relationships are closely related to similar relations between physical and mental ability.

The Relation of Physical and Mental Ability

The interrelationship between mental and physical measures in infancy was discussed previously. It will be remembered that there was found to be a relatively high degree of relationship. By the later childhood age this relationship had decreased considerably. There was however, still some degree of relationship.

In general, there is found to be a low, but positive correlation between physical and mental ability. Even physical measures such as height or weight have been found to conform to the same general rule (Paterson, 1930). In other words, there is a *slight* tendency for the taller individual to be smarter than the shorter. But the relation is such that a number of exceptions to it are found. This does not mean that the relationship is so negligible in children that it can be dismissed, merely that relationships based on it must be interpreted with extreme caution.

Abernethy (1936) studied physical and mental growth in nearly 200 boys and 200 girls. The Stanford-Binet Scales provided the measure of mental ability and a large battery of physical growth measures provided the indices of physical ability. Both kinds of measures were administered at regular intervals over an 11-year period. Comparable measures were also given college men and women in order to provide measures to serve as a terminal standard of development. Low positive correlations between the physical and mental measures were found. In the case of height and mental ability, the average correlation was .26 for boys and .22 for girls over the age range of two to eight years. There was a general trend for the correlations to decrease after 14 or 15 years of age, eventuating in negligible correlations in the adult group. This general "togetherness" of physical and mental measures in childhood has been supported by a number of researchers, for example, Olson and Hughes, (1943) and Shuttleworth (1939). Enough information has been reported here to show that there is a slight positive relationship during later childhood which tends to decrease as the child grows older.

Learning and Sensorimotor Skills

Speed of sensorimotor performance has been studied at different ages and with various tasks. The specificity of task learning seems to be less with younger than with older children. One study by Henery and Nelson (1956) involved about 70 ten-year-old and 70 15-year-old boys. One task they studied was simple in nature—throwing a celluloid ball downward into a basket and then grasping a suspended tennis ball. The stimulus was a sound; no stimulus discrimination or choice was involved. The other tasks, although essentially similar, were more complicated—one involved a discrimination between two stimuli; the other required a choice to be made between which of two activities to carry out according to the particular stimulus on a given trial. In initial performance on all three tasks, the younger boys were slower; but they learned a greater amount by practice. Correlations of the amount of learning among the tasks were greater for the younger boys. This suggests that relative specificity of motor learning increases between ages ten and 15. It would seem that the ten-year-old's final skill depends more on ability to learn. In the older boys individual differences in initial skill served more to determine final skill.

Smith and Greene (1963) gave boys 9 to 13 years old a writing task in which they were unable to see their hand, which was concealed from them behind a curtain. They could view it, however on a television screen which gave them feedback as to their performance. The picture was first normal, then reversed, then upside down, and finally upside down reversed. All subjects were able to perform adequately when they viewed the normal picture, but boys under 12 were seldom able to adjust to the reversed or inverted pictures. Older subjects seldom failed to adjust to the task. Results showed that younger subjects were not able to make the complex sensorimotor adaptation necessary to perform adequately when visual feedback is systematically distorted. This is like the childhood trick of patting one's head and rubbing one's stomach simultaneously. Younger children have some difficulty in picking up the trick, but older children and adolescents have little trouble.

The Hyperactive-Child Syndrome

There are some children, mostly boys, who have great difficulty in remaining still. They seem to have a need to be in motion at all times, a need that interferes with many kinds of activities, especially normal classroom learning. This restlessness is often accompanied by aggressiveness and destructiveness; sometimes the frustration caused by having to sit still and

First indications of adulthood

Although preschoolers play at being adults, it is during the middle years of childhood that children possess the sensorimotor coordination and the cognitive ability necessary to develop some proficiency in adultlike activities.

Playing hockey, for example, requires a high degree of speed, precision, and coordination. Learning to crochet calls for small-muscle control, coordination, working from an abstract pattern, and a great deal of patience.

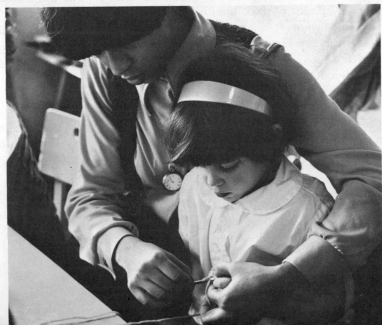

Learning to write is equally complex and demanding. Cooperative projects, like construction work, require all these qualities, as well as the ability to collaborate. Reading is the major cognitive skill learned during this period, and reading aloud in a way that commands the interest and attention of others requires social poise and empathy as well.

work on a demanding task leads the child to rebel and to turn to antisocial forms of behavior.

In recent years, pediatricians and others who work with emotionally disturbed children have come to believe that some neurological impairment or imbalance is at the basis of the hyperactive-child syndrome and use the term minimal brain dysfunction (MBD) to describe it. Mark A. Stewart (1970), a clinical psychologist, points out that hyperactive tendencies appear early, often before the child is two years old. When they occur, they develop into a pattern of symptoms that is quite different from the behavior of other children. Figure 14-2 presents the results of interviews of mothers of hyperactive children and those of a group of unselected children who were attending the first grade in suburban schools near St. Louis. Stewart also notes that a high proportion of the hyperactive children have a history of accidental poisoning in early childhood. Furthermore, a high proportion of the children have fathers who were also restless and quick-tempered.

One interesting characteristic of this hyperactivity or *hyperkinesis* is its controllability by drug therapy. Certain drugs apparently have

Figure 14-2. A comparison of the incidence of behavior symptoms commonly associated with hyperactivity among 37 children (32 boys and 5 girls) who were patients at a psychiatric clinic and a control group of children attending first grade in suburban schools. Percentages refer to the proportion of the children displaying each type of behavior, according to mothers' reports. (After Stewart, 1970.)

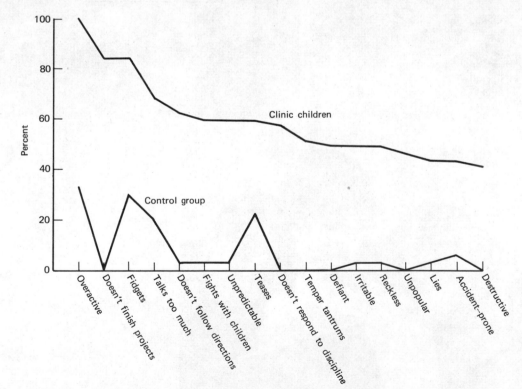

a quieting effect on the hyperactive child's behavior, thus enabling him to persevere longer with assigned tasks and to moderate the intensity of his interaction with others.

This practice has come under considerable criticism on the part of some psychologists and educators for the following reasons.

1. The drugs being prescribed are *amphetamines* (e.g., *Benzedrine*), which have a highly stimulating and energizing effect on adults, but oddly enough, a quieting effect on children thought to have MBD. Continued heavy dosage with adults is likely to have very dangerous results: extreme depression, extreme aggressiveness, and psychotic states. Counterarguments are that the drugs have no such effect on hyperkinetic children; hence it is safe to use them.

2. Although such drugs should be prescribed by physicians only after a careful analysis of all the factors in the case, it appears that sometimes prescriptions are written on the suggestion of a teacher or school official who has found a certain child "difficult to handle."

3. If one of the tasks of society in general and the school in particular is to help children establish proper emotional controls, the continued use of drugs will teach them only to depend on drugs, without learning proper self-control.

The problem is admittedly a difficult one for the school, the physician, the parents and, of course, the child. School personnel who have too many problems already and are poorly equipped to deal with hyperactive children, who are often hostile and aggressive, claim that the drugs enable the child to cope with problems that otherwise would go unresolved. The counterargument holds that it is better not to solve the problem than to solve it via the drug route.

The picture becomes further confused when one reads the comments of those who express doubts as to the diagnosis of hyperactivity and its treatment. Thomas E. Twitchell (1971) of the Department of Neurology of Tufts University Medical School, for example, questions whether hyperactivity is due to any neurological impairment and says that the use of the label MBD is misleading and probably erroneous. He says, "The whole syndrome has become so nebulous and definitions so blurred that it is becoming another diagnostic wastebasket, and it is no surprise that attempts to determine the incidence of MBD among school children yield estimates ranging from 1 to 20 percent" (p. 136). Even those who accept MBD as a valid diagnostic category admit that many children, perhaps as many as 60%, are not helped by drug therapy (Wender, 1971).

There is, however, no question that hyperactivity in all its variations poses a difficult problem for the parent, the school, and for the child himself. All we can say at present is that the dimensions of the problem are not clear, that drugs have been of assistance in some instances, and that drug treatment carries potential risks that have not adequately been assessed. In light of our inadequate knowledge, all we can do is to present this brief discussion as one item in our description of children and their developmental progress.

Emotional Development

As was the case with early childhood, emotional development in later childhood will be centered in a discussion of anger, fear, anxiety, and the affectively pleasant emotions.

Anger

A systematic study of anger of the scope of the classic Goodenough (1931) study (described in Chapter 10) concerning older children has not appeared. However, it will be remembered that the age range of her subjects extended to over seven years, thus overlapping the ages now under consideration. It will also be recalled that certain age trends seemed to be operative. Some of her major findings were that (1) the immediate causes of anger shifted with increase in age and that the older children showed an increase of problems of social relationships; and (2) developmental changes in expression of anger showed less and less random behavior and more and more aggressive behavior directed toward something or someone.

The continuing prominence of social relationships as causes for anger was studied by Hicks and Hayes (1938). In a group of older children and adolescents, 11 to 16 years of age, they found that the social situations most apt to evoke anger were being teased, being lied to, being treated unfairly, being imposed on by brothers and sisters, and other people being bossy or sarcastic. These causes of anger relate to people and the characteristics of people. Even more specifically it was the child's peers who often made him angry.

These "causes" of anger in older children can also be seen, from the perspective of the source of anger, as instances of angry behavior on the part of his peers. Although the investigators did not study the way these children directed their anger, but only what made them angry, it is not difficult to see that the instigators of the anger (often other children) were also expressing anger themselves. If this interpretation be accepted, it means that this study also throws light on how the older child expresses anger. As the child grows older, he learns to show deviousness in his expression of anger. Children become more round-about in their aggressiveness, finding that through sneers, sarcasm, and so on they are able to stir up anger in older children. Just as in adults, a whisper may take the place of a blow, a joke the place of name calling.

A derivative of anger, annoyance, becomes more prominent in later childhood. Annoyance is an emasculated form of anger and frequently expresses more aptly the general kind of emotional response given during these years than does anger itself. In addition, the older child may be observed to express his anger in sulkiness, quarreling, fussiness, and being generally disagreeable.

Fear

Fear is still very much present in the life of children of this age range. The results of a study by England (1946) bring this out dramatically. He asked about 100 seventh- and eighth-grade children of an average age of 11.8 years to make drawings of the most important events of their lives. Nothing in the instructions called for drawings depicting fear. Nevertheless, 88 of the resulting 290 drawings were identifiable as those of fear experiences. Since they were asked for drawings of their most important experiences, the relatively high number of drawings in which fear was the central element is impressive of their awareness of fear situations. Moreover, Pratt (1945), in a carefully conducted study of the fears of children living in rural areas, found that children from grades five through eight reported both more fears and more different fears than children from the four earlier grades.

The classic study of fear by Jersild and others (1933, 1941) described in connection with preschool-aged children, was extended to school-aged children as well. As might be anticipated from the growing subtlety of anger expression in children of this age, fear in its direct open sense was not the only form that was investigated. In fact, in one of the two major studies in which they used a questionnaire check list, they were directly concerned with whether each of the children they studied "often," "sometimes," or "never" *worried* about their specified situations. Their particular choice of terminology, worry, aptly expresses the shift away from overt naked fear that takes place during childhood in the direction of more complex derivatives from it. In this study over 1000 fifth-and sixth-grade children were presented with 25 one-sentence descriptions of situations and asked to express the degree to which they would worry about each one.

Apprehensions about commonplace occurrences in their own environmental situations were prominent among their worries. For example, more than four-fifths admitted that they sometimes worried about failing a test, more than two-thirds worried about the possibility of having a poor report card, and about two-fifths sometimes or often worried about being hit by rough children. In a sense, these were practical worries about realistic situations. However, many were pointless.

Almost one-fifth worried *often* about being left back in school and many hundred more *sometimes* worried about this. Analysis of promotion practices showed that less than 1% were not going to be promoted. Fear of being attacked by animals was mentioned in an interview by 18% of the children studied, yet less than 2% of this sample had been attacked by animals. Even what appear on the surface to be realistic fears are found to contain a large amount of fantasy.

An interview study by Jersild, Markey, and Jersild (1933) of 400 children aged five to twelve years bears out the contention that many fears of children of these ages are unrealistic. About 20% of all fears of the children involved fear of imaginary creatures, of the dark, and of being alone. Another 10% dealt with robbers and other criminal characters. Remote dangers, such as fear of wolves or tigers, also loomed large. In general, fears of a mundane sort were relatively low in frequency as compared to those fears of an antic-ipatory or imaginary sort. Such fears, then, are irrational in the sense that they often occur either when there is no danger or when it is very remote.

This raises the question of whether fear is useful in adjusting to daily problems. It is evident that often it is not. Many fears are restricting and fruitless wastes of energy.

A large proportion of the fears shown in childhood persists into the adult years. This was a finding of Jersild and Holmes (1935) through the study of the recall by adults of childhood fears. Over 40% of the fears they had had as children persisted in their later years. To be sure, they may have forgotten the nature of some of their childhood fears and thus failed to report them, while reporting proportionately more of those that persisted into adulthood.

Those that showed the greatest persistence were fear of animals, of bodily harm through such dangers as fire, illness, or drowning, of the supernatural, of the dark, and of being alone. These fears are presumably kept alive by circumstances in the adult's life that make them in some way indices of present insecurities and conflicts. Their persistence, however, from childhood is still an impressive indication of the importance of the emotional experiences in these earlier years.

Anxiety

The term "anxiety" has two somewhat different meanings in psychological usage: an emotional state and a personality trait. When we use the term in the emotional-state sense we are referring to the arousal that occurs when a situation is perceived as being potentially embarrassing, degrading, or guilt-provoking, and in which there is, consequently, a threat to our self-concept or self-image. The kind of pervasive apprehensiveness that we term "anxiety" is likely to occur in our interactions with others or when we are uncertain about the way things will turn out. Anxiety is a highly socialized emotion and probably serves as a prime motivator in our attempts to get along with others, to conform to their expectations, and to work with them peacefully and cooperatively. A person who lacks anxiety also lacks concern for the thoughts and feelings of others and, as a consequence, is likely to be without empathy. Too much anxiety, on the other hand, leads to an intense self-concern and interferes with good social adjustment. Inasmuch as anxiety is an uncomfortable or even painful emotion, we strive to avoid it at all costs and develop mental mechanisms in order to keep situations from provoking further anxiety. *Repression* is one of these mechanisms: it enables us to conveniently forget embarrassing or guilt-laden thoughts, experiences, or perceptions and to go about the business at hand. *Rationalization* is another mechanism: it enables us to make explanations of our own behavior that are plausible and reasonable but that conceal some embarrassing reality. The list of mechanisms is endless. Some psychologists hold that virtually any kind of activity can serve as a mechanism to prevent or reduce anxiety.

Some people are characteristically more anxious than others—that is, they are more likely to perceive psychological threats in their environment, and their general response to threats is more extreme. Such tendencies can be picked up by psychological tests designed for the purpose. These tests enable psychologists to conduct correlational research comparing anxiety test scores to other variables—social acceptance by others, or errors in learning tasks, to give two examples. When a psychologist administers such tests, he is usually attempting to measure *trait*, rather than *state*, anxiety, because he is trying to determine the level of anxiety that is characteristic of an

individual or a group of subjects and is not especially concerned with the mood of the moment.

The *state* and *trait* concepts of anxiety overlap to some degree. Most of the research studies dealing with measures of anxiety are concerned with the trait, rather than the state. One widely used self-report device is the Test Anxiety Scale for Children (TASC) developed by Sarason and his associates (1960). It consists of 30 items concerned with manifestations of anxiety in their affective, physiological, and motor forms, and placed in a setting of test or test-like situations. Illustrative items include worrying about being promoted and worrying a lot before taking a test. The researchers also developed a so-called General Anxiety Scale for Children (GASC) with items about being afraid of snakes or worrying about becoming sick. These studies demonstrated that anxious children have more difficulty with various kinds of psychological tests than do nonanxious children. Moreover, they found that anxiety adversely affected learning since low anxious subjects performed better than high anxious subjects on a verbal learning task (Waite et al., 1958).

Another popular self-report of behavior and attitudes is the Children's Form of the Manifest Anxiety Scale (CMAS) by Castenada, McCandless, and Palermo (1956). This 42-item questionnaire concerns physiological and psychological indicators of generalized anxiety, worry about such matters as blushing or angering easily, and having sweaty palms. The test has proved to be a useful measure of trait anxiety in grades three to six (Holloway, 1959; 1961). Much of the research with the CMAS compares children scoring high with those scoring low: "high-anxious" and "low-anxious" children. In contrast to low-anxious children, high-anxious children have been observed to do better on simple tasks, but poorer on more complex ones (Castenada, Palermo, and Mc-Candless, 1956; Palermo, Castenada, and Mc-Candless, 1956).

The idea that moderate levels of anxiety facilitate learning, and that levels too high or too low interfere, was tested by F. N. Cox (1960), who found that the academic performance of fifth-grade boys scoring in the middle ranges of anxiety was superior to the other two groups. The poorest performance was in the high-anxious group. The CMAS was also used by Feldhusen and Klausmeier (1962) to determine the relationship among trait anxiety, intelligence, and school achievement. Results showed that children with the lowest IQs had the highest degree of anxiety. In the middle and low IQ groups, anxiety scores were negatively correlated with intelligence and achievement, but the relationship for the high IQ group was approximately zero.

If a moderate degree of anxiety is necessary for good social relations, as we suggested earlier, then we can assume that children's anxiety would increase somewhat with maturity. Some evidence for this proposition is furnished by a study conducted by Amen and Renison (1954), who reported an increase in anxiety with the development of more mature play patterns.

Affectively Pleasant Emotions

Relatively little research has been conducted on the affectively pleasant emotions in the school-aged child. Joy-producing experiences have been studied somewhat indirectly through finding out what children consider their happiest experiences to be. Again it is the work of Arthur T. Jersild to which we turn. In collaboration with Ruth J. Tasch, he made a study of children's interests which included inquiring into what they considered to be one of the happiest days in their lives. Table 14-1

presents the results in terms of the major categories into which their responses to this inquiry could be placed for various age groups.

Younger children tended to stress a holiday or a birthday or other occasions when they received special attention and gifts more than was the case with older children. Children of all ages were apt to mention visiting friends, the return home of relatives, and the like. Girls much more than boys described joyful events as involving social relationships. The oldest-age boys had a sudden upsurge of interest in literally going places, such as parks and recreational centers and in traveling. Older children placed more emphasis on the pleasures of self-discovery and self-realization, opportunities for self-improvement, and for vocational preparation. Benefits for individuals other than themselves were mentioned more often by them than they were by younger children.

Many of the results of the Jersild and Tasch study were indirectly verified by still another study by Jersild and his associates (1933). This was a study involving interviewing 400 five-to-twelve-year-old children about their wishes, dreams, fears, dislikes, and pleasant and unpleasant happenings. The youngest child's wishes, likes, and dislikes were more specific and the older child's more inclusive and social. Girls, again, were more concerned with social relations than were boys.

With increase in age the importance of social relationships and the opportunities for self-realization loom large. The period of later childhood, in terms of the affectively pleasant emotions, is the period of self- and social discovery.

Cognitive Development

As formulated by Piaget, after the age of seven the child enters the period of *concrete* opera-

TABLE 14-1. *Percentage Frequency of Responses in Various Categories When Boys and Girls Described "One of the Happiest Days of My Life" (After Jersild and Tasch, 1949)*

Categories	Age Range and Sex							
	6–9		9–12		12–15		15–18	
	Boys	Girls	Boys	Girls	Boys	Girls	Boys	Girls
Getting or enjoying material things, money, living quarters, etc.	9	8	10	7	10	4	6	3
Holidays, festive occasions, birthdays, Christmas, etc.	39	40	32	39	6	10	1	6
Sports, games, hiking, hunting, bicycling, etc.	10	6	9	6	12	6	13	7
Visiting recreation facilities, camps, resorts, parks, traveling	10	9	10	11	10	14	30	7
Self-improvement, school, and vocational success	2	2	3	2	5	4	14	16
Happenings at school, including last day of school, attending certain schools	4	3	5	4	14	11	7	5
Relations with others, companionship, friendship, family relations, etc.	8	16	8	16	10	22	9	20
Living in or moving to a certain city or community	1	1	1	3	1	3	1	5
Benefits befalling others and mankind in general, end of a war, etc.	1	1	3	3	2	3	8	10

tions, and when he reaches the age between 11 and 15 he begins to use *formal* operations (Inhelder and Piaget, 1958). Both levels will be examined here. This will be followed by an exposition of the research findings for the development of physical causality, and then by a critique of the Piagetian levels.

Piagetian Levels of Cognition

The period of preparation for the level of concrete operations that takes place between the ages of five and seven was discussed in Chapter 10, since its characteristics seemed to have more affinity with those levels occurring during early childhood.

Before considering these levels it is necessary to examine more precisely what Piaget meant by an operation. An operation is a cognitive act which is part of some pattern of acts. It may be seen in adding, subtracting, or in placing an object in a class, a quantity, time, or space. Any of these tasks requires a prior classification. We cannot classify without having some knowledge of what we are classifying; to add to or to subtract from a classification requires a classificatory system. It is more than learning to pick up all yellow counters from a varicolored pile; the child has acquired the ability to think of yellow objects as a group. He has recognized the class "yellow objects."

Concrete operations take on stability and coherence between the age of seven and eleven through the formation of cognitive structures. Consider the problem of differently shaped containers that lead the preschool-aged child to "center" and not to understand that the short, broad container and the tall, thin container hold the same amount. By about seven, however, he recognizes that the amount remains constant regardless of the shape of the container. His first crude approximation "that one is taller, but this one is broader," is an attempt to explain that the height of the one compensates for the width of the other. At a still older age he might say that when poured from one to the other it would be similar. In so doing he has recognized that the change in quantity is invariant despite change of state. This and similar instances, when submitted to more precise scrutiny by other investigators, verified Piaget's contentions, although with greater age variation from child to child than his account would suggest (Lovell, 1961b).

In another instance of a concrete operation used by Piaget, the child is first shown two balls of clay equal in size. He is asked to flatten one ball into a pancake and, then, asked about the amount in each ball. Most five- or six-year-olds believe that necessarily a change in form produces a change in amount. (Either the pancake is larger because it is more spread out or the ball is larger because it is higher.) When older, the child acknowledges that they have the same amount of clay "because the pancake is thinner, but wider." But this level of cognitive development is still pre-operational.

A critical process in finally arriving at "conservation" is awareness of reversibility. This is shown when a child acknowledges that he can make the pancake into a ball again. He now understands that the process is reversible, that quantity is "conserved," in Piaget's usage of the term. Conservation, to Piaget, refers to a particular factor—weight, volume, and the like—remaining invariant despite changes of state. Conservation of matter becomes common at about eight to ten years of age. In short, the child at this age becomes aware that the volume of matter is constant in spite of change in shape. This attribute of the object,

not merely the object as a whole, is now invariant. Similarly, there will be understanding of conservation of weight at a later age, and that of volume still later.

Now that operations have been described it is necessary to refer to the manner in which they may be said to be *concrete*. At this stage the child uses operations but only for the manipulation of *objects* that is, concretely. For example, eight- and ten-year-olds have no trouble arranging a series of dolls or sticks according to height but fail to solve a similar problem put verbally: "Edith is taller than Susan; Edith is shorter than Lily; who is the tallest of the three?" For this principle to be comprehended, progress to the stage of *formal* operations is necessary.

Somewhere between the ages of 11 and 15 the child begins to use formal operations. They are as operational as those at the concrete level of cognition but in a different way. Concrete operations are first-degree operations; formal operations are second degree and use first-degree operations, treating them not as realities but as conditions in representational thought. As types of action they may be verbal when proportions are manipulated or they may be physical when objects are manipulated.

In one experiment five vessels containing colorless liquids are provided; liquids *A,B,C* when mixed, turn pink, *D* removes the color, and *E* has no effect. These properties can be discovered only by systematically examining mixtures of every possible pair, every trio, and so on, in turn. It is characteristic, Piaget found, for children of this age to hit on two-by-two or three-by-three combinations as the way to solve the problem.

In another experiment the subject's task is to place two vertical rings of different diameters between a candle and a screen in such manner that their shadows will coincide. The child finally discovers that the problem is solved when the ratio between the distances of the two rings from the candle is the same as the ratio between their diameters. This demands understanding of proportionality.

Another characteristic of formal operations is reversibility, or the ability to "undo," that is, to return to a starting point and begin again. A graphic illustration of reversibility in action is the child, faced with the problem of finding a balancing weight, placing one on the scale, finding it to be too heavy, taking it off, and beginning to search for a lighter one.

The young child uses formal operations (logical rules), not consciously, to be sure, since ordinarily he has not been trained in logic. Nevertheless, the application of logic becomes part of his cognitive abilities. He may not be able to formulate the rule, if A is greater than B, and B is greater than C, then A is greater than C, but he can apply it, and moreover, apply it to situations with which he is unfamiliar.

Or to put it another way, he can consider hypotheses that may or may not be true and follow the form of argument while disregarding the concrete content. This ability to be guided by the form of argument, ignoring content, gives meaning to the name, formal operations. This ability to utilize difficult logical operations in different situations is the very essence of logcal thinking.

The deductive procedures of science, as well as a host of other new intellectual procedures, become open to the child capable of formal operations. Some of these are formidable when placed in technical terminology, as, for example, the calculus of propositions which has to do with such matters as, if proposition "r" is true, then proposition "s" must be true. The rules are by no means beyond his own day-to-day use, although he does not formulate them as would the logician or mathematician.

The period of formal operations, then, is the years between 11 and 15. Although refinement, adroitness, and scope do take place

thereafter, they do so with structures of the formal sort that the adult employs when thinking logically and abstractly. This final reorganization involving new structures allows the individual to deal with reality and also with the world of pure possibility, that of abstract propositional statements.

Physical Causality

It is appropriate to turn from Piaget's general theory of levels of development to consider a more specific aspect of his views. The emergence of conceptions of physical causality is chosen for detailed exposition (Piaget, 1930). It was his work on physical causality which stimulated widespread interest in the manner in which children developed these conceptions. In studying physical causality various phenomena of nature were mentioned or demonstrated by Piaget and children were asked to explain them. Thus he would ask, "What makes the clouds move?" After the child had responded he would further question him until satisfied he had understood the child's conception. From work along these lines he arrived at a classification of 17 types of causal thinking. Five of these types, moving from relatively great to less egocentricity, were defined by Jean M. Deutsche (1937) in the following ways.

PHENOMENISTIC CAUSALITY. The fact that two events or stimuli occur together is perceived as the basis of causality. For example, a pebble is said to sink to the bottom of a pail because it is white. There is no comprehension of the true relationship of events.

ANIMISTIC CAUSALITY. Causality is explained in terms of inanimate things being alive and conscious. Clouds move, for example, because they are alive; an engine pulls a train because it is alive and wishes to do so.

DYNAMIC CAUSALITY. Events are no longer

explained animistically, but the child still sees forces inherent in objects that explain their behavior.

MECHANICAL CAUSALITY. Motion is explained by contact and transfer of movement, without the idea of an internal force. Wind pushes the clouds, and pedals make the bicycle go.

EXPLANATION BY LOGICAL DEDUCTION. Causation is explained by the principle of sufficient reason. Concepts of density, specific weight, and the like are used.

The first three types are definitely precausal (and egocentric), whereas mechanical causality may be considered as transitional, with explanation by logical definition belonging in the category of formal operations. According to Piaget these (and the remaining 12 levels) are discrete in that children's thinking proceeds in a naturalistic direction during the course of development from one level to the next higher level with relatively little overlap. In terms of the levels, a child would be phenomenistic in his thinking rather than animistic, then animistic, and so on, until logical deduction developed. A child, say at the level of dynamic causality, would when at that level be incapable of logical deduction.

Some support for Piaget's contentions may be seen in Deutsche's (1937) findings, part of which are presented in Table 14-2. She found that phenomenistic causality declined with age, while mechanical and logical causality increased with age. Dynamic causality showed no clear age trend, but this may have been due to the small number of responses observed.

Using some of the Piagetian problems, Mogar (1960) studied causal reasoning about natural phenomena in children aged five through twelve. Like Deutsche's findings, his results support Piaget's contentions in some respects. One almost incidental finding, however, is very important. To a greater degree than the control children, the experimental subjects were exposed to repeated observation of demonstrations of the phenomena about which they were questioned. At the end of the study, they were much more capable than the control subjects of working out solutions at an earlier age than the developmental levels called for. In other words, the special instruction appeared to produce an advance beyond the expected levels. The research we cited in Chapter 11 regarding the children of Mexican potters also suggests that special experiences may facilitate some kinds of cognitive development (Price-Williams, Gordon, and Ramirez, 1969).

A Critique of Piagetian Levels of Development. The apparent success achieved in teaching children more mature modes of cognition continues to raise doubts in the minds of some developmental psychologists regarding

TABLE 14-2. *Percentage of Children's Explanations of Causality Categorized According to Several of Piaget's Classifications (After Deutsche, 1937)*

Type of Causality	Ages							
	8	9	10	11	12	13	14	15–16
Phenomenistic	37	32	30	22	16	12	12	10
Animistic	1	0	1	0	0	0	0	0
Dynamic	8	6	6	6	7	7	3	6
Mechanical	32	33	37	40	41	41	40	43
Logical	11	12	14	20	28	32	36	32

the generality of Piaget's conclusions, and some even dismiss his findings on the grounds that they do not consider his research controls as adequate. This is shortsighted. Even if questions are raised on methodological grounds, his ideas are stimulating and other research has shown that they are, for the most part, basically sound.

Some of the differences between Piaget's findings together with the studies that support him and those of other investigators whose findings are in disagreement are to be found in the dissimilar methods they used. Piaget used a clinical method of adroitly questioning the children he interviewed. The method had the advantage of allowing him to trace down the particular meaning the child was giving to a word. Children, as Piaget's own work so ably shows, are in the process of developing sharpness and clarity in their use of words. There certainly is an advantage of this approach over using a group-written test where there is no follow-up of what the child meant by his answers. In a group test, the response obtained for each object or demonstration is equivalent only to the unfollowed-up first response in the interview procedure.

The group method, too, has advantages. It more readily permits a larger sampling of subjects and the application of a series of controls. Although not intrinsic to the group testing method, the use of independent observers to measure reliability is a distinct advantage. These differences in procedure between Piaget and the American research investigators undoubtedly go far in accounting for the disparities in the results obtained.

Piaget's sharp contrast between childish and adult thinking probably is an overevaluation of verbal expression as a measure of thinking and an exaggeration of the logical nature of adult thought. Just as children's thinking is not so different from adult thinking because the child is more adult than pictured by Piaget,

so, too, is the adult more childish. Children's thinking cannot be as sharply distinguished from adult modes of thought as Piaget would have it. There is confusion of fantasy with reality, as the psychoanalysts as well as followers of Piaget argue, but there is not a qualitative difference between the thinking of children and that of adults. Reality limits the child despite his creation of make-believe situations; fantasy enlivens and yet distorts the thinking of adults. A child's thinking does not differ fundamentally from an adult's by differing in kind, but rather in degree.

It is important to note that Piaget did not claim the entire absence of one form of thinking and then the full-blown appearance of another, with no residue of the earlier stage. For example, socialized speech in early childhood is recognized and accepted by Piaget. He claimed only that egocentric speech clearly predominated. Nevertheless, much more than others, he argued for relatively abrupt shifts in thinking on the part of the children at different ages. Many indications, besides the studies reported here, show that the cognitive stages of Piaget are not sharply separated, neither with quite different responses emerging at each level nor with the disappearance of those of the previous stage.

It would seem as if the weight of evidence is against the abrupt shifting from one stage of conceptualization to the next. The almost universal finding of research studies other than Piaget's own is that, instead of there being leaps from one kind of thinking to another, there is a gradual orderly change in the child's conceptualization (no matter how defined). This forces disagreement in emphasis with Piaget on this point. For example, most studies, whether of physical causality or of the narrower problem of animism, find that the categorizations of thinking they used, whatever form they may take, extend over the age range of the subjects studied. Trends of change in stages of conceptualization are found to be sure, but they are progressive and not of an "all or none" variety.

We should also note that Piaget does not dismiss training as unimportant in the development of cognitive skills. Maturation in the form of the increasing elaboration of central nervous system processes must of course take place before the child is ready to develop some form of self-regulating behavior and to have the proper experience in the form of encounters with his environment. Training comes under the heading of "social transmission," a subcategory of experience, and consists of encounters with others in formal or informal educational settings (Piaget, 1964).

Time and Space Perception

Piaget (1955) prefers to refer to time concepts rather than to time perception since he considers appreciation of time to involve not only perceptual data but also logical organization of these data. This position makes time an aspect of his general theory of cognitive development. The preoperative stage between the ages of two and seven had allowed the child to execute on the plane of thought the equivalent of the still earlier sensorimotor stage.

Up to about the age of seven the child shows a close relationship between his constructs of time and speed. Dolls are moved across a table surface at different speeds, B more rapidly than A, but stopped simultaneously. When a child is asked when they stopped, he refuses to say they stopped at the same time. This is not a perceptive error: he acknowledges when B stops; A no longer moves but he refuses to say they stopped at the same time. He may say B stopped before A because the former is "ahead" of the latter (in the spatial sense) or he may say that A stopped before B in the sense it is spatially closer. In either case

he does not understand that they stopped "at the same time," because the notion "same time" is meaningless when two objects move at different speeds.

Only gradually does the conservation of relationships of *speed* come about at around seven or eight years of age. Then, and only then, is he ready, says Piaget, to conceive of the construct of time at the concrete level. Time constructs at the formal level have not been specifically worked out. It is safe to say that they partake of the general conceptualization characteristic of that level. Many of Piaget's contentions have been verified experimentally but with more variation over wider age range than would be expected (Lovell and Slater, 1960).

Fraisse (1948) made a distinction between time perception and time estimation. He arrived at this differentiation by a study of long and short time intervals with time perception applying only to short intervals, that is, one second. He tested children aged six, eight, and ten for their ability to reproduce time intervals of .5, 1, 5, and 20 seconds, both filled with some activity and unfilled. He found only slight age differences for the short intervals. The major age difference was with the two longest intervals which were grossly underestimated by the youngest subjects, who also showed extraordinarily large variability for the longest interval. After eight the longer time intervals showed negligible time differences. Younger children are deficient primarily in time estimation, not time perception.

In summarizing the research on time perception for older children, Flickinger and Rehage (1949) concluded that the concept of past *versus* present was reached at about eight; full understanding of our system of time measurement at about 11; understanding of time-zone lines at about 13; and natural grasp of time words and dates at about 16.

Space representation, not perception, is

stressed by Piaget in order to emphasize that space is not immediately given in experience as something merely to be perceived. Organizations of actions performed in space, first through motor and later through internalized actions, give rise to operational systems.

Spatial relations are related to or coordinated with the child's own body. The child understands the elements of a spatial pattern with reference to his own body as right or left, high or low, and the rest. A factor analysis revealed that boys tended to exceed girls in spatial ability. This may possibly be due to the greater participation in construction activities during play (Michael, Zimmerman, and Guilford, 1951).

Language Development

Language is an integral aspect of cognitive development, essential as it is for perceptual-cognitive and intellectual growth. It even is to be discerned as effective in emotional development. Without the acquisition of words and some knowledge of syntactical construction, these cognitive processes would be stunted and chaotic. Without language as a means of communication, social interaction would be nearly impossible. Discussion of language is intertwined with all of these aspects of child development.

Developmental Changes in Language Skills

Growth in oral and written expression in a representative sampling of 320 children aged nine through 15 years of age has been studied by Harrell (1957). After seeing a short movie, each child told a story that was tape-recorded. After another similar movie, each wrote a story about it. With the clause as the unit of measurement, the investigators studied the length of the stories by age, sex, and oral or written means of composition. The oral stories were longer than the written ones, and both in-

creased in length with age, although repetitions and corrections decreased with age. Girls wrote longer stories than boys. It is significant that by the oldest age, 15 years, there was no indication that a mature level had been reached. Considerable increase in skill was still to be expected in the years thereafter.

Some of the complexities of language acquisition of the child should be illustrated. Consider the problem of acquisition of word meanings. An adult might use a dictionary, but this is not characteristic of the child who does not acquire meanings in this fashion. Ingeniously, Werner and Kaplan (1950) made use of 12 nonsense words, such as CORPLUM, placed in various contexts to see how children, eight through 13, would acquire their meanings. For each artificial word there were six sentences in which it was used, such as "a CORPLUM may be used for support;" "a wet CORPLUM doesn't burn;" and "you can make a CORPLUM smooth with sandpaper." After reading a sentence, one to a card, the child was asked what the word meant, and how and why the meaning he gave the word fitted into the sentence. With the first sentence card still in view, he then proceeded to the second and subsequent sentence cards, each time giving his interpretation of its meaning and how that meaning could be applied to that given to the preceding sentence. In this example CORPLUM meant wood. The major aim, however, was not correctness itself. Rather the *process* of signification was the main concern.

It was found that one major category included those instances in which children did not clearly differentiate the word from the sentence as a whole. They so confused the word and its sentence context, that instead of learning a circumscribed meaning, the word meant to them the entire context in which it appeared. Thus in the sentence, "People talk about the BURDICKS of others and don't talk about their own," one girl explained

BURDICK meant, "talk about others and don't talk about themselves." Later, the same child when given the sentence, "People with BURDICKS are often unhappy," said, "People talk about others and don't talk about themselves—they are often unhappy." It is not recorded whether she eventually found that BURDICK meant "faults."

The other major category involved instances in which children differentiated the word from the sentence, but did so in a variety of ways, most often giving too inclusive a meaning to the nonsense word. In the instance when the meaning should have been "collect" with one child it became successively, "collect ribbons," "collect autographs," and "collect information." In each instance what was collected would fit the context; to wit, people collect information quickly when there is an accident, but actually the "ribbons," "the autographs," and the "information" were entirely extraneous. "Collect" was all that was necessary. These so-called sentence-word fusions decreased most sharply at about 11 years of age, hardly to appear thereafter. Those in which there was no fusion of word meaning and context, although decreasing, were maintained through the oldest age studied. A shift in level of verbal abstraction seemed to be taking place at about the 11-year level.

The path of language acquisition is not the simple, straightforward one that adults might imagine. The child must move through difficult and devious paths of blind-alley irrelevancies to find the relevant strand of appropriate meaning.

Learning to Read. The major linguistic "leap forward" that children make during the middle years is that of learning to read. For some years, there was a controversy among reading specialists as to whether children learn best by "sounding out" the letters that compose a word or learn to recognize words by their Gestalts or overall shapes. Once one has mastered a certain degree of reading skill, words are responded to in terms of their totalities, which lends some credence to the Gestalt or "look-and-say" approach. Children who learn most efficiently, however, tend to approach new words by a form of phonic analysis, by "sounding out" each letter and guessing from the result what the word probably is.

Marchbanks and Levin (1965) conducted a study of reading approaches used by kindergarteners and first graders that tends to support the phonic analysis viewpoint. They showed the children three- and five-letter nonsense words one at a time and then asked them to pick out the word they had just been shown, or the one most like it, from a list of nonsense words. The lists were constructed so as to enable the investigators to determine which cues children were using to identify the words: the shape, the first letter, the second letter, and so forth. Their results, as Figure 14-3 indicates, showed that the words' initial letters were the most-used cues, followed by the final letters. The words' shapes were actually little used as cues. This tendency was even stronger with first graders than with kindergarteners, showing that the use of initial letters as cues was a more mature response than the use of word shapes.

Intellectual Development

Brief reference has already been made in Chapters 7 and 11 to intellectual development during infancy and early childhood. This involved consideration of the kinds of intelligent behavior observed at these particular ages, the nature of the underlying processes that seemed to account for this behavior, and the prowess of tests given at these ages for prediction of later intellectual status. Here we undertake a more detailed examination of intelligence in later childhood.

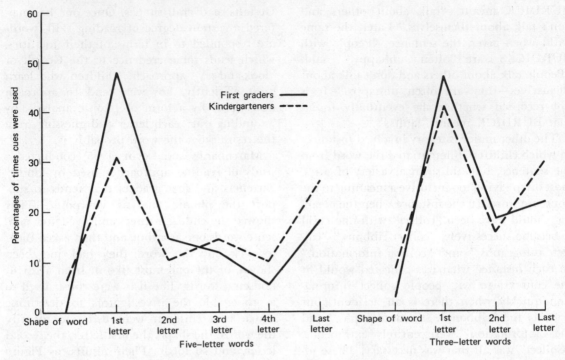

Figure 14-3. Cue preferences in word recognition: percentages of times kindergarteners and first graders used various cues in recognizing five- and three-letter nonsense words. (Marchbanks and Levin, 1965.)

The Nature of Intelligence

Intelligence becomes evident through the observing, the conceptualizing, and the thinking the child carries on. If observation, conceptualization, and thought are efficient, broad, and involve higher levels of difficulty, we speak of the individual as bright; if they are the opposite, we speak of the individual as stupid. It is only for convenience that we break down this continuum into discrete areas. Instead of there being a dichotomy of the bright and the stupid, there is a continuum from the highest degree of brightness to the lowest degree of ineptitude.

Intelligence involves all of the cognitive processes, but with emphasis on the efficiency, scope, and level of difficulty of function which

is expressed. Concepts, for example, are *used* by a child in intellectual activity—with efficiency, breadth, and hierarchical level of capabilities helping to decide what we call the intelligence of the child in question.

Woodworth (1940) once contended that intelligence is one of those nouns that should be considered a verb. A child is intelligent insofar as he acts intelligently, stupid insofar as he acts stupidly. Intelligence is always expressed in some behavior, reinforcing the necessity of considering it essentially a verb, since the emphasis is upon the behavior. Intelligence is not an entity, but a construct about ways of behavior inferred and measured indirectly. We infer from certain behaviors that are now learned that the individual will behave in this fashion.

Since the functioning of intelligence calls for a solution to a problem, there is an implication that the situation in which it functions is a new one in some particulars. Habit carries us through many activities. But before we have a habitual way of behaving, we must at some time have met what is now habitual as a new situation. Then intellectual application took place. Intelligence, then, is expressed in the application of the higher mental processes to accomplishing a task, particularly new tasks.

Intellectual development is related to learning. From the infant's first explorations of his little world to the new conception of the universe by the physicist, there is a steady background of learning. One learns more and faster because of more efficient intellectual functioning. We measure intelligence on the basis of things we have learned; for example, vocabulary, common knowledge, and school attainment. Intellectual development and learning are inextricably intertwined—intellectual development results in gaining knowledge. This is a result of learning.

Intelligence is a unified integrated way of behaving and in this sense is a function of the total personality. An individual uses it to adapt to his changing environment. Intelligence takes its place as one of the interrelated aspects of the psychological processes of the child. Consequently, intelligence is discussed not only for its own sake as an integrated way of behaving but also because it again allows stressing the interdependence of personality factors which contribute to the development of the child.

There is considerable general agreement for the assertions about intelligence made up to this point. Consideration of the more precise composition of intelligence and its changes, or lack of them, during development from infancy to adulthood reveals disagreements. Spearman (1927) held that there was a general factor, or g, influencing all intelligent behavior

while there were many special factors, or s. Some s factors were heavily dependent upon g, for example, number ability, and others were relatively independent of g, for example, musical or motor ability. He stressed abstract ability, particularly that involved in arriving at relations, as in answering the question, "Sun is to earth as earth is to what?"

Thurstone (1946), who studied the problem of intelligence for many years, disagreed with Spearman on the composition of intelligence. In contrast to g and s factors, Thurstone's position was that intelligence was made up of group factors, more or less mutually exclusive one from the other. In other words, numerical ability, or N, one of these multiple factors, is relatively unrelated to other mental abilities. He agreed with Spearman on the abstract nature of intelligence but disagreed on how it was distributed; instead of a general factor intelligence, he conceived of it as having multiple factors. Both Spearman and Thurstone tended to stress the fixed character of intelligence from infancy to adulthood.

Piaget (1950) has disagreed with this point. In his theory of cognitive development, intelligence is the adaptive aspect of cognition; its function remains invariant while the structures do not. They change in the manner analyzed in the earlier section on cognitive development.

Other psychologists also take issue with the factor theories. Lewis Madison Terman (1921) described intelligence as the ability to do abstract thinking, and David Wechsler (1958), as an "aggregate or global capacity" that enables one to deal with the environment purposefully, rationally, and effectively.

The Testing of Intelligence

The first really effective tests of intelligence were constructed for use with school children. As we noted in Chapter 1, the scales developed in 1905 by the Frenchmen, Binet and Simon, were adapted for use with American children by Terman in 1916. Both these tests were administered *individually* to children in an interview situation. The following year, the United States entered World War I, and the need to classify and train millions of recruits led to the development of the first standardized *group* tests of intelligence: the Army Alpha and the Army Beta. Following the war, a number of standardized group tests made their appearance and found ready use in schools throughout the United States and elsewhere. The testing movement was under way.

Terman had incorporated the Binet-Simon mental-age concept into his scale and, using a suggestion by the German psychologist, Wilhelm Stern (1914), reported his scores in terms of a statistic that represented the extent to which a child could be considered above, below, or at age with respect to his intelligence. This statistic, the intelligence quotient or IQ, was computed by dividing the child's mental age by his chronological age and multiplying the result by 100 in order to eliminate decimal points. The IQ became a fixture in mental tests, as well as in everyday language, but it proved to have a number of statistical problems, and today has been replaced by the "deviation IQ," which tells us how a given child's test score compares with the norms for other children his age. With both types of measures, 100 IQ represents the normal or average performance of a child at any age, and IQs higher or lower than 100 tell us the extent to which a child's performance exceeds or falls below this norm.

Table 14-3 gives the percentage of children falling in different IQ categories on the 1938 revision of the Stanford-Binet test. The IQ levels are also interpreted in terms of the possible learning attainment for individuals falling within various ranges of scores.

Mental Tests

Although the Stanford-Binet proved to be a useful test for clinicians and researchers, psychologists have often felt the need for a test that would give them additional information regarding the cognitive functioning of a child. David Wechsler developed his Intelligence Scales to meet this need. The initial versions of the scale were for use with adults and provided an overall IQ, a verbal IQ, and a performance (nonverbal) IQ, all based on the subject's performance on 11 subscales. This breakdown of scores permitted clinicians to get more information in the course of a one-hour test interview.

The Wechsler Intelligence Scale for Children (WISC) appeared in 1949. It is appropriate for use with children aged 5 to 15. In 1960, a second revision of the Stanford-Binet was published. It covers a broader age range than the WISC and is hence used more frequently with younger children. Stanford-Binet items include more verbal material than the WISC and it is a better predictor of school performance for that reason. On the other hand, the WISC is more useful in testing children who have learning problems at school or who are verbally handicapped.

Inasmuch as the Stanford-Binet and the WISC take a considerable amount of time to administer, their use is restricted to individual cases, and most of the intelligence testing in the schools is done with standardized paper-and-pencil tests like the California Tests of Mental Maturity, the Kuhlmann-Anderson Intelligence Tests, the Otis-Lennon Mental Ability Tests, and the Lorge-Thorndike Intelligence Tests. These tests tend to correlate a little higher with school success than the Stanford-Binet, because the problems they present are more similar to those encountered in school.

TABLE 14-3. IQ Classifications Commonly Used by Psychologists, Together with Reference Points for Interpretation of IQ Levels (After Merrill, 1938)

IQ	Percentage of Sample	Classification	Interpretation
160 and over	0.03	Very superior	
160–159	0.2		
140–149	1.1		
130–139	3.1	Superior	"PhD material"
120–129	8.2		
110–119	18.1	High average	"College material"
100–109	23.5	Normal or average	High school graduates
90–99	23.0		Can do some high school work
80–89	14.5	Low average	
70–79	5.6	Borderline defective	Can do fifth grade work
60–69	2.0	Mentally defective	
50–59	0.4		Educable mental retardate
40–49	0.2		Trainable mental retardate
39 and below	0.02		

The Validity of Mental Tests

The results of intelligence tests are often criticized by laymen and psychologists alike as not having much relationship to real-life behavior. Such accusations find some support in that a child who takes a number of intelligence tests over the years will show some variance in IQ, depending on the form of the test being administered; the state of the child's health, both emotional and physical; and the skill with which the test is administered. The measure of any test is, of course, its validity: do its results have any demonstrable relationship to behavior as assessed by any outside criterion? Can we, for example, use the IQ to predict a child's behavior in situations that call for the use of intelligence?

The answer is a qualified affirmative. Children's IQs are predictive of their success, for example, in school situations. In other words, if a given child has a high IQ, the chances are that he will also do well in school; there is even a greater likelihood that a child with a low IQ will do poorly. Some children with high IQs will not do well in school, because intelligence is only one of the factors essential to academic success. Other factors important for school success are motivation to achieve, self-confidence, and good social adjustment. A very few children with low IQs will do well in school not only because they have motivation and self-confidence and are well-adjusted but also because the intelligence test has failed to reflect their real mental ability.

The fact that intelligence tests lead us to make a few poor predictions does not mean that they are essentially invalid. Our ability to use them to make reliable, better-than-chance predictions in the majority of instances is sufficient reason for us to employ them as research instruments.

Intelligence Tests

The Stanford-Binet Tests of Intelligence and the Wechsler Intelligence Scales for Children (WISC) include both verbal and nonverbal tasks. In these photographs, children are being tested with nonverbal materials.

Stanford-Binet: *The child is shown a 9-bead chain and is told to copy it from memory.*

WISC: *The child assembles the parts of a horse in the Object Assembly subtest. In the Block Design subtest, the task is that of using the Kohs cubes to copy a colored design.*

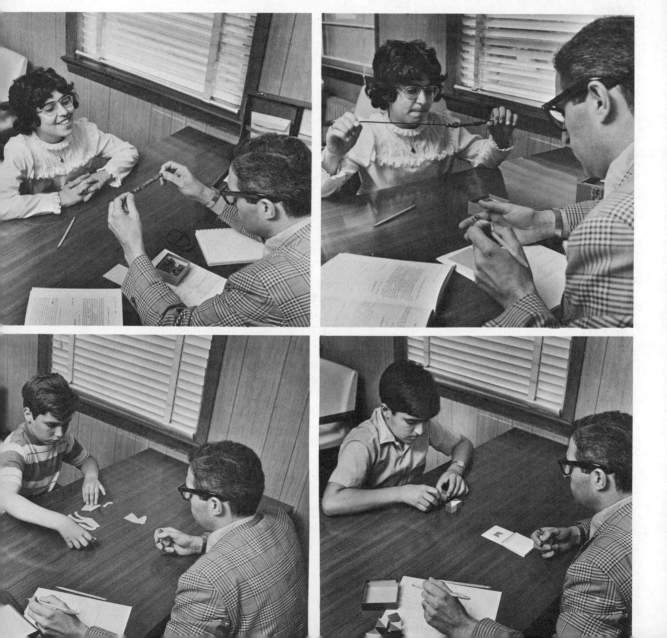

The parent, teacher, clinician, or counselor who wants to make a prediction for a single child has a special type of problem, however. Let us say that an intelligence test makes successful predictions for two-thirds of a group of unselected subjects, is equivocal for a fourth, and is definitely misleading for about 10%. Inasmuch as this is better than chance, we can use it as an instrument in research that calls for the measurement of intellectual ability. If we are considering the fate of a single child from this group, however, we will not know whether he is one of the two out of three for which the test will make a successful prediction, or the one out of three for which the test will predict not at all or incorrectly. It is because of the occasional false prediction that parents, teachers, and other nonpsychologists mistrust intelligence test scores. Clinicians and counselors are less likely to reject intelligence tests as invalid, because they understand their limitations and have recourse to a variety of

of adidtional measures on which they can base an appraisal.

As far as making predictions is concerned, as long as we continue to work with groups of subjects and not with the single case, intelligence tests should work out reasonably well. Figure 14-4 presents some typical correlations between intelligence tests and other variables. The data show that the tests have a very high correlation with school marks, marks in arithmetic, and achievement test scores in arithmetic. These results suggest that the common factor here is the ability to learn in a classroom situation: the greater the ability to learn, the better the school marks and the higher the score on intelligence and achievement tests. Motivation is undoubtedly a factor as well; without the drive to achieve, the bright studebt is unlikely to apply himself to school tasks and complete them, nor is he likely to care much about filling out the blanks in a paper-and-pencil intelligence test.

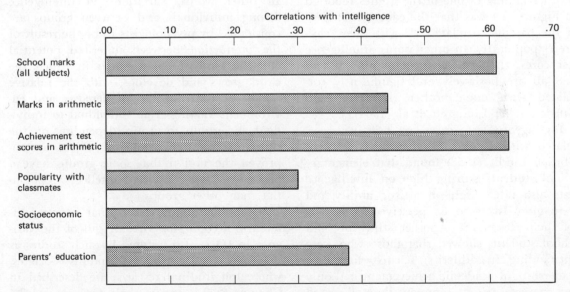

Figure 14-4. Correlations between intelligence test scores and school achievement, sociometric ratings (popularity), and indicators of socioeconomic status for two groups of elementary school children. (After Lindgren and Guedes, 1963; Lindgren et al., 1964.)

Figure 14-4 also shows that the validity of intelligence tests is not limited to classroom learning, but extends to other life activities as well. The .30 correlation with popularity (determined sociometrically) can be explained in these terms: students who are energetic, task-oriented, confident, and cooperative are the ones who make the best impressions on teachers and also eagerly tackle the problems posed by intelligence tests. In addition, it is quite probable that more intelligent children behave in a friendlier way and are more attractive to their peers than less intelligent children.

Socioeconomic status and parental education are both significantly correlated with intelligence, as Figure 14-4 shows. One explanation is genetic—namely that the intellectual potential of the parents is biologically inherited by their children. Another explanation is that better educated and more affluent parents are able to create an intellectually stimulating environment for their children. Still another finding of one of the studies reported in Figure 14-4 was that the educational level of the parents correlated .28 with their children's popularity. In other words, intelligence test scores, school achievement, popularity, and SES all are positively and significantly correlated with one another (Lindgren and Guedes, 1963; Lindgren et al., 1964).

Intelligence test scores are positively correlated with success in other fields as well. Gordon Liddle (1958) found that elementary school students scoring high on intelligence tests also rated high on artistic ability and were more likely to be perceived as leaders by their classmates. Another study of high school students showed that those who were outstanding in athletics, science, fine arts, leadership, or academic achievement had only one characteristic in common: they all scored high on intelligence tests (Clarke and Olson, 1965). Intelligence test scores also reflect over-

all adjustment, for they were found to be negatively related to measures of test anxiety (Denny, Paterson, and Feldhusen, 1964).

Intelligence and Race

The stand taken by most psychologists for many years has been that the inherited potentiality for intellectual competence varies from individual to individual, but that the extent to which this potentiality is actually developed depends on environmental factors. A child growing up in an intellectually stimulating environment, nurtured by parents who expect him to do the best he can, is likely to develop more of his potential than a child who grows up in a home where nobody cares about books and no one is expected to amount to anything. It is therefore quite possible that a child with a relatively low inherited potential living in a stimulating environment might have a higher IQ than one with a high inherited potential living in a severely restricted environment. In other words, variations in intelligence among individuals and between groups are considered by psychologists to be the result of the *interaction* between inherited potential and the kind of environment in which the child grows and develops, with the relative weight of contributions of heredity and environment varying from individual to individual and group to group, depending on the situation. Most psychologists reject as unproven the notion that some groups have a higher or lower inherited intellectual potential than other groups.

Skepticism about claims that genetic differences account for virtually all of the variance in IQ is also fostered by such studies as that of Wayne Dennis (1967) and his associates, whose longitudinal research we described in Chapter 8. To review their findings briefly, the investigators noted that the cognitive development of children who remained in the

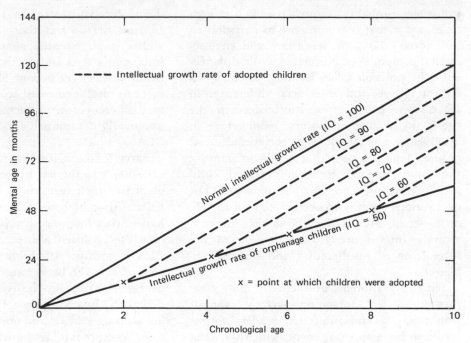

Figure 14-5. A schematic representation of the hypothetical cognitive growth pattern of adopted and non-adopted orphans from a Beirut, Lebanon crêche. (Based on data and conclusions from Dennis, 1967.) (From Lindgren, 1969, and reproduced by permission of John Wiley & Sons, Inc.)

relatively unstimulating atmosphere of a Lebanese orphanage proceeded at an abnormally low rate, as characterized by an IQ of 53. Children who were adopted, however, began to develop at a more normal rate, averaging about 80 IQ. The younger the children were adopted, the more nearly their development approached the normal rate of 100 IQ. Figure 14-5 presents a schematic diagram of the effect of adoption on the intellectual development of orphans of various ages.

Dennis' study is unique in a number of ways. For one thing, the difference of 50 IQ points attributable to environmental differences is the largest reported by any researcher to date. Most differences resulting from environmental manipulation are more modest.

Gray and Klaus (1970), in their Early Training Project, noted a maximum difference between their "best" experimental group and their "poorest" control group of only 16 IQ points, and 5 to 10 points is a more usual finding. Most children, however, do not enter experimental treatment programs until they are three or four, whereas Dennis' study began when the children were infants.

The fact that the majority of studies in which environment has been manipulated have resulted in relatively small IQ changes is taken by some psychologists, Arthur Jensen (1968a, and 1969), for example, as evidence that environment has only a minor effect on intelligence. Most of the variance in intelligence, according to Jensen, is attributable to genetic influences, probably as much as 80%, although he also says that it is nonsense to partition an individual's IQ into hereditary and environmental components. Nevertheless, he disagrees with the position taken by most psychologists on intergroup and interracial differences in IQ and maintains that differences in the "gene pools" lead to observed differences in intelligence among different social and racial groups. Jensen agrees that efforts to improve the education of the disadvantaged child should continue and even be increased, but he cautions against expecting too much. He dismisses as fatuous the notion that an individual's intelligence is the product of the interaction of his heredity and his environment.

Jensen's arguments are actually more complex than the foregoing sketchy synopsis would imply, and interested readers are referred to his major statement, which was published by the *Harvard Educational Review* in 1969 under the title *Environment, Heredity, and Intelligence*. Comments by other psychologists are also included.

One of the complications introduced by Jensen is his statement that only one type of mental ability shows variation between racial and social groups, whereas another type does not. This conclusion is based in part on some earlier research in which Jensen (1961) tested children of different SES levels with tasks that required them to memorize certain word associations. He found no differences between SES levels, with low-SES children doing as well as middle-SES children. He called the ability thus measured *basic learning ability* or BLA. Although BLA is necessary for success on intelligence tests, Jensen observes that another factor is required as well: problem-solving ability—that is, the ability to manipulate symbols, to reason inductively and deductively, and to test hypotheses. BLA does not require the use of these abilities, inasmuch as

it involves only straight rote memorization. In view of the fact that (1) problem-solving ability is an essential element in success on intelligence tests and (2) there are large differences between races and SES levels with respect to intelligence test scores, Jensen reasons that differences in problem-solving ability are genetically determined, whereas differences in BLA are not.

Barry J. Guinagh (1971) put this proposition of Jensen's to the test by setting up an experiment in which two groups of Negro children, half scoring high on a measure of BLA and half scoring low, were compared to two groups of white children also having high and low BLA subgroups. All children were third graders with low SES background. IQ was measured by the Raven's Progressive Matrices, a nonverbal test involving the selection of appropriate abstract designs and one that is considered to be "culture-fair" by Jensen.

The experiment consisted of seven half-hour sessions devoted to training the experimental groups of children in the kinds of concepts involved in the Raven test. The Raven test was administered before the experimental sessions, immediately afterward, and again after a month had elapsed, in order to determine whether the gains, if any, had been retained. Inasmuch as training is, in essence, an environmental manipulation, a finding that training had any effect on Raven test scores would provide evidence in favor of the environmentalist position and against the stand taken by Jensen.

The results, as shown in Figure 14–6, favored the environmentalist argument. Negro and white children with high BLA who had received the special training made great gains, in contrast to control groups who had no training. Low BLA Negroes in the experimental group made some gain, but it was far below that of the high BLA group. The fact that the results were not a mere coincidence was con-

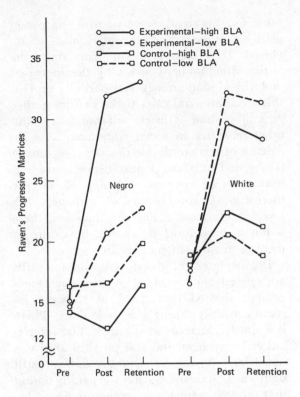

Figure 14-6. Effects of special training on Raven's Progressive Matrices scores for Negro and white low SES third-grade children who scored high or low in Basic Learning Ability (BLA). (Guinagh, 1971. Reproduced by permission.)

firmed by the scores made by the children a month later. The results for the white children also show that training improved Raven Matrices scores, but in their case, there was no relationship with BLA. Indeed, it may be that BLA is not as invariant as Jensen maintains. The fact that the gain of all the white children's groups dropped off slightly when retested a month later, whereas the Negro children's performance improved after a month, may be accounted for, according to Guinagh, in terms of personality differences between the white and Negro groups. The Negro children were more spontaneous and

affectionate and tried harder to please the trainers, whereas the white children were more emotionally controlled and more peer-oriented than teacher-oriented.

Other research evidence that raises questions about Jensen's conclusions comes from a study by Sandra Scarr-Salapatek (1971), who conducted a study of IQ and school achievement of black and white children, both twins and nontwins, in Philadelphia schools. She developed two sets of hypotheses for her study. If the genetic model as espoused by Jensen is correct, she reasoned, she should find that the IQ variance of the children in her study would be approximately equal in each social class or race, because the environment in which they grew up would have only a moderate effect. On the other hand, if the environmentalist viewpoint is correct, she should find a smaller amount of IQ variance among children from deprived homes, and a larger amount of IQ variance from those from middle-class homes, irrespective of race. The environmentalist reasoning here is that more apt children from poor homes would encounter a depressing environment that would lead them to perform little better than less apt children, whereas the more stimulating environment of middle-class homes would free children to find their own level, so to speak, and hence their IQs would vary more.

What Scarr-Salapatek found was that IQ variance, irrespective of race, was higher among children from the more advantaged homes and lower among those from poorer homes, a finding that tends to support an environmentalist interpretation of intergroup IQ differences, and she observed that "genetic factors cannot be seen as strong determinants of aptitude scores in the disadvantaged groups of either race" (p. 1292).

Man, as we have noted in our earlier discussions, is a very plastic animal. His ability to learn and adapt his behavior to his environment probably has its limits, but whatever they are, they have not been determined as yet. How much of man's variability is due to genetic factors that cannot be modified by environmental differences probably never will be known, because we have not attained that Utopia in which every child is adequately loved, nourished, and stimulated. Until such a point is reached, our only way of improving the lot of the individual and of all mankind lies in identifying the environmental elements that produce the most satisfactory results and making needed changes in the environment accordingly. Although Jensen says that he approves of such continuing research and experimentation, his conclusions unfortunately are more consistent with the idea that children are born the way they are and the way they will grow up. His findings therefore have been eagerly taken up by individuals who take a more pessimistic and fatalistic view of man and who feel that there is little point in wasting time and money on experimental programs like Operation Head Start, child-care centers, and other attempts to improve the environment of the children of poverty.

Summary

The middle and later childhood years span the period between the end of the preschool period to adolescence. In terms of age, the period runs from about 6 to 12 for girls, and from 6 to 14 for boys. The growth curve settles down to a steady rate throughout most of this period, until the prepuberal growth spurt. In recent years, scientists have become aware of what they term the "secular trend." This is the tendency for the children of each successive generation to mature sooner and grow larger than their predecessors. Evidence seems to point to improved nutrition as the cause for this trend. Some scientists have suggested that genetic factors may also be involved. If tallness is a dominant trait, the outbreeding brought about by the increased mobility of modern man may partially explain this "secular trend." Boys who mature earlier generally show greater self-confidence and more maturity in social situations. The incidence of communicable diseases rises during this period, reaching a peak between five and nine years of age, and dropping off sharply thereafter. Gastrointestinal disturbances follow a similar course. For girls, however, there is not a sharp drop-off, as with boys, but an increase to a new high at age 18.

During later childhood, sensorimotor skills are refined and extended. A study by Goodenough showed that speed of response increases steadily throughout these years. There is a similar increase in strength. The interrelation between mental and physical ability is not as large during early childhood, but is still significant. Researchers have generally found that the low correlations commonly found between these factors gradually decline after 14 or 15 years of age, eventuating in negligible correlations in the adult group. Task learning is less specific among younger children, as is indicated by the observation that the correlations between the learning of different motor tasks are higher for that age group.

In recent years, pediatricians and others who work with emotionally disturbed children have come to believe that the hyperactive-child syndrome is the result of some neurological impairment or imbalance—minimal brain dysfunction, or MBD. To support this view, they point out that hyperactive tendencies frequently appear before the child is two years old, that such children are likely to have a history of accidental poisoning or fathers who were also restless and quick-tempered. Amphetamines seem to have a calming effect on many hyperactive children, just the reverse of the effect these drugs usually have on adults. Critics of drug therapy argue that such drugs are dangerous, that they teach drug dependency, and that they are often prescribed on the mere suggestion of teachers or school officials. Furthermore, there is some question about the validity of MBD as a valid diagnostic category.

The immediate causes of anger shift with age. The older child has more problems with social relationships, especially with his peers. Although the child becomes more specific in the expression of anger and hostility, he learns to be devious and relies more on sneers, sarcasm and name-calling. Fear is still very much present in the life of children of this age range. Research has shown that a large part of these fears are unrealistic and that realistic fears of a mundane sort are relatively low in frequency. A study by Jersild and Holmes revealed that over 40% of their subjects' childhood fears persisted into adulthood. The term "anxiety" has two somewhat different meanings: an emotional state, or a personality trait. The former meaning refers to the pervasive apprehensiveness we feel when we are uncertain about the way things will turn out. It is a socialized emotion, and the person who lacks anxiety is likely to be without empathy. On the other hand, too much anxiety may lead to an intense self-concern that interferes with good social adjustment. *Repression* and *rationalization* are two of the many mechanisms that all of us use to reduce anxiety. Anxiety has also been investigated as a personality trait. In contrast to low-anxious children, high-anxious children do better on simple tasks, but more poorly on more complex ones. Moderate levels of anxiety facilitate learning, while levels either too high or too low tend to interfere. There is also an increase in anxiety as children develop more mature play patterns. Relatively little research has been conducted on the affectively pleasant emotions of

the school-aged child. The little that has been done shows that as the child grows older, his wishes and desires are less specific and more inclusive and social.

As formulated by Piaget, the child enters the period of *concrete operations* at age seven. He begins to use *formal operations* between ages 11 and 15. Before considering these stages, it is necessary to define what Piaget means by an operation. An operation is a cognitive act that is part of some pattern of acts. It may be seen in adding or placing an object in a class or space. Concrete operations are differentiated from formal operations in that they are limited to the manipulation or arrangement of concrete objects. Formal operations use representational thought and may be thought of as logical rules. One characteristic of formal operations is reversibility, the ability to return to the starting point and begin again.

Piaget was especially interested in the development of conceptions of physical causality. Five of the 17 types of causal thinking he identified are: (1) phenomenistic causality, (2) animistic causality, (3) dynamic causality, (4) mechanical causality, and (5) explanation by logical deduction. The first three types are precausal, the fourth is transitional, and the last belongs in the category of formal operations. Deutsche found a decrease in phenomonistic causality and corresponding increase in logical deduction with increasing age. Mogar found that repeated testing of causal reasoning capability improved children's performance on similar tasks. Piaget's contrast between childish and adult thinking is probably exaggerated and the bulk of the evidence is against the abrupt shifting from one stage of conceptualization to another. The child's concepts of space and time also change during middle and late childhood. The conservation of relationships of *speed* do not appear until around seven or eight years of age. Fraisse tested children aged six, eight, and ten for their ability to reproduce time intervals of .5 to 20 seconds. The major age difference was the gross underestimation of the longest time intervals by the youngest subjects.

Language is an integral aspect of cognitive development. A study of stories told by children aged 9 to 15 revealed that complexity and length increased with age and had not reached a mature level by age 15. Werner and Kaplan placed nonsense words in various contexts in an attempt to duplicate the circumstances in which language is normally acquired. Their subjects had considerable difficulty, either failing to differentiate the meaning of the word from the sentence as a whole, or giving too inclusive a meaning to the word. Research with kindergarteners and first graders shows that they tend to use the first and last letters in a word as cues for recognition, rather than the word's shape.

Intelligence, according to Woodworth, is one of those nouns that should be considered a verb. It is always expressed in some behavior. Intelligence is also related to learning and is an integrated way of behaving which the individual uses to adapt to his exchanging environment. Spearman held that there was a general factor, g, influencing all intelligent behavior, and many special factors, s. Thurstone disagreed, believing that intelligence is composed of mutually exclusive group factors. Piaget and many other psychologists take issue with such factor theories. The first effective tests of intelligence for schoolchildren were developed in 1905 by Binet and Simon, and revised by Terman in 1916. Terman also introduced the IQ, which was computed by dividing mental age by chronological age and multiplying the result by 100. This measure has proved to have statistical problems, and has been replaced by the "deviation IQ," which tells us how the child's test scores compares with the norms for children his age.

Wechsler has developed an individual intelligence test which gives more information regarding the cognitive functioning of the child than the Stanford-Binet test. Because the Stanford-Binet includes more verbal material, it is a better predictor of school performance. A number of paper-and-pencil group tests correlate even more highly with school success because they present problems similar to those encountered in school.

Many people have questioned the validity of IQ tests. Do the tests, they ask, have any demonstrable relationship to behavior as assessed by any outside criterion? Generally, IQ tests correlate with a number of other measures, such as school success, and their better-than-chance predictions are sufficient reason for their use as research instruments. For predictions for the individual child, however, some caution must be exercised. Exceptions do occur and individual scores may be misleading. With groups of subjects, intelligence tests correlate highly with school marks, tests in arithmetic, and achievement test scores. Most of these measures depend on both learning ability and motivation. Intelligence test results are correlated not only with school success but also with such diverse factors as popularity, socioeconomic status, artistic ability, leadership, and athletic ability.

There is some controversy regarding the genetic origins of intelligence. For many years, psychologists have taken the stand that inherited competence varied from person to person, but that the development of this potential depended on environmental factors. Most psychologists would agree that both factors interact and thus contribute to variations in IQ, and reject the idea as unproven that genetic differences between races lead to intelligence differences. Jensen claims that 80% of the variance is attributable to genetic influences and that some racial and social groups have lower IQs because of differences in genetic potential. He also notes that children from different SES levels and racial groups are equal in *basic learning ability* (BLA), but differ in problem-solving ability. The latter ability, he claims, is basic to IQ and is largely genetically determined. Guinagh tested Jensen's contentions by attempting to train Negro and white children with both high and low BLA in the kinds of concepts used in a nonverbal, "culture-fair" intelligence test. When the children were tested, it was found that both black and white children with high BLA benefited from the training and children with low BLA

did not, suggesting that BLA is not as invariant as Jensen maintains. Another study that raises questions about a narrowly genetic interpretation of IQ differences found no differences between intelligence scores of black children from middle class and welfare families between 18 and 24 months of age. By age three, however, the usual SES differences in IQ had appeared. Although Jensen endorses continuation of attempts to stimulate intellectual development of children, his other statements have been widely used by individuals and groups who oppose such programs.

15 Parental Influences, Behavior Tendencies, and the Self

Parental Influences

The widening social scene to which the older child is exposed renders parental influence less crucial than it is with younger children. Nevertheless, as expressed in attitudes and patterns, it requires some attention. The first matter to be considered is consistency of maternal attitudes. This will be followed by some representative findings on parental attitudes and family patterns.

Consistency of Maternal Attitudes

Consistency of maternal attitudes poses the problem of whether mothers behave differently toward older children from the way they behaved toward them when they were younger. As might be expected, both similarities and differences have been found.

In studying this problem, Schaefer and Bayley (1960) utilized data from the longitudinal Berkeley Growth Study sample. Observational data had been collected in the research center during the child's first three years. Interview data in the child's home were obtained when he was between 9 and 14. The framework for the analysis was the circumplex model which has been used by a number of researchers to classify mothers' and children's behavior. The model was developed by Schaefer (1959, 1961), who found that it reflected the *molar* or overall dimensions of mother-child interaction better than the *molecular* or piecemeal approaches used by other researchers. One of Schaefer's circumplex models is presented as

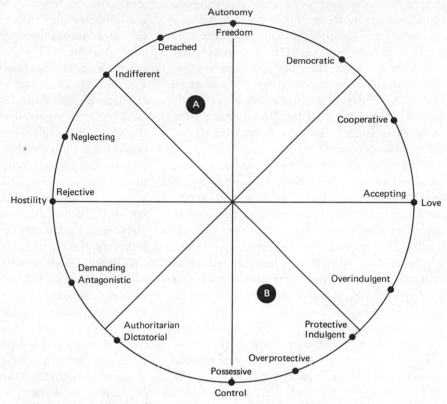

Figure 15-1. A hypothetical model of dimensions of maternal behavior. (After Schaefer, 1959.)

Figure 15-1. The various behavior descriptions represent ends of behavioral continua: *democratic*, for example, is the opposite of *authoritarian-dictatorial*, and *neglecting* is the opposite of *overindulgent*. The "ideal" maternal behavior would be found in the upper right-hand sector of the model, close to the outside of the circle. Any type of behavior can be plotted, theoretically, in terms of this model. Mother A on Figure 15-1 would be colder, more off-hand than Mother B. Mother B would be warmer than Mother A, but would at the same time permit her children less freedom. Bayley and Schaefer (1960) found a considerable degree of consistency in mothers'

behavior, using positions on the circumplex model: their ratings for love versus hostility during infancy correlated .68 with the same dimensions of the same mothers' behavior during their children's preadolescence. In other words, there was a considerable degree of consistency of affection. Those mothers who were relatively more affectionate toward their infants were also more affectionate toward them as preadolescents, whereas those who were initially less affectionate, tended to remain less affectionate.

When the many experiences of the intervening years which would blur the relationship are taken into consideration, a remarkable degree of consistency of attitude emerges. Other factors, however, might account for differences. For example, different measures were used: in the earlier period, infant observation and later, parental interview. Moreover, there were different settings: earlier, the research center and later, the child's home. The substantial correlation in affection might have been even higher had not these procedural differences occurred.

These factors are actually mentioned for another reason. The second major finding of the Schaefer and Bayley analysis was an insignificant correlation between restrictiveness, or autonomy versus control, at the two age levels. This correlation coefficient may reflect a true lack of relationship between maternal attitudes of restrictiveness at the two ages or it may be that these differences affected restrictiveness more than affection. The investigators chose to accept the former alternative.

They concluded that there were greater changes over time in autonomy versus control than in love versus hostility. On one dimension, love versus hostility, the mothers were consistent; on the other dimension, autonomy versus control, they were inconsistent. It is plausible to believe that maternal restrictiveness would change over time. The amount of restrictiveness a young child needs, say at three, is more or less constant one child to the next; that required by a 14-year-old varies according to his individual degree of maturity. Some preadolescents would need almost as much supervision and restriction as they did when much younger; others would not. Maternal affection, on the other hand, is less likely to change with time.

Parental Disposition and Children's Adjustment

The circumplex model displayed in Figure 15-1 has been shown to apply both to parental and to child behavior (Schaefer, 1961). The kind of behavior displayed by a parent appears to foster similar behavior in children, generally speaking. This is particularly true of behavior in the aggressive side of the model. Leonard D. Eron and others (1963) had 451 children in a semirural school rate each other on a scale of aggressiveness. The parents of the children were then questioned as to their policies on punishment. A comparison of the sociometric ratings with ratings of parental discipline showed that the more the punishment at home, the more the aggression at school. The results held true for boys and girls alike, and it did not matter whether the father or the mother was the punisher.

Goodwin Watson (1957) conducted a study which compared teachers' and psychologists' ratings of a sample of children from permissive homes with a sample from strict homes. An analysis of the ratings showed that those from the permissive homes tended to score higher in independence, cooperativeness, persistence, creativity (including spontaneity, originality, and the use of imagination), and friendliness. The children from the strict homes rated higher in dependence, negativism, energy level, conformity, and hostility. The children from strict homes were also rated as being more easily discouraged and more easily frustrated in learning. There was no difference between the groups with respect to self-control during frustration, passivity, or anxiety.

Another study of more than passing interest was conducted by Murray and Seghorn (1970), who investigated the background of sexually dangerous persons, men who had been convicted of forceable rape. Inasmuch as this crime rates high on a scale of antisocial aggression, we would expect, from the research findings we have cited at various points in this book, that the early life of these men would be marked by a high degree of parental aggression, and this is, indeed, what the investigators found in a sizable number of cases. In such instances, the offender's father was likely to be a physically cruel person who would often incite, support, and demand physically aggressive behavior from his son. All encounters with the father were characterized by feelings of fear and anger. The mother was likely to have been a passive woman with intense needs to nurture her son. In a number of instances, her indulgence included the giving of drugs, excusing her son's immoral and inappropriate behavior, and self-deception regarding the difficulties experienced by her children in their failures to achieve an adequate social adjustment. What such a mother did *not* give was freedom and independence. Instead, she used her passive, dependent behavior to tie her son closely to her. On the one hand, the offender saw his mother as kind, understanding, and giving, but on the other, he had a feeling of being engulfed or entangled with her. Whereas the fathers of these offenders would be placed at the far left of the circumplex model in Figure 15-1, the mothers would be placed in the lower right-hand sector, in the protective-indulgent area.

One significant variable that often emerges in studies of child rearing is the family's socioeconomic status (SES). Waters and Crandall (1964) found that the SES of a family was essentially unrelated to maternal nurturance and affection, but that it had a definite relationship with coerciveness. The higher the SES of the mothers they surveyed, the less the likelihood that the mothers would use coercive and threatening suggestions, restrictive regulations, and severe penalties for misbehavior. Their survey covered a span of 20 years, from 1940 to 1960, and their evidence showed that during that period there was a tendency for middle-class mothers to become more permissive.

Bayley and Schaefer (1960), in analyzing data from the Berkeley Growth Study, got similar results. The higher the SES of a mother, the more likely she was to be warm, understanding, and accepting, and the less likely to be controlling, irritable, and punitive. SES-related differences, incidentally, were greater for the mothers of boys than of girls.

SES differences in families were also found to be associated with the personal adjustment of children. Burchinal, Gardner, and Hawkes (1958) administered a personality questionnaire to fifth-grade children in midwestern schools. Here are the mean scores, categorized as to fathers' occupation (the higher the score, the poorer the adjustment): unskilled, 42; skilled or semiskilled, 39; professional and business, 36. One interesting finding that emerged was that children whose parents had continued in university beyond the bachelor's degree were somewhat more maladjusted than other middle-class children. Otherwise, maladjustment declined as the family's social status increased.

It seems to be a reasonable assumption that neurosis should breed neurosis—that is, parents who have more than the usual number of problems of adjustment would be likely to have poorly adjusted children. This proposition was tested by Wolking, Quast, and Lawton (1966), who administered the Minnesota Multiphasic Personality Inventory (MMPI) to parents of children referred to a clinic for psychiatric treatment. When their scores were analyzed they were found to reflect a considerable degree of maladjustment, with more signs of personal psychopathology and poor interpersonal adaptation, in contrast to scores made by the average person. A recurring personality pattern in the "clinic parent" was that of the individual who outwardly conforms, but who expresses hostile and rebellious feelings in indirect ways. Many had established friendships with marginal, highly aggressive individuals, thereby gratifying their own antisocial tendencies. The writers commented that a parent of this type "serves both as a model and a source of vicarious reinforcement for his child's unacceptable behavior, thereby shaping this type of behavior in the child by two of the most powerful methods known."

Another study compared projective test protocols of boys referred to a child guidance center with those of their brothers. If we can accept the thesis that there is something in the family situation of an emotionally disturbed child that leads him to be disturbed, it becomes quite interesting to find out why his siblings are not disturbed enough to be referred. In this study, Jarmon and Duhamel (1969) asked patients and their brothers to place two-dimensional figures representing the child, the father, mother, and the other members of a family on a dark background. The test enabled the researcher to observe the placement of the figures and the distance between them and to draw conclusions as to the relationship between the child's problems and his perception of family relations. The same test was also given to boys who were not clinic patients and not in the family, in order to secure a pool of control-group responses. The results showed that in contrast to the control group boys, both the "clinic children" and their brothers placed the family figures further apart, thus suggesting a greater degree of psychological distance among the members of the clinic families. The researchers took this to mean that the clinic children were the products of disturbed family units, marked by poor marital relationships, rather than products of any specific kind of child-parent relationship. An interesting finding was that the clinic children were more likely to place the child's figure *between* the parents, whereas their brothers were more likely to place the parents *together* and the child *apart*. This placement suggests that the clinic children were less able to avoid involvement in parental disputes and other shared maladjustments.

Dependence and Independence Tendencies

The widening scope of psychosocial relationships in later childhood has repercussions in dependent-independent behaviors. Parental influences have a lessening importance and teacher and peer influences an increasing importance, as we shall see in the next chapter. At the moment this will be reflected by a relatively short discussion of dependence-independence in relation to parental influences, which in turn indicates the relative paucity of studies concerning children of this age.

As with maternal attitudes earlier in the chapter, stability of child behavior through time is of interest. In this instance it concerns stability of dependency behavior. Using Fels Research Institute data collected on children when they were between three and six, six and nine, and again between 20 and 29, Kagan and Moss (1960) studied the amount and kind of dependence they exhibited at these three age periods. While one psychologist examined the information in the files on dependence when the subjects were children, another interviewed each one about the extent of his dependence in adulthood. Without knowledge of each other's findings, each psychologist rated 54 subjects on various aspects of passive and dependent behavior.

Correlations of dependency measures at age three with those at six and at six with those at ten were fairly high for girls, but somewhat lower for boys. General dependence at the younger of the two ages correlated .61 and .63 respectively with emotional dependence and instrumental dependence in girls when they were older, but only .37 and .38 in boys. Correlations for both sexes and both ages with the dependence behavior they showed as adults were, generally speaking, positive. This showed that there was some consistency between being more dependent or less dependent and status in this respect as adults. Even more important were two specific findings: (a) The dependence ratings for ages six to ten were much more related to adult dependency status than were those for ages three to six. (b) For girls aged six to ten there were many more significant correlations (60%) with adult dependency status than there were for boys (9%). In other words, consistency of dependency between childhood and adulthood was much greater for girls than for boys.

The relatively greater amount of dependency responses in girls has been noted on several occasions. The new finding, greater relationship of adult to past dependency in girls, fits that pattern. Greater positive relationships for girls as compared to boys are probably to be accounted for by the fact that young girls are less punished for passive and dependent behavior as children, and, that as adults, they are still encouraged to be more passive. For example, dependent women in this sample consulted their family about purchases, had strong needs to keep a close tie with their family, and lived as closely as possible to them. To put the same point another way, there is an expectancy of a shift away from dependence in boys when they become men. This is reflected in the lower correlations obtained. Individual case analysis showed that a greater proportion of men than women shifted from high dependency in childhood to relative independence as adults, which supports this interpretation.

This study is of considerable importance. To be able to collect information about six- to ten-year-old children and from it predict adult patterns of dependence with reasonable precision is something of a scientific triumph.

Anita Whiting (1971) conducted an interesting study of the relationship between child-rearing practices and school achievement. The subjects in Whiting's study were elementary school boys and their parents. The boys were all above average in intelligence, with IQs averaging between 113 and 114. Half of them were performing well, academically speaking; they were getting A's and B's, their achievement test scores were above grade level, and teachers described them as showing initiative, completing assigned work, and functioning independently. The other half were getting D's and F's, and their achievement test scores were about six months below the expected grade level. Teachers saw these boys as demanding attention, being unconcerned about failure, continually seeking help, and failing to complete assignments.

The parents of both groups of boys were seen together for interviews and testing either in their home or in the psychologist's office. (Incidentally, none of the parents whose sons were nonperformers wanted the psychologist to come to their homes, while the other parents preferred to be interviewed in their homes.) The session was taken up with each parent independently filling out a questionnaire, the Age-Independence Scale (AIS), whereupon they participated together in a standardized interview. The AIS is a list of 110 common activities and tasks, pertaining to self-care, cognitive facility, physical skills, social responsibility, autonomy, and wide experience. Each parent was asked to indicate the age at which his son should have attained mastery of each activity or task and also to indicate the ones he thought were most significant.

Whiting's results showed that, in general, parents of successful boys expected independence and mastery of tasks *earlier* than did the parents of the less successful ones. The difference was particularly marked on the Autonomy scale, where the parents of successful boys expected mastery a year earlier, on the

Parental influence

Although the peer group begins to have some effect on children's attitudes during the middle years, the fact that they are still dependent on their parents means that the latter are still the major influence in their capacities: as sources of love, as authority figures, as sources of values and as models.

average, than did the other parents. When it came to selecting items that were most important to the parent, there was no difference on Cognitive Facility; both groups thought the tasks important. Nor was there much difference on the Physical Skills scale, whose activities were not thought to be very important. There were differences on the other scales, however. Parents of the successful boys were more inclined to stress items from the Autonomy and Social Responsibility scales, whereas the other parents were more likely to emphasize those on the Wide Experience and Self-Care scales.

Another point that emerged from the interview was that the fathers of unsuccessful boys seemed unaware of the school difficulties faced by their sons, either because their wives had not told them or because they felt the problems were typical for boys that age. The fathers of the successful boys, however, enjoyed a closer relationship with their sons and were keenly aware of what was going on at school.

Achievement, independence, and self-esteem are likely to go together. Maw and Maw (1966), noted that a child who scores high on curiosity: (1) reacts positively to new, strange, or incongruous stimuli by moving toward them in order to explore or manipulate them; (2) is strongly motivated to find out more about himself and his environment; (3) seeks new experiences; (4) shows persistence in examining or exploring stimuli in order to understand them better.

Maw and Maw asked teachers to rate fifth graders on their curiosity and at the same time collected sociometric data dealing with curiosity from their classmates. The parents of children scoring the highest and the lowest on a composite of these measures were also given the Parental Attitudes Research Instrument (PARI) to complete. Differences between the two groups of parents were in the expected direction, but only in the case of boys.

Fathers of high-curiosity boys, in contrast to the other fathers, were less inclined to foster dependence on the part of their sons or to punish them harshly, and were more egalitarian or democratic in their relations with them. Mothers of high-curiosity boys, in contrast to the other mothers, also did less to foster their sons' dependency. They were, furthermore, less inclined than the other mothers to shelter their sons from outside influences and were less intrusive (meddling) in their sons' lives.

Achievement Motivation

The need to achieve in older children is closely related to independence training received from their mothers. This relationship was clearly demonstrated by Winterbottom (1958) in the following manner. She studied the role of the mother in supplying her boy with learning experiences that would develop independence and a desire for mastery, and then related these measures of independence training to measures of the boy's own needs for achievement (n Ach). Her subjects were 29 eight- to ten-year-old boys and their mothers in a small, middle-class community. The mothers were questioned concerning the number of demands they made for independent accomplishment in their children, the age at which they wanted these accomplishments to be evident, the number of restrictions they placed on independent activity on the part of their children, and the age at which they wanted the restrictions to be learned. To anticipate one aspect of her results, analysis of the items showed that the crucial discriminating ones concerning independence development centered on the child being able to "do" for himself, as in selecting clothes and choosing friends. She also collected teachers' ratings of indices of n Ach expressed by the children.

To measure n Ach, she asked each boy to tell stories after giving them brief verbal descriptions, such as "A mother and her son. They look worried." One set of four stories was given under so-called relaxed conditions in which every effort was made to put the boy at his ease. Another set of four stories was given under so-called achievement orientation; just preceding the story telling, the boy was told that he was to take a puzzle test (a form board) which would show how smart he was, and that his results would be compared with those of the others in his class. After the puzzle he told stories to the second set of verbal descriptions. The stories for both sets were scored for achievement-related imagery. Stories under achievement orientation were significantly greater in the amount of achievement imagery. Winterbottom considered this to demonstrate that the achievement orientation did, in fact, increase achievement imagery. Consequently, the method used actually measured n Ach.

Two groups of children were isolated, one high and the other low in n Ach. It was found that boys with high need for achievement were given earlier training for independence by their mothers, earlier (but fewer) restrictions on independent activity, and earlier demands for learning these restrictions. Early independence training by mothers clearly engendered stronger achievement motivation in their children. The high need achievers, as evaluated by their teachers, rated as trying harder, taking more pleasure in success, being more independent, and being more popular than low need achievers.

A rather specific aspect of achievement motivation is task mastery, a desire to complete tasks, even though failure occurred in previous attempts. Younger children have not yet developed to the point at which they manifest a desire for such mastery. In a study by Crandall and Rabson (1960), an older group of

29 six-, seven- and eight-year-olds was given the same tasks as the younger children. These consisted of two wire picture puzzles of equal difficulty. Each child was allowed to complete one puzzle, but on the second he was made to fail by being told his time was up; actually this was decided not by the time he had used, but by the fact he had five of the seven pieces of the puzzle in place. After working on both puzzles he was told that he could work again on the one of the two puzzles and that he was to choose which one. The investigators also collected ratings in free-play settings concerning such behaviors as the amount of help sought from adults and from peers, the amount of approval sought from adults and from peers, and the children's readiness to withdraw from threatening situations.

It was found that the older children preferred to repeat the previously failed puzzle, as contrasted with the younger children who preferred to repeat the successfully completed one. When the results of an earlier study of the same problem by Rosenzweig (1945), who used still older children, were related to theirs, Crandall and Rabson concluded that task mastery appears to develop gradually with age, at least through preadolescence.

A sex difference, not evident at the younger ages, was clearly present by the early grade school age. Boys were found to prefer doing the previously failed puzzle more often than were the girls. Moreover, by this same age, boys were found to be less dependent on peers and adults for help and approval and less ready to withdraw from threatening situations than were girls. It will be noted that this phase of achievement motivation shows relationship to independence-dependence striving.

These results are congruent with those of Winterbottom. She found that independence training of boys was initiated earlier and emphasized more than for girls. Girls, both studies found, seem to show more passivity and open dependence than boys and, to return to the issue under discussion, less desire for task mastery.

Parental attitudes toward 40 boys of high and of low need for achievement were assessed in the home setting by Rosen and D'Andrade (1959). These boys performed several achievement tasks while their parents observed them and commented on their performance. The investigators noted parental behavior and verbalization as their sons carried out their tasks.

In contrast to parents of sons showing low need for achievement, parents of boys with high need for achievement held higher aspirations and expectations for their sons' performances. They gave more approbation when performances were good and more readily criticized incompetent efforts. They tended to allow their sons latitude in choice of tasks to perform, but once the boys had decided, they held them to high performance in these tasks. Parents with boys showing high need for achievement, then, showed high aspiration and allowed freedom of choice, but once a task was selected, maintained high performance expectations.

The stability and validity of achievement fantasy in the same children at different ages has been studied by Kagan and Moss (1960), who used data gathered from parents and children associated with the Fels Research Institute. Achievement fantasy was measured by the TAT at approximately ages 9, 11 and 14. As age increased, the achievement themes increased for both boys and girls. Moreover, a fair degree of stability of achievement fantasy was also found. Amount of achievement fantasy themes on the first testing was significantly associated with that on the second and third testings. In other words, the children showed some tendency to retain their relative position in the group on amount of achievement fantasy despite its general increase over the age period studied.

Degree of maternal concern with achievement during the first three years of the child's life had been rated on the home visits by the staff. It was found that girls, whose mothers showed greater concern, had higher achievement fantasy scores six years later. Moreover, mothers with greater concern for their daughters' achievement actually had girls showing significant IQ *gains* from tests given on the semiannual testing during the years in question.[1] For boys no correlation was found between degree of maternal concern at age three and later achievement fantasy, or IQ gain. Both among girls and boys there was a generally positive (although nonlinear) relation between the amount of achievement fantasy and the gain in IQ. In other words, boys and girls who showed increased achievement strivings at age 14, as compared to that shown at eight or nine years of age, tended to reveal a greater increase in IQ than children not showing this increase in striving. It would seem as if "trying" does make a difference.

The researchers also found some indications that when the education of the same-sex parent was relatively greater, there was an increase in their children's achievement fantasy. It is plausible to believe a more highly educated parent would be more concerned with achievement and would communicate this concern to his child. Overall it would seem that achievement fantasy serves as an index of the children's tendency to seek achievement goals.

Need for achievement expressed between the ages of six and ten has proven to be highly predictive of similar adult tendencies. As children, the subjects had been evaluated for

[1] This finding is particularly significant because other Fels Institute data show that IQs of boys are generally more likely to increase during childhood years, whereas most of the decreases occur with girls (Sontag, Baker, and Nelson, 1958).

achievement behavior (tendency to persist with challenging tasks, and degree of involvement in tasks to which a standard of excellence was applicable). An investigator who had no knowledge of the results obtained in childhood interviewed and rated 71 Fels subjects again when they were between 20 and 30 years of age. Two areas on which he made evaluations were achievement behavior (attempts to master tasks for which self-satisfaction rather than social recognition was the goal) and concern for intellectual competence (value placed on intelligence, knowledge, and academic achievement regardless of whether goal is inner standards or social recognition). Ratings on achievement behavior at six to ten correlated with similar ratings in adulthood, .46 for males and .38 for females. Ratings on achievement behavior at six to ten correlated with concern for intellectual competence, .69 for males and .49 for females. Relationships at younger ages (first three years and ages three to six) were either unrelated or much less closely related to adult behavior. To translate chronological age into the corresponding school years, the measures taken during the first five years of schooling proved prognostic of adult mastery (Moss and Kagan, 1961).

Overall, the Fels investigators consider the period between the ages of six and ten to be crucial for the development of motivation to master intellectual tasks. If the child's experiences during these years are self-reassuring and give him freedom from too strong dependence on his parents, this desire develops. Since it proves to be highly correlated with achievement behavior in adulthood, it makes for an effective, problem solving, successfully competitive adult (Sontag and Kagan, 1963).

It is a routine finding that SES differences are related to achievement motivation. Rosen (1962), for example, found a consistent relationship between SES and the amount of

achievement and independence training received by boys in both Brazil and the United States, even though the overall mean for n Ach was lower in Brazil than in the United States. In another study, Rosen (1964) analyzed children's perceptions of their parents and found that middle-class boys saw their parents as more competent, accepting, emotionally secure, and interested in their achievements than did boys from lower-class homes. As the research cited in this section has shown, it is the parental expectations for achievement that has the most powerful effect on the extent to which a boy develops n Ach. If his parents do not express confidence in him, it is difficult for him to have confidence in himself.

The Development of Self- and Social Awareness

Each child in his own way, as he moves through infancy and childhood, reaches some sort of understanding of himself and of other persons. He acquires knowledge about and attitudes toward himself and others. Certainly, the older child has increased self-awareness, often expressed in self-consciousness. Entering school exposes each child to the always sharp, often critical, and sometimes unfriendly eyes of his classmates. Every foible, every weakness is open to them, and their comments range from such direct appellations as "Fatso," "Skinny," "Dopey," and "Four-eyes" to more individual and subtle, but equally critical, comments. A sharpening of the sense of self could hardly fail to develop under this regime.

Consideration of the self will center on self-esteem (self-acceptance), the ego-ideal (ideal self), and an issue closely related to the self, empathy (ability to take the other person's role). Despite the essential privateness of the child's self-concept, it is at least partially revealed in his behavior. It is only because of this that it is possible to suppose that poor or good self-concepts would have correlations in good or poor adjustment and that empathy might be measurable.

Studies of Self-Esteem

The antecedents of self-esteem were studied by Stanley Coopersmith (1967, 1968) who administered a 50-item Self-Esteem Inventory to children in fifth- and sixth-grade classes. Teachers were also asked to rate the children on behaviors presumed to be related to self-esteem; this enabled Coopersmith to secure two ratings on each child: one subjective and one behavioral. Background data were gathered in the course of a 2½-hour interview with each child's mother, and each child was also queried as to parental attitudes and practices. In addition, projective tests of personality were administered to each child. In more than 80% of the cases, the children's self-ratings were confirmed by the data from outside sources.

A part of the research dealing with boys showed that those who had a high degree of self-esteem were active, expressive children who were successful both academically and socially. In discussions, they played active roles, eagerly expressed their opinions, did not avoid disagreement, were not especially upset by criticism, showed little destructiveness, and were little troubled by anxiety.

Boys in the middle ranges of self-esteem were quite similar to the high-self-esteem boys, but with more conventional values and behavior patterns. They tended to be somewhat uncertain in their self-ratings and were more dependent on social acceptance than were the high-self-esteem boys.

The low-self-esteem boys tended to be discouraged, depressed, timid, and convinced of their inferiority. In social groups, they were the listeners, easily upset by criticism, self-

conscious, and preoccupied with emotional problems. Eager for social contact, they were unable to secure it; their bungling attempts at socializing only served to alienate them further from the peer group.

Some flavor of the differences between the three types of boys are shown by the sketches in Figure 15–2. The instructions were: "Draw a person and complete the drawing in 10 minutes." The drawing on the left is by a low-self-esteem boy; it seems to reflect feelings of tentativeness and inadequacy. The second drawing, by a middle-self-esteem boy, is bolder and more definite. When it is compared to the third drawing, done by a high-self-esteem boy, it seems conventional and uninteresting. The third drawing has considerable interest and energy, as well as a touch of humor—all characteristics of the high-self-esteem boys.

Coopersmith noted that his data contradicted a number of popular clichés about child rearing. He found no consistent relationship between children's self-esteem and height, physical attractiveness, size of family, early traumatic or upsetting experiences, breast- or bottle-feeding during infancy, or mother's employment outside the home. The amount of time parents spent with their children was not significant, but what was important was their interest in the children's welfare, concern about their companions, availability for the discussion of problems, and participation in family fun.

Another surprising finding was that the parents of high-self-esteem children were stricter and less permissive than those with medium and low self-esteem. They insisted on high standards of behavior and were firm and consistent in the enforcement of rules. Their discipline was not harsh, however, and they were less punitive than other parents in the survey. The parents of low-self-esteem children tended to be extremely permissive but inflicted harsh punishment when their

Figure 15-2. Drawings made by low-, medium-, and high-self-esteem boys as part of a draw-a-person test. (Coopersmith, 1968. Reprinted by permission.)

children gave them trouble. The latter children considered their parents to be unfair, and they interpreted the absence of definite rules and limits as indicating that their parents were not interested in them.

Although the parents of high-self-esteem children set limits, there was considerable latitude for individual variation. The limits thus established were reasonable, rational, appropriate to the child's age, and not arbitrary and inflexible. At the same time, these parents exerted greater demands than the other parents for academic performance and excellence. The parents themselves were active, poised, self-assured individuals, who led active lives outside the context of the family and did not rely on the family for sole and necessary sources of gratification. It seems clear that in this they served as social learning models for their children.

With respect to other correlates of self-esteem, Lipsitt (1958) found that low-self-esteem children were more troubled by anxiety, as measured by the Children's Manifest Anxiety Scale. Another set of studies demon-strated that early onset of puberty was associated with the development of favorable self-concepts. In a comparison of physically accelerated boys and girls with those who were late in maturing, the latter consistently showed less favorable self-concepts in their responses to TAT pictures. It seems that slower physical development exposed the child to an environment that had an adverse effect on his conception of his own personality development, whereas more rapid physical development led to an environment that enhanced the self-concept (Mussen and Jones, 1957; Jones and Mussen, 1958).

The self-concepts of children whose achievement at school is higher than would ordinarily be expected from their IQ (overachievers) have been compared with those whose achievement is lower than that which would be expected (underachievers). In a study by Ann M. Walsh (1956), two such carefully matched groups of elementary school pupils were compared. She found that underachievers showed distinctly more signs of inhibition, insecurity, and defensiveness.

The middle years of childhood

Influences on the development of the self come from diverse sources: imitation of adult models, cooperative and collaborative relations with adults, fantasy playing of adult roles, participation in games and rituals, relationships with other children in a closely knit peer group.

In still another study, this time involving high school boys, the underachievers and over-achievers differed little in self-described emotional and school adjustment, but considerably more underachievers described themselves as restless, undependable, and as belonging to cliques who showed negative attitudes toward school and opposition to authority. The investigators interpreted their findings as supporting a view that underachievers' behavior was "asocialized," that is, a mild form of delinquency which takes its major focus from the groups with which these particular children associate, the peer clique groups (Morrow and Wilson, 1961).

The usual finding that underachievers tend to have a poorer emotional and social adjustment than children who achieve more adequately does not hold true in all cultures. Lindgren and Mello (1965) administered a Portuguese version of the Bell Adjustment Inventory and a sentence-completion test measuring adjustment to fourth-grade overachievers and underachievers in a school in São Paulo, Brazil. Unexpectedly, overachievers reported significantly more problems than did underachievers, particularly in emotional adjustment.[2] The extent to which a child is able to meet the demands of the school is likely to be crucial for children's adjustment in the United States and other industrialized countries. The child who succeeds in school is functioning in a way that is more consistent with the values and expectations of his culture than the child who does poorly. Hence the relationship between emotional adjustment and school success is likely to be positive for children in urbanized, industrialized societies. This is less likely to be so in developing countries like Brazil. The authors observed that there seems to be a culturally determined "adjustment norm" in Brazil, probably stronger with lower-class children, that is characterized by such traits as agreeableness and acceptance, low levels of hostility and anxiety, and a low drive to achieve and compete academically. The child who deviates from this norm by setting high academic goals for himself is likely to deviate in other ways—that is, he is likely to have more anxiety and experience poorer relations with his peers than the child who conforms to the cultural norm.

The Ideal Self or Ego-Ideal

The psychological importance of peer group norms to the preadolescent child was shown by a study by Rae Carlson (1963), who compared sixth graders' descriptions of their self-ideal and their parents' description of an "ideal child." An analysis of responses showed that the self-ideals of the children were closer to those of their classmates than they were to those held by their parents for them. Carlson concluded that parental expectations for their children are likely to be outweighed by the fact that peer and community norms have a greater appeal. In other words, by the time a child is 12 years old, the social world outside the family potentially possesses a greater influence on his personality development than his parents do.

Carlson also observed, as have other researchers, that children rating higher in self-esteem were more likely to be accepted by their peers. An additional and unexpected finding was that the parents were more approving and accepting of boys than of girls and that this tendency was even greater for mothers than for fathers. All mothers overes-

[2] Somewhat similar results were reported by Oetting and Dinges (1971), who were perplexed to find that Navajo first graders, who were judged by their teachers to have a high degree of adjustment, actually scored higher on a scale of anxiety than did other Navajo children judged to have a low degree of adjustment.

timated the similarity of their sons to their ideal child, but only two-thirds of the mothers made similar overestimates for their daughters.

A number of studies have focused on differences perceived between an individual's ideal self and what he considers to be his "real self." A common technique in such studies is to have subjects fill out a personality questionnaire once in terms of "the kind of person you really are" and again in terms of "the kind of person you would like to be." The difference between the two sets of ratings thus serves as an index to the disparity between the real and the ideal self. The usual interpretation of the results is that the greater the real-ideal-self disparity, the more the anxiety, guilt, and self-depreciation. Indeed, one of the goals of psychotherapy with adults has traditionally been that of closing the gap between the two self-percepts (Rogers and Dymond, 1954; Friedman, 1955; Turner and Vanderlippe, 1958).

More recent research, however, has raised some questions about such conclusions. A study of the progress of former mental patients, for example, showed that those who were more self-depreciating tended to be more successful in completing a program of rehabilitation (Neff and Koltuv, 1967). It may well be that the individual who is too complacent about himself is the one who is less willing to become involved in self-improvement, and that some degree of self-criticism is necessary for progress in socialization and self-improvement.

The study that is relevant here is one by Phyllis Katz and Edward Zigler (1967) who asked children in the fifth, eight, and eleventh grades to fill out questionnaires in terms of what was true about themselves and what they wished were true of them. The results, as shown in Figure 15-3 show that there was an increasing degree of real-ideal-self

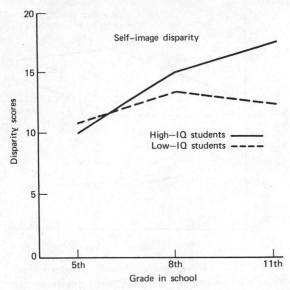

Figure 15-3. Disparity between students' concepts of their "real self" and their "ideal self." (After Katz and Zigler, 1967.)

disparity with age and, furthermore, that children with high IQs had a greater degree of disparity than did low-IQ children. This finding is particularly interesting in view of the fact that one might expect low-IQ children to be more dissatisfied with themselves. Figure 15-4 shows, however, that high-IQ eleventh graders actually thought less well of themselves than did low-IQ students in the same grade and high-IQ students in lower grades. The data suggest, in other words, that more intelligent students become more critical of themselves with age and experience a greater disparity with respect to how they see themselves and what they would like to be, in contrast to low-IQ students, who show little change over the years.

Empathic Ability

Empathic ability, it will be remembered, is the ability to predict the feelings and actions

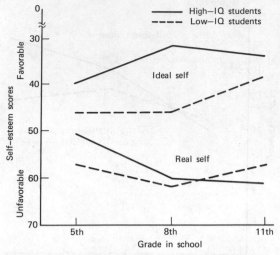

Figure 15-4. Scores for students' ratings of their "real self" and their "ideal self" on a questionnaire measuring self-esteem. (After Katz and Zigler, 1968.)

of others. Studies use the method of comparing a child's estimate of another child's attitudes with the actual attitudes as reported by this other child. Empathy, then, is sensitivity to the attitudes of others.

With younger children empathic ability increases with age as we noted in Chapter 13. For children of the age under discussion, a similar increase in empathic ability with age (or at least with grade) has been demonstrated by Dymond and her associates (1952). As a first step, cards, similar to those in the TAT, but adapted to the children's ages, were given to small groups of second- and sixth-graders with mean ages, respectively, of about 7 and 11. After being told a simple story that accompanied each picture, each child was asked a standard series of questions about the thoughts and feelings of the characters in the story. Potential for empathy was measured by the ease (lack of prodding or of the necessity for asking specific questions) with which the child could voice opinions about a pictured individ-

ual's thoughts and feelings, that is, what is he thinking and feeling. The mean score in "empathy" was significantly higher in the sixth than in the second grade. These results demonstrated that older children, as compared to younger, could express themselves more easily about others' thoughts and feelings. This potential for empathy had no objective reference as to correctness in their expressions. This was studied in the second phase of the study.

A second measure, the social insight test, was given. After judging sociometrically whom in the class he would like to sit with, invite home to a party, and so on, each child judged the extent to which he was liked or disliked by each other member of the class. As a consequence, there was a measure of how the child thought he was liked and another of how he was actually liked. The empathy score was based on the degree of correspondence between the two. The children whose measures indicated agreement between how much they thought they were liked and how much they were actually liked showed high empathy. The children who showed a discrepancy showed low empathy. There was a clear difference that indicated greater empathy on the part of the sixth-graders than the second graders.

Within a grade, the sociometric and empathy scores correlated .26 for the second and .50 for the sixth grade. If every child expects himself to be well-liked, only actually popular children can get a high score on empathy or insight. Hence the relation is about as high in the sixth grade as we might expect. The correlation is so low for the second graders it appears that they show relatively little relation between sociometric or popularity status and empathy or social insight. It will be found from the discussion in the section on friendships that Dymond and her associates observed that second-graders were choosing friends on the basis of external qualities, such as money and a nice home. Certainly, these are not qualities which emphasize understanding or empathy, so it is hardly surprising that those who were most popular were not high in empathy at this age grade level. But, by the sixth grade, children become more aware and better able to assess the feelings of others accurately, as shown by the increased correlation at that age.

Social Attraction

Another facet of the self-social perception problem is the question of a relationship between perceived similarity and the valuation given another person. Davitz (1955) found that the highest sociometric choices tended to be perceived as more similar to the self than the lowest sociometric choices, indeed, more similar to self than they actually were. He did this in a summer camp with a small group of boys and girls of an average age of about 10. They had been together 11 days when the study was conducted. Rankings gave sociometric choices, whereas social perception was measured by an activity inventory, with items consisting of two activities, such as dodge ball and ping pong; the subject was required to make choices between the pairs.

Each child filled out this measure (1) for his own preferences; (2) for his highest sociometric choice; and (3) for his lowest sociometric choice. Perceived similarity was the degree of correspondence between his own responses and his prediction of the responses of the other child, both high or low sociometric choice arrived at by counting the agreements between them. Actual similarity was the degree of correspondence between the child's responses and those predicted for him. As mentioned, Davitz found that the highest sociometric choices were perceived as those more like oneself than the lowest choices. In fact, these highest choices were perceived as

more similar to oneself than they actually were.

This may be interpreted as a tendency to wish to be similar to valued persons—in this case one's peers. One way this is expressed is in the usual pattern of identification, that of trying to make oneself more like others. Here we have another way of being similar—trying to make the other person more like oneself. That is what seems to have been happening in this study. It bears witness to the importance of the peer group.

It is often observed that strong desires to be liked by others actually may interfere with social adjustment. Lahaderne and Jackson (1970) found that sixth-grade girls who scored high on a questionnaire measuring wanting-to-be-liked tendencies were likely to withdraw from classroom activities generally. They tended to be inattentive and had poorer academic achievement than girls scoring low on the questionnaire. Very likely such tendencies go along with general feelings of inferiority and inadequacy, which in turn interfere with one's ability to interact with others.

Sex-role Behaviors

An important dimension of the developing self-concept of the child is his increasing awareness of himself as a male or female. As we noted previously, even in infancy girls and boys are biologically "programmed" to behave in ways characteristic of their sex. These early behavior patterns tend to be reinforced, and the young child normally models his behavior after that of the appropriate parent.

There are some differences between boys and girls with respect to the extent to which they accept their sex roles. Sex-role preference over the age range 5½ to 11½ was investigated by Brown (1957), who found: (a) girls of all ages were significantly more variable in their sex-role preferences than boys; (b) boys show much stronger preference for the masculine role than girls did for the feminine role. Indeed, girls at the kindergarten level showed equal preference for masculine and feminine roles and an even strong preference for the masculine role from the first through the fourth grades. Only in the fifth grade did girls show a stronger preference for the feminine role.

It should be emphasized that Brown's results are stated in terms of averages. Some girls at all ages preferred the feminine role. Nor do his results imply that the girls' identifications may not be feminine. Girls, after all, are more encouraged than boys to engage in activities typical of the opposite sex.

Taking on of adult roles by children is considered by Maccoby (1961) to be an aspect of identification. Role taking is a class of behavior that the child learns from his interactions with his parents, such as the behaviors they perform toward him when carrying out their adult role. They establish rules, apply discipline, scold him, give him medicine, and the like. Whereas the child himself seldom performs these activities overtly for reasons that should be obvious, they do occasionally appear in his play and it is likely that he performs them in fantasy. All children presumably practice some of the adult-role behavior that characterizes their parents. There should be differences from child to child in the amount learned. It is plausible to expect that in social interaction with their peers some children will employ the same kinds of behavior the parents used toward them in similar situations.

Maccoby set herself the task of discovering what conditions lead children to take on adult-role behavior. The specific task she selected was the child's tendency to enforce rules when another child deviated from them. Material about the children from the "pattern" study and the follow-up data when they were in the sixth grade utilized by Sears (1961) in his study of aggression were studied. The 160 sixth-grade children still available from the original preschool sample were given a so-called role-taking questionnaire. Among the scales included was the rule enforcement scale, which contained such items as that of asking whether he would say nothing or tell a boy to pick up the pieces if he saw him break a bottle on the sidewalk while both were walking to school. Scores on this scale supplied information about the amount of rule enforcing the children showed. Antecedents of rule enforcement were sought in the information obtained six years earlier about the parents' behavior toward their children.

Boys high in rule enforcing had parents who had been restrictive (nonpermissive) about their children's impulsive behaviors in the earlier years. Hence, the parents were fairly strict rule enforcers themselves. If the boy was relatively dependent, and if the parents were relatively warm during early childhood, the son's present rule enforcing tendencies became even more closely matched to earlier parental behavior toward him.

Rule-enforcing girls tended to have relatively punitive parents and the match became significantly greater when the child was more, rather than less, dependent on the parents. It would seem that boys and girls, although showing different forms of interrelationships, had both acquired during early childhood some adultlike behavior tendencies manifested in connection with role-taking about rule enforcing.

Remarkable stability has been demonstrated in sex-role related behavior. By extending the data already available at the Fels Research Institute, Kagan and Moss (1962) had material on the same individuals from infancy through adulthood. Their findings became so extensive as to require a tightly written, full-length book. So striking were certain findings that two of the five major topics around which their summary is organized concern matters relevant to the present issue: (a) that an intimate relation exists between behavior change or stability of behavior and the traditional standards for sex-role characteristics; and (b) that sex-role identification is a major governor of behavior.

The basic subject pool consisted of 35 boys and 35 girls who were followed in a longitudinal study in which many variables were observed and analyzed. Of interest here is the relationship between observations of the subjects' behavior when they were between the ages of six and ten and again when they were adults aged 19 to 29. Some of the findings

are presented in Figure 15-5, which graphically summarizes correlations between child behavior and similar adult behaviors.

Inspection of the figure will show that at the left are two pairs of variables—passivity-withdrawal and dependence-dependence on family—in which the correlation is relatively higher in females than in males. The next two pairs—behavior disorganization-anger arousal and heterosexuality-sexuality behavior—show the reverse, that is, higher correlations for males than for females. Male dependence between six and ten is uncorrelated with dependence on the family as an adult but in females these two phenotypically similar behaviors at the two ages correlate positively at .30. This finding is one among the various

Figure 15-5.   Correlations between the behavior of children aged six to ten, and similar forms of behavior displayed by the same individuals as adults. (Kagan and Moss, 1962. Reproduced by permission.)

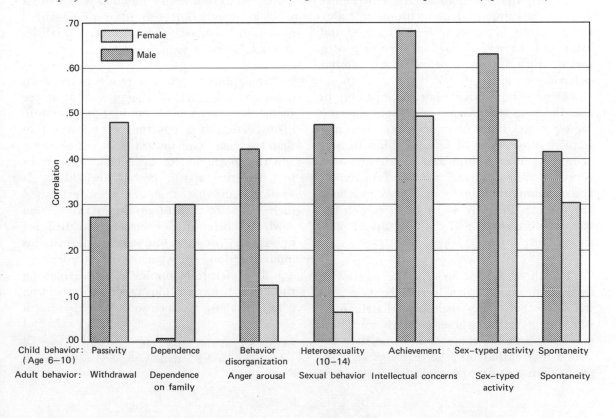

correlations that led to the earlier conclusion that a greater proportion of men than women shifted from high dependence in childhood to relative independence as adults. It is now seen as exemplifying differential sex-typing. Passivity in childhood and withdrawal in adulthood show the same trend, again reflecting the influence of differential cultural pressures. Passivity and dependency are both subject to consistent cultural disapproval in men but not in women. The differential correlations obtained on both relations presumably reflect the rewards and punishments the children received, which differentially reinforced these tendencies in boys as compared to girls.

Behavior disorganization (anger and tantrums) in childhood and anger arousal (aggressive behavior) in adulthood, and heterosexuality in childhood and sexual behavior in adulthood, the next two relations in Figure 15-5, show substantial correlations in males, but relatively low ones in females. Anger and tantrum behaviors in boys were better predictors of adult aggressive behavior than similar behaviors in girls.

The remaining three relations, appearing in the right in the figure, although showing higher correlations in males, also show substantial correlations in females. They involve achievement as a child and intellectual concerns as an adult, and sex-related activities and spontaneity at both ages. These relations are also explained by Kagan and Moss on the basis of differential and similar cultural pressures. They write:

"A low threshold for anger, direct aggressive retaliation, and frequent sexual behavior, on the other hand are disproportionately punished in females, whereas males are given greater license in these areas. The data revealed that childhood rage reactions and frequent dating during preadolescence predicted adult aggressive and sexual predispositions, respectively, for men but not for women. . . .

Intellectual mastery and adoption of appropriate sex-typed interests are positively sanctioned for both sexes, and both of these behaviors showed a high degree of continuity for males and females from the early school years through adulthood" (P. 268).

They go on to summarize:

"The preceding discussion places the construct of sex-role identification in a central position in directing the selective adoption of maintenance of several behavior domains. The expression of aggression, competitiveness, passivity, dependency, or sexuality is determined, in part, by the individual's assessment of the congruence of the behavior with traditional sex-role standards. For many individuals are motivated to behave in a way that is congruent with a hypothetical ego ideal or idealized model that embodies the essential qualities of masculinity or femininity" (P. 271).[3]

The significance of these results at this even more general level, as Kagan and Moss see them, is worthy of examination. Sex-role identification is a governor of behaviors in that the goal state toward which they strive and the incentives for these behaviors are in the cognitive system of the individual. It would seem that these children evaluated their behavior against an internalized standard and behaved not merely as called for by external situation but weighed against this internalization. Each person has an idealized cognitive picture of himself against which he checks his behavior. This model, they believe, is ranged along a dimension of highly mascu-

[3] From Kagan and Moss (1962). Copyright 1962 by John Wiley and Sons and published with permission.

line to highly feminine and is a prime determinant of an adult's behavior.

Perceptions of Parents

Although parental influence begins to wane during the middle years of childhood and the influence of the peer group grows, parents are still psychologically important to children in this age span, as is indicated by their views about the treatment they receive from their parents. Kagan (1956) questioned 217 children about who would be on their side in an argument (friendliness), who would punish them (punitiveness), and who was boss (dominance). The majority of both boys and girls perceived their mothers as friendlier, less punitive, and less dominant than their fathers.

L. Pearl Gardner (1947) studied the perception of the father and of the mother through reports of about 400 boys and girls. She used a questionnaire approach which asked which parent was easier to get along with, who would punish them, and who was the bigger boss. The correspondence to friendliness, punitiveness, and dominance of mothers and fathers as studied by Kagan is apparent. Mothers were perceived as friendlier, less dominant, and about equally punitive. The studies, then, are in essential agreement about friendliness and dominance. Only in connection with punitiveness is there same difference in results.

This discrepancy about punitiveness is easily accounted for when age differences are taken into consideration. The children studied by Kagan ranged from six to ten years of age. The older children of about nine or ten in his sample, both boys and girls, tended to view the same-sex parent as more punitive and dominant than did the younger children. The differential handling of boys and girls as they begin to assume more definitive sex roles is suggested to account for this finding. The children Gardner studied were almost all 10

through 13, thus extending Kagan's age group. Kagan found that as age increased within his sample, punitiveness of the same sex parent increased. In Gardner's group, this had increased to such an extent that the parents were equally punitive. Thus, there is no discrepancy between the results of the two studies. The answer to the question with which these studies were introduced, which qualities are parents perceived as having, appears to be that the father is seen as the source of authority and the mother the source of affection; however, as age increases the same-sex parent assumes more and more a punitive role.

Children's attitudes toward their parents show changes with age. In a study of 3000 children, about equally divided as to sex, ranging in grade from the third to the twelfth, Harris and Tseng (1957) had them reply to sentence completion items with the stems, "My father ———" and "My mother ———." The completions were classified as showing positive, negative, or neutral attitudes toward the particular parent. Illustrative would be "My father is mean" (negative), "My mother is a teacher" (neutral), and "My father is the best in the world" (positive).

Younger boys in grade three were more favorable to their mothers and slightly less so to their fathers. Boys' attitudes toward both parents became steadily less favorable up to the fifth grade where attitudes more or less leveled off with a shift toward slightly greater favorable attitudes in the late high school years.

Lest this gives an incorrect impression, it should be indicated that for these boys even at the point of least favorable attitudes toward the mother, it never went as low as 50% and toward the father never as low as 35%. Girls showed about the same pattern, except, in general, they were throughout somewhat more favorable toward both mothers and fathers. Starting at grade seven, they showed a rather dramatic increase in favorable attitudes toward fathers, but never to the same level as toward their mothers. Through the years of the study the small proportion of boys showing negative attitudes toward mothers or fathers decreased steadily, whereas the small proportion of girls showing negative attitudes increased steadily.

Children are still very much under parental authority. But this authority can be expressed differently and with different outcomes in the perceptions of the children. Basically, authority means restricting and checking behavior. Although having this essential effect, the motivations for wielding authority may stem from different sources on the part of the parents. Exercising authority may arise from restrictive motivation on the part of the parent for authority's sake itself, or it may come from rational motivation on his part for the sake of the child's welfare. Further, either of these motivations may be expressed *concretely* by parents, having reference to restrictions concerning particular objects or events, or either may be expressed *abstractly* in terms of more general relations in which a principle is advanced rather than some sort of dictate laid down.

With these principles to guide him, Pikas (1961) studied several hundred Swedish children by using a variety of specially constructed projective and nonprojective tests. He established that children's perception of parental rational motivation in an abstract form was correlated positively with the children's age and intelligence. In other words, the older and smarter the child, the more ready he was to accept rational, abstractly stated authority. Authoritarian motivations, especially when stated concretely, were negatively correlated with age and intelligence. The older and smarter the child, the more he rejected these ways of expressing authority. It would seem that as children get older, use of rationally imposed, abstractly stated authority is more acceptable and the smarter they are, the sooner this should be instigated.

These findings may well be related to those of Harris and his associates (1954) who showed that responsibility is fostered when they perceive their parents as taking a constructive orientation toward them. Constructive, rational, parental motivation seems to be the most healthful way in which the still necessary authority over children may be expressed if children's perceptions are to be a criterion.

Moral Development

In our discussion so far we have said little about the development of behavior standards that are basic to all forms of social behavior. We have mentioned the emergence of the superego or conscience during the preschool years and shall say more about its development during the middle and final years of childhood. Moral standards, in their more mature form, however, consist of more than the superego's "Thou shalt not's," for they also include prosocial acts as well. Broadly conceived, moral standards cover not only the control of antisocial impulses but the imperative to be concerned about the welfare and feelings of others.

In a review of the research relating to this topic, Martin L. Hoffman (1970) noted that there are three major theories bearing on the moral development of children: (1) the "original sin" doctrine, which assumes that each child has inborn antisocial impulses that adults must teach him to curb; (2) the "innate purity" doctrine, that assumes that children are innately good and that adult society has corrupting influences from which children should be protected, particularly during their early years; and (3) the *tabula rasa* or "clean slate" doctrine, which assumes that children are born neither good nor bad, but become what their environment causes them to become. Hoffman characterized Freudian theory as basically an original-sin doctrine, in the sense that the young child is held to be possessed by a bundle of drives (the id) that adults must help him master if he is to become a functioning member of society. Jean Piaget and Lawrence Kohlberg represent the innate-purity doctrine. They see morality as generated largely by the child's cognitive powers as they develop within the context of peer society. This process occurs quite naturally, and the less interference in the form of training by adults, the better. The *tabula rasa* doctrine is represented by the various learning theory schools—the classical learning theorists, the operant conditioners, and the social learning theorists—all of whom view moral development as a product of the child's social environment.

The original-sin/Freudian doctrine is probably most consistent with everyday practice and is essentially derived from what might be called "common sense." Child rearing in the majority of families throughout the world—certainly in the Western world—usually operates on principles consistent with this formulation. Moral development, according to psychoanalytic theory, takes place through the development of the superego, a process we described in Chapter 4. The child identifies with his parents, takes on their values, and suffers guilt when he transgresses. Guilt feelings emanating from the superego hence enable him to behave in a socially acceptable way, even when his parents are neither visible nor likely to discover his transgressions.

Research evaluating this theory has been concerned with comparative studies of families that, to some degree, conform to or deviate from conventional child-rearing norms, and with experiments that test the efficacy of other theories, especially those of the *tabula rasa*

type. There has also been a considerable amount of research attempting to relate child-rearing practices to children's developing guilt feelings and other mechanisms of self-restraint, but is has been difficult to identify any kind of precise relationship. It is to the credit of this basically common-sense doctrine that we have turned out as well as we have; it is to the discredit of the doctrine that we have turned out as badly as we have. It is largely because of the failures of common-sense doctrine that the other two competing doctrines have been developed.

Piaget's Approach

Piaget (1948) holds that there are basically two stages in moral development. Before age three and preceding these two stages, there is also an early period in which the child resolves conduct problems in a ritualistic fashion, without any understanding of the moral issues. The child at this age is unable to do any thinking about what is involved.

From about age three or four to eight or so, the child uses what Piaget terms *objective morality* in his dealings with others. This period is marked by (1) *objective responsibility*, the literal evaluation of an act in terms of its exact conformity to a rule, rather than the intent of the rule; (2) *unchangeability of rules*; (3) *absolutism of value*, the child's belief that everyone shares the same ideas of right and wrong; (4) *moral wrongness defined by sanctions*, whereby a child defines the wrongness of an act by the fact that he is punished; (5) *duty defined as obedience to authority*; (6) *immanent justice*, the belief that violations of social norms are followed by accidents or misfortunes inflicted by nature or God (Kohlberg, 1963a). This earlier stage of morality is also called the stage of *moral realism*, *morality of constraint*, or *heteronomous morality*. The second stage is variously termed *subjective morality, autonomous morality, morality of cooperation,* or *reciprocity,* and is marked by giving up the earlier fixed ideas of morality in exchange for a system of beliefs that takes into account the intentions of the individual and the possibility of human error. This appreciation of the feelings, attitudes, needs, and values of others is developed in the context of playing and interacting with others, especially in children's games. In fact, much of Piaget's research into morality was conducted in the course of playing marbles. The rules for such games and the children's attitudes toward the rules provided the raw material from which Piaget shaped his theories of the development of moral judgment.

In his review of the research on moral development, Hoffman (1970) observed that studies conducted in Western societies strongly supported Piaget's sequence of stages, but that children's progress through the sequence was related to IQ and to social class. In other words, the middle-class child or the child with an above-average IQ is more likely to move earlier and more definitely into the morality of cooperation and reciprocity than is the lower-class child or the child with a low IQ. Both SES and IQ are highly intercorrelated, as we have noted previously.

Lawrence Kohlberg (1963b) has extended Piaget's sequence into a six-stage system, divided into three levels (see Table 15-1).

TABLE 15-1. Stages in Children's Moral Development (Kohlberg, 1963b)

Level   I. Premoral level

Stage 1. *Obedience and punishment orientation*
Defers to a superior power because of dislike of punishment

Stage 2. *Naive hedonistic and instrumental orientation*
Rightness of conduct determined by extent to which action satisfies self and, occasionally, others; some reciprocity.

Level II. Morality of conventional role-conformity

Stage 3. *"Good-boy" morality of maintaining good relations*
Oriented toward seeking approval and to pleasing and helping others; some consideration of intentions.

Stage 4. *Authority and social-order-maintaining morality*
Oriented toward "doing one's duty," respect for authority, and maintaining the social order for its own sake; takes perspective of those who have legitimate rights; believes that virtue must be rewarded.

Level III. Morality of self-accepted moral principles

Stage 5. *Morality of contract, individual rights, and democratically accepted law*
Right and wrong defined in terms of laws and regulations, which are seen as having rational bases; duties and obligations seen in terms of abstract concept of contract, which take precedence over individual needs.

Stage 6. *Morality of individual principles of conscience*
Orientation that considers laws and regulations, but also bases decisions on mutual respect and trust, internalized ideals, and broader moral principles.

Kohlberg's first level is an expansion of Piaget's moral-realism stage, and his latter two expand Piaget's autonomous stage. Kohlberg maintains that at age seven most of the statements made by children are at Level I (premoral), with a few statements at Level II (conventional morality), and none at Level III (self-accepted moral principles). Figure 15-6 shows how Stage 1 (the lower stage in the premoral level) statements decline sharply from the middle years of childhood until adolescence for three groups of boys: American urban, Mexican urban, and Mexican rural (an isolated village on the Yucatan Peninsula). Note how concepts in the rural setting lag behind development in the urban centers. Conversely, development of Stage 4 concepts (doing one's duty, showing respect for authority, and maintaining the social order) increases during the years between 10 and 13, and levels off thereafter. Once again, the development of moral concepts on the part of rural boys lags behind that of boys in the urban centers.

Kohlberg's formulations have been tested by Elliot Turiel (1966), who attempted to get seventh-grade boys to move up or down the scale in the direction of greater or lesser maturity. Results showed some tendency to move in the direction of the experimenter's arguments. Turiel maintained that inasmuch as a control group actually regressed to a more immature level, the result supported the idea that the general movement was in a more mature direction. The tendency toward greater maturity also appeared in a study by Rest, Turiel, and Kohlberg (1969). Hoffman (1970) maintains that this research does not necessarily substantiate the Piaget-Kohlberg theory, because subjects may have merely been rejecting less mature concepts that they had already abandoned.

Some question regarding the validity of stage theories of moral development has been raised as a result of other experiments in which children were placed under various kinds of pressures to modify their thinking regarding proper moral behavior. The classic experiment of this type was conducted by Albert Bandura and Frederick J. McDonald (1963), who used two groups of children aged 5 to 11 years, half of whom were making moral judgments characteristic of Piaget's less mature or "objective" stage and the other half who

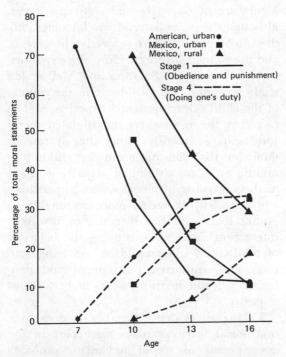

Figure 15-6.   Changes in moral concepts between middle childhood and adolescence, as reflected by statements made by three groups of boys: American urban, Mexican urban, Mexican rural (Yucatan village). Two types of statements are contrasted: (1) those at the most elementary level, as characterized by an orientation toward obedience and punishment, and (2) those at a more mature level, as characterized by a willingness to "do one's duty" with respect to those in authority and to the social order in general. (After Kohlberg, 1963b, and Kohlberg and Kramer, 1969.)

were making more mature judgments of the "subjective" type. Children were presented with pairs of descriptions of incidents. Each pair consisted of one incident in which material damage was great, but there was little intent to be injurious or destructive, and one incident in which the amount of destruction was small, but the individual concerned was guilty of some kind of wrongdoing. Children were asked to determine which incident in each pair was the more serious crime. Children in the "objective" stage tended to judge the wrongdoing in terms of the extent of the damage caused, whereas those in the "subjective" stage tended to judge in terms of the intentions of the individual concerned.

The subjects were divided into three groups and in each instance were exposed to a treatment designed to change their style of moral judgment. In one treatment, they watched adult models making judgments counter to the children's orientation, and the children themselves were then reinforced for adopting the model's style of evaluation. In a second treatment, the children watched the models, but were not themselves reinforced for matching their behavior. In a third treatment, the children had no exposure to models, but were merely reinforced for expressing judgments that ran counter to their dominant tendencies. Results showed that watching the model was the most effective way of getting children to change their orientation. Reinforcement alone produced little change and, furthermore, added little to the effect of the model on the children's behavior.

The researchers concluded that their results were strong evidence in favor of a social-learning explanation of the development of moral behavior. When their findings are extrapolated to everyday life, they suggest that the example set by a parent is a more powerful teacher of moral judgment than is anything he might do *to* a child by way of direct en-

couragement or even rewarding him for adopting this or that judgmental style. The fact that the experimental treatments could so readily cause children to progress or regress in the maturity of their moral judgment also raises some doubts as to whether Piaget's moral stages stand up as well as his cognitive stages. Additional data gathered by the researchers as part of their study raised further questions about stage theories, for children at all age levels in their sample were using a mixture of objective and subjective styles, although the general trend was for older children to be making more subjective judgments, and the younger children, more objective ones.

As impressive as Bandura and McDonald's study is, it must be considered in the context of the child's developmental experiences. The fact that the researchers manipulated moral judgments so readily shows that it can be done, but that does not mean that children in middle and late childhood actually do most of their learning of moral values by watching adult models. It seems more reasonable to assume that a number of modes are involved: interaction with peers, copying the behavior of adults and older children, resolving conflicts with authority, punishment and reinforcement, and learning when to be anxious or guilty.

Taking all evidence together, it does seem that social learning plays some part in the development of moral judgment, probably more in the initial stages than the later ones. Hoffman (1970) suggests that as the child develops his cognitive abilities and interacts with his peers, he reevaluates and shifts his view of authority and regulations, so that they are no longer arbitrary and external, but are internalized and rational. During this period, too, children are learning to control antisocial impulses. In effect, this means learning to be anxious and guilty when social norms are violated, even when authority figures are absent. Hoffman notes that a fourth process is needed to help the child develop strong prosocial feelings. Empathy plays a key role here, because it is through becoming aware of the feelings and needs of others that the child grows up to become a truly socialized —and civilized—adult.

Summary

Parental influences are less crucial for the older child annd different from those which come to bear on younger age groups. To study this problem, Schaefer and Bayley used a circumplex model to classify the dimensions of maternal behavior. The behavioral continua with which these investigators were concerned were *autonomy-control* and *love-hostility*. They found a considerable degree of consistency of maternal affection between infancy and preadolescence, but an insignificant correlation between maternal restrictiveness measures taken at the two age levels.

The kind of behavior displayed by a parent appears to foster similar behavior in children, especially in terms of aggressive responses. Watson found that children from strict homes rate high in dependence, negativism, conformity, and hostility. Murray and Seghorn investigated the background of sexually dangerous persons and discovered that the offender's father was often cruel and the mother passive and indulgent.

SES is another significant variable in child rearing. Although unrelated to maternal nurturance and affection, SES is closely related to coerciveness and restrictive regulations. The higher the SES of a mother, the more likely she is to be warm and accepting. Higher SES children also tend to be better adjusted, with the exception of children whose parents continued their education past the bachelor's degree. Children who have been referred to a clinic for psychiatric treatment often have parents who outwardly conform, but express hostile and rebellious feelings in indirect ways. Such children also tend to place the two-dimensional representations of family figures used in projective tests farther apart, suggesting greater psychological distance between members of their families.

Kagan and Moss studied the amount and kind of dependence shown at several age levels. They found that dependence ratings for ages six to ten were much more related to adult dependency status than were those for ages three to six, and that the consistency of dependency between childhood and adulthood was much greater for girls than for boys. Whiting investigated the relationship of child-rearing practices to school achievement. Her findings showed that the parents of successful boys expected independence and mastery of tasks earlier than did the parents of unsuccessful boys. Achievement, independence, and self-esteem are likely to go together. Studies have indicated that the parents of high-curiosity boys are more democratic in their relations with them and less likely to foster dependence.

Independence training is also related to the need to achieve (n Ach). Generally speaking, earlier independence training by mothers engenders stronger achievement motivation in their children. High-need achievers tend to try harder, take more pleasure in success, and are more popular than low-need achievers. The desire to complete tasks is another aspect of achievement motivation. Crandall and Robson noted that, when given a choice between puzzles that had been successfully completed and puzzles that had not been completed, older children preferred to repeat the previously failed puzzle. Boys also seemed to be more concerned with task mastery than girls. These results are consistent with Winterbottom's finding that independence training begins earlier for boys than for girls. The need for achievement is closely related to parental expectations and concern. There are also indications that achievement strivings are associated with gains in IQ, and the education of the same-sex parent. Need for achievement as expressed between the ages of six and ten has proven to be highly predictive of similar adult tendencies. This period is thought to be crucial for the development of motivation to master intellectual tasks. It is a routine finding that SES differences are related to achievement motivation.

The antecedents of self-esteem were investigated by Coopersmith, who found that children with high self-esteem were little troubled by anxiety, showed little destructiveness, actively expressed their opinions, and were not upset by criticism. Low-self-esteem boys tended to be discouraged, timid, and convinced of their inferiority. Contrary to a number of popular clichés about child rearing, Coopersmith found no relationship between self-esteem and height, physical attractiveness, traumatic experiences, feeding method in infancy, or maternal employment. Children with high self-esteem also were more likely to have strict parents who administered discipline consistently but not harshly. The parents of high-self-esteem children were also active and self-assured, suggesting that they serve as social learning models for their children. Walsh observed that academic underachievers show more signs of inhibition and insecurity. The usual finding that underachievers tend to have poorer emotional and social adjustment does not hold true in all cultures. The norms of developing countries like Brazil tend evidently to deemphasize achievement, and the child who sets high academic goals for himself very likely deviates from his cultural norms in others ways as well.

By the time the child reaches the sixth grade, his "ideal self" probably conforms more closely to the ideals of his peers than to those of his parents. The reduction of the discrepancy between the individual's ideal self and what he considers to be his "real self" has traditionally been one of the goals of psychotherapy. Recent research, however, has indicated that the disparity increases along with age and IQ. Empathic ability also increases with age during later childhood. Dymond and her associates found that sixth-grade children were more aware and better able to assess the feelings of others than second graders. Children's perceptions of others are influenced by how well they like them. Davitz found that high sociometric choices were perceived as more similar to oneself than they were in fact. It is often observed that strong desires to be liked by others actually interfere with social adjustment.

The child's increasing awareness of himself as a male or female is another important dimension of the child's self-concept. Generally, boys show a stronger and earlier preference for the masculine role than girls do for the feminine role. Maccoby considers the taking on of adult roles by children to be an aspect of identification and has collected evidence to support her view. She found that sixth graders who were likely to enforce rules tended to have parents who were strict rule-enforcers themselves. Remarkable stability has been demonstrated in sex-role related behavior. Measures of dependence and passivity taken between the ages of six and ten are highly predictive of equivalent adult behavior for girls but not for boys. Measures of male heterosexuality and behavior disorganization (anger) are equally predictive, while intellectual concerns, sex-related activities and spontaneity seem to be equally predictive for both sexes. These results suggest that sex-role identification is a governor of behavior and that children check their behavior against idealized internal models ranging from highly masculine to highly feminine.

Although parental influence begins to wane during middle childhood, it is still important. Mothers are generally seen as less dominant and punitive than fathers. However, as age increases, the same-sex parent assumes more and more of a punitive role. Boys' attitudes toward both parents become steadily less favorable up to the fifth grade when they level off until they improve again in the late high school years. Girls show the same pattern except for the fact that they are generally more favorable toward both parents. A study of Swedish children conducted by Pikas established that older and more intelligent children were more likely to reject authoritarian expressions of authority. Related findings show that responsibility in children is fostered if they perceive their parents as taking a constructive orientation toward them.

Moral standards in their mature form include prosocial acts as well as "thou shalt nots." Hoffman noted that there are three major theories bearing on the moral development of children: (1) the *original sin* doctrine; (2) the *innate purity* doctrine and (3) the *tabula rasa* doctrine. Freudian theory is characterized as representing the first doctrine, Piaget the second. The *tabula rasa* doctrine is represented by the learning theory schools. According to Freudian doctrine, moral development is a matter of superego development which, in turn, is the result of the child's identification with his parents.

Piaget holds that moral development is separated into two basic stages. The first stage, *objective morality*, lasts approximately from age three until age eight, and is characterized by rigid conformity to rules that are thought of by the child as arbitrary and universal. The second stage, *subjective morality*, is marked by a system of beliefs that take into account the intentions of the individual and the possibility of human error. Studies conducted in Western societies strongly support Piaget's sequence of stages, but also make reference to environmental factors such as IQ and SES.

Kohlberg has extended Piaget's sequence into a three-level system. Turiel tested Kohlberg's formulation by attempting to get seventh-grade boys to move up and down the scale of stages. The results showed some tendency to move in the direction of the experimenter's arguments. Bandura and McDonald conducted a similar study in which children were presented with pairs of descriptions of incidents. In one of these incidents the material damage was great, but there was little malicious intent. In the second incident the damage was slight, but the individual involved was guilty of some wrongdoing. Children in the *objective* stage tended to judge the wrongdoing in terms of the extent of damage. The *subjective* stage children judged in terms of intentions. Bandura and McDonald used several methods to change the children's various styles of moral judgment. They found that reinforcement had little effect and that the exposure to adult models was the most effective way of changing the children's orientations. The fact that the children's moral judgments were so easily changed raises some question as to whether Piaget's moral stages are as valid as his cognitive stages. All evidence considered, it seems that social learning plays some role in moral development, especially in the early stages.

16 Peer Influences and School Relationships

The major influences during the middle- and late-childhood period come from the peer group and the school in the North American culture.[1] These two sources of influence do not operate independently, because the school plays a large part in bringing the child and the peer group together. Most children, to be sure, have had some interaction with peer groups before entering school, but school provides maximum exposure to this type of social stimulation. The groups children are involved in during the preschool years are likely to be loose, informal, and less stable. During the elementary school years, groups tend to become more highly structured and, in the classroom at least, highly formalized.

School children can be said to leave home, literally and figuratively, to a much greater degree than younger children. Wright (1956) studied the average number of hours per day spent by the children and adults in the family and in community settings in a midwestern town. As shown in Figure 16-1, infants and preschoolers spent, on the average, about one hour a day outside the home. An increase to six or seven hours outside the home occurred in the age period now under consideration (referred to as young-middle and old-middle

[1] This qualification is added because in more traditional cultures—for example, European or Latin American—family influences are stronger and peer group influences weaker during the childhood years than they are in the United States and Canada.

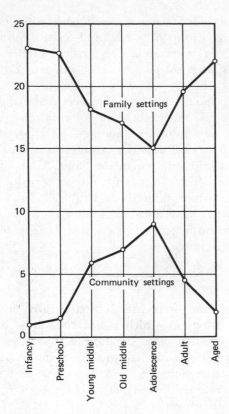

Figure 16-1. Average amount of time spent in family and community settings. (Wright, 1956. Copyright 1956 by the Society for Research in Child Development, and published with permission.)

childhood in the figure). During these hours away from home the children were in school and at play. Most of this time they spent in the company of their age mates.

The Peer Group

Although the parents are the first socializing agents for the child, the more complex social skills are learned in peer groups. How a child will react to the social forces within peer groups will depend partly on his temperament and the basic personality trends set during preschool years and partly on the character of the peer groups to which he is exposed.

How does the peer group influence a child? It supplies norms, roles, and models with which he can identify; it provides rewards, reinforcements, both negative and positive; and and it constitutes a source of information, stimulation, and emotional support. A peer-age child sees in the behavior of other children that which he may model himself upon—a model for characteristics no adult can serve. He cannot model himself after his mother and father in seeking social acceptability—they are popular or unpopular in their own adult fashion through cocktails, bridge, or conversation on the latest novel (or through beer, pinochle, and the latest racing results). These forms of behavior are not yet within a child's ken. Other children must serve as models.

To be accepted by the group is a reward. So the child learns the way of the group in order to be accepted by that group. Once in the group he develops new needs—he acquires new secondary drives. No longer a means to an end, approval of the agents of socialization now becomes an end in itself. Thus, the peer group provides rewards. The peers also provide an identity of and for the child himself —not Mr. Brown's son Bob, but *Bob*. He also takes on successive identities provided by the group from a first-grader, to a Cub Scout, and so on up through the years. The group offers support through sheer numbers in presenting requests to do what others do or have what others have because "all the kids do (or have) it."

Although all of these positive, group-cohesive factors are present, we must also remember that groups and grouping carry within their very structure a measure of exclusiveness. Boys cannot have an airplane model club with a membership without excluding someone. Moreover, even in loosely knit groups, such as those that form on the playground, there still will be "outsiders." These are the recessive children (listless, lacking in vitality, below normal in intelligence, and careless); the socially uninterested; and the socially ineffective (the noisy, rebellious, boastful, and arrogant). Negative influences from the peer group will also be very evident in the discussion to follow.

Peer groups in their purer form show characteristic difference from groups at home, at school, or as imposed by other adults. They involve individuals of the same age centered about some immediate and short-term concern. They are loosely organized and change their composition rapidly. What the child learns is apt to be picked up and made his own uncritically and without examination. He feels reassured if he behaves like all the others without quite knowing why something is "in" or "out."

This tendency to adopt the values and attitudes of others can lead to acceptance of views that are wrong. Ruth Berenda (1950) conducted a classic study in which children were shown a single black line which was to serve as standard, along with three other black lines of differing lengths. Their task was to state which of the three lines was equal in length to the standard. When alone, most children judged correctly. These same children when judging in a group made errors. Why? The child who erred did not know that the five children, who gave their judgments aloud before his turn came, were confederates of the experimenter who had been told to report the wrong answer. When his turn did come, this child tended to go along with the group and made an inaccurate judgment. Younger children (ages seven to ten) were more influenced in this regard than older children (ages ten to 13).

In a second experiment with different children, the teacher was the accomplice, giving her judgment first. Again the children were influenced, but not as much as they had been by the group of peers, and again, younger children were relatively more influenced. Peers seem to be even more important than the teacher in influencing judgment.

We should note that the effect that the peer group has on the behavior of children varies from one culture to another. Urie Bronfenbrenner (1970) found vast differences between 12-year-old children in the Soviet Union and in the United States with respect to values to which they subscribed. Children in both countries were asked what they thought they would do in ten hypothetical situations. Here is an example.

"The Lost Test

You and your friends accidentally find a sheet of paper which the teacher must have lost. On this sheet are the questions and answers for a quiz that you are going to have tomorrow. Some of the kids suggest that you not say anything to the teacher about it, so that all of you can get better marks. What would you really do? Suppose your friends decide to go ahead. Would you go along with them or refuse?" (p. 182).

Responses to problems like these were scored on a scale that ranged from −2.5 (going along with peers) to +2.5 (responding to adult-approved standards of behavior). A score of −25 for the ten items would thus represent the ultimate in peer-oriented values, whereas +25 would represent the most extreme adult-oriented outlook. Children took different versions of the test under three different conditions: (1) the *baseline* condition, in which they were told that no one would see their responses except the investigators; (2) the *adult* condition, in which they were told that each child's responses would be posted on a chart and displayed at a parents' meeting

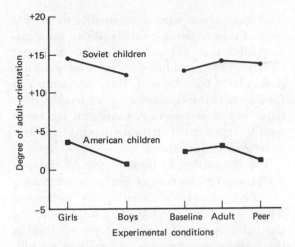

Figure 16-2. Differences in degree to which Soviet and American children give adult-oriented (in contrast to peer-oriented) responses in conflict situations involving possible misdemeanors. (After Bronfenbrenner, 1970.)

to be held the following week; and (3) the *peer* condition, in which the chart would be displayed a week later to the class itself.

The results, as shown by Figure 16-2, indicate first of all that there was the usual difference between boys and girls, with both American and Soviet boys expressing values that are somewhat more peer-oriented, and girls in both nations being more adult oriented. Second, and more significant, Soviet children were a great deal more adult-oriented than American children.

Third, although both Soviet and American children responded in ways that were slightly more adult-oriented when told that their parents would learn of their responses, knowledge that their *peers* would hear of them had quite a different effect on the two groups of children: in contrast to their baseline position, American children moved to a more peer-oriented response mode, whereas Soviet children became slightly more adult-oriented. In other words, Soviet children wanted their peers

to think that they were more accepting of adult standards than they really were, whereas American children wanted their peers to think that they *rejected* adult standards more than they actually did. The peer norm for Soviet children is apparently much more *pro*adult than it is for American children.

Bronfenbrenner explains this large difference between Soviet and American children as an indication that the American family, because of urbanization and of technological changes in the larger society, "has been losing power as a major socializing agent in the lives of children, and the resulting vacuum has been filled by the age-segregated peer group." (p. 182). Ties between Soviet children and their parents, on the other hand, have remained strong. Other evidence reported to Bronfenbrenner suggests similar trends in Western and Eastern Europe, with Western European children expressing attitudes quite similar to those of American children, and children from Hungary and Poland expressing attitudes similar to those of Soviet children.

Aggressive Tendencies

In cultures like ours, in which children tend to be ambivalent toward or even rejecting of adult values, it is to be expected that peer groups will encourage the expression of aggressive behavior to some degree. Adults come to symbolize restraint, routine, and boredom, and the child is attracted to the peer group because of its ability to generate excitement, tension, and adventure. The aggressive behavior fostered by the peer group is not only a way of rebellion against adults' constraints but the instability of the peer group itself also sets child against child in hostile encounter.

The investigation of aggressive behavior can be related in a variety of ways to the peer group within which they take place. McNeil (1962) conducted a study concerned with the interrelationships among patterns of aggressive behavior with other facets of social behavior as observed in a summer camp for emotionally disturbed and delinquent boys, ranging in age from seven to 15. For each cabin there was a high counselor-child ratio of eight boys to six counselors. The latter supplied the observational ratings, working morning, afternoon, or evening shifts in teams of three. The three counselors completed collective behavior checklists after each shift with their eight boys. With three shifts per day and 45 days, it would appear that the combined ratings on any one child's behavior pattern could be based on as many as 135 collective ratings. An adequate number of 59 subjects and a lengthy 45-day period of observation made the study especially noteworthy.

The rated behaviors involved swearing, sulking, fighting, fighting to protect self or others, competing without aggression, following others into trouble, seeking leadership, and friendliness with others. In addition to these child-initiated behaviors, the responses of other children to each child were rated in terms of the latter's being accepted and rejected or being made the scapegoat.

The children who fought frequently, often needing no justification, were also the ones who fought to protect others. Lest the altruistic note be too strong here, it is rather clear the boys in the present study championed others not so much for their sake, as they did to get in the fight for its own sake.

One very notable correlate with high fighting was what might be expected, namely swearing and calling names. Another was less expected, namely, that children who fought a great deal were neither the best nor the worst in staying within the rules in organized competition. Indeed, those who fought the

least were those who were unable to handle competition without hostility. As to the characteristics that did not distinguish the boys clearly, subjects addicted to fighting were not particularly friendly with their peers nor did they seek visible positions of leadership. Perhaps, as the investigators comment, the camp sample represented delinquent children who were leadership failures.

The interaction of these personal behaviors with the acceptance, rejection, or scapegoating of peers showed interesting relationships. Those who were rejected most were made the butt of severe and continued persecution in the form of scapegoating. There was no philosophy of live and let live which would be compatible with rejection as such. It follows, as they found, that scapegoated boys had little opportunity for leadership. The converse seems to occur for those accepted—they were rarely scapegoated and were freer to seek and attain leadership.

This study suggests clearly that aggression is not a unitary phenomenon, captured by one global estimate; instead, it appears in a pattern reflected in a child's interaction with his peers. Aggressive tendencies have been shown to be instigated in the peer group by characteristic relationships within that group.

Direct training within the peer group may bring about increased aggressiveness. A specific study of aggression training was made by Davitz (1952) in the setting of peer interaction of 40 children aged seven to nine. He hypothesized that a child's response to frustration would be affected by his previous experiences in situations similar to that in which frustration was encountered. More specifically, he studied the differing effects of aggressive training and of constructive training on later responses to frustration.

In order to carry this out properly, several steps were necessary: (a) Free play for ten groups of children in the experimental play-room. (b) Five groups received ten-minute aggressive training sessions, involving playing games designed to incite aggression, such as one in which each tried to break everyone else's ping pong ball while protecting his own, and another in which each tried to secure everyone else's "scalp" (a piece of cloth tied around the arm) while protecting his own. During the games, aggressive behavior was praised and encouraged, and individual stars were awarded for winning. Five other training groups received constructive training sessions, involving drawing murals and completing jig-saw puzzles as a group. Throughout aggression was discouraged, and cooperation praised and encouraged. (c) A frustration session for each group, aggressive and constructive alike, fol-lowed. The children were told they were to see movies just outside the playroom, five reels of film were brought out, the first was shown, and at the start of the second reel they were given candy, but at the climactic point of this reel, without explanation the experimenter stopped the film and took back what candy remained. (d) They were then led back into the playroom and told they could play with anything they wished.

Unknown to the children, their behavior in the earlier prefrustration period had been photographed and now in the postfrustration session was photographed again. Their behav-ior in the film was reduced to behavioral de-scriptions which were given to judges who had no knowledge whether a given behavior pro-tocol was from pre- or post-frustration play. Judges were asked to rank the protocols in order of aggressiveness (20 out of 80 protocols showed no aggression at all). Now the data was divided into pre- and postfrustration be-havior, and for each subject it was recorded whether there was a gain or a loss in rank.

The constructively trained subjects showed 6 gains, 11 losses, and 3 ties. The aggressively trained subjects showed 14 gains, 5 losses, and 1 tie. These differences were shown not to be due to chance alone. Constructively trained subjects when faced thereafter by a frustrating situation nevertheless behaved more construc-tively. Aggressively trained subjects faced with the same frustrating situation behaved more aggressively. Previous training, it was con-cluded, is a significant determiner of a child's postfrustration reaction to a frustrating situa-tion. It is not merely the frustrating situation that determines the child's behavior. Stimulus conditions are not the only determinants of how one reacts to a frustrating situation; pre-vious experience in the peer group must also be taken into account.

Behavior Tendencies

Earlier child-parent relations also have a sig-nificant effect on the amount of aggressiveness a child expresses toward others, and there is a tendency for patterns of aggression to con-tinue from the preschool period on into the preadolescent years. Sears (1961) did a follow-up of his "pattern" study that shows how these earlier trends tend to persist between the ages of five and twelve. Of the original population of 379 five-year-old children, 160, now 12 years of age, were still in the schools from which they had originally been drawn. These children each filled out several self-administering scales concerned with aggressive attitudes. Their classmates, totaling 377, also completed these forms. As compared to boys, aged twelve, girls showed significantly higher scores on *aggression anxiety* (fear and dislike of aggression, such as being uncomfortable when seeing two friends argue) and *prosocial aggression* (aggression used in socially ap-proved ways, as advocating punishing of some-one who has clearly broken a rule). The boys, as compared to girls, exhibited higher scores on *antisocial aggression* (socially unacceptable forms of aggression, as settling an argument by a fight).

Current antisocial aggression was found to be related to high permissiveness and low punishment from their mothers seven years before. As related to high permissiveness, antisocial aggression repeats the findings at age five; as related to low punishment it is the reverse of what it was at the earlier age. At the early age, punishment seemed to produce aggression; at the later age punishment tended to have an inhibiting effect not present when the children were younger. Punishment, in this instance, did seem to work.

Current prosocial aggression and aggressive anxiety were also related to earlier high maternal permissiveness as before. This time, however, they were found to be associated with high punishment, quite the opposite of the relation to antisocial aggression. High permissiveness and high punishment promote prosocial aggression and aggression anxiety; high permissiveness and low punishment incite antisocial aggression.

Sex differences appeared to such an extent in the antecedents of the degree of anxiety over aggressiveness that different dynamics must be attributed to boys and girls. Severity of parental punitiveness for aggression during early childhood correlated significantly with aggression anxiety in older girls but not in older boys. It seems as if the boys' aggression anxiety arises when socialization is experienced in a love-oriented atmosphere; here there are dictates against aggression. In short, there is conformity. In girls, on the other hand, anxiety is induced by conflict. A forced conformity seems to occur, despite girls' being less aggressive than boys either overtly or in fantasy. In girls, incipient aggressive tendencies are nipped in the bud and anxiety develops. Under most circumstances, aggression in girls is not acceptable in their sex-role training. In her sex role a girl is not supposed to show aggressiveness, does not do so, and becomes anxious.

Finney (1961) also obtained information about maternal-child characteristics as related to aggressiveness. Particularly interesting is his finding on so-called *covert hostility*. This is not direct, overt aggression, but resentment expressed in bitterness, sulking, and easily hurt feelings. He found mothers who were hostile, rigid, or lacking in nurturance to have covertly hostile children.

Covert hostility can express itself in a number of ways. Evelyn Morrison (1969) investigated the correlates of over- and underachievement in a group of fifth-grade boys. She found that the underachievers showed more hostility toward authority, as revealed by the TAT stories they wrote, and were also rated as more passive aggressive (i.e., stubborn) by their teachers. Incidentally, there was no difference between the under- and the overachievers when their achievement was measured by standardized tests of achievement: they differed only in the marks they received from their teachers. In other words, the underachievers were learning as much as the overachievers but were unwilling to give teachers the evidence that would have got them better grades.

Another dimension of aggression that has attracted much attention throughout the last century is the effect of fantasy materials on behavior. Mothers and teachers confiscated "penny dreadfuls" and "dime novels" 60 or more years ago, saying such reading matter poisoned the minds of youth and aggravated criminal tendencies. In more recent years, comic books, radio thrillers, and now television crime programs have been similarly accused of corrupting the young. This viewpoint has been supported by some psychiatrists, but a number of psychologists have argued against it, saying that such material may actually have a positive effect on children's emotional and social development by giving them a healthy outlet for normal aggressive tendencies.[2] Research findings are somewhat contradictory. Bandura, Ross, and Ross (1963) showed preschool children films in which two male adults engaged in aggressive or vigorous nonaggressive play. In one version, aggression was rewarded; in another it was punished. Although the viewing of the rewarded aggressive model was followed by a higher degree of aggressive behavior on the part of the young viewers, there were some confusing results, especially for boys, who also behaved aggressively after seeing the nonaggressive model. Seymour Feshbach (1970) interprets these findings as suggesting that perhaps any kind of vigorous stimulus, aggressive or otherwise, may incite aggressive responses in boys, who are more prone to such behavior than girls are.

The possibility that aggressive fantasy material may actually have the opposite effect on the behavior of boys was explored by Feshbach and Singer (1970), who enlisted the cooperation of parents and private schools and were thus able to control the television viewing behavior of several groups of boys aged 9 to 15 over an extended period of time. Some groups watched more violent and aggressive programs involving gangsters, outlaws, and the FBI, while others watched nonviolent, nonaggressive programs, such as family situation comedies, variety shows, and *Lassie*. Records were kept of the number of aggressive acts the two groups engaged in. Here are some of the findings.

1. There were no significant differences be-

tween the two groups with respect to cursing and swearing, destruction of property, and breaking of rules.

2. The group that watched the nonviolent programs were involved in more than twice as many fistfights as those who watched the violent programs.

3. The nonviolent-program group participated in 859 loud, angry arguments, in contrast to 407 for the other group.

4. The nonviolent-program group engaged in 973 instances of criticizing or insulting others, whereas the violent-program group engaged in only 456.

5. With respect to feelings of jealousy, the group watching the nonaggressive films reported 254 instances versus 87 for the other group.

With respect to comic books, objectionable or otherwise, a study by W. Paul Blakely (1958) found that they had no effect on children's behavior, except that seventh graders who read more comic books tended to read more library books as well.

The relationship between fantasy violence and aggressive behavior is far from clear, however. Common sense would lead to the conclusion that exposure to fantasy violence in the form of television programs and the like *should* incite aggressive behavior. This view is expressed by Leonard Berkowitz (1971), who cites an impressive array of studies to support his position.

Findings typical of much research in fantasy aggression are reported by Cameron and Janky (1971), who asked all parents of kindergarten children in a Michigan school district to cooperate in an experiment in which children were placed on a three-week "diet" of violent television, passive television, or some combination (first period violent, and second period passive, or vice versa). Parents' obser-

[2] In Chapter 10 we discussed the research of Ames (1966), whose data suggest that even very young children are fascinated by violent and aggressive themes in fantasy material.

vations of children's behavior disturbances were the dependent variable.

Results showed that children watching violent programs showed the greatest number of behavior disturbances, and some of the effects still persisted a month later. Findings were not clear-cut, however. Only one-third of the children seeing all-violent programs showed any change. Furthermore, the least change was shown by children who were exposed to a diet first of passive films and then of violent ones, a finding that is contrary to what would be expected. The authors also point out that the controls in the study were of necessity quite loose: children were able to watch television at neighbors' homes, where parents were unable to monitor the programs; parents were not 100% vigilant; many television commercials were violent; and so forth. What is more important, however, is that parents who controlled the stimuli were also asked to judge their children's behavior—another opportunity for unconscious bias to slip in. Although the results of the study are consistent with common sense and with Berkowitz's position, they can be accepted as only suggestive. Obviously more research is needed before we can say that we understand the relationship between fantasy violence and the subsequent appearance of aggressive behavior in children.

Social Acceptance

We noted earlier that one of the major functions of the peer group, as far as the child is concerned, is that of supplying a means whereby he may find emotional support through social acceptability. The task is now to examine what are the correlates of social acceptability. Sociometric status, popularity, and leadership are treated as more specific aspects of social acceptance in what follows.

Constancy of social acceptability with increase in age during the peer-group ages has

been established. Merl E. Bonney (1943) used the sociometric technique to differentiate socially accepted from socially unaccepted children in the second through the fifth grades in three schools. The bases of choice of acceptability varied from grade to grade, but in each there were from five to six bases of choice, including with whom to have their pictures taken, partner for a party, and to whom to give Christmas presents. The children were also asked the names of their best friends. A composite score was derived for each child. Bonney used a semilongitudinal approach, with most of the subjects tested in successive grades (although there was pupil population turnover). Consequently, correlation between general social acceptance at successive age levels was possible, giving him a measure of social acceptance constancy.

Between the sociometric measure of the second and third grades the correlation was .84; between the third and fourth and fourth and fifth grade it was, respectively, .77 and .67. A high degree of constancy in degree of social acceptability is exhibited from grade to grade. To emphasize this point, the magnitude of the correlations in social acceptability was approximately as large as that between intelligence test scores for the same grades (.75 to .86). In other words, social acceptability is almost as constant as intelligence.

This constancy of social acceptability was checked by a study of children who transferred from one school to another where, naturally, they were unknown. Although the group was small, in every instance their social acceptance scores at the end of the year in the new school gave them very much the same degree of social acceptability they had had in their previous schools.

In spite of constancy of social acceptability, the peer-group members shift in their evaluation of desirable and undesirable personality characteristics over the years of this period.

In other words, personality characteristics responsible for social acceptability change as the children grow older. This may be illustrated from data of the longitudinal study reported by Jean Walker Macfarlane (1942) using a "Guess Who" technique. This involves short sketches of children about whom the subjects are to guess who is being described as in "Guess who it is that is always bossing other children?"

In the first grade "quiet" was given the highest mark by the children for what makes a real boy. By the third grade being "quiet" had almost dropped out of the pattern. If a given boy had maintained stability in the personality characteristic from the first grade to the third grade by remaining "quiet," he would thereby suffer change in reputational status as a "real boy." (Whether this bothered him or not is a different matter, dependent on whether he wanted this form of prestige.)

These findings were extended with a larger sample by Read D. Tuddenham (1952), using the same "Guess Who" technique. Popularity in first-grade girls was associated with "acting like a little lady," "being quiet," and "not being bossy or quarrelsome." In the fifth grade "acting like a little lady" had little to do with social acceptability. By this age characteristics such as good looks, being a good sport, friendliness, and tidiness were most highly correlated with social acceptability. The evidence seems clear that the children evaluate other children's social acceptability somewhat differently at different age levels in the light of standards and values characteristic of that age level.

At first, it may appear that there is a contradiction between the constancy of social acceptability found by Bonney, and the shifts in characteristics making for social acceptability found by Macfarlane and Tuddenham. This is not the case. Bonney dealt with *constancy of individual acceptability status;* Macfarlane and Tuddenham with *shifts in characteristics making for social acceptability.* So there is no contradiction between their results. Characteristics may shift in the socially acceptable child so that he maintains his acceptability, but through different characteristics.

Social adaptability, whether deliberate or not, seems to be characteristic of the socially acceptable. The child maintains his acceptability while changing his characteristics.

In peer-aged children popularity is also associated with the traits that are characteristic of sex typing. Popular boys are regarded by their peers as athletic, daring, friendly, and leaders; popular girls are regarded by their peers as docile and unassertive. High prestige is related to conforming to sex typing (Tuddenham, 1951).

There are also age differences with respect to the extent to which the two sexes are attracted to each other. Children during the earlier preschool years pay relatively little attention to the sex of their playmates: boys often play house with little girls, while girls frequently work out on the jungle gym. As the years go by, however, play activities become more sex-typed, and affiliations become less heterosexual. By the time children are about ten years old, patterns of acceptance have pretty much sorted themselves out along sex lines. Figure 16–3 consists of a sociogram of a typical fourth grade. It shows a strong tendency for boys to choose boys as friends, and girls to choose girls. Although four of the boys—Mort F., Victor, Brian S., and Mort D.—are chosen by girls, no boy chooses a girl. The boys chosen by girls are also popular with other boys, but two of the girls who choose boys are isolates in their own group. Joan is a tomboy and the teacher reports that she is very quiet. When she is approached by the teacher and prodded into a conversation, she can talk very intelligently.

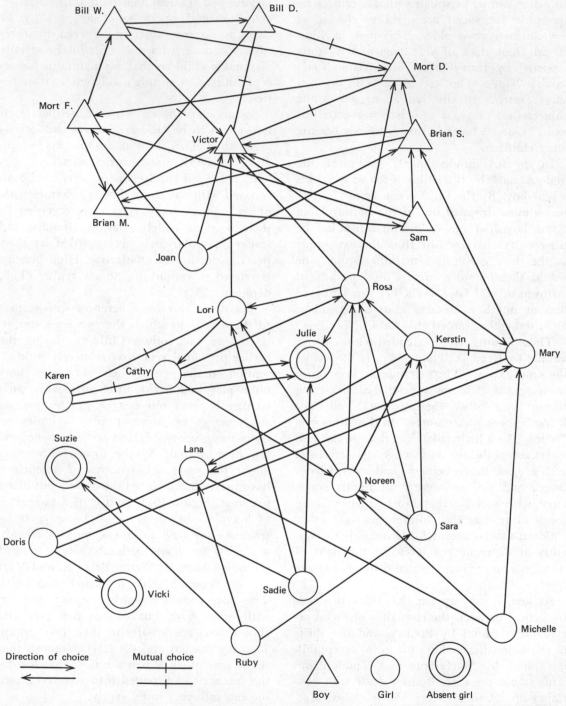

Direction of choice   Mutual choice

Boy   Girl   Absent girl

Figure 16-3. *Sociogram of a fourth grade, showing preference for own sex typical of this age.* (After Burke, 1971.)

Social acceptance patterns also vary with SES. In studying this matter, Pope (1953) used one group from the lower-lower (LL) class and another from the upper-middle (UM) class. The children came from different schools in different areas of a large city. Both groups averaged 12 years in age, but it was impossible to avoid an IQ discrepancy of 104 for the UM group as compared to 96 for the LL group. A variation of the "Guess Who" type of test yielded a reputational score for each child. The nature of the items may be inferred from the description of results that follow. Each of the 25 traits on which information was obtained was intercorrelated for the UM and LL groups, separately for boys and girls. Cluster analysis (a modification of factor analysis) was then performed. Inspection revealed clusters of traits which were interrelated, yielding characteristic patterns of social behavior.

Among the LL boys three major patterns could be discerned. The members in the first pattern, in which only a few boys fell, were the leaders who had the homage of the other boys and the companionship of the girls. They were aggressive, belligerent, and domineering. The second pattern for LL boys was the one involving most of the boys who were happy, sociable, able to enjoy a good joke, and considerably less aggressive than their leaders. The third pattern, the sissy, was the one the rest could not tolerate. This pattern included the studious and classroom conforming boys as well as what other groups would call "sissy."

Among the UM boys, the group leader, although active and skilled in competitive games, was not expected to be aggressive; in fact, being bossy and pugnacious tended to make him unpopular. Somewhat more numerous were instances of the pattern of the friendly, personable, good-looking boy who was accepted by both boys and girls. Instances of another pattern would be described as the

classroom intellectual. He was not actively rejected; in fact, he enjoyed a certain respect. The sissy, in the narrower sense, belonged to still another pattern. He was no more acceptable than he was among low socioeconomic boys, however. Along with the bossy, the unkempt, and the fighter, he was not accepted.

Among the LL girls, the type widely accepted was "the little lady" who was likable, friendly, good, tidy, and a good student. She was, however, not likely to be a leader nor did she associate with boys. Another pattern that enjoyed considerable prestige, but was less frequently encountered, was the somewhat rowdy, talkative, attention-getting, aggressive girl. She, rather than the little lady, associated with boys in the LL group.

UM girls, instead of having two contrasting patterns of prestige, as did the LL group girls, had but one, that of the "little lady" pattern, but with certain differences. Although good-looking, friendly, and tidy, this girl was more vivacious than her low socioeconomic counterpart and she was the one most likely to go out with boys. The tomboy had no place in the group, since any form of aggressiveness or bossiness was rejected. From these results it is apparent that there are distinct differences in the value systems in the two peer cultures. In other words, the members of the groups face different socialization pressures as shown by their differing criteria of what makes for acceptance. But in both, the peer group plays a direct role in personality formation.

The correlates of social power or influence among second and fifth graders was found to differ between boys and girls. Boys acquired influence through general intimidation; girls through decorous behavior and special social skills. Both intelligence and physical attractiveness were assets in the acquisition of power for boys and girls. The manner in which they used this power was dependent on individual personality characteristics. Just as an illustration, boys of lower intelligence tended to be frankly coercive and at the same time, inconsistent (Zander and Van Egmond, 1958).

Davids and Parenti (1958) found evidence that popular children, as determined by sociometric choice, tended to be relatively well-adjusted emotionally and to possess greater amounts of socially desirable personality traits (such as less anxiety, less resentment, optimism, and trust, as judged by professional personnel). The results have to be spoken of in relative terms since one of the samples studied was from a home for disturbed children. In this home population, the "disliked" group showed poorer adjustment than the "ignored" group.

Role playing skill is positively associated with sociometric status. Popular children are described as low in frustration, clear in expression, assured, and unhesitant. Twenty-six preadolescent Negro boys and girls from the sixth grade were subjects. Information to study this problem was supplied by a combination of sociometric selection by fellow students and judgments by adults who watched these children play "spur of the moment" roles. Each child played different scenes extemporaneously, in which they were assigned roles: (a) a friend who is sad, talking to an adult about not being invited to a party, (b) a playmate who is angry at another boy, and (c) a mischievous student sent to the principal's office for misconduct. Their role-playing ability seemed to be a social skill which contributed to their popularity with their classmates. Those children who were most skillful were also the most popular with their peers (Mouton, Bell, and Blake, 1956).

Friendships

Among older children a variety of factors seem to help to decide which particular peers will be chosen as friends. Peer-aged children as they become older show greater stability in their choice of friends, according to a series of studies by Horrocks, Thompson, and their associates. The data were collected simply. They asked about 350 suburban children from five through ten years of age and 900 rural and 900 urban children from 11 to 18 years of age to write down the names of their three best friends. Two weeks later the same request was made of them. The investigators worked out an index of constancy of friendship, extending from identity of names and order on the two lists, on the one hand, to no similarity between the two lists, on the other. They also presented data on whether the first choice of best friend on the two occasions remained the same.

Both methods of analysis showed essentially similar results. As age increased, stability of friendships increased from years five through 18. For example, among urban children only about 40% of the 11-year-old girls chose the same best friend two weeks later, but by age 15 the stability of choices over the same length of time had increased to over 60%. Similar figures for the same ages in urban boys were 50% and 60%. These trends toward greater stability continued to the oldest age studied, that of the 18-year-old. The more fluctuating friendships of the younger child steadily gave way to relatively more permanent friendships of the mature person (Horrocks and Buker, 1951; Horrocks and Thompson, 1946; deGroat and Thompson, 1949; Thompson and Horrocks, 1947).

Dymond and her associates (1952) examined the differences in friendship qualities chosen by second and sixth graders. Drawing on a list of descriptive phrases to characterize their friends, second graders stressed externals, such as a nice home, being good-looking, and having lots of spending money. The sixth graders, on the other hand, shifted to an emphasis on personality characteristics such as friendliness, cheerfulness, tidiness, and cleanliness. As they indicate, these changes in characteristics emphasized show an increase in socialization through the internalization of middle-class norms.

The causes of disruption of friendships have also been investigated. After finding the three best friends of a group of 400 sixth-grade children, they checked on changes two weeks later. Sixty percent changed in their choice of at least one of these friends. The major reasons for changing friends, in decreasing order of importance, were lack of recent contact, a quarrel, incompatibility, judgment that they were now conceited or bossy, disloyal or underhanded, bullying or quarrelsome, or dishonest or untruthful. Sheer physical unavailability in lack of recent contact was thus a major factor.

The second major factor, embracing all the rest of the reasons mentioned, is fluctuation in the child's social needs. In order for a friendship to endure, it must be mutually satisfying. Quarreling, incompatibility, and the like means that it is not, and the friendship is broken. If one or the other of the pair of friends gets nothing from it, or finds it frustrating, that friendship is headed toward dissolution (Austin and Thompson, 1948).

Cooperation and Competition

The peer group provides opportunities for both cooperation and competition. Children may work together toward a common goal and, hence, cooperate, or they may vie with one another and, hence, compete. Often, of course, both cooperation and competition simultaneously are present. In a basketball game a boy cooperates with his teammates in trying to beat his opponents, hence, he is cooperating with his own team and competing with the other one. But even among those

with whom he cooperates, he is also competing in that he tries to be a better player than his teammates. In classrooms the same confusing admixture occurs. Teachers ask that children cooperate and then place only a few in the best reading group, or hang only selected paintings on the wall. This is not meant as a criticism for behaving one way or the other—both cooperation and competition seem necessary to us. However, this does make it difficult to appraise their relative influence, since the same behavior may be motivated by either cooperation or competition.

An older study by Maller (1929) is still relevant today. He compared cooperation and competition in various groups of children, aged from eight to 17, from different schools and different socioeconomic levels. The task was simple one-place addition. Various forms of cooperation and competition were arranged. For example, competition was measured in an individual speed contest; from this result a list showing their ranks was to be posted. In addition, prizes for those scoring highest were offered. Cooperation was measured by staging a contest between classrooms.

Efficiency of work under competition was significantly and consistently higher than work under cooperation. When offered the choice between working for themselves or working for the group, the children selected the group only 26% of the time. In a contest between boys and girls, however, boys preferred to work for their own group rather than by themselves. Nevertheless, in the overall results, girls were more cooperative, choosing more often than boys to work for the group (though still predominantly in favor of competition).

It would appear that competition on behalf of the self improved performance over cooperation on behalf of the group. Moreover, with only one exception, competition was chosen by the children over cooperation. But as Doob (1952) suggested, however, certain qualifications seem indicated. There is the fact that there were quite different rewards in the two situations. In competition, both the prestige and prize were acquired. In cooperation, there was no prize, and the given child could feel rewarded only if he belonged to a victorious group and was also strongly attached to the group. Classrooms of children are not necessarily conducive to *esprit de corps*.

Moreover, competition was organized in a particular situation. Certain competitive versus cooperative aspects of many other situations were absent. Interaction among children was minimal. For example, competition often meant that one tried to prevent competitors from reaching a goal, and cooperation required constructive assistance of one another rather than merely contributing to a common goal. Any or all of these factors may contribute to different results concerning the relative influence of cooperation and competition. Hence, although Maller's study indicates competition was favored over cooperation, which may even be typical of many situations, it does not prove that competition is always favored over cooperation.

Phillips and D'Amico (1956) found that members of groups working together for the good of the group actually increased their liking for one another. On the other hand, groups where one competed with another did not necessarily decrease their liking. In competing groups, decrease in liking seemed to occur only when one or two members of the group got disproportionate shares of the rewards. When the individual rewards were fairly evenly distributed, then the effect might be similar to that holding in cooperating groups.

These results were obtained by dividing 40 fourth-grade children into eight groups of five,

with four high and four low "cohesive" groups. The groups had been derived by presenting a sociometric questionnaire. This was then used to divide groups so that some groups were composed of members who liked one another and other groups of members who did not.

The questionnaire was again administered at the end of the study to see what changes were brought about by cooperation or competition. In cooperating groups members shared equally in the rewards; in the competitive groups they received them only according to their contributions to correctness. A form of the game "Twenty Questions" used for identifying animals was the task. Two high cohesive groups worked under cooperative conditions; two under competitive conditions. Low cohesive groups were similarly composed. The increase in cohesiveness even under competition, unless rewards were disproportionately distributed, was encouraging evidence of the ability of children to get along with one another.

The School Age

There is no question of the importance of the influence of the peer group on the child. But there is the equally uncontrovertible fact that social behavior takes place under the watchful eye of adults, other than parents, who constantly impose on the child their own standards of socialization.

Wright (1956), who studied the amount of time spent by children in community settings, also investigated who were the leaders in these settings. Almost all leaders were adults—in only 8% of community settings had children assumed leadership. In effect, this means that adults were almost always on hand to look after the children. Every Boy Scout troop has its scoutmaster. To be sure, in other communities, especially in the large cities and in lower socioeconomic groups, children are much more "on the loose." Too little supervision can have a pernicious effect, but it also is possible that these findings imply that too much supervision is being given these children.

Teachers, recreation leaders, clergymen, group workers, and the like are intent upon teaching the child forms of behavior which they consider proper. They wish to bring about an increase in cooperation, a diminution of conflict, and the other social values of our society. In what follows, teachers in school settings and their effect upon school-age children will be made central.

Socialization and the Teacher

The school, expressed through teacher practices, reflects educational philosophy and practices. The amount of time a North American child spends in school attests to its importance. To state it in terms of the shortest minimum range, from six to 18 years of age a child spends from four to six hours a day, five days a week, 36 weeks a year in the classroom. This amounts to about 180 days a year, and in Northern Europe the school year may run to 220 days and more. The number of years students spend in school are increasing, as well. Although the figures vary from one state to another and are higher in urban areas, the typical adolescent graduates from high school and also spends some time in college or technical training.[3]

In North America, the school's task has also broadened tremendously during the last hun-

dred years or so. During the last century, schools were concerned largely with imparting certain information and skills. Today, the educator's concern for the "whole child" has permeated the educational program to the point where it is involved in students' personal, social, economic, political, and health development, and programs concerned only with the imparting of information and skills are now considered to be "less than minmial."

Robert J. Havighurst (1953) noted that the American middle class uses the school for a wider variety of purposes than any other society. American schools are expected to cooperate with the other training institutions of society—the family, the church, industry, and youth-serving organizations—in helping young people learn physical and recreational skills, select and prepare for occupations, prepare for marriage, and learn a scale of values. Basic to all these are the tasks of social development, and American educators consider the teaching of these tasks a major part of the school's responsibility.

Havighurst observed that there is no developmental task of children or adolescents that the school can completely ignore, inasmuch as these tasks are so interrelated that difficulties in classroom tasks often cause difficulties in tasks that are less obviously the responsibility of the school. Failure in academic tasks, for example, may result in failure in achieving a satisfactory vocational adjustment.

It is common knowledge that teachers not only share the views that Havighurst delineated but also that they are actively engaged in implementing them in the classroom. How the teacher serves as an agent of socialization as reflected by a sample of certain relevant research results concerns us here.

The teacher chooses certain activities in preference to others. She sets up certain standards and not others; thus, she is giving direc-

---

[3] Current Population Survey data from the U.S. Census Bureau estimate that in 1970 more than three-fourths of persons aged 25 to 29 had at least finished high school, and about one-sixth of this age group had completed four years of college or more.

tion to the group. She, of course, makes her choices on the basis of her conception of what children are like, how they should behave, and what they should learn; also involved is her own system of values—most often that of the middle class. The desirability of correct speech, politeness, cleanliness, neatness, and respect for property and thrift are imparted along with more academic information.

The teacher proceeds to socialize the child, using much the same methods as does the mother. She sets up standards of conduct to which the child is expected to conform. In addition to teaching subject matter, the teacher performs a variety of socializing practices. For example, she helps individual children in the school group by a variety of consciously recognized devices—creating situations in which it would be possible to see a previously objectionable child in a new role, getting a child previously ignored to contribute a talent which the other children have not recognized, helping a child to accept her as a person by accepting him as a person of worth, hoping these will lead to peer acceptance.

The teacher uses rewards and punishments in her socialization efforts. Not only are these used at the formal level epitomized by the "gold star" or "staying after school," but also in a variety of more subtle and much broader ways. Any teacher behavior that students regard positively may become a reinforcement that helps socialize children—a nod, a smile, a "that's fine," or merely giving a student full attention and listening to what he is saying. Some teachers, of course, seem unaware that the subtle approach works best and attempt to use more direct methods that hinder more than they help.

"The teacher looked up at Richard and said: 'Richard, stop that talking.' Following this,

she changed her focus from Richard and started to talk to the entire class. 'Some of you are cooperating and some of you aren't. Mary is cooperating and doing her work and so is Jimmy. Mabel was not listening. Now you know this is not a playground. This is a classroom and we're supposed to be learning. Good citizens don't bother other children who are trying to learn, do they? So let's all cooperate and be good citizens and not disturb other children. You know it's hard to learn when there's a lot of noise.'" (Kounin, 1971, pp. 102–103. Reprinted by permission.)

This type of admonition helps socialize some children, others take it as a matter of course, and still others rebel openly. Some classes, in fact, respond negatively to any of the usual methods of socialization and control. Terry Borton (1970) described a class

". . . in which eighteen children seemed to be devoting all their energies to massacring one another, destroying school equipment and breaking the sound barrier. They were not only oblivious to observers but did not even acknowledge the existence of their teacher. The teacher could not prevent the children from disassembling desks, tearing up classmates' papers, hurling books across the room, and running around the halls at will. I saw no evidence of friendship among the children. In fact, during one half-hour's observation each of the eighteen children was hit or kicked at least once. ten of the children being aggressors."[4]

The observer who made these comments took over this class and placed it on a "behavior modification" schedule, using principles of operant learning. The regimen she used called for the rewarding of socialized and socializing

4 Page 137. Reprinted by permission.

behaviors and the ignoring of misbehavior. (The rationale for ignoring misbehavior is that any kind of attention, positive or negative, is recognized by misbehaving children as a form of reinforcement that only serves to strengthen it.) Acceptable behavior was reinforced with points that could be traded in at a "store," which stocked a range of tangible rewards, such as candy, puzzles, model planes, comics and outings. The "prices" of rewards at the store were scaled in proportion to their educational relevance, as well as their attractiveness to the children: lollipops and gum were 10 points, and a trip to the zoo was 450 points. Children earned points for doing their assigned work, raising their hands when they wanted to talk, being on time, and following rules. A child typically earned between 20 to 100 points a morning, plus extra "teacher reinforcements" in the form of verbal praise and hugs.

Immediately the room became calmer and began to change, as most of the children busily began to accumulate points.

Some children rebelled, however. One boy strutted up and down, shouting: "I don't want any more points; stop giving them to me!" The other children ignored him completely, and, after a period of engaging in this unreinforced behavior, he sneaked into his seat and began to work furiously in order to accumulate points.

The experience described above is not an isolated incident. Operant conditioning and other behavior-modification methods have been used successfully in many other classrooms to bring order out of chaos and to get children back on the educational track. They have also been employed to eliminate or reduce the severity of a wide range of behavior problems in children and adults, as reports in the *Journal of Applied Behavior Analysis* attest.

Praise and Criticism

Behavior modification is a special skill that can be acquired by teachers and parents who wish to set up the proper controls and follow through with appropriate reinforcements. It is not clear, however, how it can be integrated with a regular school program on a routine basis. A busy teacher who has two, three, or more activity groups going on simultaneously in his classroom is likely to have all he can do to manage and direct the complex situation for which he is responsible and get his reinforcing done when he can. Still another problem is that children react in different ways to rewards (positive reinforcements). Cotler and Palmer (1971) discovered a considerable degree of variability among fourth, fifth, and sixth graders when they used positive reinforcement (Praise), negative reinforcement (Criticism), or No Reinforcement in test situations in which the children read printed material aloud. Children were divided into groups in terms of their test-anxiety scores, and were further subdivided in terms of whether their school achievement was higher than would be expected from their IQ (overachievers) or lower than would be expected (underachievers).

As might be expected, girls generally made fewer errors in oral readings than boys, and boys' performances showed the highest degree of variability. Although one might expect that the poorest performances would occur with children in the Punishment condition, the No Reinforcement condition actually produced the most errors for about half the children, and most of the boys in the Criticism condition did better than those in the Praise condition, as Figure 16–4 shows. This suggests that for some children, negative attention actually may stimulate learning better than positive attention or no attention at all. The

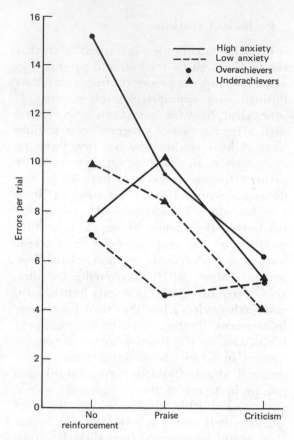

Figure 16-4. Effect of three experimental conditions in eliminating reading errors for elementary school boys, classified according to their test anxiety and their records of school achievement. (After Cotler and Palmer, 1971.)

results of a single study are not enough to base a philosophy of education on, of course, but they do show that there are no hard-and-fast rules with respect to the "best way to teach."

The Need to Achieve

Quite apart from its contribution to academic skills, the material the school selects for assignments or background reading also

influences children's values, beliefs, and attitudes, as well as their general behavior. This is done in ways that are often obvious, but even more often subtle.

David C. McClelland (1961) has shown that the kind of stories that appear in school textbooks can be used as an index to the stress a culture places on the need to achieve (n Ach). Here is a brief paraphrase of an example he cites that comes from a third-grade reader used in the Soviet Union and that rates high in n Ach.

The family had been working all morning harvesting the rye crop and were having a nap after lunch. Peter and his friend Bob were not sleeping, but were out in the field. Bob was bragging that he knew how to use the big scythe, and Peter challenged him to prove it. As Peter watched Bob mow, he became jealous, because Bob was obviously very skillful. Although Bob was older and larger, Peter felt he could do as well. Bob warned him that mowing was not as easy as it looked, but Peter was determined to have a go at it.

He picked up his father's scythe and began to swing it against the standing grain. At first he kept running the point into the ground. Then, on Bob's advice, he raised the tip, whereupon the scythe did not cut the rye but only flattened it. With more advice from Bob, he began to improve. His success led him to be overconfident, and on one particularly wide sweep, the scythe became tangled in the grain, and the handle broke.

At this point his father came up and asked who had broken the scythe. Peter confessed, saying that he had been trying to learn to mow. His father considered the possibility of boxing Peter's ears and then decided against it. He then said that he would make Peter a scythe that was lighter, more his size, to practice with. When Bob laughed at that, Peter's father asked him how many of *his* father's scythe blades he had broken in learning to mow.

This story rates high in n Ach because it shows the chief character taking initiative for self-improvement, attempting to compete with someone older and more skillful, succeeding at first and then failing, and his father approving of his trying to learn a new skill. McClelland has found that countries whose children read stories like these showed greater gains in economic production in succeeding years than did countries whose children read stories that lacked n Ach emphasis.

Teachers' Attitudes Toward Children's Behavior

In view of the fact that teachers play parent-like roles in their interaction with students, teacher attitudes are considered very important. In a classic study of this topic, Wickman (1928) secured ratings of mental hygiene specialists and teachers on the relative seriousness of various specified child behavior symptoms. The specialists and the teachers rated the relative seriousness of the same behavior item quite differently. The results were interpreted as showing that teachers rated as more serious those symptoms associated with noisier, more rebellious, disobedient, outgoing behavior which threatened the orderliness of the classroom, whereas the specialists rated as more serious the less threatening symptoms associated with withdrawal, anxiety, and sensitivity, while attaching little importance to almost all of those stressed by teachers.

It is evident that teachers were defining seriousness in terms of a moralistic point of view, with stress on aggressiveness against persons and property. Many of the problems the teachers placed as most serious were, in one way or another, challenges to their authority in the classroom. Evidently, seriousness was

equated with seriousness as a threat to the smooth-running functioning of the classroom. Moreover, before we become too critical of the attitude expressed by the teachers it is well to remember the mental hygienist had a different frame of reference, being much more concerned with behavior which had an ominous implication for the child's future emotional and personal development. The withdrawing type of symptom, unsocialness, as well as depression, suspicion, fearfulness, and sensitiveness have been demonstrated to be most difficult to overcome in treatment and sometimes to be the precursors of a more serious form of maladjustment.

The results seemed to reflect discredit on the acumen of the teachers, or so it was widely interpreted. Actually, the Wickman study had many serious defects, as Beilin (1959) and Beilin and Werner (1957) have shown, which render the results much less conclusive than they were interpreted to be. It should be noted that if the teacher is to do her job of communicating skills and values, this can be done only in an orderly environment. The aggressive child disrupts the class, the withdrawing child at least does not do this.

The attitudes and values of teachers in recent years have become more like those of the clinicians. This is particularly true for the more experienced teachers (Tolor, Scarpetti, and Lane, 1967). The need to impose structure and order on a classroom group, however, does lead teachers to adopt a nonsense approach to their work that is quite different from the nonteacher's view of what the ideal teacher-pupil relationship should be and that probably varies considerably from views held by students who enroll in teacher-education programs. Supervisors of practice teachers are, of course, highly aware of the personal qualities needed for classroom management. In one study, they tended to characterize the ideal female elementary teacher as being *dominant*, *persevering, persistent, serious, opinionated, ambitious, demanding, logical, rigid, clear-thinking, determined,* and *responsible.* This view was in marked contrast to students in introductory education courses, who were more likely to characterize the ideal teacher as being *curious, affectionate, careless, easy-going, unconventional, dreamy, understanding, irresponsible, cheerful, natural, individualistic,* and *thoughtful.* Those students who had some experience in practice teaching, however, had an image of the ideal teacher somewhat closer to that held by their supervisors. This finding suggests that their attitudes had been shaped by the give-and-take of the actual classroom situation or that they had been using their supervisors as models. Probably both explanations apply (Uchiyama and Lindgren, 1971).

Children's Reactions to the School Experience

Entrance into school is an experience that is exciting, thrilling, stressful, and anxiety-provoking. For many children, it is the first time that they have had to conform to a group pattern imposed by a single adult who is in charge of too many children to react to each child as an individual. Children are told to listen and not all speak at once. When the time comes for art, each child gets paper and crayons whether he feels like drawing or not. As one child said, "It is awful; all you do is mind all day long," and on another day he commented, "It is really awful. All you do is sit and sit and sit" (Murphy, Murphy and Newcomb, 1937, p. 652).

This new pattern of group conformity is moderated somewhat in some schools, but no teacher, no matter how humane and how sympathetic, can respond to or even be aware of each individual child simultaneously. As a consequence, she must make use of teacher-to-group rather than teacher-to-child methods.

The school is a source of frustration as well

as satisfaction. The child must conform or suffer the consequences. If his experiences are too painful, if he is unable to satisfy at least some of his needs, he will reject the school and do everything he can to fight off its influence, awaiting only the day he is of age to leave. In the meantime, he struggles against the teachers, and those children who accept the school become his natural enemies.

How do children react to the demands and pressures of the school? Any school is likely to have things to enjoy and things to complain about. Perhaps the best way to get some perspective on this matter is to look at data comparing American children's experiences with children in another culture. Berk, Rose, and Stewart (1970) replicated a study done in England with nine- and ten-year-old children, who had been asked how they felt about their relationship with their teachers, their class, doing well in school, school work, themselves, conforming or nonconforming behavior in class, and school in general. Results showed that American children, in general, expressed more positive attitudes about school than British children did. This was true of both middle- and lower-class students, and students at all ability levels. As might be expected, girls in both countries tended to express a more positive attitude toward school than boys, especially with respect to these factors: relationship with the teacher, attitude toward the class, importance of doing well, and conforming behavior in class. These sex differences were more marked with American children.

Differences in social class and ability were more likely to affect the attitudes of British rather than American children. Middle-class or high-IQ British children were more favorable toward school than were working-class children, but there were virtually no SES differences with American children.

The explanation for differences seems to lie in the fact that British schoolchildren have to cope with a much more rigid and more academic school curriculum and are also segregated fairly early according to their academic ability. The best-qualified children (most of whom are middle class) are oriented toward the more academically prestigious secondary schools, whereas those in less-qualified "streams" are shunted into schools that lead directly into employment and technical training. At the end of elementary school, British children take the famous 11+ examinations, which are used to decide their educational, vocational, and social fate thenceforward. As a consequence, children in the lower-ability streams (most of whom are working class) tend to feel some degree of jealousy and hostility toward children in the higher streams and reject the academic interests and values that characterize the successful ones—a kind of a defense mechanism to protect their diminished self-esteem.

Although children in American schools are often segregated by ability-grouping schemes, the arrangement tends to be much looser than it is in Britain, and the practice is far from universal. In America there is more shifting from one stream to another, and a child who is ability-grouped for some subjects (e.g., mathematics or English) may not be grouped for others (e.g., general science, art, social studies, music). The rather haphazard American system is better suited to permit the emergence of academic "late bloomers," whereas late blooming in the British system, though technically possible, is less likely to occur. The net effect, whether by accident or design, is for the American system to be more open and democratic, and the British system to be more closed, structured, and aristocratic. One should also add that it is much easier for American secondary school graduates to go on to higher education, and that most of them take advantage of the opportunity, as we have noted. Students who enter British universities and technical colleges are more

rigorously selected and admission is more of a signal honor, particularly when the government stands ready to subsidize almost all the students who are admitted.

The fact that SES differences in attitudes toward school are not as great in the United States as in Britain does not mean that they do not exist. Indeed, a number of studies with American children have focused on these differences. The reason why Berk, Rose, and Stewart found only slight ones may be explained in terms of the questionnaires they used, which were designed initially for a study of British children and were not aimed at following through on hypotheses based on comparative studies of psychological differences between social classes in America. Furthermore, only one city school system was included in their survey, the other five districts being suburban. This suggests that lower-class children may have been somewhat underrepresented in their study, although their finding that American working-class children have more favorable attitudes toward school than British working-class children is probably a valid one.

A study by James A. Dunn (1968) is worth reviewing here, not only because he found some differences in attitudes toward school among children at different levels of SES but also because some of his findings were contrary to what might ordinarily be expected.

Dunn surveyed over 700 fifth-, seventh-, and ninth-grade children, fairly equally divided as to sex and social class, from suburban and "inner city" schools. He asked them to indicate the degree to which they liked eight different school activities, ranging from learning about science and nature to playing games and sports. Four activities were concerned with the academic aspects of the school, and four with its social aspects.

His findings showed that with increasing age, students' attitudes toward both academic and social aspects of school became more

Responses to the school experience

Although the school is a highly structured, formalized and, to some extent, artificial situation, it nevertheless represents society's major attempt to bring children into the mainstream of life. The attempts of teachers to carry out their tasks in this undertaking meet with variable success. Some children respond with enthusiasm, others with apathy. Some respond with diligence, others with anxiety. Some respond with interest and involvement, or eagerness and warmth, and still others, with boredom.

negative. This was, however, truer of the middle-class students, who expressed increasing dislike and gave lower ratings in value for all aspects of school, whereas lower-class children not only expressed fewer negative feelings but also tended to value school activities higher. In view of the fact that lower-class children have more problems in school and are also more likely to drop out before graduation, this finding is surprising and paradoxical: middle-class children come to like and value school less, but are more successful; lower-class children like and value school relatively more, but are more likely to fail.

One explanation for this apparent paradox is this: the fact that academic success is more elusive to the lower-class individual may make it more attractive. The lower-class approach to institutionalized authority, represented in this instance by teachers and administrators, is that of taking their pronouncements unquestioningly and literally, whereas the middle-class student is more likely to assert his independence and raise challenging questions. As we noted in our earlier discussion of SES differences, lower-class children are trained by their parents to obey authority figures, whereas middle-class children are trained to think for themselves. Other research supports this interpretation of the results, as we shall see shortly.

The children in this study also took a test to measure anxiety about school success. Results showed more anxiety for lower-class children, particularly at the elementary school level. Girls expressed more anxiety than boys, but not at the fifth grade level. Again we have a paradox: girls, who get better grades than boys, express more anxiety about school work. The explanation may be found in the attitudes girls report: at the fifth-grade level, girls also are much more positive about academic activities than boys, and are also less anxious; from the seventh grade onward, girls'

interest in academics drops, but their anxiety about school success increases. Seen in this light, the relationship seems to be a logical one. What was earlier a pleasure has become a threat.

Another study comparing the attitudes of children of various grades and at various SES levels was conducted by Neale and Proshek (1967), whose findings were in some respects similar to those of Dunn. They found a general decline in positive attitudes toward the school during grades four, five, and six, the more significant drop being in attitudes favorable toward *my teacher, my classroom, my school books, following rules, working arithmetic problems, talking in front of class, having to keep quiet, fighting with other children,* and *stealing things.* In fact, the attitudes expressed by the sixth graders were *generally* more negative than those of fourth graders: even *mother* and *father* were regarded less favorably. It is interesting to note that *reading a book* suffered the least decline of any of the stimulus variables toward which children expressed attitudes. Except for *fighting with other children* and *stealing things,* boys' attitudes toward school were less favorable than those of girls— a routine finding.

There were a number of differences in the reactions of students in the two SES levels tested. As Figure 16-5 shows, there was no overall difference in attitude toward *mother,* but middle-class children regarded *father* and *college student* more favorably. These differences are in the expected direction: in the more democratic middle-class families, fathers are less of a threat, and the expectation that one go to college is not only accepted but is looked forward to eagerly. Except for *my teacher* and *reading a book,* however, lower-class children regard school more positively than middle-class children. Some of the differences deserve comment. The visible aspects of education are valued by lower-class children

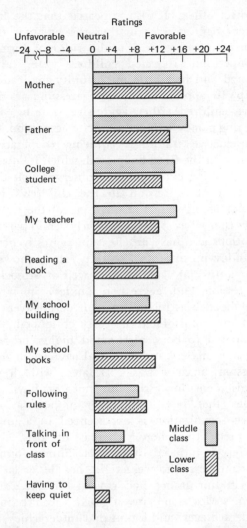

Figure 16-5. Social-class differences in elementary school children with regard to their attitudes toward mother, father, *and a number of stimulus variables representing the school and its activities.* (After Neale and Proshek, 1967.)

more than some of its activities: *my school books* gets a higher rating than *reading a book*. Conforming to discipline is also more attractive to lower-class children: *following rules* and *having to keep quiet* are valued positively.

This latter finding supports our explanation of why lower-class children are more favorably disposed to school than middle-class children, even though they are more likely to fail.

One can also add that the lives of lower-class children are more likely to be chaotic and unpredictable; for many of them, school is the only place where they can count on the security of an orderly, dependable routine.

Although children's evaluations of school decline somewhat with increasing maturity, their reactions are generally positive. Berk, Rose, and Stewart noted that their American subjects, by and large, responded postively to questions about their school and were willing to give it the benefit of the doubt, irrespective of SES and IQ differences. The ratings in Figure 16-5 are also almost entirely positive. Even *following the rules* gets a favorable endorsement. This should be heartening and supportive to teachers who find themselves being stricter than they would like to be, who work hard at the task of making their classrooms interesting "laboratories for learning," and generally try their best to live up to everyone's expectations for them.

To end this discussion on an even more positive note, we can cite a particularly interesting survey by Greenfield and Finkelstein (1970), who compared the reactions of junior high school students in the early 1930s with those of students at the same school 30 years later. The students of the 1960s, they found, were spending much more time on their studies than those of the 1930s: 48% studying two hours or more a day, in contrast to only 17% in the 1930s. Students in the 1960s were also more humanistic and less materialistic in their values. What is of particular interest, however, is that children in the 1960s of both sexes and all ability levels reported better relations with teachers than did children in the 1930s.

To be sure, this is a single study about two

sets of students removed in time in a single school, but it is one solid bit of evidence suggesting that the increasing democratization of the school may be having some positive results.

Summary

In North American culture, the major influence during middle and late childhood comes from the peer group. Children in this age group leave home (literally and figuratively) to a much greater degree than younger children. The time spent at home declines to its lowest level during adolescence. The peer group teaches the child complex social skills he could not acquire at home. It provides norms, roles, and models with which the child can identify. Peer groups in their purest form may be characterized by their loose organization and the fact that they are centered around short-range concerns rather than long-term goals. The child's susceptibility to the pressures of the group is reflected in a classic study by Berenda. Asked to judge the relative length of lines, children were induced to make errors by the false answers of other "subjects" who were actually confederates of the experimenter. Younger subjects were the most influenced, and a group of peers had a greater effect as confederates than a teacher had. Comparative studies of Soviet and American children show that Soviet peer groups are likely to reinforce adult behavior standards, whereas American peer groups are likely to be less accepting of adults and more ambivalent.

Peer groups often encourage the expression of aggressive behavior. McNeil investigated the aggressive patterns of behavior in a group of emotionally disturbed and delinquent boys. He found that the children who fought frequently were also the ones who fought to protect others. It also appeared that the frequent fighters were neither the best nor the worst at staying within the rules of formal competition. Rejected children were scapegoated and had little opportunity for leadership. In another study of aggression, Davitz gave children either aggressive training, involving games designed to incite aggression, or constructive training, requiring cooperative efforts. In the free-play period, which followed a frustrating experience, he observed that the amount of aggression in the children's behavior changed in the direction of the training that they received. Early child-parent relations also have an effect on aggressiveness. A follow-up of Sears' "pattern" study showed that antisocial aggression, as well as prosocial aggression and aggression anxiety in later childhood, was related to high permissiveness and low punishment in early childhood. As compared to boys, girls rated higher on aggression anxiety and prosocial aggression. Aggression anxiety was correlated with high punishment for girls, but not for boys. It seems that boys' aggression anxiety arises when socialization is experienced in a love-oriented atmosphere, whereas in girls, the anxiety is induced by conflict. Finney found that mothers who were rigid, hostile, or lacking in nurturance had covertly hostile children. Morrison investigated over- and underachievers and found that underachievers were covertly hostile. She also found no difference between the groups' scores on standardized achievement tests. A great deal of current interest has been directed toward the influence of violence and aggression in the mass media. Bandura, Ross and Ross showed children films of adult aggression and vigorous nonaggressive play. Their results suggest that any kind of vigorous stimulus may incite aggressive responses in boys, who are more prone to such behavior than girls are. Feshbach and Singer noted the opposite effect when they controlled the television viewing behavior of several groups of boys. The boys who saw violent and aggressive programs had fewer fights of all kinds. Berkowitz cites research that comes to conclusions opposite to those of Feshbach and Singer and more consistent with common sense. One study of kindergarteners showed that those who saw violent programs displayed more disturbed behavior than those who saw "passive" programs, but the nature of the study made it difficult to maintain adequate controls and the results are more suggestive than definitive. More research is obviously needed to clarify the ambiguous relationship between fantasy violence and aggressive behavior.

Sociometric measures of individual social acceptability remain as constant as intelligence test scores. In spite of this constancy, however, the characteristics responsible for social acceptibility change as the children grow older. This suggests that the popular child is consistent in his social adaptibility. Popularity is also associated with the traits that are characteristic of sex typing. Popular boys are regarded by their peers as athletic and daring and popular girls as docile and unassertive. There are also age differences with respect to the extent the two sexes attract each other. Preschoolers pay little attention to the sex of their playmates, but affiliations become less heterosexual as the children grow older. Social acceptance patterns also vary with SES. Pope compared a group of lower-lower (LL) class youngsters with another from the upper-middle (UM) class and found a number of different patterns of social behavior. The leaders of the LL group were domineering and belligerent, whereas the leaders of the UM group were athletic but not aggressive. Although the LL group boys could not tolerate studious or classroom-conforming boys, this same type was not rejected by the UM group. In contrast to the UM group, where girls of

the "little lady" type are popular with the boys, LL boys preferred girls who were rowdy and aggressive. The correlates of social influence differs between boys and girls. Boys acquire influence through intimidation, girls through decorous behavior and social skills. High sociometric status is also related to role-playing ability and emotional adjustment. Throughout middle and late childhood the stability of friendships increases. Dymond and her associates found that friendship qualities also change with time. Younger children stress external characteristics, such as having a nice home, while older children emphasize personality characteristics.

The peer group provides opportunities for both cooperation and competition. An older study by Maller revealed that children preferred to work competitively, and the efficiency of work under competition was higher than work under cooperation. The only exception to this general finding was a situation in which boys and girls were allowed to work for their own sex group. Phillips and D'Amico found that children working together for the good of the group actually increased their liking for one another. This was also the case in competing groups unless one or two members got disproportionate shares of the rewards.

In North America, the school's task has broadened tremendously during the last century. Schools are expected to help young people learn physical and recreational skills, prepare for marriage, and learn a scale of values. The teacher serves as an agent of socialization, reinforcing certain activities in preference to others. Any teacher behavior that students regard positively, from a smile to a gold star, may become a reinforcement that helps socialize children. Some contemporary methods, notably the "behavior modification" technique, make use of this fact and attempt to extend control over all such sources of reinforcement. By ignoring misbehavior, rewarding acceptable behavior, and sometimes establishing an "economy" or system of tangible rewards as well, psychologists and teachers can reduce the severity of a wide range of classroom behavior problems. Some research, however, shows considerable variability among children, especially boys, in the way they re-respond to various reinforcements. In one study, boys tended to make the most errors in reading under No Reinforcement conditions, fewer errors under Praise conditions, and the fewest under Criticism conditions. For one subgroup of boys, Praise produced the greatest number of errors.

Quite apart from its contribution to academic skills, the materials the school selects for study also influence the child's values, attitudes and behavior. McClelland has shown that the kind of stories that appear in school textbooks can be used as an index to the stress that culture places on the need to achieve. Countries whose children read stories stressing the need to achieve show greater gains in economic production in succeeding years. The attitudes held by teachers are also important to the child's development. Wickman compared the ratings of what teachers and mental hygiene specialists considered to be serious child behavior symptoms. It seemed that teachers felt that behavior which interfered with the smooth-running functioning of the classroom was serious, whereas the clinicians were most concerned with symptoms of depression or withdrawal. In recent years, however, teacher attitudes have become more like those of the clinicians. The supervisors of practice teachers tend to characterize the ideal female elementary school teacher as being persevering, dominant, ambitious, rigid, and responsible. This is in contrast to the view of students in introductory education courses, who characterize the ideal teacher as curious, affectionate, individualistic, easy-going, and understanding.

The entrance into school is both exciting and anxiety-provoking. The child is forced to conform to group standards, perhaps for the first time. Berk, Rose, and Stewart compared the feelings expressed by American and British youngsters about school. American children proved to have a more positive attitude than British children did. One explanation for this difference is the fairly inflexible structure of the British system of ability grouping. The children in the lower ability group "streams" may display their feelings of jealousy and hostility toward the children in higher streams by rejecting academic interests and values. The fact that SES differences in attitudes toward school are not as great in the United States as in Britain does not mean that they do not exist at all. Dunn found that, with increasing age, middle-class children expressed increasing dislike for all aspects of school. In view of the fact that lower-class children have more problems with school, this finding is paradoxical. A possible explanation is that middle-class children and older children are encouraged to raise challenging questions while lower-class children are trained not to question authority. Dunn also found that girls expressed more anxiety about school work, even though they got better grades. Neal and Proshek conducted a study with findings similar to those of Dunn. Some specific observations were that middle-class children regarded *father* and *college student* more favorably than did lower-class children, although they did not differ in attitude toward *mother*. The lower-class children also seemed to value the visible aspects of education more than some of its activities. Greenfield and Finklestein compared the reactions of junior high school students in the early 1930s with those of students at the same school 30 years later. The students of the 1960s were found to be more humanistic, less materialistic, studied harder, and got along better with their teachers.

Photo Credits

page 131 left		Ken Heyman
	right	Suzanne Szasz
page 150 left		Ken Heyman
	right	George Roos
page 151 top left		Burt Glinn/Magnum
	top right	Mimi Forsyth/Monkmeyer
	bottom	Ken Heyman
page 158 top		Abe Halperin/Monkmeyer
	bottom	Suzanne Szasz
page 159 left &		Ken Heyman
	top right	
	bottom right	Mimi Forsyth/Monkmeyer
page 170		Courtesy Dr. Richard D. Walk
page 172 top left		Lew Merrim/Monkmeyer
	top right	George Roos
	bottom	Susanne Szasz
page 173 top left		Michael Heron/Monkmeyer
	top right	Ken Heyman
	bottom	Sybil Shackman/Monkmeyer
page 206 left &		Ken Heyman
	top right	
	bottom right	Henry Clay Lindgren
page 207		Ken Heyman
page 216 top left		Suzanne Szasz
	top right &	Ken Heyman
	bottom	
page 217 top left		Michael Heron/Monkmeyer
	bottom left &	Ken Heyman
	right	
page 242 top		David S. Strickler/Monkmeyer
	bottom left	Ken Heyman
	bottom right	Henry Clay Lindgren
page 243		George Roos
page 246 left		Ken Heyman
	right	Sybil Shelton/Monkmeyer
page 247		Suzanne Szasz
pages 266 & 267		George Roos
page 278 top left		Suzanne Szasz
	top right	Ken Heyman
	bottom	George Roos
page 279 top left		Ken Heyman
	bottom left	Robert S. Smith/Rapho Guillumette
	right	Harvey Barad/Monkmeyer
page 300		Ken Heyman

page 301 top		Michael Heron/Monkmeyer
	bottom	Ken Heyman
page 314 top left		Henry Clay Lindgren
	top right &	Ken Heyman
	bottom left	
page 315 top left &		Ken Heyman
	bottom left	
	right	Henry Clay Lindgren
page 344 top &		Ken Heyman
	bottom left	
	bottom right	George Roos
page 345 left		George Roos
	top right	Wayne Miller/Magnum
	bottom right	Ken Heyman
page 350 left		Ken Heyman
	right	David Hurn/Magnum
page 351 top		George Roos
	bottom	Dan Nelken/Monkmeyer
page 368 top		Mimi Forsyth/Monkmeyer
	bottom	Irene B. Bayer/Monkmeyer
page 369 top left		Hugh Rogers/Monkmeyer
	top right	Sybil Shackman/Monkmeyer
	bottom	George Roos
page 388		George Roos
page 404 top left		Sybil Shackman/Monkmeyer
	top right &	Ken Heyman
	bottom	
page 405 left		Sybil Shelton/Monkmeyer
	top right &	Ken Heyman
	bottom right	
page 412 top left		Ken Heyman
	top right &	Michael Heron/Monkmeyer
	bottom	
page 413 left		Bruce Davidson/Magnum
	right	Michael Heron/Monkmeyer
page 452 top left		Ken Heyman
	top right	Joe Molnar
	bottom left	Pro Pix/Monkmeyer
	bottom right	Eric L. Brown/Monkmeyer
page 453 top left		George Roos
	top right	Michael Heron/Monkmeyer
	bottom	Joe Molnar

References and Author Index

Works cited in this book are listed alphabetically by author and year of publication.
Numbers following each citation refer to the text pages on which the works are cited.

Abbott, L., *see* Wilson et al.

Abernethy, E. M., Relationships between mental and physical growth. *Monogr. Soc. Res. Child Develpm.,* 1936, 1, No. 7. 366

Abrams, N., & Pieper, W., Experiences in developing a preschool program for neurologically handicapped children— a preliminary report. *J. Learn. Disabil.,* 1968, 1, 394-402. 52-53

Adams, A. O., *see* Holt et al.

Adams, G., *see* Brackbill et al.

Aldrich, A. A., Sung, C., & Knop, C. A., The crying of newly born babies: II. The individual phase. *J. Pediat.,* 1945, 27, 89-96. 182

Alexander, G. J., Miles, B. E., Gold, G. M., & Alexander, R. B., LSD: Injection in early pregnancy produces abnormalities in off-spring of rats., *Science,* 1967, 157, 459-460. 116

Alexander, R. B., *see* Alexander et al.

Allen, K. D., *see* Blatz et al.

Allen, V. L., *see* Asher & Allen.

Alpert, R., *see* Sears, Rau, et al.

Ambrose, J. A., The age of onset of ambivalence in early infancy: Indications from the study of laughing. *J. child psychol. Pschyiat.,* 1963, 4, 167-181. 257

Amen, E. W., & Renison, N., A study of the relationship between play patterns and anxiety in young children. *Genet. psychol. Monogr.,* 1954, 50, 3-41. 253, 375

Ames, E. W., *see* Brennan et al.

Ames, L. B., The constancy of psycho-motor tempo in individual infants. *J. genet. Psychol.,* 1940, 57, 445-450. 182, 244

Ames, L. B., The development of the sense of time in the young child. *J. genet. Psychol.,* 1946, 68, 97-125. 270

Ames, L. B., Children's stories. *Genet. psychol. Monogr.,* 1966, 73, 337-396. 254-255, 437

Anastasi, A., Intelligence and family size. *Psychol. Bull.,* 1956, 53, 187-209. 42, 228

Anderson, J. E., Methods of child psychology. In L. Carmichael, Ed., *Manual of child psychology.,* 2nd ed. N. Y.: Wiley, 1954. 37

Anthony, E. J., The behavior disorders of childhood. In P. H. Mussen, Ed., *Carmichael's manual of child psychology,* 3rd ed. N. Y.: Wiley, 1970. 98

Apgar, V., Proposal for new methods of evaluation of newborn infants. *Anesth. Analg.,* 1953, 32, 260-267. 122

Aries, P., *Centuries of childhood.* N. Y.: Knopf, 1962. 4

Arsenian, J. M., Young children in an insecure situation. *J. abnorm. soc. Psychol.,* 1943, 38, 235-249. 214, 330

Asher, S. R., & Allen, V. L., Racial preferences and social comparison processes. *J. soc. Issues,* 1969, 25(1), 157-165. 346

Austin, M. C., & Thompson, G. C., Children's friendships: A study of the bases on which children select and reject their best friends. *J. educ. Psychol.,* 1948, 39, 101-116. 443

Ausubel, D., Negativism as a phase of ego development. *Amer. J. Orthopsychiat.,* 1950, 20, 796-805. 332

Babson, S. G., Henderson, N. B., & Clark, W. M., Jr., Preschool intelligence of oversized newborns. *Amer. Psychol. Assn. Proc.,* 1969, 4, 267-268. 123

Baer, D. M., *see* Bijou and Baer.

Baker, C. T., *see* Sontag et al.

Baldwin, J. M., *Social and ethical interpretations in mental development.* N. Y.: Macmillan, 1906. 227

Ball, W. & Tronick, E., Infant responses to impending collision: Optical and real. *Science,* 1971, 171, 818-820. 171

Balsbaugh, C., *see* McCandless et al.

Bandura, A., Social-learning theory of identificatory processes. In D. A. Goslin, Ed., *Handbook of socialization theory and research.* Chicago: Rand McNally, 1969. 84-85, 86

Bandura, A., & McDonald, F. J., Influence of social reinforcement and the behavior of models in shaping children's moral judgments. *J. abnorm. soc. Psychol.,* 1963, 67, 274-281. 425-426

Bandura, A., Ross, D., & Ross, S. A., Transmission of aggression through imitation of aggressive models. *J. abnorm. soc. Psychol.,* 1961, 63, 575-582. 340

Bandura, A., & Walters, R. H., *Social learning and personality development.* N. Y.: Holt, Rinehart, & Winston, 1963a. 72-73

Bandura, A. & Walters, R. H., Aggression. *Yearbook Nat. Soc. Stud. Educ.,* 1963b, **62**, Part I, 384-415. 339

Banham, K. M., The development of affectionate behavior in infancy. *J. genet. Psychol.,* 1950, **76**, 283-289. 215

Bates, H. D. & Katz, M. M., Development of the verbal regulation of behavior. *Amer. Psychol. Assn. Proc.,* 1970, **5**, 299-300. 282

Baumrind, D., Harmonious parents and their preschool children. *Develpm. Psychol.,* 1971a, **4**, 99-102. 54-55

Baumrind, D., Current patterns of parental authority. *Develpm. Psychol.,* 1971b, **4**, No. 1, Part 2. 302-303

Bayer, L. M., & Snyder, M. M., Illness experience of a group of normal children. *Child Develpm.,* 1950, **21**, 93-120. 238, 365

Bayley, N., Mental growth during the first three years: A developmental study of sixty-one children by repeated tests. *Genet. psychol. Monogr.,* 1933, **14**, No. 1. 180

Bayley, N., The development of motor abilities during the first three years. *Monogr. Soc. Res. Child Develpm.,* 1935, **1**. 145-146

Bayley, N., Development and maturation. In H. Nelson, Ed., *Theoretical foundations of psychology.* N. Y.: Van Nostrand, 1951. 244

Bayley, N., On the growth of intelligence. *Amer. Psychologist,* 1955, **10**, 805-818. 180

Bayley, N., Value and limitations of infant testing. *Children,* 1958, **5**, 129-133. 182

Bayley, N., Consistency of maternal and child behaviors in the Berkeley Growth Study. *Vita Humana,* 1964, **7**, 73-95. 305-306

Bayley, N., Learning in adulthood: The role of intelligence. In H. J. Klausmeir & C. W. Harris, Eds., *Analyses of concept learning.* N. Y.: Academic, 1966. 288

Bayley, N., Development of mental abilities. In P. H. Mussen, Ed., *Carmichael's manual of child psychology,* 3rd ed., N. Y.: Wiley, 1970. 288, 305

Bayley, N., & Schaefer, E. S., Relationships between socioeconomic variables and the behavior of mothers toward young children. *J. genet. Psychol.,* 1960, **96**, 61-77. 399-401

Bayley, N., & Schaefer, E. S., Correlations of maternal and child behaviors with the development of mental abilities: data from the Berkeley Growth Study. *Monogr. Soc. Res. Child Develpm.,* 1964, **29**, (6, Whole No. 97). 303-304

Bayley, N., *see also* Cameron et al.; Jones & Bayley; Rheingold & Bayley; and Schaefer & Bayley

Bee, H. L., et al. Social class differences in maternal teaching strategies and speech patterns. *Develpm. Psychol.,* 1969, **1**, 726-734. 318

Behrens, M. L., Child rearing and the character of structure of the mother. *Child. Develpm.,* 1954, **25**, 225-238. 195

Beilin, H., Teachers' and clinicians' attitudes toward the behavior problems of children: a reappraisal. *Child Developm.,* 1959, **30**, 9-26. 449

Beilin, H., & Werner, E., Sex differences among teachers in the use of the criteria of adjustment. *J. educ. Psychol.,* 1957, **48**, 426-436. 449

Bell, R. L., Jr., *see* Mouton et al.

Bell, R. Q., Relations between behavior manifestations in the human neonate. *Child Develpm.,* 1960, **31**, 463-477. 134-135, 182

Bell, R. Q., *see also* Schaefer & Bell

Beller, E. K., Dependency and independence in young children. *J. genet. Psychol.,* 1955, **87**, 25-35. 329

Beller, E. K., Dependency and autonomous achievement striving related to orality and anality in early childhood. *Child Develpm.,* 1957a, **28**, 287-315. 329

Beller, E. K., Dependency, socialization and emotional disturbance in early childhood. Unpublished paper, *Amer. Psychol. Assn.,* convention, 1957b. 329

Beller, E. K., A study of dependency and perceptual orientation. *Amer. Psychologist,* 1958, **13**, 347. (Abstract). 330

Beller, E. K., Exploratory studies of dependency. *Trans. N. Y.: Acad. Science,* 1959, **21**, 414-426. 329, 330

Beller, E. K., & Turner, J. le B., Dependency and aggression: sex differences in "normal" and "emotionally disturbed" preschool children. Unpublished paper, *Amer. Psychol. Assn.* convention, 1962. 335

Bellugi, V., *see* Brown & Bellugi; and Bronowski & Bellugi

Benjamin, J. D., Further comments on some developmental aspects of anxiety. In H. Gaskill, Ed., *Counterpoint.* N. Y.: International University Press, 1963. 221

Bennett, E. L., Diamond, M. C., Krech, D., & Rosenzweig, M. R., Chemical and anatomical plasticity of brain. *Science,* 1964, **146**, 610-619. 189

Bennett, H. L., *see* McCandless et al.

Bereiter, C. & Engelmann, S., *Teaching disadvantaged children in the preschool.* Englewood Cliffs, N. J.: Prentice Hall, 1966. 286

Berenda, R. W., *The influence of the group on the judgments of children.* N. Y.: King's Crown Press, 1950. 432

Bergman, P., *see* Escalona & Bergman

Berk, L. E., Effects of variations in the nursery school setting on environmental constraints and children's modes of adaptation. *Child Develpm.,* 1971, **42**, 839-869. 15, 41

Berk, L. E., Rose, M. H., & Stewart, D., Attitudes of English and American children toward their school experience. *J. educ. Psychol.,* 1970, **61**, 33-40. 450-451, 455

Berkowitz, L., The contagion of violence: An S-R mediational analysis of some effects of observed aggression. In W. J. Arnold & M. M. Page, Eds., *Nebraska Symposium on Motivation,* 1970. Lincoln,: U. of Nebraska Press, 1971. 437-438

Berkson, J., *see* Norval et al.

Berlyne, D. E., Recent developments in Piaget's work. *Brit. J. educ. Psychol.,* 1957, 27, 1-12. 226

Berlyne, D. E., Curiosity and exploration. *Science,* 1966, 153, 25-33. 189

Berlyne, D. E., Arousal and reinforcement. In D. Levine, Ed., *Nebraska Symposium on Motivation.* Lincoln: U. of Nebraska Press, 1967. 88, 89

Bernstein, B. A., Sociolinguistic approach to socialization: with some reference to educability. In J. Gumperz & D. Hymes, Eds., *Directions in sociolinguistics.* N. Y.: Holt, Rinehart, & Winston, 1972. 276

Bibring, G. L., Dwyer, T. F., Huntington, D. S., & Valenstein, A. F., A study of the psychological processes of pregnancy and of the earliest mother-child relationship: II. Methodological considerations. *Psychoanalyt. Stud. Child,* 1961, 16, 25-72. 140

Bijou, S. W., & Baer, D. M., *Child development: a systematic and empirical theory.* N. Y.: Appleton-Century-Crofts, 1961. 29

Biller, H. B., *see* Blanchard & Biller

Blake, R. R., *see* Mouton et al.

Blakely, W. P., A study of seventh grade children's reading of comic books as related to certain other variables. *J. genet. Psychol.,* 1958, 93, 291-301. 437

Blanc, W. A., *see* Naeye et al.

Blanchard, R. W. & Biller, H. B., Father availability and academic performance among third-grade boys. *Develpm. Psychol.,* 1971, 4, 301-305. 309-310

Blase, B., *see* Solkoff et al.

Blatchley, M. E., *see* Ottinger et al.

Blatz, W. E., Allen, K. D., & Millichamp, D. A., A study of laughter in the nursery school child. *Univ. of Toronto Stud. Child Develpm. Series,* 1936, No. 7. 257

Bloom, B., *Stability and change in human characteristics.* N. Y.: Wiley, 1964. 61

Blum, W. L., *see* Bresnahan & Blum

Bonney, M. E., The constancy of sociometric scores and their relationship to teacher judgments of social success, to personality self-ratings. *Sociometry,* 1943, 6, 409-424. 438, 439

Boring, E. G., The nature and history of experimental control. *Amer. J. Psychol.,* 1954, 67, 573-589. 54

Borton, T., *Reach, touch, and teach.* N. Y.: McGraw-Hill, 1970. 446-447

Bowlby, J., *Maternal care and mental health.* Geneva: World Health Organization, 1951. 198, 199

Brackbill, Y., Extinction of the smiling response in infants as a function of reinforcement schedule. *Child Develpm.,* 1958, 29, 115-124. 227

Brackbill, Y., Continuous stimulation and arousal levels in infants: Additive effects. *Amer. Psychol. Assn. Proc.,* 1970, 5, 271-272. 134, 188

Brackbill, Y., Adams, G., Crowell, D. H., & Gray, M. L., Arousal level in neonates and older infants under continuous auditory stimulation. *J. exper. child Psychol.,* 1966, 4, 178-188. 134

Brackett, C. W., Laughing and crying of preschool children. *Child develpm. Monogr.,* 1934, No. 14. 256-257

Braine, M. D. S., Piaget on reasoning: a methodical critique and alternative proposals. In W. Kessen & C. Kuhlman, Eds., *Thought in the young child. Monogr. Soc. for Res. in Child Develpm.,* 1962, 27, 41-61. 265

Braine, M. D. S., The ontongeny of English phrase structure: The first phase. *Language,* 1963, 39, 1-13. 276

Brandt, E. M., *see* Mitchell & Brandt

Brennan, W. M., Ames, E. W., & Moore, R. W., Age differences in infants' attention to patterns of different complexities. *Science,* 1966, 151, 354-356. 170

Bresnahan, J. L., & Blum, W. L., Chaotic reinforcement: a socioeconomic leveler. *Develpm. Psychol.,* 1971, 4, 89-92. 317

Bridges, K. M. B., A genetic theory of the emotions. *J. genet. Psychol.,* 1930, 37, 514-527. 155-156

Bridges, K. M. B., *Social and emotional development of the preschool child.* London: Kegan, Paul, 1931. 251, 255

Bridges, K. M. B., Emotional development in early infancy. *Child Develpm.,* 1932, 2, 214-341. 155-156, 220

Brill, S., *see* Honig & Brill

Brockman, L. B. & Ricciuti, H. N., Severe protein-calorie malnutrition and cognitive development in infancy and early childhood. *Develpm. Psychol.,* 1971, 4, 312-319. 140-141

Brodbeck, A. J. & Irwin, O. C., The speech behavior of infants without families. *Child Develpm.,* 1946, 17, 145-156. 179

Bronfenbrenner, U., Reaction to social pressure from adults versus peers among Soviet day school and boarding school pupils in the perspective of an American sample. *J. pers. soc. Psychol.,* 1970, 15. 179-189

Bronowski, J. & Bellugi, U., Language, name, and concept. *Science,* 1970, 168, 660-673. 284

Brophy, J. E., *see* Laosa & Brophy

Brotemarkle, R. A., Clinical psychology 1896-1946. *J. consult. Psychol.,* 1947, 11, 1-4. 23

Brown, D. G., Masculinity-femininity development in children. *J. consult. Psychol.,* 1957, 21, 197-202. 417-418

Brown, R. & Bellugi, U., Three processes in the child's

acquisition of syntax. *Harvard educ. Rev.,* 1964, **34,** 133-151. 276

Bruner, J. S., et al., *A study of thinking.* N. Y.: Wiley, 1956. 269

Buhler, C., The social behavior of children. In C. Murchison, Ed., *Handbook of child psychology,* 2nd ed., rev. Worcester: Clark U. Press, 1931, 374-416. 220-230

Buker, M. C., *see* Horrocks & Buker

Burchinal, L., Gardner, B., & Hawkes, G. R., Children's personality adjustment and the socio-economic status of their families. *J. genet. Psychol.,* 1958, **92,** 149-159. 401

Burchinal, L. G., *see* Gardner, Hawkes & Burchinal

Burke, E. J., III, Sociogram of a fourth-grade class. Unpublished paper, San Francisco State College, April, 1971. 439-440

Burns, N. & Cavey, L., Age differences in empathic ability among children. *Canad, J. Psychol.,* 1957, **11,** 227-230. 347

Buss, A. H., *The psychology of aggression.* N. Y.: Wiley, 1961. 335

Caldwell, B. M., et al., Mother-infant interaction in monomatric and polymatric families. *Amer. J. Orthopsychiat.,* 1963, **33,** 653-664. 208

Caldwell, B. M., *see* Honig et al.; and Graham, Matarazzo, et al.

Cameron, J., Livson, N., & Bayley, N., Infant vocalizations and their relationship to mature intelligence. *Science,* 1967, **157,** 331-333. 42, 181

Cameron, P. & Janky, C., Effects of TV violence on children: a maturalistic experiment. *Amer. Psychol. Assn. Proc.,* 1971, **6,** 233-234. 437-438

Campos, J. J., Langer, A., & Krowitz, A., Cardiac responses on the visual cliff in prelocomotor human infants. *Science,* 1970, **170,** 196-197. 170

Capra, P. C., & Dittes, J. E., Birth order as a selective factor among volunteer subjects. *J. abnorm. soc. Psychol.,* 1962, **64,** 302. 322

Caputo, D. V., & Mandell, W., Consequences of low birth weight. *Develpm. Psychol.,* 1970, **3,** 363-383. 123

Carlson, R., Identification and personality structure in preadolescents. *J. abnorm. soc. Psychol.,* 1963, **67,** 566-573. 414

Carpenter, A., The differential measurement of speed in primary school children. *Child Develpm.,* 1971, **12,** 1-7. 245, 366

Carmichael, L., Ontogenetic development. In S. S. Stevens, Ed., *Handbook of experimental psychology.* N. Y.: Wiley, 1951. 75

Carmichael, L., The onset and early development of behavior. In L. Carmichael, Ed., *Manual of child psychology,* 2nd ed. N. Y.: Wiley, 1954. 63

Castenada, A., McCandless, B. R., & Palermo, D. S., The children's form of the Manifest Anxiety Scale. *Child Develpm.,* 1956, **27,** 317-326. 374

Castenada, A., Palermo, D. S., & McCandless, B. R., Complex learning and performance as a function of anxiety in children and task difficulty. *Child Develpm.,* 1956, **27,** 328-332. 375

Castenada, A., *see also* McCandless et al.; and Palermo et al.

Cattell, P., *The measurement of intelligence of infants.* N. Y.: Psychol. Corp., 1940. 179, 181

Caudill, W., & Weinstein, H., Maternal care and infant behavior in Japan and America. *Psychiatry,* 1969, **32,** 12-43. 81

Cavey, L., *see* Burns and Cavey

Chance, J. E., Independence training and first graders' achievement. *J. consult. Psychol.,* 1961, **25,** 149-154. 334

Charlesworth, R., & Hartup, W. W., Positive social reinforcement in the nursery school peer group. *Child Develpm.,* 1967, **38,** 993-1002. 352

Charlesworth, R., *see* Hartup et al.

Child, I. L., *see* Whiting & Child

Chomsky, N., Review of "Verbal behavior," by B. F. Skinner. *Language,* 1959, **35,** 26-58. 177

Chomsky, N., Current issues in linguistic theory. In J. A. Fodor and J. J. Katz, Eds., *The structure of language.* Englewood Cliffs, N. J.: Prentice Hall, 1964. 178

Chomsky, N., *Aspects of the theory of syntax.* Cambridge, Mass: M. I. T. Press, 1965. 275

Chomsky, N., The formal structure of language. In E. H. Lenneberg, Ed., *Biological foundations of language.* N. Y.: Wiley, 1967. 178

Chomsky, N., *Language and mind.* N. Y.: Harcourt Brace and Jovanovich, 1968. 275

Clark, K. B., & Clark, M. K., Racial identification and preference in Negro children. In T. Newcomb & E. L. Hartley, Eds., *Readings in social psychology.* N. Y.: Holt, 1947. 346

Clark, K. E., *see* Harris et al.

Clark, M. K., *see* Clark & Clark

Clark, W. M., Jr., *see* Babson et al.

Clarke, H. H., & Olson, A. L. Characteristics of 15-year-old boys who demonstrate various accomplishments of difficulties. *Child Develpm.,* 1965, **36,** 559-567. 390

Clausen, G. T., *see* Schwartz & Clausen

Coates, B., *see* Hartup & Coates

Coffield, K. E., Research methodology: a possible reconciliation. *Amer. Psychologist,* 1970, **25,** 511-516. 43

Coghill, G. E., *Anatomy and the problems of behavior.* N. Y.: Macmillan, 1929. 63-64

Cohen, M. B., *see* Wenner et al.

Cohen, M. L., & Seghorn, T., Clinical and research experience with sexually dangerous persons. Unpublished paper, Amer. Psychol. Assn. convention, Miami Beach, Sept., 1970. 400-401

Coleman, D., *see* Minard et al.

Coleman, J. S., et al., *Equality of educational opportunity.* Washington; U. S. Dept. of Health, Educ., & Welfare, 1966. 318, 319

Conner, R., *see* Stith & Conner

Conrad, H. S., *see* Jones & Conrad

Conrad, R., The chronology of the development of covert speech in children. *Develpm. Psychol.,* 1971, 5, 398-405. 274

Coopersmith, S., *Antecedents of self-esteem.* San Francisco: Freeman, 1967. 410

Coopersmith, S., Studies in self-esteem. *Scient. American,* 1968, 218(2), 96-106. 410-411

Corner, G. W., *Ourselves unborn.* New Haven: Yale Univ. Press, 1944. 110

Cotler, S., & Palmer, R. J., Social reinforcement, individual difference factors, and the reading performance of elementary school children. *J. pers. soc. Psychol.,* 1971, 18, 97-104. 447-448

Courtney, R. G., *see* Rothenberg & Courtney

Cox, F. N. Correlates of general and test anxiety in children. *Aust. J. Psychol.,* 1960, 12, 169-177. 375

Craft, M., *see* Graham, Ernhart, et al.

Crandall, V., & Rabson, A., Children's repetition choices in intellectual achievement situations following success and failure. *J. genet. Psychol.,* 1960, 97, 161-168. 407

Crandall, V. J., *see also* Waters & Crandall

Cronbach, L. J., The two disciplines of scientific psychology. *Amer. Psychologist,* 1957, 12, 671-684. 43

Crowell, D. H., *see* Brackbill et al.

da Rocha, N. S., *see* Lindgren et al.

Dahms, L., *see* Walters et al.

D'Amico, L. A., *see* Phillips & D'Amico

D'Andrade, R. G., *see* Rosen & D'Andrade

Darley, F. L., & Winitz, H., Age of first word: Review of research. *J. speech hear. Dis.,* 1961, 26, 272-290. 176

Darwin, C., A biographical sketch of an infant. *Mind,* 1877, 2, 285-294. 11

Davids, A., & Parenti, A. N., Personality, social choice, and adults' perception of these factors in groups of disturbed and normal children. *Sociometry,* 1958, 12, 212-224. 442

Davidson, K. S., *see* Waite et al.

Davies, E. A., *see* Holt et al.

Davis, C. M., Self-selection of diet by newly-weaned infants. *Amer. J. Dis. Child.,* 1935, 36, 651-679. 147

Davis, C. M., Results of the self-selection of diets by young children. *Canad. Med. Assn. J.,* 1939, 41, 257-261. 147

Davitz, J. R., The effects of previous training on posfrustration behavior. *J. abnorm. soc. Psychol.,* 1952, 47, 309-315. 434-435

Davitz, J. R., Social perception and sociometric choice of children. *J. abnorm. soc. Psychol.,* 1955, 50, 173-176. 417

deGroat, A. F., & Thompson, G. C., A study of the distribution of teacher approval and disapproval among sixth grade children. *J. exper. Educ.,* 1949, 18, 57-75. 442

Dellinger, W. S., *see* Naeye et al.

Dement, W., The effect of dream deprivation. *Science,* 1960, 131, 1705-1707. 127

Denenberg, V. H., The mother as a motivator. In W. J. Arnold & M. M. Page, Eds., *Nebraska symposium on motivation, 1970.* Lincoln: Univ. of Nebr. Press, 1971. 209-210

Denenberg, V. H., *see* Ottinger et al.

Dennis, M. G., *see* Dennis & Dennis

Dennis, W., A description and classification of the responses of the newborn infant. *Psychol. Bull.,* 1934, 31, 5-22. 132

Dennis, W., An experimental test of two theories of social smiling in infant. *J. soc. Psychol.,* 1935, 6, 214-223. 160

Dennis, W., Mental growth of certain foundlings before and after adoption. Unpublished paper, Amer. Univ. of Beirut, 1967. 192. 390-391

Dennis, W., & Dennis, M. G., The effect of cradling practices upon the onset of walking in Hopi children. *J. genet. Psychol.,* 1940, 56, 77-86. 143

Dennis, W., & Dennis, M. G., Development under controlled environmental conditions. In W. Dennis, Ed., *Readings in child psychology.* N. Y.: Prentice Hall, 1951. 191, 256, 257

Denny, T., Paterson, J., & Feldhusen, J., Anxiety and achievement as functions of daily testing. *J. educ. Measmt.,* 1964, 1, 143-147. 390

Detwiler, S. R., *see* Matthews & Detwiler

Deutsche, J. M., The development of children's concepts of causal relations. *Univ. Minn. Child Welf. Monogr.,* 1937, No. 13. 378-379

Diamond, M. C., *see* Bennett et al.

Diener, M. M., *see* Naeye et al.

Ding, G. F., & Jersild, A. T., A study of the laughing and smiling of preschool children. *J. genet. Psychol.,* 1932, 40, 452-472. 257

Dinges, N. G., *see* Oetting & Dinges

Dittes, J. E., *see* Capra & Dittes

Dixon, J. C., Development of self recognition. *J. genet. Psychol.,* 1957, 91, 251-256. 226

Dollard, J., & Miller, N. E., *Personality and psychotherapy.* N. Y.: McGraw-Hill, 1950. 153-154, 254

Dollard, J., *see also* Miller & Dollard

Dolto, F., French and American children as seen by a French child analyst. In M. Mead & M. Wolfenstein, Eds., *Childhood in contemporary cultures.* Chicago: Univ. of Chicago Press, 1955. 6

Doob, L. W., *Social psychology.* N. Y.: Holt, 1952. 444

Doty, B. A., Relationships among attitudes in pregnancy and other maternal characteristics. *J. genet. Psychol.,* 1967, 111, 203-217. 119-120

Dowart, W., Ezerman, R., Lewis, M., & Rosenhahn, D., The effect of brief social deprivation on social and non-social reinforcement. *J. Pers. soc. Psychol.,* 1965, 2, 111-115. 92

Drach, K., Kobashigawa, B., Pfuderer, C., & Slobin, D., The structure of linguistic input to children. Univ. of Calif., Berkeley, Language-Behavior Res. Lab., Working Paper, No. 14. 275

Dreyer, A. S., & Wells, M. B., Parental values, parental control, and creativity in young children. *Journal of Marriage and the Family,* 1966, 28, 83-88. 305

Duhamel, T. R., *see* Jarmon & Duhamel

Dunn, J. A., The approach-avoidance paradigm as a model for the analysis of school anxiety. *J. educ. Psychol.,* 1968, 59, 388-394. 451

Dwyer, T. F., *see* Bibring et al.

Dymond, R. F., Hughes, A. S., & Raabe, V. L., Measurable changes in empathy with age. *J. consult. Psychol.,* 1952, 16, 202-206. 416, 442-443

Dymond, R. F., *see* Rogers & Dymond

Early, C. J., Attitude learning in children. *J. educ. Psychol.,* 1968, 59, 176-180. 83

Eckerman, C. O., *see* Rheingold & Eckerman

Edwards, N., The relationship between physical condition immediately after birth and mental and motor performance at age four. *Genet. psychol. Monogr.,* 1970, 78, 257-289. 122, 123

Eichenwald, H. F., & Fry, P. C., Nutrition and learning. *Science,* 1969, 163, 644-648. 140

Elkind, D., Children's discovery of the conservation of mass, weight, and volume: Piaget replication study. *J. genet. Psychol.,* 1961, 98, 219-227. 265

Elkind, D., Discrimination, seriation, and numeration of size and dimensional differences in young children: Piaget replication study IV. *J. genet. Psychol.,* 1964, 104, 275-296. 265

Elkind, D., Cognition in infancy and early childhood. In Y. Brackbill, Ed., *Infancy and early childhood.* N. Y.: Free Press, 1967. 196

Elkind, D. & Sameroff, A., Developmental psychology. In P. H. Mussen & M. R. Rosenzweig, Eds., *Annual review of psychology,* vol. 21. Palo Alto: Annual Reviews, 1970. 30

Emerson, P. E., *see* Schaffer & Emerson

Engelmann, S., *see* Bereiter & Engelmann

England, A. O., Non-structured approach to the study of children's fears. *J. clin. Psychol.,* 1946, 2, 364-368. 372

Erikson, E. H., *Childhood and society,* 2nd ed. N. Y.: Norton, 1963. 97-98, 196-197, 226

Erikson, E. H., *Identity, youth, and crisis.* N. Y.: Norton, 1968. 97-98

Eron, L. D., Walder, L. D., Toigo, R., & Lefkowitz, M. M., Social class, parental punishment for aggression, and child aggression. *Child Develpm.,* 1963, 34, 849-867. 400

Ernhart, C. B., *see* Graham, Ernhart, et al.

Escalona, S., Emotional development in the first year of life. In M. J. Senn, Ed., *Problems of infancy and childhood: Transactions of the sixth conference.* N. Y.: Macy, 1953. 193

Escalona, S. & Bergman, P., Unusual similarities in very young children. *Psychol. Stud. Child,* 1949, 3, 333-352. 182

Ezerman, R., *see* Dowart et al.

Fales, E., Genesis of level of aspiration in children from one and one-half to three years of age. Reported in Lewin, K. et al. Level of aspiration. In J. Mc. V. Hunt, Ed., *Personality and the behavior disorders,* vol. 1. N. Y.: Ronald, 1944. 333

Fantz, R. L., Pattern vision in newborn infants. *Science,* 1963, 140, 296-297. 128

Fantz, R. L., Visual perception from birth as shown by pattern selectivity. *Annals of the New York Academy of Science,* 1965, 118, 793-814. 169

Fantz, R. L., Ordy, J. M., & Udelf, M. S., Maturation of pattern vision in infants during the first six months. *J. compar. physiol. Psychol.,* 1962, 55, 907-917. 168, 190

Faraco, I., *see* Lindgren et al.

Fatheree, D., Play patterns in preschool children. Unpublished student report, San Francisco State College, 1971. 348-349

Faust, M. S., Developmental maturity as a determinant of prestige of adolescent girls. *Child Develpm.,* 1960, 31, 173-184. 365

Fearing, J. M., *see* Wenner et al.

Federov, V. K., Cited in H. L., Rheingold and W. C. Stanley, Developmental psychology. *Ann. Rev. Psychol.,* 1963, 14, 1-8. 224

Felder, J. G., Some factors determining the nature and frequency of anger and fear outbreaks in preschool children. *J. juv. Res.,* 1932, 16, 278-290. 254

Feldhusen, J. F., & Klausmeier, H. J., Anxiety, intelligence, and achievement in children of low, average, and high intelligence. *Child Develpm.,* 1962, 33, 403-409. 375

Feldhusen, J., *see also* Denny et al.

Ferreira, A., The pregnant woman's emotional attitude and its reflection on the newborn. *Amer. J. Orthopsychiat.,* 1960, 30, 553-561. 119

Feshbach, S., Aggression. In P. H. Mussen, Ed., *Carmichael's manual of child psychology,* 3rd ed. N. Y.: Wiley, 1970. 220, 437

Feshbach, S., & Singer, R. D., *Television and aggression.* San Francisco: Jossey-Bass, 1970. 437

Finch, H. M., Young children's concepts of parent roles. *J. home Econ.,* 1955, 47, 99-103. 347

Finkelstein, E. L., *see* Greenfeld & Finkelstein

Finney, J. C., Some maternal influences in children's personality and character. *Genet. psychol. Monogr.,* 1961, 63, 199-278. 436

Fischer, A., *see* Fischer & Fischer

Fischer, J. L., & Fischer, A., The New Englanders of Orchard Town, U. S. A. In B. Whiting, Ed., *Six cultures: Studies of child rearing.* N. Y.: Wiley, 1963. 152

Flavell, J. H., *The developmental psychology of Jean Piaget.* Princeton: Van Nostrand, 1963. 164, 262, 268

Flickinger, A., & Rehage, K. J., Building time and place concepts. In *Improving the reading of world history.* National Council for Social Studies, 20th yearbook, 1949. 381

Fowler, W., Cognitive learning in infancy and early childhood. *Psychol. Bull.,* 1962, 59, 116-152. 143

Fraisse, P., Étude comparée de la perception et de l'estimation de la durée chez les enfants et les adultes. *Enfance,* 1948, 1, 199-211. 381

Franks, C., *see* O'Connor & Franks

Freeberg, N. E., & Payne, D. T., Dimensions of parental practice concerned with cognitive development in the preschool child. *J. genet. Psychol.,* 1967, 111, 245-261. 324

Freeman, F. N., *see* Newman et al.

Freeman, M., *see* Kagan & Freeman

Freshley, H. B., *see* Wispe & Freshly

Freud, A., *The psychoanalytical treatment of children.* London: Imago, 1946. 21

Freud, A., *The ego and mechanisms of defense.* N. Y.: Intl. Universities Press, 1946. 95

Freud, A., Some remarks on infant observation. *Psychoanalyt. Stud. Child,* 1953, 8, 9-19. 225

Freud, S., Mourning and melancholia. In *Collected papers,* vol. IV. London: Hogarth, 1925. 85-86, 93-97

Freud, S., *Civilization and its discontents.* London: Liveright, 1930. 93

Freud, S., *New introductory lectures on psychoanalysis.* N. Y.: Norton, 1935. 94

Freud, S., *The problem of anxiety.* N. Y.: Norton, 1936. 94

Freud, S., *An outline of psychoanalysis.* N. Y.: Norton, 1949. 94

Friedman, I., Phenomenal, ideal and projected concepts of self. *J. abnorm. soc. Psychol.,* 1955, 51, 611-615. 415

Friedrich, U., *see* Nielsen et al.

Fries, M. E., & Woolf, P. J., Some hypotheses on the role of the congenital activity type in personality development. *Psychoanalyt. Stud. Child,* 1953, 8, 48-62. 182

Fry, P. C., *see* Eichenwald & Fry

Fuller, J. L., Experimental deprivation and later behavior. *Science,* 1967, 158, 1645-1652. 209

Furth, H. G., Linguistic deficiency and thinking: research with deaf subjects. *Psychol. Bull.,* 1971, 76, 58-72. 274

Galfo, A. J., A pilot study of relationships between the sex of culturally disadvantaged children and maternal perceptions of the child and his environment. *Amer. Psychol. Assn. Exper. Publ. System,* April 1971, Ms. No. 405-435. 308-309

Gallimore, R., Howard, A., & Jordan, C., Independence training among Hawaiians: A cross-cultural study. In H. C. Lindgren, Ed., *Contemporary research in social psychology.* N. Y.: Wiley, 1969. 333-334

Gallimore, R., Tharp, R. G., & Kemp, B., Positive reinforcing function of "negative attention." *J. exper. child Psychol.,* 1969, 8, 140-146. 92

Garai, J. E., & Scheinfeld, A., Sex differences in mental and behavior traits. *Genet. psychol. Monogr.,* 1968, 77, 169-299. 183

Gardner, B., *see* Burchinal et al.

Gardner, B. T., & Gardner, R. A., Two-way communication with an infant chimpanzee. In A. Schrier & B. Stollnitz, Eds., *Behavior of non-human primates.* N. Y.: Academic, 1969. 76

Gardner, D. B., Hawkes, G. R., & Burchinal, L. G., Noncontinuous mothering in infancy and development in later childhood. *Child Develpm.,* 1961, 32, 225-234. 208

Gardner, D. B., & Pease, D., & Hawkes, G. R., Responses of two-year-old children to controlled stress situations. *J. genet. Psychol.,* 1961, 98, 29-35. 208, 227

Gardner, L., An analysis of children's attitudes toward fathers. *J. genet. Psychol.,* 1947, 70, 3-28. 421

Gardner, R. A., *see* Gardner & Gardner

Geber, M., The psychomotor development of African children in the first year and the influence of maternal behavior. *J. soc. Psychol.,* 1958, 47, 185-195. 146

Gellermann, L. W., Form discrimination in chimpanzees and two-year-old children: 1. Form (triangularity) *per se. J. genet. Psychol.,* 1933, 42, 3-27. 171-174, 274

Gesell, A., Maturation and the patterning of behavior.

In C. Murchison, Ed., *A handbook of child psychology,* 2nd ed. Worcester: Clark Univ. Press, 1933. 75

Gesell, A., et al., *The first five years of life: A guide to the study of the preschool child.* N.Y.: Harper, 1940. 224, 227, 239-240

Gesell, A., & Ilg, F. L., *Child develpm.,* 2nd ed. N.Y.: Harper, 1949. 126, 146, 152, 239, 269, 270

Gesell, A., & Thompson, H., *Infant behavior.* N.Y.: McGraw-Hill, 1934. 143, 175, 221

Gewirtz, J. L., A learning analysis of the effects of normal stimulation privation and deprivation on the acquisition of social motivation and attachment. In B. M. Foss, Ed., *Determinants of infant behavior.* London: Methuen, 1961a. 203

Gewirtz, J. L., A learning analysis of the effects of affective privation in childhood. *Acta Psychologica,* 1961b, 19, 404-405. 203, 205

Gewirtz, J. L., *see* Rheingold et al.

Gibson, E. J., *see* Walk & Gibson

Ginzberg, E., et al., *The ineffective soldier. Vol. 3. Patterns of performance.* N.Y.: Columbia Univ. Press, 1959. 44

Glazer, J. A., *see* Hartup et al.

Gold, G. M., *see* Alexander et al.

Goldfarb, W., The effects of early institutional care on adolescent personality. *J. exper. Educ.,* 1943, 12, 106-129. 198, 285

Goldfarb, W., Psychological privation in infancy and subsequent adjustment. *Amer. J. Orthopsychiat.,* 1945, 15, 247-255. 285

Goldman, R., Psychosocial development in cross-cultural perspective: A new look at an old issue. *Developm. Psychol.,* 1971, 5, 411-419. 310-311

Golman, B., *see* Jersild, Golman, & Loftus

Goodenough, F. L., Anger in young children. *Univ. Minn. Inst. Child Welf. Series,* 1931, No. 9. 220, 245, 254, 336-337, 371

Goodenough, F. L., Expressions of the emotions in a blind-deaf child. *J. abnorm. soc. Psychol.,* 1932, 27, 328-333. 160

Goodenough, F., The development of the reactive process from early childhood to maturity. *J. exper. Psychol.,* 1935, 18, 431-450. 366

Goodenough, F. L., *Mental testing, its history, principles and applications.* N.Y.: Rinehart, 1949. 13

Gordon, M., *see* Green & Gordon

Gordon, W., *see* Price-Williams et al.

Gottesman, I. I., Heritability of personality: a demonstration. *Psychol. Monogr.,* 1963, 77, No. 9 (Whole No. 572). 61

Gottesman, I. I., & Shields, J., Contributions of twin studies to perspectives on schizophrenia. In B. A. Maher, Ed., *Progress in experimental personality research,* vol. 3.

N.Y.: Academic, 1966. 61

Goulet, L. R., Verbal learning in children: Implications for developmental research. *Psychol. Bull.,* 1968, 69, 359-376. 277

Graham, F. K., Behavioral differences between normal and traumatized newborns: I. The test procedures. *Psychol. Monogr.,* 1956, 70, No. 427. 122

Graham, F. K., Ernhart, C. B., Thurston, D., & Craft, M., Development three years after perinatal anoxia and other potentially damaging newborn experience. *Psychol. Monogr.,* 1962, 76, No. 522. 122

Graham, F. K., Matarazzo, R. G., & Caldwell, B. M., Behavioral differences between normal and traumatized newborns: II. Standardization, reliability, and validity. *Psychol. Monogr.,* 1956, 70, No. 428. 122

Grant, G., *see* Hraba & Grant

Gray, M. L., *see* Brackbill et al.

Gray, P. H., Theory and evidence of imprinting in human infants. *J. Psychol.,* 1958, 46, 155-166. 205

Gray, S. W., & Klaus, R. A., The Early Training Project: A seventh year report. *Child Develpm.,* 1970, 41, 909-924. 287-288, 316-317, 391

Green, P. C., & Gordon, M., Maternal deprivation: its influence on visual exploration in infant monkeys. *Science,* 1964, 145, 292-294. 204-214

Green, R. L., & Hoffmann, L. J., A case study of the effects of educational deprivation on Southern rural Negro children. *J. Negro Educ.,* 1965, 34, 327-341. 287

Greene, P., *see* Smith & Greene

Greenfeld, N., & Finkelstein, E. L., A comparison of the characteristics of junior high school students. *J. genet. Psychol.,* 1970, 117, 37-50. 455-456

Gross, M., *Learning readiness in two Jewish groups.* N.Y.: Center for Urban Educ., 1967. 319

Guedes, H. de A., *see* Lindgren & Guedes

Guilford, J. P., *see* Michael et al.

Guinagh, B. J., An experimental study of basic learning ability and intelligence in low socio-economic-status children. *Child Develpm.,* 1971, 42, 27-36. 392

Gutteridge, M. V., A study of motor achievements of young children. *Arch. Psychol., N. Y.,* 1939, No. 244. 240-244

Habenstein, R. W., *see* Queen & Habenstein

Haddad, R. K., *see* Rabe & Haddad

Hagman, E. R., A study of fears of children of preschool age. *J. exper. Educ.,* 1932, 1, 110-130. 252

Haith, W. W., *see* Kessen et al.

Hall, C. S., & Lindzey, G., *Theories of personality,* 2nd ed. N.Y.: Wiley, 1970. 273

Hall, G. S., The contents of children's minds on entering school. *Ped. Sem.,* 1891, 1, 139-173. 12

Halverson, H. M., An experimental study of prehension in

infants by means of systematic cinema records. *Genet. psychol. Monogr.,* 1931, **10**, 107-286. 143

Halverson, H. M., Infant sucking and tensional behavior. *J. genet. Psychol.,* 1938, **53**, 365-430. 154

Halverson, H. M., The development of prehension in infants. In R. G. Barker et al., Eds., *Child behavior and development.* N. Y.: McGraw-Hill, 1943. 128

Harlow, H. F., The nature of love. *Amer. Psychologist,* 1958, **15**, 675-685. 201-202, 214

Harlow, H. F., The heterosexual affectional system in monkeys. *Amer. Psychologist,* 1962, **17**, 1-9. 201, 308

Harlow, H. F., & Suomi, S. J., Nature of love—simplified. *Amer. Psychologist,* 1970, **25**, 161-168. 201-202, 204

Harrell, L. E., A comparison of the development of oral and written languages in school-age children. *Monogr. Soc. Res. Child Develpm.,* 1957, **22**, No. 3. 382

Harris, D. B., Clark, K. E., Rose, A. M., & Valasek, F., The relationship of children's home duteis to an attitude of responsibility. *Child Develpm.,* 1954, **25**, 103-109. 422

Harris, D. B., & Tseng, S. C., Children's attitudes toward peers and parents as revealed by sentence completion. *Child Develpm.,* 1957, **28**, 401-411. 421

Harris, C. W., *see* Sewell et al.

Hartman, D. M., The hurdle jump as a measure of the motor proficiency of young children. *Child Develpm.,* 1943, **14**, 201-211. 244

Hartup, W. W., Nurturance and nurturance withdrawal in relation to the dependency behavior of preschool children. *Child Develpm.,* 1958, **29**, 191-201. 330

Hartup, W. W., Peer relations. In T. D. Spencer & N. Kass, Eds., *Perspectives in child psychology.* N. Y.: McGraw-Hill, 1970. 228, 352, 355

Hartup, W. W., & Coates, B., Imitation of a peer as a function of reinforcement from the peer group and rewardingness of the model, *Child Develpm.,* 1967, **38**, 1003-1016. 352

Hartup, W. W., Glazer, J. A., & Charlesworth, R., Peer reinforcement and sociometric status. *Child Develpm.,* 1967, **38**, 1017-1024. 355-356

Hartup, W. W., *see also* Charlesworth & Hartup; and Rosekrans & Hartup

Hasselmeyer, G., *see* Holt et al.

Havighurst, R. J., *Human development and education.* N. Y.: Longmans, Green, 1953. 66-67, 98, 445

Havighurst, R. J., Minority subcultures and the law of effect. *Amer. Psychologist,* 1970, **25**, 313-322. 318-319

Hawkes, G. R., The child in the family. *Marriage fam. Liv.,* 1957, **19**, 46-51. 346

Hawkes, G. R., *see* Burchinal et al.; Gardner, Hawkes, & Burchinal; and Gardner, Pease, & Hawkes

Hayes, C., *The ape in our house.* N. Y.: Harper, 1951. 76

Hayes, M., *see* Hicks & Hayes

Haynes, H., White, B. L., & Held, R., Visual accommodation in human infants. *Science,* 1965, **148**, 528-530. 128

Heathers, G., Emotional dependence and independence in nursery school play. *J. genet. Psychol.,* 1955, **87**, 37-57. 214, 332, 334

Heider, E. R., Style and accuracy of verbal communications within and between social classes. *J. pers. soc. Psychol.,* 1971, **18**, 33-47. 320

Heinstein, M. I., Influence of breast feeding on children's behavior. *Children,* 1963, **10**, 93-97. 195

Heinstein, M. I., *Child rearing in California: A study of mothers with young children.* Bureau of Maternal & Child Health, California State Department of Public Health, 1965. 194

Held, R., *see* Haynes et al.

Hendry. L. S., & Kessen, W., Oral behavior of newborn infants as a function of age and time since feeding. *Child Develpm.,* 1964, **35**, 201-208. 183

Henderson, N. D., Brain weight increases resulting from environmental enrichment: A directional dominance in mice. *Science,* 1970, **169**, 776-778. 189-190

Henery, F. M. & Nelson, G. A., Age differences and interrelationships between skills and learning in gross motor performance of ten- and fifteen-year-old boys. *Res. Quart. Assn. Hlth. Phys. Educ.,* 1956, **27**, 162-175. 367

Hepner, R., Maternal malnutrition and the fetus. *J. Amer. med. Assn.,* 1958, **169**, 1774-1777. 5, 13

Hess, E. H., Two conditions limiting cultural age for imprinting. *J. comp. physiol. Psychol.,* 1959a, **52**, 515-518. 204

Hess, E. H., Imprinting: An effect of early experience, imprinting determines later social behavior in animals. *Science,* 1959b, **130**, 133-141. 204

Hetherington, E. M., Effects of paternal absence on sex-typed behaviors in Negro and white preadolescent males. *J. pers. soc. Psychol.,* 1966, **4**, 87-91. 309

Hicks, J. A., The acquisition of motor skill in young children: a study of the effects of practice in throwing at a moving target. *Child Develpm.,* 1930, **1**, 90-105. 240

Hicks, J. A. & Hayes, M., Study of the characteristics of 250 junior high school children. *Child Develpm.,* 1938, **9**, 219-242. 372

Hilgard, E. R., Human motives and the concept of self. *Amer. Psychol.,* 1949, **4**, 374-382. 342

Hilton, I., Differences in the behavior of mothers toward first- and later-born children. *J. pers. soc. Psychol.,* 1967, **7**, 282-290. 322

Hinde, R. A. & Spencer-Booth, Y., Effects of brief separation from mother on rhesus monkeys. *Science,* 1971, **173**, 111-118. 199

Hoffman, M. L., Moral development. In P. H. Mussen,

Ed., *Carmichael's Manual of child psychology,* 3rd ed. N.Y.: Wiley, 1970. 422-427

Hoffman, M. L., Father absence and conscience development. *Develpm. Psychol.,* 1971, 4, 400-406. 309

Hoffmann, L. F., *see* Green & Hoffmann

Hofstaetter, P. R., The changing composition of "intelligence:" A study technique. *J. genet. Psychol.,* 1954, 85, 159-164. 180

Hohle, R. H., *see* Spears & Hohle

Holloway, H. D., Reliability of the Children's Manifest Anxiety Scale at the rural third grade level. *J. educ. Psychol.,* 1959, 49, 193-196. 374

Holloway, R. D., Normative data on the Children's Manifest Anxiety Scale at the rural third grade level. *Child Develpm.,* 1961, 32, 129-134. 374

Hollenberg, E. & Sperry, M., Some antecedents of aggression and effects of frustration in doll play. *Personality,* 1951, 1, 32-43. 337, 338

Holmes, F. B., *see* Jersild & Holmes

Holt, L. E., Jr., Davies, E. A., Hasselmeyer, E. G., & Adams, A. O., A study of premature infants fed cold formulas. *J. Pediatr.,* 1962, 61, 556-561. 129

Holzinger, K. J., *see* Newman & Holzinger

Honig, A. S., & Brill, S., A comparative analysis of the Piagetian development of twelve month old disadvantaged infants in an enrichment center with others not in such a center. Unpublished paper, Amer. Psychol. Assn. Convention, Miami Beach, 1970. 166, 180

Honig, A. S., Caldwell, B. M., & Tannenbaum, J., Patterns of information processing used by and with young children in a nursery school setting. *Child Develpm.,* 1970, 41, 1045-1065. 231

Hooker, D., Reflex activities in the human fetus. In R. G. Barker, et al., Eds., *Child behavior and development.* N.Y.: McGraw-Hill, 1943. 64

Horrocks, J. E., & Buker, M. E., A study of the friendship fluctuations of preadolescents. *J. genet. Psychol.,* 1951, 78, 131-144. 442

Horrocks, J. E., & Thompson, G. C., A study of the friendship fluctuations of rural boys and girls. *J. genet. Psychol.,* 1946, 69, 189-198. 442

Horrocks, J. E., *see also* Thompson & Horrocks

Houston, K. B., Review of the evidence and qualifications regarding the effects of hallucinogenic drugs on chromosomes and embryos. *Amer. J. Psychiat.,* 1969, 126, 251-254. 116

Howard, A., *see* Gallimore et al.

Howells, T. H., The obsolete dogmas of heredity. *Psychol. Rev.,* 1945, 52, 23-34. 75

Hraba, J., & Grant, G., Black is beautiful: A reexamination of racial preference and identification. *J. pers. soc. Psychol.,* 1970, 16, 398-402. 346

Huang, I., & Lee, H. W., Experimental analysis of child animism. *J. genet. Psychol.,* 1945, 66, 69-74. 264

Hughes, A. S., *see* Dymond et al.

Hughes, R. D., *see* Olson & Hughes

Hull, C., *Principles of behavior.* N.Y.: Appleton-Century-Crofts, 1943. 29

Huntington, D. S., *see* Bibring et al.

Hymes, D. H., On communicative competence. In R. Huxley & B. Ingram, Eds., *The mechanism of language development.* London: CIBA Foundation, 1972. 285

Ilg, F. L., *see* Gesell & Ilg

Inhelder, B., & Piaget, J., *The growth of logical thinking: From childhood to adolescence.* N.Y.: Basic Books, 1958. 376

Inhelder, B., & Piaget, J., *The early growth of logic in the child.* N.Y.: Harper & Row, 1964. 274

Inhelder, B., *see also* Piaget & Inhelder

Irons, N. McC., & Zigler, E., Children's responsiveness to social reinforcement as a function of short-term preliminary social interactions and long-term social deprivation. *Develpm. Psychol.,* 1969, 1, 402-409. 89-92

Irwin, O. C., Research on speech sounds for the first six months of life. *Psychol. Bull.,* 1941, 38, 277-285. 175

Irwin, O. C., Infant speech: effect of systematic reading of stories. *J. speech hear. Res.,* 1960, 3, 187-190. 179

Irwin, O. C., *see also* Brodbeck & Irwin

Jackson, C. M., Some aspects of growth. In W. J. Robbins, et al., Eds., *Growth.* New Haven: Yale Univ. Press, 1929. 125

Jackson, P. W., *see* Lahaderne & Jackson

Janky, C., *see* Cameron & Janky

Jarmon, H., & Duhamel, T. R., Interpersonal distance in families with emotionally disturbed boys. *Amer. Psychol. Assn., Proc.,* 1969, 5, 555-556. 402

Jensen, A. R., Learning abilities in Mexican-American and Anglo-American children. *Calif. J. educ. Res.,* 1961, 12, 147-159. 392

Jensen, A. R., Social class, race, and genetics: implications for education. *Amer. J. educ. Res.,* 1968a, 5, 1-42. 391

Jensen, A. R., Patterns of mental ability and socioeconomic status. Unpublished paper, Natl. Acad. of Science, Washington, April, 1968b. 391

Jensen, A. R., How much can we boost IQ and scholastic achievement? *Harvard educ. Rev.,* 1969, 39, 1-123. 23, 391-392

Jersild, A. T., Research in the development of children. *Teach. Coll. Rec.,* 1936, 38, 129-143. 251

Jersild, A. T., Studies of children's fears. In R. G. Barker et al., eds., *Child behavior and development.* N.Y.: McGraw-Hill, 1943. 252

Jersild, A. T., *Child psychology,* 6th ed. Englewood Cliffs,

N. J.: Prentice Hall, 1968. 98

Jersild, A. T., Golman, B., & Loftus, J. J., A comparative study of the worries of children in two school situations. *J. exper. Educ.*, 1941, 9, *323-326. 372*

Jersild, A. T., & Holmes, F. B., Children's fears. *Child develpm. Monogr.*, 1935, No. 20. 250-252, 373

Jersild, A. T., Markey, F. V., & Jersild, C. L., Children's fears, dreams, wishes, daydreams, likes, dislikes, pleasant and unpleasant memories. *Child develpm. Monogr.*, 1933, No. 12. 372, 373, 375

Jersild, A. T., & Tasch, R. J., *Children's interests and what they suggest for education.* N. Y.: Teachers College, Columbia Univ., 1949. 375-376

Jersild, A. T., *see also* Ding & Jersild

Jersild, C. L., *see* Jersild et al.

Johnson, R. C., Similarity in IQ of separated identical twins as related to length of time spent in same environment. *Child Develpm.*, 1963, 34, 745-749. 61

Jones, H. E., & Conrad, H. S., The growth and decline of intelligence: A study of a homogeneous group between the ages of ten and sixty. *Genet. psychol. Monogr.*, 1933, 13, 223-298. 43

Jones, M. C., The later careers of boys who were early—or late—maturing. *Child Develpm.*, 1957, 28, 113-128. 364

Jones, M. C., & Bayley, N., Physical maturing among boys as related to behavior. *J. educ. Psychol.*, 1950, 41, 129-148. 364

Jones, M. C., & Mussen, P. H., Self-conceptions, motivations, and interpersonal attitudes of early—and late—maturing girls. *Child Develpm.*, 1958, 29, 491-502. 365, 411

Jones, M. C., *see* Mussen & Jones

Jordan, C., *see* Gallimore et al.

Jordan, T. E., & Spanner, S. D., Biological and ecological influences on development at 12 months of age. *Hum. Develpm.*, 1970, 13, 178-187. 139-140

Justin, F., A genetic study of laughter provoking stimuli. *Child Develpm.*, 1932, 3, 114-136. 256, 257

Kagan, J., The child's perception of the parent. *J. abnorm. soc. Psychol.*, 1956, 53, 257-258. 421

Kagan, J., Attention and psychological change in the young child. *Science*, 1970, 170, 826-832. 222-224

Kagan, J., *Change and continuity in infancy.* N. Y.: Wiley, 1971. 167, 275

Kagan, J., & Freeman, M., Relation of childhood intelligence, maternal behaviors, and social class to behavior during adolescence. *Child Develpm.*, 1963, 34, 899-911. 305, 312

Kagan, J., & Moss, H. A., Stability and validity of achievement fantasy. *J. abnorm. soc. Psychol.*, 1959, 58, 357-364. 408

Kagan, J., & Moss, H. A., The stability of passive and de-

pendent behavior from childhood through adulthood. *Child Develpm.*, 1960, 31, 577-591. 402

Kagan, J., & Moss, H. A., *Birth to maturity: a study in psychological development.* N. Y.: Wiley, 1962. 418-421

Kagan, J., *see also* Moss & Kagan; Sontag & Kagan; Tulkin & Kagan

Kahn, M. A., *A polygraph study of the catharsis of aggression.* Unpubl. doctoral dissertation, Harvard University, 1960. 254

Kaplan, E., *see* Werner & Kaplan

Karelitz, S., et al., Relationship of crying activity in early infancy to speech and to intellectual development at age three years. *Child Develpm.*, 1964, 35, 769-777. 181

Katz, M. M., *see* Bates & Katz

Katz, P., & Zigler, E., Self-image disparity: A developmental approach. *J. pers. soc. Psychol.*, 1967, 5, 186-195. 415

Katz, P. A., *see* Ostfeld & Katz

Kaufman, I. C., & Rosenblum, L. A., Depression in infant monkeys separated from their mothers. *Science*, 1967, 155, 1030-1031. 199-200

Kaye, K., Unpublished research ms., 1969. Cited by Kagan (1971). 183

Kendler, T. S., & Kendler, H. H., Reversal and nonreversal shifts in kindergarten children. *J. exper. Psychol.*, 1959, 58, 56-50. 290

Kendler, T. S., Kendler, H. H., & Wells, D., Reversal and non-reversal shifts in nursery school children. *J. comp. physiol. Psychol.*, 1960, 53, 83-88. 290

Kendler, H. H., *see* Kendler & Kendler; and Kendler et al.

Kemp, B., *see* Gallimore et al.

Kennedy, J. F., Message from the President of the United States relative to mental illness and mental retardation. House of Representatives, 88th Congress, 1st Session. Document No. 58. Feb. 5, 1963. 114-115

Kennedy, R. L. J., *see* Norval et al.

Kessen, W. Research design in the study of developmental problems. in P. H. Mussen, Ed., *Handbook of research methods in child development.* N. Y.: Wiley, 1960. 77

Kessen, W., *The child.* N. Y.: Wiley, 1965. 11

Kessen, W., Haith, W. W., & Salapatek, P. H., Human infancy: A bibliography and guide. In P. H. Mussen, Ed., *Carmichael's manual of child psychology*, 3rd ed. N. Y.: Wiley, 1970. 129

Kessen, W. E., Williams, J., & Williams, J. P., Selection and test of response measurement in the study of the human newborn. *Child Develpm.*, 1961, 32, 7-24. 133

Kessen, W., *see also* Hendry & Kessen; and Nelson & Kessen

Kinsey, A. C., et al., *Sexual behavior in the human female.* Philadelphia: Saunders, 1953. 258

Kinsey, A. C., Pomeroy, W. B., & Martin, C. E., *Sexual behavior in the human male.* Philadelphia: Saunders, 1948. 154, 258

Klaus, R. A., *see* Gray & Klaus

Klausmeier, H. J., *see* Feldhusen & Klausmeier

Kluckhohn, C., The influence of psychiatry on anthropology during the past one hundred years. In J. K. Hall, Ed., *One hundred years of American psychiatry.* N. Y.: Columbia Univ. Press, 1944. 25

Kluckhohn, C., *Mirror for man.* N. Y.: McGraw-Hill, 1959. 60

Kluckhohn, C., Murray, H. A., & Schneider, D. M., Eds., *Personality in nature, society, and culture.* N. Y.: Knopf, 1953. 80

Knobloch, H., & Pasamanick, B., Seasonal variations in the birth of the mentally deficient. *Amer. J. publ. Health,* 1958, 48, 1201-1208. 114

Knop, C. A., *see* Aldrich et al.

Kobashigawa, B., *see* Drach et al.

Koch, H. L., Some personality correlates of sex, sibling position, and sex of sibling among five- and six-year-old children. *Genet. psychol. Monogr.,* 1955, 52, 3-50. 322

Koff, R. H., Systematic changes in children's word-association norms 1916-1963. *Child Develpm.,* 1965, 36, 299-305. 283

Kogan, N., Stephens, J. W., & Shelton, F. C., Age differences: A developmental study of discriminability and affective response. *J. abnorm. soc. Psychol.,* 1961, 62, 221-230. 269

Kohl, H. R., *36 children.* N. Y.: New American Library, 1967. 319

Kohlberg, L., Moral development and identification. In H. W. Stevenson, et al., Eds., *Child psychology,* 62nd yearbook, Natl. Soc. Stud. of Education. Chicago: Univ. of Chicago Press, 1963a. 423

Kohlberg, L., The development of children's orientations toward a moral order. 1. Sequence in the development of moral thought. *Vita Humana,* 1963b, 6, 11-33. 424-425

Kohlberg, L., & Kramer, R., Continuities and discontinuities in childhood and adult moral development. *Hum. Develpm.,* 1969, 12, 93-120. 425

Kohlberg, L., *see also* Rest et al.

Kohn, M. L., Social class and parent-child relationships: An interpretation. *Amer. J. Sociol.,* 1963, 68, 471-480. 312

Koller, K. M., Parental deprivation, family background and female delinquency. *Brit. J. Psychiat.,* 1971, 118, 319-327. 310

Koltuv, M., *see* Neff & Koltuv

Kooistra, W. H., *Developmental trends in the attainment of conservation, transivity, and relativism in the think-ing of children.* Unpubl. doctoral dissertation, Wayne Univ., 1963. 72

Korner, A. F., Relationship between overt and covert hostility—economy and dynamics. *Personality,* 1951, 1, 20-31. 337

Kounin, J. S., *Discipline and group management in classrooms.* N. Y.: Holt, Rinehart, & Winston, 1971. 446

Kramer, R., *see* Kohlberg & Kramer

Krech, D., *see* Bennett et al.

Kreitler, H., & Kreitler, S., Dependence of laughter on cognitive strategies. *Merrill-Palmer Q.,* 1970, 16, 163-177. 258

Krowitz, A., *see* Campos et al.

Krugman, M., Orthopsychiatry and education. In L. G. Lowrey, Ed., *Orthopsychiatry 1923-1948: Retrospect and prospect.* N. Y.: Amer. Orthopsychiat. Assn., 1948. 24

Kvarnes, R. G., *see* Wenner et al.

LaCrosse, E. R., Lee, P. C., et al., The first six years of life: A report on current research and educational practice. *Genet. psychol. Monogr.,* 1970, 82, 161-266. 237, 265

Lahaderne, H. M., & Jackson, P. W., Withdrawal in the classroom: A note on some educational correlates of social desirability among school children. *J. educ. Psychol.,* 1970, 61, 97-101. 417

Lampl, E. E., *see* Tennes & Lampl

Landauer, T. K., & Whiting, J. W. M., Infantile stimulation and adult stature of human males. *Amer. Anthropol.,* 1963, 66, 1007-1028. 190

Lane, P. A., *see* Tolor et al.

Langer, A., *see* Campos et al.

Laosa, L. M., & Brophy, J. E., Sex x birth order interaction in measures of sex-typing and affiliation in kindergarten children. *Amer. Psychol. Assn. Proceedings,* 1970, 5, 363-364. 322

Laurendeau, M., & Pinard, A., *Causal thinking in the child: A genetic and experimental approach.* N. Y.: Intl. Universities Press, 1963. 72

Lawton, J. J., *see* Wolking et al.

Lee, H. W., *see* Huang & Lee

Lee, P. C., *see* LaCrosse et al.

Lefkowitz, M. M., *see* Eron et al.

Lenneberg, E. H., On explaining language. *Science,* 1969, 164, 635-643. 178

Leuba, C., Tickling and laughter: Two genetic studies. *J. genet. Psychol.,* 1941, 58, 201-209. 256, 257

Levin, H., & Sears, R. R., Identification with parents as a determinant of doll play aggression. *Child Develpm.,* 1956, 27, 135-153. 337, 339

Levin, H., & Wardell, E., The research uses of doll play. *Psychol. Bull.,* 1962, 59, 27-56. 337

Levin, H., *see also* Sears, Maccoby, et al., and Marchbanks & Levin

LeVine, R. A., Cross-cultural study in child psychology. In P. H. Mussen, Ed., *Carmichael's manual of child psychology*, 3rd ed. N. Y.: Wiley, 1970. 208

Levine, S., Stimulation in infancy. *Scient. American*, 1960, 202, 81-87. 189

Levison, C., Levison, P. K., & Norton, H. P., Effects of early visual pattern deprivation on later motor development in chair-reared rhesus monkeys. *Amer. Psychol. Assn. Proc.*, 1970, 5, 193-194. 190

Levison, P. K., *see* Levison et al.

Levy, D. M., Psychsomatic studies of some aspects of maternal behavior. *Psychosom. Med.*, 1942, 4, 223-227. 117

Levy, D. M., In J. Kasanin (chm.), Research in orthopsychiatry. *Amer. J. Orthopsychiat.*, 1943a, 13, 230-232. 53

Levy, D. M., *Maternal overprotection.* N. Y.: Columbia Univ. Press, 1943b. 54

Levy, D. M., The early development of independent and oppositional behavior. In R. R. Grinker, Ed., *Mid-century psychiatry*. Springfield: Thomas, 1953. 227

Levy, N., *see* Lipsitt & Levy

Lewis, M., *see* Dowart et al.

Liddle, G., Overlap among desirable and undesirable characteristics in gifted children. *J. educ. Psychol.*, 1958, 49, 219-223. 390

Liebert, R. M., & Poulos, R. W., Eliciting the "norm of giving": Effects of modeling and presence of witness on children's sharing behavior. *Amer. Psychol. Assn. Proc.*, 1971, 6, 345-346. 86-87

Lighthall, J. J., *see* Waite et al.

Lindgren, H. C., *An introduction to social psychology.* N. Y.: Wiley, 1969. 391

Lindgren, H. C., & Guedes, H. de A., Social status, intelligence, and educational achievement among elementary and secondary students in São Paulo, Brazil. *J. soc. Psychol.*, 1963, 60, 9-14. 42, 389-390

Lindgren, H. C., & Mello, M. J., Emotional problems of over- and underachieving children in a Brazilian elementary school. *J. genet. Psychol.*, 1965, 106, 59-65. 414

Lindgren, H. C., Silva, I., Faraco, I., & da Rocha, N. S., Attitudes toward problem solving as a function of success in Brazilian elementary schools. *J. educ. Res.*, 1964, 58, 44-45. 41-42, 389-390

Lindgren, H. C., *see also* Uchiyama & Lindgren

Lindzey, G., *see* Hall & Lindzey

Ling, B.-C., Form discrimination as a learning cue in infants. *Comp. psychol. Monogr.*, 1941, 17, No. 2. 171-174

Lipsitt, L. P., A self-concept scale for children and its relationship to the children's form of the Manifest Anxiety Scale. *Child Develpm.*, 1958, 29, 463-472. 411

Lippsitt, L. P., & Levy, N., Electrotactual threshold in the neonate. *Child Develpm.*, 1959, 30, 547-554. 124

Livson, H., *see* Cameron et al.

Loftus, J. J., *see* Jersild, Golman, & Loftus

Long, L., Conceptual relationships in children: The concept of roundness. *J. genet. Psychol.*, 1940, 57, 289-315. 171

Lorenz, K. Z., *King Solomon's ring: A new light on animal ways.* N. Y.: Crowell, 1952. 204

Lovell, K., A follow-up study of Inhelder and Piaget's "The growth of logical thinking." *Brit. J. Psychol.*, 1961a, 52, 143-153. 265

Lovell, K., A follow-up study of Inhelder and Piaget's "The growth of logical thinking." *Brit. J. Psychol.*, 1961b, 52, 153-193. 377

Lovell, K., & Slater, A., The growth of the concept of time: A comparative study. *J. child. psychol. Psychiat.*, 1960, 1, 179-190. 381

Lowrey, G. H., *see* Watson & Lowrey

Lunt, P. S., *see* Warner & Lunt

Luria, A. R., *The role of speech in the regulation of normal and abnormal behavior.* N. Y.: Liveright, 1961. 282

Lustman, S. L., Rudiments of the ego. *Psychoanal. stud. Child*, 1956, 11, 89-98. 127

Lynn, D. G., & Sawrey, W. L., The effects of father-absence on Norwegian boys and girls. *J. abnorm. soc. Psychol.*, 1959, 59, 258-262. 309

McCall, R. B., Addendum. The use of multivariate procedures in developmental psychology. In P. H. Mussen, ed., *Carmichael's manual of child psychology*, 3rd ed., vol. 2. N. Y.: Wiley, 1970. 256

McCandless, B. R., Child socialization. In D. A. Goslin, Ed., *Handbook of socialization theory and research.* Chicago: Rand McNally, 1969. 336

McCandless, B. R., Balsbaugh, C., & Bennett, H. L., Preschool-age socialization and maternal control techniques. *Amer. Psychologist*, 1958, 13, 320. (Abstract) 355

McCandless, B. R., & Marshall, H. R., Sex differences in social acceptance and participation of preschool children. *Child Develpm.*, 1957b, 28, 421-425. 355

McCandless, B. R., & Marshall, H. R., A picture sociometric technique for preschool children and its relation to teacher judgments of friendship. *Child Develpm.*, 1957c, 28, 139-147. 355

McCandless, B. R., *see also* Castaneda et al.; Marshall & McCandless; and Palermo et al.

McCarthy, D., *The language development of the preschool child.* Univ. Minn. Inst. Child. Welf. Monogr., 1930, No. 4. 277, 280

McCarthy, D., Language development in children. In. L.

Carmichael, ed., *Manual of child psychology,* 2nd ed. N. Y.: Wiley, 1954. 176, 277, 280, 283, 285

McClelland, D. C., *The achieving society.* Priceton: Van Nostrand, 1961. 448-449

MacDonald, A. P., Jr., Manifestations of differential levels of socialization by birth order. *Develpm., Psychol.,* 1969a, 1, 485-492. 322

MacDonald, A. P., Jr., Anxiety, affiliation, and social isolation. *Develpm. Psychol.,* 1969b, 3, 242-254. 322

McDonald, F. J., *see* Bandura & McDonald

Macfarlane, J. W., Study of personality development. In R. G. Barkerm et al., Eds., *Child behavior and development.* N. Y.: McGraw-Hill, 1943. 439

McGraw, M. B., *Growth: A study of Johnny and Jimmy.* N. Y.: Appleton-Century-Crofts, 1935. 66

McGraw, M. B., Neural maturation as exemplified in a-chievement of bladder control. *J. Pediat.,* 1940, 16, 580-589. 153

McGraw, M. B., Maturation of behavior. In L. Carmichael, Ed., *Manual of child psychology.* N. Y.: Wiley, 1946. 63

McGuire, D., *see* Zimmerman et al.

McLendon, P. A., *see* Simsarian & McLendon

McNeil, E. B., Patterns of aggression. *J. child Psychol. Psychiat.,* 1962, 3, 65-77. 434

McNemar, Q., *The revision of the Stanford-Binet Scale: An analysis of the standardization data.* N. Y.: Houghton Mifflin, 1942. 285

McNemar, Q., *Psychological statistics,* 2nd ed. N. Y.: Wiley, 1955. 42

Maccoby, E., The taking of adult roles in middle childhood. *J. abnorm. soc. Psychol.,* 1961, 63, 493-503. 418

Maccoby, E. E., *see also* Sears, Maccoby, et al.

Maller, J. B., Cooperation and competition: An experimental study of motivation. *Tech. Coll. Contr. Educ.,* 1929, No. 384. 443-444

Mandell, W., *see* Caputo & Mandell

Marchbanks, G., & Levin, H., Cues by which children recognize words *J. educ. Psychol.,* 1965, 56, 57-61. 383-384

Markey, F. J., *see* Jersild et al.

Marquis, D. G., The criterion of innate behavior. *Psychol. Rev.,* 1930, 37, 334-349. 75

Marquis, D. P., A study of frustration in newborn infants. *J. exper. Psychol.,* 1943, 32, 123-138. 147-148, 156

Marshall, H. R., & McCandless, B. R., A study in prediction of social behavior of preschool children. *Child Develpm.,* 1957a, 28, 149-159. 355

Marshall, H. R., & McCandless, B. R., Relationships between dependence on adults and social acceptance by peers. *Child Develpm.,* 1957d, 28, 413-419. 355

Marshall, H. R., *see also* McCandless & Marshall

Martin, C. E., *see* Kinsey et al.

Maslow, A. H., *Motivation and personality.* N. Y.: Harper, 1954. 87-88

Matarazzo, R. G., *see* Graham, Matarazzo, et al.

Matthews, S. A., & Detwiler, S. R., The reaction of Amblystoma embryos following prolonged treatment with chlorotone. *J. exper. Zool.,* 1926, 45, 279-292. 66

Maudry, M., & Nekula, M., Social relations between children of the same age during the first two years of life. *J. genet. Psychol.,* 1931, 39, 393-398. 229

Maw, W. H., & Maw, E. W., Children's curiosity and parental attitudes. *J. Marriage and the Family,* 1966, 28, 343-345. 406

Maw, E. W., *see* Maw & Maw

Mead, G. H., *Mind, self, and society.* Chicago: Univ. of Chicago Press, 1934. 227

Mead, M., *Coming of age in Samoa,* N. Y.: Morrow, 1928. 25

Mead, M., *Growing up in New Guinea.* N. Y.: Morrow, 1930. 25

Mead, M., Investigation of thought of primitive children with special reference to animism. *J. roy. anthrop. Inst.,* 1932, 62, 173-190. 25

Mead, M., Research on primitive children. In L. Carmichael, Ed., *Manual of child psychology,* 2nd ed. N. Y.: Wiley, 1954. 25

Meredith, H. V., A descriptive concept of physical development. In D. R. Harris, Ed., *The concept of development.* Minneapolis: Univ. of Minn. Press, 1967. 238

Merrill, B. A., Measurement of mother-child interaction. *J. abnorm. soc. Psychol.,* 1946, 41, 37-49. 336

Mello, M. J., *see* Lindgren & Mello

Metheny, E., Breathing capacity and grip strength of pre-school children. *Univ. Iowa Stud. Child Welf.,* 1941, 18, No. 2. 366

Michael, W. B., Zimmerman, W. S., & Guilford, J. P., An investigation of the nature of the spatial-relations and visualization factors in two school samples. *Educ. psychol. Measmt.,* 1951, 11, 561-577. 382

Miles, B. E., *see* Alexander et al.

Miller, N. E., & Dollard, J., *Social learning and imitation.* New Haven: Yale Univ. Press, 1941. 273

Miller, N. E., *see also* Dollard & Miller

Millichamp, D. A., *see* Blatz et al.

Minard, J., Williams, G., & Coleman, D., A change of possible neurological and psychological significance within the first week of neonate life: Sleeping REM rate. *Amer. Psychol. Assn. Proc.,* 1969, 4, 271-272. 127

Mischel, W., Preference for delayed reinforcement: An experimental study of a cultural observation. *J. abnorm. soc. Psychol.,* 1958, 56, 57-61. 309, 310

Mitchell, G., & Brandt, E. M., Behavioral differences related to experience of mother and sex of infant in the rhesus monkey. *Develpm. Psychol.,* 1970, 3, 149. 307-308

Mogar, M., Children's causal reasoning about natural phenomena. *Child Develpm.,* 1960, 31, 59-65. 379

Montagu, M. F. A., Constitutional and prenatal factors in infant and child health. In M. J. E. Senn, Ed., *Symposium on the healthy personality.* N. Y.: Josiah Macy Found., 1950. 110-111, 116

Moore, R. W., *see* Brennan et al.

Moreno, J. L., *Who shall survive? A new approach to the problem of human interrelations.* Washington: Nerv. & Ment. Dis. Publishing Co., 1934. 355

Morgan, G. A., & Ricciuti, H. N., Infants' responses to strangers during the first year. In B. M. Foss, Ed., *Determinants of infant behavior.* London: Methuen, 1963. 221

Morrison, E., Underachievement among preadolescent boys considered in relationship to passive aggression. *J. educ. Psychol.,* 1969, 60, 168-173. 436

Morrow, W. R., & Wilson, R. C., The self-reported personal and social adjustment of bright high-achieving and under-achieving high school boys. *J. child psychol. Psychiat.,* 1961, 2, 203-209. 414

Moss, H. A., & Kagan, J., Stability of achievement and recognition seeking behaviors from early childhood through adulthood. *J. abnorm. soc. Psychol.,* 1961, 62, 504-513. 409

Moss, H. A., *see also* Kagan & Moss

Mouton, J. S., Bell, R. L., Jr., & Blake, R. R., Role playing skill and sociometric peer status. *Group Psychother.,* 1956, 9, 7-17. 442

Mowrer, O. H., A stimulus-response analysis of anxiety and its role as a reinforcing agent. *Psychol. Rev.,* 1939, 46, 553-565. 253

Munn, N. L., Learning in children. In L. Carmichael, ed., *Manual of child psychology,* 2nd ed. N. Y.: Wiley, 1954. 74

Murphy, G., Murphy, L. B., & Newcomb, T. M., *Experimental social psychology.* N. Y.: Harper, 1937. 227, 450

Murphy, L. B., *see* Murphy et al.

Murray, A. H., *see* Kluckhohn et al.

Mussen, P. H., & Jones, M. C., Self-conceptions, motivations, and interpersonal attitudes of late- and early-maturing boys. *Child Develpm.,* 1957. 28, 242-256. 411

Mussen, P. H., *see also* Jones & Mussen; Sewell & Mussen; and Sewell et al.

Myklebust, H. R., Language disorders in children. *Except. Child,* 1956, 22, 163-166. 174

Myrianthopoulos, N. C., *see* Willerman et al.

Naeye, R. L., Diener, M. M., Dellinger, W. S., & Blanc, W. A., Urban poverty: Effects on prenatal nutrition. *Science,* 1969, 166, 1026. 114

Naylor, A. F., *see* Willerman et al.

Neale, D. C., & Proshek, J. M., School-related attitudes of culturally disadvantaged elementary school children. *J. educ. Psychol.,* 1967, 58, 238-244. 454-455

Neff, W. S., & Koltuv, M., Toleration of psychiatric rehabilitation as a function of coping style. *J. consult. Psychol.,* 1967, 31, 364-370. 415

Neill, B. M., *Perception by preschool children of parental roles in selected home situations.* Unpubl. master's thesis, Iowa State Coll., Ames, Iowa, 1946. 346

Neilon, P., Shirley's babies after fifteen years. *J. genet. Psychol.,* 1948, 73, 175-186. 183

Nekula, M., *see* Maudry & Nekula

Nelson, G. A., *see* Henery & Nelson

Nelson, H. W., *see* Rheingold et al.

Nelson, K., & Kessen, W., Visual scanning by human newborns: Responses to complete triangle, to sides only, and to corners only. *Amer. Psychol. Assn. Proc.,* 1969, 4, 273-274. 128

Nelson, V. L., *see* Richards & Nelson; and Sontag et al.

Newberry, H., *see* Richards & Newberry

Newcomb, T. M., *see* Murphy et al.

Newman, H. H., Freeman, F. N., & Holzinger, K. J., *Twins.* Chicago: Univ. of Chicago Press, 1937. 61

Nielsen, J., Friedrich, U., & Tsuboi, T., Chromosome abnormalities in patients treated with chlorpromazine, perphenazine, and lysergide. *Brit. med. J.,* 1969, 3, 634-636. 116

Norton, H. P., *see* Levison et al.

Norval, M., Kennedy, R. L. J., & Berkson, J., Biometric studies of the growth of children of Rochester, Minn. *Hum. Biol.,* 1951, 23, 273-301. 139

Nourse, A. E., et al. *The body.* N. Y.: Time-Life, 1964. 111

Nowlis, V., *see* Whiting et al.

O'Connor, N., & Franks, C., Childhood upbringing and other environmental factors. In H. J. Eysenck, Ed., *Handbook of abnormal psychology: An experimental approach.* NY: Basic Books, 1961. 198

Oetting, E. R., & Dinges, N. G., An anxiety and mood scale for young Navajo children. *Amer. Psychol. Assn. exper. publ. System,* June, 1971, 12, Ms. No. 472-35. 414

Ohaneson, E. M., *see* Wenner et al.

Olson, A. L., *see* Clarke & Olson

Olson, W. C., Developmental theory in education. In D. B. Harris, Ed., *The concept of development: An issue in the study of behavior.* Minneapolis: Univ. of Minn. Press, 1957. 76

Olson, W. C., & Hughes, R. O., Growth of the child as a

whole. In R. G. Barker et al., Eds., *Child behavior and development*. N. Y.: McGraw-Hill, 1943. 367

Ordy, J. M., *see* Fantz, R. L., et al.

Orlansky, H., Infant care and personality. *Psychol. Bull.*, 1949, 46, 1-48. 194

Osser, H., Language development. In G. S. Lesser, Ed., *Psychology and educational practice*. Chicago: Scott Foresman, 1971. 275, 285, 286

Ostfeld, B., & Katz, P. A., The effect of threat severity in children of varying socioeconomic leveks. *Develpm. Psychol.*, 1969, 1, 205-210. 313

Ottinger, D. R., Blatchley, M. E., & Denenberg, V. H., Stimulation of human neonates and visual attentiveness. *Amer. Psychol. Assn. Proc.*, 1968, 3, 355-356. 190

Owens, W., Age and mental abilities: A longitudinal study. *Genet. psychol. Monogr.*, 1953, 48, 3-54. 43

Palermo, D. S., Castaneda, A., & McCandless, B. R., The relationship of anxiety in children to performance in a complex learning task. *Child Develpm.*, 1956, 27, 333-338. 375

Palermo, D. S., *see* Castaneda et al.

Palmer, R. J., *see* Cotler & Palmer

Parenti, A. N., *see* Davids & Parenti

Parten, M. B., Leadership among preschool children. *J. abnorm. soc. Psychol.*, 1932-33, 27, 430-440. 348

Parten, M. B., Social play among preschool children. *J. abnorm. soc. Psychol.*, 1933, 28, 136-147. 348

Pasamanick, B., *see* Knobloch & Pasamanick

Paterson, D. G., *Physique and intellect*. N. Y.: Century, 1930. 366

Paterson, J., *see* Denny et al.

Payne, D. T., *see* Freeberg & Payne

Pearce, D., *see* Walters et al.

Pease, D., *see* Gardner, Pease, & Hawkes

Pfuderer, C., *see* Drach et al.

Phillips, B. N., & D'Amico, L. A., Effects of cooperation and competition on the cohesiveness of small face-to-facegroups. *J. educ. Psychol.*, 1956, 47, 65-70. 444

Piaget, J., *The language and thought of the child*. N. Y.: Humanities Press, 1926. 174, 264, 277

Piaget, J., *The child's conception of the world*. N. Y.: Harcourt Brace, 1929. 73

Piaget, J., *The child's conception of physical causality*. N. Y.: Harcourt Brace, 1930. 378

Piaget, J., *The moral judgment of children*. Glencoe, Ill.: Free Press, 1948. 49-50, 423-425

Piaget, J., *Psychology of intelligence*. N. Y.: Harcourt Brace, 1950. 74, 165, 385

Piaget, J., *Play, dreams, and imitation in childhood*. N. Y.: Norton, 1951. 224-225

Piaget, J., *The origins of intelligence in children*. N. Y.: Intl. Universities Press, 1952. (Trans. by M. Cook; ori-

ginal, 1936). 69, 75, 165

Piaget, J., The development of time concepts in the child. In P. H. Hoch, & J. Zubin, eds., *Psychopathology of childhood*. N. Y.: Grune & Stratton, 1955. 381

Piaget, J., *Logic and psychology*. N. Y.: Basic Books, 1957. 165

Piaget, J., Cognitive development in children. In R. E. Ripple and V. N. Rockcastle, eds., *Piaget rediscovered*. Ithaca: Cornell Univ. Press, 1964. 381

Piaget, J., *The child's conception of number*. N. Y.: Norton, 1965. 265

Piaget, J., *The child's conception of time*. N. Y.: Basic Books, 1969. (Trans. by A. J. Pomerans; original, 1946). 271

Piaget, J., Piaget's theory. In P. H. Mussen, ed., *Carmichael's manual of child psychology*, 3rd ed., vol. 1. N. Y.: Wiley, 1970. 68

Piaget, J., & Inhelder, B., *The child's conception of space*. London: Routledge & Kegan Paul, 1956. 270

Piaget, J., & Inhelder, B., *Le genèse des structures logiques élémentaires: Classifications et sériations*. Neuchâtel, Switzerland: Delachaux & Niestlé, 1959. 268

Piaget, J., *see also* Inhelder & Piaget

Piddington, R., *The psychology of laughter: A study of social adaptation*. N. Y.: Gamut Press, 1963. 257

Pieper, W., *see* Abrams & Pieper

Pikas, A., Children's attitudes toward rational versus inhibiting parental authority. *J. abnorm. soc. Psychol.*, 1961, 62, 315-321. 422

Pinard, A., *see* Laurendeau & Pinard

Pinneau, S. R., The infantile disorders of hospitalism and anaclitic depression. *Psychol. Bull.*, 1955, 52, 429-452. 198

Pomeroy, W. B., *see* Kinsey et al.

Pope, B., Socio-economic contrasts in children's peer culture prestige values. *Genet. psychol. Monogr.*, 1953, 48, 157-220. 441

Poulos, R. W., *see* Liebert & Poulos

Prader, A., Tanner, J. M., & von Harnack, G. A., Catch-up growth following illness or starvation. *J. Pediat.*, 1963, 62, 646-659. 239

Pratt, K. C., The neonate. In L. Carmichael, ed., *Manual of child psychology*, 2nd ed. N. Y.: Wiley, 1954. 125, 128

Preyer, W., *Die Seele des Kindes*. Leipzig: T. Grieben, 1882. 11

Price-Williams, D., Gordon, W., & Ramirez, M., III, Skills and conservation: A study of pottery-making children. *Develpm. Psychol.*, 1969, 1, 769. 268, 379

Proshek, J. M., *see* Neale & Proshek

Quast, W., *see* Wolking et al.

Quay, L. C., Language dialect, reinforcement, and the

intelligence-test performance of Negro children. *Child Develpm.*, 1971, 42, 5-15. 286

Queen, S. A., & Habenstein, R. W., *The family in various cultures*, 3rd ed. Philadelphia: Lippincott, 1967. 4

Raabe, V. L., *see* Dymond et al.

Rabe, A., & Haddad, R. K., Response of micrencephalic rats to environmental complexity. *Amer. Psychol. Assn. Proc.*, 1970, 5, 195-196. 190

Rabin, A. I., Behavior research in collective settlement in Israel: Infants and children under conditions of "intermittent" mothering in the kibbutz. *Amer. J. Orthopsychiat.*, 1958, 28, 577-586. 205

Rabin, A. I., *Growing up in the kibbutz*. N. Y.: Springer, 1965. 205

Rabson, A., *see* Crandall & Rabson

Ramirez, M., III, *see* Price-Williams et al.

Raynor, R., *see* Watson & Raynor

Rau, L., *see* Sears, Rau, et al.; and Winder & Rau

Read, G. D., *Childbirth without fear*, 2nd ed. N. Y.: Harper, 1959. 120

Regan, R. A., *see* Tuckman & Regan

Rehage, K. J., *see* Flickinger & Rehage

Renison, N., *see* Amen & Renison

Rest, J., Turiel, E., & Kohlberg, L., Relations between level of moral judgment and comprehension of the moral judgment of others. *J. Pers.*, 1969, 37, 225-252. 425

Rheingold, H. L., The modification of social responsiveness in institutional babies. *Monogr. Soc. Res. Child Develpm.*, 1956, 21, No. 2. 191-192, 227

Rheingold, H. L., The measurement of maternal care. *Child Develpm.*, 1960, 31, 565-575. 44

Rheingold, H. L., The social and socializing infant. In D. A. Goslin, ed., *Handbook of socialization theory and research*. Chicago: Rand McNally, 1969. 228

Rheingold, H. L., & Bayley, N., Later effects of an experimental modification of mothering. *Child Develpm.*, 1959, 30, 363-372. 192

Rheingold, H. L., & Eckerman, C. O., The infant separates himself from his mother. *Science*, 1970, 168, 78-83. 215-218

Rheingold, H. L., Gewirtz, J. L., & Nelson, H. W., Social conditioning. *J. comp. physiol. Psychol.*, 1959, 57, 68-73. 178

Ribble, M. A., *The rights of infants*. N. Y.: Columbia Univ. Press, 1943. 125, 197, 199, 201

Ricciuti, H. N., *see* Brockman & Ricciuti; and Morgan & Ricciuti

Richards, T. W., & Nelson, V. L., Abilities of infants during the first eighteen months. *J. genet. Psychol.*, 1939, 55, 299-318. 180

Richards, T. W., & Newberry, H., Studies in fetal behavior: III. Can performance test items at six months postnatally

be predicted on the basis of fetal activity? *Child Develpm.*, 1938, 9, 79-86. 114

Rogers, C. R., & Dymond, R., *Psychotherapy and personality change*. Chicago: Univ. of Chicago Press, 1954. 415

Rose, A. M., *see* Harris et al.

Rose, M. H., *see* Berk et al.

Rosekrans, M. A., & Hartup, W. W., Imitation influences of consistent and inconsistent response consequences to a model on aggressive behavior in children. *J. pers. soc. Psychol.*, 1967, 7, 429-434. 341

Rosen, B. C., Socialization and achievement motivation in Brazil. *Amer. sociol. Rev.*, 1962, 27, 612-624. 409

Rosen, B. C., Social class and the child's perception of the parent. *Child Develpm.*, 1964, 35, 1147-1153. 409

Rosen, B. C., & D'Andrade, R. G., The psychosocial origins of achievement motivation. *Sociometry*, 1959, 22, 185-218. 408

Rosenblum, L. A., *see* Kaufman & Rosenblum

Rosenhahn, D., *see* Dowart et al.

Rosenthal, M. K., *The generalization of dependency behaviors from mother to stranger*. Unpubl. doctoral dissertation, Stanford Univ., 1965. 253

Rosenthal, M. K., The generalization of dependency behavior from mother to stranger. *J. child psychol. Psychiat.*, 1967, 8, 117-133. 253

Rosenzweig, M. R., *see* Bennett et al.

Rosenzweig, S., Further comparative data on repetition choice after success and failure as related to frustration tolerance. *J. genet. Psychol.*, 1945, 66, 75-81. 407

Rosenzweig, S., Available methods for studying personality. *J. Psychol.*, 1949, 28, 345-368. 48

Ross, D., *see* Bandura et al.

Ross, S. A., *see* Bandura et al.

Rothbart, M. K., Birth order and mother-child interaction in an achievement situation. *J. pers. soc. Psychol.*, 1971, 17, 113-119. 323-324

Rothenberg, B. B., & Courtney, R. G., Conservation of number in very young children. *Develpm. Psychol.*, 1969, 1, 493-502. 265

Rousseau, J.-J., *Émile, or on education*. (Trans. by B. Foxley). London: Dent, 1911. Cited by W. Kessen (1965). 10

Routh, D. K., Conditioning of vocal response differentiation in infants. *Develpm. Psychol.*, 1969, 1, 219-226. 175, 178

Russell, R. W., Studies in animism: II. The development of animism. *J. genet. Psychol.*, 1940a, 56, 353-366. 264

Russell, R. W., Studies in animism: IV. An investigation of concepts allied to animism. *J. genet. Psychol.*, 1940b, 57, 83-91. 264

Salapatek, P. H., *see* Kessen et al.

Salk, L., The effects of the normal heartbeat sound on the behavior of the newborn infant: Implications for mental health. *World ment. Health,* 1960, 12, 168-175. 133

Salk, L., The importance of the heartbeat rhythm to human nature: Theoretical, clinical, and experimental observations. *Proc. 3rd World Cong. Psychiat.* vol. 1. Montreal: McGill Univ. Press, 1961. 133

Salmon, M., *see* Sayler & Salmon

Sameroff, A. J., Can conditioned responses be established in the newborn infant: 1971? *Develpm. Psychol.,* 1971, 5, 1-12. 133

Sameroff, A., *see also* Elkind & Sameroff

Santrock, J. W., & Wohlford, P., Effects of father absence: Influence of the reason for and the onset of the absence. *Amer. Psychol. Assn. Proc.,* 1970, 5, 265-266. 310

Sarason, S. B., et al., *Anxiety in elementary school children: A report of research.* N.Y.: Wiley, 1960. 374

Sarason, S. B., *see also* Waite et al.

Sawrey, W. L., *see* Lynn & Sawrey

Sayler, A., & Salmon, M., Communal nursing in mice: Influence of multiple mothers on the growth of the young. *Science,* 1969, 164, 1309-1310. 209

Scammon, R. E., The measurement of the body in childhood. In J. A. Harris, et al., *The measurement of man.* Minneapolis: Univ. of Minn. Press, 1930. 141

Scarpetti, W. L., *see* Tolor et al.

Scarr-Salapatek, S., Race, social class, and IQ. *Science,* 1971, 174, 1285-1295. 393

Schachter, S., *The psychology of affiliation.* Stanford: Stanford Univ. Press, 1959. 321-322

Schaefer, E. S., A circumplex model for maternal behavior. *J. abnorm. soc. Psychol.,* 1959, 59, 226-235. 398-399

Schaefer, E. S., Converging conceptual models for maternal behavior and child behavior. In C. Glidewell, ed., *Parental attitudes and child behavior.* Springfield, Ill.: Thomas, 1961. 398-399, 400

Schaefer, E. S., & Bayley, N., Consistency of maternal behavior from infancy to preadolescence. *J. abnorm. soc. Psychol.,* 1960, 61, 1-6. 398-400

Schaefer, E. S., & Bell, R. Q., Development of a parental attitude research instrument. *Child Develpm.,* 1958, 29, 339-361. 50

Schaefer, E. S., *see* Bayley & Schaefer

Schaffer, H. R., Some issues for research in the study of attachment behavior. In B. M. Foss, ed., *Determinants of infant behavior,* vol. 2. London: Methuen, 1963. 161

Schaffer, H. R., The onset of fear of strangers and the incongruity hypothesis. *J. child psychol. Psychiat.,* 1966a, 7, 95-106. 161

Schaffer, H. R., Activity level as a constitutional determinant of infantile reaction to deprivation. *Child Develpm.,* 1966b, 37, 595-602. 179

Schaffer, H. R. & Emerson, P. E., The development of social attachments in infancy. *Monogr. Soc. Res. Child Develpm.,* 1964a, 29, No. 3. 196

Schaffer, H. R. & Emerson, P. E., Patterns of response to physical contact in early human development. *J. child psychol. Psychiat.,* 1964b, 5, 1-13. 215

Schaie, C. W. & Strother, C. R., A cross-cultural study of age changes in cognitive behavior. *Psychol. Bull.,* 1968, 70, 671-680. 43

Scheinfeld, A., *see* Garai & Scheinfeld

Schneider, D. M., *see* Kluckhohn et al.

Schwartz, S. H. & Clausen, G. T., Responsibility, norms, and helping in an emergency. *J. pers. soc. Psychol.,* 1970, 16, 299-310. 353

Sears, P. S., Doll play aggression in normal young children: Influence of sex, age, sibling status, father's absence. *Psychol. Monogr.,* 1951, 65, No. 323. 51, 337

Sears, P. S., *see also* Sears, Whiting, et al.

Sears, R. R., *Survey of objective studies of psychoanalytic concepts.* N.Y.: Social Science Research Council, 1943. 29

Sears, R. R., Relation of fantasy aggression to interpersonal aggression. *Child Develpm.,* 1950, 21, 5-6. 337-338

Sears, R. R., A theoretical framework for personality and social behavior. Amer. Psychol., 1951, 6, 476-483. 338

Sears, R. R., Personality development in the family. In R. F. Winch & R. McGinnis, eds., *Marriage and the family.* N.Y.: Holt, 1953. 250

Sears, R. R., Relation of early socialization experiences to aggression in middle childhood. *J. abnorm. soc. Psychol.,* 1961, 63, 466-492. 418, 436

Sears, R. R., Maccoby, E. E., & Levin, H., *Patterns of child rearing.* Evanston: Row, Peterson, 1957. 117, 147, 148, 149, 154, 219, 258, 331, 335

Sears, R. R., Rau, L., & Alpert, R., *Identification and child rearing.* Stanford Univ. Press, 1965. 255

Sears, R. R., Whiting, J. W. M., Nowlis, V., & Sears, P. S. Some child-rearing antecedents of aggression and dependency in young children. *Genet. psychol. Monogr.,* 1953, 47, 135-236. 219, 221

Sears, R. R., *see also* Levin & Sears

Seghorn, T., *see* Cohen & Seghorn

Senn, M. J. E., Pediatrics in orthopsychiatry. In L. G. Lowrey, ed., *Orthopsychiatry 1923-1947: Retrospect and prospect.* N.Y.: American Orthopsychiatric Assn., 1948, 300-309. 24

Sewell, W. H., Infant training and the personality of the child. *Amer. J. Sociol.,* 1952, 58, 150-159. 97

Sewell, W. H. & Mussen, P. H., The effect of feeding, weaning, and scheduling procedures on childhood adjustment and the formation of oral symptoms. *Child Develpm.,* 1952, 23, 185-191. 194

Sewell, W. H., Mussen, P. H., & Harris, C. W., Relationship among child training practices. *Amer. sociol. Rev.*, 1955, 20, 137-148. 194

Shelton, F. C., *see* Kogan et al.

Sherman, M., The differentiation of emotional responses in infants. I. Judgments of emotional responses from motion picture views and from actual observations. *J. comp. Psychol.*, 1927, 7, 265-284. 157

Shields, J., *Monozygotic twins.* London: Oxford U. Press, 1962. 61

Shields, J., *see* Gottesman and Shields

Shirley, M. M., *The first two years: A study of twenty-five babies, Vol. I. Postural and locomotor development.* Minneapolis: Univ. of Minn. Press, 1931. 144, 182-183

Shirley, M. M., *The first two years, Vol. II. Intellectual development.* Minneapolis: Univ. of Minn. Press, 1933. 144, 176, 177, 182-183

Shuttleworth, F. K., The physical and mental growth of girls and boys age six to nineteen in relation to age at maximum growth. *Monogr. Soc. Res. Child Develpm.*, 1939, 4, No. 3. 367

Siegel, A. E., Editorial. *Child Develpm.*, 1967, 38, 901-907. 41

Silva, I., *see* Lindgren et al.

Simsarian, F. P. & McLendon, P. A., Feeding behavior of an infant during the first twelve weeks of life on a self-demand schedule. *J. Pediat.*, 1942, 20, 93-103. 126

Singer, R. D., *see* Feshbach & Singer

Siqueland, E. R., Reinforcement patterns and extinction in human newborns. *J. exp. child Psychol.*, 1968, 6, 431-442. 133

Skeels, H. M., et al., A study of environmental stimulation: The orphanage preschool project. *Univ. Iowa Stud. Child Welf.*, 1938, 15, No. 4. 192

Skinner, B. F., *The behavior of organisms: An experimental analysis.* N.Y.: Appleton-Century-Crofts, 1938. 29

Skinner, B. F., *Verbal behavior.* N.Y.: Appleton-Century-Crofts, 1957. 177, 275

Slater, A., *see* Lovell & Slater

Slobin, D., *see* Drach et al.

Smith, K. U. & Greene, P., A critical period in maturation of performance with space-displaced vision. *Percept. & Mot. Skills,* 1963, 17, 627-639. 367

Smith, K. U., Zwerg, C., & Smith, N. J., Sensory-feedback analysis of infant control of the behavioral environment. *Percept. & Mot. Skills,* 1963, 16, 725-732. 213

Smith, M. E., An investigation of the development of the sentence and the extent of the vocabulary in young children. *Univ. Iowa Stud. Child Welf.*, 1926, 3, No. 5. 281-282

Smith, N. J., *see* Smith et al.

Solkoff, N., Yaffe, S., Weintraub, D., & Blase, B., Effects of handling on the subsequent developments of prema-ture infants. *Develpm. Psychol.*, 1969, 1, 765-768. 133

Sontag, L. W., Baker, C. T., & Nelson, V. L., Mental growth and personality development: A longitudinal study. *Soc. Res. Child Develpm. Monogr.*, 1958, 23, No. 68. 408

Sontag, L. W. & Kagan, J., The emergence of intellectual achievement motives. *Amer. J. Orthopsychiat.*, 1963, 33, 532-535. 409

Spanner, S. D., *see* Jordan & Spanner

Spear, P. S., Motivational effects of praise and criticism on children's learning. *Develpm. Psychol.*, 1970, 3, 124-132. 38

Spearman, C. E., *The abilities of man.* N.Y.: Macmillan, 1927. 385

Spears, W. C. & Hohle, R. H., Sensory and perceptual processes in infants. In Y. Brackbill, Ed., *Infancy and early childhood.* N.Y.: Free Press, 1967. 129

Spencer-Booth, Y., *see* Hinde & Spencer-Booth

Sperry, M., *see* Hollenberg & Sperry

Spitz, R. A., Hospitalism. *Psychoanal. Stud. Child,* 1945, 1, 54-74. 201

Spitz, R. A., Hospitalism: A follow-up report. *Psychoanal. Stud. Child,* 1946, 2, 113-117. 201

Spitz, R. A., The importance of the mother-child relationship during the first year of life: A synopsis in five sketches. *Ment. Health Today,* 1948, 7, 7-13. 197, 199

Springer, D., Development in young children of an understanding of time and the clock. *J. genet. Psychol.*, 1952, 80, 83-96. 271

Staub, E., The use of role playing and induction in children's learning of helping and sharing behavior. *Child Develpm.*, 1971a, 42, 805-816. 353

Staub, E., A child in distress: The influence of nurturance and modeling on children's attempts to help. *Develpm. Psychol.*, 1971b, 5, 124-132. 353-354

Steinschneider, A., Developmental psychophysiology. In Y. Brackbill, Ed. *Infancy and early childhood.* N.Y.: Free Press, 1967. 237

Stephens, S. W., *see* Kogan et al.

Stern, W., *The psychological methods of testing intelligence* (Trans. by G. M. Whipple). Baltimore: Warwick & York, 1914. 386

Stevenson, H. W., *see* Weir & Stevenson

Stewart, D., *see* Berk et al.

Stewart, M. A., Hyperactive children. *Sci. Amer.*, 1970, 222(4), 94-99. 370

Stith, M. & Conner, R., Dependency and helpfulness in young children. *Child Develpm.*, 1962, 33, 15-20. 331

Stone, L. J., A critique of studies of infant isolation. *Child Develpm.*, 1954, 25, 9-20. 191

Stott, D. H., An empirical approach to motivation based on the behavior of the young child. *J. child psychol. Psychiat.*, 1961, 2, 97-117. 224

Strobel, D. A., *see* Zimmerman et al.

Strother, C. R., *see* Schaie and Strother

Sullivan, H. S., *Conceptions of modern psychiatry.* Washington, D. C.: William Allison White Psychiatric Foundation, 1947. 343

Sung, C., *see* Aldrich et al.

Sunley, R., Early nineteenth-century literature on child rearing. In M. Mead & M. Wolfenstein, Eds. *Childhood in contemporary cultures.* Chicago: U. Chicago Press, 1955. 4

Suomi, S. J., *see* Harlow & Suomi

Takaishi, M., *see* Tanner et al.

Tannenbaum, J., *see* Honig et al.

Tanner, J. M., *Growth at adolescence,* 2nd ed. Philadelphia: Davis, 1962. 141

Tanner, J. M., The regulation of human growth. *Child Develpm.,* 1963, 34, 817-848. 141

Tanner, J. M., Physical growth. In P. H. Mussen, ed. *Carmichael's manual of child psychology,* 3rd ed. N.Y.: Wiley, 1970. 42, 141, 238, 239, 264

Tanner, J. M., Whitehouse, R. H., & Takaishi, M., Standards from birth to maturity for height, weight, height velocity, and weight velocity: British children, 1965. *Arch. dis. Childhood,* 1966, 41, 454-471; 613-635. 140

Tanner, J. M., *see* Prader et al.

Tasch, R. J., *see* Jersild & Tasch

Templin, M. C., *Certain language skills in children.* Minneapolis: Univ. of Minn. Press, 1957. 282, 283, 285

Tennes, K. H. & Lampl, E. E., Stranger and separation anxiety in infancy. *J. nerv. ment. Dis.,* 1964, 139, 247-254. 221

Terman, L. M. & Merrill, M. A., *Measuring intelligence.* Boston: Houghton Mifflin, 1937. 42

Terman, L. M. et al., Symposium: Intelligence and its measurement. *J. educ. Psychol.,* 1921, 12, 123-147, 195-216, 271-275. 385

Tharp, R. G., *see* Gallimore et al.

Thomas, D. S. et al., Some techniques in studying social behavior. *Child Develpm. Monogr.,* 1929, No. 1. 44

Thompson, G. G. & Horrocks, J. E., A study of the friendship fluctuations of urban boys and girls. *J. genet Psychol.,* 1947, 70, 53-63. 442

Thompson, G. C., *see also* Austin & Thompson; deGroat & Thompson; and Horrocks & Thompson

Thompson, H., Physical growth., In L. Carmichael, ed. *Manual of child psychology,* 2nd ed. N.Y.: Wiley, 1954. 139

Thompson, H., *see* Gesell & Thompson

Thompson, J., Development of facial expression of emotion in blind and seeing children. *Arch. Psychol. (NY),* 1941, 37, No. 264. 160

Thurston, D., *see* Graham, Ernhart, et al.

Thurstone, L. L., Theories of intelligence. *Scientific Monthly,* 1946, 62, 101-112. 385

Tizard, J., *Community services for the mentally handicapped.* London: Oxford Univ. Press, 1964. 92

Toigo, R., *see* Eron et al.

Tolor, A., Scarpetti, W. L., & Lane, P. A., Teachers' attitudes toward children's behavior revistied. *J. educ. Psychol.,* 1967, 58, 175-180. 449

Torrance, E. P., Peer influences on preschool children's willingness to try difficult tasks. *J. Psychol.,* 1969, 72, 189-194. 352

Torrance, E. P., Influence of dyadic interaction on creative functioning. *Psychol. Reports,* 1970, 26, 391-394. 352

Tronick, E., *see* Ball & Tronick

Tseng, S. C., *see* Harris & Tseng

Tsuboi, T., *see* Nielsen et al.

Tuckman, J. & Regan, R. A., Size of family and behavioral problems in children. *J. genet. Psychol.,* 1967, 111, 151-160. 229

Tuddenham, R. D., Soldier intelligence in World Wars I and II. *Amer. Psychol.,* 1948, 3, 54-56. 321

Tuddenham, R. D., Studies in reputation: III. Correlates of popularity among elementary school children. *J. educ. Psychol.,* 1951, 42, 257-276. 439

Tuddenham, R. D., Studies in reputation: I. Sex and grade differences in school children's evaluation of their peers. II. The diagnosis of social adjustment. *Psychol. Monogr.,* 1952, No. 333. 439

Tuddenham, R. D., Jean Piaget and the world of the child. *Amer. Psychol.,* 1966, 21, 207-217. 68, 72

Tulkin, S. R., Race, class, family, and school achievement. *J. pers. soc. Psychol.,* 1968, 9, 31-37. 320

Tulkin, S. R. & Kagan, J., Mother-child interaction: Social-class differences in the first year of life. *Amer. Psychol. Assn. Proc.,* 1970, 5, 261-262. 178

Turiel, E., An experimental test of the sequentiality of developmental stages in the child's moral judgments. *J. pers. soc. Psychol.,* 1966, 3, 611-618. 425

Turiel, E., *see* Rest et al.

Turner, J. leB., *see* Beller & Turner

Turner, R. H. & Wanderlippe, R. H., Self-ideal congruence as an index of adjustment. *J. abnorm. soc. Psychol.,* 1958, 57, 202-206. 415

Turnure, C., Response to voice of mother and stranger by babies in the first year. *Develpm. Psychol.,* 1971, 4, 182-190. 36-37

Twitchell, T. E., A behavioral syndrome. *Science,* 1971, 174, 135-136. 371

Tylor, E. B., *Primitive culture.* London: J. Murray, 1871. 25

Uchiyama, A., & Lindgren, H. C., Ideal teacher concepts:

Attitude shift after practice teaching. *Psychol. Rep.,* 1971, 28, 470. 450

Udelf, M. S., *see* Fantz et al.

Uzgiris, I. C., Situational generality of conservation. *Child Develpm.,* 1964, 35, 831-841. 265

Valasek, F., *see* Harris et al.

Vanderlippe, R. A., *see* Turner & Vanderlippe

Van Egmond, E., *see* Zander & Van Egmond

Valenstein, A. F., *see* Bibring et al.

von Harnack, G. A., *see* Prader et al.

Waite, R. R., Sarason, S. B., Lighthall, J. J., & Davidson, K. S., A study of anxiety and learning in children. *J. abnorm. soc. Psychol.,* 1958, 57, 267-270. 374

Walder, L. O., *see* Eron et al.

Walk, R. D., & Gibson, E. J., A comparative and analytical study of visual depth perceptions. *Psychol. Monogr.,* 1961, 75, No. 15. 170

Walsh, A. M., *Self-concepts of bright boys with learning difficulties.* N.Y.: Bureau of Publications, Teachers Coll., Columbia Univ., 1956. 411

Walters, C. E., Prediction of postnatal development from fetal activity. *Child Develpm.,* 1965, 36, 801-808. 114

Walters, J., Pearce, D., & Dahms, L., Affectional and aggressive behavior of preschool children. *Child Develpm.,* 1957, 28, 15-26. 337

Walters, R. H., *see* Bandura & Walters

Wardwell, E., *see* Levin & Wardwell

Warner, W. L., & Lunt, P. S., *The social life of a modern community.* New Haven: Yale Univ. Press, 1941. 311

Warren, J. M., *see* Wilson et al.

Washburn, R. W., A Study of smiling and laughing of infants in the first year of life. *Genet. psychol. Monogr.,* 1929, 6, 397-537. 256, 257

Waters, E., & Crandall, V. J., Social class and observed maternal behavior from 1940 to 1960. *Child Develpm.,* 1964, 35, 1021-1032. 401

Watson, E. H., & Lowrey, G. H., *Growth and development of children.* Chicago: Yearbook Publishers, 1958. 238

Watson, G., Some personality differences in children related to strict or permissive parental discipline. *J. Psychol.,* 1957, 44, 227-249. 400

Watson, J. B., & Raynor, R., Conditioned emotional reactions. *J. exper. Psychol.,* 1920, 3, 1-4. 18, 157

Watson, R. I., *see* Zemlick & Watson

Wechsler, D., *The measurement and appraisal of adult intelligence,* 4th ed. Baltimore: Williams & Wilkins, 1958. 385

Weigert, E. V., *see* Wenner et al.

Weinstein, H., *see* Caudill & Weinstein

Weintraub, D., *see* Solkoff et al.

Weir, M. W., Children's behavior in probabilistic tasks. *Young Children,* 1967, 23, 90-105. 289

Weir, M. W., & Stevenson, H. W., The effects of verbalization in children's learning as a function of chronological age. *Child Develpm.,* 1959, 36, 173-178. 274

Welch, L., The genetic development of the associational structures of abstract thinking. *J. genet. Psychol.,* 1940, 56, 175-206. 271

Welch, L., A behaviorist explanation of concept formation. *J. genet. Psychol.,* 1947, 71, 201-222. 271-272

Wells, D., *see* Kendler et al.

Wells, M. B., *see* Dreyer & Wells

Wender, P. H., *Minimal brain dysfunction in children.* N.Y.: Wiley-Interscience, 1971. 371

Wenner, N. K., Cohen, M. B., Weigert, E. V., Kvarnes, R. G., Ohaneson, E. M., & Fearing, J. M., Emotional problems in pregnancy. *Psychiatry,* 1969, 32, 389-410. 119

Werner, E. E., Sex differences in correlations between children's IQs and measures of parental ability, and environmental ratings. *Develpm. Psychol.,* 1969, 1, 280-285. 316-317

Werner, E. E., *see also* Beilin & Werner

Werner, H., *Comparative psychology of mental development.* N.Y.: Harper, 1940. 269

Werner, H., The concept of development from a comparative and organismic point of view. In D. B. Harris, Ed., *The concept of development: An issue in the study of human behavior.* Minneapolis: Univ. of Minn. Press, 1957. 74

Werner, H., & Kaplan, E., Development of word meaning through verbal context: An experimental study. *J. Psychol.,* 1950, 29, 251-257. 382

Wertheimer, M., Psychomotor coordination of auditory and visual space at birth. *Science,* 1961, 134, 1962. 129

White, B. L., Child development research: An edifice without a foundation. *Merrill-Palmer Q. Behav. Developm.,* 1969, 15, 47-48. 146

White, B. L., *see also* Haynes et al.

White, R. W., Motivation reconsidered: The concept of competence. *Psychol. Rev.,* 1959, 66, 297-333. 123

White, S. H., The learning theory tradition and child psychology. In P. H. Mussen, ed., *Carmichael's manual of child psychology,* 3rd ed. vol. 1. N.Y.: Wiley, 1970. 28-29

White House Conference on Children, *Profiles of children.* Washington: Govt. Printing Off., 1970. 115, 121, 122, 142, 312

Whitehouse, R. H., *see* Tanner et al.

Whiting, A., Parental expectation for independent behaviors and achievement of elementary school boys. In H. C. Lindgren & F. Lindgren, Eds., *Current readings in educational psychology,* 2nd ed. N.Y.: Wiley, 1971. 403-406.

Whiting, B. B., ed., *Six cultures: Studies of child rearing.* N.Y.: Wiley, 1963. 149

Whiting, J. W. M., The frustration complex in Kwoma society. In C, Kluckhohn & H. A. Murray, Eds., *Personality in nature, society, and culture.* N.Y.: Knopf, 1948. 219

Whiting, J. W. M., & Child, I. L., *Child training and personality: A cross cultural study.* New Haven: Yale Univ. Press, 1953. 333

Whiting, J. W. M., *see also* Landauer & Whiting; and Sears, Whiting et al.

Wickman, E. K., *Children's behavior and teachers' attitudes.* N.Y.: Commonwealth Fund, 1928. 449

Willerman, L., Naylor, A. F., & Myrianthopoulos, N. C., Intellectual development of children from interracial matings. *Science,* 1970, *170,* 1329-1331. 318

Williams, G., *see* Minard et al.

Williams, J. P., *see* Kessen et al.

Wilson, M., Warren, J. M., & Abbott, L., Infantile stimulation, activity and learning by cats. *Child Develpm.,* 1965, *36,* 843-853. 189

Wilson, R. C., *see* Morrow & Wilson

Winder, C. L., & Rau, L., Parental attitudes associated with social deviance in preadolescent boys. *J. abnorm. soc. Psychol.,* 1962, *64,* 418-424. 41-42

Winitz, H., *see* Darley & Winitz

Winterbottom, M. R., The relation of need for achievement to learning experiences in independence and mastery. In J. W. Atkinson, ed., *Motives in fantasy, action, and society.* Priceton: Van Nostrand, 1958. 406-407

Wispe, L. B., & Freshley, H. B., Race, sex, and sympathetic helping behavior: The broken bag caper. *J. pers. soc. Psychol.,* 1971, *17,* 59-65. 353

Wohlford, P., *see* Santrock & Wohlford

Wolins, M., Young children in institutions: Some additional evidence. *Develpm. Psychol.,* 1970, *2,* 99-109. 198

Wolking, W. D., Quast, W., & Lawton, J. J., Jr., MMPI profiles of the parents of behaviorally disturbed children and parents from the general population. *J. clin. Psychol.,* 1966, *22,* 39-48. 401

Woolf, P. J., *see* Fries & Woolf

Woodworth, R. S., *Psychology,* 4th ed. N.Y.: Holt, 1940. 384

Wright, H. F., Psychological development in Midwest. *Child Develpm.,* 1956, *27,* 265-286. 430-431, 444

Wright, H. F., Observational child study. In P. H. Mussen, ed., *Handbook of research methods in child development.* N.Y.: Wiley, 1960. 44

Yaffe, S., *see* Solkoff et al.

Yarrow, L. J., Maternal deprivation: Toward an empirical and conceptual reevaluation. *Psychol. Bull.,* 1961, *58,* 459-490. 198

Zander, A., & Van Egmond, E., Relation of intelligence and social power to the interpersonal behavior of children. *J. educ. Psychol.,* 1958, *49,* 257-268. 442

Zemlick, M. R., & Watson, R. I., Maternal attitudes of acceptance and rejection during and after pregnancy. *Amer. J. Orthopsychiat.,* 1953, *23,* 570-584. 117-118

Zigler, E., Social class and the socialization process. *Rev. educ. Res.,* 1970, *40,* 87-110. 320

Zigler, E., *see also* Katz & Zigler, and Irons & Zigler.

Zimmerman, R. R., Strobel, D. A., & McGuire, D., Neophobic reactions in protein malnourished infant monkeys. *Amer. Psychol. Assn. Proc.,* 1970, *5,* 197-198. 141-142

Zimmerman, W. S., *see* Michael et al.

Zunich, M., Child behavior and parental attitudes. *J. Psychol.,* 1966, *62,* 41-46

Zwerg, C., *see* Smith et al.

Subject Index

Achievement motivation (n Ach), 287, 406-409, 448-449
Adolescence, cultural relativity of, 25
Age, as index to development, 77
Aggressiveness, anxiety about, 436
  in infancy, 220-221
  maternal control of, 209-210
  in middle childhood, 433-435
  in preschool years, 335-342
  and punishment, 338
  and social learning, 339-341
Allantois, 109
Altruism, in children, 86-87, 353-354
Amnion, 109, 111
Amphetamines, 371
Anaclitic depression, 197, 201
Anal stage, 96-97
Anger, in infancy, 220-221
  in middle childhood, 371-372
Animism, 264
Anorexia nervosa, 239
Anoxia, 39, 121-122
Anthropology, cultural, 25-27
Anxiety, 95, 414
  about aggressiveness, 436
  in infancy, 221-222
  in middle childhood, 373-375
  in newborns, 123
  in preschool years, 253
Apgar test, 122, 139
Arousal, need for, 88-89
Attention, reward value of, 88-89
Attitudes, mother's prenatal, 117-120
Auditory stimuli, reactions of neonates to, 129
Authoritarian parents, 54-55, 302
Authoritative parents, 302

Babinski reflex, 130
Basic learning ability (BLA), 392-393
Basic trust, in infancy, 196
Behavior modification, 446-447
Behaviorism, beginnings of, 15-18
Binet, A., 13, 18, 24, 45-48, 386
Birth-order effects, 321-324

Birth size, and intelligence, 123
Birth trauma, 121-123
Black English, 286
Blastocyst, 109
Blastula, 108-109
Bleuler, E., 68
Brain damage, and prenatal malnutrition, 114-115
Brazil, 409, 414
Breast-feeding, 148, 194-195
Butler, Samuel, 34

Cattell, J. McK., 45
Causality, physical, 378-379
Centering, 264-268
Cephalocaudal trends, in growth and development, 62, 113, 139, 145
Character development, Freudian interpretation of, 67
Child development, early theories of, 7-12
Child guidance clinics, early, 21-23
Child psychology, beginnings of, 11-18
  and clinical psychology, 23
  in Europe, 6
  modern period of, 27-31
  in the 1920s and 1930s, 18-21
  and self-understanding, 6
Child-rearing practices, American, 6, 149, 296, 333, 432-433
  Asian and Mediterranean, 218
  authoritarian, harmonious, and permissive, 54-55
  democratic tradition in, 5-6
  French, 6
  Hawaiian, 333-334
  Hopi, 142-143
  in India, 149
  Israeli, 205-208
  Japanese, 81
  in Kenya, 149
  Kwoma, 219
  in Mexico, 149
  in New England, 149
  in Okinawa, 149
  in the Philippines, 149
  in the Rajput, 149

485